P9-EDV-961

Central America

FODOR'S TRAVEL GUIDES

are compiled, researched, and edited by an international team of travel writers, field correspondents, and editors. The series, which now almost covers the globe, was founded by Eugene Fodor in 1936.

OFFICES
New York & London

Fodor's Central America

Editor: Alice Thompson
Area Editors: Robert Braaton, John Chater, Philip Finnegan, Helena de Gutiérrez, Neville Hobson, Tito del Moral, Michael Shawcross
Contributing Editor and Consultant: A. R. Williams
Editorial Contributors: Ellen Caldwell, María Elena del Valle, Michael Hutchison, Susan Lindeman, John Mitchem
Drawings: Sandra Lang
Maps: Jon Bauch, Pictograph
Cover Photograph: Jacques Jangoux

Cover Design: Vignelli Associates

SPECIAL SALES

Fodor's Travel Publications are available at special discounts for bulk purchases (100 copies or more) for sales promotions or premiums. Special editions, including personalized covers, excerpts of existing guides, and corporate imprints, can be created in large quantities for special needs. For more information, write to Special Marketing, Fodor's Travel Publications, 201 East 50th Street, New York, NY 10022. Enquiries from the United Kingdom should be sent to Merchandise Division, Random House UK Ltd, 30–32 Bedford Square, London WC1B 3SG.

Central America

FODOR'S TRAVEL PUBLICATIONS, INC.
New York & London

Copyright © 1988 by Fodor's Travel Publications, Inc.

Fodor's is a trademark of Fodor's Travel Publication, Inc.

All rights reserved under International and Pan-American Copyright Conventions. Published in the United States by Fodor's Travel Publications, Inc., a subsidiary of Random House, Inc., New York, and simultaneously in Canada by Random House of Canada Limited, Toronto. Distributed by Random House, Inc., New York.

No maps, illustrations, or other portions of this book may be reproduced in any form without written permission from the publisher.

ISBN 0–679–01613–9

MANUFACTURED IN THE UNITED STATES OF AMERICA
10 9 8 7 6 5 4 3 2 1

CONTENTS

CONTENTS

FOREWORD

Central America comprises some of the world's most beautiful countries. The political situation of recent years may have made many travelers wary of venturing here, but, in truth, Central America remains an area of magnificent beaches, fascinating relics of the Mayan civilization, fine national parks, and wonderfully warm people. For sophisticated travelers who want to see the largely undiscovered beauty here, for journalists, political scientists, and business people who need a first-hand look at the change and development of these nations, Central America is a fascinating destination.

Fodor's Central America is designed to help you plan your own trip based on your time, your budget, your interests—your idea of what this trip should be. Perhaps, having read this guide, you'll have some new ideas. We do not attempt to gloss over the political realities of these countries; we do try to be realistic about the dangers, as well as the pleasures, of a trip to Central America. We also stress that the situations here are *constantly* changing—and you must keep apprised of current events before you begin your travels. Additionally, we emphasize the need for you to inquire locally whenever our guide does not seem to reflect the situation you're seeing.

Based on the situation at press time, we have tried to offer you the widest possible range of activities and, within that range, selections that will be safe, worthwhile, and of good value. The descriptions we provide are designed to help you make your own intelligent decisions from among our selections.

While every care has been taken to assure the accuracy of the information in this guide, the passage of time will always bring change, and consequently the publisher cannot accept responsibility for errors that may occur.

All prices and opening times quoted here are based on information available to us at press time. Hours and admission fees may change, however, and the prudent traveler will avoid inconvenience by calling ahead.

Fodor's wants to hear about your travel experiences, both pleasant and unpleasant. When a hotel or restaurant fails to live up to its billing, let us know and we will investigate the complaint and revise our entries where the facts warrant it.

Send your letters to the editors of Fodor's Travel Publications, 201 E. 50th Street, New York, NY 10022, or 30–32 Bedford Square, London WC1B 3SG, England.

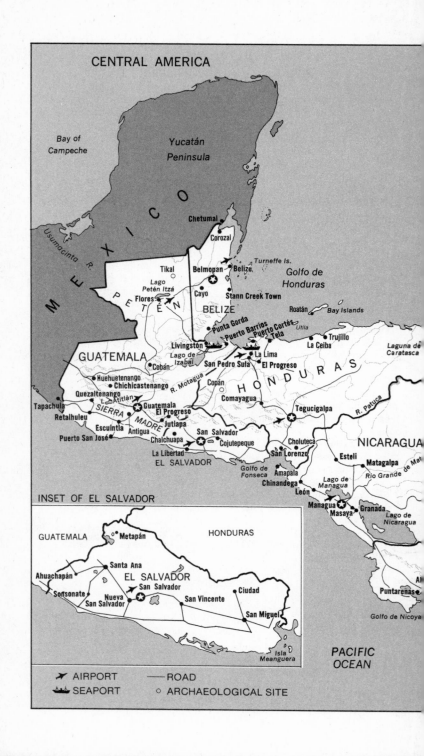

CENTRAL AMERICA

Bay of
Campeche

Yucatán
Peninsula

MEXICO

Usumacinta R.

Chetumal

Corozal

Tikal

Belmopan
Belize

Turneffe Is.

Golfo de
Honduras

Lago
Petén Itzá
Flores

PETÉN

Cayo

BELIZE

Stann Creek Town

Roatán

Bay Islands

Utila

Punta Gorda

Puerto Barrios

Puerto Cortés
Tela

Trujillo
La Ceiba

Laguna de
Caratasca

GUATEMALA

Livingston

Cobán

Lago de
Izabal

San Pedro Sula

La Lima

El Progreso

Huehuetenango
Chichicastenango

Copán

HONDURAS

R. Motagua

Comayagua

R. Patuca

Quezaltenango

L. Atitlán

Guatemala
El Progreso

Tegucigalpa

Tapachula
Retalhuleu

SIERRA
MADRE

Jutiapa

Escuintla
Antigua
Puerto San José

Chalchuapa

San Salvador

Cojutepeque

Choluteca

NICARAGUA

La Libertad
EL SALVADOR

San Lorenzo

Estelí

Matagalpa

Golfo de
Fonseca

Amapala

Chinandega

León

Lago de
Managua

Río Grande de Mat

Managua
Masaya

Granada

Lago de
Nicaragua

INSET OF EL SALVADOR

GUATEMALA

Metapán

HONDURAS

Ahuachapán

Santa Ana

EL SALVADOR

Sonsonate

Nueva
San Salvador

San Salvador

San Vincente

Ciudad

San Miguel

Al

Puntarenas

Golfo de Nicoya

Isla
Meanguera

PACIFIC
OCEAN

✈ AIRPORT   —— ROAD
⛴ SEAPORT   ○ ARCHAEOLOGICAL SITE

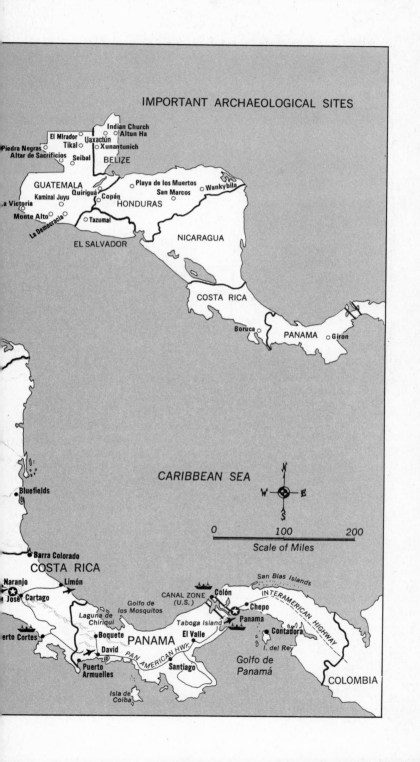

IMPORTANT ARCHAEOLOGICAL SITES

Indian Church
El Mirador   Altun Ha
Piedra Negras   Tikal   Uaxactún
Altar de Sacrificios   Xunantunich
Seibal   BELIZE

GUATEMALA   Playa de los Muertos
Kaminal Juyu   Quiriguá   San Marcos   Wankybila
La Victoria   Copán
Monte Alto   HONDURAS
La Democracia   Tazumal
EL SALVADOR   NICARAGUA

COSTA RICA

Boruca   PANAMA   Giron

CARIBBEAN SEA

N
W   E
S

0   100   200
Scale of Miles

Bluefields

Barra Colorado

COSTA RICA
San Blas Islands
Naranjo   Limón
San José   Cartago
CANAL ZONE   Colón
(U.S.)   Chepo
Golfo de   INTERAMERICAN HIGHWAY
los Mosquitos   Panama
Laguna de   Taboga Island
Chiriqui   Contadora
Puerto Cortes   Boquete   PANAMA   El Valle   I. del Rey
David
Puerto   PAN AMERICAN HWY.   Golfo de
Armuelles   Santiago   Panamá
Isla de   COLOMBIA
Coiba

FACTS AT YOUR FINGERTIPS

FACTS AT YOUR FINGERTIPS

by
A. R. WILLIAMS

TO GO OR NOT TO GO. If you're thinking about traveling to Central America these days, you also may be secretly wondering whether it's all that good an idea. But how dangerous will it really be? And how crazy do you have to be to do it? Not as much as you might think, on either count. You'll just need a healthy sense of adventure in some places, a good dose of patience everywhere, and a practical no-nonsense streak to keep you out of trouble.

Aficionados of Central America will tell you that the trip is more than worth the effort, and many return year after year to their favorite spot. One woman, for instance, has been back and forth so many times on vacations that the visa section of her passport is a solid block of immigration stamps, and the silver eagle has been worn off the front cover after many heavy handlings at border crossings. Among other attractions, the world's second-longest barrier reef—after the Great Barrier Reef of Australia—brings skin divers to the offshore islands of Belize and Honduras. Ruins of Mayan settlements such as Tikal in Guatemala and Copán in Honduras are rated as spectacular even by veteran Mesoamerican pyramid climbers. Textile collectors bargain for brilliantly colored weavings with Guatemalan Indians (called *indígenas* there, never *indios*) speaking softly sibilant native languages, or for intricate reverse appliqué *molas* from Panama's Cuna Indians. The trains that link Costa Rica's capital of San José to the coastal city of Puerto Limón, and the Panama Railroad that links Panama City on the Pacific with Colón on the Atlantic, are classic railroad adventures, The Panama Canal, that country's number one tourist attraction, is still a wonder of engineering. Bird-watchers add to their life lists in Panamanian jungles and Costa Rica's extensive national parks. High rollers revel in Panama City's sizzling nightlife. Students of socioeconomic and political change (100,000 of them in 1987) check things out in Nicaragua.

Sure, there are risks in some of this. Hardly a day goes by when Central America doesn't appear in the news, and reports usually are not cheery. You've got to expect that traveling through countries involved in seething political confrontations will pose some dangers, but then if you wanted complete security, you'd still be reading *National Geographic* in front of the fireplace. Actually risk to life and limb through armed conflict is not great. Certainly there are dangerous places, but, in general, host governments are not about to let tourists anywhere near potential or real hot spots, and you're unlikely to get into serious trouble unless you insist on being where you're not supposed to be and doing what is forbidden.

The present unrest is more likely to have an impact on your trip in the form of inconveniences—increased border security, military checkpoints along highways, disrupted public transport, and so forth. How inconvenient things get depends greatly on what country or countries you'll be traveling in—places with grave political problems don't have much time or patience for the niceties of the tourist trade, of course. Predicting what areas those will be by the time you read this book is impossible. Things are changing so quickly in Central America these days that even people who travel around the region frequently on business are finding it difficult to keep current. We have tried in this section, though, to provide you with basic information on how to plan and prepare for your trip and how to maneuver yourself through what you find once you get there. But in a region where rules, regulations, and the specifics of a given situation are liable to shift suddenly, nothing can or should be taken for granted. It is recommended that you check with your State Department for current travel advisories before departure. Once you arrive, keep your wits about you, and if something looks dangerous or different from what you expected, ask about it. Things may have changed just yesterday.

TRAVEL AGENTS. The chances of finding a travel agent who counts Central America among his or her specialties is slim. Nevertheless, a good one can be a tremendous boon to your trip, saving you time and money by guiding you through the complex maze of foreign travel. Agents can arrange transportation, accommodations, auto rentals, tours, and package deals. They can advise you on how to obtain a passport and can get necessary visas for you (usually for a separate fee). They have information about U.S. Department of State travel advisories and what sort of inoculations you are likely to need. As a middleman, the agent may also be able to sell you different kinds of insurance offered by a variety of specialty companies.

Insurance is a good thing to consider when planning a trip to Central America, for obvious reasons. Baggage insurance against loss or damage depends on the length of your trip and the coverage you want—a 30-day $1,000 policy may run you about $50. (Check first to see if your homeowner's personal property policy already covers some of your belongings.) Health insurance also depends on the length of your stay, with fees and options varying widely. (Again, check current coverage. What you already have may be sufficient.) Comprehensive packages are also available, and may include coverage for trip cancellation or interruption, baggage problems, accidental death, medical expenses, personal liability, or emergency evacuation.

You might consider planning your trip through a vast agency like *American Express* or *Thomas Cook* or through a smaller one with an affiliate in the country or countries where you will be traveling. You will be their client, and they can take care of you all along the way. Bear in mind, though, that travel agents are much more likely to be able to help someone who wants to fly in and out of Central America, stay at upscale hotels, and see the sights from a rental car or a guided tour. They may not know much about local transport, land border crossings, or charming, cheap (but clean and comfortable) *pensiones* in converted colonial houses. The more unusual your plans and off the beaten track your itinerary, the more you're on your own.

If you don't know of a good travel agent, consult the Yellow Pages for a travel agency that displays the *American Society of Travel Agents* (ASTA) logo, or contact ASTA directly (Box 23992, Washington, DC 20026–3992, tel. 703–739–2782); for a small fee they can provide listings of their members in your area. See if the initials CTC appear after your agent's name, too. These stand for Certified Travel Counselor and indicate that the person has had at least five years' experience and has completed a two-year graduate-level program on the travel industry. Complaints against a travel agency should be addressed to the Consumer Affairs Dept. at the above address. *(ASTA Canada* can be contacted through Chapter President Lise Shearaer, Cabie House of Travel Ltd., 511 W. 14th Ave., Suite 101, Vancouver, BC V5Z 1P5; the *Association of British Travel Agents* (ABTA) can be contacted at 55–57 Newman St., London W1P 4AH (tel. 01–637–2444).

OFFICIAL PAPERS AND PAMPHLETS. You will need some sort of documentation to enter all Central American countries. A few require a passport stamped with a visa granted for a specific purpose and period of time. Embassies and consular offices of the countries you plan to visit issue visas, and you can arrange to obtain the ones you need at home, or one or two countries ahead on the road (at the Guatemalan Embassy in Mexico City, for instance, if you're traveling down that way). There is sometimes a fee for obtaining a visa (it can run to $10 or so), you may need one or more photographs, and the process is a slow one, so start well in advance. If you're negotiating this through the mail, be sure to send your passport registered and insist that it be sent back the same way.

It is wise to obtain all visas you think you will need before you leave home. Foreign consular offices abroad may have hours that are very inconvenient for your traveling schedule, and the offices may be difficult to find in a strange city. Failing this, on the road you should try to keep at least one visa, if not two, ahead of your travels. It's also a good idea to take a half dozen passport-style photographs in case additional documentation is required for anything from a fishing license to a tourist-card extension.

Other countries in the region let tourists from certain countries visit with a tourist card and proof of citizenship (birth certificate or naturalization papers, for instance; other documents may be accepted, but that varies from country to country, and it's best to check that out with an embassy or consulate). Some tourist cards are issued free, some cost money, most last for just a few months. Many travelers to Central America pick them up in the airport at the counters of airlines serving the region, but embassies and consulates issue them as well, and they can usually be obtained at land border crossings.

The U.S. Department of State publishes a pamphlet entitled *Visa Requirements for Foreign Governments,* which can be obtained by writing to the DOS, Passport Services Correspondence Branch, Room 386, 1425 K St., N.W., Washington, DC 20524; or call 202–523–1673. The Department of State also maintains an information line for visitors who wish to check on any official travel advisories for the region at 202–647–5225. Central America is in such a state of flux these days, though, that details may quickly become out of date. You had best double-check what you'll need by contacting embassies or consulates directly. You can then inquire about other requirements as well. Some countries require an ongoing or return airline or bus ticket, and some ask visitors to show money to prove they can support themselves. The amount often depends on the particular traveler, the immigration officials, and the length of stay. Most countries charge an entrance and/or exit fee, but payment configurations may be unusual. Belize, for example, charges a $13 departure tax. In Guatemala, visas are free, but tourist cards must be purchased for $1 and departing visitors pay an $8 fee. Also, if you arrive at land borders at off hours, you may be asked to pay extra. If you're planning on doing anything out of the ordinary, ask about it. (Example: if one parent is traveling with a minor child in Guatemala, he/she needs a written authorization from the other parent, notarized and in triplicate.) Embassies and consulates sometimes can provide you with general tourist information as well, or they will refer you to national tourist offices that can.

Although a number of Central American countries do not require that U.S. citizens have a passport, it is a good idea to carry one anyway. It is *the* internationally accepted form of personal identification and is recognized everywhere—at airport immigration, at land border crossings, at military checkpoints on the roads, at banks when you want to cash traveler's checks. (A birth certificate is much less recognized and will be unintelligible to a non-English speaker anyway.) Make sure you fill in on page 4 of the passport the name, address, and phone number of next of kin or a close friend. If you lose your passport, or if it is stolen, notify the nearest U.S. consular office or passport agency immediately.

If you are planning to travel among several Central American countries, a passport bearing multiple-entry visas may be more convenient than tourist cards. Small border crossings in particular may present difficulties if you're traveling on a tourist card. At the crossing closest to the Mayan ruins of Copán, for instance, Guatemalan officials may refuse to allow travelers with tourist cards to cross the border out of Guatemala and visit the site—even if Honduran officials directly across the way give the go-ahead. Conversely, if you're coming from Honduras into Guatemala, the Guatemalan officials at that same crossing do not issue tourist cards, and you won't be able to enter Guatemala there without a visa in a passport. Farther north, Guatemala doesn't recognize Belize as a country, so border crossings between the countries may be dicey without a passport and visa. In addition to border problems, getting extensions on tourist cards can be difficult, requiring a lot of time and red tape.

TOURIST INFORMATION. The publications these offices send you will give a fair idea of how competitive the tourist industry is in each country. On the high end of the scale is **Costa Rica,** with *National Tourist Bureaus* in Miami (200 S.E. 1 St., Suite 402, Miami, FL 33131; 800–327–7033) and Los Angeles (3540 Wilshire Blvd., Suite 1707, Los Angeles, CA 90010; 800–762–5909). People answering the phones know their country and the tourism business well, and they send out a splendid package of country and city maps and brochures on almost every tourist experience you might want to have in Costa Rica. At the other end of the scale is **El Salvador,** which is just hanging onto the political status quo by its fingernails. Other countries fall somewhere in between—**Panama** and **Guatemala,** for instance. You can contact the *Panama Government Tourist Bureau* at 2355 Salzedo St., Suite 305, Coral Gables, FL 33134, 305–442–1892 or 1893. The *Guatemala Tourist Commission* may be contacted at Box 144351, Coral Gables, FL 33114–4351, 305–358–5110. For information on Honduras, send an SASE to *Honduras Information Service,* 501 Fifth Ave., Suite 1611, New York, NY 10017, 212–490–0766 or 683–2136. Not a government agency, the information service provides maps and news and sells guidebooks. They can also give you information on Guatemala.

The cultural attachés at the following embassies may be useful when you're making travel plans:

Belize: 3400 International Dr. NW, Suite 2-J, Washington, DC 20008, 202–363–4505.

El Salvador: 2308 California St. NW, Washington, DC 20008, 202–265–3480.

Guatemala: 2220 R St. NW, Washington, DC 20008, 202–745–4952.

Nicaragua: 1627 New Hampshire Ave. NW, Washington, DC 20009, 202–387–4371.

TOURS. Your travel agent should be able to get you information on tours to Central America that match your means and interests. The variety of what's available within the region is considerable, though tours are concentrated in countries that are most popular (and considered safest). Archeological tours abound, of course, since Central America was the home of the Maya empire and ruins lay scattered across the northern part of the region. *(The Complete Visitor's Guide to Mesoamerican Ruins,* written by Joyce Kelly and published by the University of Oklahoma Press, is a good site-by-site primer complete with maps and photographs.) *Far Horizons* (Box 1529, 16 Fern Lane, San Anselmo, CA 94960; 415–457–4575), for instance, offers a 10-day tour of the Mayan ruins in Belize, with an optional four-day extension to visit Tikal in Guatemala. *Holbrook Travel* (3540 N.W. 13 St., Gainesville, FL 32609; 904–377–7111), has tours of Belize and nature tours of Costa Rica, among others. The more adventurous might want to try the Costa Rican white-water rafting, volcano climbing, and nature hiking tours put together by *Wilderness Travel* (801 Allsto Way, Berkeley, CA 94710; 415–548–0420) and *SOBEK Expeditions* (Box 1089, Angels Camp, CA 95222; 209–736–4524). Michael S. Kaye, president of *Costa Rica Expeditions* (Apartado 6941, San José, Costa Rica) will send you a complete pack of information on tours that range from white-water rafting and kayaking to tarpon, snook, and trout fishing to nature walks through that country's superb national park system. His company also has a "design-your-own-adventure" feature that allows you to assemble different modules into a three- to six-day trip for as few as two people. (Travelers planning an adventurous trip to Central America should read Hilary Bradt and Rob Rachowiecki's *Backpacking in Mexico and Central America,* which includes detailed accounts of hiking through rain forests and climbing an active volcano; it costs $11.95, plus $1 postage, and can be obtained from Bradt Enterprises, 93 Harvey St., Cambridge, MA 02140.) Kaye also will include a list of companies in the United States and Europe through which you can book tours with CRE.

If can't make up your mind about what you want to see before you go, you can always arrange to take a local tour. Travel agencies in every capital city will be delighted to help you put together a travel itinerary for their country—and they're likely to know more than your agent at home, since they're on their own turf.

STAYING HEALTHY. Before you set off on your trip, make sure immunizations for measles, mumps, rubella, polio, diphtheria, tetanus, and pertussis are up-to-date. You might also consider a typhoid vaccination and a gamma globulin shot against hepatitis as well as a yellow fever vaccination (for travelers planning to be off the beaten track in infected areas). None of these is required except the yellow fever vaccinations, and that only for Panama's provinces of Bocas del Toro and Darién. Nevertheless, it is a good idea to keep an official record of your vaccinations. The booklet *International Certificates of Vaccination* (# PHS-731), is an internationally recognized form that serves this purpose and can be obtained for $2 from the Superintendent of Documents, U.S. Government Printing Office, Washington, DC 20402; telephone 202–783–3238. Keep the booklet with your passport. If you are subject to severe allergic reactions or have some other unusual health problem, you should wear a medical-alert bracelet and carry an appropriate warning card along with your passport as well.

If you take prescription medicines, keep them in their original bottles and carry a copy of your doctor's prescriptions to make passage through customs easier. (Panama is particularly strict about this because of widespread drug trade in neighboring Colombia.) Take whatever you need in the way of medical supplies. In many Latin American countries you can obtain medicines over the counter just by knowing what to ask the pharmacist for, but shortages are not unknown. (At this writing, for example, the shelves of Nicaraguan drugstores are all but bare, and aspirin is selling for a hefty sum by the *tablet* in local markets. If you do purchase medicine from a local pharmacy, make sure that it has been refrigerated, if needed, and that the expiration date hasn't passed.

When you're packing, put in an extra pair of eyeglasses and contact lenses and enough contact lens fluid to see you through the trip, as well as a copy of the prescription for your glasses or lenses. Travelers planning to spend time in coastal areas should include a pair of sunglasses and an appropriate sunscreen. (Bear in mind that the sun is strong in the tropics. You can get a burn before you realize it, so take it slow. Reflection off the water or off a light-colored building will fry you doubly quick.) Women should take along feminine hygiene products. Tampons, in particular, tend to be scarce, expensive, and of dubious quality. The same goes for birth control devices. You might also make up a small first-aid kit of basics: Band Aids, antiseptic cream, aspirin or stronger pain killer, diarrhea medicine, decongestant–antihistamine, motion sickness pills, lip balm with a sunscreen, topical sunburn remedy, hand and body lotion against chapping, throat lozenges, dental floss, antifungal foot powder (for the steamy coastal areas), insect repellent, and anything else your doctor suggests.

Before you leave, make sure you treat, or have treated, even the smallest injury. Cuts and stings fester quickly in the tropics.

Medical insurance is a must. Double-check that you are covered, and if not, take out a policy.

Once you're off on your travels, it's the food and water that are most likely to do you in. Until your body gets used to local bacteria, it's best to think before you put anything into your mouth. And if hands are involved (in eating, dental flossing, etc.), scrub them first. They can easily transmit street bugs into your digestive tract.

In general water systems in the larger Central American cities are fairly safe, whereas water in the small towns and villages is likely not to be. It is best to use bottled water for the first few weeks, or for your entire trip if you're not staying long. Hotels where tourists stay are usually quite honest about the quality of their water and will gladly bring you bottled (*aqua de botella*) or purified water (*aqua purificada*) if you ask. Some hotel rooms are automatically stocked with it. If you generally feel nervous about drinking water in foreign countries or plan to be out backpacking where you know the water will be consistently bad, you can stock up on Sterotabs or Halazone tablets before you leave home. When dissolved in the water, they will purify it after about a half hour. If you have the proper equipment, you can always boil water for about 15 minutes. Remember that ice cubes are simply frozen water and might be contaminated. Make sure that plates and glasses on which you are served are completely dry. Residual water on a recently washed plate may be bad as well.

Unless you are on a long trip and your body can adjust slowly to the local food, it's best to avoid eating on the street or in markets. Even after adjusting, it's a risky proposition. Carelessly washed glasses in market restaurant sections have been known to pass on the cold-sore type of herpes virus, among other things. You should also avoid salads, fresh fruits or vegetables that you haven't peeled yourself, milk or custard products of suspicious appearance or origin, and mayonnaise and creamed foods (which spoil quickly in the tropics). Meat, poultry, seafood, and vegetables should be cooked thoroughly and served hot. Pork is best avoided entirely. Bottled soft drinks, beer, wine, and hot coffee and tea are safe beverages.

Despite the best precautions, you may come down with a case of diarrhea. Some travelers prefer to let nature take its course for a few days. Others swear by over-the-counter medication such as Pepto-Bismol tablets. Still others prefer to plug everything up right away with a prescription remedy like Lomotil (though this can be toxic if the indicated dosage is exceeded). If you've traveled a lot, you know what works for you. If not, you should ask your doctor for suggestions before you leave home. If you are stricken, stick to a bland diet of foods like rice, mashed potatoes, bananas, papayas, and lots of liquids. Latin American mothers set great store by chamomile tea (*tée de manzanilla,* or just *manzanilla*) as a treatment for upset stomachs.

If the diarrhea persists or if it is accompanied by fever, cramps, and blood in the stool, you may have dysentery. Don't try to treat it yourself. See a doctor, who will figure out which sort it is and prescribe proper medication to clear up the problem. Central American doctors may be better at treating tropical gastrointestinal maladies than their colleagues in the United States, since they see patients with such complaints all the time. U.S. embassies often have lists of local English-speaking doctors.

Malaria is a serious health problem around the world, especially since the disease itself is becoming resistant to medicines and mosquitoes are increasingly resistant to insecticides. Virtually every Central American country has infected areas, particularly in low-lying coastal regions. If you know you will be traveling where malaria is a risk, ask your doctor at home to prescribe the appropriate antimalarial medicine before you leave. (Chloroquine is still good for most of Central America, but malaria strains in Panama are becoming Chloroquine-resistant, so Fansidar may be prescribed for that country.) The medicine should be taken before, during, and after your trip, either daily or weekly. It is not prophylactic, but simply suppresses the symptoms. Once you've contracted the disease, you're stuck with it, and bouts of fever and chills may reoccur for years. Prevention, of course, is best.

Malaria mosquitoes feed between dusk and dawn, and they don't have the high-pitched whine that alerts you to swat them. You can protect yourself after sunset by avoiding perfume or aftershave, covering as much of your body as possible with clothing (preferably light-colored), applying insect repellent to exposed skin, and sleeping under a mosquito net unless your hotel is air-conditioned and the windows are sealed.

If you develop a high fever and extreme exhaustion once you have returned home, you may have contracted malaria. See your doctor immediately and tell him/her where you have been and when.

Travelers should be aware that the incidence of dengue, a viral disease transmitted by mosquitos, has increased in Central America over the last few years. Although visitors are considered at low risk for severe dengue infection, extra precautions against mosquito bites are advised.

Backpackers, bird-watchers, and other travelers who expect to be in the boonies should be aware of Chagas' disease. It is caused by parasites borne by the barbar bug, or *vinchuca.* This nocturnal critter hitchhikes on opossums, armadillos, and various rodents of the countryside, and usually bites humans on the face as they sleep. The resulting disease is inevitably fatal. The nooks and crannies of native huts are favorite hiding places of the *vinchuca,* so if you're planning to accept local hospitality, bring a hammock (or buy one—they're one of Central America's best handicrafts) and string it up outside. Though not all that common, cases of Chagas' disease occur in all countries covered in this book except Belize.

Rabies is a much bigger health problem in Latin American countries than it is in the United States. Loose dogs on the street obviously should be avoided, but be careful of domestic animals that are behaving peculiarly as well. If you are bitten, the offending animal should be kept under observation for signs of the disease. Treatment for humans, begun within three days of the bite, is a series of injections given over a two-week stretch.

If you want to read up on any of the above diseases and health problems before you set out, the *Health Guide for Travellers to Warm Climates,* published by the Canadian Public Health Association, 1335 Carling Ave., Suite 210, Ottawa, Ontario, Canada, K1Z 8N8, is highly recommended by many tropical travelers. *Health Information for International Travel* is comprehensive and updated yearly, though slanted toward health-care professionals. Your doctor should be able to get it for you free from the Centers for Disease Control, Center for Prevention Services, Division of Quarantine, Atlanta, GA 30333; or it can be purchased for $5.50 from the Superintendent of Documents, U.S. Government Printing Office, Washington, DC 20402. The International Association for Medical Assistance to Travellers (IAMAT for short) publishes a wide variety of pamphlets with health information, including one on Chagas' disease, a *World Malaria Risk Chart,* a *World Immunization Chart,* one on *How to Adjust to the Heat,* and another on *How to Avoid Traveller's Diarrhea.* Its *World Climate Charts* contain information on appropriate clothing and the sanitary conditions of water, milk, and food. And it puts out a list of IAMAT affiliates around the world that will find you an English-speaking doctor (a specialist, if you need one) who has agreed to provide services for a set fee ($20 for an office visit, $30 for a house or hotel call, and $35 for Sundays, holidays, and nights). To obtain any of the IAMAT's publications, write to 736 Center St., Lewiston, NY 14092, in the United States; 188 Nicklin Rd., Guelph, Ontario, N1H 7L5, in Canada; and 17 Gotthardstr., CH 6300 Zng, Switzerland, in Europe.

CLIMATE. The clothing you decide to take with you will depend on where you will be traveling in Central America and what time of year it is. Climate generally depends on altitude. Coastal areas tend to be hot and humid, and low-lying Panama in the south can be quite a steam bath. Cities of the highlands and central plateaus are mild all year round. Some, like Guatemala City and Antigua in Guatemala, Tegucigalpa in Honduras, and San José in Costa Rica, are known as cities of eternal spring. There, the middle part of the day is usually warm and sunny—sometimes even hot—but evenings are chilly enough for a jacket or a sweater. Towns at higher altitudes, such as Chichicastenango, Guatemala, are cooler during the day and can be downright nippy at night. (The Hotel Santo Tomás in Chichicastenango even has a working fireplace in each room.) Climate variations, though, are nowhere near as drastic as the change from winter snow to summer heat up north. Central America is a temperate region, and the clothing you pack can be reasonably homogeneous, even if you plan to spend some time in the mountains and some time on the coast.

The region's rain cycle will be the overriding climate factor that will shape your trip. The rainy season runs from about April or May to October. It moves north, so while Panama's Darién province may be dripping in April, northern countries may still be waiting for the first rains in May. Rain falls part of almost every day, with brief afternoon showers during the first part of the season giving way to downpours (often still in the afternoon) later on, and finally rain and more rain well into the season. It turns the land to an emerald green bursting with flowers. It also brings a steamy 100 percent humidity to the coasts, makes unpaved roads virtually impassable, and breeds mosquitoes—not big problems if you're sticking to large cities.

During the dry season, from November to April or May, rainfall is unusual except along the coasts. The land is generally parched and brown, the air may be dusty and unpleasant to breathe at times.

Many people try to plan their trips to Central America during the transition periods, which are the most pleasant parts of the year. In June and July the rains have just started, the dust has settled, and the countryside has begun to bloom again. And in October and November the land is still lush and the air still fresh, although the rain has slackened off. Travelers have to break out the umbrella for rain in either case, but showers are bracketed by clear weather, and nothing gets too wet or too dry.

WHAT CLOTHING TO PACK. U.S. spring-weight clothing is a good basis for a Central American wardrobe. It is appropriate for the central plateaus, and you can add layers if you're going up into the highlands or subtract layers if you'll be on the coasts.

Although wash-and-wear fabrics are convenient, natural fibers are apt to be more comfortable—and healthy—in either cold or heat. Cotton is a good fiber for the tropics. It is marvelously absorbent and allows perspiration to evaporate as well as air to circulate. Synthetics can be hot and sticky on the coasts, cold and clammy in the mountains. This is true all the way down the line, from shirts to underwear to socks. Don't worry about keeping the cotton pristine. Labor is relatively cheap in Central America, and you can get clothes washed and ironed for very little money. Dry cleaning is quite another matter. Quality in this part of the world is *very* uneven.

If you're going to be on the coasts a lot, lighter colors will be cooler, since they reflect rather than absorb light. Bring a straw or cotton sun hat if you plan to be outdoors a lot as well as at least one long-sleeved shirt and a pair of trousers to fend off the sun in case you get burnt. Remember your bathing suit, too.

You might pack a water-repellent raincoat (waterproof won't let the air circulate), which will keep the rain off in general and over a woolen sweater will keep you warm in the highlands. Bring a fold-up umbrella as well.

Shoes are important, especially if you will be walking a lot. Make sure they're comfortable and sturdy, and take a couple of pairs. Tuck in sandals for warm days. You certainly don't want to overpack, but don't count on being able to purchase satisfying replacements for shoes—or any other item of clothing—that you have forgotten. For one thing, quality may not be up to U.S. standards. But more important, you may be much larger and proportioned quite differently than local customers, so finding something that fits in a useful fashion may be difficult. Tailors are still pretty cheap compared with those in the U.S., and they do beautiful work, but having something custom-made is practical only if you're staying put for a while. Good tailors often have quite a backlog of orders to fill, and you'll have to go back for fittings if you've asked for something complicated like a suit.

It is quite all right for women to wear trousers in Central America, but shorts on either sex are definitely out of place anywhere outside coastal resorts and archeological sites. (And they're not such a great idea when you're pyramid climbing. If you have to sit down to get down steep, shallow stairs, you're liable to get your legs scraped.) Women should be particularly careful not to draw attention to themselves with their clothing. Wearing sarongs, strapless sundresses, or tube tops outside of a resort setting is frowned upon. Always wear a bra, whether you need it or not, unless you deliberately mean to provoke. *Under no circumstances* should anyone of either sex wear army khaki or camouflage jungle attire or carry or use anything that smacks of the military. You're setting yourself up as a target if you do.

Central America has gotten used to the disheveled backpacker style by now, but in general you'll have a much better traveling experience if you're clean and tidy. Latin Americans are very appearance-conscious, and people there take great pains with personal grooming and attire. The logic behind someone having enough money for international travel, yet looking like a waif in patched jeans, escapes them. Border guards and other officials may be particularly unsympathetic. If you look especially scruffy, penniless, and powerless and act at all disoriented, you run the risk of having drugs planted on you, and perhaps being denied entry into a country. Nicaragua is the exception to the above. Although Nicaraguans do seem to be making the distinction between the U.S. government and U.S. citizens, the less like a member of U.S. officialdom or the business establishment you look, the better you are likely to get on there.

On the other end of the scale, if you're planning to dine in good restaurants, attend cultural events, or go to a nightclub, your dress should be reasonably formal. Women should bring at least one nice dress and appropriate shoes, while men will want a lightweight suit, or trousers and sports jacket. Men in Central America often wear collars open at the neck, but you should bring a tie just in case. The *guayabera* shirt is standard apparel for men in Central America and is accepted in all but the most elegant situations. Always worn open-necked and with the hem outside of the waistband, it may have plain vertical tucks or lots of embroidery done in the same color thread as the shirt (usually white, cream, pale yellow, pale blue). Short-sleeved varieties are more sporty, long-sleeved more appropriate for evening wear. If you like that sort of thing and want to go native, it's one local item of clothing that is a good buy.

Other Necessities

Each traveler has a different list of things he or she absolutely cannot live without on a trip. Here's a list of suggestions in case you go blank when it's time to pack. A penknife, complete with scissor, screwdriver, and bottle opener elements. A flashlight. An alarm clock. (Wake-up calls are unreliable.) A sewing kit and safety pins. A manicure kit with tweezers and nail file. Scotch or adhesive tape. Rubber bands. A good supply of toilet tissue and facial tissues. (Hotels outside of big cities may provide toilet tissue only sporadically, and you are unlikely to find any at all in public places; so carry a small packet of facial tissue in your purse or pocket for emergencies.) Zip-lock plastic bags in various sizes and a couple of big garbage bags. (They're good for separating wet things from dry, clean from dirty.) A flat rubber plug for baths and sinks. A small spiral notebook, for use as a journal as well as a record book for expenses and photos taken. Ballpoint pens. (These make good gifts to children who have a hard time getting school supplies.) Business cards. (It is very Latin to exchange business cards with someone you have just met socially.) A few paperback books you can leave along the way for the times you have to sit and wait for something. (Keep it light, though; literature deemed revolutionary, subversive, or otherwise politically sensitive may be confiscated in a number of countries.) Addresses of people you want to send postcards to. Special soaps, shampoos, and conditioners that might not be available locally. Handiwipes, for use as disposable washcloths. Individually packaged moistened towelettes. (Marvelously refreshing for face and neck when traveling in the tropics.) Earplugs. (Dogs bark at night, roosters crow early in the morning, and traffic tends to be loud, especially if it's a large truck revving its engine or a motorcycle without a muffler.) A small Spanish dictionary–phrasebook. Small packages of snack food (especially good during long car or bus rides). Light bulbs, if you're traveling to Nicaragua. (No fooling—they're scarce, as are batteries, cigarettes, razor blades. . . .)

Leave valuables at home. They may pose a great temptation to potential thieves, and it's not worth the worry of constantly looking after them or the hassle of (futilely) filling out a police report after a theft. But if you do bring something that needs to be locked up in the hotel safe, make sure you can get at it when you need it. You don't want to be running to make an 8 A.M. flight only to find that hotel personnel in charge of the safe are not available.

LUGGAGE. If you are flying to Central America, ask about the baggage allowance of the airlines you'll be using when you make your reservation. Most regulations are pretty standard, but details can change from airline to airline. Generally you are allowed two bags, with the length and width of the larger not to exceed 62 inches and the total dimensions of both not to exceed 106 inches. You can also bring aboard one carry-on, as long as you can stow it under the seat in front of you. Under this arrangement, no bag should weigh more than 70 pounds. As long as the volume of what you're bringing is under regulation, most airlines won't bother about the weight unless you've packed something extraordinarily heavy. Also, if the flight isn't that full, you can probably sneak on a little extra without being charged for excess baggage—but that's taking a chance.

If you're not flying, consider the possibility that you might end up toting your own bags more frequently than you had planned, notwithstanding the availability of all manner of baggage carriers all over Latin America. Take only what you can manage with two hands.

It is best not to bring expensive or brand-new luggage on a Latin American trip. Thieves figure that if the outside looks good, what's on the inside might be even better. Suitcases should have some sort of lock. Combination is best, since a key lock may be opened with *any* key from that series. Luggage should certainly be locked while in transit. Some travelers feel safer if they keep it locked when they're not in their hotel room, too, but this may serve as an advertisement that there's something inside worth taking. All luggage should bear a tag on the outside with the address and phone number of your destination as well as your home address and phone. A slip of paper with this information on the inside will identify the bag as yours if the outside tag is lost.

A carry-on bag should have a sturdy shoulder strap as well as a handle so you can hang on to it closely when you're not actually on a flight. Zippered compartments *inside* a main chamber are best on the theory that the more a thief will have to go through before finding what he's after, the less likely he is to bother. Important documents, such as your passport, airline tickets, medical prescriptions, vaccination booklet, credit cards, and driver's license, should be carried in an inside compartment, but you should be able to get at them fairly easily when you need them. They should never be locked inside checked baggage. Neither should one person carry all the documents (especially passports) for a group. Each person should carry his or her own. Toiletries, cosmetics, medicines, and jewelry also belong in your carry-on, as well as clean underwear, if not an entire change of clothing, in case your main luggage goes astray (not an unusual occurrence).

How you decide to carry your money and traveler's checks may depend on the kind of trip you're taking. Backpackers who are camping and staying in cheap *pensiones* may prefer a money belt, which can be worn while sleeping and taken into the shower if necessary. But this does make getting at one's valuables difficult, if not downright embarrassing, at border crossings or in banks and restaurants. Some packers and other super safety-conscious travelers use a pouch that can be carried inside the front of one's trousers or slung over one's neck and under the armpit. Many travelers find that a thick leather bag (difficult to slit open) with a strap that can be looped over the neck and *interior* compartments to hold money and important documents is safe enough. If not too large, the bag can be tucked inside the carry-on.

You might also take along a French net shopping bag, which scrunches down to a light handful but expands to hold great quantities of Latin American market purchases. A nylon tote bag that folds and zippers down to a small square may also be useful. If you've made more purchases than you planned, for instance, you can jettison dirty laundry into the tote to make room, then pack valuable purchases in your lockable suitcase for the flight home.

Never ever let your baggage out of your sight. You only need to turn your back once and it may be gone. Don't let the airport taxi drivers run off with your things in their effort to hustle business. Hang on to your bags and tell them to wait a sec—*un momento, por favor.*

MONEY AND OTHER LEGAL TENDER. Gone are the days when all Central American currencies were pegged at a fixed rate against the dollar. A number have been devalued recently or are in the process of being devalued. Also, with the current economic problems, there is often a better parallel rate in addition to an official one. To complicate things even further, Nicaragua recently replaced its national currency, the córdoba (which had been trading for several thousand to the dollar in the country's active black market), with a new córdoba valued at 10 to the dollar at press time. Its black market value is anyone's guess.

Exchange regulations vary from country to country. In Nicaragua,for instance, you must change $60 into córdobas at the official rate when you come into the country, whether or not you intend to spend $60 there. And in Costa Rica, changing money anywhere but at a bank or your hotel is punishable by a jail term or a heavy fine. The exchange rate at press time can be found in the *Practical Information* sections for each country, but do check out current rates and regulations before you leave.

The traveler's checks you take should be from an internationally recognized company, perferably one that will cash a personal check for you or be similarly helpful if you run short. You should get them in U.S. dollars and in as small denominations as possible. Most Central American currencies are virtually worthless outside their country of origin, since they are generally impossible to exchange once you leave. You want to exchange as little money as possible and spend all the local currency you've got before you leave (putting aside just enough for the departure tax).

Carrying cash is risky, but it does have its advantages. For one thing, traveler's checks are difficult to cash in some places, and the process may involve lengthy paperwork in countries like Costa Rica and El Salvador. For another, you're likely to get a much better exchange rate, and you won't have to pay a commission. In addition, U.S. dollars are welcome just about anywhere; for example, you can usually pay for a taxi from the airport to your hotel in dollars when you first arrive, then worry about changing money and figuring out the local currency later. Bring some cash, and make it small bills. One-dollar tips are easy for you and welcomed by maids and bellhops. (Save your quarters. U.S. coins can't be exchanged abroad.) Veteran travelers to Latin America often carry a wad of 20 or 30 one-dollar bills for just such purposes. In Nicaragua you may be asked to pay for hotels, international phone calls, international bus tickets, and guided tours in U.S. dollars. Also, when you're bargaining for textiles in Guatemala, you're likely to get a much better buy if you offer U.S. dollars. And you may be asked to pay entry or exit fees in dollars if you're crossing land borders.

Keep track of local holidays and weekends. You don't want to run short of money, only to find that the bank is closed. Also, ask when the local payday is. Banks are likely to be mobbed then.

If you're traveling outside of large cities, take lots of small bills in the local currency. Bear in mind that what may be a small bill in the city may be an unchangeable fortune in the countryside.

Because of currency controls, it may not be a good idea to have money sent from home. You may not be able to acquire dollars in the transaction, and you'd hate to end up with, say, $500 worth of Salvadorean colones. Still, if you think you may need to do this, ask your bank at home for the name of a correspondent bank where you'll be. When you're traveling, you can then telex your bank at home and get it to send funds to that local bank.

If you're planning to put a lot of your trip on plastic, bring a couple of credit cards. Major ones are widely used, but some business establishments won't accept all of them.

BACKGROUND READING. The U.S. Department of State publishes and periodically updates pamphlets called *Background Notes* on just about every country on earth. They cover people, geography, history, government, and economy and include a reading list, travel notes, and a map. You can purchase the ones for Central America for $2 apiece from the Superintendent of Documents, U.S. Government Printing Office, Washington, DC 20402; 202–783–3238.

The Department of State's Bureau of Consular Affairs puts out a booklet entitled *Your Trip Abroad,* which discusses everything from how to get a passport to clearing U.S. customs when you return home. It's a handy reference and is available for $1 from the Superintendent of Documents.

If you want to keep up with the news in Central America before you go or once you return, you can subscribe to English-language newspapers such as *The Tico Times,* Apartado Postal 4632, San José, Costa Rica (a weekly covering Central America, at $15 for three months); the *El Salvador News-Gazette,* Apartado Postal CG No. 225, San Salvador, El Salvador (a weekly covering El Salvador, at $25 a year); and the *Times of the Americas,* 910 17 St., N.W., Suite 632, Washington, DC 20006 (a biweekly covering all of Latin America, at $25 a year).

PHOTOGRAPHY. Central America is a wonderfully photogenic part of the world, and you will want to take a camera with you. Polaroids are great fun and good ice breakers if you don't mind giving away snap shots, but that can be expensive. For the traveler who wants pictures for an I-was-there album, an instamatic-type camera is a good idea. It will fit in your purse or pocket and won't attract the attention of thieves. If it wasn't too expensive, you won't worry about its being stolen if you leave it behind in your hotel.

The serious amateur will want to take a camera body with strap, a 28mm wide-angle lens for landscapes and crowded marketplaces, a 50mm f/1.8 lens for low-light situations, and some sort of telephoto. (Consider the difference in weight between a 100mm and a 400mm if you'll be walking a lot.) All lenses should have protective skylight filters and lens caps. If you're shooting in color, you might bring a polarizing filter to darken blue skies and an 81B to warm up dull days, but only take them if you know how to use them. Otherwise, they're just dead weight. Most of the action and color here is out of doors, but if you do a lot of indoor photography and don't mind carrying it all, pack a flash, tripod, and cable release. Bring two fresh batteries, and a typewriter eraser to clean oxidation from terminals. You might also tuck in a blower brush, lens tissues, and cotton swabs for cleaning, as well as several sizes of zip-lock bags and Silicagel packets to protect against moisture.

Estimating how much film you will need is always difficult, but whatever you figure, take more. (Each country has its own limit on how much film you can bring in, but customs officials are usually lenient about this if you are a tourist.) Film is terribly expensive in Central America, some kinds may be unavailable, and what is for sale may not be fresh or have been stored under improper conditions. Unless you're doing something special, most of your film should be medium speed (ASA 64 to ASA 125). Take along a few rolls of faster film for low-light situations (ASA 200 to ASA 400) and a few slow rolls (ASA 25) for bright light. Wildlife and bird photographers should concentrate film in the fast range, since many spectacular species live in dimly lit cloud forests. Keep your film as cool as you can, and don't take it out of its inner container until you're ready to use it, even if you've jettisoned the outer box to save on space.

To avoid problems leaving the country you are visiting and clearing customs on your return home, you should take purchase receipts or a list of all your equipment and its serial numbers to a U.S. customs office and register it before you leave. Foreign countries don't want you to sell the cameras and lenses you've brought with you, and the U.S. customs doesn't want you to sneak home without paying duty on a great photo equipment bargain you got abroad.

One time through a low-dose X-ray machine at an airport probably won't do your film any harm, but if you're taking a number of flights and film is X-rayed several times, your pictures may indeed be spoiled. You can protect film by putting it in a lead-lined film shield bag, which you can purchase at most camera stores. You might also put film in carry-on luggage and ask for a hand inspection. You should not travel with film in your camera, in case it accidentally gets sent through the X-rays or an overzealous customs agent insists on opening it. If you take rolls of 12 or 20 exposures, you can finish a roll of film before traveling without throwing away too many shots.

A camera bag is a definite target for thieves, but it's the best way to carry your equipment. If you're carrying an expensive camera, you're a temptation anyway, so just hang on to everything. Unbreakable metal straps may foil slash-and-run artists. There are some places it may not be wise to take your camera at all, and your hotel should be able to give you advice on this score. Do not leave photographic equipment in your hotel room. Have it locked up in the hotel safe if you can't take it with you.

The act of photographing in Central America is an educational experience these days. For one thing, the region is no longer as innocent as it once was, and you may be asked to pay anyone who appears as a subject in your pictures. Cuna Indians on Panama's San Blas Islands, for example, charge 25 cents per person per photo; natives of Santiago Atitlán in Guatemala charge one quetzal per click—and they count. In addition, photographing military subjects is almost out of the question. Even an innocent shot of a marine taking down the flag at the end of the day outside a U.S. Embassy may incense local army guards at the embassy entrance. When in doubt, move slowly, raise your eyebrows and ask with your eyes before you even focus.

Film processing in Central America, where available, often is not of the best quality. Wait till you get home. If you are on a lengthy trip and can't bear to haul all that film around, you can mail it back. Don't use film company mailers. Stamps reportedly don't stick to them very well, and they draw thieves' attention. Use a strong padded mailer, certify the package, and send it airmail. (Surface mail for this sort of thing might as well be sent by burro, it's so slow.) If you bought the film in the United States, you can send it home duty free. Just mark the package for customs: *Undeveloped photographic film of U.S. manufacture—Examine with care.*

BEFORE YOU GO. Leave your passport number, traveler's checks numbers, airline ticket data, credit card numbers, and any other information you might lose and need in a hurry, along with a copy of your itinerary, with a friend or relative.

GETTING THERE AND GETTING AROUND. By plane. Most visitors fly to Central America. International flights connect the United States with all the region's capitals and some large cities as well. New York, Miami, New Orleans, Houston, and Los Angeles are the U.S. gateway cities to the region. Many flights originate in Mexico City, too, and a whole network of intraregional flights connects Central America's major cities. Latin American airlines are generally the ones that serve this part of the world, and they include *Taca, Tan-Sahsa, Copa, SAM, Aviateca, Lacsa, Aerónica,* and *Mexicana. Pan Am* flies into Guatemala City, San José, and Panama City, *Eastern* into Guatemala City, San Salvador, Panama City, and San José, Costa Rica, and *KLM* and *Iberia* serve all three capitals. Panama is the odd country out here, with connections to more U.S. cities as well as to South American and European countries on a variety of international carriers.

Airline fares are in a great state of flux these days. They change daily—literally. And how much you pay will depend on a number of factors, such as your point of departure and destination, the time you are traveling, whether your trip is part of a package, and whether the airline you are using has a special fare offer. Be aware, also, that if a carrier drops a route for any reason, there is automatically less competition, and other airlines that fly to the same destination may boost prices precipitously. Nevertheless, we have included here a list of round-trip fares out of Miami to each Central American capital, valid as of this writing, to give a rough idea of how much you can expect to pay. Lower fares, of course, often carry more restrictions.

Belize City, Belize	$285	Tan-Sahsa and Taca
Tegucigalpa, Honduras	$350	Tan-Sahsa and Taca
Guatemala City, Guatemala	$424	Tan-Sahsa
	$394	Pan Am
	$299–$376	Eastern

San Salvador, El Salvador	$390	Tan-Sahsa
	$390	Eastern
Managua, Nicaragua	$390	Tan-Sahsa
San José, Costa Rica	$352	Tan-Sahsa
	$345	Lacsa
	$345	Pan Am
	$289	Eastern
Panama City, Panama	$339	Pan Am
	$307	Air Panama
	$289	Eastern

If you are planning to travel from one Central American country to the next by plane, you should think carefully about whether you want to purchase your tickets ahead of time in the States. If you do so and later decide to alter your arrangements—leave at a different time, say—and need to change carriers, you may have trouble getting one airline to endorse the ticket over to the next. On the other hand, if you wait till you're on the road, you may have to pay a local sales tax (5 percent in Honduras, 10 percent in Costa Rica, for instance).

Latin airlines are chronically overbooked. Make sure you reconfirm your reservation within 72 hours of your departure, then check again 24 hours before flight time. Arrive at the airport with *plenty* of time to spare.

Don't book flights back to back on the same day or expect to fly into a Central American country and make quick connections to ground transport. Leave yourself enough time for Latin time. Baggage handling may not be nearly as fast as in the United States, and clearing customs and immigration can be agonizingly slow.

Most Central American countries have internal airlines that serve larger cities and popular tourist spots. In Guatemala, for example, tourists choose between the national airline Aviateca or air-taxi service to the town of Flores to visit the nearby Mayan site, Tikal. El Salvador and Nicaragua have no local airlines, but charter flights are easy to arrange. (The service is still private in Nicaragua and is called *Alas.* Don't panic. That means "wings" in Spanish.)

By ship. Costa Rica and Panama appear on the itineraries of a number of luxury cruises. Panama City, or the port of Balboa, is especially popular because many ships sail to or through the Panama Canal on their routes. One trip might leave from Tampa, Florida, for instance, calling at Playa del Carmen on the island of Cozumel off Mexico, cruising to and from Gatún Lake in the Panama Canal, then stopping at Aruba, La Guaira, Grenada, Martinique, and Saint Thomas before returning to Tampa. Many round-the-world cruises travel through the Panama Canal, and some put in at Puerto Limón, Costa Rica, or, most likely, Balboa, Panama. Other cruises—out of San Diego, for example—might include stops at Mexican ports on the way down to Central America as well as land connections to San José, Costa Rica, a tour of Panama's San Blas Islands, and transit of the Panama Canal with stops at each end in Colón and Panama City. Still other ships sail from Alaska, stopping in Balboa, Panama, and transversing the Panama Canal on their way to Europe. It all depends on what you want and how much you can pay. Some short cruises cost as little as $2,000. The more monumental ones can run into the tens of thousands.

Cruise lines serving Costa Rica or Panama include *Holland America-Westours,* 300 Elliott Ave. W., Seattle, WA 98119, 800–426–0327; *Royal Viking Line,* 750 Battery St., San Francisco, CA 94111, 800–422–8000; *Cunard Line,* 555 Fifth Ave., New York, NY 10017, 212–880–7500; *Exploration Cruise Lines,* 1500 Metropolitan Park Bldg., Olive Way at Boren Ave., Seattle, WA 98101, 800–426–0600; and *Sitmar Cruises,* Century City, 10100 Santa Monica Blvd., Los Angeles, CA 90067, 800–421–0880.

Ford's International Cruise Guide, published quarterly, gives details about a great number of U.S. cruises going to all sorts of places. It costs $9.95 an issue and can be obtained from Ford's Travel Guides, 19448 Londelius St., North Ridge, CA 91324.

The same company puts out *Ford's Freighter Travel Guide* semiannually for $8.95. Travel on a passenger-carrying freighter is much cheaper than on a luxury liner, but it does depend on the commercial considerations of trade routes and cargo.

By bus. A brochure put out by Panama's Tourist Bureau notes that a bus ride from Panama City to San José, Costa Rica, "costs about one-fifth of the air fare, takes about 16 times as long." That about sums up bus travel in Central America, but in a region where money is scarce and time is no object, it is *the* method of transportation par excellence.

If you're coming down through Mexico by bus, *Greyhound* travels as far south as Laredo, Texas. They will sell you a through ticket to Mexico City, but since they feel the Mexican connection is unreliable, they won't quote a schedule. You have to cross the border and get on the Mexican bus yourself.

A company called *Ticabus* used to run Greyhound-style buses to all the Central American captials, but it reportedly has suspended most services. Now it connects only Costa Rica and Panama. Other lines are still making the long runs between countries, but no one seems to be going everywhere, the way Ticabus did.

If you are traveling by bus, you should arrange all your visas ahead of time. You cannot hop out of one of these buses at the border and try to negotiate a tourist card. In fact, the bus driver will probably run everyone's passport and personal identification by the border guards en masse. These are popular routes, so you should also book your passage well in advance of when you want to leave and be prepared for layovers of a couple of days in capital cities until you can get another passage to the next capital.

The local bus network in Central America is vast. Schedules may be erratic, buses are slow and often crowded with passengers standing in the aisle, and you may have to share a seat with a chicken or two. Buses are also extraordinarily cheap and go just about everywhere, not only stopping at various locations within large cities but also going off the highways down dirt roads to tiny towns.

On all Latin American buses, you will want to sit toward the front of the bus. The rear is quite a bit more bouncy, and the engine is located there, so it can be hot and noisy. Rest stops are few and far between and may not be even close to U.S. standards, so go easy on liquids beforehand and take Lomotil for diarrhea.

We do not recommend traveling alone at night on buses; inquire locally about the safety of this.

By taxi. All Central American capitals, and some large cities, have taxis. They are much less expensive than those at home, running not more than a dollar or two for a normal ride and certainly less than $10 an hour. Taxis traveling to and from airports may charge more. In addition to the flexibility they offer over city buses, they also remove you from the theft and sexual harassment (if you're a woman) fostered by the close confines of public transport. They are often not metered, so agree on a price before you get in. You'll get a better deal, of course, if you speak Spanish and are familiar with local customs. Nicaragua is somewhat of an exception, since all its taxis have been converted to *colectivos*—vehicles shared by a group of people all going more or less in the same direction or to the same part of the city.

By car. Other forms of transportation can't beat being able to throw your gear into a car and take off whenever you want to wherever strikes your fancy. Flying into your destination and renting a car locally is the quickest and least arduous way of acquiring wheels during a trip. Major car rental companies, and sometimes local ones, have facilities in all Central American capitals, especially at airports and in large hotels. But they tend to be expensive, as is gasoline, almost all over the region.

In Nicaragua company rental cars are awful, because the bad roads have beaten them into rattletrap condition. Your best bet is to rent a car from a private person. Ask around outside the *Intercontinental Hotel* in Managua. Prices vary according to how many journalists on expense accounts are in town, but in Nicaragua they run something like $50 a day for a car (paid in dollars, you supply the gas), and $100 a day for a four-wheel-drive vehicle. A driver will cost you an extra $20 a day, but if he can double as a mechanic, he'll be worth every cent. In Belize, several companies offer cars for $50–$100 per day.

People with a good chunk of vacation time who genuinely enjoy driving may consider taking their own car down. It's a long haul, but you can get all the way down to Panama's Darién Gap on the Pan-American Highway. (The route stops in the Darién about 200 miles short of the border with Colombia. The official reason the highway has not been completed is that it would encourage the transmission of South America's hoof-and-mouth disease northward. It also, obviously, impedes the northbound drug trade. When the road will be finished, if at all, is anyone's guess.)

Before you set off on such a safari, you should have a mechanic check your car from top to bottom. Mechanics in Central America can be quite good and cheap (they'll do 10 hours of work on your car for about $60 in Honduras, for example), but you would hate to get stuck in some out-of-the-way place over something you could have prevented at the outset.

Precautions notwithstanding, things do go wrong. Make sure you're prepared. Take a jack, and know how to use it, as well as a kit of standard car tools. You may not know what to do with all of them, but mechanics along the way will. A repair manual with diagrams may be similarly useful. Good tires are a must in this part of the world, as is a spare. Tires take a beating over potholes, mud and gravel, and cobblestones. Pack as many spare parts as you can. Things like a fan belt, an extra diaphragm for the gas pump, a spare condenser and rotors for the distributor, spark plugs, an extra set of points, a washer for the gas filter, and fuses for the lighting system may not always be available along the way. (Latin American mechanics are wonderfully inventive, since they often can't get proper parts and have to come up with novel solutions to keep local vehicles on the road. There are limits, however, and you should prepare yourself for the possibility of having to wait for a part to be flown in from the States if something major gives out.) Jumper cables are a good idea, and also flares, a water jug (radiators often boil over at highland altitudes, and you may have to make a water run to the nearest house or village), electrical tape, and a flashlight, as well as a funnel, length of hose, and gas container for siphoning gas. (In some countries, like Guatemala, it is considered a normal courtesy to give a bit of gas to motorists who have run out along the road. And you may run short, yourself.)

A U.S. driver's license is generally recognized in Central America, but an international driving permit issued by the American Automobile Association is a good thing to take along as well. It's valid in all countries in the region and has an explanatory page in Spanish, so there will be no doubts or misunderstandings. It costs $5, and you'll need two passport-size photos.

Good maps are essential for this sort of venture. Bradt Enterprises (95 Harvey St., Cambridge, MA 02140; 617–492–8776) is reputedly the best source of Latin American maps in the United States, though proprietor George Bradt admits that Central American maps are particularly difficult to come by these days because of current political difficulties. Maps put out by Exxon and Texaco are good but also may be hard to find. Failing those possibilities, you may have to pick maps up as you go along. National geographic institutes in the capital cities of many Central American countries often have splendid maps that show types of roads, the size of towns (and, hence, an indication of the quality of food and lodging), the location of gas stations, and points of interest (such as archeological sites).

Since you will be driving through Mexico, you will need to get in touch with the nearest Mexican consulate to negotiate a transit visa for your car. If you don't do this ahead of time, Mexican border officials may send you back to the nearest consulate in the United States, thus adding an extra day to your trip, or may charge you whatever fee they feel like, which may be far in excess of the official rate.

You can purchase car insurance for your trip through Mexico at the U.S.–Mexico border, and if you get it from *Sanborn's,* they will supply you with detailed road logs that take you town by town, street by street, through Mexico on the route you have planned. You can write ahead for more information and a list of their offices to Box 1210, McAllen, TX 78501.

Some countries, like Belize, require you to have an internationally valid car insurance policy. Even in countries where it is not mandatory, it's a good idea. People are generally not cautious behind the wheel, and accidents are frequent. It's a macho society—Costa Ricans *boast* that they have the region's highest rate of auto accident fatalities. You may be able to arrange a policy before you leave home from a U.S. company dealing in international insurance, but as of March 1, 1986, AAA discontinued its Central American coverage. Policies issued in Guatemala are often good for the whole region, or you can negotiate the matter country by country.

Border crossings are the bane of driving in Central America. Countries are small, so crossings are frequent—and they often seem to take forever, although it may only be hours. You will need vehicle registration papers as well as a passport so that officials may stamp a car entry permit into it. (They want to make sure you leave with a vehicle if you enter with it.) You will have to clear immigration as well as customs (two stops), and you may be asked to take just about everything out of your car. Your car probably will be fumigated as well. (Central American economies are heavily based on agriculture, and countries can't afford to have devastating pests spread across the region.) All of this usually requires a series of fees. And even when you think you've left it all behind, there may be more customs officials down the road double-checking the honesty of those at the border. Look and act your best at border crossings. There is no international audience at these border crossings, as there is at airports, and *everything* is up to the discretion of the border authorities. Try to cross during the normal workday, and bear in mind that the hours officials work on each side of a contiguous border may be different. After-hours crossings may cost more. If your Spanish isn't good, border crossings may be even more difficult; keep this in mind before deciding to drive through Central America at all.

Road conditions vary widely here, and even in the same country you may find they range from perfectly fine highways (usually well-traveled routes such as the Guatemala City–Antigua run) to rock and mudhole swaths that don't look like much more than wide cowpaths (the road through Guatemala's Petén to Tikal, for instance). The Pan-American Highway is in *great* disrepair in spots, so if you're traveling on that route, ask as you go along. Locals may know better and faster ways of getting to where you want to go. Roads are the main transport arteries through the region, so highways are likely to be filled with exhaust-belching, road-hogging passenger buses and freight trucks.

Many road signs nowadays are done in pictures, and the ones below are fairly common. Still, many directions are given in Spanish. Even if you don't speak the language, you should be able to recognize them if you are driving. The ones you're most likely to see are the following:

alto	stop
bajada	downgrade
bajada frene con motor	steep hill; brake with engine
camino angosto	narrow road
camino cerrado	road closed
camino en reparación	road under repair
carril izquierdo sólo para rebasar	left lane for passing only
ceda el paso	yield
conserve su derecha	keep right
cruce	crossroad, crossing
cuidado	be careful
curva forzada	sharp turn
curva peligrosa	dangerous curve
despacio	slow
desviación	detour
dirección única	one way
escuela	school
grava suelta	loose gravel
hombres trabajando	men at work
no estacionarse	no parking

no hay paso	road closed
parada obligatoria	full stop
peligro or *peligroso*	danger or dangerous
pendiente peligrosa	dangerous grade
poblado próximo	town nearby
puente angosto	narrow bridge
siga en fila	follow single file
topes	traffic control bumps
una vía	one way
un solo carril	one lane
viraje obligatorio	obligatory turn
zona de derrumbes	landslide zone

The *puente angosto* sign is often found in the countryside, sometimes hand-lettered. It means not only that the bridge is narrow, but also that it will accommodate only one vehicle at a time. Such structures are negotiated on a first-come, first-serve basis.

A circular sign bearing two crossed black lines and FC (for *ferrocarril*) indicates a railroad crossing.

Topes or *túmulos* are a series of washboardlike bumps designed to make vehicles slow down, often at the entrance to a town or to a residential neighborhood in the city. They can be quite wicked, so take them very easy.

Shoulders of the roads are often narrow, and pedestrians use them as sidewalks, night and day. Also, livestock is often unpenned and may stroll across the road toward the grass that's greener on the other side. Piles of rocks or tree branches that signaled a breakdown may be left on the highway after vehicles have finally moved on. All this, plus dubious road conditions, make night driving extremely dangerous and something to avoid. If you must travel at night, try to follow a local car (at a distance). The driver will be familiar with the road and may react to anything out of the ordinary more quickly than you can.

It's a good idea to slow down and beep your horn before you take sharp curves in the mountains. If you barrel on through, you may get halfway around and come face to face with another vehicle that has careened into your lane.

If you're going up into the mountains or on unpaved roads, use a four-wheel-drive vehicle with high suspension. Even the road to Chichicastenango, Guatemala, may stall an ordinary car with four gears.

Unleaded gas may be hard to find in Mexico, and it does not exist farther south, so you will have to unhook your catalytic converter. Never let your gas tank fall below the half-full mark. There may be a gas station marked up ahead on the map, but it may be waiting for a shipment and not have a drop. Nicaragua is the only country in Central America (so far) where gas is rationed, though you can usually buy coupons from taxi drivers or small boys who have managed to acquire them under dubious circumstances. If you run out of gas along the road, sometimes the local army commander can be convinced to give you a few gallons to get you on your way.

Unscrew your U.S. license plates and put them *inside* the car, showing through the back window. They tend to disappear, since they are great souvenirs. And in countries with political problems, they may be lifted

Highway Signs

STOP

NO PASSING

HORIZONTAL CLEARANCE

MAXIMUM WEIGHT (METRIC TONS)

PEDESTRIANS KEEP LEFT

SPEED LIMIT (IN K.P.H.)

NO BICYCLES

NO PEDESTRIANS

PARKING LIMIT

ONE-HOUR PARKING

NO LEFT TURN

NO U TURN

NO PARKING

USE RIGHT LANE

NO TRUCKS

INSPECTION

CONTINUOUS TURN

KEEP RIGHT

DO NOT ENTER

TRAILER CAMP

AIRPORT

HOSPITAL

MECHANIC

FERRY

GAS STATION

RESTAURANT

RESTROOMS

TELEPHONE

SLIPPERY ROAD LOOSE GRAVEL

VERTICAL CLEARANCE

YIELD RIGHT-OF-WAY

STEEP HILL

LANDSLIDE AREA

CATTLE

SCHOOL CROSSING

MEN WORKING

TWO-WAY TRAFFIC

TRAFFIC CIRCLE

SIGNAL

R.R. CROSSING

BUMPS

NARROW BRIDGE

DIP

by unsavory characters who put them on their own cars, which they then use to commit dastardly deeds.

Take everything that is easily removable off the outside of your car and stash it in the trunk. Likewise, use a gas cap with a lock. And don't leave anything of value in your car, locked or not. At night leave your car only in an attended lot (*estacionamiento*) or in your hotel parking space. If you park on the street during the day and someone offers to watch your car for you (usually a small boy or an old man), agree and let him know you'll pay a few units of local coin when you return. If he knows he's getting paid, at least he won't steal anything.

Theft of car parts is particularly bad in Nicaragua, since that country has absolutely no spare parts for any kind of car. (They're making oil gaskets out of paper these days.)

If you are going to Central America for a substantial stretch of time and want to ship your car down, you will need a freight forwarder to book your car on a ship and deal with the copious paperwork. Such agents are listed in the telephone yellow pages of port cities, and the port authority may be able to help you find one as well. Cost will vary according to how heavy your car is and how far you're sending it, but a Baltimore–Costa Rica shipment, for instance, might run $1,500.

By rail. Railroads generally transport bananas, not people, in Central America. There are two well-known exceptions that tourists might be interested in: the train linking San José and Puerto Limón, Costa Rica, and the one that runs across the Isthmus of Panama between Panama City and Colón. Both have regular daily schedules.

CREATURE COMFORTS AND COSTS. There are hotels and restaurants to fit almost every taste and pocketbook in Central America, but the selection, as well as the price, will depend very much on where you are, both within a given country, and from country to country within the region. Deluxe international-name hotels with pools, room service, air-conditioning, televisions—the works—are mostly in capital cities, though hotels in the Belize cays and the resort islands off the Honduran coast can be just as luxurious and expensive. A room in a Honduras Bay Island hotel, including boating, snorkeling, and three meals a day, may run $150 a day, double occupancy. A double at the Marriott in Panama City is around $125 a day. It all depends where you are.

Capitals and large cities have the widest selection of hotels, ranging from the top of the line noted above to spartan pensiones or *casas de huéspedes* (guest houses) where a room and a shared bath may go for $5 or so. Mid-range hotels can be found for around $25 to $35 (in Belize City, $25–$100 per day). They may lack the pool and air-conditioning, but you probably will get your own bath. What they lack in amenities, they may well make up for in charm—some are lovely Colonial-style buildings with cool tile floors and bougainvillea-decked patios.

Outside big cities, the selection—and the luxury—are more limited, but prices are quite a bit lower as well. In the colonial town of Antigua, just a 45-minute drive outside Guatemala City, a double room in a quiet, clean small hotel that was once an old Spanish house built around a garden courtyard may cost $15. The farther you stray from modern bustle, the fewer creature comforts you are likely to find.

Restaurants tend to reflect the situation of hotels. In capitals and large cities, there is generally a wide selection of domestic and international cuisines at a range of prices. In San José, Costa Rica, for instance, you can get a filet mignon for two for $25. At the other end of the scale, a meat stew with tortillas and beans might be a couple of dollars. Smaller towns may have only one or two less expensive restaurants, and the menu will be limited to local dishes—sometimes written each day on a chalk board—depending on the produce available.

Within the region as a whole, Panama is probably the most expensive. The prices of hotel accommodations, restaurant meals, and evening entertainment are definitely on the high side, since this is an international business and banking center, and prices are what the market will bear. Department store price tags are about on par with those in the United States, and you probably won't do any better with the bargains in duty-free stores than you would in a weekend of shrewd shopping in New York.

On the other end of the scale, El Salvador is quite inexpensive. Dinner at El Bodegón, one of San Salvador's best restaurants, runs about $15 a person. (That used to include French or Chilean wine, but the government's recent ban on luxury imports will probably dry up the foreign spirits.)

A few additional notes about hotels and restaurants. Some hotels do not have hot water all the time. Inquire about hours when you check in, or you may be surprised with a cold shower in the morning.

At times some places may not have water at all. In Santa Elena, the closest town to Tikal in Guatemala, for instance, there is no water during certain hours of certain days. The hotel management will let you know. In Managua, to pick another example, water is shut off for one day a week all over town during the dry season. If you're staying in the Intercontinental, maids will fill your bathtub with water the night before the dry day and instruct you on how to flush the toilet. (You, as a dollar-toting foreigner, will have access to items in dollar stores which ordinary Nicaraguans can't easily purchase. You might consider tipping your hotel maid in such merchandise—aspirin, razor blades, cigarettes, etc.—rather than money.)

Power failures black out many parts of Central America fairly frequently, particularly in Managua. Bring a flashlight.

Motels and autohotels rent by the hour in this part of the world and are no place for weary tourists.

Before you plan your trip, find out when major holidays and local fiestas are celebrated. They are often fun to see and participate in, but the rest of the country may be on the move, too, and hotel reservations may be hard to get. Holy Week is particularly bad for accommodations all over the region, and Panama is mobbed by shoppers before Christmas, so make sure you have a hotel room waiting for you before you set off from home.

Taxes and tipping. A number of countries charge a tourism tax on hotel room bills—usually 5 to 10 percent. Also, a value-added tax, or IVA (*impuesto de valor agregado*), may be tacked on to your restaurant check. A typical IVA is that of Belize, which ranges from 7–10 percent, depending on the article or service purchased. In Costa Rica, a 10-percent gratuity will automatically appear on your restaurant check. Elsewhere in the region, 10 percent is a reasonable tip, except in Panama, where the constant stream of high rollers from around the world has boosted tipping to an international 15 to 20 percent.

SPORTS. Central America offers all sorts of participatory and spectator sports for the athletically minded or competitive traveler. In many instances equipment can be rented, but if you prefer your own, pack it. A partial list includes: golfing, tennis, bowling, swimming (in pools, Atlantic and Pacific oceans, lakes, and thermal springs), volcano climbing (with the Club de Andinismo in Guatemala, for instance), fishing (sport fishing tackle is reportedly in short supply in Costa Rica, so bring your own), skin diving and snorkeling (you might want to bring your own mask, fins, and snorkel), sailing, waterskiing, hang gliding (at Lake Atitlán in Guatemala), surfing (supposed to be good off Puerto Quepos in Costa Rica, and so spectacular off El Salvador that surfers continued to visit even through the worst of that country's troubles), wildlife and bird-watching (bring binoculars), hiking (wear high-topped boots against snakes in the back country), bullfighting (strictly a spectator sport), horseback riding, baseball (popular all over the Caribbean, and the national sport of Nicaragua, believe it or not), spelunking (in Belize), cricket (also in Belize), and whitewater rafting (in Costa Rica). For those of you who like a friendly wager, there is horse racing in Panama (all of the Panamanian jockeys now working in the United States got their start at the President Remon Racetrack there), cockfighting and gambling (roulette and a type of blackjack in some hotels in Costa Rica; roulette, dice games, blackjack, and slot machines in Panamanian casinos).

SPEAKING SPANISH. The shape that your trip ultimately takes will depend on how much Spanish you speak. Although Belize is an English-speaking country, some Indian groups still speak original native tongues, and English is the compulsory second language in schools in Panama, the region as a whole is Spanish-speaking. In capitals and large cities many people, including tourism professionals such as hotel receptionists, speak excellent English and will, in fact, prefer speaking that with you if your Spanish is less than fluent. Many more people in spots frequented by tourists speak a passable variety of English, and they'll have as much fun practicing with you as you will trying your Spanish out on them. If you have come to Central America on a guided tour or are spending most of your vacation at a large hotel in a capital city and taking local tours to see the sights, the vocabulary you will need is minimal.

If, however, you plan to be a bit more adventurous and perhaps try out local public transport, you should know enough Spanish to at least get you back to your hotel. (Remember to keep the name and address of your hotel in a purse or pocket. If you get hopelessly lost, you can always hop a taxi, show the driver your cheat sheet and be deposited safely back where you started.) A basic vocabulary of maybe 500 words that will allow you to order food in a restaurant and inquire about transportation routes, fares, and schedules—Where does it go? How much does it cost? When does it leave?—will help enormously, and you might tote a pocket dictionary or phrasebook along so you can look things up as you go. As some travelers point out, though, it's not formulating the question that's the hard part. It's understanding the answer.

The farther off the beaten tourist track you get, the more heavily you will have to rely on Spanish. Most people in small towns in the countryside will not speak or understand English at all—and if their first language is an Indian dialect, they may not speak much Spanish either. If your Spanish is similarly weak, you may find yourself incommunicado, and although you may be able to mimic your way through a meal, fixing a car breakdown is another matter entirely. In fact, it is inadvisable to drive down to Central America or to drive extensively around parts of the region with serious political problems if you speak no Spanish. You can't count on border guards or personnel at civilian and military road checkpoints to speak much English at all, and a trouble-free passage through those spots depends on your doing precisely what they tell you to. (This is not to say that you might not get by those spots more easily if you pretend to speak less Spanish than you do, if you're fluent. Exceptional ability in Spanish may indicate to a soldier that you have been trained by the U.S. government.)

When you're learning a language, there is no substitute for being in a country where it is spoken, and many travelers find that a session or two of Central American Spanish classes helps them polish what they already have learned in the States or gives them a good foundation for future study. Language schools are numerous in Latin America, and you should be able to find an intensity and a schedule that suits you. Programs in Guatemala have a reputation for being particularly good at total immersion, with students housed in non-English-speaking homes and paired one-on-one with a tutor during the day so they are obliged to speak Spanish all the time.

ELECTRICITY. Electrical current in most of Central America is 110 volts–60 cycles, and U.S. plugs are used. There is usually not a third opening for a grounding prong, however, so bring an adapter if your appliances need it. Electricity in some countries (Belize and Honduras, for example) may run at 220 volts in places, but that's usually in private homes. Blackouts are not unusual all over the region, so your razor, travel alarm, hair dryer, curlers, and radio–cassette player should be battery-powered unless you don't mind waiting till the current comes back on. You should have no problem clearing customs with any of those appliances if it is obvious they are for your personal use. Officials at land borders may take longer to sift through it all, though. Larger appliances may require more red tape, so check with embassies or tourist offices before you set off.

MEASUREMENTS. Central American countries function under the metric system. Aside from buying food by the kilo at the market, you are most likely to have to deal with this when you're keeping track of your car speed on highways in kilometers per hour (about double miles per hour) and filling the tank with liters of gasoline (about four per gallon). The following chart should help you keep it all straight.

CONVERTING METRIC TO U.S. MEASUREMENTS

Multiply:	by:	to find:
Length		
millimeters (mm)	.039	inches (in)
meters (m)	3.28	feet (ft)
meters	1.09	yards (yd)
kilometers (km)	.62	miles (mi)

Multiply:	by:	to find:
Area		
hectare (ha)	2.47	acres
Capacity		
liters (L)	1.06	quarts (qt)
liters	.26	gallons (gal)
liters	2.11	pints (pt)
Weight		
gram (g)	.04	ounce (oz)
kilogram (kg)	2.20	pounds (lb)
metric ton (MT)	.98	tons (t)
Power		
kilowatt (kw)	1.34	horsepower (hp)
Temperature		
degrees Celsius	9/5 (then add 32)	degrees Fahrenheit

CONVERTING U.S. TO METRIC MEASUREMENTS

Length		
inches (in)	25.40	millimeters (mm)
feet (ft)	.30	meters (m)
yards (yd)	.91	meters
miles (mi)	1.61	kilometers (km)
Area		
acres	.40	hectares (ha)
Capacity		
pints (pt)	.47	liters (L)
quarts (qt)	.95	liters
gallons (gal)	3.79	liters
Weight		
ounces (oz)	28.35	grams (g)
pounds (lb)	.45	kilograms (kg)
tons (t)	1.11	metric tons (MT)
Power		
horsepower (hp)	.75	kilowatts (kw)
Temperature		
degrees Fahrenheit	5/9 (after subtracting 32)	degrees Celsius

TIME ZONES. Central America is six hours behind Greenwich Mean Time, the same as U.S. Central Standard Time. Panama is five hours behind GMT, the same as U.S. Eastern Standard Time. There is no daylight savings in Central America, so calculate accordingly.

COMMUNICATIONS. Central America is connected to the rest of the world by long-distance telephone, cable, and telex lines. You may have to wait awhile in some countries for an international phone call to go through, and calls are liable to be expensive—about $13 for a three-minute call from Guatemala to Alabama, for instance. Calls from your hotel room may end up being quite a bit more expensive than normal long-distance rates, so inquire before dialing. You may also only be able to make collect calls to North America, not Europe.

Sending mail home is no problem, though it's best to use airmail rather than the slow surface service. Getting mail sent down to you is another matter. If you know where you'll be staying, you can have it sent to your hotel. Tell the sender to mark it "hold for arrival" in case it gets there before you do. If a letter is mailed to you in care of a U.S. embassy or consulate, it probably will be returned to the sender, though other countries' officials may be more helpful for their citizens. And although American Express offices were once *the* place for international wanderers to pick up mail sent to them abroad, it is an expensive service that the company would rather not continue. If you're interested, ask your local representative whether the office in your destination country is still in the mail business. If so, you'll have to have an American Express credit card or traveler's checks to use the service. The main post office of each city will hold mail for you as long as it is addressed care of the *lista de correos* at the *oficina central de correos*. If the postal worker can't find something you know should be there, have him look under your middle name. Latin last names are compounded differently, and it may be filed under that. Usually you will be charged a small fee for each letter you pick up. Do not have cash or checks sent through the mail. They probably won't make it. Do not have packages sent to you and do not send down packages to friends once you return home. Customs duties are often many times what the contents are worth.

SAFETY. Theft is a big problem for tourists all over Central America. Foreign visitors are the haves traveling in a have-not part of the world, and of course their possessions will represent a great temptation to certain segments of the population. We have given advice on how to protect yourself in various sections above, but it really is not all that different from what you would do in a big city in the United States. There's no need to spoil your trip with paranoia. A healthy case of caution will do. Violent crimes are rare here. You may get your purse snatched, but it is unlikely that you will be physically assaulted in the process. Belize City (dubbed Pirate City by some), Panama City, and the Darién are probably the most dangerous spots as far as crime is concerned.

Drivers are crazy throughout the region. Exercise *extreme* caution when you are crossing streets.

Political turmoil and the dangers it presents are of great concern to travelers, of course, but these are precisely the subjects it is most difficult to give definite advice about. Situations vary greatly from country to country, and things are changing so quickly that a hot spot one day might be safe the next. Still, the whole region is not out in the streets shooting at one another the way it sometimes seems in newspapers and TV news. You can travel quite comfortably and quietly through much of Central America, and danger is the exception rather than the rule. The following, as general rules of thumb, may help you stay clear of those exceptions.

The places where everyone else is working, playing, and traveling are the safest. The farther you get away from population centers and into mountains and jungles, the more likely you are to run into something scary. Border areas are particularly bad. The Guatemala–Belize border isn't very friendly, since Guatemala doesn't recognize Belize as a country. The Guatemala–Mexico border has a great Guatemalan refugee problem. The Honduras–Nicaragua and Costa Rica–Nicaragua borders are tense for political–ideological reasons. In addition, specific areas within a country should be avoided. As of this writing, for instance, northwestern Guatemala sees sporadic guerrilla action and army "sweeps," and there is still conflict in the eastern part of El Salvador. The danger in these areas is not so much that you would be a target of attack as that you might blunder into something unknowingly. The U.S. Department of State's Office of Overseas Citizens Emergency Center (2201 C St. NW, Washington, DC 20520; 202–647–5225) issues travel advisories that evaluate dangerous situations around the world. You can write for copies on Central American countries, and travel agents, airlines, and passport agencies should have them as well. Once you're on your trip, local people you meet will be able to fine-tune that information, telling you exactly where to say away from and what roads have been closed. They will also be able to fill you in on local quirks that you wouldn't otherwise know about. In El Salvador, for instance, tying a white handkerchief to the antenna of your car indicates that it is a civilian vehicle and the guerrillas know to leave it alone.

A number of countries have set up military and civilian checkpoints along the roads. As a tourist, you should be able to pass through quite easily as long as you do what you are told. Usually you will be waved on without even being asked for your passport if it's obvious that you're a tourist. In general while traveling in the region, but specifically at these checkpoints, never make derogatory remarks in English. People may understand more than they let on.

Officials are very document-minded here. Make sure your papers are in order and always carry them with you. It is against the law not to have proper documentation with you in Costa Rica, and you may be jailed if you don't.

Bribing authorities is common in many parts of Latin America. But don't try it unless you know what you're doing.

If you're concerned about conditions where you will be traveling, you might consider registering with the nearest U.S. embassy or consulate so that officials can get hold of you in an emergency. If things go amiss, friends and relatives at home can call the Department of State's Office of Overseas Citizen Services at 202–647–5225 to find out if you're all right.

Consular officials can be of great help to you if you run into trouble, though they do have their limits. They can't get you out of jail, but they can help find you a lawyer, try to get you relief from inhumane or unhealthy conditions, and arrange for loans for a dietary supplement. They can help you wire friends or relatives for money if you run short or are robbed. The Department of State doesn't like to advertise it, but consular officials can make you a small *reimbursable* loan to tide you over while you wait for funds from home, and they can make you a *reimbursable* repatriation loan to get you back to the United States (*not* to continue your trip) if you can't arrange to get more money from home. They also deal with medical emergencies, deaths, missing persons, and various types of legal matters, such as notarizing documents that you hope you'll never need. If you want to know about this kind of assistance in detail, you can write for the *Handbook of Consular Services* from the Public Affairs Staff, Bureau of Consular Affairs, U.S. Department of State, Washington, DC 20520.

ILLEGAL ACTIVITIES. Drugs are not the problem in Central America that they are in Mexico and South America, but several countries in the region are being used as trans-shipment areas, so illegal substances are around. Penalties in drug cases are stiff (*years* in jail under unsavory conditions, to say the least), and generally no distinction is made between hard and soft drugs and between possession and trafficking. If you are caught with illegal drugs, you will receive no special quarter or treatment simply because you are a foreigner. You will be handled like any other person in that country arrested in a similar situation. The legal process is a long one, and you may be imprisoned without bail for years until your case is heard, on the theory that you are guilty until proven innocent. Don't count on being able to serve part of your sentence in a U.S. jail either. Panama is the only country in the region that has a prisoner transfer treaty with the United States.

As we have pointed out previously, appearance has a lot to do with how officials treat you on this score. If you look scruffy and act at all disoriented, officials may tend to suspect that you are carrying drugs with you—and may plant some on you for good measure. If you roll your own cigarettes, officials may view you as suspect, too. Leave the rolling papers at home.

Conducting unauthorized archaeological excavations or trafficking in antiquities are illegal in many parts of the region. Stick to reproductions. A variety of other activities are illegal in various countries, too. In Belize, for instance, it is against the law to remove from a reef, and export, black coral as well as to pick orchids in forest reserves. Tourist literature supplied by embassies and tourist boards usually includes appropriate warnings.

CLEARING U.S. CUSTOMS. U.S. residents who are out of the country at least 48 hours and have claimed no exemption during the previous 30 days are entitled to bring home duty-free up to $400 worth of gifts or items for their personal use. If you buy clothing abroad and wear it during your travels, it is still dutiable when you return to the United States. For the next $1,000 worth of goods beyond the initial $400, customs inspectors will assess a flat 10 percent duty across the board, rather than hit you with different percentages for different types of goods.

The $400 duty-free allowance is based on the full fair retail value of the goods, and you must have those goods with you. You may make an oral declaration if items don't exceed the $400 allowance, but it's best to keep all your purchase receipts together and handy in case you are asked to produce them. Every member of a family is entitled to the same $400 exemption, regardless of age, and members of a family can pool their exemptions.

You may include 100 cigars (not Cuban) and 200 cigarettes in your $400 exemption as well as 1 liter (33.8 fluid ounces) of alcoholic beverages if you are 21 or older—all subject to the laws of the state in which you are arriving. If you exceed these limits, you must pay duty, the internal revenue tax, and possibly a state tax.

The U.S. Customs Service *Know Before You Go* pamphlet includes all the information above and more. You can get a copy by writing to U.S. Customs Service, Box 7407, Washington, DC 20044, or by calling 202–566–8195.

Since 1976, under the Generalized System of Preferences (GSP), approximately 2,800 items from developing countries may be brought into the United States duty-free. The purpose of this is to help the economic development of such countries by encouraging exports. All the Central American countries and Panama benefit from the GSP, so many items you buy there will be exempt from duty. Write to the Department of the Treasury, U.S. Customs Service, Washington, DC 20229, for the latest edition of the pamphlet *GSP and the Traveler,* which explains the system and lists types of products exempted.

Gifts that cost less than $50 may be mailed to friends or relatives at home, but not more than one per day of receipt to any one addressee. Mark the package "unsolicited gift" and list its contents and retail value. These gifts must not include tobacco, liquor, or perfumes containing alcohol that cost more than $5.

Packages mailed to yourself are subject to duty. Your best bet is to carry everything with you, even if you have to pay for excess baggage. Mail out of Central America can be slow and unreliable.

Do not bring home any agricultural items. They can spread destructive pests and diseases, and it is illegal to import them. For details contact APHIS, Department of Agriculture, 6505 Belcrest Rd., Federal Bldg., Room 732, Hyattsville, MD 20782; 301–436–7776.

In recent years many plants, birds, animals, and marine mammals have come under protection as endangered species. They and their products cannot be brought into the United States. For details contact the U.S. Fish and Wildlife Service, Department of the Interior, Washington, DC 20240; 202–343–9242.

CENTRAL AMERICA

An Introduction

by
JOHN MITCHEM

John Mitchem has covered Latin America for a variety of publications, including the Philadelphia Inquirer, *the* Denver Post, *and* Américas Magazine.

For centuries the tropics have held a unique allure. Something clicks in the mind of Europeans or North Americans—particularly during their respective winters—when the tropics are considered as an ideal vacation spot. The tropics are paradise.

Central America has all the attributes needed to fulfill dreams of equatorial bliss. A languid pace of life; compelling, polychromatic landscapes; hundreds of miles of coast where the sea meets beaches lined with coconut trees, and jungle foliage crashes down nearby mountains. From the rain forests of Costa Rica to the high-mountain volcanic lakes of Guatemala and to the offshore cays and islands strung like jewels from Panama to Belize, Central America has always been a sensory paradise of color and climate.

But new images of Central America have begun to circulate, supplanting the romanticized visions of the past. And these images are every bit as much a part of Central America as the more traditional views—but they are not nearly as pleasant. They are images of war—of tooth-and-nail conflicts, of divided loyalties and pitched confrontations between philosophies, between families. A new language, too, has emerged to describe these new images. New words and phrases need to be learned to articulate the events of the region: *lucha:* struggle; *fusil:* rifle; *escuadrón de muerte:* death squad. More familiar phrases require less memorization: *imperialismo; communismo; opresión; revolución.* Some terms have become internationally accepted and are seldom translated: *CIA; Sandinista.*

Central America today is a region that can fulfill any vision. If one goes looking for the conflict, one will find it—in the mass political rallies of Managua, in the cold stare of uniformed troops in Guatemala, or among the guerrillas of El Salvador. But if one is looking for a place to lay back and luxuriate in the pleasures of an earthly paradise, Central America can offer this—in the cloud forests of Costa Rica, on Honduras's Bay Islands, the San Blas Islands of Panama, or the offshore cays of Belize.

Central America is a compelling, fascinating part of the world. It is a place where the texture and electricity of history-in-the-making is felt every moment of the day. In many ways, Central America is working through a lot of the same growing pains that Europe and North America experienced only a generation ago. Here, as elsewhere in the world, a certain common-sense caution is in order. But there is no reason to avoid the region, or in any way abandon it.

The Geography of Influence

Central America, from Guatemala to Panama, has a total area of 196,000 square miles, which makes it about one-fourth the size of Mexico, its northern neighbor. But this area is packed with a variety of terrain that rivals the continent of South America. Mountain peaks at over 14,000 feet; areas of jungle in the Darién and the Mosquito Coast have never been surveyed; there are deserts, plains, and vast pine barrens; high-altitude hardwood forests resemble northern Europe more than the tropics.

The narrow isthmus, as narrow in some places as 50 miles, is, in its entirety, smaller than Texas. But the placement of the isthmus has opened the area up to incredible amounts of foreign influence. It has always tended to stand between things: between the gold and silver of Peru and Spain; between the East Coast of the United States and California (during the California Gold Rush, Nicaragua was the preferred transit route for westward migration); between Mexico and South America—and, at least politically, between the United States and the Soviet Union. The Panama Canal is an added factor, raising the strategic stakes in the region and bringing to bear incredible political pressure.

Economically, culturally, and politically, Central America has been washed over by repeated waves of foreign influence. Never isolated like Africa or the jungles of the Amazon Basin, its great ancient cultures were in decline before the European Conquest and were easy prey for the economic and cultural exploitation of Spain. It is today a mélange of various African, Amerindian, and European cultures with, for the most part, only the Spanish language and the Catholic church to give it a sense of unity. And even Spanish is not universal, as thousands of Central Americans prefer to speak the English language or indigenous dialects. And as the coasts of Central America and its placement on the globe have exposed it to the outside world, its mountains have hindered communication within.

The Barrier Mountains

The overwhelming geographic fact of life in Central America is the continuous, relentless chain of mountains that dominate nearly every republic. The mountains that run the north–south length of the isthmus are volcanic and young. There are over 20 active volcanoes in the region. These pressure points of geothermal energy constantly threaten havoc, but ironically it is the rich ash of volcanic eruptions that have given Central American soil its legendary fertility. Virtually the entire region is an active earthquake zone, and on numerous occasions (as recently as 1972 for Managua and 1976 for Guatemala City), capital cities have had to be rebuilt from the ground up.

Over the centuries the mountains have served to divide population groups to the degree that today the cultural landscape of the region is more of a quilt than a melting pot. The terrain of the isthmus, which made roads and communications problematic right into the 1980s, can still be blamed for much of the economic underdevelopment of the region. Trade among the Central American republics has always been difficult, and attempts at regional political integration have failed repeatedly. It was only under President Kennedy's Alliance for Progress that a highway linking the republics of Guatemala, Honduras, El Salvador, Nicaragua, Costa Rica, and Panama was constructed. Belize is still cut off from the rest of Central America with poor mountain roads across to Guatemala and irregular shipping down the coast to Honduras. Even within nations the mountains and jungles of Central America have kept populations separate to the degree that mountain Indians in Guatemala often speak no Spanish, and the peoples of the Caribbean coasts of Honduras and Nicaragua generally have more relatives in New Orleans or Miami than they do in Tegucigalpa or Managua.

The ocean has always been a more reliable transit route for the Central American economies, and as a result, Europe and the United States have overwhelmingly influenced the isthmus. Intraregional contact remains a deeply problematic goal. An extractive, agricultural economic system has developed in which most economic activity involves the export of commodities and the import of goods and services from outside the region. These foreign economic powers have brought their cultural and political influences with them, and thus, Central America today has profound difficulties with regional unity.

The mountains have also stood as a barrier to social equality and the development of the Central American people. When the riches of the Maya were looted and the gold and silver mines played out, the Spanish conquerors turned to export-oriented agiculture as the primary economic activity of the Central American colonies. To put it bluntly, the indigenous inhabitants of the land were driven to the mountains or barren coasts, where they scratched out whatever subsistence could be had. Even today it is on the coasts and in the highest mountains that one finds concentrations of native inhabitants. The Spanish built their plantations on the best areas of rich soil, and the Indians came down to work these fields as day laborers. Indigo, cacao, and then sugar, cotton, coffee, tobacco, and bananas were the primary crops. It is ironic to note that few of these products are actually designed to feed the people of Central America.

The struggle over land has been at the root of most Central American conflicts in the 500 years since the arrival of the first Europeans, and it remains the principal cause of the struggle today. Early in its history, Central America divided into two distinct classes of people—those who had the land, and those who worked the land on their behalf. The mountains predestined this division from the very earliest days of Central America's history.

The Receding Forests

It is a serious understatement to describe the landscapes of Central America as beautiful. The Caribbean and Pacific coasts, the high mountain cloud forests, even the supernatural desolation of the volcanoes in Central America have a transcendent quality. The popular conception is of jungle, dense with color and the omnipresent roar of insects, reptiles, and multi-colored birds. (Movies and popular lore have given a kind of Tarzan image to the isthmus. And a Tarzan movie was indeed once set in Guatemala—a Guatemala with elephants.)

Despite the popular view, the hand of man is everywhere apparent. Central America has a dense and rapidly growing population. Beyond the agroindustrial tracts of bananas, cotton, and coffee, most agriculture is of a rudimentary subsistence nature. The principal method of planting is of the slash-and-burn type—the most primitive form of planting on earth. Land is cleared, trees cut down, and the vegetable mass is burned. The soil, often deceptively meager under the canopy of natural growth, rapidly loses its nutrients as minerals are leached away. The patch of land is then abandoned for another. Scrub weeds take over and underfed cattle graze where forests once stood. This type of destruction is complicated by the need to cultivate even extremely steep tracts of land to keep up with the demands of a rapidly growing population. The slash-and-burn technique produces alarming erosion and land destruction in mountain areas, and the natural recovery process is extremely slow.

Belize was once a logging colony where fine hardwoods like mahogany were harvested for nearly two centuries. Today virtually the entire expanse of the nation is covered by a meager scrub of gnarled trees and undergrowth. The great stands of mahogany have been turned into furniture for North American and European drawing rooms. In Honduras and El Salvador overcultivation and erosion are complicated by rocketing populations, which further tax the exhausted soil. Water tables are dropping at dangerous rates and international aid agencies finance the digging of ever-deeper wells to perform rudimentary irrigation. The rain forests that once characterized the isthmus are, sadly, vanishing. In northern Costa Rica the pressure comes from large-scale cattle ranching, which produces cheap meat for American fast-food chains. In northern Guatemala and southern Mexico simple population pressures are driving subsistence farmers farther and farther into the wilderness in search of new land to slash and burn. The destruction of natural habitats for wildlife in the region are driving many species of animals, notably exotic birds and wildcats, to the brink of extinction.

A political dimension is introduced into the mix when it is remembered that the struggle over land continues to be the essence of the Central American conflict. Since the best lands are occupied by the tiny minority of the population that controls the national economies, it is politically expedient to encourage peasant occupation of unused wilderness lands. In Nicaragua, Honduras, Belize, El Salvador, and Guatemala there are still vast areas under no form of cultivation.

Central American People

Central America is an ethnic patchwork—a blend of virtually every racial type known to the New World. A foundation of indigenous population built upon by waves of European, Afro-Caribbean, Middle Eastern, and even Asian immigration has created a modern mixture of races known as the *mestizo.*

The indigenous population of pre-Conquest Central America was in itself a blend of Indians from North and South America. Mezoamerican Indians were the product of highly developed, stratified, often urban cultures. The Olmecs, Toltecs, and Aztecs of Mexico and the Maya of Guatemala, Belize, Honduras, and El Salvador are examples of advanced Indian groups living in developed, hierarchical states. Indians migrating northward from South America included the Chibcha of Colombia; the Cuna, Chocó, and Guayamí of Panama; the Huetares, Borucas, and Chorutegas of Costa Rica; the Rama, Suma, and Mosquito, or Miskito, of Nicaragua. These groups lived in less complex societies based on hunting, primitive agriculture, and fishing. Between these two distinct groups were the Lenca, Jicaque, and Paya of Honduras and El Salvador.

The Spanish that came to settle in Central America soon subdivided into various social strata founded on degrees of racial purity and even place of birth. The Spanish crown dictated that only the *peninsulares* born in Spain could occupy key posts such as governors, judges, and administrators, and these Spaniards came to monopolize wealth and power. The *Creoles,* born in the colonies, were relegated to inferior positions, but eventually had their day when independence destroyed the peninsular aristocracy.

Continuing down the social ladder of colonial Central America were the mestizos, who soon came to represent the majority. The mestizos fell in where the "pure" bloods left off—in small business and small-scale plantation farming. The mestizos, for the most part, spoke Spanish and culturally embraced Europe. The mestizos in turn passed social aggression down the scale to the full-blood Indians, who were held in contempt by all. The Indians served as serfs and slaves, oppressed and put down by every religious, political, and economic institution created by colonialism.

Indians in Central America, even in the present day, have had to make a bitter choice in their lives—to live in Indian communities and withdraw from advancement along the economic scale or to ignore their cultural heritage by assuming the Spanish language and European dress, abandoning traditional lands and moving to urban areas, and even discarding their indigenous names. This choice between isolation and assimilation is increasingly evident in Central America as Indian communities continue to languish at the most basic levels of social and economic poverty.

Africa also lives in Central America—in the thousands of black Central Americans, the vast majority of whom live on the Caribbean coast of the isthmus. Blacks were first brought to the region in the sixteenth century when indigenous slave populations working the mines and plantations of the colonies needed to be replenished. These older black populations were augmented by groups of blacks from the West Indies brought to the isthmus in later centuries for plantation work or, in the case of Panama, for large-scale engineering projects. Many of these black Central Americans speak English as their primary language.

Blacks in the coastal region have intermingled with indigenous groups to the degree that today many tribal peoples in Nicaragua and Honduras appear Negro in their physical aspect. The Miskito, Suma, and Rama Indians of Nicaragua are examples of this. A smaller subgroup are the Black Caribs of Belize, Honduras, and Nicaragua. The Black Caribs are the product of a racial mix of Africans and Carib Indians on the island of Saint Vincent who were exported en masse by the British and deposited on the coast of Central America in the late eighteenth century.

Various new strains have been added to this mixture. Asians are evident in virtually every Central American city. European-descended Jews are a small but economically dynamic ethnic group, as are the Palestinians sprinkled throughout the region—with a particular concentration in Honduras, where they are active in industrial development. Cubans and Eastern Europeans are active in the administration of Nicaragua's Sandinista government. North Americans of various ethnicities are evident in every Central American nation.

Central America's geography is a mirror of its multiracial history. Guatemala today is overwhelmingly indigenous, with the minority of mestizos and whites concentrated in the cities. Belize is primarily black with various blends in the principal cities and Maya communities in the south. The coast of Honduras has a strong Afro-Caribbean influence, with the rest of the country populated by various formulas of *mestizaje*. Costa Rica is the only country in Central America with a largely "pure" European ethnicity. Panama has the color and feel of the Caribbean or Brazil—a kaleidescopic blend of numerous races and colors.

A HISTORY OF CONFLICT

by
JOHN MITCHEM

Central America's history is the history of exploitation—exploitation of mineral wealth, of agricultural produce, and of people. There was never the spectacular influx of immigrants that produced the high level of industry and the varied economies in North and South America. What resources were available were squabbled over, and authoritarian rule and military conquest were favored methods of controlling the resources.

Any culture is the product of its traditions and history, but in Central America the ancient and the modern live side by side every day, often overlapping, often operating simultaneously. The methods of cultivation employed by the *campesino,* or peasant (the word doesn't carry the pejorative implications of its English translation), in Central America are identical to those employed thousands of years ago. The social and political systems of the isthmus today share the same traditions of deference to authoritarian rule, military resolution of conflicts, and politically powerful religion found in the ancient cultures of the Maya. Central America has walked uneasily into the modern world, and ancient traditions appear to die hard.

The Preclassic Period

Central America's first highly developed culture evolved among the Olmec, in the area of what is today Veracruz, Mexico, near the Tuxtla

Mountain range, from 1200 B.C. to A.D. 100. The Olmec are known for their art objects, notably anthropomorphized jaguars and massive, round-headed busts of mysterious figures with thick lips, wide noses, and some kind of helmetlike cap. Some anthropologists have broadly speculated the possibility of these sculptures representing some African visitors, but given the importance of fertility and virility in Olmec myth, the heads probably represent healthy overfed children or men.

Olmec society was highly artistic and employed advanced mathematics. Their villages had crafts specialists who never worked in agriculture, and large pools of available labor were used for urban engineering projects. Olmec society had a highly organized leadership, able to direct numerous workers and oversee sophisticated commerce. It was a society of village agriculturalists ruled by high priests who inherited their power at birth. The Olmec explored far and wide, and Olmec-style carvings, paintings, ceramics, and figurines have been found from Central Mexico to El Salvador and Costa Rica. It was also a society, like those that followed it, founded on military conquest and colonization.

The Classic Maya

While Europe was still mired in the Dark Ages, the Maya civilization reached its peak. The empire covered all of Guatemala and Belize and parts of Honduras, El Salvador, and Mexico. The classic Maya were a people of great intellectual dynamism and wide-ranging, vivid creative activity. They enjoyed great public architecture and an explosion of energy in the arts, commerce, mathematics, and astronomy. They were a people who witnessed the rise of urbanization and sophisticated engineering. They possessed an intricate written literature based on pantheistic religions and elaborate myth. They had a complex system of theocratic government and a multilayered social system.

The greatest intellectual achievements of the ancient Maya were in mathematics, astronomy, and the development of written language. The Maya had sophisticated, interlocking religious and secular calendars; a mathematic system based, like our decimal system, on the zero; and an intricate knowledge of astronomy, directly inherited from the Olmec. Mayan astronomers predicted solar eclipses and mapped out the cycles of Venus. The Maya were the only people in the pre-Columbian Americas to possess a developed writing system. The other ancient cultures of Mesoamerica—including the Aztec of Mexico, who postdated the Maya—used only rudimentary symbols. The most famous example of their written language is the Dresden Codex, a 24-foot-long book of folding screens now housed in the State Library of Dresden. The Dresden Codex was a divinatory treatise on astronomy with tables of eclipse dates and five panels devoted to the revolutions of the planet Venus.

But despite their complex intellectual greatness, the Maya were curiously inept. The Maya never developed the wheel—they had no wheeled vehicles and no potter's wheel. They had no beasts of burden or draft animals. And the Maya civilization was a stone-age culture. The ancient cultures of the Old World had their iron and bronze ages, whereas the Maya used only stone blades and tools. Indians of South America were working in gold for 2,000 years before the Spanish Conquest, but the Mezoamerican waited until A.D. 1000.

The exploitive nature of the Maya culture should not be forgotten. Whatever greatness there was was achieved through outrageous oppression. The great levels of education in the sciences and mathematics reached by the priestly classes were at the expense of thousands who toiled the land so that others could live in luxury. The magnificent architectural monuments created by the Maya were built by slaves.

The rise of the Maya cities centered in the Petén of Guatemala and adjacent lowlands; the areas of Chiapas, Tobasco, and southern Campeche in Mexico; Belize and western Honduras. For the most part, Maya cities were located on rivers or in uplands between river systems. By the fifth century B.C. village farming communities had formed in the Petén, and by the time of Christ, buildings were already being constructed on top of the ruins of previous structures.

The greatest Maya center was at Tikal, near the present town of Flores, in the Guatemalan department of Petén. The site is dominated by ceremonial buildings in the form of truncated pyramids, arranged around central plazas that served ceremonial and athletic functions. The largest of the central lowland Maya cities, it is estimated to have had a population of more than 50,000 at its peak (some say as high as 100,000) with a population density of 600 per square mile. The site was surrounded by suburbs extending three or four miles in every direction.

Tikal's Temple IV is the highest Mayan pyramid standing, at 212 feet. The pyramids were constructed of limestone blocks, carved with obsidian blades and set with mortar. The truncated tops of the pyramids served astronomical and religous functions, and ceremonial fires burned on the broad stairs leading upward. Some human sacrifices took place on the top of the pyramids, but anthropologists today conclude that human sacrifice was practiced on special religious occasions, not as a matter of common practice.

By A.D. 900 the great Maya ceremonial centers were quiet. To this day, historians can't target the reason for the Maya decline, although a rapid, dramatic decrease in population and activity seems to have taken place. It is thought that the social structure centered around the powerful high priests broke down completely since there is evidence that the palaces were occupied by peasants, who cooked food on the once-sacred steps, discarding garbage in a haphazard manner.

The Maya today number about two million, and they live alongside the overgrown ruins of their ancient monuments. They have mingled to a great degree with the Latin, and most speak Spanish, although 15 dialects of Maya are still spoken. The Maya are often short and sturdy of build, with broad heads, flat noses, and copper-colored skin. Many are extremely religous; Catholicism as practiced in the Maya areas of Central America has deeply animist overtones reflecting religions that predate Christianity here. The Maya are open and friendly but they are in many ways a humbled people. For the most part they do not seem to share their ancestors' passion for learning or leadership. They are today a people threatened with cultural decimation as modernization, war, migration to Spanish-speaking urban centers, and the exhaustion of the land conspire to break the patterns of their ancient lifestyle.

The Conquest

> Eat, eat, thou hast bread
> Drink, drink, thou hast water
> On that day, dust possess the earth
> On that day, a blight is on the face of the earth
> On that day, a cloud rises
> On that day, a mountain rises
> On that day, a strong man seizes the land
> On that day, things fall to ruin
> On that day, the tender leaf is destroyed
> On that day, the dying eyes are closed
> On that day, three signs are on the tree
> On that day, three generations hang there
> On that day, the battle flag is raised
> And they are scattered afar in the forest

—*The Seventh Prophecy of Chilam Balam,* 15th-century Mayan book of prophecy. Translated by D. G. Brinton.

Central America was not settled by the Europeans; it was conquered. The men who came from Spain weren't religious puritans looking for land to farm. They did not come to create a representative democracy of hard-working farmers. They did not come to create anything. They were soldiers looking for riches to loot. The conquistadores came to Central America to extract whatever they could (gold, principally), as rapidly as possible, and then return to Spain. The early first decades of the Conquest are characterized by vicious bickering, arguments over conquered territories, claims, counterclaims, and accusations. Whatever misfortunate Indians got in the way were quickly eliminated, but there was almost always a priest handy to baptize them before they died.

Partly as a result of the feudal tradition in Spain, all measures of social or economic prestige in the colonies were a function of land—how much was owned and what it produced. Secondary to land ownership was labor ownership, and the conquistadores divided up the Indian communities in a merciless system of forced labor.

Central America was first claimed by Columbus, in July 1502, when he set foot on the island of Guanaja, in the Bay Islands off Honduras, on his fourth voyage to the New World. The principal activity of the Conquest's first decade was the capturing of thousands of Indians in order to bring them to work in the mines of the Caribbean island of Hispaniola, where natives were dying from overwork in large numbers. The first Spanish settlements in the isthmus, in the Darién of Panama, were beset by disease, shipwrecks, and hostile Indians. The Pacific was discovered in 1513 by Vasco Núñez de Balboa, who had stowed away on a ship from Hispaniola. Balboa came back with gold and legends of a great empire, almost certainly the Inca, somewhere to the south. A rival conqueror, Pedro Arias de Avila, commonly known as Pedrarias, explored north up the isthmus, while Balboa explored the south. Pedrarias founded the original settlement of Panamá in 1519, but not before he had Balboa convicted of treason and beheaded by a hastily gathered court.

By 1521, Hernán Cortés had defeated the Aztecs in Mexico. The Maya of the Yucatán were subdued by Francisco de Montejo in 1527. (The complete destruction of the Maya empire would not come about until 1697, when the last Maya leaders of the Petén were captured.) A second in command to Cortés, Pedro de Alvarado, established the kingdom of Guatemala in 1524. Guatemala City was founded in the Almolonga Valley in 1527. In Honduras, to the south, Alvarado linked up with Pedrarias, and the inevitable territorial squabble forced the Spanish to divide the territories of the isthmus. Spain's priority was on safe passage across the isthmus for the incredible fortunes in precious metal being looted from the Inca, and by 1520, Central America was already one of the world's most strategically vital areas.

Gold and silver mines were established early in the century, and when these were played out, settlers streamed in and established an agricultural base for the colonial economy. But from Panama to Mexico, the sixteenth century was violent with conflict—Indian revolts, followed by Spanish massacres in reprisal. Where the Indians lived in elaborate hierarchical societies, such as in Guatemala or parts of Mexico, the Conquest was simply a matter of removing tribal leadership and putting the masses to work. These are the regions of Mesoamerica in which one sees the greatest concentration of Indian populations today. But where the Indians were nomadic and stubborn in their refusal to be enslaved, they were massacred en masse. For example, the Indians of Costa Rica were so fierce that they delayed Spanish settlement until 1561. Costa Rica today has the smallest Indian population of any Central American republic.

Once the initial violence of the Conquest was out of the way, the colonization of Central America became more economic than military. The Spanish took all the best Indian lands, destroying the system of cooperative farming, and reduced the natives to landless serfs. The *encomienda* was designed to replace slavery. It began as a tribute-collecting system, but eventually became a device for the steady, organized usurpation of all Indian lands and the enslavement of indigenous populations.

The Conquest also had its religious side. A voice of benevolence in this century of genocide was Farther Bartolomé de Las Casas, a Dominican priest who tried to institute less violent, more productive forms of Conquest. He convinced Spain to promulgate the New Laws of the Indies in 1542, which officially abolished the *encomienda*. The colonists vigorously opposed the New Laws. They considered Las Casas a troublemaker and a dangerous impediment to progress. The *repartimiento*, created in place of the *encomienda*, replaced tribute with forced part-time labor. Indians were supposed to work one week a month for the Spaniards, with the rest of their time free to tend their own land. But in practice, the Indians were still little more than slaves. Migrant, landless Indians still constitute the backbone of much of Central American agricultural production today.

From the very beginning of the colonial period, a sense of unity among the Central American territories proved elusive. Problems of geography and rivalry were so severe that by 1530, Guatemala, Chiapas (now part of Mexico), Honduras, Nicaragua, and Panama functioned under separate royal orders. It was not until 1543 that the crown unified the region by creating the Audiencia de los Confines. This administrative unit fell apart in 1560, with Panama, Costa Rica, and Nicaragua under one *audiencia*, and Honduras, Guatemala, and Chiapas ruled by Mexico. By 1570, Guatemala was again independent of Mexico. Continuity of government also proved elusive, since the colonial administrators were, for the most part, a rotating corps of Spanish bureaucrats, few of whom remained in the colonies.

Economic development in the sixteenth century established patterns that are still evident today. The vast majority of early agricultural production was for domestic consumption, but indigo and cacao were exported. For the first 50 years, productive mines ensured considerable economic activity, but once these precious metals played out, Central America became something of a backwater in the Spanish empire.

In a move that would prove fateful for the region's development, Spain also actively discouraged intercolonial trade. The colonies were used as productive engines that shipped raw materials to Europe, imported finished products in return, and little else. Individual provinces within the colonies were isolated from each other. Transportation was developed to link the productive plantation lands to the ports, not with each other.

Economic and social and political power in the colonies lay in the hands of a small number who owned productive lands, controlled substantial numbers of Indians, and exhibited fidelity to Spain. What wealth was evident was spent on government buildings, religious institutions, and magnificent plantation homes, not on the general welfare.

The Decline of Spanish Power

The defeat of the Spanish Armada in 1588 marked the end of Spanish naval hegemony and the consequent inability of Spain to protect imperial power abroad. Other European powers stepped up their activities in the Caribbean, with France, Holland, and England vigorously trading in cacao, tobacco, and indigo. They could sell goods to the Central American colonies for much less than the Spanish could, and by the 1660s the British were so bold as to establish a settlement to cut lumber at the mouth of the Belize River.

The Caribbean coasts of Central America were subjected to devastating raids by pirates, who wreaked havoc on the Incan treasure routes. Rival European colonies were established at Jamaica (England), the Netherlands Antilles, and Haiti (France), and these territories served as bases of piracy. In 1642 the British attacked and seized Roatán, in the Bay Islands off Honduras, and with the complicity of Miskito Indians they soon were raiding the Caribbean coast as far south as Costa Rica.

In 1643 the Dutch sacked Trujillo, and the Spanish reacted by building a series of fortresses along the Caribbean coast. Fort San Felipe on the Río Dulce in Guatemala and Castillo Viejo on the Río San Juan in Nicaragua are still standing today. In 1665 and 1670, English buccaneers penetrated Nicaragua as far as Grenada, and the arch pirate Henry Morgan sacked Panama City in 1671. By 1680 the British controlled the entire Mosquito Coast (the Caribbean coast), and added slave hunting to their list of atrocities. The general underdevelopment of the Caribbean coast of the isthmus today can be traced back to this period, as can the thousands of English-speaking people who now live on the Caribbean coasts of Costa Rica, Nicaragua, Honduras, and Belize.

The ascent of the Bourbon Philip V plunged the Spanish empire into the War of the Spanish Succession. The eighteenth century would be a period of profound conflict. It was a period in which the European powers carved Central America up into spheres of influence and used the isthmus as a battleground for European strategic conflicts and economic rivalries.

The close relationship between the Bourbon monarchs of Spain and France pumped French ideas into the Spanish world and modified Spain's colonial policies. Anticlerical measures reduced the power of the church; commercial reform boosted trade; administrative reforms brought increased colonial efficiency; and a new emphasis was placed on the military defense of Spanish commerce in the isthmus. The Spanish Bourbons, aided by the French, sought to rid Central America of British influence, and new forts were constructed from Panama to the Yucatán. Britain countered by solidifying their grasp on the Mosquito Coast, and by 1748 the English had significant settlements at Black River, Cape Gracias a Dios, Bluefields, Roatán, and Belize. Spain's military responses were not effective. In 1754 the British stopped a Spanish expeditionary force of 1,500 in the Petén, and Belize remained in the British camp. In 1756, British-sponsored Miskito Indians captured and murdered the governor of Costa Rica.

By signing the Treaty of Paris in 1763, the British recognized Spanish sovereignty over Central America and agreed to dismantle their forts. In return, the British were allowed to continue their woodcutting settlement at Belize. But the British did not dismantle their forts, and Belize soon had a quasi-colonial administration that was approving private land titles. The Miskito Indians, acting on behalf of their British clients, continued to harass the Spanish, and in 1779 Spain retaliated by routing the British from Roatán and Belize. The British then focused all their efforts on the Mosquito Coast, in an attempt to cut the isthmus in half. However, preoccupied with their insurrection in the newly declared United States, the British eventually ran out of steam, and the Treaty of Paris in 1783 ended the American Revolution and reaffirmed the 1763 treaty. The British left the Mosquito Coast and settled permanently in Belize after 1787. In 1796 the British again seized and reoccupied the Bay Islands of Honduras and increased their plunder of the Caribbean coast.

While Europe convulsed through the changes brought by the French Revolution, shifts of a more subtle but still profound sort were going on in the Central American colonies. The Creole aristocracy of the isthmus developed a new view of Spain—a view not founded in the idealization of the Spanish past that had previously characterized the colonies. These Creoles still elevated the cultural and spiritual values of the Spanish Conquest, but in the Spanish officials who administered the colonies, they saw scheming, calculating bureaucrats threatening their interests with taxation and plans for new land-hungry immigration. A new bitterness emerged against the Spanish, and a deep, parochial conservatism was born that survives in the Central American upper classes today.

These changes were underscored by the growth of the mixed Latin–Indian, or *Ladino* population in the region. The *Ladinos* emerged as merchants, artisans, and tradesmen, forming guilds and creating a petit bourgeoisie that served as a precursor of the middle classes that would play such a vital role in the nineteenth and twentieth centuries. In larger towns *Ladinos* were the majority of the population, but in the principal cities they often performed menial jobs or endured a new social malady— unemployment. In the cities crime among the *Ladinos* became a concern, and laws were promulgated by the aristocracy that forbade the bearing of arms by Indians or *Ladinos*. In 1806 laws were passed that outlawed knives, with violators subject to 200 lashes and six years of hard labor.

At the end of the eighteenth century, Indians were still a definite majority of the population in Guatemala (as they are today), but *Ladinos* and Spanish were the majority everywhere else in the region. Blacks, sprinkled in various concentrations up and down the length of the Caribbean coast, remained more a part of the British empire than of the Spanish.

By the time of the Spanish–French alliance against England in 1796, the British controlled the Atlantic. Spain had to turn to neutrals to carry on their Central American trade, and the United States was the logical choice. Capitalizing on their new opportunity, American shipping in the region increased radically. Madrid, seeing that the "neutrals" were seriously chipping away at its monopoly, revoked these rights in 1800, but American trading in the region would continue.

In 1804 war resumed between Spain and England. The Miskito Indians received renewed military aid from the British and privateering again increased. The Treaty of London in 1809 allied England and Spain against the French, and Central American trade boomed. Belize grew with new construction and increased shipping traffic. The Americans, their foot in the door, began to be seen as a long-term threat to the Spanish monopoly.

By the end of the eighteenth century, foreign ideas had permanently altered the order of Spanish reign. There were new calls for freer economic institutions, a more open political process, and some form of representative colonial government. New questions were raised about trade monopolies, the landed aristocracy, special privileges, and clerical power.

Independence

> The states of the isthmus from Panama to Guatemala will perhaps form a confederation. This magnificent location between the two great oceans could in time become the emporium of the world. Its canal will shorten the distances throughout the world, strengthen commercial ties with Europe, America, and Asia, and bring that happy region tribute from the four quarters of the globe. Perhaps some day the capital of the world may be located there, just as Constantine claimed Byzantium was the capital of the ancient world.
>
> (Simón Bolívar, *Jamaica Letter*)

Agustín de Iturbide's Plan de Igual in Mexico forced the topic of independence onto Guatemala in 1821. Indications were that an army of independent Mexico might invade Guatemala and annex Central America, so the question was not purely one of tearing away from Spain but a choice between annexation to Mexico and independence. Guatemala declared its independence on September 15, 1821. The abdication of Iturbide in Mexico led to the declaration of independence for Central America on July 3, 1823. Only the colony of Chiapas elected to become a state of Mexico.

The rest of Central America (with the exception of Panama, which was still part of Colombia) formed the United Provinces of Central America.

Independent Central America got off to an unstable, turbulent beginning. New political labels were invented to replace the old, but the same issues divided Central Americans. The Conservatives opposed reforms, stubbornly demanding the continuance of royalist institutions. The Liberals, inspired by the Enlightenment philosophers and the Spanish Bourbons, advocated free trade, economic liberalization, republicanism, and clerical reform. They advocated "radical" ideas like public education and the end of forced labor. The new political divisions also had a geographic dimension. The Liberals, largely representing the provinces, advocated a federation of states as had been created in North America. The Conservatives, strongest in Guatemala, wanted a centralized government similar to that of the colonial era. The Liberals gained control of the government and adopted the Constitution of 1824, which abolished slavery and noble titles, limited monopolies, encouraged immigration, and limited tax revenue.

When Conservatives gained power in Guatemala in 1826, a bloody civil war erupted. The Liberals, led by the Honduran Francisco Morazán, won the war in 1829. They quickly imprisoned Conservative leaders and gave state governments broad powers to crush insurrection, and Morazán moved the federal capital to Liberal stronghold San Salvador. In Nicaragua the dispute was particularly acute, with the Conservatives of Granada and the Liberals of León in perpetual conflict. Costa Rica, remote throughout the colonial epoch, remained to one side, avoiding the conflict and quietly becoming the first state to export coffee in the 1830s.

The revolt of 1837 was the beginning of the end for the United Provinces. This revolt wasn't just another violent rivalry—it was a peasant uprising throughout the isthmus. The rebellion was chiefly a reaction to the Liberal reforms, modeled after England and the United States. Private acquisition of titles was encouraged as a stimulus to production. A major side effect of this legislation was the swallowing up of new lands by the wealthy few who already possessed substantial holdings. Formerly landed peasants became sharecroppers, and, most important, foreigners snapped up substantial tracts of land, especially in Guatemala. The revolution was particularly hostile to foreign elements.

Popular uprisings against the Liberal reforms stretched from Costa Rica to Quezaltenango during the first half of 1837, but the nucleus of the war surrounded Guatemala's peasant hero, Rafael Carrera. The governor of Guatemala, Mariano Gálvez, failed in his efforts to arrest Carrera. The war began to take on the image of a race war, with Indians, *Ladinos,* and blacks joining to fight the landed white Creoles and foreigners. Guatemala City fell to Carrera's forces on January 31, 1838. A fragile peace soon fell apart, and by March, Carrera had resumed warfare.

Through all this, the federation over which Morazán governed was dissolving. Nicaragua seceded on April 30, 1838, and a month later the Congress in San Salvador followed suit. By the end of the year Honduras and Costa Rica had left the federation. In March 1839, Carrera again entered Guatemala City. For the rest of the year he fought off Liberal resistance, consolidating his grip over Guatemala. Conservatives meanwhile had gained power in Honduras and Nicaragua, and in March 1840 the showdown came. Morazán invaded Guatemala, entering the capital city on

March 18. The next day Carrera's Conservative forces routed his army. Morazán escaped to Panama by sea and would reenter Central America only once more. In 1842 he briefly seized power in Costa Rica, only to die before a firing squad in San José.

A new power structure of Conservative *caudillos,* or strongmen, was born in Central America. The Liberals' unsuccessful experiment with federalism had dashed the Conservatives' plans for centralized government in the isthmus. Conservatives now embraced a divisive form of nationalism. Braulio Carrillo in Costa Rica, Francisco Ferrera in Honduras, Francisco Malespín in El Salvador, and Carrera in Guatemala solidified the formation of the new independent nations, thus permanently destroying any dreams of lasting unity. In 1842 all these nations except Costa Rica entered into a defensive pact dedicated to their individual sovereignty, preventing the restoration of the Constitution of 1824. Free trade was encouraged, but they all produced the same commodities and had little to sell one another.

The idealism of the Liberals was abandoned. Carrera and his allies arrived in power as a reaction to the Liberals' efforts to impose economic and social systems that flew in the face of three centuries of Spanish tradition. The Conservatives now supported a strengthened church, a society run by elite landholders and merchants, a deep suspicion of foreigners, and a respect (bordering on romantic glorification) of the region's Spanish heritage. The Conservatives' emphasis on nationalism and autonomous government, coupled with their paternalistic concern for the rural masses, established attitudes that are the bedrock of modern Central American nationalism.

The Age of Imperialism

International economic pressures played as large a role as internal political dynamics in the development of nineteenth-century Central America. The decline of Spain and the simultaneous rise of the modern industrial powers put Central America under a microscope of world attention not experienced since the treasure flows of the sixteenth century.

Since the days of the conquistadores, a canal had been seen as the key to the economic future of the isthmus. All through the nineteenth century, English, Dutch, French, and North American interests encouraged plans for a canal—usually through Nicaragua. As the leading world trading nation, Britain took the lead.

After 1830 Britain established military garrisons and colonial settlements in the Bay Islands. Central Americans retook the islands almost immediately, lost them again in 1839, and finally reoccupied them in 1841. Britain's economic imperialism continued apace. Belize became the principal port for Central American import and export, and by 1846 all Central American products except coffee entered England duty-free.

Debt also solidified the British influence. Numerous loans from British financial institutions to Central American governments created a morass of debt that is not resolved even today. As an example of the imperialistic nature of these loans, the Carrera government of Guatemala negotiated with the firm of Isaac and Samuel in 1856 to pay off previously encountered debts. Under the terms, the Carrera government pledged 50 percent of its customs receipts to service the debt. Trade, like loans, furthered the

British interests. By 1840 nearly 60 percent of Guatemala's imports came from England via Belize, with another 20 percent coming directly from England. By contrast, only 15 percent came from Spain.

The United States had little direct contact with Central America before 1850. The Americans had recognized Central American independence promptly, but did little to discourage British designs in the area. It was not until the end of the Mexican War and the acquisition of California and Oregon that U.S. interests were turned southward. The Bidlack Treaty of 1846 guaranteed U.S. rights of transit across Panama, and a U.S. company used the treaty to construct the Panama railroad between 1850 and 1855.

Anglo-American rivalries were grafted onto domestic Central American frictions as respective commercial and political spheres of interest were carved out. Great Britain tended to ally with Conservative forces, encouraging the division of the territories as a hedge against their dominance in the region, while the Americans ardently supported the Liberal cause of unification.

British gunboat diplomacy once again became commonplace along the Caribbean coast. In 1848 the British seized the settlement at the mouth of the Río San Juan in Nicaragua. The Americans, predictably, protested vigorously. U.S. interests in the region, and in the possibility of a canal, were steadily expanding. The U.S. Pacific territories were separated from the east coast by thousands of miles of trackless wilderness and hostile Indians, and the Central American isthmus was looked to as the most expeditious east–west route available.

The Clayton-Bulwer Treaty of 1850 called for joint U.S.-British control of any route across the isthmus. It stepped lightly around the questions of colonization and military presence. While it seemed on the surface to guarantee parity of influence, two years later the British declared the Bay Islands a British colony. Honduras protested with U.S. backing, and the British withdrew in 1859. By a treaty with Nicaragua in 1860, the British likewise agreed to abandon the Mosquito Coast. In 1859 the question of sovereignty over Belize was dealt with in a treaty with Guatemala. Guatemala agreed to recognize British sovereignty in return for the construction of a road between the port and Guatemala City. The road was never built, and the issue was never adequately settled. Guatemala reluctantly agreed to Belizean independence in 1981, but a British garrison is still based in the former colony.

Liberal–Conservative conflicts continued in the form of civil wars and open conflicts between the Central American republic. The use of exile forces and international support for internal conflicts became common in the nineteenth century, and this tradition is seen vividly today in Nicaraguan support for revolutionary forces in El Salvador, and Honduran assistance to insurgent Nicaraguan Contras. This ongoing meddling has severely impeded regional unification and has been dramatically compounded by the participation of extra-regional forces—British and American and now Cuban and Soviet influences.

William Walker

The story of William Walker is one of the most bizarre episodes in Latin American history. Not accidentally, every Central American schoolchild knows all about Walker and his adventures, while few North American children even know his name.

The alliance of the Conservatives in Nicaragua with the aggressive British had largely discredited them in the eyes of many Central Americans. For much of the 1840s, Nicaragua effectively had two governments, with Conservatives and Liberals respectively operating out of Granada and León. This simmering civil war had carried on without relief since independence, and Nicaragua was divided and weak. The British had their eye on the territory as the site of a possible canal, and in many ways the country was up for grabs with various players—the Liberals and Conservatives within Nicaragua, Conservatives from Honduras and Costa Rica, the British and the North Americans—all jockeying for position.

North American stakes in the game were raised precipitously by the discovery of gold in California in 1848. This fact, coupled with the absence of convenient transcontinental routes in North America, placed Nicaragua squarely at the center of the principal route for California-bound traffic. In 1849 Cornelius Vanderbilt and his associates established a service in which passengers traveled by boat from New York to San Juan del Norte in Nicaragua, boarded riverboats for travel up the Río San Juan and Lake Nicaragua, and then rode stagecoaches for a brief land journey to the Pacific coast, where they boarded other ships to the San Francisco Bay area. Vanderbilt juggled the books to rob the Nicaraguans of taxes on his substantial profits, and by 1851 his service needed loans to finance expansions required by the thousands demanding transit to California. Vanderbilt borrowed from British financiers, thus coming into direct conflict with American interests involved in building a railroad across Panama. (Once this railway was completed, Vanderbilt's company went out of business, but by this time Vanderbilt had neatly bought into the Panama route and continued to profit.)

William Walker was the gifted son of a Tennessee frontier family who completed college at age 14 and who by age 23 had obtained a medical degree from the University of Pennsylvania; studied at Paris, Heidelberg, and Edinburgh; and opened a law practice. He drifted into journalism, and became a controversial editor at the *New Orleans Crescent.* When the only woman he would ever love died in a Gulf Coast yellow fever epidemic, he took off for California via Panama. No great wealth or success awaited him there, and he took up the career of the filibuster. At this time of expansion and growth the United States was acquiring new territories in a variety of ways. Some were bought, some conquered, some wrested from Indian nations, and some the object of private initiative. Such was the case when, in 1853, Walker and a group of hastily gathered gold-field losers invaded the northern Mexico department of Sonora, comically declaring the short-lived Republic of Lower California. They were soon routed by Mexican *federales* and surrendered to American border authorities after a devastating march across the scorched desert.

In Nicaragua the Liberals had gained ground in the ongoing conflict, but in 1854 Carrera dispatched aid from Guatemala, which substantially strengthened the Conservative position. The Liberals looked abroad for assistance, offering Byron Cole, an associate of Walker's from San Francisco, huge tracts of land in return for military assistance. Walker gathered his forces in San Francisco and took off south with a motley band of 57 Californians of various nationalities, inadequate weaponry, and a boat that was more an embarrassment than a ship of war. U.S. authorities, flushed with the acquisition of new territories and the Monroe Doctrine, looked the other way.

Walker and his mercenaries landed at Realjo in June 1855. At his first encounter his forces were routed by Conservative troops under Honduran command. Walker successfully retreated to Chinandega, eventually emerging as commanding general of the Liberal forces. In October he took Granada, and the Conservatives agreed to a truce. A coalition government, headed by a Conservative, Patricio Rivas, was established with Walker named chief of the armed forces. Formal recognition came from Washington in May 1856.

Cornelius Garrison, Cornelius Vanderbilt's San Francisco manager, was, meanwhile, conspiring with New York financier Charles Morgan to undercut Vanderbilt's interests in Nicaragua. They sent arms, money, and additional mercenaries to Walker. Veterans of the Mexican War flooded into the territory and the Walker army soon numbered over 2,500 men. Walker, who had been philsophically opposed to slavery, departed from these views as his ranks swelled with American southerners who allegedly wanted to annex Nicaragua as a slave state.

The British had opposed Walker's activities all along, and they fanned Costa Rican, Honduran, and Guatemalan fears of American designs on the isthmus. Liberals throughout Central America supported Walker, agreeing with him that the region needed democratic values, destruction of the aristocracy, public education, and increased trade. But Liberals were out of power in every territory, and by February 1856 the Conservative governments of Costa Rica, Honduras, El Salvador, and Guatemala were sending troops to dislodge Walker. On March 1 of that year, Costa Rica declared war and the British provided them arms, munitions, and equipment.

By May, Walker was on the ropes. Guatemalan, Honduran, and Salvadoran troops arrived in Nicaragua to aid the Costa Ricans, and Rivas quit the government. In June 1856 a rather dubious election recognized Walker as president of Nicaragua. He desperately tried to consolidate his power, offering large land grants to Americans who would join him, making English the official language, and legalizing slavery. As Americans with visions of annexing a slave state arrived, support for Walker among Nicaraguans dwindled. Costa Ricans soon had Walker on the defensive and his retreating forces burned Granada, ravaging its architectural beauty. At the end of the year additional reinforcements from the United States were stopped by a British blockade. In April 1857, 2,000 Guatemalans defeated Walker's exhausted and diseased forces. When the Costa Ricans promised surrendering Americans medical attention and passage home, most deserted Walker, leaving him with only 200 troops. Walker surrendered to a U.S. warship sent by President Buchanan.

In New Orleans, Walker received a hero's welcome. He vowed to return to Central America, and in 1860 he did, when British residents in the Bay Islands, furious over British surrender of the islands to Honduras, approached him with the plan of declaring the islands' independence from Honduras. Walker developed plans to join a group of Liberals then rebelling in Tegucigalpa, and in June 1860 he set sail for Roatán. He landed instead at Trujillo, only to be captured by British marines and handed over to the Hondurans. He was promptly executed and is today buried in Truji-llo.

The Walker misadventure discredited Liberals throughout the isthmus and consequently extended Conservative power. Also discredited was the United States, which had demonstrated its new imperial role in the region. The Civil War and completion of the Union Pacific Railroad in 1869 di-minished U.S. interest in Central America., and the French thought to step into this void and contracted to build a canal through Nicaragua in 1858. Failing in this, they contracted with Colombia in 1878 for a canal through Panama. Ferdinand de Lesseps, builder of the Suez Canal direct-ed the effort, which failed during construction. The emergence of the Unit-ed States as a naval power focused new interest on the strategic signifi-cance of the isthmus, and the U.S. stepped in to finish the canal in 1914, securing Panamian independence from Colombia and carving out a U.S. colony—and a permanent military presence—in the Panama Canal Zone.

The shift of power from Conservatives to Liberals at the end of the cen-tury accelerated trends toward modernization and dependence upon coffee and other export commodities. Politically, resurgent Liberalism meant a reaction against the Conservative *caudillos,* but dictatorship continued as the principal method of government. The new Liberals had lost some of the idealism of their predecessors in the days of Morazán, but they did not abandon dreams of progressive government. Rather they had conclud-ed that material economic growth was a priority that needed to precede political democracy. Long-term patterns emerged in their obsession for development: anticlericalism, faith in technical education, a rejection of the metaphysical, a "postponement" of democracy, imitation of European and North American values, and an insensitivity to the working classes.

Age of Dictatorship

Between 1870 and 1900 commerce boomed in the region, but capital flight also began as wealthy plantation owners deposited their funds abroad. (This export of wealth is still a critical problem in the region today.) Foreigners played vital roles in the development of the export economies, but a large-scale influx of hardworking immigrants never took place in Central America as it did in North and South America. Rather a small foreign entrepreneurial class created an elite partnership with wealthy Liberals and skimmed their fortunes off the top of the economy.

Politically historians call this period an Age of Dictatorship. The boom-ing export trade required centralized, executive-managed economies, with the military as a guarantor of labor peace and political stability. These so-called Republican dictators from the Liberals' stronghold—Justo Ru-fino Barrios, Manuel Estrada Cabrera, and Jorge Ubico of Guatemala; Tomás Guardia of Costa Rica; José Santos Zelaya and Anastasio Somoza of Nicaragua; Marco Aurelio Soto, Luis Bográn, Policarpo Bonilla, and Tiburcio Carías Andino of Honduras; and Santiago González and the infa-mous Maximiliano Hernández Martínez of El Salvador—all created politi-cal machinery founded on rigged elections and military might, with an elite of coffee producers and foreigners as their patrons. Only in Costa Rica, where an election transferred power successfully in 1889, did voting rights mean anything at all.

On the face of it these Liberal dictators were similar to their Conservative predecessors, but several changes were evolving: personal cliques of cronies were replaced by permanent administrative bureaucracies; the church lost much of its privileged status; the armies, previously bully gangs faithful only to local *caudillos,* became professional and institutional in nature; and most of the elite families of the Conservative period lost their fortunes. But the new oligarchy would soon become as inbred and aristocratic as their predecessors, and plans for reforms that would spread the wealth evaporated. Public education had always been a rallying issue for Liberals, but the only nation that made any headway during this period was Costa Rica, where literacy rose from 11 percent in 1864 to 76 percent in 1927 and 85 percent in 1963.

Rural peasants and Indians remained where they had always been—at the bottom of society in every category of development. Throughout the region planters ruled entire villages through debt patronage, forced labor, and naked intimidation. Whenever Indians or workers made efforts to organize, they were ruthlessly suppressed by the army. Communal Indian lands were steadily gobbled up, and a landless serfdom was created. The material advances championed by the Liberals—new roads, ports, bridges, expanded agricultural production, and exports—were provided by the backbreaking labor of shamelessly exploited peasants.

The twentieth century found Central America in the same colonial, dependent position from which it had supposedly liberated itself in the previous century. In the modern era, however, the tune would be called by the United States of America.

The Continuing Struggle

It was the United States participation in the Cuban War of independence, and the subsequent acquisition of Puerto Rico and a string of Pacific island colonies that focused new interest in a Central American canal at the turn of the century. The United States, always with the consent of local authorities, had sent troops to Panama (then a department of Colombia) numerous times in the second half of the nineteenth century to protect the American transisthmus railroad.

In 1902, however, U.S. troops entered in response to disturbances in Colombia and aided Panama in gaining independence. A treaty was signed, granting the United States construction rights for a canal, U.S. control of the 10-mile-wide Canal Zone—and permanent military presence.

The canal exponentially raised the economic and strategic stakes in the Caribbean Basin and Central America. The U.S. rose to the challenge with military interventions in Haiti in 1915, the Dominican Republic in 1916, and, perhaps most significantly, in Nicaragua in 1912. While U.S. fiscal agents seized control of the national treasury, the marines occupied the principal cities, towns, ports, and railroads. The Bryan-Chamorro Treaty of 1916 formalized the client–state status of Nicaragua, and granted the U.S. exclusive rights to the construction of a Nicaraguan Canal, 99-year leases to the Corn Islands off the Caribbean coast, rights to the construction of a navy base in the Gulf of Fonseca, and carte blanche to intervene in Nicaraguan affairs whenever so inclined. As a trade-off, Nicaragua received all of $3 million—to be subtracted from its substantial foreign debt.

The U.S. occupation was essentially low-key. Showing the flag seemed enough to maintain the Conservative governments of Emiliano Chamorro and his succesor Diego Manual Chamorro. The marines were there to protect U.S. economic interests, not to police the turbulent nation. Banditry and political strife continued in the countryside, but stability was sufficient for the marines to withdraw in 1925.

When new revolutionary action broke out in 1926—with support from Mexico—the marines returned. In 1927, State Department official Harry Stimson negotiated a compromise that would maintain Aldofo Díaz in power through 1928, when a U.S.-supervised election would take place. The Stimson agreement also provided for the U.S. creation of a National Guard to police the countryside. In 1928, Liberal army chief José María Moncada won the presidency. However, a military ally of Moncada's, Augusto César Sandino, didn't cooperate, and took to the hills as a guerrilla fighter. U.S. and Nicaraguan forces (led by American officers) pursued Sandino into Nicaragua's northern mountains, but the geography and guerrilla tactics of Sandino's army stymied their efforts. In desperation U.S. forces began aerial bombardment—which did more damage to civilian mountain villages than to Sandino's soldiers—and intimidation of the peasant population sympathetic to the rebels. Sandino was a profound anti-imperialist, and leftists the world over rallied to his cause; however, he resisted their support, publicly rejecting the solidarity of the Communist International. Sandino, contrary to modern historical revision from both Havana and Washington, was certainly never a Marxist.

In 1932 an election placed the Liberal Juan Bautista Sacasa in the presidential palace, and in January 1933, U.S. forces left Nicaragua. In February 1934 Bautista Sacasa met with Sandino, ostensibly to discuss reconciliation. After their dinner together, however, Sandino was murdered by National Guardsmen led by Bautista Sacasa's nephew, Anastasio Somoza García, who was the head of the National Guard. Somoza García would not formally assume the presidency until 1936, but from the murder of Sandino onward, the Somozas ruled the Nicaraguan Republic—the strongest family dynasty in Latin American history. In 1950, "Tacho" Somoza pushed a constitution through congress that gave him indefinite dictatorial powers.

The stock market crash of 1929 and the subsequent Depression was disastrous for all the commodity-exporting economies of Central America. The collapse of the region's economies led to an embracing of authoritarian regimes (and, in many cases, flirtations with fascism and communism) throughout the isthmus. In addition to Nicaragua, strong-arm dictators assumed power in Guatemala, El Salvador, and Honduras. Even democratic Costa Rica endured strikes and riots.

In El Salvador the military installed Maximiliano Hernández Martínez into the presidency in December 1931. Hernández Martínez crushed the mildly socialist opposition, further polarizing the nation's two incredibly disparate have and have-not classes. El Salvadoran communists decided that the times were right for revolution, and on January 22, 1932, a peasant insurrection was launched in the western coffee-growing region. As an eerie backdrop, that evening volcanoes throughout Guatemala and El Salvador erupted, filling the air with an ashen haze. Rebels marched on the town of Sonsonate, pillaging and terrorizing the various ranches of the countryside. The army garrison in town managed to drive them back, and the revolutionaries—some 5,000 strong—retreated to a nearby town to regroup. Martínez responded with a demonic frenzy of violence. Today it is called simply the *matanza*—the massacre. In villages all over the region, troops marched civilians to mass graves and executed them. A scorched-earth policy was pursued and entire villages were wiped out. Estimates today are that up to 30,000 people were systematically executed by Martínez's army and a hastily assembled civil guard composed of wealthy landowners and their loyal peasants.

Tiburcio Carías Andino was the dictator of Depression-era Honduras. Carías Andino was considerably less ruthless than his fellows in Guatemala and El Salvador, but where Martínez in El Salvador, and Jorge Ubico in Guatemala lasted until 1944, Carías held onto power until 1948.

Guatemala

In Guatemala, General Jorge Ubico became the prototypical tyrant. Freely elected in 1931, Ubico turned suddenly brutal, ordering a wave of assassinations, executions, prison terms, and exile for communists, labor organizers, and any others who seriously questioned his rule. With all opposition silenced, Ubico bore down on the financial front, stabilizing the national economy and granting generous concessions to foreign (usually United States) economic interests. Although the Guatemalan economy actually expanded under Ubico, Guatemalans as a whole did not profit. Ubico, his cronies, and the foreign capitalists banked the national wealth abroad, while a pernicious secret police kept the peace at home.

When railroad workers joined a nationwide strike to paralyze Guatemala's transportation system, Ubico fled to New Orleans exile. The resultant power struggle was brief. Professional men gathered to form the new National Renovation Party (PRN), backing Juan José Arévalo Bermejo, an exiled university president. Ubico's military staff turned power over to a military junta headed by military officer Frederico Ponce Vaides. When a respected newspaper editor was assassinated, reportedly on Vaides's orders, students, workers, and rebel military officers seized power. A revolutionary junta allowed for the election of the exiled Arévalo.

Arévalo, who had been teaching philosophy in Argentina, called for a new political movement, "spiritual socialism," which focused on a substantial restructuring of Guatemalan political and economic life. Marxists, encouraged by Arévalo's leftist leanings, became very dynamic in the country's substantial labor movement. By 1950 virtually every union had communist-influenced leadership. Urban workers saw wages increase, the establishment of a social security program, new public works, hospitals, and schools.

Arévalo counted on the backing of much of Guatemala's new, expanding urban middle class, but his populist policies put him squarely in conflict with the class of planters and foreign investors who had profited so handsomely during the Ubico years. During five years in office, Arévalo withstood no less than 22 military revolts. In late 1949 rebellious forces murdered Fransisco Arana, Arévalo's chief supporter in the military, and Arévalo responded by arming a civilian militia.

Leftist elements were active in the preelection period in 1950. Communist student groups campaigned openly, the government news bureau and radio station were dominated by leftists, as was the government newspaper. The communists in and out of government actively supported the presidential candidacy of Jacobo Arbenz, Arévalo's 36-year-old defense minister.

After Arbenz won the presidency by a commanding majority, his government promoted mass organizations, land reform, collectivization, and union rights. Though Arbenz himself was not a communist, his government forged a close relationship with the Soviet Union, vociferously opposing U.S. intervention in Korea. Labor unions and mass organizations provided the foot soldiers for a crackdown against anticommunists, which resulted in hundreds of arrests, tortures, and assassinations.

Arbenz's principal pillar of support were leftist labor unions; his opposition, the army. In 1952 leftists urged that Arbenz begin arming the unions against possible army opposition to the land reform program. Ernesto ("Che") Guevara, then working in the land reform administration, was a particularly strident advocate of arming the masses. The Arbenz movement, like the Sandinistas 30 years later, was conceived as a movement without borders. The communist Guatemalan Labor Party (PGT) was active in propaganda and agitation in El Salvador and Honduras. In 1954, Guatemalan and Honduran workers joined in striking the principal American agroindustrial operation in Central America, the United Fruit Company.

The United Fruit Company, with 550,000 acres (of which only 77,000 acres were cultivated), was the largest landowner in Guatemala. The government proposed to expropriate nearly 400,000 acres, indemnifying the company through long-term bonds. Washington was not compliant. If the confiscation of United Fruit lands and opposition to U.S. activities in the United Nations were not enough, the Guatemalans pushed Washington over the brink when they imported a leaky boatload of aging Czechoslovakian rifles. When attempts at securing international condemnation of the Guatemalan regime proved fruitless, Secretary of State John Foster Dulles and John E. Puerifoy, the U.S. ambassador to Guatemala, entered into a conspiracy with exiled Guatemalans Carlos Castillo Armas and Miguel Ydígoras. The U.S. air-lifted arms into Honduras and Nicaragua (where the Somozas were more than willing to assist) and laid down plans for an invasion to be disguised as a popular insurrection.

When rebel forces, backed by the CIA and elements of the United State Marine Corps, entered the country from Honduras, the Guatemalan army refused to defend the Arbenz regime. Arbenz fled and Castillo Armas was placed at the head of the new junta. Arrests and assassinations followed as part of a general purge of leftists. Under Castillo Armas, the old power structure of coffee planters and foreign capitalists was established anew. Castillo Armas was assassinated in 1957. His partner in the overthrow of Arbenz, Miguel Ydígoras, promptly assumed the presidency—his reward for assisting in the overthrow of Arbenz.

Ydígoras rule was a turbulent one. In November 1960 he quelled a rebellion at the Matamoros military barracks which led to his ordering B-26 bombing runs over the rebellious provinces. Survivors of the rebellion, led by Lieutenant Marco Antonio Yon Sosa, began a guerrilla insurgency that would last a decade. Throughout the 1960s these and other rebels kept up a low-level bush war, supported by many in the universities, that confounded the military. Right-wing reaction took the form of new shadowy organizations like Mano Blanca ("The White Hand") and Ojo por Ojo

("An Eye for an Eye"), which began 20 years of death-squad activity in Guatemala and nearby El Salvador.

Ydígoras was ousted by the military in 1963. His successor, Enrique Peralta Azurdia, plunged the nation into a dark military dictatorship. U.S.-trained counterinsurgency forces quelled the rural rebellion, while death squads targeted urban political leaders. By 1966, Peralta had stabilized the country and permitted a free election, won by Julio César Méndez Montenegro, a successor to Arévalo's movement. Méndez lived in the palace, but the military did not let him rule.

In 1970 the military's candidate, Colonel Carlos Arana Osorio breezed to an easy presidential victory after leftist elements had been forbidden from campaigning. In 1974, General Kjell Laugerud García, the son of Norwegian immigrants, assumed the presidency in a nakedly rigged election. While Arana and Laugerud were making a mockery of the democratic process, business boomed. The military elite took advantage of the good times and began acquiring private companies, banks, and large land holdings, amassing substantial fortunes.

In the mountains the 10-year-old insurgency continued. The Guatemalan army's counterinsurgency training was paying off though, and the rebels remained only an irritant. In 1978 the infamous General Romeo Lucas García became president after an election marred by open fraud and voter abstention. Lucas bore down on opposition with almost pathological intensity. In the cities death squads wiped out a generation of political and intellectual leadership. In the countryside military sweeps seized huge tracts of land and systematically murdered thousands of Indian peasants thought to be sympathetic to Marxist-Leninist guerrillas. By 1984 nearly 200,000 Guatemalan Indians would be living in Mexico as refugees.

International outrage was rapidly isolating Guatemala, as foreign capital dried up and the United States cut off military aid. Young military officers, seeking to limit the damage, ousted Lucas García in March 1982, placing in his stead retired General Efraín Ríos Montt. Ríos Montt, who had been President Arana's military chief of staff, was by this time a born-again Christian through the efforts of the evangelical protestant, California-based Christian Church of the Word. Ríos endeavored to discipline the greedier military capitalists, and to some degree he restrained the army, whose rural massacres reportedly declined, though they did not stop. Ironically, Ríos's pressure on the military was not his undoing; rather it was his annoying evangelical preaching and his imposition of an unpopular sales tax.

In August 1983, Ríos was replaced by his defense minister, General Oscar Humberto Mejía Victores. Mejía returned to the generals their special financial privileges, and army violence flared in the countryside. Mejía was just a caretaker, though, until new elections could be formulated. Guatemala desperately needed to renew international faith and funding, and in 1986 the Christian Democrat Vinicio Cerezo Arévalo was allowed to assume the presidency after an internationally supervised election.

El Salvador

In El Salvador, Maximiliano Hernández Martínez went quietly in 1944, followed by a series of military officers who put into place an alliance of landowners and the army which would govern for 30 years. Notable among these officers was Major Oscar Osorio, who ascended to the presidency in 1948, enacting the first social security legislation, public health programs, and women's suffrage. Osorio's Revolutionary Party of Democratic Union (PRUD) dominated the country until 1960, when Osorio broke away to form the Social Democratic Party (PDS). In January 1961 the military imposed a junta along the lines of the reactionary government in Guatemala, formally breaking relations with Castro's Cuba.

Throughout the 1960s, El Salvador had numerous political parties, but the government was essentially a military regime. In 1964 a Christian Democratic Party (PDC) was formed by José Napoleón Duarte, who served as mayor of San Salvador from 1964 to 1970. The charismatic Duarte offered a moderate, though still anticommunist, opposition to the governing conservative National Conciliation Party. In 1972, Duarte ran for the presidency, only to see his evident victory snatched away by a recount. Duarte organized a general strike, which was followed by an aborted coup attempt. Although Duarte denies complicity in the coup, he was arrested by security forces and beaten unconscious. Three days later he fled to exile in Guatemala.

When General Carlos Humberto Romero won a fraudulent election to the presidency in 1977, right-wing death squads, underwritten by wealthy landowners and organized by shadowy elements of national security forces, began systematic assassinations of opposition political leaders. Leftist and moderate leftist parties abandoned the electoral process, heading into the mountains to organize armed opposition. The Catholic church, led by Archbishop Oscar Romero, boycotted Romero's inauguration. The People's Revolutionary Army (ERP) began activity in the country's eastern mountains, and open civil war was on.

A revolutionary junta seized power in 1979 with Duarte serving as chief of state. Although moderate middle-class leaders and progressive young officers made up the junta, they could not restrain the accelerating activities of the death squads. In January 1980, Guillermo Ungo and Román Mayorga, the junta's most important progressive civilians, quit the junta and went into exile. Ungo assumed the leadership of the Revolutionary Democratic Front (FDR), a new union of leftist political and military organizations. In March the much-loved Archbishop Romero was murdered while saying mass. In April the Farabundo Martí Front for National Liberation (FMLN), named for the communist leader of the 1932 uprising that led to the *matanza*, unified the country's guerrilla forces. As centerleft and centrist politicians began to be targeted by the death squads, they joined the guerrillas in increasing numbers.

Meanwhile, Duarte was virtually a puppet president, held captive by the military and landowners, who frustrated his attempts at gradual change and land reform. In 1982, Duarte was defeated by a right-wing coalition led by Roberto D'Aubisson, a retired army major described by U.S. Ambassador Robert White as a "pathological killer" responsible for the murder of Archbishop Romero. Alvaro Magaña was named provisional president in 1982. Magaña was a moderate but beholden to the reactionary coalition that had secured his election. In many ways Magaña was a compromise lesser-of-two-evils, acceptable to the military and to the powerful U.S. Embassy, which was determined to keep D'Aubisson out of the Presidential Palace.

When Duarte was elected to the presidency in 1984, narrowly defeating Roberto D'Aubisson, El Salvador was in many ways an exhausted nation. The guerrillas had mounted a premature "final offensive" in 1981 and, after failing to inspire an insurrection, settled in for a long, bitter struggle with the military, which continues today.

Nicaragua

Throughout the twentieth century, when nationalistic strikes and social-ist-inspired reforms swept over Central American countries, Nicaragua was America's most faithful and docile ally. A special relationship was formed between the government and American business interests, which guaranteed stability, continuity, and profit—at the expense of democracy, social evolution, and welfare. The Somoza family dynasty ruled a Nicaragua that lived out social and economic patterns forged in the previous century. A tiny minority of the population profited from close association with the Somozas, while the majority toiled in the agricultural export industries, owned by the oligarchy, that was the foundation of the economy.

While disenchantment with the Somozas grew, only one party, the Conservatives, stood as an alternative—and they were deeply divided over whether to collaborate with the dictatorship. When an earthquake flattened Managua in 1972 and the Somozas made off with much of the international aid that poured into the nation, the appalled people of Nicaragua began to think seriously about alternatives to Somocismo.

The Sandinista Front for National Liberation (FSLN) was founded in the 1960s by university students convinced that Marxist-Leninist revolution was the only option for getting rid of the Somoza dynasty. The FSLN was considered the radical left of the Nicaraguan political spectrum until events of the late 1970s forced an alliance of the Sandinistas with other sectors in opposition to the dictatorship. Among these sectors to ally with the Sandinistas were opposition business people frustrated at the graft and avarice of the Somozas, the Catholic church, active in social issues since the declaration of Vatican II, independent unions, political parties, and the independent press, particularly the influential daily *La Prensa*.

In January 1978, *La Prensa* publisher Pedro Juaquín Chamorro was assassinated—many feel on orders from Somoza. The people of Nicaragua rose up in insurrection. Somoza struck back with fury, unleashing his palace army, the National Guard. The United States fretted back and forth, alternately supporting and condemning the dictatorship. Weapons and material support flooded to the Sandinistas from Costa Rica, Venezuela, and Panama. As the war marched through the towns of Nicaragua and as thousands died in the crossfire, the United States sought to ease Somoza out of power through resolutions from the Organization of American States; pointedly leaving out the Sandinistas.

When a national strike—coupled with the flight of capital out of the country—paralyzed the nation in the spring of 1979, the Sandinistas launched a final offensive from Costa Rica. Somoza retreated to his bunker overlooking Managua as his National Guard, in disarray, turned to aerial bombing of the city in an effort to hold back the tide of revolution. International opinion, already behind the Sandinistas, pushed Somoza over the edge when National Guard troops murdered U.S. journalist Bill Steward—on camera, for all the world to see. On July 19, 1979, the Sandinistas marched into Managua, and Somoza's National Guard fled.

Over 40,000 Nicaraguans had died in the vicious civil war, and the national economy was a shambles. The United States set out to assist the shattered nation with generous loans, aid, and the renegotiation of existing debt. But as Cuban advisers and Soviet-supplied weaponry poured into the nation, it became clear that the broad spectrum of dissent that had forced the Somoza regime out was largely powerless—and that true power lay in the national directorate of the FSLN and in the Sandinista Army.

When Ronald Reagan entered office in 1981, the U.S. ceased aid and adopted a decidedly adversarial position. The CIA began meeting with exiled officers of Somoza's National Guard, and the Nicaraguan Democratic Force (FDN) was created to harass the Sandinistas. The Contras allied with insurgent Mosquito Indians from the Caribbean coast and with exiled Nicaraguans in Costa Rica under the leadership of Eden Pastora— the legendary Commander Zero—who had bravely served with Sandinista Forces during the insurrection, only to find himself edged out of power by hard-line Marxist Sandinistas.

In Nicaragua the Sandinistas embarked on a revolutionary program, much of it modeled on the social and political experiments of the Cuban revolution. The people were quickly mobilized into mass organizations, government-dominated unions, and a militia that by 1984 brought the Sandinistas' total military force to over 100,000. Opposition unions, political parties, and the clergy were harassed, and censorship was decreed. Neighborhood Committees for the Defense of the Revolution, modeled on the block spies of Castro's Cuba, kept watch for suspicious behavior among the citizenry.

The Sandinistas' efforts toward positive social transformation included new housing and health facilities for the poor and a celebrated literacy campaign that combined basic reading skills with political propaganda. The Sandinistas created a hybrid economic system of state-controlled industry (largely created from the vast expropriated holdings of the Somozas), cooperative farming, and private enterprise that has thus far seen production dramatically plummet. The United States cut off all economic relations, and the ongoing counterrevolutionary war further bled the economy.

In 1984, Nicaragua's de facto chief of state, Daniel Ortega Saavedra, was elected president in elections marred by censorship, limits on opposition campaign activities, and a state-mobilized organization in favor of the FSLN.

Central America Today

Ten years have passed since the murder of Pedro Juaquim Chamorro in Nicaragua unofficially launched a decade of social and political tumult in Central America. Every economy in the region has felt the financial strain of the conflict, and the issues that divided Central Americans then continue today. In the fundamental struggle—the striving of the Central American people for social, economic, and political human rights—little has changed.

A notable cause for optimism, however, is the ascension of Costa Rican President Oscar Arias to the world stage as a Nobel prize-winning peacemaker. His plan for the region, which calls for political rights, freedom of expression, the cessation of armed conflict, and the use of neighboring countries as sanctuaries for insurgent groups, along with the expulsion of foreign military influence from the isthmus, stands as the best hope yet for peace. Arias seems to have the stature, the credibility, and the charisma to galvanize the forces of peace. But while every Central American state and insurgent organization has endorsed the plan, none seem anxious to live by it.

Guatemala, although ruled by democratically elected President Cerezo, remains little more than a cosmetic democracy. The military machine that accounted for over 100,000 political killings and 40,000 disappearances in the early 1980s is essentially still in place. In most measurable areas of national affairs, Guatemala is seeing good times. Political violence in the countryside has ebbed and the nation's agricultural production is back on track. Death-squad activity in the cities has also been reduced, and tourists are visiting again in large numbers. But Cerezo has not managed any program of land reform; the Indian majority still languishes in poverty with little hope for opportunity in the future. While it remains a country of astounding natural beauty and culture, Guatemala is in many ways a sociopolitical relic of an earlier century.

In El Salvador, the war grinds on. Despite a flow of U.S. military and economic aid that, according to a recent count, amounted to $30,000 per guerilla, per annum, the FMLN still controls vast areas of the countryside with impunity. They regularly sabotage national electrical grids (recently plunging 80 percent of the country, including the capital city, into darkness), and, by threatening public servants, can effectively freeze public transportation and other essential services.

The government of President Duarte came to power with a promise to bring peace to El Salvador through a combination of peace talks, amnesties, and reformist policies. Instead, his party has been accused of widespread corruption, including the theft of American aid funds. The military, staffed by an unmotivated officer corps and a fighting force of conscripts, has been unable to secure several provinces.

Results from the National Assembly and municipal elections held in the spring of 1988 promise continuing conflict. The Christian Democrats, in a stunning defeat, lost their legislative majority to the right-wing Nationalist Republican Alliance (ARENA), which has been implicated—for eight years—in death-squad violence. ARENA also enjoyed sweeping mayoral victories in all of El Salvador's major cities, including the capital of San Salvador, which has seen Christian Democrat mayors for 24 years.

The guerillas of the FMLN demonstrated contempt for the election by murdering one mayor and kidnapping four others. Under threat of death, citizens in several provinces chose not to vote. Those that did walked to the polls following a guerilla-enforced ban on public transportation.

The FMLN has stepped up a new policy of attacks on civilian targets, including randomly selected automobiles on the nation's highways. Guerillas detonated three car bombs in the capital city—the first such incident employed against civilians. With ARENA in control of the National Assembly and a lame-duck President (Duarte is constitutionally forbidden an additional term), any hope of reform or reconciliation in El Salvador has been stalled for the indefinite future. The combination of a Marxist insurgency in the provinces and a far-right National Assembly in the capital city promises little more than enduring hostilities.

In Nicaragua, the sheer weight of the war—on the ruling Sandinistas, on the Contras, and on the people—has raised the hope of compromises that would have been unthinkable a few years ago. The central fact of Nicaraguan life today is a wartime economy reeling under inflation that reached 1,800 percent in 1987, and was projected for an astounding 10,000 percent in 1988. Shortages of electricity, gasoline, and cooking gas, and never-ending lines for everything from buses to beans are everywhere apparent. In a gesture more symbolic than practical, the Sandinistas replaced the national currency, the cordoba, which had been trading at 20,000 to the dollar, with a *new cordoba,* trading at 10 to the dollar. The new currency has neither slowed inflation nor increased the supply of basic commodities. The war continues to hemorrhage Nicaragua's economy.

But if the war has taken a toll on the Sandinistas and their supporters, it has likewise worn down the Contras. In five years of U.S.-financed guerilla war the Contras are still based in Honduras (in open violation of the Arias' plan) and utterly dependent on the United States Congress for funding. The congressional vote to cut Contra funding has had a chilling effect on the Contras, curtailing airlifts from Honduras that allow the projection of guerilla power into the Nicaraguan interior. Unlike the largely self-sufficient FMLN of El Salvador, the Contras evidently cannot live off the largess of the civilian population nor capture their weaponry from the Sandinistas. Theirs is an insurgency based on the lobbying floor of Congress.

When a March 1988 offensive routed the financially strapped Contras from their forward bases in the Bocay region of northern Nicaragua, the Sandinistas pursued the fleeing Contras across the Honduran border, destroying base camps and ammunition supplies as they went. It was a dazzling military victory for the Sandinistas. The response from Washington was swift, if theatrical. Over 3,000 U.S. troops were quickly airlifted to Honduras in a show of force. Most of the Sandinistas were back across the border before the Americans landed, and the Americans were back in the United States within two weeks without a shot being fired. As an epilogue to the melodrama, news reports revealed that officials of the Reagan Administration had in fact requested that the Honduran President José Azcona Hoyo request the U.S. response in the face of the invading Sandinista army.

The next chapter of the drama unfolded in the tiny Nicaraguan town of Sapoa, near the Costa Rican border, where Sandinista and Contra leaders sat down only days later for peace talks. This spectacular series of meetings resulted in cease-fire zones for the Contras within Nicaragua, an agreement for the Contras to participate in a national dialogue with other political parties, and the recognition of the Sandinista constitution and Daniel Ortega as the nation's President.

With an economy crippled by ten years of civil war and a Soviet government reluctant to increase economic aid, the Sandinistas have swallowed their pride. The Contras have likewise learned the value of compromise: their rout at the hands of Sandinista forces laid bare their dependence on a regular check from Uncle Sam. In an irony that must make political purists on both side wince, it is evident that the combatants are talking peace—after a war that has claimed some 25,000 lives—because neither can *afford* to fight indefinitely.

With regular elections, a standard of living that rivals some United States communities, booming business in international trade and finance, a free (if self-censoring) press, and a permanent American military presence of 10,000 troops, Panama for years seemed insulated from its squabbling neighbors. Recently, however, it became evident that the good life in Panama was built on a foundation of corruption, deceit, and the cocaine trade.

General Manuel Antonio Noriega rose to prominence as the right hand of Omar Torrijos, whose 1968 populist coup broke the grip that a few chosen families had maintained over Panamanian life since the turn of the century. When Torrijos mysteriously died in a 1981 plane crash, Noriega assumed the mantle of military strongman behind the throne of the Panamanian presidency.

The cracks in the facade emerged in early 1987 when discontented military officers went public with accusations that Noriega had laundered funds and taken bribes from Colombian cocaine smugglers. Noriega, it was said, had for years supplied information to the Central Intelligence Agency while passing information and restricted U.S. high-tech exports in the other direction to Cuba. Opposition to the General coalesced around a civil crusade reminiscent of the people power demonstrations of the Philippines. Thousands of middle-class citizens, many in new German and Japanese automobiles, gathered in anti-government motorcades.

Early in 1988 U.S. grand juries in Tampa and Miami indicted Noriega for conspiring to ship four thousand pounds of cocaine and one million pounds of marijuana to the United States. When José I. Blandon, Panamanian consul general in New York, broke with the Noriega government, the floodgates parted. Blandon detailed to a Senate investigative subcommittee an incredible tale that included accusations that Noriega had regularly accepted bribes from the dreaded Medellin Cartel cocaine mafia; that Noriega had converted the national customs and passport offices, as well as the railroad, ports, and airports, into a huge kickback scheme; that cocaine dealers laundered $200 million per month in Panamanian banks, and that between $200 million and $600 million found its way into Noriega's personal bank accounts.

When Panamanian President Eric Arturo Delvalle demanded Noriega's resignation on national television he was placed under house arrest and later escaped into hiding somewhere within Panama. Noriega put down a coup attempt led by the head of the national police and enacted state of urgency laws that suspend habeas corpus and allow the government to confiscate businesses taking part in national strikes.

Due to Panama's dependence on its financial industry and its use of the U.S. dollar as an official currency, the country proved uniquely vulnerable to U.S. economic pressure. Washington instructed the Federal Reserve to cease shipping cash to Panama's financial organizations, and within days banks had closed. Public servants unable to cash their checks took to the streets.

What is perhaps most remarkable about the Panama situation is that to date only a handful of citizens have been killed or seriously wounded in daily disturbances. It seems clear that the people of Panama have had enough, and the insurrection is intended to wash away corruption, not to radicalize a political and economic system that is fundamentally pro-Western and democratically inclined.

By the time you read this, there may well be more significant events to add to an overview of Central American history. The stories of these countries are still very much unfolding.

GUATEMALA

Land of Eternal Spring

by
MICHAEL SHAWCROSS

Michael Shawcross is a writer and editor who has worked on numerous publications. He lives in Antigua.

Guatemala is considered by many to be one of the world's most beautiful countries. Volcanos, mountain lakes, and jungles combine with a population that is mostly of Indian descent to make this a unique land.

The main attractions for visitors are the highland Maya, descendants of the original Maya of centuries ago. Awesome ruined cities overgrown by jungle speak of a civilization that lasted some 2,000 years, a civilization whose history and culture are still not totally understood, whose sudden decline is not completely explained, and whose descendants still persist, planting and harvesting their corn, and worshiping the ancient gods, as they have done for centuries. Scores of weathered, magnificent old churches hidden away in isolated mountain villages, and charming old colonial towns, with their central squares, fountains, government buildings, and cobblestone streets, recall the days of the Conquest, when the Spaniards tried to re-create their homeland in the threatening wilderness of a new world. Hundreds of picturesque Indian villages, with their colorfully clad inhabitants, who still speak languages descended directly from the Maya, who still live much as they did a thousand years ago, who still adamantly and proudly refuse to become a part of the culture that conquered their forefathers, offer glimpses into a fascinating world and a way of life that, while it remains strong and vital here, has all but disappeared in the rest of the world. The land itself, like a dream of some romantic painter, with its chains of rocky mountains, smoking volcanos, pine forests, hot mineral springs, vast jungles, and isolated lakes, is like nothing else on earth. And set among those mountains, beside those lakes, are modern hotels and resorts offering modern comforts and services. It is an enchanting and mysterious land, in which even the most seasoned traveler will find experiences, sights, and pleasures that are new, strange, and exciting.

The Land

The approximately 42,000 square miles of Guatemala are remarkable for their beauty and variety. The country is crisscrossed by chains of towering mountains cut by *barrancas* or ravines thousands of feet deep; 33 volcanos, some almost 14,000 feet high, several still active, are constant reminders of the seismic activity beneath the surface of the land; lush jungles adjoin scorched, arid desert land; frosty highlands sweep down to steaming lowland swamps; broad savannahs and vast hardwood forests cover hundreds of square miles; highlands are dotted with deep, crystalline volcanic lakes, which flow through rushing mountain streams and sluggish jungle rivers to the white sands of the Atlantic or the black volcanic sands of the Pacific Coast; steaming mineral springs and geysers spurt out of the earth, while limestone caverns stretch out below the earth; high plateaus of incredible fertility, nourished by millennia of volcanic ash, are edged by volcanic wastelands of black tumbled rocks and lava. It is as if someone had tried to jam the topographical features of an entire world into the confines of a country about the size of the state of Ohio.

The dominant feature of Guatemala's topography is its dense, rugged, central mountain chain, part of that immense *cordillera* that runs from the Rocky Mountains in the north to the Andes in the south. Transversing the country like a spine, the peaks of the Sierra Madres, Cuchumatanes, and other related mountain ranges have had an immeasurable effect on every aspect of Guatemala's history. The fertile mountain slopes and plateaus, with their variety of climates, proved perfect breeding grounds for a wide variety of flora and fauna—it is said that in Guatemala alone there are more varieties of plants, birds, and other animals than in the entire United States, an example of biological diversity caused by geographical diversity.

The constant springlike climate of the mountains encouraged the growth of early human cultures, but at the same time, the rugged and wild terrain made communication difficult and discouraged the growth of unified or centrally governed societies. The mountains provided strongholds for the Indians, enabling them to hold out against attacking enemies and retain their cultural diversity. With the conquest, the mountains also provided bastions against the threat of invasion by other European nations, but made travel, trade, and communication difficult, causing a sense of separatism and isolation which Guatemala is still trying to overcome.

Today, the mountains still play a major role in all aspects of Guatemalan life—more than two-thirds of the populace lives in less than one-third of the land's total territory: in the cool, fertile lands at elevations of over 3,000 feet, the Tierra Templada.

Running along the southern edge of the central mountain chain is a jagged string of thirty-three volcanos, the tallest in Central America, with several of them (Pacaya, Fuego, Santiaguito) still active. From Tajumulco, the highest volcano in Central America (13,812 feet) near the Mexican border, into El Salvador, these volcanos run along a major fault line almost parallel to the Pacific Coast, at an average distance from the coast of forty-five miles. The ash from these volcanos has made the surrounding lands some of the most fertile and productive in the world; but on the other hand, their eruptions, with their great flows of lava and rains of fire, have again and again destroyed the towns and crops that surround them, making the land both desirable and dangerous, and giving rise to a deep fatalism in the cultures that flourish "under the volcano."

South of the volcanic highlands, the terrain slopes steeply toward the Pacific, leaving between the mountains and the sea a thin strip of hot, fertile lowland. Once covered with impenetrable jungles and swamps, disease-ridden, and all but uninhabitable, this land was cleared away in the late nineteenth and early twentieth century and has now become Guatemala's agricultural center. Cotton, sugar cane, cattle, and bananas are raised on vast ranches, and moved to ports on the Atlantic and Pacific for shipment abroad.

To the north of the central highlands, the land slopes away more gently, through the rainy, verdant coffee lands of Alta and Baja Verapaz, into the vast rolling lowlands known as El Petén. Once the center of the Maya civilization, this immense territory remained virtually empty for hundreds of years, and remains almost empty today—but its dense hardwood forests, jungles, swamps, and savannahs, which form more than one-third of Guatemala's total territory, are beginning to show the impact of colonization motivated by Guatemala's growing population.

To the northeast, the highlands near Guatemala City drop into the desert-like valley of the Motagua River, shut off from rain by the Sierra de las Minas range. But as the river flows toward the Caribbean, the climate becomes hotter, the rains more frequent, until it reaches the lush, tropical Caribbean lowlands. Here the rains are heavy, almost incessant, the weather simmering, the lands prodigiously fertile. It was in these lowlands, between Lake Izabal and the border of Honduras, that the first great banana plantations were planted toward the end of the nineteenth century by the United Fruit Company—plantations that were to have such a profound effect, economically, politically, and culturally, on everything that has happened since.

A good way to get acquainted with Guatemala and to get oriented is to visit the relief map in the Hipodromo del Norte located at the north end of 6 Avenida in Zona 2 of Guatemala City. This huge map presents a dramatic image of the geological diversity of the country.

The History

Archaeologists now believe that humans have inhabited Guatemala for at least 15,000 years, and perhaps as much as 25,000 years. By 1000 B.C.

there were highly developed and organized societies, sharing a common way of life, throughout all of what is now Guatemala. These societies, centered around stepped pyramids, which must have served as places of worship, were to become the greatest pre-Columbian civilization in the western world, the Maya.

The achievements of the Maya are well known. They took a system of hieroglyphic writing and mathematics from the earlier Olmecs and developed them into subtle, efficient, and sophisticated means of conveying and storing wisdom. Their use of the zero predates its use in European society by more than a thousand years. Their calendar was more accurate than the one we use today. Their knowledge of astronomy was staggering; their astronomical observations almost incredibly accurate when it is remembered they had no telescopes or metal instruments. Their skills as architects, engineers, sculptors, and painters can be seen at numerous archaeological sites throughout Guatemala, and in museums all over the world. The cities they built are still overwhelming in their immensity, majesty, and mystery; and when they were flourishing, they must have been some of the most beautiful and awesome cities the world has known.

Then, in the 9th century A.D., classic Maya civilization collapsed and the great cities were abandoned. The exact cause of this collapse remains unknown.

The Spanish Victory

The conquest of Guatemala was assured with the death of the Maya-Quiché warlord Tecún Umán, in hand-to-hand combat with the brash young Spanish officer, Pedro de Alvarado, near present-day Quezaltenango in 1524. Alvarado, Cortés's chief lieutenant in the battles against Montezuma, had been sent south by Cortés to (as one historian puts it) "subdue and seduce the lands and the people." Ambitious, cunning, ruthless, cruel, complex, and colorful, and driven by dreams of empire as vast as those of Cortés, Alvarado was bold and imaginative both as subduer and as seducer—he had found the role he was born to play and never turned back. With the help of an epidemic of smallpox, which preceded his army's advance, decimating the Indian population, by cleverly taking advantage of the bitter enmities between the tribes and playing them off against each other, and by ruthlessly exterminating any Indian rulers who stood in his way, Alvarado was able to subdue almost all of Guatemala in a few years.

The Indians were defeated, but were not reconciled to slavery. In the decades that followed, spontaneous Indian revolts broke out everywhere, and most of the energies and resources of the Spaniards were needed to put down these rebellions. The suppressions were brutal, and it is estimated that between 1524 and 1650 as many as six-sevenths of the Indian population in Mesoamerica (more than 10 million people) were wiped out by the fighting and diseases. Ultimately, the most efficient means of bringing the Indians under control was found to be ideological—Maya ceremonial centers were torn down, churches erected in their places, and the Indians were forcibly converted to Christianity. But though they were pacified, the Indians of Guatemala remained defiantly apart from the culture of the conquerors. While the Indian populations of other Central American nations were slowly absorbed into colonial civilization by intermarriage, forming a new people known as mestizo, the highland Maya of Guatemala doggedly and with fierce determination retained their own cultural identity.

The capital city of Santiago de Los Caballeros de Guatemala was first established in Tecpán, near the Cakchiquel capital of Iximché, in 1524. When the Cakchiquel rebelled against the Spaniards' voracious demands for gold, the capital was moved to the Almolonga valley, at the foot of volcano Agua. The city and Alvarado's widow Beatriz (who had only hours before declared herself ruler of Guatemala) perished in a great earthquake and flood in 1543.

The capital was then moved to the nearby Panchoy Valley, where it remained for over 200 years, growing into one of the most magnificent cities in the New World. Destroyed by earthquakes in 1773, the city's ruined palaces, cathedrals, and monasteries are still lovely, and the once-majestic town is now known as Antigua.

Seeking land that would be free of earthquakes, in 1776, the Guatemalan leaders moved the capital to La Ermita Valley, which was severely damaged by a strong earthquake in 1917. In the last two hundred years, this city, now known as Guatemala City, has grown into the largest metropolis in Central America, with a population of well over two million.

In the centuries that followed the conquest, Guatemala became the most important province in Central America, and its capital was the capital of the Kingdom of Guatemala, which extended over Chiapas, El Salvador, Honduras, Nicaragua, and Costa Rica. Guatemala was not just the political, but also the religious, cultural, economic, and social center of the kingdom, and those with ambitions, talents, and a taste for power naturally gravitated there from the other provinces. As Guatemala grew more powerful, the other provinces became increasingly resentful over discriminations they suffered at the hands of the rulers, landowners and merchants of the capital. These jealousies, resentments, and rivalries have continued to smoulder through the centuries, destroying several times attempts to unify the nations of Central America into a single republic.

But just as Guatemala was resented by the provinces, Spain was bitterly resented by the colonists. Creoles (people of Spanish descent born in the colonies) were ruled by bureaucrats from Spain, and were discriminated against, receiving only minor governmental posts. Spain's restrictions on what the colonies could grow and export (they were not allowed to grow anything that would compete with Spanish products; they could carry on trade only with Spain), were increasingly irritating to the merchants and landowners. With the American and French Revolutions as examples, emboldened by Spain's decreasing power, rebellion was in the air.

On September 15, 1821, 12 men, now hailed as the *Próceres de la Independencia* —Heroes of the Independence—gathered in Guatemala City to sign the Act of Independence of Central America. Soon after, the other nations of Central America declared their independence from Guatemala. Emperor Agustín de Iturbide of Mexico then sent troops south, forcing Guatemala to become a part of its Mexican Empire. The empire lasted less than a year, however, and the nations united as the Federal Republic of Central America in 1823. The republic was a noble dream, but it never really got off the ground, as jealousies, rivalries, greed, treachery, and almost constant warfare plagued it until it fell apart completely in 1839.

Since then, the political life of Guatemala has been marked by continuing struggles between liberals who have sought to reduce the power of the church, to build roads and schools, and to distribute the nation's wealth more equitably, and conservatives, who have represented the old families, the large landowners, the wealthy, and the church. Strongman dictators, both liberal and conservative, have ruled the country for most of its post-Independence history. Some of the most colorful were Rafael Carrera, a charismatic, illiterate peasant who seized power and ruled as a conservative for almost thirty years; Justo Rufino Barrios, known as The Reformer, who confiscated church property, tried to distribute wealth more fairly, developed plans for a railroad, ports, and a national school system, and was killed in battle in 1885 while struggling to reestablish the Central American Republic; Manuel Estrada Cabrera, who ruled with an iron hand for twenty years until he was declared insane and overthrown in 1920; and General Jorge Ubico Castañeda, who modernized the country, encouraged industrial growth, increased foreign trade, and instituted public works programs. When Ubico was deposed in 1944, Juan José Arévalo tried to improve the conditions of the poor, increasing the number of schools and improving the education system. President Jacobo Arbenz Guzman attempted to begin a program of land reform, making unused land available to the landless poor. This disturbed the large landowners, particularly the United Fruit Company, which owned large portions of Guatemala. With the help of the U.S. Central Intelligence Agency, Arbenz was overthrown in 1954 by the right-wing Colonel Carlos Castillo Armas, who was assassinated three years later.

Guatemala remained a political hotbed, and for most of the last thirty years the army has been the ruling power, selecting each new president from among its ranks. The leaders of the left generally had to remain in exile or temper their opinions, and there were frequent assassinations of those espousing liberal opinions. In the late 1970s and early 80s, tens of thousands of Indian peasants were reported murdered as a result of the government's "antiterrorist" campaign. Hundreds of thousands of Indians fled to Mexico. On March 23, 1982, a coup by young army officers overthrew the military government of Lucas García, after a fraudulent election, and invited General Ríos Montt to head the junta who would run the government. During Lucas García's regime tourism had dropped off sharply, and it was during Ríos Montt's time that the political and social systems began to change.

A serious attack on corruption and bribery was carried out, and there was much less conflict in the highlands. The number of guerrillas fighting there diminished considerably, and after six months of Montt in power, massacres by government soldiers stopped almost completely. However, on August 8, 1983, there was another coup, and Mejía Victores became chief of state. During 1984 and 1985 the quetzal was unofficially devalued, and during one period in late 1985 you could exchange $1 for up to 4 quetzales, causing many problems during the economic chaos of Mejía Victores' government.

Vinicio Cerezo Arévalo, of the Cristian Democrat party, easily won the internationally supervised presidential elections in December 1985, and on January 14 he was inaugurated as the first civil president of Guatemala for many years. He has a large number of social, political, and economic problems to resolve during his presidency. However, with discoveries of petroleum and a new hydro-electric plant, the country seems well on the way to self-sufficiency in energy. Its traditional strong exports of coffee, beef, cotton, sugar and bananas, increasing foreign investment, and its tourist industry all combine to make Guatemala's future seem economically promising. If the country can somehow bring the Indian majority into the economy, lower its birth rate, and bring about a more equitable distribution of the nation's land and wealth, most of its present problems will be well on the way to being solved.

As of this writing northwestern Guatemala is experiencing sporadic guerrilla actions and army "sweeps." The Guatemala–Belize and Guatemala–Mexico borders are also currently problematic. Inquire locally about the current safety situations in Guatemala.

GUATEMALA CITY

Because it was leveled in 1917 by earthquakes, Guatemala City has few points of historic interest. But there is lots of activity here: crowded streets, deluxe hotels and gourmet restaurants, active nightlife, many shops and boutiques.

The city is divided into zones; any address that isn't in Zona 1 is probably some distance from the center of town.

Parque Central is the city's center. The National Palace on the north side houses the offices of the executive branch of government. East of the park is the Metropolitana Cathedral. Begun in 1782, it suffered heavy damage in the earthquake of 1976. Much of the colonial and religious art within was brought from Antigua when Guatemala City was inaugurated as the new capital in 1776. The General Archives of Central America are housed across from the park to the west in the Biblioteca Nacional.

A short walk northeast of the park, is Cerrito del Carmen, a small church surrounded by pleasant gardens, situated on a hill with a grand view of the city. The church contains the gold and silver statue of Nuestra Señora del Carmen brought from Spain around 1600. Miraculous powers have been attributed to her.

Another church of particular interest is La Merced, 11 Avenida and Calle 5, Zona 1—a gracefully domed church containing numerous examples of colonial art. Another church, San Francisco (6 Avenida and Calle 13, Zona 1), has a famous sculpture of the Sacred Heart.

On the western outskirts of the city are the Mayan ruins of Kaminal Juyu. The area is not fully excavated, but there are sites open to the public and a sculpture display. Public buses go right to the ruins (take the number 7), and the site is included on a number of city tours.

PRACTICAL INFORMATION FOR
GUATEMALA AND GUATEMALA CITY

Because Guatemala City is often the gateway to the country of Guatemala we are including general facts for the country as a whole in this section.

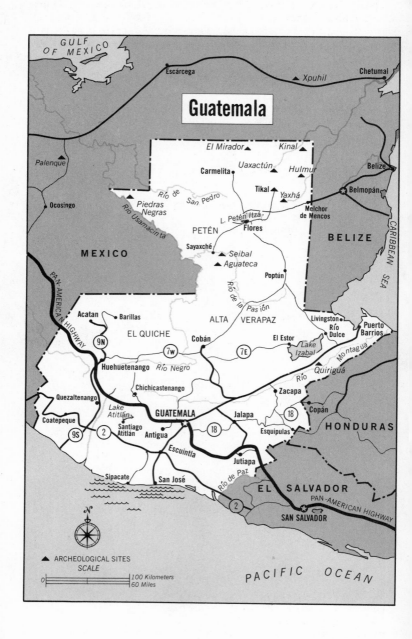

Guatemala

GULF OF MEXICO

Escárcega

Xpuhil

Chetumal

Palenque

El Mirador ▲   Kinal ▲

Carmelita •   Uaxactún ▲   Hulmur ▲

Ocosingo •

Río de San Pedro

Piedras Negras ▲

Tikal ▲   Yaxhá ▲

Belize •

Belmopán ⊙

Río Usamacinta

L. Petén Itzá   Melchor de Mencos

PETÉN   Flores •

BELIZE

MEXICO

Sayaxché •

Seibal ▲

Aguateca ▲

Poptún •

CARIBBEAN SEA

Río de la Pasión

ALTA   VERAPAZ

Livingston •

Río Dulce

Puerto Barrios

Acatan •   • Barillas

EL QUICHE

Cobán •   El Estor •

Lake Izabal

Montagua

⑨N

⑦W   ⑦E

Huehuetenango •   Río Negro

Río   Quiriguá ▲

• Chichicastenango

Zacapa •   Copán ▲

Quezaltenango •

GUATEMALA ★

Jalapa •   ⑱

HONDURAS

Coatepeque •

⑨S   ②   Santiago Atitlán   Lake Atitlán

Antigua •   ⑱

Esquipulas •

Escuintla •

Sipacate •   San José •

Jutiapa •

Río de Paz

EL SALVADOR

PAN-AMERICAN HIGHWAY

②

SAN SALVADOR ✪

PAN-AMERICAN HIGHWAY

N

▲ ARCHEOLOGICAL SITES

SCALE

0   100 Kilometers
       60 Miles

PACIFIC   OCEAN

HOW TO GET THERE. La Aurora airport in Guatemala City in serviced by the national airline, *Aviateca,* as well as by *Taca, Pan Am, Mexicana, Lacsa,* and *Eastern,* which fly to Guatemala from Miami, New Orleans, Houston, Los Angeles, Washington, and New York. *Taca, Copa, Tan/Sahsa, Sam, Mexicana,* and *Lacsa* fly into the country from El Salvador, Belize, Honduras, Nicaragua, Costa Rica, Panama, and Colombia; *Iberia* from Madrid; and *KLM* from Lisbon and Amsterdam.

TRAVEL DOCUMENTS. This information is subject to change. Before traveling obtain the latest information. Guatemalan consulates in the U.S. are New York: 57 Park Ave., New York, NY 10016; (212) 686–3837. Washington: 2220 R St. NW, Washington, DC 20008; (202) 745–4952/4. Miami: 300 Sevilla Ave., Suite 210, Coral Gables, FL 33134; (305) 443–4828/9. Los Angeles: 548 South Spring St., Suite 1030, Los Angeles, CA 90013; (213) 489–1891/2. Houston: 9700 Richmond Ave., Suite 218, Houston, TX 77042; (713) 953–9531/2.

Visitors from the U.S. (and from the U.K. and Canada) need to obtain a tourist card, which is valid for up to six months, from their nearest consulate or embassy. Tourist cards for these nationalities can also be obtained from the immigration office at La Aurora airport, though we recommend obtaining them before you leave.

CURRENCY. The Guatemalan currency is the quetzal (Q), issued in the following color-coded denominations: brown—50 centavos; green—1 quetzal; purple—5 quetzales; red—10 quetzales; blue—20 quetzales; orange—50 quetzales; brown—100 quetzales. Guatemalan coins are issued for 1 centavo, 5 centavos, 10 centavos, and 25 centavos. At press time the exchange rate has stabilized around U.S. $1 = Q2.50. **Prices quoted in this chapter are in U.S. dollars at an exchange rate of U.S.$1 = Q2.50.**

Dollars or traveler's checks can be converted into quetzales in most banks, at about 1 percent commission on the day's exchange rate, or on the black market at a better rate. Best to change in Guatemala City since banks in other towns may not wish to change dollars or will offer a lower rate.

The safest way to carry money is by traveler's checks in U.S. dollars. Many banks have English-speaking cashiers at the exchange *(cambio)* counter and all are open from 9 A.M. to 3 P.M., with a few open later than this. The *Banco de Guatemala* has its headquarters in the Centro Civico, 7 Avenida 22–01, Zona 1, with branches in the International Airport; the GUATEL building, 7 Avenida 12–39, Zona 1; and in major towns throughout the country. Other banks: *Bank of America,* 5 Avenida 10–55, Zona 1; *Lloyds Bank International,* 8 Avenida 10–67, Zona 1; *Banco Granai & Townson,* 7 Avenida 1–86, Zona 4; *Banco Internacional,* 7 Avenida 11–20, Zona 1.

Major credit cards are accepted at most large hotels, car rental agencies, and large retail stores. The Central Bank of Guatemala has stabilized the official exchange rate for business transactions at $1 = Q2.50, and this includes credit card transactions.

Warning: Guatemala has its share of pickpockets, especially in large markets, on buses, and in other crowded places. Men should carry money in a front pants pocket—never in the hip pocket—and women should keep a strong hand on the bottom of their bag, since thieves can easily slit the bottom and remove money, documents, and other valuables. Never flash large amounts of money in public.

HOW TO GET AROUND. In Guatemala City and other large towns avenues run north-south and streets *(calles)* run east-west; the city is divided into zones *(zonas)*. It is important to check carefully the zone number of any address since the same avenues and streets occur in other zones miles away. A map of Guatemala City can be obtained from *INGUAT* and for $1 from the *Instituto Geográfico Militar,* Avenida Las Américas 5–76, Zona 13.

From La Aurora airport you can hire a **taxi** to get to your hotel but fares are very high: $4 to Camino Real and El Dorado hotels, and $8 to Zona 1. Taxis in Guatemala do not have meters so you should bargain over the price quoted and check with other taxi drivers also. Explain to the taxi driver exactly where you want to go. A taxi from the airport to Antigua will cost approximately $30. Buses run to and from the airport—though you may have to change to another bus on the way—for 3 cents. Many of the buses are very dilapidated and from your hotel in Zonas 9 or 10 it will take 15 minutes or more to reach Zona 1 through crowded, smoke-polluted streets.

Some of the buses to other towns are in much better shape than city buses and one can ride across the country from Huehuetenango to Guatemala City and from there to Puerto Barrios for less than $4. From Guatemala City the following buses are recommended: to Huehuetenango—*Los Halcones,* 7 Avenida 15–27, Zona 1, 81–979; *Rápidos Zaculeu,* 9 Calle 11–42, Zona 1, 22–858. To Quezaltenango—*Galgos,* 7 Avenida 19–44, Zona 1, 23–661, 534–868. To Puerto Barrios—*Litegua,* 8 Avenida 15–42, Zona 1, 27–578; *Fuente del Norte,* 9 Avenida 18–60, Zona 1, 27–041. To Talisman (Mexican Border)—*Galgos* (as above). To Esquipulas—*Rutas Orientales,* 19 Calle 8–18, Zona 1, 537–282, 512–160. To Cobán—*Monja Blanca y Escobar,* 7 Avenida 20–07, Zona 1, 511–878, 81–409.

Some of the major **car** rental agencies in the U.S. have offices in Guatemala City, and a good way for the short-term visitor to get to areas of particular interest is to rent a car. Check very carefully what types of cars are available, particularly if you require four-wheel drive or manual transmission, and also phone other rental agencies to check which have the most competitive rates for the car you want to drive. Several agencies have branch offices at the airport, and reservations can be made by phone from abroad:

Budget, Avenida La Reforma 15–00, Zona 9; 316–546, 67–669, 322–591, 310–273 (airport).

Avis, 12 Calle 2–73, Zona 9; 316–990, 67–469, 321–263, 310–017 (airport).

Hertz, 7 Avenida 14–76, Zona 9; 680–107, 681–217, 312–222, 312–421, 322–242, 311–711 (airport).

Dollar, 6 Avenida "A" 10–13, Zona 1; 67–796, 23–446, 317–185 (airport).

National, 14 Calle 1–42, Zona 10; 680–175, 683–057, 318–365, 318–218 (airport).

Tabarini, 2 Calle "A" 7–30, Zona 10; 316–108, 319–814, 322–161, 322–555/66, 314–755 (airport).

Tally, 7 Avenida 14–60, Zona 1; 514–113, 23–327.

The major road going east from Guatemala City is the Ruta al Atlántico (CA9). For visits to Cobán and the departments of Baja Verapaz and Alta Verapaz, you turn north at km. 86 at El Rancho; for Poptún, Flores, and Tikal, you turn north just after Morales at km. 247; for the road to Estanzuela, Copán, Esquipulas, and Honduras, you turn south at Río Hondo at km. 133; continue straight on the Ruta al Atlántico to visit Quirigua, Puerto Barrios, and Livingston. To drive directly to El Salvador, you can take CA1 and then CA8 from Guatemala City, through Cuilapa to the frontier. The easiest way to reach the Ruta al Atlántico from the city is to drive north on 11 Avenida until you meet Calle Martí, 12 blocks from the central square. Turn right and after a few miles you will leave the city and be on the Ruta al Atlántico. There are toll stations on this road and you should indicate where you are turning off the road and pay the toll (maximum toll: 25 cents).

The drive to Puerto Barrios, 185 miles from Guatemala City, will take about five hours; to Cobán—135 miles from the city—about four hours; and to Tikal, depending on the clearance of your vehicle and the state of the road, part of which is unpaved, fifteen hours or so.

TELEPHONES. From Guatemala City to other towns in Guatemala dial 0 plus the six-figure number you have, except for calls to Quezaltenango where you dial 061 plus a four-figure number. (For calls to Guatemala City from outside the capital dial 02 plus the five- or six-figure number.) Pay phones—when functioning—are available in most large towns, and a one-minute call will cost a maximum of 10 cents. Place a 5-, 10-, or 25-cent coin in the slot at the top of the pay phone, dial the number, and when the call is answered the coin will drop into the box. Have a lot of coins ready if you are making a long call. Overseas calls can be made from GUATEL offices in the larger towns. GUATEL in Guatemala City is at 7 Avenida 12–39, Zona 1. Other offices of GUATEL are located at: 7 Avenida 3–44, Zona 4; Avenida Bolivar 40–42, and Avenida la Castellana 6–66, Zona 8; Avenida la Reforma 6–29, Zona 9. Collect calls can be made to Mexico, the other countries in Central America, U.S., Canada, Italy, Sweden, and Spain. To call the international operator dial 171. Direct calls to the U.S. cost $2.50 to $3.75 for three minutes ($3.25 to $5 person-to-person); to Canada, $3.25 to $4 ($4.80 to $6 person-to-person); to Great Britain, $7.25 ($9.75 person-to-person). These rates are reduced from 15 to 30 percent if you call at night or on the weekend. The country code for Guatemala is 502.

MAIL AND COMMUNICATIONS. An airmail letter or postcard costs 8 cents for five grams, 12 cents for 10 grams to the U.S., 12 cents and 16 cents to Canada, and 24 cents and 28 cents to the U.K. Mail to and from the U.S. usually takes from seven to 10 days, and less than that to and from the U.K. Internal cables are sent from the post office *(correos)* at a cost of 3 cents per word; international cables are sent from GUATEL offices at a cost of 45 cents per word to the U.S., 65 cents to Canada, and 70 cents to Great Britain. (These charges include the name and address of the recipient as well as the message.) *Jet Express International Courier,* 11 Calle 5–16, Zona 1, tel. 514–185, will deliver documents up to one pound in weight to the U.S. for $16 to $22 and to Europe for $30. Under the current regulations parcels weighing more than 2 kgs. (4.4 lbs.) have to be mailed from the post office in Guatemala City. Parcels weighing less than 2 kgs. can be mailed from most rural post offices. You'll need to obtain a box (sold for 5 or 10 cents in many foodstores), wrapping paper, string, and adhesive tape, and take the parcel to the post office before wrapping it, and fill in a customs declaration. Surface mail will take up to six months to the U.S. and Canada, and longer than that to the U.K. You can send parcels airmail *much* cheaper if they are not certified: an unregistered parcel to the U.K. will cost $2.25 for 2 kgs., and $20 if it is sent registered.

USEFUL ADDRESSES. *American Express,* Avenida la Reforma 9–00, Zona 9, 311–311, 311–463. Mon.–Fri., 8 A.M.–5 P.M. *U.S. Embassy,* Avenida La Reforma 7–01, Zona 10, 311–541/55. *Canadian Embassy,* 7 Avenida 11–59, 6th Floor, Zona 9, 321–411, 321–413. *U.K. Consulate,* British Interests Section, Centro Financiero Torre 11, 7 Avenida 5–10, Zona 4, 321–602/04/06. Swiss Embassy, 4 Calle 7–73, Zona 9, 65–726, 313–725. *Mexican Consulate,* 13 Calle 7–30, Zona 9, 66–504, 63–573. *Honduran Consulate,* 16 Calle 8–27, Zona 10, 373–921. *Consulate of El Salvador,* 12 Calle 5–43, Zona 9, 325–848. *Nicaraguan Consulate,* 2 Calle 15–95, Zona 13, 65–613. *Costa Rican Consulate,* Avenida La Reforma 8–60, Oficina 320, Zona 9, 320–531. *Consulate of Panama,* Edificio Maya, Via 5 4–50, 7th floor, Zona 4, 320–763. *INGUAT,* the National Tourist Office, is located at 7 Avenida 1–17, Zona 4, Centro Civico, 311–333/37. INGUAT offices are also located in Antigua (see *Practical Information for Antigua*), 320–763; in Flores, at the airport, 811–595; in Panajachel, Calle Principal, 621–393; in Quezaltenango, in the Casa de la Cultura (on the north side of the square), tel. 4931 and at La Aurora International Airport.

READING MATTER. Magazines, newspapers, and books in English are available in the major hotels. The *Miami Herald* (dated the day it arrives but actually the previous day's news), the *New York Times* (the same day's edition), *USA Today, The Wall Street Journal,* and other English-language papers are available in the bookshops of the major hotels and at *Importación General de Publicaciones,* 12 Calle 5–42, Zona 1, which also has some magazines (*Time, Newsweek,* etc.) in English. The IGA *(Instituto Guatemalteco Americano)* has a library of English-language books and magazines and long-term visitors can obtain a library card for a nominal sum. It is located on Ruta 1 and Vía 4, Zona 4, just behind the tourist office. Those interested in more in-depth anthropological or archaeological information on the country will want to visit Cirma located at 5 Calle Oriente No. 5 in Antigua.

Several bookstores specialize in books and magazines in English and other languages: *Arnel,* 9 Calle 6–65, Zona 1 (books and magazines in English, German and French); *Bremen,* Pasaje Rubio, between 6 Avenida and 9 Calle, Zona 1 (books and magazines in German); *Cervantes,* Avenida La Reforma 13–70, Zona 9; *Géminis,* 6 Avenida 7–24, Zona 9; *La Plazuela,* 12 Calle 6–14, Zona 9 (including used books); *Tuncho Granados,* at the Plaza del Sol on 12 Calle, Zona 9; and *Vista Hermosa Book Shop,* 2 Calle 18–48, Zona 15. *Asociación Tikal,* Avenida La Reforma 8–60, 3rd floor, Zona 9, has a small selection of archaeological books in English and a reading library.

HEALTH. Tap water in Guatemala is purified only by putting chlorine in the water supply, so it is wiser to drink only pre-boiled or bottled water. Many first-class restaurants use water that has been boiled previously, but one should be sure of that before drinking fresh water. In rural areas either boil the water yourself or use Halazone or similar water purification tablets.

Milk served in first-class restaurants is usually pasteurized, though milk and cheese sold in cheap restaurants, *comedores,* or markets *(mercados)* are usually not pasteurized. The adventurous may wish to try some of the city's great variety of "street food." A few rules of thumb are: 1) avoid ceviches made with raw seafood; 2) stick to foods cooked on the spot; 3) check the hygiene of the person serving the food.

If you suffer from diarrhea during your stay, try staying off food for a day or two, or ask a pharmacist for the best of the stomach remedies. If diarrhea continues, visit a doctor. If you have been eating fruit with the peels on, raw vegetables, or meat that is not well cooked you may come down with amoebic dysentery and should visit a doctor immediately.

The best hospitals in Guatemala City are the *Herrera Llerandi,* 6 Avenida 8–71, Zona 10, 66–771/5; *Centro Médico,* 6 Avenida 3–47, Zona 10, 65–061/3, 323–555/9; *Bella Aurora,* 10 Calle 2–31, Zona 14, 681–951/5.

The Red Cross has a 24-hour emergency service. It is located at 3 Calle 8–40, Zona 1. In an emergency dial 125.

Klee drugstores have 10 branches in the city and one of them is open 24 hours a day. All drugstores have a sign indicating which pharmacy is *en turno* (open at night) that week.

For some drugs you will need a prescription from a local doctor and some drugs are difficult to find in Guatemala. It will be better to bring with you any drugs and vitamins you will need during your visit.

ACCOMMODATIONS. Guatemala City has a large number of hotels and pensiones ranging from several deluxe or first class hotels to a multitude of inexpensive hotels and pensiones. Many visitors to Guatemala spend very little time in the capital, since many of the most interesting sites (and sights) in the country are to the west, east, and north of Guatemala City, and by visiting the towns and villages in the country you avoid the bustle, noise, and pollution of the capital. Visitors staying more than a couple of days in the city should visit some of the moderate and inexpensive hotels, which, while lacking the facilities of the deluxe and first-class establishments, are nonetheless clean, well run, friendly, and much less expensive. Be aware that the deluxe and first-class hotels have different prices for foreigners and Guatemalans, and that some of the moderate hotels—which do not raise their prices for foreigners—are very good hotels.

Prices for hotels and pensiones listed are per night for a double room: *Deluxe,* from U.S.$60 to U.S.$100; *First Class,* from U.S.$30 to U.S.$60; *Moderate,* from U.S.$10 to U.S.$30; *Inexpensive,* from U.S.$5 to U.S.$10; *Budget,* less than U.S.$5. A 10 percent tourism tax and a 7 percent sales tax will be added to posted prices.

Deluxe

Camino Real. 14 Calle and Avenida La Reforma, Zona 10; 374–402, 374–406. Guatemala's largest hotel with 416 rooms and 19 suites. Facilities include two swimming pools, tennis courts, sauna and health club,

La Ronda and *El Cafetal* restaurants, bars, nightclub, barbershop, beauty salon, bank, travel and car rental agencies, bookstore, and two jewelry shops.

Conquistador-Sheraton. 5 Vía 4–68, Zona 4; 312–222/30. 186 rooms and 4 suites. Swimming pool, *Las Espadas* restaurant, *El Refugio* bar, *La Cueva de los Capitanes* nightclub, beauty salon, bank, travel and car rental agencies, shops, and bookstore.

Cortijo Reforma. Avenida La Reforma 2–18, Zona 9; 66–712/6. 150 large rooms with color TV, private bars, refrigerators, and living rooms. 4 conference rooms. *El Regidor* restaurant, live music in *Bar Sarambo,* piano bar, 2 floors of underground parking, 2 travel agencies, art gallery, florist, beauty salon, dress boutiques, typical stores, jewelry store, bookstore. The hotel has an arrangement with the country club in which guests can use their swimming pool, tennis court, and golf course. Reservations for the hotel can be made with the chain of Golden Tulip hotels or with KLM airline.

El Dorado. 7 Avenida 15–45, Zona 9; 317–777/88. 249 rooms and suites. Swimming pool, *El Parlamento* bar, *El Galeón de Oro* restaurant, cafe-bar open 6 P.M.–1 A.M., beauty salon, travel agency, jewelry shop and bookstore. Guests can use the facilities of the hotel's *Club Cabana,* which include a sauna, gym, swimming pool, and tennis, squash, and racquetball courts.

Guatemala Fiesta. 1 Avenida 13–22, Zona 10; 322–555/66. 205 rooms and 25 suites. Swimming pool, Finnish sauna, steam baths, gym and massage, *La Comparsa* restaurant, *Fiesta Brava* bar, beauty salon, shops, car rental, and travel agencies. Guests can use the facilities at *Club La Villa,* 5 minutes from the hotel, including tennis, racquetball, and squash courts, swimming pool, and games room.

First Class

Pan American. 9 Calle 5–63, Zona 1; 268–07/9. 60 rooms. Dining room, central dining lounge, conference room, laundry, and shop. On Thursdays the hotel offers an excellent local cuisine buffet.

Ritz Continental. 6 Avenida "A" 10–13, Zona 1; 519–803, 82–513, 80–889. 250 rooms. Restaurants, *Taberna de Don Pedro de Alvarado* bar, cocktail lounge, swimming pool, games room (chess, backgammon, pool), reading room, conference room, parking.

Moderate

Alameda Guest House. 4 Avenida 14–10, Zona 10; 680–152. 7 rooms. Fine old house in residential district.

Apart-Hotel Alamo. 10 Calle 5–60, Zona 9; 65–411, 319–914. 15 suites with cable TV. Laundry. Daily or monthly rates.

Del Centro. 13 Calle 4–55, Zona 1; 812–81/2, 25–547. 60 rooms and 5 suites. Rooftop terrace. Live music Mon.–Sat. in *Los Arcos* bar, *Candilejas* restaurant. Request rooms away from street.

Guatemala Internacional. 6 Avenida 12–21, Zona 1; 84–441/5. 40 apartments with private bar, TV, kitchenettes. Daily or monthly rates.

Plaza. Vía 7 6–16, Zona 4; 63–173, 310–396. 63 rooms. Restaurant, bar, swimming pool, squash court.

Residencial Carillon. 5 Avenida 11–25, Zona 9; 324–267. 15 suites with TVs and private bars in quiet residential neighborhood.

Residencial Reforma, La Casa Grande. Avenida La Reforma 7–67, Zona 10; 65–723, 67–900. 28 rooms in quiet, pleasant district near U.S. Embassy.

Villa Española. 2 Calle 7–51, Zona 9; 65–417, 65–611, 323–381. 63 rooms, 3 suites. Restaurant, cafeteria, laundry.

Inexpensive

Centenario. 6 Calle 5–33, Zona 1; 80–381/3. 43 rooms with private bath and telephone. Laundromat, parking.

Colonial. 7 Avenida 14–19, Zona 1; 26–722, 22–955, 81–208. 42 rooms, some with private baths. Cafeteria.

Hogar del Turista. 11 Calle 10–43, Zona 1; 25–522. 10 rooms. Breakfast can be included in room price if required.

Lessing House. 12 Calle 4–35, Zona 1; 513–891. 8 rooms. Friendly proprietors.

Mansion San Francisco. 6 Avenida 12–62, Zona 1; 25–125/8. 45 rooms and apartments. Restaurant, bar, conference room. TV in room at extra cost.

Posada Belen. 13 Calle "A" 10–30, Zona 1; 29–226, 513–478, 534–530. 9 rooms. Restaurant, cafeteria. Proprietors speak English, have a good library of books and are a fount of information about Guatemala. Travel agency (Maya Tours). Highly recommended.

Posada Real. 12 Calle 6–21, Zona 1; 81–092, 25–257. 13 rooms.

Spring. 8 Avenida 12–65, Zona 1; 26–637. 30 rooms, 2 cafeterias, TV room.

Budget

Capri. 9 Avenida 15–63, Zona 1.

Centro America. 9 Avenida 16–38, Zona 1.

Fenix. 7 Avenida 15–81, Zona 1.

Pension Chalet Suizo. 14 Calle 6–82, Zona 1; 513–786. Recommended.

Ritz. 6 Avenida 9–28, Zona 1.

There are many other budget hotels and *pensiones* in Zona 1, some good and some not, and the budget traveler should obtain impressions from other visitors of the hotels and pensiones they stayed at.

RESTAURANTS. Due to its population of more than two million and to the fact that most of the upper-class and many of the middle-class Guatemalans live in the capital, Guatemala City has a large variety of restaurants. The cost of a meal (not including wine or liquors) ranges as follows: *Deluxe,* $5 to $10; *Moderate,* $2 to $5; *Inexpensive,* less than $2.

Typical

Los Antojitos. *Moderate.* Three locations: Calle Montúfar and 4 Avenida, Zona 9; 15 Calle 6–28, Zona 1; Calzada Roosevelt 30–50, Zona 7.

El Cafetal. *Moderate.* At the Camino Real hotel.

El Parador. *Moderate.* Three locations: Avenida La Reforma 6–70, Zona 9; 12 Calle 4–09, Zona 9; Calzada Roosevelt 30–92, Zona 7.

Arrin-Cuan. *Inexpensive.* 5 Avenida 3–27, Zona 1.

Ranchon Antigüeño. *Inexpensive.* 13 Calle 3–50, Zona 1.

Los Tecomates. *Inexpensive.* 6 Avenida 15–69, Zona 1.

French

Petit Suisse. *Deluxe.* Avenida La Reforma 6–67, Zona 10; 316–804. Next to the U.S. Embassy.

La Belle Epoque. *Moderate.* 1 Avenida 13–27, Zona 10. Opposite the Guatemala Fiesta hotel.

Chez Pierre. *Moderate.* 2 Calle 15–92, Zona 13; 319–215.

German

Kloster. *Moderate.* Tívoli Plaza and 6 Calle, Zona 9.

Bremen. *Inexpensive.* 3 Calle 6–39, Zona 9.

Delicadezas Hamburgo. *Inexpensive.* 15 Calle 5–28, Zona 1. On Parque Concordia, a block from where the buses leave for Antigua.

International

All major hotels have *deluxe* restaurants serving international cuisine. Others include:

Martin's. *Deluxe.* 13 Calle 7–65, Zona 9.

Estro Armonico. *Moderate.* Vía 4 4–36, Zona 4. Opposite the Conquistador-Sheraton hotel.

Lai Lai. *Moderate.* 12 Calle 5–27, Zona 9.

Multirestaurantes. *Moderate.* 6 Avenida and 10 Calle, Zona 1, and Avenida La Reforma 13–59, Zona 10.

Nais. *Moderate.* 5 Avenida 12–31, Zona 9 and 7 Avenida 6–65, Zona 9.

O.K. Corral. *Moderate.* 12 Calle 6–40, Zona 9. Video, bar.

Paulo Alto. *Moderate.* 4 Avenida 13–59, Zona 10.

Vivaldi. *Moderate.* 3 Avenida 10–41, Zona 10.

Los Tylos. *Inexpensive.* Located at kilometer 18½ on Calzada Roosevelt (the Pan-American Highway) on the way to Antigua.

Italian

Las Palmas. *Moderate.* 7 Avenida 7–30, Zona 9.

Mario's. *Moderate.* 13 Calle and 1 Avenida, Zona 10.

Pizzeria Cozzoli's. *Moderate.* 7 Avenida 14–88, Zona 9.

Bologna. *Inexpensive.* 10 Calle 6–20, Zona 1.

Franco's. *Inexpensive.* 7 Avenida 4–40, Zona 4.

Giovanni Canessa. *Inexpensive.* 12 Calle 6–23, Zona 1.

Mexican

El Alamo. *Moderate.* 12 Calle 2–04, Zona 9. Near Montúfar shopping center.

El Gran Pavo. *Moderate.* 13 Calle 4–41, Zona 1 and 12 Calle 5–54, Zona 9.

Los Cebollines. *Moderate.* 12 Calle 6–36, Zona 9; 6 Avenida 9–65 and 13–22, Zona 1; Calzada Roosevelt 19–02, Zona 7.

Tacomex. *Inexpensive.* 12 Calle 5–54, Zona 9, Local 14.

North American

American Doughnuts. *Inexpensive.* Six locations: 5 Avenida 11–47, Zona 1; 6 Avenida 2–73, Zona 4; 12 Calle and 6 Avenida, Zona 9; Centro Comercial Aguilar Batres, Zona 11; Avenida Las Américas 17–78, Zona 13; Supermercado La Torre, Vista Hermosa II, Zona 15.

Danny's Pancakes. *Inexpensive.* Three locations: 6 Avenida 9–45, Zona 1; 6 Avenida 0–60, Zona 4; 6 Avenida and 12 Calle, Zona 9.

Oriental

Celeste Imperio. *Moderate.* 7 Avenida 9–99, Zona 9. Near major hotels.

China Queen. *Moderate.* 6 Avenida 14–04, Zona 9.

Excellent. *Moderate.* 13 Calle and 2 Avenida, Zona 10.

Palacio de Oro. *Moderate.* 8 Calle 6–01, Zona 9.

Palacio Royal. *Moderate.* 7 Avenida 11–00 and 11–32, Zona 9. Near major hotels.

Real Capitol. *Moderate.* 6 Avenida 9–11, Zona 9.

Shogun. *Moderate.* 1 Avenida 13–27, Zona 10.

Teppanyaki. *Moderate.* 11 Calle 7–45, Zona 9.

Canton. *Inexpensive.* 6 Avenida 14–29, Zona 1. Facing Parque Concordia.

El Encanto. *Inexpensive.* 7 Avenida 8–31, Zona 4.

Fu Lu Sho. *Inexpensive.* 6 Avenida 12–09, Zona 1.

El Mandarin. *Inexpensive.* 7 Avenida 6–62, Zona 4.

Seafood

Costa Brava. *Deluxe.* 15 Avenida 7–79, Zona 13.

Hola. *Deluxe.* Avenida de las Americas, Zona 14.

Puerto Barrios. *Deluxe.* 7 Avenida 10–65, Zona 9.

Baja Mar. *Moderate.* 6 Avenida and 10 Calle, Zona 9.

Mediterraneo. *Moderate.* 7 Avenida 3–31, Zona 9.

Delicias del Mar. *Moderate.* Vía 5 3–65, Zona 4.

Estro Mariscos. *Moderate.* 13 Calle 1–55, Zona 10.

Las Brisas. *Moderate.* 12 Calle and 1 Avenida, Zona 10.

Ler's. *Moderate.* 16 Calle 7–29, Zona 9.

Mar y Flores. *Moderate.* 1 Avenida 13–42, Zona 10.

Variedades Sureñas. *Moderate.* 7 Avenida 14–44, Zona 9.

Auto Mariscos. *Inexpensive.* Vía 9 5–04, Zona 4.

Spanish

Altuna. *Inexpensive.* 5 Avenida 12–31, Zona 1.

La Barraca Valenciana. *Inexpensive.* Ruta 5 8–42, Zona 4.

Isaias. *Inexpensive.* 9 Calle 3–59, Zona 1.

Steakhouses

La Estancia. *Deluxe.* Avenida La Reforma 6–89, Zona 10.

El Ganadero. *Deluxe.* 20 Calle 2–19, Zona 10.

Hacienda De Los Sanchez. *Deluxe.* 12 Calle 2–19, Zona 10.

Gauchos. *Moderate.* 13 Calle 1–20, Zona 10.
Nim-Guaa. *Moderate.* Avenida La Reforma 8–01, Zona 10.
El Rodeo. *Moderate.* 7 Avenida 14–84, Zona 9.
Tambasco. *Moderate.* 7 Avenida 9–15, Zona 9 and 7 Avenida and 9 Calle, Zona 1.
La Villa. *Moderate.* 20 Calle 3–50, Zona 10.

Vegetarian

Arbol de la Vida. *Inexpensive.* Avenida La Reforma 12–01, Zona 10.

Fast Food

These are all *inexpensive.*
Chevere Hot-Dogs. 12 locations including 10 Avenida 9–79, Zona 1; 10 Avenida 17–34, Zona 1; 6 Avenida 11–76, Zona 1.
Frankfurt Mixta. 15 branches in different zones.
Grizzly Bear Pizza. 5 locations including: Calzada Roosevelt 13–66, Zona 7; Centro Commercial Vista Hermosa, Zona 15.
McDonalds. 10 Calle 5–30, Zona 1; 7 Avenida and 14 Calle, Zona 9; Calzada Roosevelt 31–55, Zona 11.
Pizza Hut. 6 locations including Avenida La Reforma 15–54, Zona 9; Calzada Roosevelt and Periférico, Zona 7; 24 Calle and 6 Avenida, Zona 4; Novicentro, Zona 5.
Pollo Campero. Many locations in different zones.
Rostipollo Chapin. 8 locations including: 5 Avenida 10–26, Zona 1; 6 Avenida 1–76, Zona 4; 12 Calle 0–60, Zona 9.
Wimpy. 6 locations including: 6 Avenida 12–00, Zona 1; Centro Comercial Montserrat, Zona 7.

Cafés

Cafe La Crepe. Avenida Las Américas and 11 Calle, Zona 13; 14 Calle 7–49, Zona 9.
Cafe Milot. Avenida La Reforma 13–70, Zona 9.
Cafe Terraza. Avenida La Reforma 14–34, Zona 9.
El Gran Comal. Vía 7 6–71, Zona 4. Reggae music nightly.
Pasteleria Los Alpes. 10 Calle 1–09, Zona 10.
Pasteleria Las Americas. 9 Calle 5–04, Zona 1; 12 Calle 0–93, Zona 9; Avenida La Reforma 8–60, Zona 9; Avenida Las Américas 17–40, Zona 13; 4 Calle 14–26, Zona 13; Avenida Hincapié 28–29, Zona 13.
Pasteleria Austria. 12 Calle 6–58, Zona 1. Near the post office.
Pasteleria Bohemia. 11 Calle 8–48, Zona 1; 6 Avenida 0–60, Zona 4.
Pasteleria Jensen. 14 Calle 0–53, Zona 1; 10 Calle 6–66, Zona 1; 7 Avenida 12–13, Zona 9.
Pasteleria Lins. 11 Calle 6–12, Zona 1; 7 Avenida 10–76, Zona 9.
Pasteleria Milano. 7 Avenida 7–22, Zona 4; 16 Calle 8–41, Zona 14.
Pasteleria Palace. 12 Calle 4–37, Zona 1; 7 Avenida 7–22, Zona 4; 10 Calle 3–40, Zona 10.
Pastelerias Los Tilos. 11 Calle 6–54, Zona 1; 7 Avenida 15–67, Zona 9.
Pasteleria Zurich. 4 Avenida 12–09, Zona 10. Excellent chocolates.

Siriacos. 1 Avenida 12–16, Zona 10. Good atmosphere.
Tertulia. Avenida Reforma 10–31, Zona 10.

TOURS. Many tour agencies in Guatemala City offer trips from a half-day sightseeing in the city, a full day to Antigua, Lake Atitlán or Chichicastenango, to tours of a week or more to the western highlands. Visitors with a special interest—bird-watching, archaeology, fishing, etc.—should contact several of the following agencies to find out what they offer.

Alfa Tours. Avenida La Reforma 12–01, Zona 10; 318–488, 318–008.

Clark Tours. 7 Avenida 6–53, Edificio El Triángulo, 2nd floor, Zona 4; 10 Calle 6–34, Zona 1 and in the lobbies of the Camino Real and the Conquistador-Sheraton; 310–213/6, 682–056, 320–443, 514–172.

ECA Tours. 5 Avenida 13–16, Zona 9; 310–540.

Hayter Travel. 9 Calle 4–69, Zona 1; 519–673, 85–215.

Jerry's Tours. 9 Calle 6–36, Zona 1; 85–731.

Maya Tours. 6 Avenida 9–62, Zona 1; 84–479.

Ney's. 13 Calle 0–56, Zona 10; 680–959, 370–883/4.

Panamundo Guatemala Travel Service. 7 Avenida 14–44, Zona 9; 319–116.

S.T.P. 3 Calle 10–58, Zona 10; 61–920, 319–870.

PARKS. *Aurora Park,* Diagonal 12 and 7 Avenida, Zona 13. This large park contains the Museum of Archaeology and Ethnology, the Museum of Natural History, and the Museum of Modern Art (see "Museums," below), as well as the International Airport, the Hippodrome and the bull-fight ring (where horse races and bullfights occasionally take place), the zoo, an amusement park, the Artesan's Market, a restaurant, and numerous food stands. At the entrance you will note a huge statue of the national hero Tecún Umán and to the north the partially repaired remains of the colonial aqueduct.

Central Park, 8 Calle between 5 and 7 Avenidas, Zona 1. There are actually two parks—Parque Centenario to the west of 6 Avenida and the Plaza de Armas to the east. Here was the old market in colonial times; the Palace of the Captains-General, where the Declaration of Independence was signed in 1821; the Supreme Court; and the Royal Mint, but all these colonial structures were destroyed in the 1917 earthquake. The Plaza de Armas has just been remodeled and now has underground parking. On the east side of the park is the Catedral Metropolitana, which contains colonial altars and religious art, much of it brought from Antigua when the new capital was inaugurated in 1776. The cathedral was heavily damaged by the 1976 earthquake but has now been repaired. Directly across from the park to the west is the Biblioteca Nacional (National Library), which houses the General Archives of Central America. On the north side of the park is the National Palace, constructed in green stone between 1939 and 1943 at the orders of dictator Jorge Ubico. To the south is the arched shopping arcade *(Portal del Comercio),* colonial in style, where many vendors sell their wares. The park has an acoustical bandshell, where concerts by a military band or orchestra are held several days a week, as well as fountains, trees, benches, and small gardens.

Minerva Park, 11 Calle and 6 Avenida, Zona 2. Known for the huge relief map of Guatemala, constructed in 1904 by Francisco Vela. Two towers enable you to see the whole country from above; best to bring a good map of Guatemala with you. The park also contains a public swimming pool, a baseball park, picnic grounds, and amusement park, and gardens. Be advised that this is not a very safe place for young women to visit late at night.

Smaller parks are situated throughout the city, each with busts or statues of historical figures, a fountain, benches, and, as in the central park, a crew of shoeshine boys, photographers, food vendors, and beggars. These include the *Parque Morazán,* north of Parque Central; *Parque Concordia,* between 5 and 6 Avenidas and 14 and 15 Calles, Zona 1; *Parque Centro América,* at 8 Calle and 5 Avenida, Zona 9, with gardens, a modern exhibition hall for trade fairs and other public events; and the *Ciudad Olímpica,* a sports complex built for the Central American and Caribbean Olympics of 1950, which includes tennis courts, a swimming pool, a gymnasium, and a huge stadium, and is situated in a ravine that cuts through the center of the city in Zones 4 and 5.

MUSEUMS. *Museo Nacional de Historia Natural.* 7 Avenida 7–30, Zona 13; 720–468. Collections of Guatemalan minerals, plants, snakes, butterflies, birds, animals, and insects. Admission free. Mon.–Fri., 9 A.M.–4 P.M.

Museo Nacional de Arqueología y Etnología. Salón 5, La Aurora Park, Zona 13 (next to Natural History Museum); 720–489. Exhibits of archaeological artifacts from many sites, native weavings, and Maya culture. Small admission charge. Tues.–Fri., 9 A.M.–4 P.M.

Museo Nacional de Arte Moderno. Salón 6, La Aurora Park, Zona 13; 720–467. Museum closes for a few days when exhibitions are changed. Admission free. Tues.–Sun., 9 A.M.–4 P.M.

Museo Ixchel del Traje Indígena. 4 Avenida 16–27, Zona 10; 680–713. Dedicated to the collection and conservation of traditional Indian textiles. Exhibits of weavings, ceramics, jewelry, paintings, and Indian customs. Small admission charge. Mon.–Sat., 9 A.M.–5:30 P.M. Admission free to store selling books, cards, and handicrafts.

Jardín Botánico (Botanical Garden) and *Museo de Historia Natural* (of the Department of Biology, San Carlos University). Calle Mariscal Cruz 1–56, Zona 10 (just off Avenida La Reforma); 310–904. Stuffed and mounted animals and plants, plus collections of minerals and snakes from Guatemala. Admission free. Mon.–Fri., 8 A.M.–noon, 2–3:30 P.M. *(Museo),* 2–6 P.M. *(Jardín Botánico).*

Exposición de Artes y Artesanías Populares de Guatemala (at the Center for Folkloric Studies). Avenida La Reforma 0–09, Zona 10 (near *Jardín Botánico,* above); 319–171. Collection of Guatemalan handicrafts. Admission free. Mon.–Fri., 8 A.M.–4 P.M. (usually).

Museo Popol Vuh. Avenida La Reforma 8–60, 6th floor, Zona 9; 318–921. Exhibits of archaeological artifacts, folklore, colonial art. Library of books on history, archaeology, art—scholars welcomed. Small admission charge. Admission free to store selling books on Guatemala, handicrafts. Mon.–Sat., 9 A.M.–5:30 P.M.

Museo en Ruinas de Kaminal Juyú (archaeological project). Colonia Kaminal Juyú, Zona 7. Free admission on working days Mon.–Sun., but a permit is required from IDAEH (Instituto de Antropología e Historia), 12 Avenida 11–65, Zona 1; 531–570, 25–571, 25–948.

Museo Nacional de Artes e Industrias Populares. 10 Avenida 10–72, Zona 1; 80–334. Small admission charge. Tues.–Fri., 9 A.M.–4 P.M.; Sat. and Sun., 9 A.M.–noon, 2–4 P.M.

Museo Nacional de Historia. 9 Calle 9–70, Zona 1; 536–149. Exhibits of antiquities, paintings, documents, stamps, furniture, and arms from Independence onward. Admission free. Tues.–Sun., 8 A.M.–4 P.M.

Museo de Armas y Escudos. Centro Cultural de Guatemala Miguel Angel Asturias, 24 Calle 13–81, Zona 1. Located in the Castillo de San José, this museum houses a permanent collection of artillery pieces and coats of arms from Guatemala's past. Admission free. Mon.–Fri., 8A.M.– 4P.M.

SHOPPING. Guatemalan Indians are famed for the quality and variety of their handicrafts, and many travelers in Guatemala visit the markets of Chichicastenango and Sololá and bargain for the very inexpensive folk art. Many of the textiles and artifacts sold in the market towns are available in Guatemala City, though you will miss the pleasure of visiting these towns and villages on market days and may pay more for them in the city. In the expensive stores in Guatemala City very little bargaining is possible, but in the market towns if you don't bargain you may pay more than twice what you could have bought the article for. You should also go from stall to stall in the markets both to decide what articles you want to purchase and to find out what the different prices are.

If you have enough time, tailor-made clothing is one of the best buys in Guatemala. A suit, pants, shirt, dress, or a pair of shoes or boots, can be handmade very inexpensively, and after you've chosen the material and discussed the design, the tailor or shoemaker can will have it ready for you in a week or two. Visit the tailor or shoemaker frequently to make sure that it's going to be ready before you leave.

Markets. The *Central Market* was destroyed by the earthquake in 1976 and is now located in a new building behind the Cathedral between 7 and 8 Avenidas. It's only worth a visit if you don't have time to get to one of the market towns. The *Terminal Market,* recently renovated, is located between 4 Avenida and 9 Calle in Zona 4. Beware of pickpockets and robberies. To the west of the market is the bus terminal from which local buses leave to small towns and villages throughout the country.

The *Mercado Nacional de Artesanías* (National Handicrafts Market) is located at 6 Calle and 11 Avenida in La Aurora Park near the International Airport. Prices will be higher here than at the stalls in Zona 1 or at the local markets. There are small stalls selling a wide variety of produce on 18 Calle in Zona 1.

Tiendas Tipicas (handicraft shops). Many shops in Guatemala City offer a wide variety of native handicrafts from all over Guatemala, including jewelry, textiles, ceramics, and carvings. The following is only a small selection of those available: Sombol, Avenida La Reforma 14–14, Zona 9, offers modern clothing made with traditional textiles. *La Tinaja.* 12 Calle 4–80, Zona 1; *Típicos Reforma Utatlán,* 14 Calle 7–77, Zona 9; *4 Ahau,* 11 Calle 4–53, Zona 1; *La India Moderna,* 9 Calle 6–25, Zona 1; *Maya Exports,* 7 Avenida 10–55, Zona 1; *Mayatex,* 12 Calle 4–56, Zona 1; *La Regional,* 7 Avenida 9–34, Zona 1; *El Tocoyal,* 7 Avenida 13–56, Zona 9; *Típica Maya Quiché,* 11 Calle 6–60, Zona 1; *Lin-Canola,* 5 Calle 9–60, Zona 1; *La Momosteca,* 7 Avenida 14–48, Zona 1; *Galerías La Mon-*

taña, 14 Calle 7–71, Zona 9; *Silver Shop,* International Airport, Zona 13; *Jimmy Tex,* 1 Avenida 30–80, Zona 12. Some of the shops listed will accept major credit cards.

Antiques. Colonial furniture, Maya artifacts, statues, ceramics, old coins, carved chests, candelabra, and antique objects of all kinds are available in Guatemala City. Try one of the following, but remember that the export from Guatemala and import to the U.S. of archaeological artifacts is prohibited: *Antigüedades Barrientos,* Avenida La Reforma 12–01, Zona 10 and 5 Avenida 9–3, Zona 1; *Rodas Antiques,* 5 Avenida 8–42, Zona 1; *Antigüedades Estoril,* 12 Calle 4–64, Zona 1; *El Patio,* 12 Calle 3–39, Zona 1; *Casa Colonial,* 5 Avenida 9–34, Zona 1; *Pat and Olga Andrews,* 7 Avenida 8–02, Zona 9; *Joyeria Los Chachales,* Pasaje Rubio #38 (6 Avenida and 9 Calle), Zona 1; *Antigüedades San Francisco,* 11 Calle 3–56, Zona 1; *Antiques Santa Clara,* 7 Avenida 15–51, Zona 9.

Jewelry. Jade carvings, mostly reproductions of ancient Maya and Olmec designs, and silver and gold jewelry are produced in many parts of Guatemala, and several shops in Guatemala City offer these and other items. *Jades S.A.* and *La Esmeralda* at the Camino Real Hotel; *Devaux Jade,* 7 Avenida 3–22, Zona 1; *Pierpont Jewelers,* Avenida Las Américas 7–20, Zona 13; *La Perla,* 6 Avenida 8–83, Zona 1; *Lazzari,* 12 Calle 1–25, Zona 10; *El Sol,* 12 Calle 2–04, Zona 9; *El Angel Diamantino,* 7 Avenida 13–01, Zona 9; *F.S. Richard,* 6 Avenida 12–52, Zona 1; *La Marquesa,* Avenida La Reforma 13–70, Zona 9, and 6 Avenida 10–45, Zona 1.

Leather. Many handicraft shops carry leather goods—hats, belts, sandals, etc.—and two establishments each have three shops: *Arpiel,* Avenida Las Américas 7–20, Zona 13; Avenida La Reforma 15–54, Zona 9; 11 Calle 5–38, Zona 1. *Boutique Mariano Riva,* Avenida La Reforma 15–54, Zona 9; 12 Calle 1–28, Zona 9; 2 Calle 22–65, Centro Comercial Vista Hermosa, Zona 15.

ART AND FOLK ART GALLERIES.

Artists find Guatemala an irresistible subject for painting, and collectors of art soon note the vibrant colors in the paintings, weavings, and handicrafts, such as ceramics and carvings, done by native artists, who are heavily influenced by the striking colors and topography of the country. There are a number of galleries in Guatemala City that carry a wide range of these works of art.

Fortuny César. 48 Avenida "B" 3–74, Zona 11; 913–406. Open 8 A.M.– 6 P.M. Mon.–Sat.

Galerías Arriola. 7 Avenida 8–22, Zona 4; 316–932. Paintings by Víctor Manuel Arriola. Mon.–Fri., 9 A.M.–12:30 P.M., 3:30–7:30 P.M.

Galería El Dzunun. 1 Avenida 13–29, Zona 10; 682–569. Opposite the Guatemala Fiesta Hotel.

Galerías De León Campos. 13 Calle 7–20, Zona 9; 65–334.

Galería El Tunel. 16 Calle 5–30, Zona 1; 83–021.

Galería Rios. 7 Avenida 9–31, Zona 1; 535–191. 12 Calle 0–85, Zona 9; 317–095, 317–071.

Galería Fórum. 7 Avenida 14–44, Zona 9.

Galería Santa Lucia. 12 Calle 1–25, Local 016, Zona 10; 319–719. Mon.–Fri., 9 A.M.–1 P.M., 3–7 P.M. Wicker products—trays, chairs, bookcases, lampshades, etc.—made by the blind. Recommended.

Sombol. Avenida La Reforma 14–14, Zona 9; 312–906, 312–685. Large selection.

NIGHTLIFE AND ENTERTAINMENT. The place to go for nightlife is the "Zona Viva," a 16-block area around the Camino Real and Fiesta hotels that contains many of the city's most popular restaurants, bars, and nightclubs. Most night spots don't open until 8 P.M. or later, and many remain open until the wee hours of the morning.

Cocktail Lounges/Bars

ALTUNA. 5 Avenida 12–31, Zona 1.
Cheers. Close to Edificio Géminis (12 Calle and 1 Avenida, Zona 10). Terrace.
El Establo. Avenida La Reforma 14–32, Zona 9.
El Mostachon. 12 Calle 5–54, Zona 9.
El Optimista. Avenida La Reforma 12–01, Zona 10.
El Zocalo. 18 Calle 4–39, Zona 1. Marimba music.
Las Sillas. 7 Avenida 13–01, Zona 9. Near the major hotels in Zonas 9 and 10.
O.K. Corral. 12 Calle 6–40, Zona 9. Darts, backgammon, video movies.
Sherlock's Home. Avenida de las Americas and 1 Avenida, Zona 13.
Shakespeares. 13 Calle 1–51, Zona 10
There are also bars in most of the major hotels in the city.

Nightclubs

After Eight. Edificio Galerías España, Plazuela España, Zona 9.
Friends. 7 Avenida 7–07, Zona 4.
Kaluha. 1 Avenida 13–29, Zona 10.
Kayuco Pub. 10 Calle 6–12, Zona 9.
Manhattan. Opposite the El Dorado Hotel.
Restaurante la Peña de los Charangos. 6 Avenida 13–62, Zona 9.
Safari. 3 Avenida 11–65, Zona 10.
There are also nightclubs at the *Ritz Continental* and *Conquistador-Sheraton* hotels.

Discos

Baco's. Avenida Reforma and 16 Calle, Zona 10.
Dash Disco. 12 Calle 1–25, Zona 10.
Le Pont. 13 Calle 0–48, Zona 10.
There are also discos at the *Camino Real* and *Guatemala Fiesta* hotels.

Theaters, Concerts, Cinemas

Most plays are in Spanish—though you might be lucky enough to see one in English; check the advertisements in the local newspapers. Theater prices are much lower than in the U.S. Call the following theaters to ask if they have any plays in production: *Teatro Universidad Popular,* 10 Calle 10–32, Zona 1; 28–433; *Teatro Gadem,* 8 Avenida 12–15, Zona 1, 80–011; *Teatro IGA,* Ruta 1 and Vía 4, Zona 4; 310–022, which sometimes presents English-language productions. The *Universidad Popular* theater runs the *Festival de Teatro Guatemalteco* from Sept. to Jan. and is open all year on weekends showing plays by European and Latin American authors. *Gadem* theater participates in the *Festival de Teatro Guatemalteco,* shows plays by European and Latin American authors, and is open Thurs.–Sun. *Teatro Abril,* 9 Avenida 14–22, Zona 1; 81–141. Completely remodeled, this theater presents Vegas-style shows and plays with international casts.

The *Teatro Nacional* is located where the San José fortress once stood, between 21 and 24 Calles in Zona 1, overlooking the Civic Center. The structure itself is worth a visit, and you could check there, in the local newspapers, or at the tourist office (INGUAT) to find out what productions are in the works.

Concerts of classical music, ballet, and dance are presented at *Teatro IGA, Teatro de Bellas Artes* (Fine Arts Theater), Avenida Elena 14–75, Zona 1, 513–735, *Conservatorio Nacional de Música,* 3 Avenida 4–61, Zona 1, 28–726 and at the *Teatro al Aire Libre* and *Teatro Cámara* at the National Theater.

There are many movie theaters in Guatemala City, a number of which show movies in English with Spanish subtitles. The new theaters are clean and comfortable and admission is much less than what you would pay in the U.S. Many of these theaters are in Zona 1, on or near 6 Avenida, and many of the new theaters are in zones 4 and 9. Advertisements in the daily papers will show you what is playing. The *Alianza Francesa,* 4 Avenida 12–39, Zona 1, 24–827, has movies on Mondays and Wednesdays (as well as exhibitions and lectures on other days), and the *Instituto de Idioma Alemán,* 11 Calle 3–27, Zona 1, has movies, lectures, or concerts on Wednesdays at 6:30 P.M., 511–463.

ANTIGUA

From 1543 to 1773 the capital city of the Kingdom of Guatemala—which comprised the Mexican department of Chiapas, and Guatemala, Belize, El Salvador, Honduras, Nicaragua, and Costa Rica—was called the *Muy Noble y Muy Leal Ciudad de Santiago de los Caballeros de Goathemala* (the Most Noble and Most Loyal City of St. James of the Knights of Guatemala). Today it is known as Antigua. Its wealth, splendor, sophistication, power, and size was rivaled only by Mexico City and Lima. In 1773 it contained 32 churches, 18 convents and monasteries, 15 hermitages, 10 chapels, a university and seven colleges, five hospitals, an orphanage, exquisite fountains set in carefully tended parks and gardens, beautiful private mansions, and some of the most beautiful buildings constructed in the New World. An estimated population of nearly 80,000 lived in Antigua when it was destroyed by an earthquake that same year and the capital was moved to present-day Guatemala City in 1776.

Today Antigua has a population of more than 30,000 and many of its cobblestone streets have changed little since 1773. There are no signs jutting out across the streets, few buildings are more than one-story high, and the center of town is full of colonial-style homes with metal grilles; ornate, metal-studded doorways; whitewashed walls; and tile roofs. And everywhere still stand the churches and palaces, mansions, fountains, convents, and other monuments—some in ruins after the earthquake of 1976, some looking much as they did before 1773—reminders of Antigua's past, of the pride, wealth, and love of beauty that were colonial Spain at its best.

The previous capital—now known as Ciudad Vieja (old city), though recent research has shown that the center of the old capital city was actually at San Miguel Escobar—had been established in 1527 in the Almolonga Valley, between the volcanoes Agua and Fuego, and was ruled over by Don Pedro de Alvarado, the *conquistador,* and his new wife, Doña Beatriz de la Cueva. On an expedition to Mexico in 1541 Don Pedro was crushed under the horse of his own secretary, remarking laconically as he died, "This cannot be helped, and should happen to fools like myself who take with them people like Montoya."

When the news of his death reached Almolonga in early September, his wife ordered such excessive displays of mourning that the people were disturbed, fearing that her blatant show of mourning was sacrilegious and would bring disaster to them all. Doña Beatriz demanded that she be appointed as governor to replace her husband, and ordered all who opposed her arrested and jailed. Only 36 hours after she became the first female ruler in the Americas the 22-year-old Beatriz was in the chapel when, after several days of torrential rain, a flood of water and mud crashed down on the capital from the slopes of Volcán Agua, destroying the city and killing many of its inhabitants, including Doña Beatriz.

The new capital was established in the Panchoy Valley, a few miles away. Antigua was the first planned city in the Americas and was carefully laid out by Juan Bautista Antonelli. The cathedral and government buildings were situated around a spacious central plaza which was the center of a rectangular grid pattern: *calles* running east–west and *avenidas* north–south. Antigua was susceptible to earthquakes and volcanic eruptions and during the next 230 years was severely damaged by earthquakes many times.

Each time the buildings were flattened the structures were rebuilt, more massive than before, with buttresses placed against thicker walls to protect them against earthquakes. The buildings were solid and low to the ground with large courtyards containing spacious gardens and fountains.

During these years many now-famous people lived in Antigua, including Hermano Pedro de Betancourt, whose grave in a San Francisco church has become a shrine; Bernal Díaz del Castillo, who fought with Cortés and Alvarado and wrote his *True History of the Conquest of New Spain* in a house that was located where the *Compañía de Jesús* church now stands; Thomas Gage, the Jesuit priest who wrote a famous account of his travels; Francisco Marroquín, the first bishop of Guatemala, buried somewhere in the cathedral; Rafael Landivar, one of Guatemala's finest poets, expelled with his fellow Jesuits in 1767, but whose tomb and house can still be seen in Antigua; Diego de Porres, the great architect, whose works include some of Antigua's finest buildings (City Hall, the Archbishop's Palace, the Royal Mint, the churches of Escuela de Cristo and Santa Clara, Convento de Capuchinas, and many others); Bartolomé de Las Casas, the priest who denounced Spanish policy toward the Indians and whose missionary work brought peace to Alta and Baja Verapaz (the departments of Upper and Lower True Peace). These and scores of other illustrious scholars, painters, sculptors, writers, and builders made Antigua one of the most vital, active, and cosmopolitan cities in the New World.

Then, at the peak of its power, Antigua was destroyed. The church authorities resisted moving from Antigua but the governor, backed by the king of Spain, ordered the city to be abandoned in 1775 and the new capital to be located on the Ermita Valley, site of the present-day Guatemala City. The wealthier people were forced to leave Antigua and after stripping the ruined buildings of everything that could be used—doors, furniture, church altars, and art—only the poorest people remained. More than a century later, as the population increased, people found it easier to renovate old houses rather than build anew, and Antigua today remains quite similar in style, ambience, and layout to the colonial capital it once was.

Semana Santa

Holy Week—from Palm Sunday to Easter Sunday—is without doubt the biggest occasion of the year in Antigua, and possibly the biggest Easter celebration in the New World. Thousands of people from Antigua and the nearby villages take part, and the streets become a vast stage on which is reenacted the entire spectacle, starting with processions over palm-lined streets, symbolizing Christ's entry into Jerusalem, and ending with processions of the resurrection on Easter Sunday. If you like to stay up *very* late or to get up *very* early don't miss the sight of armor-clad Roman soldiers charging through the streets on horseback early on Good Friday, demanding the sentence of death for Jesus, or the local people working through the night creating the exquisite rugs *(alfombras)* of sawdust and flowers over which the processions pass. Thousands of men clad in purple robes, accompanied by Roman soldiers, take turns (changing every two blocks) carrying the *andas* (floats, the biggest of which—from La Merced church—weighs 8,000 pounds) for several hours through the streets of town. There are several *andas,* carried by men and women, from different churches during Holy Week, and information on the routes and times is available at the tourist office. One procession stops at the city jail, where a prisoner is released. After the crucifixion all the participants in the processions wear black robes.

This massive piece of religious theater is witnessed by thousands of people from all over the world and is one of the most remarkable, colorful, spectacular, and—for Christians—religiously moving experiences imaginable. Be warned that in Antigua (and elsewhere in Guatemala) hotels, and even pensiones, are booked far in advance for Semana Santa.

At other times of the year, the experience of Antigua will be one of more quiet beauty. A one-day tour of the ruins will be impressive and informative, but long strolls through the cobbled streets, resting by a fountain in a tree-shaded plaza, observing people from all walks of life, and visiting nearby Indian villages will give you a clearer feeling of the culture and tradition of Antigua and its people. The longer you stay, the more you will understand why the city was declared "Monumental City of the Americas" by the Pan American Institute of History and Geography.

People who have lived in Antigua for years never stop discovering new surprises—a sunrise or sunset over the volcanoes unlike the hundreds you'd seen before, a door, facade, or chimney that is worth another look. Not to mention works of art, fountains, volcanoes, pillars on street corners, and the Indians from the villages nearby.

The Plaza de Armas

The social and economic center around which the city was organized in 1543 is the Plaza de Armas. It was a place of constant activity: market vendors selling their wares, bullfights, tournaments, whippings, hangings, horseraces, pageants, and processions. The major fountain, La Sirena, was originally constructed in 1738, but was broken by the earthquake of 1773. For years it was not restored, but in 1936 it was reconstructed and only the shaft between the nubile women on the four sides and the top bowl is not original.

From the Parque Central (as it is known now) one can get a fine view of the volcanoes Fuego and Acatenango to the southwest, get a shoeshine, hire a taxi, or listen to a lay preacher. Near the cathedral Indian weavers lay out their wares and adorn the park with the beauty of their weavings and other handicrafts.

The Palace of the Captains-General

Originally built in 1558, the the Palace of the Captains-General was damaged by successive earthquakes and almost completely rebuilt in 1761. Then heavily damaged by the great earthquake in 1773, it has been largely restored and its great size and purity of design make it one of the most magnificent structures in colonial America.

The building housed royal offices and courts, great rooms for balls and ceremonies, the royal treasury, tax offices, the council chambers, the barracks of the palace guards, offices for all the bureaucrats, and much more. High officials and their guests would observe hangings, celebrations, and other ceremonies in the central plaza from the second-floor balcony. It now houses the offices for the department of Sacatepéquez, police offices, the tourist office, and other government offices.

City Hall (Ayuntamiento)

Built in 1740 City Hall, on the north side of the central park, compliments in style and beauty the Palace of the Captains-General to the south and houses the city government of Antigua as it did in 1773. It was badly damaged by the earthquake of 1976, but has now been completely restored and contains the Museo de Santiago, in which are displayed artifacts from the colonial period, and the Museo del Libro Antiguo, displaying originals and replicas of some of the early documents published by the first printing press in Central America, started in 1660. Under its arcade poor people who have come to market unroll their *petates*—woven reed mats—and sleep the night.

Cathedral of San José

The first cathedral in Antigua was begun in 1542, but after constant repairs it was demolished in 1669 and construction of the present cathedral was started in the same year. The structure was intended to be the most majestic cathedral in Central America, with a great dome, five naves, and 18 chapels in a main chamber measuring 300 by 170 feet, with statues and paintings executed by such masters as Quirio Cataño, Antonio Montúfar, and Alonso de Paz. The present church is only two chapels of the original, which was destroyed in the great earthquake of 1773 and damaged by the earthquake of 1976. Behind it are columns, broken arches, and tumbled walls—the only reminders of its former magnificence.

Buried somewhere beneath the floors are Don Pedro de Alvarado and Doña Beatriz, Bishop Marroquín, Bernal Díaz de Castillo, and other illustrious figures, but the location of their graves was lost when the cathedral was destroyed.

Universidad de San Carlos de Borromeo

The university was founded in 1681 but this building, facing the south side of the cathedral, was not erected until around 1760. With deep-set hexagonal windows, an exquisite arched corridor surrounding the patio, and ornate plaster work, the building is as strong as it is harmonious, and has survived the centuries with little damage. Note the fine view of Volcán Agua from the south side of the patio.

The building now houses the Museum of Colonial Art, with rooms exhibiting religious paintings and sculpture, murals depicting the life of colonial scholars, a map of Antigua drawn by seventeenth-century historian Antonio de Fuentes y Guzmán, and a library of old, as well as recent, scholarly books.

Convento de las Capuchinas

One of the most interesting and best-preserved ruins in Antigua, the convent of the Capuchin nuns was built between 1726 and 1736. The Torre del Retiro (Tower of Retreat) contains several "cells," each with a sewage system and private bathroom. Below the tower is a large circular vault with a massive central pillar, and there are several speculations on its raison d'être: was it a warehouse, a wine cellar, a laundry or choir room . . . or a torture chamber?

The ruins also house the offices of the Consejo Nacional para la Protección de Antigua Guatemala (National Council for the Protection of Antigua Guatemala), a small archaeological museum, an exhibit of photographs and site plans of the ruins, and a small bookstand selling books on Antigua and the council's newsletter.

La Recolección

Begun in 1701 on the outskirts of town, La Recoleccíon was completed shortly before it was severely damaged in the 1717 earthquake. Rebuilt even more magnificently, the church, with its refectories, cells, cloisters, study and music rooms, and gardens, was one of the largest architectural gems of Antigua. Destroyed in 1773, some of its stones were used to build other structures nearby, and the huge arch collapsed in the earthquake in 1976. Set among coffee fields and feet deep in rubble, the ruins are away from the noise of the traffic and its great columns and broken arches, and beautiful gardens, are a fine place to spend a few quiet hours.

Santa Clara

Much work has been done by the National Council to repair the ruins of Santa Clara and particularly notable are the tiered arches and the excellently preserved central fountain in the patio.

San Francisco

Begun in 1543, the church of the Franciscans became larger than even the Cathedral of San José. With its hospital, monastery, college, cloisters, library, music rooms, printing press, and chapel, it covered four city blocks. Destroyed in 1773, large-scale reconstruction was started in 1960, and it is interesting not only as a remarkable structure but also for the opportunity it offers us to see what the church must have looked like more than 200 years ago.

Hermano Pedro de Betancourt is buried in the Chapel of the Third Order and pilgrims from all over Central America come to seek miracles from—and to give thanks to—the beloved, and now beatified, Hermano Pedro.

La Merced

Completed just six years before the 1773 earthquake, this church is highlighted by the finest stucco work in Antigua. Flowers, vines, geometric patterns, and graceful figures seem to cover every inch of the facade, giving the massive structure a lacy, gossamer appearance. In the plaza outside the church is a (non-functioning) fountain and a huge stone cross, and in the gardens of the church is the cloister fountain, known as Fuente de Pescados (Fountain of Fish) because of the fish-breeding experiments done by the Mercedarian brothers. The fountain is one of the largest and most elaborate in the city—a symmetrical, ornate masterpiece.

Among other ruins worthy of attention in Antigua are San Jeronimo, with its octagonal fountain and double-arched cloister; Escuela de Cristo, containing works by Quirio Cataño; and Compañía de Jesús, the Jesuit religious-educational complex, abandoned when the order was expelled from Guatemala and damaged again during the 1976 earthquake. Restoration of the ruins by the National Council for the Protection of Antigua Guatemala continues. El Carmen, known for its Ionic columns and fine plaster work, is worth visiting, as are San José El Viejo, near the Hotel Antigua and El Calvario—a lovely walk down a tree-lined road starting at the church of San Francisco and passing small, enclosed altars for each station of the cross.

Also well worth seeing are some of the restored colonial houses, such as the Casa de los Leones (now the Posada de Don Rodrigo), the facade of Convento de la Concepción—note the date of construction above the facade; and, especially, the Casa Popenoe (Popenoe House), 1 Avenida Sur between 5 and 6 Calles. This early seventeenth-century house was lovingly restored by Dorothy Popenoe, who filled it with authentic colonial furnishings and works of art. Half-hour tours of this exceptional house are offered at 3 and 3:30 P.M. from Monday to Saturday, except on national holidays. Wilson Popenoe wrote a small pamphlet on the house in the

1940s (in Spanish and English) and Dorothy wrote a book entitled *Santiago de los Caballeros de Guatemala,* first published by Harvard University Press in 1933 and republished in 1973 and 1975 under the title *The Story of Antigua Guatemala.*

Cerro de la Cruz

This hill to the north of town is reached by car or by a footpath that starts near the ruins of Candeleria. From the top you can see Antigua spread out below you like a map (bring a map of Antigua with you to find out which ruin is which), as well as the volcanoes Agua (to the south) and Fuego and Acatenango (to the southwest), and Ciudad Vieja in the distance. A beautiful panorama and a pleasant place for a picnic—though you should be aware that a couple of years ago several people were robbed here.

Nearby Villages

San Antonio Aguas Calientes is a Cakchiquel farming community, known for the quality of its weavings. This Indian village now depends heavily on tourism, as evidenced by the string of *tiendas* (shops) selling textiles along the road into the village. The colors, as always, are incredible, and you will be offered fine tablecloths and napkins, wall hangings, women's belts, *huipiles* (long blouses), and shirts at very low prices. You should check from shop to shop, and bargain if you find two similar pieces that interest you.

Santa María de Jesús is located on the slopes of Volcán Agua. This village cultivates corn and vegetables far up the steep slopes of the volcano. Native *trajes* (suits) are still worn by some of the men, and the weaving is excellent. On a clear day there is a fine view of Antigua far below, and this is the starting point for hikes up Agua. There is a small pensión (Hospedaje El Oasis) in the village.

The church in the village San Felipe de Jesús, located on the outskirts of Antigua, was destroyed in the 1976 earthquake, but has since been completely restored. On the first Sunday of Lent, pilgrims arrive here from all over Central America, hundreds of them walking 30 miles from Guatemala City; the church is famous for its Black Christ. There is a silver factory two blocks from the central square, where you can watch the craftsmen at work.

Ciudad Vieja is the capital city where Pedro de Alvarado and Beatriz lived until 1541. The ruins that were thought to be part of the original palace are now known to be only the remains of a small monastery.

San Juan del Obispo is the site of Bishop Marroquín's mansion and church, just over a mile south of Antigua. With some of the oldest altars and paintings in Guatemala, still in their original sixteenth-century condition, the church is an important historical structure and is sometimes open to the public.

Other villages you can drive or walk to near Antigua, more off the beaten track, are San Pedro Las Huertas, the ruined church at San Gaspar Vivar, San Miguel Dueñas, Santa Catarina Barahona, San Bartolomé Becerra, Magdalena Milpas Atlas, and Santo Tomás Milpas Altas.

PRACTICAL INFORMATION FOR ANTIGUA

HOW TO GET THERE. By bus. Buses leave from 15 Calle between 3 and 4 Avenidas and from 18 Calle between 4 and 5 Avenidas in Zone 1 in Guatemala City, from 7 A.M. to about 8 P.M. every day. They depart about every half-hour, and are very crowded late in the afternoon, particularly on Fri. Buses from Antigua to the capital leave about every half-hour from 6 A.M. to 7 P.M. or later from the bus terminal, in front of the post office, 3 blocks west of the central park.

To reach Antigua from the western highlands, take any bus to Guatemala City and get off at Chimaltenango and catch one of the buses near the Pan-American Highway (two blocks from the town square) for the 30-minute trip to Antigua. If you arrive in Chimaltenango later than 6 P.M., continue to San Lucas Sacatepéquez and stop a bus coming from Guatemala City for the 20-minute trip to Antigua.

By car. Leave Guatemala City on Calzada Roosevelt (the Pan-American Highway). The road winds uphill, passing a *mirador* that has a panoramic view of Guatemala City, until it reaches San Lucas where you take the bridge to the right (north) at the edge of town. Driving time to Antigua is about 45 minutes.

From the western highlands, drive along the Pan-American Highway to Chimaltenango and turn right (south) a few blocks after the town for the short drive to Antigua.

From the Pacific Coast you can drive to Antigua by way of Escuintla. Take route 14 from Escuintla, a gravel road which climbs into the mountains past volcanoes Agua and Fuego and through the towns of Alotenango and Ciudad Vieja, before entering Antigua. Note that this road is not in good condition.

A shuttle now operates between Antigua and the Airport in Guatemala City. It makes five trips a day and stops at all the major hotels in Antigua before departing for the city. Check at the airport for information.

TOURIST INFORMATION. The Tourist Office (INGUAT) is located on the south side of the central park and is run by the most charming, helpful, and knowledgeable Benjamín García López (Don Benjamín). He is a fount of information on Antigua, past and present, and can be counted on to answer—or find the answers to—any questions you have. Legitimate tour guides are licensed by the tourist office, and will be able to show you their certification. You can find guides at the central park and near the bridge at the entrance to Antigua. Don't be misled by hustlers.

COMMUNCATIONS. GUATEL, located at the southwest corner of the square, is open 7 days a week, from 7 A.M. to 9 P.M., for international and national phone calls. International cables are made from the GUATEL office, and national cables are made from the Post Office *(Correos)* at the corner of 4 Calle Poniente and Calzada de Santa Lucía, which is open 24 hrs. a day, 7 days a week. Letters can be mailed, 8 A.M.–4:30 P.M., Mon.–Fri., and parcels and registered letters, 8 A.M.–3:30 P.M., Mon.–Fri.

Public telephones for local calls are available—when functioning—at *Funerales Figueroa,* 4 Avenida Norte No.4, on the northwest side of the square; at *Arnold's,* on the west side of the square; outside the *Los Capitanes* hotel; and at the gas station on 4 Calle Oriente and 1 Avenida.

AUTO REPAIRS. At most gas stations, including the Chevron and Shell stations on 4 Calle Oriente. *Taller Mecánico Libélula,* 6 Avenida Sur No.6. *Caribe Motor,* Calle Real de Jocotenango No.34. Owner Jorge Vobejda speaks English. Car insurance is available at *Seguros Granai & Townson,* 6 Avenida Norte No.14A.

ACCOMMODATIONS. *Deluxe,* $70 to $100; *First-Class,* $25–$70; *Moderate,* $10 to $25; *Inexpensive,* $5 to $10; *Budget,* less than $3.

Deluxe

Hotel Antigua. Callejón San José El Viejo, between 4 and 5 Avenidas; 320–288, 320–331. 58 rooms and 2 suites. Conference room for 400 people. Fireplaces and cable TV in rooms. Landscaped gardens, swimming pool, restaurant, bar, outdoor Sunday buffet.

Ramada Inn. 9 Calle, on the road to Ciudad Vieja; 320–011/5. Reservations from the U.S.: 1–800–2RAMADA, or from any airline. 156 rooms and 12 suites, with fireplaces and cable TV. Four conference rooms. 2 swimming pools, playground, wheelchair facilities, bar with live music, restaurant with live music on weekends, tennis courts, saunas, gym, disco, tour and car rental agencies. Rental of horses and bicycles.

First-Class

Posada de Don Rodrigo. 5 Avenida Norte No.17; 320–291, 320–387. A restored colonial mansion, *La Casa de los Leones.* 33 rooms, some with fireplaces, each unique and furnished with antiques. Gardens, patios, fountains. Large restaurant, bar, marimba music daily, conference room. Good service.

Moderate

Palacio de Doña Leonor. 4 Calle Oriente No.8; 320–226. Colonial-style hotel with 68 rooms. Pool, disco, parking, restaurant, bar.

Suites Santa Isabel. 1 kilometer south on the road to Santa María de Jesús; 320–652. 12 suites, all with fireplaces and living rooms, with 1 or 2 bedrooms. Special rates by the week or month.

Inexpensive

Aurora. 4 Calle Oriente No.16; 320–217. 17 rooms. Family-run colonial mansion which opened in 1923. Large patio, fountain, restaurant serving breakfast, cafeteria, laundry, parking.

Casa El Patio. 5 Avenida Norte No.37; 320–003. 12 rooms, 2 with fireplaces. 2 living rooms and dining room for guests, solarium, large patio, parking. Will arrange laundry service and offer large discounts for stays of 2 weeks or more. Old colonial home.

El Rosario. 5 Avenida Sur No.36, just south of Hotel Antigua; 320–336. 10 rooms. Set in orange groves and a coffee *finca,* with gardens and a small swimming pool. Fireplaces in some of the rooms, bar service, good and inexpensive restaurant attached.

Budget

Los Capitanes. 5 Avenida Sur No.8. 36 rooms. Next to movie theater. Restaurant.

La Casa de Santa Lucia. Calzada de Santa Lucía No.5. 10 rooms. Bathrooms in some rooms; clean.

El Descanso Guest House. 5 Avenida Norte No.9.

El Pasaje. Calzada de Santa Lucía No.3. 9 rooms. Recommended.

Pension el Arco. 5 Avenida Norte No.32.

El Placido. Avenida del Desengaño No.25. 13 rooms. Private bathrooms in some rooms.

There are many other pensiones, including **Posada El Refugio** and **Posada de Doña Angelina,** on 4 Calle Poniente; **Posada Las Rosas,** on 6 Avenida Sur; **Antigüeñita,** on 2 Calle Poniente; **Posada San Francisco,** on 3 Calle Oriente; and **Posada San Agustín,** on 7 Avenida Norte.

RESTAURANTS. As one of Guatemala's most popular tourist attractions, and with a large population of foreign residents, Antigua has new restaurants and cafés opening constantly. The following is but a sampling of the best in operation at this time, though you may find others have opened when you visit. The major hotels have quality restaurants, but you should try some of those listed below, which are less expensive and, in some cases, very good.

Angeletti. 5 Calle Poniente #4. Italian cuisine.

El Capuchino. 6 Avenida Norte No.10. Italian and international meals. Owner speaks English.

Casa de Cafe Ana. 5 Avenida Sur No.36, next to the El Rosario lodge. Closed Wed.

El Churrasco. 4 Calle Poniente No.16. Small, basic restaurant with good meat dishes.

Don Miguel. Road to San Felipe #97. Interesting gardens.

La Estrella. 5 Calle Poniente No.6. Chinese restaurant. Good food and service.

Fonda de la Calle Real. 5 Avenida Norte No.5. The main dining room is on the second floor, with a view of the beautifully lit street. Guitar music occasionally on weekends.

Pasteleria y Panaderia Doña Luisa Xicotencatl (Doña Luisa's). 4 Calle Oriente No.12. Homemade breads, cakes, and pies. Great for breakfast or for a filling sandwich. The major meeting place for local and visiting foreigners. Very crowded on weekends when many Guatemalans from the capital visit Antigua. *El Tarro* bar behind the restaurant.

Panza Verde. 5 Avenida Sur in Front of El Rosario. Lovely Colonial house, dining inside or on the patio. Good food and atmosphere.

Portada Del Palomar. 5 Calle Oriente #3. Colonial house with restaurant, art gallery, and antiques.

El Sereno. 6 Calle Poniente No.30. A beautifully restored colonial house. Dining inside or on the patio. Excellent food and service. Open Wed. to Sun.

Welten. 4 Calle Oriente No.21. Beautifully decorated restaurant and cafe in old colonial-style house. International menu. Expensive.

Zen. 3 Avenida Norte No.3, behind the cathedral. Japanese restaurant. International food. Closed Wed.

Also: **La Casa de las Gárgolas,** 5 Avenida Norte No.14; **Martedino,** 4 Calle Poniente No.18; **Angeletti,** 5 Calle Poniente No.4; **Emilio,** 4 Calle Poniente No.2; **San Carlos,** northwest corner of the square; **Las 3 Puertas D'Rino,** 5 Avenida Norte, just off Parque Central.

Cafés

Cafe Jardin. West side of Parque Central.
Cafe Roble. 3 Avenida Sur No.15A. Open 2 P.M. to 8 P.M.
La Cenicienta. 5 Avenida Norte No.7. Good pies and cakes.
Mio Cid. 5 Calle Oriente and 3 Avendia Norte. Cafe and bar.
Ice cream is available at **Topsy,** 5 Avenida Norte, right near the square; **Kandy,** 4 Calle Poniente, a few yards from the square; **Arnold's** and **Helados Sarita** (also a cafe), west side of Parque Central.

HOW TO GET AROUND. Since the central part of Antigua is only 8 blocks by 8 blocks, there is no better way of seeing the town than walking through it. Walk to the nearest villages—good maps of the area will show you the routes with least traffic. You can also rent a bicycle, at a cost of 25¢ an hour, from *Taller Mecánico Libélula* (no sign) at 6 Avenida Sur No.6.

Taxis are available on the north side of the park and in front of the market. A full day visiting the nearby villages should not cost more than $10 or $15.

Buses leave from the market every 45 minutes or so from 6:30 A.M. to 5:30 P.M. for connections from Chimaltenango to the western highlands. Buses go to Ciudad Vieja and San Antonio Aguas Calientes and buses or minivans *(ruleteros)* go to Santa María de Jesús, for the hike up Volcán Agua, about every hour or so until 5 P.M. Frequent buses to other small villages—inquire for times—leave from the bus terminal at the market.

SPORTS. The **swimming pools** at the *Ramada Inn,* the *Hotel Antigua* and *El Viejo Club,* 5 Calle Oriente No.22, are open to the public for a nominal fee. The hot springs at *Baños de San Lorenzo El Tejar,* about 6 miles from Antigua (turn right for a mile at San Luis Las Carretas) has a swimming pool and private cubicles.

If you plan to **climb any of the volcanoes,** make sure that you have sturdy hiking shoes, lots of water, and warm clothes. If you plan to sleep at the top you'll need a good sleeping bag. Volcán de Agua is the most-often climbed volcano, and will take 3 to 5 hours going up and much less coming down. Take a bus to Santa María de Jesús, about 7,000 feet, and from the village take trails for about a mile until you hit the road that winds about half-way up the volcano from Santa María. The top is at 12,336 feet. Volcán de Acatenango, 13,044 feet high, is reached by taking a bus going to Yepocapa or Acatenango villages from the market in Antigua, or by hiring a taxi and getting off at Finca La Soledad. The hike will take 5 hours or more, and if you want to stay the night, there is a small hut 700 feet below the summit. Volcán de Fuego—which is still active—is more than 12,000 feet high, and you have to descend more than 2,000 feet from the summit of Acatenango before climbing to the top of Fuego. The *Asociación Andinismo,* 6 Avenida Norte No.34, arranges trips to these and the other volcanoes in Guatemala. *Casa Andinista,* 4 Calle Oriente No.5A, sells copies of the topographic maps of the area, and Mike Shawcross's guide to Antigua and area has more information on climbing these volcanoes. You could also ask Don Benjamín at the tourist office to recommend a guide.

MUSEUMS. *Casa Kojom,* Calle de los Recolectos No. 55. Museum of indigenous musical instruments. Admission 20 cents; Mon.–Fri. 9A.M.–5 P.M. *Convento de las Capuchinas,* 2 Avenida Norte between 1 and 2 Calles. Open daily 9 A.M.–5 P.M. Admission 10 cents, Wed.–Mon.; free on Tues.

Museo de Arte Colonial, south of the Cathedral on 5 Calle Oriente. Open Tues.–Fri., 9 A.M.–4 P.M., Sat. and Sun., 9 A.M.–noon, 2–4 P.M. The museum library is open Tues.–Fri., 2 P.M.–4 P.M. Admission to the museum Tues.–Sat. is 10 cents; Sun., free.

Museo del Libro Antiguo, north side of the square. Open the same times as the *Museo de Arte Colonial.* Admission free.

Museo de Santiago, north side of the square. Open the same times as the Museo de Arte Colonial, and with the same admission costs.

GALLERIES AND STUDIOS. Artists from all over the world make their home in Antigua and their original works are on display in several places in town. There are also some very talented local artists whose work is well worth a look. See also "Shopping," below.

Un Poco de Todo, west side of the square. Displays paintings, drawings, and photographs by Guatemalan and foreign artists, plus rubbings and posters.

Utatlán, 5 Avenida Norte No.18. Primitive paintings, plus handicrafts and weavings.

El Prisma, 4 Calle Oriente No.5. Guatemalan paintings. They also make frames.

El Sereno, 6 Calle Poniente No.30. Occasional exhibits of paintings; check if there is an exhibit of Anita Storck's works.

Klaske, 5 Avenida Sur No.34. Photographs. Knock if the studio is not open.

Sombra y Luz, Calle de San Luquitas No.20 (near the Ramada Inn). Photographs by Daniel Chauche. Examples of his fine photographs are sold at *Casa Andinista,* 4 Calle Oriente No.5A.

Rafael Blanco, 7 Calle Poniente No.2. Beautiful works on Antigua by a local artist; pyrogravure on wood.

Guillermo Blanco, Avenida del Desengaño No.17. Illustrations of Antigua; ink on wood.

Portada del Palomar, 5 Calle Oriente No. 3. Exhibits by different artists.

SHOPPING. Because of earthquake damage in 1976 to the old market, the recently constructed **market** is located at the end of 4 Calle Poniente, three blocks from the central square. It is open daily, with Mon., Thurs., and Sat. being the main market days. Indian artisans are currently located at the *Compañía de Jesús* church, entrance on 7 Avenida Norte between 3 and 4 Calle.

Antigua has a very large number of shops selling quality work by **Guatemalan artisans.** Prices are usually fixed, though you can always try to bargain. *El Tecolote,* 5 Avenida Norte No.14; *El Quetzal,* 4 Calle Oriente No.3; *Casa de Artes,* 4 Avenida Sur No.11 (a large selection of quality

100　　　　　　　　　GUATEMALA

items); *Concha's,* 7 Calle Oriente No.14; *Casa de los Gigantes,* 7 Calle Oriente No.18; *Plateria Típica Maya,* 7 Calle Oriente No.9 (silver); *Utatlán,* 5 Avenida Norte No.18 (large selection); *La Casa de las Gárgolas,* 5 Avenida Norte No.14; *Plateria y Joyeria M.& W.,* Callejón de la Animas No.3; *La Casa de Jade,* 4 Calle Oriente No.3; *Jades, S.A.,* 4 Calle Oriente No.34; *Evelia del Pinal,* 6 Calle Oriente, between 6 and 7 Avenidas, (candles); *Don Carlos,* 5 Avenida Sur No.4; *Un Poco de Todo,* west side of Parque Central (paintings, rubbings); *Colibri,* 4 Calle Oriente No.3B; *Típica Nebajense,* 3 Avenida Norte No.1; *Harlon* (no sign), 5 Avenida Norte No.25B; *Ixchel,* 4 Calle Oriente No.13 (blankets and rugs); *Alex,* 4 Calle Oriente No.6; *Mary's Originals,* 3 Avenida Norte No.7; *Casa El Carmen,* 3 Avenida Norte No.8; *Papier Maché.* 8 Calle Oriente No.19.

Antiques. *Antigüedades,* Alameda de Santa Lucía No.15; *Antigüedades Concepción,* 4 Calle Oriente No.38 (expensive); *Antigüedades La Unión,* 2 Avenida Sur No.12 (Mayan ceramics, bronze items).

Three **bookdealers** live in Antigua: *Shawcross Book Service,* tel. 320–161; *Casa El Carmen,* tel. 320–207; *Libros Centroamericanos,* tel. 320–274, weekday mornings only.

Bronze. *Juárez Hermanos,* 6 Calle Poniente No.36; *Forja-Bronze,* 7 Avenida Norte No.64.

Ceramics. *Amalia Rodenas,* 1 Avenida del Chajón No.26; *Cerámica Rodenas,* 1 Calle del Chajón No.28; *Florencio Rodenas,* 1 Calle del Chajón No.24; *Jesús Rodenas,* Colonia El Manchén No.79; *Víctor Rodenas,* Colonia El Manchén No.11; *Manuel Francisco Rodenas,* 7 Calle Poniente No.43; *Eben-Ezer (Piedad García Rodenas),* 1 Avenida del Chajón No. 9; *Juan José Pellecer,* Colonia El Manchén No.8; *Enrique España,* San Felipe de Jesús No.58, Zona 1; *Marcelino Monroy,* Calle de los Pasos (south of plaza opposite Escuela de Cristo church); *Fabrica Montiel,* No.20 on the old road to San Felipe.

Colonial-style furniture. *Antigua Colonial,* 5 Avenida Norte No.38; *Fidel Guerrero,* Calzada de Santa Lucía No.4; *Rogelio Morales,* 4 Calle Oriente No.15; *Joaquín Gaytán,* 2 Calle Poniente No.46; *Heriberto Valle,* Calzada de Santa Lucía No.1; *Virgilio Castillo,* 4 Calle Oriente No.36; *Juan García López,* Avenida del Desengaño No.20; *Manuel Antonio Arzú,* 7 Avenida Norte No.72. *Rubén Miranda Pérez,* 6 Avenida Norte No.53, makes wood carvings. *Portada del Palomar,* 5 Calle Oriente No. 3 (good selection of antique furniture and reproductions).

Jade. *Jades, S.A.,* 4 Calle Oriente No.34 (reproductions of Colonial coins, jade, textiles, and Mayan rubbings; tourist prices); *La Casa del Jade,* 4 Calle Orient No.3 (good jade selection and Mayan rubbings; reasonable prices); *El Jade Maya,* 7 Calle Oriente, Calle Jon Lopez No.12; *Jades, J.C.,* 9 Calle Oriente No. 2A.

NIGHTLIFE AND ENTERTAINMENT. Movies. Antigua's 2 movie houses offer a selection of English-language movies with Spanish subtitles, Spanish-language movies and a few films dubbed into Spanish. The films change daily, and prices are low (about 25 cents). Check the posters at the theaters or obtain a handbill to see what the weekly movies will be. Don't sit below the balcony, particularly on Sun. *Teatro Colonial,* 5 Avenida Sur No.8. *Cine Imperial,* on the west side of the square. The *Alianza Francesa,* 3 Calle Oriente No.19A, shows movies in French, with Spanish subtitles, at 7 P.M. on Fridays. Admission free.

Bars. *El Tarro,* 4 Calle Oriente No.12. Closed Mon.; *Los Encuentros,* 4 Calle Oriente No.290; *La Fiesta,* a disco lounge, 4 Calle Oriente No.39, open Tues.–Thurs. 8–11 P.M., Sat. and Sun. 9 P.M.–2 A.M. There are also bars in most of the major hotels.

Music and Dancing. There is a discotheque at the *Ramada Inn;* marimba playing daily at noon at the *Posada de Don Rodrigo* and outside the *Hotel Los Capitanes* on Sun.; marimba or rock music some weekends at the *Manhattan Club,* 4 Calle Poniente No.34, and occasionally at *Salón Señorial,* 2 Calle Poniente No.46; marimba and band music at night on the north, south, and occasionally, east side of the central square, particularly on Fri. nights.

Cultural Events. There are several places in Antigua that offer exhibitions, concerts, and lectures. Best to visit, or telephone, to find out what events are planned. *El Sereno,* 6 Calle Poniente No.30 (concerts, exhibitions); tel. 320–073. *C.I.R.M.A. (Centro de Investigaciones Regionales de Mesoamérica),* 5 Calle Oriente No.5 (concerts, exhibitions, lectures). They also have a fine library; tel. 320–126. *C.N.P.A.G. (Consejo Nacional para la Protección de Antigua Guatemala),* 2 Avenida Norte and 2 Calle (lectures, exhibitions); tel. 320–743, 320–184, 320–157. *Alianza Francesa,* 3 Calle Oriente No.19A (concerts, exhibitions, lectures); tel. 320–223; *Casa de la Cultura,* northeast side of the square (lectures, exhibitions, concerts). Open 4–8 P.M.; *Instituto Italiano,* 4 Calle Oriente No.21 (concerts).

LAKE ATITLÁN

In 1840, John L. Stephens wrote about Lake Atitlán: "We both agreed that it was the most magnificent spectacle we ever saw." Almost half a century ago Aldous Huxley called it the most beautiful lake in the world; 450 years ago the great conquistador Don Pedro de Alvarado was also awed by the sheer majesty of the lake and its surrounding mountains and volcanoes.

The verdict throughout history has been the same—Lake Atitlán, with its pure blue waters, its towering volcanoes, its ever-changing colors, its powerful and mysterious aura, and its abundance of exotic flowers, fruits, birds, and animals, is not simply a beautiful place but something altogether unique—a spot in which the earth's forces have been brought together to such a concentrated degree that the effect is nothing less than sublime.

The lake itself is remarkable. It measures some 11 by 8 miles and is more than 1,000 feet deep—some say as deep as 1,600 feet, though in fact its deepest point has not yet been found. Seen from a vantage point on one of the trails that wind through the mountains surrounding the water, these currents appear as huge swaths of lapis lazuli, deep green or purple—patches of color that are always changing, as the colors of the lake itself change from hour to hour.

At times clear and placid, the aspect of the lake can change when a gusty wind known to the Indians as the *xocomil (sho-ko-meel)* sweeps across its surface, ruffling up white choppy waves and making travel by boat dangerous.

Rising above the southern rim of the lake in almost perfect cones are volcanoes San Pedro (9,920 feet), Tolimán (10,340 feet), and Atitlán (11,560 feet), which can be seen from every village.

Panajachel is a tropical resort on the shores of Lake Atitlán, some 70 miles from Guatemala City. Lodging here ranges from luxury hotels to the most basic accommodations. The food here is very good.

At just over 5,000 feet, the weather here is just about perfect year-round, with temperatures in the low 70s during the day and in the 40s at night. The dry season runs from November to April, while the rainy season spans from late April to early June and is heaviest in September and early October. The *canícula* (Indian summer) is—sometimes—in July and August. During the dry season the skies are generally clear, though for a month before the rainy season starts, humidity increases and the air becomes quite hazy, both from farmers burning the *milpas* (cornfields) in preparation for planting and from the cloudy skies of the upcoming rainy season. Toward the end of the dry season the green colors fade to brown, and everyone awaits the start of the rains.

There is usually a week or more of intermittent showers before the rainy season really starts, and when it does you'll find it is not a continuous drizzle, but a well orchestrated series of showers in the afternoon, with mornings usually clear and sunny. Driving on unpaved roads and hiking on trails are more difficult during the rainy season due to the muddy surfaces.

During *Semana Santa* (Holy Week) all the hotels, and even many of the pensiones, are booked up well in advance—and prices are sometimes higher. Early reservations are advised. Summer months (June, July, August) are the most popular for foreign visitors, as well as Holy Week and Christmastime.

Santiago Atitlán

The ancient capital and religious center of the Tzutuhiles, this is still the most fascinating village on the lake. Lately, however, perhaps because of frequent mass invasions by tourists, the Indians have taken to capitalizing on their reputation. On Sundays (the famous market, run by the women of the town, is open daily, but Sundays are the big days when everyone comes to town) you can walk toward the dock shortly before the tourist boat from Panajachel arrives and you'll see colorfully dressed women and carefully groomed children sitting stolidly by their rock and bamboo huts, waiting.

Set on the slopes of Atitlán amid great chunks of lava, its stone streets winding past stone or cactus-fenced compounds and thatched-roof stone and bamboo huts, it is surrounded by water and volcanoes and mountains. The women wear vibrant red *cortes* and *huipiles* of white and purple, intricately embroidered; their unique headdresses are long (over 30 feet) red bands wrapped around and around their heads like halos (you can see it pictured on the Guatemalan 25 centavo coin). The men's purple and white striped *pantalones* with embroidery around the knees are also lovely, both in the colors and the quality of the work (though nowadays the men wear their *pantalones* and bright sashes with western-style shirts and cowboy hats) and in fact the weavings of Santiago, especially the *huipiles,* are admired and prized throughout the world as works of art. Perhaps the most delightful way to spend an afternoon is to take a lunch, sit on the huge boulders by the lake, and watch the women doing their washing in the lake—scrubbing and drying their beautiful clothes on the rocks, the colors shining and dancing in the clear sunlight—as men glide by in *cayucos,* or cut reeds in the shallow water, children play on the shore, young girls carry water and baskets of laundry on their heads, and volcano San Pedro towers massively in the background. This, and not the frantic bustle of the Sunday market, is the Santiago that is worth seeing.

There are basic accommodations in Santiago for the hardy budget traveler, but most visitors will come either via San Lucas or take one of the launches that leave daily from Panajachel. The bus ride from Guatemala City—a four-and-a-half hour, jouncing and frequently hair-raising trip—is only for those who specifically want to avoid Panajachel.

PRACTICAL INFORMATION FOR LAKE ATITLÁN

HOW TO GET THERE. By car. Take Calzada Roosevelt (the Pan-American Highway) northwest out of Guatemala City, passing through Chimaltenango (km. 56) to Los Encuentros (km. 127). On the way there is a turnoff to the south, at km. 89, to Tecpán and the ruins of the first capital of Guatemala, Iximché, 4 miles away. (Iximché is open 9 A.M.–4 P.M. daily; small admission.) On the right, just before the turnoff, is the *Katok* restaurant, and on the left, just after the turnoff, is the *La Montaña* restaurant. On the left, at km. 102, is the *Café Chichoy,* where you can get a snack and look at the weavings sold by the local widows' cooperative. A few miles farther on, a new road to the left goes to Godínez (and continues to San Lucas Tolimán), from which you can drop down to Panajachel on a poorly paved road. At km. 120, at an altitude of 8,000 feet, there is a *mirador* (lookout), with an excellent view of the lake.

At Los Encuentros there is a gas station and a small restaurant, and a road leading north to Santo Tomás Chichicastenango, 11 miles away. Two miles after Los Encuentros, at km.130, turn left to Sololá and Panajachel, 11 miles from the junction, descending the winding mountain road to the lake. Total distance from the capital to Panajachel: 92 miles; driving time about 2½ hours.

By bus. *Transportes Rébuli,* 20 Calle 3–42, Zona 1, and 3 Avenida 2–36, Zona 9, 516–505, go to Panajachel at 5:45, 6:20, 7, and 8:30 A.M. and hourly, 10 A.M.–3 P.M., leaving Panajachel on the same schedule. *Transportes Higueros,* 17 Calle 6–25, Zona 1, 24–794, go to Panajachel at 4 A.M., and at 3:30 P.M. to Panajachel and Quezaltenango. Fares to Panajachel: $1. You can also take any bus that is going farther than Los Encuentros, and change there to take a *ruletero* (minivan—usually very crowded) to Sololá and Panajachel.

ACCOMMODATIONS. Since it is a favorite vacation spot for middle-class Guatemalans, Panajachel has a number of fine but moderately priced hotels. There are also several deluxe and first-class hotels. Prices quoted are for double accommodation: *Deluxe,* from $25 to $100; *First-Class,* from $15 to $25 for a double; *Moderate,* from $5 to $15; *Inexpensive,* from $3 to $5. Unless noted, all hotels are in Panajachel.

Deluxe

Atitlán International Country Club. Entrance at hospital in Solola. Reservations in Guatemala City: 12 Calle 1-25, Zona 10, of. 1801; 320–584. Spectacular view of lake from 1,000 feet up. All rooms (6) are suites. Pool, Jacuzzi, bar and restaurant.

First-Class

Hotel Atitlán. A mile to the northwest of the center of town; 0–621–429, 0–621–441. Colonial-style hotel. 45 rooms, each with balcony and many with fireplaces. Heated pool, private beach, tennis courts, restaurant, cafeteria, bar.

Hotel del Lago. Overlooking the lakeshore; 0–621–555, 0–621–564; in Guatemala City: 317–461, 316–941. 100 rooms, each with balcony and view of the lake. Pool. Bar and restaurant service only at weekends.

Hotel Tzanjuyu. On the lakeshore at the entrance to town; 0–621–317 (ask for Don Alfonso); in Guatemala City: 310–764. 40 rooms, some with terraces overlooking lake. Beautiful gardens, pool, bar, restaurant, private beach. Boats available for hire.

Moderate

Bungalows el Aguacatal. 100 yards from the beach; in Guatemala City: 761–582. 8 bungalows, 4 with kitchens. Hot water, bathroom, 2 bedrooms in each bungalow. Cheaper rates weekends.

Bungalows Guayacan. In a nice garden across the river on the road to Santa Catarina Palopó; 0–621–479. 6 bungalows with fully equipped kitchens.

Cacioue Inn. Just as you enter town; 0–621–205. 33 large rooms, each with fireplace. Good restaurant, bar, pool, beautiful garden. No credit cards.

Galindo. On main street in lovely garden; 0–621–168. 30 rooms, each with fireplace. Restaurant, bar.

Monterrey. On lakeshore; 0–621–126. 28 rooms. Private beach, restaurant, bar.

Playa Linda. On the public beach; 0–621–159. 20 suites and rooms, each with terraces facing the lake and fireplaces—somewhat noisy. Restaurant, bar.

Rancho Grande. A short walk from the lake; 0–621–554. 3 bungalows and 4 double rooms. 1 double room with fireplace. Breakfast included in price.

Regis. 200 yards from the lake; 0–621–149, 0–621–152. 20 rooms, most with fireplaces. Delightful gardens. Play area for children, excellent for families. Lower rates by week and month.

Terrazas del Lago. In San Antonio Palopó, reached by dirt road. Small hotel. Boats available. Restaurant, bar.

Vision Azul. Northwest of town, before *Hotel Atitlán;* 0–621–426. 15 rooms, each with fine view of lake. Private beach. Restaurant, bar. Boating available.

Inexpensive

La Fonda del Sol. On main street; 0–621–162. 15 rooms, 5 with private bathrooms. Restaurant.

Riva Bella. On main street; 0–621–348. 6 rooms, with private bathrooms.

Budget

There are many low-cost hotels and *pensiones,* including **Santander, Hotel Panajachel, Maya Kanek, Casa Suiza, Las Casitas, Casa Loma, Mario's Rooms, El Rosario.**

CAMPERS. Recreational vehicles and people with tents may use the public beach, but don't leave equipment unattended at night; you may be robbed.

RESTAURANTS. Some of the best food is served in the major hotels, many of which offer a fixed-price lunch *(almuerzo)* or dinner *(cena)* for less than $3. Recommended is the restaurant at the *Cacique Inn,* and you should also try the restaurants at *Hotel Atitlán, Hotel Tzanjuyu,* and the *Galindo.* Other restaurants are listed below.

El Bistro. *Moderate.* Past GUATEL, on the way to the lake. Italian Cuisine, recommended.

El Cisne. *Inexpensive.* Near the beach, opposite *Hotel del Lago.*

La Fontana. *Moderate.* On Main Street, at corner of the back road to the post office.

La Fonda del Sol. *Moderate.* On the main street. International and local dishes.

Gebel Gran Chaparral. *Inexpensive.* On road to beach. Recommended.

La Laguna. *Moderate.* On main street, at corner of back road to post office. Good steaks, local foods, pastries. Eat inside or on the front porch.

Pajaro Azul. *Inexpensive.* Just after *La Posada del Pintor.* Good local dishes.

The Pie Shop (Casa de Pays). *Inexpensive.* Just before market. Meals and pastries.

La Posada del Pintor. *Moderate.* On back road to post office. Restaurant, bar. Italian cuisine.

Restaurante Vegetariano Hsieh. *Inexpensive.* On the back road to the post office.

El Ultimo Refugio. *Inexpensive.* On the street to the left after GUATEL. Restaurant, bar. Good salads. Darts.

Zanahoria Chic. *Inexpensive.* Near *Hsieh.* Mostly vegetarian.

HOW TO GET AROUND. Visiting the lake villages is easiest done by launch, though you can drive from San Lucas Tolimán to Santiago Atitlán and San Pablo La Laguna on a poor, unpaved road. Buses on this route are infrequent. The mailboat to Santiago Atitlán leaves every morning at 9 A.M. from the Hotel Tzanjuyu, and boats to other villages leave from the public beach. The mailboat leaves Santiago Atitlán at noon, so if you want to spend more time there, or visit other villages, you could hire a boat yourself. Inquire at the Hotel Tzanjuyu, Hotel Atitlán, on the public beach, or at the tourist office. If you hire a boat, you'll have to bargain hard! There are also canoes running between some of the villages; the fare depends on whether you want to row or not!

There are constant *ruleteros* running up to Solola and Los Encuentros, for connections to Chichicastenango, and points west and east, and there are a few buses that go directly to Guatemala City; inquire at the tourist office for the schedule.

Taxis are available across the street from the post office; you'll have to bargain for the best price.

MONEY. There is a bank on the main street where you can change traveler's checks, though you can also change money at the major hotels or on the street.

COMMUNICATIONS. GUATEL phone offices are located on Calle Santander, and national and international calls and cables can be made here daily, 7 A.M.–midnight. For mail, the *Oficina de Correos* is located on a side street near the market, and is open Mon.–Fri. 8 A.M.–4:30 P.M. (3:30 P.M. for parcel post).

USEFUL ADDRESSES. *Tourist Office* (INGUAT). Manuel Salguero, who runs the office, is very helpful and can provide tourist information and personal advice. INGUAT is on the main street, near the Texaco station, and is open 8 A.M.–noon Mon., and 8 A.M.–noon, 2–6 P.M., Wed.–Sun.

Car repairs. The Texaco station, 621–272, has a mechanic on duty. Ask at INGUAT for the address of Carlos Gordillo, who is a mechanic.

SPORTS. Bicycles, motorbikes. These are available in front of *Farmacia Nuevo Mundo.* Bikes can be rented on Calle 14 de Febrero and in front of the Riva Bella hotel.

Bird-watching. Scores of species of birds exist in the lake area. The famous *poc* is flightless, exists only on Lake Atitlán, and is a protected species. It lives near San Lucas Tolimán, and since it is now illegal to hunt the bird, it is hoped that the population will increase.

Boating, fishing. Most of the major lake-front hotels offer boat rentals and some equipment for fishing. The major game fish in the lake is the small-mouth black bass, which the natives catch by spearfishing, and there are also bluegill, perch, carp, crabs, and local fish. Boats can also be rented from the *Selta* company (near the Hotel Tzanjuyu) and from Manuel Crespo's *Lake Recreation Services,* near the public beach. There are rowboats for rent, but one should remember the dangerous currents of the *Xocomil* and not go too far from shore in the afternoon.

Climbing. The best time to climb the volcanoes is during the dry season—though it will be a dusty descent—as rain clouds reduce visibility. You'll need good hiking shoes, lots of water, warm clothing for the summit, and sufficient food. A topographic map is invaluable, but the ones covering the volcanoes are restricted (as are many of the topos of highland areas) by the *Instituto Geográfico Militar,* Avenida Las Américas 5–76, Zona 13 in Guatemala City. You can obtain six-page copies of these and other maps from Casa Andinista in Antigua, but if you don't have them, a knowledgeable guide, or explicit instructions from someone who has made one of the climbs, are recommended. Note that guerrilla forces are sometimes camped on the southern slopes of volcanoes Tolimán and Atitlán.

Volcán San Pedro. The smallest (9,908 feet), closest to the lake, and easiest to climb. Start from the village of San Pedro La Laguna, where you can hire a guide, if desired. You can make the ascent and descent in a day.

Volcán Tolimán. 5 miles southwest of San Lucas Tolimán and 10,360 feet high, the 2 cones of this volcano make a challenging climb. Starting from the village, the ascent of more than 5,000 feet will take about 5 or 6 hours.

Volcán Atitlán. 11,604 feet high and 7 miles from San Lucas Tolimán, the ascent will take all day to complete, so it will be necessary to spend the night on the volcano. There is a hut below the summit, and on a clear night you can make the final climb just before dawn to see the sunrise from the top. Guides can be arranged in San Lucas.

Hang-gliding. National, and occasionally international hang-gliding championships are held here. Ask around if you're interested in lessons.

Hiking. The best way to get to know the lake villages, its people and its wildlife, is to walk. You can walk round the lake in less than a week, and there are footpaths from where the roads end: San Antonio Palopó to the road leading to San Lucas Tolimán, and from San Pablo La Laguna to Panajachel, though sometimes you can find a trail away from the road. You can start your walk by taking a bus to San Lucas Tolimán, Santiago Atitlán, or San Pedro La Laguna, or hire a boat to or from any point you would like to start or end your hike. (See "How to Get Around," above.)

Swimming. The lake is chilly and fairly clean away from the drainage ditches emptying into it. The best time for swimming is in the morning, before the *Xocomil* starts about noon. Be warned that the underwater currents can be treacherous, and one could be in trouble swimming out too far. The are good beaches around the lake, and you could try driving or walking to San Antonio Palopó on the east side of the lake, or drive to San Juan La Laguna and walk to Cristalinas on the west side of the lake, or hire a boat to get there. Hotel del Lago, Cacique Inn, Hotel Tzanjuyu, and Hotel Atitlán all have chemically treated swimming pools.

Tennis. There are tennis courts at the Hotel Atitlán.

GALLERIES. *La Galería,* past the Rancho Grande Hotel, on the way to the public beach, features original paintings and prints by Nan Cuz and other local artists. Ask around for other talented artists in Panajachel.

SHOPPING. There are a large number of *tiendas* (shops) that carry native handicrafts from villages around the lake. The shops in the hotels have fixed prices, and the stalls along the main street and the shops on the road to the beach are cheaper, though you will have to bargain diligently. Some of the better shops are: *Mundo Real,* and *Tienda Mayan Palace* (more expensive), on the main street, *Mercado de Artesanías,* on the road to the beach, and *Mario's Creations.* There are many more, and new *tiendas* appear constantly, so walk around and check them out before buying.

The best bargains are to be found in the local markets—though you will have to haggle constantly. Market days are as follows. Every day: Santiago Atitlán (biggest on Sunday). Tuesday: San Andrés Semetabaj, Santa Clara La Laguna, San Lucas Tolimán, Sololá. Thursday: Santa Lucía Utatlán, Panajachel. Friday: San Lucas Tolimán, Sololá. Saturday: Santa Clara La Laguna, the Gringo Market in Panajachel. Sunday: San Lucas Tolimán, Panajachel.

NIGHTLIFE. *Past Ten* is a bar, disco, and pub in the Casa Loma Hotel near the public beach, opposite the Hotel del Lago. *La Posada del Pintor* (also known as Circus Bar), on the back road to post office; live entertainment on weekends, good atmosphere. *Molino Viejo* is a disco bar, *El Patio* is a video bar, and *Tex Saloon* is a bar. There are other bars in the major hotels, and in some of the restaurants.

THE WESTERN HIGHLANDS:

CHICHICASTENANGO, QUEZALTENANGO,

HUEHUETENANGO

Chichicastenango is a Maya village about 90 miles from Guatemala City. Every Thursday and Sunday morning one of Guatemala's most colorful markets is held here: for sale are blankets and *huipiles,* jewelry and leather goods, pottery, and much more.

The Church of Santo Tomas is on the main plaza and was built in 1540. It is still an active religious center for the Maya. Near the church is a collection of thousands of Maya pieces brought by the Indians to Father Rossbach, priest of Santo Tomas for almost forty years—until his death in 1944.

Quezaltenango, known to all Guatemalans as Xela (pronounced *shayla*), is a major industrial center and the focal point for trade for the Indian villages of the western highlands. The center of Quezaltenango's commercial and social life is Parque Centroamerica—a central square full of trees, benches, statues, and shoeshine boys. Around the park are several small restaurants, banks, taxis, the city hall, and many stores.

A larger park is Parque Minerva. Located in Zona 3, it can be reached by local bus, or by driving north on 14 Avenida and turning left on Calle Rodolfo Robles.

Also in Zona 3 is the big, bustling market on 15 Avenida. In the market building and on the streets around it, you can find handicrafts from all over the western highlands.

The best way to see the small highland villages in the area is by hiking. In a day you can visit a number of villages around Quezaltenango and take a bus, or hitchhike back. Carry water and carefully ask directions before you go.

Huehuetenango, surrounded by small Indian villages, is another good base for excursions into the highlands. Todos Santos has a good Saturday market and a number of Indian weavers who sell *huipiles.* It can be reached by bus. Aguacatán has its own language—Aguateca—and is the garlic center of the highlands. Its market is on Thursdays and Sundays. Also with a fine Thursday and Sunday market is San Mateo Ixtatán.

PRACTICAL INFORMATION FOR
THE WESTERN HIGHLANDS

HOW TO GET THERE. Most of the towns discussed in this section can be reached by bus from major cities. See "How to Get Around" in *Practical Information for Guatemala and Guatemala City* and *Practical Information for Antigua.*

From Cobán. There are no buses going directly to Huehuetenango, though there are buses to Chichicastenango. There are buses as far as Uspantán, and this trip will take several hours on an unpaved road, so you will probably want to stay the night at one of the pensiones there. Since it is only 25 miles to Sacapulas, you may want to try and hitch a ride there and stay in the small pension to the west of the bridge (where you will be asked for your identification) over the river. Market days in Sacapulas are Thurs. and Sun. If you stay in Uspantán, check if there is a direct bus to Nebaj, though you may find that buses only go to Sacapulas. Buses to Nebaj—usually 2 a day—pass through Sacapulas before 2 P.M., and you'll arrive in Nebaj, 25 miles away, after 4 P.M.

There is sometimes—when it's not broken down—a bus from Nebaj or Sacapulas to Huehuetenango, 40 miles from Sacapulas. You'll pass through Aguacatán on the way, and it is worthwhile getting off just before this village and walking a mile to the resurgence of the Río San Juan. You can camp here and eat in the small restaurant, or get one of the fairly frequent buses to Huehuetenango, 15 miles farther.

Chichicastenango

ACCOMMODATIONS. We classify the hotels in this Indian town as follows (rates are for double rooms): *Deluxe,* $45; *First-Class,* $15; *Moderate,* $6.

Mayan Inn. *Deluxe.* Tel. 0–56–1176; in Guatemala City: 60–213. One of the oldest rural hotels, furnished with colonial artifacts. 31 rooms; restaurant; bar. Marimba on Wed. and Sat. Rooms with a view of the mountains slightly more expensive.

Santo Tomas. *First-Class,* Tel. 0–561–061. Colonial-style hotel, furnished with colonial artifacts and Indian handicrafts. 43 rooms. Patios/gardens with fountains and parrots. Good restaurant, bar. Gift shop.

Mayan Lodge. *Moderate.* Tel. 0–561–167. Old colonial inn on central plaza. 8 rooms, with fireplaces. Restaurant, small gift shop. Some rooms have bathrooms.

Pension Chuguila. *Moderate.* Tel. 0–561–134. 20 rooms of different quality around a courtyard. Some rooms have fireplaces—extra cost for firewood. Restaurant. Some rooms have bathrooms.

There are also several budget pensiones near the center of town.

RESTAURANTS. All the hotels have restaurants, and there are a number of *comodores* (eateries) within a few blocks of the plaza. Just explore.

MUSEUMS. Father Rossbach, the priest of Santo Tomas Chichicastenango for almost 40 years until his death in 1944, was brought antiques and family heirlooms by Indians grateful for his services. The collection of thousands of pieces, some from Classic Maya times, is housed in a building on one side of the plaza, near Santo Tomas church.

NIGHTLIFE. There are a few local bars, but the most interesting thing to do at night is to take a walk through the plaza the night before market days (market on Thurs. and Sun.) and watch the Indians set up their stalls. They will offer you their wares by candlelight.

Huehuetenango

ACCOMMODATIONS. Lodging in Huehuetenango is very inexpensive. Double rooms run as follows: *Moderate,* $4 to $7; *Inexpensive,* $2 to $3; *Budget,* less than $1.

Centro Turístico Pino Montano. *Moderate.* Km. 259, just more than a mile after the junction to Huehuetenango. 3 Avenida 1–37, Zona 1. 18 rooms, each with bathroom. Very inexpensive restaurant. Reservations only necessary at Christmas and during Holy Week. Swimming pool being constructed.

Hotel Mary. *Moderate.* 2 Calle 3–52, Zona 1; 0–641–569. 25 rooms, 11 with private baths. Brand-new hotel. Restaurant on second floor.

Hotel Zaculeu. *Moderate.* 5 Avenida 1–14, Zona 1; 0–641–086. 17 rooms, some with private bath. Colonial-style inn around flower-filled courtyard. Quality of room varies—ask for one away from the street, where the El Condor buses leave at 4 A.M.! Restaurant, common room with TV.

Robert's. *Inexpensive.* 2 Calle 5–49, Zona 1; 0–641–526. 10 rooms, some with private baths. Restaurant.

Auto Hotel Vasquez. *Inexpensive.* 2 Calle 6–67, Zona 1; 0–641–338. 20 rooms, some with private baths.

Gran Hotel Shinula. *Inexpensive.* 4 Calle 2–34, Zona 1; 0–641–225. 30 rooms, with cold-water bathrooms.

Hospedaje del Viajero. *Budget.* 2 Calle 5–20.

Hotel Central. *Budget.* 5 Avenida 1–33, Zona 1 (opposite the Hotel Zaculeu). Good restaurant with limited menu.

Hotel Maya. *Budget.* 3 Avenida 3–55.

Mansión El Paraiso. *Budget.* 3 Avenida and 2 Calle.

Pensión Asturia. *Budget.* 4 Avenida, north of the plaza.

RESTAURANTS. Good restaurants are hard to find in Huehuetenango, but after eating at *Pino Montano, Zaculeu, Mary,* and *Central* hotels, you could try one of the following: *Pizza Hogareña,* 6 Avenida between 4 and 5 Calles, for good pizza. *Las Brasas,* around the corner from GUATEL at 2 Calle. *Rico Mac Pollo,* 3 Avenida 3–55. *Los Alpes,* 2 Calle, a few yards west of the square. *Ebony,* opposite Los Alpes. *Las Vegas,* next to the gas station at the turnoff to Huehuetenango. *Las Magnolias,* 4 Calle and 6 Avenida. *La Pradera,* next to Rico Mac Pollo, sells yogurt, ice cream, etc. (pasteurized). *Helados Snoopy,* on the northwest corner of the square, sells ice cream. There are many other restaurants and cafeterias that you'll find on your strolls round the town.

SHOPPING. Handicrafts of all kinds from the villages of Huehuetenango can be found in the covered market, and at *Artexco,* the government cooperative store, on 4 Calle near the market. The market, between 1 and 2 Avenidas and 3 and 4 Calles, is open daily.

COMMUNICATIONS. Telephones, telegraph, post office are all located a block east of the square at 2 Calle 3–54.

ENTERTAINMENT. *Ciné Lili,* west of the square at 3 Calle 5–35, sometimes has English-language movies. You might catch a band concert one night in the acoustical bandshell in the central park.

Quezaltenango

ACCOMMODATIONS. Though there are no deluxe hotels in Quezaltenango, there are a number of good hotels at cheaper prices than in Guatemala City. *First-Class,* $15; *Moderate,* $10; *Inexpensive,* $5; *Budget,* less than $3.

Pensión Bonifaz. *First Class.* On the north side of Parque Centroamérica; 061–2959, 061–4241. 63 rooms. Very good restaurant, bar, roof garden. Highly recommended.

Hotel Centroamericana Inn. *Moderate.* Boulevard Minerva 14–09, Zona 3; 061–4901. 14 rooms, some with fireplaces. Restaurant, bar.

Hotel del Campo. *Moderate.* 3 miles out of town near the junction to Cantel and Zunil; 2–064. 108 rooms and suites. Covered, heated pool; restaurant; bar; discotheque (*El Grillo*).

Hotel Modelo. *Moderate.* 14 Avenida "A" 2–31, Zona 1; 061–2529, 061–2715, 061–4074. 20 rooms. Good restaurant; bar.

Casa Kaehler. *Inexpensive.* 13 Avenida 3–33, Zona 1. 061–2091. Very pleasant house, Swiss-owned, full of plants.

Hotel Canadá. *Inexpensive.* 4 Calle 12–22, Zona 1; 061–4045. 30 rooms.

Kiktem-Ja. *Inexpensive.* 13 Avenida 7–18, Zona 1; 061–4304. 20 rooms.

Pensión Casa Suiza. *Inexpensive.* 14 Avenida "A" 2–36, Zona 1; 061–4350. 11 rooms. Restaurant.

There are many *budget* pensiones in Quezaltenango, including: **Hotel Colonial,** 3 Calle 9–48; **Hospedaje Belén,** 15 Avenida 0–25; **Pensión Maya,** 10 Calle 9–19; **Casa del Viajero,** 8 Avenida 9–17; **Radar 99,** 13 Avenida 3–27—all in Zona 1.

RESTAURANTS. If you've eaten at the **Pensión Bonifaz,** or at the other major hotels, and want to have a meal in one of the city restaurants, try one of the following: **Café and Taberna de Don Rodrigo.** 14 Avenida between 1 and "C" Calles, Zona 1. **El Chaparral.** Centro Comercial Delco. Steakhouse. **El Maruc's.** 23 Avenida A–16, Zona 1. Local dishes. Live music on Sat. nights. **Panchoy.** A steakhouse on the road to San Marcos at km. 205. **La Oropéndola.** 3 Calle between 14 and 14"A" Avenidas. Seafood, yogurt, granola. **El Potrero.** Calle Rodolfo Robles 17–23, Zona 1. **Restaurante y Acuario Zurich.** 14 Avenida 3–11, Zona 1. Swiss restaurant. **El Rincón Valenciano.** 7 Calle 5–89, Zona 2. **La Rueda.** 4 Calle 27–73, Zona 3. Steakhouse. Opposite sports complex. **El Mexicano.** 7 Avenida 2–13, Zona 3. Good authentic Mexican food. **Don Benito's,** Calzada de la Revolucion and 15 Avenida. Possibly the best pizza in Guatemala, also good steaks. **Pocholo's,** 7 Avenida 10–17, Zona 5. Good Steakhouse.

There are many other small cafeterias and restaurants you'll pass on your trips round town.

COMMUNICATIONS. The GUATEL office is at 6 Calle and 13 Avenida, Zona 1, the southwest corner of Parque Centroamerica. The post office is located at 4 Calle 15–06, Zona 1. The telephone company is open 7 A.M.–midnight 7 days a week, and the post office *(correos)* 8 A.M.–4:30 P.M., Mon.–Fri.

TOURS. *SAB Tours,* 1 Calle 12–35, Zona 1, 061–2042, offer daily tours around the city and the surrounding villages, and they will arrange tours for a week or more to any part of the country, for groups of 5 or more.

SPORTS. *Tennis, swimming,* and *bowling* facilities are available at the *Tennis Club Quezalteco,* and courtesy passes are given to guests at the *Pensión Bonifaz.* One can also swim—or soak—in the hot mineral waters at *Fuentes Georginas,* located in a lush valley just 20 minutes by car from Zunil, at *Villa Alicia* in Almolonga, and at *El Chirriez* and *Hotel del Campo* in Quezaltenango.

Volcán Santa María can be *climbed* in a day, or with camping equipment you can spend the night on top. Take a bus on 17 Avenida at 1 Calle, Zona 3, to Llanos del Pinal, and from there it is about 3 to 4 hours to the summit. Topographic maps for climbing Santa María, or any other mountains, are very useful. You can obtain copies at Casa Andinista in Antigua and at the Instituto Geografico Militar, Avenida de las Americas 5–76, Zona 13, Guatemala City. (Maps of certain areas are currently restricted.)

MUSEUMS. The *Casa de la Cultura de Occidente,* south side of the Parque Centroamerica, has occasional painting exhibits. The *Museo de Historia Natural,* near the Casa de la Cultura, contains a strangely classified collection of stuffed birds, dried plants, pre-Columbian artifacts, and Indian costumes and artifacts. Currently open from Mon.–Fri.

SHOPPING. The big and bustling market *(mercado)* is located at 15 Avenida and 1 Calle in Zona 3. In the market building, and in the streets around it, you can find handicrafts from all over the western highlands—though if you have enough time it would be less wearing to visit the villages in which the weavings, carvings, and ceramics are made.

Artexco, a federation of artisan cooperatives that focus on export, is located on the east side of the city at 7 Avenida 15–97, Zona 5, and can be reached by bus or by driving east on 5 Calle and turning north on 7 Avenida. The prices in Artexco may be slightly higher than in the market, but the quality is consistent and you can find handcrafted items from all over the country, away from the frenzy of the *mercado*.

Salsa, Ltd., 14 Avenida "A" 2–53, Zona 3, sells handwoven textiles; *Vitra, S.A.,* 13 Avenida 5–27, Zona 3, makes fine items of handblown glass; *Kamal Be,* 14 Avenida 3–36, Zona 1, offers local handicrafts.

If you want to purchase custom-made clothes, shoes, or boots there are a number of fine tailors *(sastrerias)* and shoemakers *(zapaterias)* in Xela. Buy the cloth *(tela),* explain or show a picture of what you want made, and within a week or so you can pick it up at a much lower price than store-bought items in the U.S.

THEATER AND ENTERTAINMENT. The *Teatro Municipal,* 14 Avenida and 1 Calle, Zona 1. Check at the tourist office for information on musical or theatrical productions. If there are no events when you're there you may be able to tour through the theater 9 A.M.–5 P.M. The *Casa de la Cultura de Occidente,* south side of the Parque Centroamérica, organizes concerts and other events, which take place there or at the Municipal Theater.

THE PACIFIC COAST

For the great majority of the Guatemalans who live in the highlands, the country fully lives up to its reputation as "The Land of Eternal Spring." But for travelers whose idea of paradise is beaches, roaring surf, palm trees, and bamboo cabanas under a tropical sun, Guatemala's Land of Eternal Summer is only an hour and a half from Guatemala City.

Between the string of mountains and volcanoes that line southern Guatemala from Mexico to El Salvador, and the Pacific Ocean, is a thin strip of land—never more than thirty miles wide—known as "La Costa Sur," or the South Coast. Flat, humid, simmering in the intense sunlight, the land is also extraordinarily fertile—in its hothouse atmosphere, luxuriant vegetables, tropical flowers, trees, and lush jungle foliage grow to incredible sizes, with birds and flowers so bright they seem to vibrate against the background of deep, always-changing green. Here, for example, in the department of Escuintla alone, are produced more than four-fifths of Guatemala's total production of sugar and cotton, more than three-fourths of its cattle, and one-fifth of its coffee.

Between these sweltering lowlands and the blue Pacific, from west of Puerto San José to the border of El Salvador, runs a manmade intracoastal waterway, the Chiquimulilla *(chickie-moo-lee-ya)* Canal. Lined with mangrove trees that send their tangled roots into the water, coconut palms, and impenetrable walls of jungle vegetation; inhabited by herons, egrets, motmots and other bright-plumed birds; creeping, crawling and swimming with iguanas, alligators, frogs, fish and crustaceans; populated by shirtless natives who cruise through the maze of overgrown passageways in dugout canoes, casting out great circular nets, the canal is dense, mysterious, and a challenge to explore.

Between the canal and the Pacific lies a thin strip of land—often not more than a hundred yards wide—made up of fine, black volcanic sand. And for the seekers of surf, sand, suntans, and seafood, these last 100 yards are the most important territory between the highlands and the ocean. On this thin strip of sand and palms are the resorts—ranging from tiny bamboo huts to modern, self-contained resort communities, complete with bars and swimming pools. None of these beaches are more than two hours by car from Guatemala City. So it's easy to drive down, spend the day swimming, boating, fishing, or loafing, and be back in the capital by suppertime.

As you near the coast the smell of sugar is mixed with an odor of salt and swamp and fish, the houses become even more ramshackle—sagging, with wallpaper of old newspapers and walls of unpainted and unmatching boards—and there is a Caribbean ambience to the people as well as the land and houses. And then you are in Puerto San José, the most important Pacific port of Guatemala, and the epitome of a dusty, sun-baked tropical seaport. Seemingly the set for a 1930s Hollywood movie or an O. Henry or Somerset Maugham short story, the dirt streets are lined with battered little thatch-roofed *comedores,* rotting shacks, and scores of raunchy sailors' bars. During the day, panting dogs lie in the shade snapping lazily at flies, pigs and chickens root for food among the garbage in the shimmering streets, old men squat in front of *cantinas* watching and saying nothing. At night the music from a dozen competing jukeboxes in the bars mixes in the street, and noisy sailors move from bar to bar, each one as dilapidated and dimly lit as the next, with slowly moving fans, garish faded colors, and exotic names. Free-flowing rum, aguardiente, and beer, hardworking houses of ill repute, now and then a desultory fight—some will find it fascinating, exotic, or adventurous, others merely hot, dirty, and depressing. Everyone will at least want to take a stroll down the main street.

The main street crosses a small bridge over the Chiquimulilla Canal and leads in a few steps to the black sand beach and a fine view of the port itself.

But of the towns along the coast, Puerto San José is the exception, rather than the rule. Spread out along the canal from west of San José to the border of El Salvador are a number of charming towns and superb beaches where one feels not in the dusty tropics of honky-tonk port towns but in a kind of South Sea Island paradise where one can spend lazy afternoons in a hammock under coconut palms, smell the clear wind off the sea, or just search for shells and make footprints in the sand on miles of virtually deserted beaches. There are small towns with streets made of sand where one can buy a fat coconut for a dime, watch as the smiling salesman nimbly chops it open, complete with drinking spout, with his machete; there are towns made up of grass huts and friendly people; there are towns of luxurious homes and condominiums, where every house has its yacht and the discotheque goes until the early hours of the morning.

One of the most interesting of these coastal towns is Iztapa, only a few miles from San José. Take a left on the well-marked road just as you enter San José and in a few minutes you will arrive in a pleasant village fronting on the canal.

Iztapa, like the other coast towns, is a favorite weekend spot for Guatemalans. If you arrive on a weekday, the beaches will be almost deserted, the string of large dormitory-like cabanas empty, the place feeling like a ghost town. During the weekends, however, the hordes from the highlands arrive in waves and by Saturday afternoon the beaches are swarming, the *comedore* jukeboxes are blaring, and a party atmosphere takes over.

A half-hour boat trip will take you to Puerto Quetzal beach, less crowded on weekends than Iztapa. You can also get there by walking along the Iztapa beach.

Other tiny ocean front villages set on the narrow strip of land between the Chiquimulilla Canal and the sea, each with idyllic dark-sand beaches, thatched bamboo cabanas, broiled seafood, abundant and cheap coconuts and fruits, and excellent surf, are La Avellana, east of Iztapa, and Las Lisas, near the El Salvador border. Both can be reached by turning left at Escuintla onto the Pacific Highway (CA2) and driving toward El Salvador until you reach Taxisco (paved road leading 11 miles south to La Avellana) and the turnoff to Las Lisas about 10 miles beyond (paved road leading 11 miles south to the town).

Like most coastal resorts, these towns have cheap cabanas with only the most basic accommodations (generally a rope bed or a hammock, with a shared bath or none at all), and comfortable bungalows that are fairly expensive, and almost nothing in between. Those who want the comforts of hotel living should head directly to Turicentro Likín. Located only two miles from San José on the road to Iztapa, this lovely resort is an entire resort community, with beautiful homes built along an interconnected grid of canals, supermarket, condominiums, hotel, bungalows, restaurant, swimming pools, and more. Visitors leave their cars in a protected lot and are ferried through mangrove-lined canals to the modern, squeaky-clean hotel near the beach. There are also neat and sizable bungalows with kitchens, that can be rented for a night, a weekend, or longer. Between the hotel and bungalows and the beach are swimming pools (both salt water and fresh water) and an open-air restaurant overlooking the sea. The resort is set in lovely landscaped gardens, with palm trees, flowers, and exuberant jungle foliage.

All along this coast the surf can be big and powerful, and those not used to heavy surf should be careful and watch out for the strong undertow. Look down the beach at night and see the lights of the ships lying offshore at San José—a lovely sight.

Chulamar, with similar facilities and similar prices, is situated just three miles west of Puerto San José.

PRACTICAL INFORMATION FOR
THE PACIFIC COAST

WHEN TO GO. Hot and damp at all times of the year, the Pacific Coast is at its hottest and dampest during rainy season, from May to November. While not common, malaria does exist in these swampy lowlands when the heavy rains create breeding grounds for the disease-carrying mosquitoes. Travelers to the lowlands during the wet months should take precautions: stay in hotels with good screens or use mosquito nets, and take antimalaria pills such as Aralen (Chloroquine).

HOW TO GET THERE. By bus. Buses to the coastal towns are frequent, reliable, crowded, and hotter than hell. A 110-degree afternoon bus ride with 3 people to every seat through the coastal lowlands can be truly miserable. Concentrate on the cool blue Pacific, into which you will soon be plunging.

San José, Iztapa: Frequent buses leave from the terminal in Zona 4, Guatemala City, until 7 P.M. every day. Most of the buses pass the railroad station at 19 Calle and 9 Avenida, Zona 1, before leaving the city.

Likín: The bus to Iztapa passes by the entrance gate to Likín. A regular ferry takes you from there to the beach and hotel.

Las Lisas, Taxisco: The *Cubanita* leaves the terminal in Zona 4 several times a day.

Escuintla: Numerous buses leave for Escuintla every day from the terminal in Zona 4; also, *Mirtala, Charras,* and *Rutas Lima* buses from Zona 1. *(Mirtala* and *Charras,* 9 Avenida 18–50, Zona 1; *Rutas Lima,* 8 Calle 3–63, Zona 1.) In Escuintla you can make connections to many of the small villages, up and down the coast.

Santa Lucía Cotzumalguapa: The *Mirtala, Charras,* and *Rutas Lima* buses leave frequently, stopping in Escuintla and Santa Lucia on their way west via the Coastal Highway. Or take any bus to Escuintla and transfer there for Santa Lucía.

By car. Take CA9 out of Guatemala City to Escuintla, where it crosses CA2, the Coastal Highway, which runs from the Mexican to the El Salvador border parallel with the coast. Turn west or east onto CA2, and frequent roads drop from the highway to the small coastal villages and beaches. Campers with their own vehicles should explore as many of these as possible, as there are frequent stretches of deserted, sandy, palm-tree lined beach where one can camp for days of undisturbed, idyllic peace.

To reach San José, continue past Escuintla on CA9. Just as you enter San José a road turns off to the left, leading past Likín to Iztapa.

You can also reach CA2 from Quezaltenango by taking the good road (9S) that leads past Cantel, Zunil, and hits the Coastal Highway a few kilometers before Retalhuleu. By continuing on 9S you will reach the seaport of Champerico.

A new road (route 11) drops from Lake Atitlán down to the Coastal Highway, passing San Lucas Tolimán. This scenic route joins CA2 not far from Santa Lucía Cotzumalguapa.

ACCOMMODATIONS. Without a doubt the 2 best hotels on the Pacific Coast of Guatemala are the **Turicentro Likín** and **Club Palmeras de Chulamar.** In many ways they are quite similar: both are self-contained resort communities, both have beaches, fresh water and salt water swimming pools, beautifully landscaped grounds with flowers and palm trees, excellent restaurants overlooking the ocean, and moderate rates. Chulamar is a few miles west of Puerto San José, Likín is a few miles east, on the road to Iztapa. Both are less than 2 hours from Guatemala City, and both are absolutely packed on weekends; reservations for weekend stays are a must.

Turicentro Likín. In Guatemala City: 512–190, 518–490. Bungalows for 2: $20; for 6: $35. Double room: $17. Air-conditioned. Boat rental, with pilot, $7 for 5 passengers. Admission to Likín for non-guests: $3.50 per person. Hardly any beach left; expensive; little food available (non-guests not allowed to take in food), slow service in restaurant. Supermarket at the entrance.

Club Palmeras de Chulamar. In Guatemala City: 313–782. 52 rooms, no air-conditioning, most rooms have fans. Rooms for 4: $12, Sun.–Thurs.; $35, Fri./Sat.

Balneario Chulamar. In Guatemala City: 23–836. Next to Club Palmeras de Chulamar. 12 bungalows, $18 for 6 people on weekends.

Those traveling the Coastal Highway by car will find several nice hotels along the way. Rates run $12 to $15 for a double. Facilities include air-conditioning, private baths, pools, bars, and restaurants. A few such accommodations are: **Tropicana,** Km. 183 near Retalhuleu; **Colonial,** Km. 178 at the entrance to Retalhuleu; **Santiaguito,** Km. 90 in Santa Lucia Cotzumalguapa.

COBÁN AND THE VERAPACES

During the early days of the conquest, the lands immediately to the north of the central highlands of Guatemala came to be known as the Land of War. Three times the Spaniards tried to conquer these lands, and three times they were defeated by its fierce Indian inhabitants. At this time Bartolomé de las Casas was preaching his doctrine that only through peaceful conversion to Christianity, not through war, could the Indians be integrated into the society. Sneered at and told to put his words into practice, he asked for and was given five years to convert the Indians of the Land of War by his own methods. He then composed hymns in the Kekchí language that told of the Creation, the Fall, Jesus, and the Gospel. These songs aroused the interest of one of the chiefs, Don Juan, who asked them to explain to him in detail what they meant. The result was that the Indians were converted, the lands pacified, and the area was renamed the Verapaces (Land of the True Peace).

The capital city founded by de las Casas was Cobán, and through the centuries, before first airplanes and then paved roads connected it with Guatemala City, Cobán existed as an almost independent nation, shipping its coffee to and dealing directly with the capitals of Europe, via the railway down the Polochic Valley to Lake Izabal, and down Río Dulce to Livingston.

Coming with (and contributing to) the coffee boom of the nineteenth century were numerous Germans, who arrived from Europe to create vast coffee *fincas.* The German "coffee barons" created a cosmopolitan, cultured society in Cobán, and made it a city completely unlike any other in Central America. However, though they profited from the land, many of the Germans felt themselves to be colonists rather than immigrants, with their loyalties belonging to Germany, and, ultimately, Hitler, rather than to Guatemala. With the coming of W.W. II (and under pressure from the United States), the government of Guatemala expelled the Germans from the Alta Verapaz and seized their lands. Most of these fincas are still owned by the government.

Now, with the completion of the highway from the Alta Verapaz to Guatemala City, Cobán is no longer a shipping center. Most people will find the city of interest mainly as a center for exploring outlying Indian towns or as a stop on the way to hiking and cave-exploring expeditions.

A few miles outside Cobán, the Ruta al Atlántico descends sharply for many miles and crosses a river just before El Rancho. If you want a snack or to fill up your gas tank, there are several small restaurants and two gas stations. The road to Cobán ascends for 30 miles, and on the left you will see below you the Salama Valley. At the junction here your car will be fumigated, and you then continue on towards Cobán. At km. 156, 14 miles after the junction, situated on the right-hand side of the road is the Posada de la Montaña del Quetzal, a very good hotel to stay at if you want to visit the Quetzal Reserve (Biotopo del Quetzal) just ahead—one of the last places that the rare bird can be found.

The Quetzal reserve is a few miles past the posada, on the left-hand side of the road. There are three trails through the reserve, ranging in length from 500 yards to more than 2 miles, and since you'll be hiking to a height of more than 6,000 feet (the entrance is at more than 5,000 feet), use good shoes and take warm and rainproof clothing.

The village of Tactic is situated a few miles after the Biotopo, and has two small pensiones: Pensión Central and Hospedaje Pocomchi. A double room costs less than $2; the Central has a restaurant and hot showers. Tactic has a market on Tuesdays and Sundays, but you should look at the beautiful huipiles for sale here whatever day you arrive. Twenty miles after Tactic, beyond the junctions to Santa Cruz Verapaz and San Cristóbal Verapaz, you'll reach Cobán.

The Alta Verapaz, the lush land surrounding Cobán is kept always always green by the chipi chipi, a light but constant drizzle that keeps up through many months of every year.

The area contains a wealth of pre-Columbian sites, and was apparently much more heavily populated a thousand years ago than it is now. Scattered through the Alta Verapaz are numerous fascinating Indian villages.

San Pedro Carchá is located four miles east of Cobán, easily reached on a paved road by car, taxi, or regular local buses. On the route to the village are several small shops selling silver handicrafts, and there are many shops in the village offering weavings, pottery, and wooden masks. The major market day is Tuesday. There are small pensiones in the village, and the Pensión Central serves good meals.

Lanquín is 40 miles past San Pedro Carchá on a rough, unpaved road. Lanquín is famous for its cave, from which the Río Lanquín emerges. With a four-wheel-drive or other high-clearance vehicle it will take about three hours to reach the village. Transportes La Esmeralda, 2 Calle 4–66, Zona 1 in San Pedro Carchá (tel. 0–511–726), leaves daily at 5:30 A.M. from Cobán and arrives, often after breakfast on the way, in Lanquín six hours later. The fare is 70 cents, and you can catch the bus on the north side of the cathedral. But be there early, as it's usually very crowded. Another bus from the same company leaves San Pedro Carchá daily at 2 P.M. The bus returns from Lanquín at 5:30 A.M.

There are roofed shelters near the cave entrance a mile before the village, and if you have camping gear you should ask the bus to stop at the Grutas de Lanquín. In the village there are two small basic pensiones and small restaurants. The cave has a metal gate at the entrance, and you should go to the municipal hall to hire an official guide who will open the gate and turn on the lights. There's good swimming in the deep, fast-flowing river outside.

If you are somewhat disappointed in your visit to the Lanquín cave, you definitely will not be disappointed in your visit to the natural bridge of Semuc Champey. This writer considers this to be the most beautiful place in Guatemala, and you may well agree once you get there. It is about a 7-mile walk, slightly more if you drive, from Lanquín, and if you are not going to stay the night, you should start early in the morning if you hike there. From the center of Lanquín an unpaved road winds upward and then sharply downward to a cleared parking area near a new bridge over the Río Cahabón. Walk across the bridge, turn to your right, and it's a 20-minute walk on a narrow up-and-down trail to Semuc Champey. If you are walking from Lanquín, you will have to hike to the top on the road, and then you should ask people directions there, because it is much shorter and more enjoyable to take local trails down to the bridge over the Cahabón river.

Semuc Champey is a natural bridge 500 yards long below a canyon that is up to 200 yards deep. The Río Cahabón sinks at the top (west) end of the bridge, and resurges below, and on top of the bridge are beautiful, clear pools, several feet deep, which are a delight to swim in. Tennis shoes are advisable, since the edges of the travertine pools are sharp. There is a large roofed shelter on the bridge, and since you are at very low altitude here you will need only a minimal sleeping bag. Domingo Pop Tut, who lives in the last thatched hut before the bridge,will cut firewood, and bring you water or soda pop, for less than $1.

PRACTICAL INFORMATION FOR
COBÁN AND THE VERAPACES

HOW TO GET THERE. See also "How to Get Around" in *Practical Information for Guatemala and Guatemala City.* **By bus.** Two bus lines have services to Cobán from Guatemala City several times a day. The road is paved, and the trip will take a little more than 4 hours on a pullman, and about 5 hours on the regular buses, which sometimes visit the towns of Santa Cruz Verapaz and San Cristóbal Verapaz on the way. The pullman buses go daily, but the companies operating the regular buses each go on alternate days, so you should phone to find out which company is going the day you want to visit Cobán on the regular *(corriente)* bus. Contact *Transportes Monja Blanca y Escobar,* 8 Avenida 15–16, Zona 1, 511–878, 81–409, for pullman or regular bus information, or *Transportes La Cobanerita,* 9 Calle 11–46, Zona 1, 20–257, to get to Cobán by regular bus. Their offices in Cobán: Monja Blanca y Escobar, 2 Calle 3–77, Zona 4, 0–511–952; La Cobanerita, 3 Avenida 1–07, Zona 4, 0–511–172. The pullman bus will pick up outside La Posada, but make sure they write this down when you are buying your ticket.

ACCOMMODATIONS. There are no first-class hotels in Cobán, but there are some that are quite acceptable. **La Posada.** 1 Calle 4–12, Zona

2; 0–511–495. 14 rooms in 2 buildings. Double room: $11, including 3 meals. Good restaurant, with daily menu, open to nonguests. Rooms vary in quality. Terraces outside rooms overlook pleasant gardens.

Oxib Peck. 1 Calle 12–11, Zona 1; 0–511–039. 11 rooms. Double room: $12 with private bathroom and meals; $11 with general bathroom and meals; $2 without meals. Restaurant for guests only.

Cobán Imperial. Half a block north of Banco de Guatemala on 1 Calle; 0–511–113. 6 rooms with private baths, TV. Double room: $7 without meals. Restaurant, cafeteria.

El Recreo. 10 Avenida 5–01, Zona 3; 0–512–160, 0–512–333. 13 rooms with private baths. Double: $12 with meals; $4 without meals. Restaurant.

Hotel Motor Inn San Vicente. Diagonal 3 11–20, Zona 2, about a mile from the center of Cobán, where you turn to the right on the road from Guatemala City; 0–511–549. 7 rooms. Double room: $3.

Tico's Hotel and Cafeteria. On the corner of the road turning left to Santa Cruz Verapaz. Double room: $7.

Other small hotels, at less than $4 for a double room, include the **Central, La Paz, Monterrey, Chipi Chipi,** and **Santo Domingo.**

A good place to stay if you want to visit the Quetzal Reserve is **Posada de la Montaña del Quetzal.** Km. 156, 14 miles after the junction of the Ruta al Atlántico and the road to Cobán; in Guatemala City for reservations: 314–181. 8 rooms and 8 bungalows (which have fireplaces). Double room: $6: small bungalows: $8; large bungalows: $12. Restaurant, cafeteria, swimming pool, playground, gardens. Book in advance if you plan to visit the Biotopo del Quetzal on the weekend. A friend saw quetzales nesting right by his bungalow!

RESTAURANTS. The best meals would be at **La Posada** or, perhaps, **The Oxib Peck,** but there are several other small restaurants and cafeterias you might want to try: **El Refugio,** 2 Calle 1–34, Zona 2, offers international and local dishes; the restaurant at the **Hotel Santo Domingo** offers local dishes, and was recommended in Cobán; **San Jorge,** in the Hotel Central.

COMMUNICATIONS. *GUATEL,* 1 Calle between 2 and 3 Avenidas; 0–511–498, 0–511–598. Telephone calls and international cables, 7 A.M. to midnight, 7 days a week. *Post Office (Correos),* 3 Calle 2–02, Zona 3; 0–511–140. The post office is open Mon.–Fri., 8 A.M.–4:30 P.M. Local cables, 24 hours a day.

TIKAL AND THE PETÉN

Though it is the most populous nation of Central America, there are still vast sections of Guatemala that remain uninhabited and in some cases virtually unexplored. Those who visit the giant relief map in Guatemala City's Minerva Park will have noticed first the towering sawtooth chain of mountains and volcanoes that forms the spine of the country. On these jagged highlands the markers that indicate cities and towns bristle like porcupine quills. Here are the Indian villages, the market towns, the lakes, the cities, and almost three-quarters of Guatemala's total population. But then, the eye is unconsciously drawn to a low, featureless, ominously empty stretch of land thrusting north, into the Yucatán peninsula. This is the Petén, Guatemala's equivalent to America's frontier territories of the eighteenth and nineteenth centuries (and with more than a touch of the Wild West to it). These lowlands, making up more than one-third of Guatemala, are covered by jungle, hardwood forests, vast dry savannahs, and little else.

Only recently has the Petén been connected by roads to the outside world. Now the government of Guatemala has instituted a program to lure people from the highlands by giving free land in the Petén (much like the North American Homestead Act), and in the last few years deposits of nickel and petroleum have been discovered there. As a result, new bamboo-hut settlements are springing up everywhere in fields that were jungle only weeks before, and one is as likely to meet a hardhat, a road engineer, a poor corn farmer recently arrived from the mountains, or a construction worker, as he is to meet a *chiclero* or a native of the Petén.

New roads are being built, corn fields are planted on cleared jungle land, an intense search for minerals and petroleum is going on, and the government is pursuing plans to develop a number of Mayan ruins into major tourist attractions. The Petén is far away from the rest of Guatemala, in mind as well as miles of unpaved roads. There are towns like San Benito—across the lake from Flores—that can be as rough-and-tumble as old Dodge City. But far away as it is, the Petén is only 60 minutes from the capital by plane. And what was once thought to be a vast wasteland is now emerging as a great wonderland, not only for archaeologists, but for hunters, fishermen, botanists, ornithologists, hikers, spelunkers, canoers, and many others. But despite all the activity, the Petén is still a very empty place.

Uninhabited and undeveloped for so many years, the Petén still teems with peccary (a type of wild boar), jaguar, ocelot, rare varieties of flowers, plants, butterflies, and hundreds of species of birds that are now rare or nonexistent elsewhere. Archaeologists have found hundreds of Maya sites, and more are turning up constantly. Spelunkers explore the caves of Jobitzinaj, near Flores, some of the most beautiful in the world. Canoe voyages up the Río de la Pasión and the Río Usumacinta—former Maya trade highways, lined with remarkable sites—can be easily arranged, as can the rental of jeeps for day trips or longer excursions to some of the more isolated archaeological sites. And in clearing trails, opening up sites, the archaeologists have created for the rest of us lovely jungle gardens—rampant with orchids, lush foliage, huge trees, an endless variety of wildlife, and yet open enough for visitors to stroll through and explore without needing high boots, machete, and compass. Although the principal roads and towns are safe, check with locals before venturing, into remote areas, guerrillas operate in certain areas of the Petén.

Flores

The best town from which to explore the Petén is also its most uncharacteristic. Built on a small raised island in Lake Petén-Itzá, the town of Flores has a population of about 1,500, and can't get any larger, since it completely fills its circular island. (The growth cities of the area are just across the lake from Flores—San Benito, with its fine Sunday market, its active nightlife, rowdy bars, and cheap hotels; and Santa Elena, which has several quality hotels and the local airport.) Picturesque, capped by the double domes of its local church, surrounded by the beautiful lake, Flores is an enchanting place to visit in itself. Though a causeway has now been built connecting the town with the mainland, for hundreds of years it could only be reached by launch, and the long, thin, dugout-modeled canoes still glide back and forth between island and shore, taxiing people to market in San Benito or smaller villages around the lake. These launches can be hired for cruises on the lake, which is quite extensive (20 miles long, 5 miles wide), for fishing, for exploring the other small lake islands, and for visiting the Maya ruins that lie along its shores.

On the north side of the lake is El Petencito, a small zoo containing many of the fauna of Petén. On the northeast shore of the lake is El Gringo Perdido, where you can camp or stay in one of the cabins. If you are driving—or want to catch the bus going to Tikal—you should turn east at El Remate, just after the junction of the road that heads to Belize, and drive or walk 2 miles to the campsite. A restaurant overlooks the lake.

Near Flores was the last Maya city of Tayasal. Unconquered, almost forgotten, Tayasal went its own way until 1697 when Martín de Ursúa and his army stumbled on it by accident, thus defeating the last independent Maya tribe. By 1700 Flores had been built, but for hundreds of years—with no roads to connect it to the outer world—it remained a backwater, its economy based on gathering *chicle*.

Today, as the face of the Petén changes, Flores remains much as it has for decades—its narrow cobbled streets, small-town atmosphere, and provincial disdain for the cares and innovations of the modern world, make it a comfortable, charming, and convenient place to spend a few days while exploring the more isolated sections of the Petén.

The single place that no visitor to the Petén will want to miss, for any reason, is Tikal, only an hour's drive from Flores. Many who find Tikal's accommodations too rudimentary can return to quite nice hotels in or near Flores for the night, and go back to Tikal in the morning.

Tikal

The ancient city of Tikal is perhaps not the most beautiful, most colorful, or most pleasant place in Guatemala; there are no resort hotels, no souvenirs or native crafts to take home, no swimming pools. But Tikal may be the most visceral, physically affecting, mentally challenging, unforgettable place that exists in Central America.

What is it about Tikal that makes it so powerful an experience? Perhaps in part it's the mere immensity of the city and its structures—only 6 square miles have been explored closely, while archaeologists believe it might have covered more than 25 square miles; its population probably reached as high as 75,000 to 100,000; and even after many days of exploring it's still hard to grasp the beauty and grandiose scale of the city—steep pyramids higher than 20-floor buildings, complex multileveled palaces built like mazes around countryards, ball courts, great market buildings, acres of flat plaster plazas surrounded by temples, terraces, shrines, sweat baths, paved causeways as wide as a superhighway and running for miles, a series of reservoirs each holding millions of gallons of water, a protective moat more than 6 miles long, hundreds of enigmatically carved stelae and altars, and literally thousands of other structures.

Perhaps, too, it's the jungle that surrounds and covers much of Tikal that makes the experience special. The ruins stand in the midst of 222 square miles of carefully preserved jungle—Tikal National Park—an area of richly various, exotic and abundant wildlife. The forest is roofed with great ceiba trees (sacred to the Maya) that tower more than 150 feet overhead, along with thick-trunked mahogany trees, Spanish cedars, zapotes (from which were carved the lintels over the doors of many of Tikal's temples—soft when first cut, upon exposure to air the zapote wood becomes harder than iron, and at more than 70 pounds per cubic foot, just about as heavy; also from the zapote comes the *chicle* for chewing gum, which the ancient Maya enjoyed as much as we do). Other trees include the copal, from which the Maya made (and in the highlands still make) a powerful incense to be used on religious occasions for communicating with the gods; tall arching palm trees; and the allspice tree, from whose fruit is ground a clove-like spice. Ropey lianas are looped and hung throughout the jungle, and great leafy ferns of all varieties grow so fast you can almost see them move. There are more than 200 species of birds, including parrots, motmots, blue and white herons, hawks, buzzards, hummingbirds, and wild turkeys. Jaguar, puma, ocelot, and peccary still prowl the forest, along with a variety of snakes (including the deadly coral snake and the *barba amarilla*, "yellow beard," also known as the fer-de-lance). Spider monkeys swing through the trees overhead near the central plaza, and often stop to shout and throw twigs at passersby. That all these plants and animals were used by, and represented in art by the Maya, adds a feeling of continuity—the jungle environment that today covers Tikal is the same one the builders of the city had to cope with throughout their history.

And perhaps, again, what makes Tikal such a mind-stretching experience is the utter mystery of it all. The Maya came mysteriously—no one knows why or when—and disappeared into mystery. In fact, though archaeologists are constantly uncovering, learning, piecing together facts, we really don't know much of anything about the essential nature of Maya life. Most great world civilizations have risen and fallen; but they have generally done so in the same arena, leaving behind records, histories, remnants, myths, and legends. The Maya rose and fell, and to a large extent disappeared. And with the coming of the Spaniards—who burned their books of history, killed their rulers, priests and wise men, and ruthlessly stamped out their religion—a way of life was forever eradicated. Mysterious, mystical, obsessed with blood and death, brutal, beauty loving, beauty fearing, wise, religious, grandiose, humorous, incomprehensible—the civilization that built Tikal is gone forever. William R. Coe, who was in charge of the University of Pennsylvania Tikal Project for many years, has written a guide, *Tikal: A Handbook of the Ancient Maya Ruins,* which is not only indispensible but excellently done. Michael Cole's *The Maya* is still the best general introduction.

Tikal's Dramatic Past

Though there are signs of inhabitants at Tikal around 600 B.C., it's known people lived by nearby Lake Petén-Itzá as early as 2000 B.C. Archaeologists wonder if Tikal—because of the lack of a certain water sup-

ply—had to wait to be developed until there arose a leader strong enough
to impose his will on the people and create labor gangs to build the necessary water storage systems. Or was it vice versa? Cultures, it seems, reach
a sort of critical mass, when either a leader emerges with strength sufficient to force people to undertake mass projects—and thus begin to create
true cities—or perhaps the growing population densities create the *need*
for more water (or food, etc.), which in a sense creates the need for such
a ruler, who then emerges.

In any case, by the time of Christ, Tikal was a thriving city, with a growing system of clay-lined reservoirs, a large complex of ceremonial temples
and pyramids—many of which now lay beneath the surface of later structures—and most of the cultural characteristics which would emerge most
fully in the classic period, from A.D. 250 to 900. At some point around
then, something happened that turned the lowland Maya from just another mesoamerican culture into a people who developed the most complex
and advanced civilization the hemisphere had ever known. Perhaps it was
because Tikal is situated on the short overland portage linking the two
great trade routes of the time—the Usumacinta/Pasión river system, flowing into the Gulf of Mexico, and the Belize River, flowing into the Caribbean—and thus became a focal point for all the knowledge of the time. Perhaps it was the introduction of hieroglyphic writing from Kaminal Juyú
that set off the innate spark in the lowland Maya. Whatever the cause,
by A.D. 300, Maya scientists had made mathematical and astronomical
discoveries and calculations that equaled or surpassed those of ancient
Egypt, and in some cases surpassed even those of contemporaneous European culture. They had developed hieroglyphic writing into an elaborate,
expressive, and beautiful means of recording information. They had per-
fected a calendar more accurate (and useful) than ours today, and by using
a complex calendrical system in which each day (and each citizen) was
ruled by a certain combination of gods and influences, were able to control
the social, religious, cultural, and agricultural activities, day by day, of
an entire civilization. They made use of the zero, something that was not
introduced into European mathematics until the Middle Ages. They calculated the orbit of Venus with an error of only fourteen seconds a year,
something astronomers of Europe weren't able to do until a thousand
years later, using precision telescopes. In ceramics, painting, sculpture, architecture and weaving, they were masters, showing a unique and subtle
esthetic sensitivity.

That they were sophisticated engineers goes without saying for anyone
who has seen their massive feats of building with stone. But perhaps the
most amazing examples of their engineering skills are barely visible today.
These are the huge, clay-lined reservoirs—as many as twelve of them—
scattered about the city, each holding millions of gallons of water. And
to ensure the rains flowed into the reservoirs, they constructed their great
raised causeways with a dual purpose. These wide plastered highways—
which must have been impressive highroads for processions and approaching traders or peasants from the surrounding country—were lined on both
sides with high walls, which were broken by periodic exit points. However,
the causeways were also carefully constructed so that during rains they
would also serve as aqueducts, funnelling the flowing waters into nearby
reservoirs.

In light of such advanced engineering feats, archaeologists are beginning to realize that Tikal's agricultural system was hardly based completely on primitive techniques such as slash-and-burn (which are effective but produce too low a yield to support a city Tikal's size), but rather was highly organized, intensive, based on advanced forms of irrigation, and carried out on a large scale. In fact, there are signs in the great *bajos,* or low swampy lands, of "raised field" cultivation—great earth platforms, fertile and highly productive, built on the waterlogged terrain, enabling them to grow crops on the seasonally flooded lowlands.

These are some of the accomplishments of the classic Maya of Tikal. We also know some of their failures. For example, they failed to develop labor-saving machines (unlike the early cultures of the Near East). Though they knew of the wheel (it has been found on childrens' toys, and of course their masterful calendar is based on a system of wheels within wheels), they never made use of it to carry loads or to create pottery. They never learned to extract metals from the earth and make iron tools or weapons: all their cutting and carving was done with stone. They had no domesticated animals, depending entirely on human labor to carry their great loads of building and trade materials. In fact, as we realize what they were able to accomplish *despite* these lacks, the Maya civilization comes to appear even more incredible and exotic.

Tikal, we're now told, was as much if not more an administrative center as a religious center. Maya art frequently depicts an extensive bureaucracy at work—judges, civil servants, rulers are all seated on their raised platforms as others sit below them, bringing gifts of tribute, pleading their cases. Tikal, it appears, was a bustling cosmopolitan city, with administraters, priests, artisans, the elite, and the royal family all living close to the center. And in almost every case, those magnificent pyramids were built not as sermons in stone or to glorify or reach the gods, but as burial monuments. Each royal family glorified itself and its ancestors by erecting these massive tombstones—at once venerating the dead patriarch or matriarch, and displaying the continuing wealth and power of the dynasty.

The classic period of Maya culture has been divided by archaeologists into early classic (A.D. 250 to 550) and late classic (A.D. 550 to c.900). The fact that most buildings now visible in Tikal date from the late classic is due to the Maya practice of tearing down or covering over one building and erecting another on top of it. From the hundreds of early classic and preclassic structures found by archaeologists in Tikal (mostly concealed under later edifices), it seems evident that Tikal was almost as extensive and magnificent in A.D. 300 as it was in A.D. 850.

However, during the early classic, there was extensive contact between Tikal and that giant to the northwest, Teotihuacán. This city, which had a population of more than 125,000 and extended its influence all over Mesoamerica, including making a colony out of even then ancient Kaminal Juyú, must have been an overpowering influence on Tikal. After its sudden destruction around A.D. 700, it is as if the genius latent in the Tikal culture was at last freed. With the removal of the influence of Teotihuacán there was a flowering in Tikal of all the arts, science, architecture, crafts, and calendrics. The sculptures and buildings seem to become fully what they had been only potentially.

So, reaching full bloom in the late classic, Maya culture flowered magnificently for some two hundred years, and then something went wrong.

Within a short period of time, the city which seemed to be at its peak was dead, deserted by its elite, buildings left unfinished, inhabited by only a few people who, as the jungle inexorably covered the monuments and temples, probably forgot the meaning of the hieroglyphs, the purpose of the temples, the history of the city, the glory of the race.

What in fact had happened was the collapse of lowland Maya civilization. About this collapse archaeologists are certain of only one thing—that it really did happen. Cities were abandoned, population densities all over the lowlands dropped sharply, people left and went somewhere else. Why, no one knows, though many give tentative answers. Some have been disproven—there is no real evidence that agricultural production declined, whether because of erosion, soil depletion or the spread of savannahs. Nor does it appear that the culture simply reached a high point and then, through cultural exhaustion or decadence, simply declined naturally.

What is known is that late classic society became progressively more rigid and highly stratified, with the ruling elite separated from the rest by power, wealth, and control of the trade networks (research shows that the elite were taller, i.e., better fed, than the commoners of the late classic). Perhaps, as access to the high levels of society became closed to all but the members of the ruling elite, the top levels became too conservative or unresponsive to pressures from below, or unable to find new answers to unprecedented problems. This, combined with rising population densities and even a slight decrease in agricultural production, could have led to widespread dissatisfaction and even rebellion.

Also, there is evidence (especially in the Mexican styles of ceramics, figurines and stelae found in frontier river cities like Seibal, Piedras Negras, and Yaxchilán) of a great movement of new peoples down from Mexico. Whether these intruders were warlike is not known. However, after the destruction of Teotihuacán there could have followed disruptions in the north and west that ultimately led to disruptions or the cutting of crucial Maya trade routes. These intrusions could have put a strain on an already inflexible, out-of-touch elite and an overextended economy, and perhaps led to power struggles and dynastic political wars in the lowland cities. Circumstantial evidence of this is now turning up.

Though the reason for the collapse is not clear, there is no reason to assume it has to be attributed to any simple or single cause. It does seem probable that, whatever the essential causes, the collapse took the form of a popular uprising by an increasingly alienated and dissatisfied peasantry against an elite whose concerns they could not understand and whose demands had become oppressive.

The Structures of Tikal

There are literally thousands of structures at Tikal. If you have a car, you can drive from plaza to plaza, but the walking is delightful, under the cover of the high hardwood trees. Some of the main structures are:

The Great Plaza. Over 2½ paved acres, this gigantic artificial platform consists of four superimposed plaster floors, the first from as early as 150 B.C., the last from around A.D. 700. Bounded by the two great pyramid-temples on the east and west, by the multitiered array of temples known as the North Acropolis to the north, and by the complex system of "palaces" in the Central Acropolis to the south, this plaza was undoubtedly the heart of the city of Tikal, the great stage on which the thousand-year drama of Tikal was played out.

Temple I. Known as the Temple of the Giant Jaguar (after the jaguar carved into one of its door lintels), this is the most famous image of Maya civilization. Its thrusting, beautiful proportions achieve a simultaneous appearance of massiveness and power, and of lightness and fragility. Its nine terraces are mounted on the front by a steeply sloping stairway (the stairway now in use is only a "construction stairway" used by workers to carry up the great amounts of limestone blocks, rubble, and mortar needed to build the structure—over it was later constructed a wide stairway which the priests or leaders used, and of which a few steps are preserved at ground level). It is a burial monument, constructed over a burial chamber with a corbeled vault—the Maya never used the true arch, instead creating a blunt, pointed arch by overhanging blocks more and more until they were close enough together to be bridged by a capstone. The skeleton found in the chamber was surrounded by ceramics, jewelry, and other marks of wealth and power—it can be seen in the Tikal Museum. Under the rearmost of the three thick-walled, corbel-vaulted rooms at the top was found another important burial. On top of everything is a hollowed-out, heavily decorated "roof-comb"—built for decorative purposes and to add impressive height. The structure is 145 feet high and was built around A.D. 700.

Temple II. Known as the Temple of the Masks after the grotesque masks on its facade, this three-terraced pyramid faces Temple I across the Great Plaza. Though it now stands 125 feet high, when its roof comb was intact it was almost as tall as Temple I. The large masonry block in front of the temple atop the pyramid is thought to have been a reviewing stand, where some powerful personage could see and be seen by all those gathered below. Notice the interesting graffiti—including some captive being speared by a masked man—that date from the late classic. For the less ambitious, this one is easier to climb than Temple I.

The North Acropolis. Elevated over the Great Plaza by a wide series of stairs, this amazing group of structures is, says William Coe, "the single most complex feature, from the standpoint of growth and content, yet excavated in the Maya area." Under the 12 visible temples lie about one hundred other structures, some dating back as far as 200 B.C. Probably the oldest ceremonial center of Tikal, there was a whole complex of structures here by 100 B.C. Archaeologists have removed late classic facades in some places to reveal the early classic structures still intact beneath, including two great long-nosed masks over 10 feet high.

The Central Acropolis. This maze of multileveled, interconnected buildings, structured around a series of six courtyards, is one of the more puzzling structures in Tikal. The small rooms with their low platforms can be seen as family homes, priestly retreats, administrative chambers, judicial chambers, throne rooms, or clubhouses. They seem dank and dark for homes, but then dankness and darkness must have been the norm for the jungle-dwelling Maya, and who knows whether 1,200 years ago the rooms weren't snug and cheery? Also, the location, overlooking the Great Plaza, must have had great prestige value—people put up with certain discomforts to live in the right neighborhood. Again, the frequent changes made—doorways opened, other doorways sealed, stairways constructed, back passageways created—seem to indicate the shifting nature of family or clan living, with marriage, birth, and death always changing the shape of the group. Note the numerous fine graffiti, especially in the building known as Maler's Palace.

Temple III. Known as the Temple of the Jaguar Priest because of a carving of a fat man in a jaguar skin on a door lintel (which is still intact and worth seeing), it is 180 feet high, and was built in the late classic. Still unrestored and covered with vegetation, it appears much as Temples I and II appeared to the early explorers of Tikal.

Temple IV. This is the tallest known building in the Mayan world, measuring 212 feet high. More squat than the other temples, this structure is incredibly immense, and surrounded by limestone quarries from which the rocks were dug to build it. Its massive front stairway is visible from a distance, but overgrown with trees and vegetation, like the rest of the pyramid. The climb, from the northeast corner, entails struggling up using roots for handholds, but the view is worth it. You have a superb look not only at the whole layout of Tikal, but of the vast forest stretching away to infinity in all directions. The Temple was built in A.D. 741.

Temple V. This is the least visited of the great temples. Separated from the Great Plaza and its surrounding structures by the ravine of the huge Palace Reservoir, it stands next to the massive, but as yet unexcavated, South Acropolis. Almost 190 feet high, it was built around A.D. 700. It too is still covered with earth and trees, but you can still make out the bulk of its stairway (uniquely, with raised edges or moldings up each side). The climb is not difficult, the trail is worn, the roots making fine hand and foot holds. At the top you'll find a room only 2½ feet in breadth, but with a rear wall fifteen feet thick.

The truly adventurous can climb through a hole in the roof to the top of the roof comb. From here, or from the front door of the temple, you have an extraordinary panoramic view of the city spread out below you. While from Temple IV you see the peaks of the pyramids above the trees, from Temple V the smaller structures are also visible—Temple IV to the far left, Temple III to the left, and in front of you an incomparable vista of Temples I and II facing each other, with the North Acropolis in the background and the Central Acropolis in all its complexity spread out before you.

At least a couple of hours should be spent at the Tikal Museum, which contains much of the material discovered in the excavation of the North Acropolis, as well as such interesting items as delicately carved human bones (on one, a badger, a priest, a laughing iguana, a chattering monkey, a supercilious parrot, and two blithe, bored oarsmen voyage enigmatically downstream in a big canoe); polychrome ceramics (including one that shows a fat dancing Maya puffing on a cigarette); the incomparable Stela 31, showing the great king Stormy Sky, the Sun God on his belt, flanked by two warriors dressed in the style of Teotihuacan; and a reconstruction of the tomb beneath Temple I.

Many visitors fly in from the capital in the morning, spend the day seeing the ruins and museum, and fly back in the late afternoon. If this is the only way you can do it, by all means do it. However, try to spend at least one night at Tikal (or if the facilities are too basic, spend the night in Flores and return in the morning), as almost two days are required just to *see* the most important structures. But you may want to spend several nights at Tikal, if only because this is the only way you can get up to the

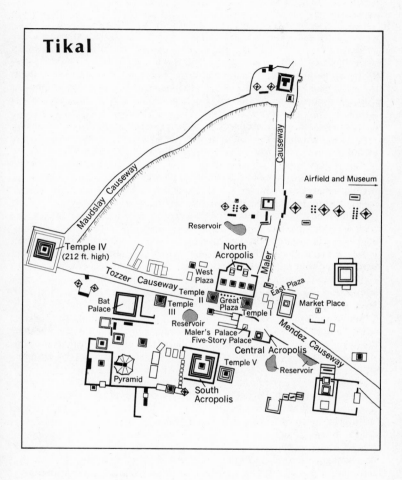

Tikal

Maudslay Causeway

Causeway

Airfield and Museum →

Reservoir

Temple IV
(212 ft. high)

North
Acropolis

Maler

Tozzer Causeway

West
Plaza

Temple
II

East Plaza

Bat
Palace

Temple
III

Great
Plaza

Temple I

Market Place

Reservoir

Maler's Palace
Five-Story Palace

Mendez Causeway

Central Acropolis

Pyramid

Temple V

Reservoir

South
Acropolis

ruins early enough to see dawn from the top of a pyramid, or stay late enough to watch the sun go down behind Temple II. Ultimately Tikal is indescribable.

Other Lowland Maya Sites Nearby

The Maya have been known to most of us through Tikal, Copán, Uxmal, Palenque—the cities that were discovered early or extensively excavated and reconstructed, or simply easily accessible. However, they built scores of cities that were as magnificent as these. El Mirador, in the northern Petén, is said to have "more and larger monumental architecture than any other site known in the Maya lowlands." It has over 200 mounds, a dozen great pyramids, one of which is probably greater than Tikal's Temple IV. Yet because it is inaccessible to all but the hardy adventurers, it is not even on many archaeological maps. El Mirador can be reached from Carmelita and Dos Lagunas, but is a several-day trek and you will need a permit from the FYDEP offices near Flores. You may be able to drive or hitchhike to Carmelita or part-way to Dos Lagunas. Take camping gear, mosquito nets, and flashlights, plus lots of food and water, and hire a guide in Carmelita or Dos Lagunas. At El Mirador, the guards will show you around the site and provide wood for a fire.

Yaxhá was, after Tikal and El Mirador, the third largest Maya city. Its ruins are extensive and almost untouched by archaeologists. It is particularly interesting for its Solstice Observatory, and its massive pyramid complexes and acropolises. It can be reached (in dry season preferably) by turning off the road between Flores and Melchor de Mencos at km. 61. Walking to the site from the road will take several hours and a guide will be essential. Nakum is only 20 km. farther north, but hard to find and harder to reach. Naranjo lies just to the south.

Uaxactún, a day's walk from Tikal has great stone palaces that cover acres; its majestic temples sit atop immense terraces. In Group E is another Solstice Observatory, where buildings and stelae are arranged so the sun rose over one stela at the winter solstice, and over another at the summer solstice.

Seibal is perhaps the most impressive Petén site after Tikal, not for its size but for its beauty. Partially cleared, it stands among the loveliest flowers, trees, and scenery imaginable—wild orchids, water vines, great palms arching together to form natural cathedrals, philodendrons blossoming red and purple. Easily reached by car or bus from Flores, you go first to Sayaxché, where a little ferry takes you across the Río de la Pasión, and the townspeople sit on the banks of the river watching, desperate for any distractions. At Seibal, you'll find stelae in excellent, almost mint condition. Made out of harder rock than the stelae at Tikal, they are beautifully carved, and some show Mexican influences (note the beards and long hair on some of the figures). There is also a circular temple (built like a wedding cake), one of only two known in the entire Maya world. There are several other nicely restored temples, and many buildings and pyramids still unexcavated. A lovely place for camping, Seibal was probably the earliest Maya center in the Petén, and also the first place taken over by the foreign invaders c. A.D. 800 (note the non-Maya faces on the stelae).

Seibal lies along the Río de la Pasión, just below Sayaxché. There are a number of small hotels in Sayaxché, including Hotel Guayacán, owned by Julio Godoy, who is a fount of information on the area. Godoy can advise you where you can hire a boat for a visit to Lago Petexbatún, several miles south of Sayaxché. The boat trip will take two or three hours, and you can camp on the lakeshore. The boat owner can tell you where you can hire a guide to the ruins of Aguateca and Dos Pilas, the latter several hours' walk through the jungle.

A number of other sites border the Usumacinta, including the great Yaxchilán in Mexico and Piedras Negras, and near the soon-to-be-developed Lake Petexbatún, lie Dos Pilas (beautifully preserved stelae) and several other unexcavated sites such as Aguateca and Tamarindito. The area is known as a fishermen's and hunters' paradise, and the banks of the rivers are teeming with wildlife of all kinds. Just as the Río de la Pasión and the Rio Usumacinta, flowing into the Gulf of Mexico, were lined with Maya cities, so was the Belize River, which flows into the Caribbean. The serious archaeology student will want to see some of these sites as he passes from the Petén into Belize. The most important are Xunantunich (Benque Viejo) and Altun Ha. It is important to remember that archaeologists today are only beginning to come to terms with the incredible number of cities that once covered the Petén. The ones that have been mentioned are only a fraction of the known sites, and more are turning up all the time. There is simply not enough time or money to even roughly catalog the known Maya sites in the Petén, and the big battle now is against looters. Many fine stelae and other artifacts have disappeared, been moved or destroyed by looters, thus depriving archaeologists of what might have been important clues in the continuing effort to understand more about this elusive and remarkable civilization.

In the far northeastern part of the Petén are the ruins of Río Azul, about which *National Geographic* magazine published a major article in April 1986. It can probably be reached from Dos Lagunas, but would be a long trek, and it would be worthwhile discussing your plans to visit the site with the director of the Museum of Archaeology and Ethnology in Guatemala City.

PRACTICAL INFORMATION FOR
TIKAL AND THE PETÉN

HOW TO GET THERE AND HOW TO GET AROUND. Also see "How to Get Around" in *Practical Information for Guatemala and Guatemala City.* **By plane.** Two airlines fly from Guatemala City to Santa Elena, the airport on the outskirts of Flores. Flights are from the national airport, *not* the International Airport. Reservations should be made at least 2 days in advance, and tickets should be purchased at least a day before you wish to fly. The round-trip fare is $40. Since schedules are constantly changing you should check current flight times before you plan to go. *Aviateca,* 10 Calle 6–30, Zona 1; 81–372, 81–415, 81–479, 81–579. Reservations can be made at the airport, 321–884/7. *Aerovias,* 8 Avenida 16–11; Zona 1; 537–885. Reservations at the airport, 316–935, 319–663.

By car. Most of the road north to Flores is unpaved, so you will need a reliable high-clearance vehicle, and should check carefully the road conditions if you plan to go during the rainy season. Take the Ruta al Atlantico and turn north just after Morales at km. 247. The paved road continues north for 20 miles to El Relleno, the impressive new bridge over the Río Dulce (toll: 35 cents), and from there you are mostly on unpaved, sometimes rocky and rutted, road to Flores. It is just over 300 miles from Guatemala City to Flores, and Tikal is 45 miles on a new paved road from there. Top up your gas tank at El Relleno, and anywhere else where you have less than half a tank of fuel left.

By bus. *Fuente del Norte,* 17 Calle 9–08, Zona 1; 513–817, 86–094, has daily service to Flores from Guatemala City. Fare: $3. The trip will take at least 10 hours, and considerably more during the rainy season. People returning from the Caribbean coast may be able to pick up a bus at midday at El Relleno. Buses leave from Flores and Santa Elena for the 1½-hour trip to Tikal, turning north at the junction with the road to Melchor de Mencos on the Belizean border. Fare about $1.

There are hotels at El Relleno and on the Río Dulce, and you can hire a launch to take you to the Fortress of San Felipe *(Castillo San Felipe),* constructed in the 17th century and now restored. Fare about $1. If you want to stay the night there is a small pension. The fortress is located where the Río Dulce exits from Lago Izabal.

Two miles before reaching Poptún is the Finca Ixobel, where you can camp or stay in the small guest house. Good food is served in the house, and several small caves can be visited near the Finca. The owners of the guest house can arrange trips to a Maya cave, a few miles east of Poptún, which is famous for its Maya hieroglyphs. The Finca has a natural swimming pool, and provides free firewood for campers. The farm is a few hundred yards to the west of the traffic control post just before Poptún, and accommodation costs just $1.

There are buses traveling south on the unpaved road to Sayaxché, 40 miles from Flores. From there you can rent a boat, drive, hitchhike,or perhaps get a bus or taxi to the ruins of Seibal, 10 miles east, where there is a small pensión.

Another, longer, way to get to Sayaxché and Flores is by bus and boat from Gautemala City of Sebol, in Alta Verapaz. *Transportes Ramos* at the Bus Terminal in Zona 4, 31–9317, or at 9 Avenida 16–20, Zona 1, 80–735, has daily buses from Guatemala City via Morales to Modesto Méndez (on the road to Flores), where they turn west to Sebol (which you can also reach by bus from Cobán), Raxrujá, and Playa Grande. They leave Guatemala City at 2 A.M., the trip takes 12 hours or more to Raxrujá, and the fare is $4. From Sebol you can get a ride on a boat to El Pato, but you may have to wait a while (days?) there to find a boat returning to Sayaxché. In Raxrujá, there is *supposed* to be a vehicle driving to Sayaxché twice a day. The trip takes 3 hours and the fare is $1. *La Pinita* bus company at the bus terminal in Zona 4 in Guatemala City has a service direct to Sayaxché, passing the junction to El Pato, but you should check in advance if the bus is running during the rainy season.

Buses leave Flores for Melchor de Mencos 2 or 3 times a day, and if you are coming from Tikal you can catch the bus at El Cruce, the junction for the roads to Tikal and Melchor de Mencos. If you get the early bus you might reach Belize City in the day; otherwise you should stay in Melchor de Mencos or one of the nearest towns in Belize. *Batty Bros.* Bus Service runs several times a day from San Ignacio, 10 miles from the border, to Belmopan and Belize City.

ACCOMMODATIONS. Budget travelers, and people who want to be near the ruins of Tikal at dawn and dusk, can stay at 1 of the 3 basic hotels in Tikal, though most visitors—particularly those who have their own vehicles—stay in Flores. The following is a sample of the hotels and pensiones near Flores, and information on the three hotels in Tikal.

Flores

Yun Kax. 0–811–386. 35 rooms. Double: $6. Restaurant, bar. Private baths in rooms.

Monja Blanca. 0–811–340. 39 rooms. Double: $4. Restaurant, cafeteria. Rooms with private baths.

Itzá. Double room: $5. Same owners as the Yun Kax.

There are several basic hotels and pensiones, including **Guayacán, Santana,** and **Petén** (tel. 0–812–392; double room: $6).

Santa Elena

Tziquina-há. 0–811–216, 0–811–216, 0–811–359; in Guatemala City: 20–528. 24 airconditioned rooms. Double: $14. Restaurant, bar. Cable TV, pool, tennis courts.

Costa Del Sol. 0–811–336. 11 rooms. Double: $14. Restaurant, bar, and pool. Some rooms have air-conditioning and TV.

Maya International. 0–811–276; in Guatemala City: 61–920. 22 rooms. Double: $12. Restaurant, bar. Can arrange tours, and rental of jeeps (though these are expensive).

There are also several basic pensiones, including **San Juan III,** near the bus terminal, **Don Quijote,** and **El Diplomático.**

Tikal

Camino Real - Tikal
800 327-3573 #132
Double) — Triple A?

Jaguar Inn. Very few bungalows, but you should reserve if one is available. Double: $15. Good restaurant.

Jungle Lodge. Reservations in Guatemala City: 760–294. 13 bungalows with private baths. 12 rooms with shared bath. Bungalow for 2: $11; double room: $7. Restaurant, bar. Can arrange guides for tours of the ruins, and tours of other sites in Petén.

Tikal Inn. 6 bungalows. Double: $15. No electricity.

TOURS. *Panamundo,* 7 Avenida 14–44, Zona 9, Guatemala City, runs tours to archaeological sites to the Petén, traveling by boat down the Río San Pedro or the Río de la Pasión. The telephone numbers in Guatemala City are: 313–188 and 312–525. See also "Tours" in *Practical Information for Guatemala and Guatemala City.*

Near the hotels in Tikal in in the central areas of the ruins guides offer their services. Ask around to see what other visitors have paid and bargain.

TIKAL. If you plan to stay the night in Tikal and haven't reserved a room, do so immediately or you may have to return to Flores (or El Gringo Perdido). If you are camping, bring additional food and water, with you, plus mosquito repellant if you are using a hammock, and book a camping site when you arrive.

Admission to the ruins of Tikal is 70 cents, and entrance to the museum, near the old airstrip, is free. If you want to see sunset or sunrise at the ruins, ask for a special permit to enter before dawn or after dusk. It is usually very hot in the middle of the day, so it is better to go early in the morning or late in the afternoon, and take a long siesta after your lunch.

THE ATLANTIC AREA

The little town of Livingston (pop. about 3,000) is like nothing else in Guatemala. Set on a low bluff overlooking the Caribbean and the mouth of the Río Dulce, it was once the busiest seaport in Guatemala and one of the busiest in all of Central America. When coffee became Guatemala's largest export in the second half of the nineteenth century, it was shipped from the highlands and Alta Verapaz down the Río Polochic, Lake Izabal, and the Río Dulce to Livingston, where it was loaded onto freighters for shipment to all parts of the world. Later, in the early twentieth century, came the banana boom, and huge quantities of the fruit came down the river from the vast plantations around Lake Izabal. But soon good roads and the development of trucks made it easier to ship coffee out of Pacific ports. And in 1939 the United Fruit Company moved its headquarters from Livingston to Puerto Barrios. Now the town is just a sleepy backwater, cut off from the rest of Guatemala, not just culturally and economically, but also topographically—the only way it can be reached is by boat. And of course, once you get there, there's nothing to do at all—nothing, that is, except kick back and relax, go swimming from one of the sandy beaches, fish or snorkel, take the mail boat up to Río Dulce to Lake Izabal, hire a dugout canoe, and explore the jungle or paddle up one of the rivers, or get to know the friendly people and observe the colorful, easy-going life of the town. In fact, having risen and fallen, the city is now once again much like it was described by John Lloyd Stephens on his journey of 1839 described in *Incidents of Travel in Central America, Chiapas and Yucatán,* "The site . . . was occupied by another tribe of Caribs. . . . Their leaf-thatched huts were ranged along the bank, shaded by groves of plantain and cocoanut trees; canoes with sails set were lying on the water, and men and women were sitting under the trees gazing at us. It was a soft and sunny scene, speaking peace and freedom from the tumults of a busy world."

One reason for this easy-going air is the town's people. About 95 percent of the population is Black Carib (also known as Garífuna, or Moreño). The people are friendly, and many speak English with a lilting, rhythmical, British-tinged accent. There's good swimming near town, although you shouldn't expect endless beaches. The little beach at the Río Blanco, across the bay and reached by boat, is clean, with white sand. You can paddle quite a way into the Río Blanco, for bird-watching and exploring the jungle. In the rainy season, try the Siete Altares to the north of town, a series of seven 10- to 20-foot-high waterfalls and pools that flow into the bay by a sandy beach. Even without water in the falls, the walk through

Carib fishing compounds and jungle is fascinating. With its mellow Caribbean atmosphere and quiet pleasures, it's little wonder Livingston has become a word-of-mouth favorite spot for travelers from all over the world. Also available; good rum, superb seafood prepared in the Carib style, and little bars playing reggae music.

Lake Izabal and Río Dulce

Twelve miles wide and 30 miles long, Lake Izabal is the largest in Guatemala, and quite different from the mountain-ringed lakes of the highlands. Surrounded by lush tropical foliage, its warm blue waters teem with an incredible variety of life—fish, lizards, alligators, colorful tropical birds, and the great blubbery manatee, or sea cow. Izabal is the only fresh-water lake in the world inhabited by this gentle sea mammal that gave rise to sailors' legends of mermaids. Izabal is a superb lake to fish, to explore, to photograph, or simply to cruise and observe, whether by yacht or rented *cayuco.*

The fact that Lake Izabal was once an important trade route, linking the riches of Alta Verapaz to the Atlantic and Europe via the Río Polochic and Río Dulce, is attested to by the stone fortress that lies at the Río Dulce end of the lake. Built in 1652 for protection against the French, English, and Dutch pirates who roamed the Caribbean in search of Spanish gold, the Castillo de San Felipe seems never to have served its purpose very well—it was captured by pirates three times, sacked and burned down once, and destroyed by an earthquake in its short, ineffectual history. In addition to being almost useless as a fortress, San Felipe was inexplicably built more than 20 miles from the Atlantic, allowing pirates to raid the coastal ports with impunity. In the seventeenth century, the castle was turned into a prison. Deserted now for over a hundred years, the fortress still makes an interesting stop for those cruising Lake Izabal and Río Dulce, and can be visited by those crossing the El Relleno bridge on their way into the Petén.

Quiriguá

Because its massive, deep-relief stelae and altars, with florid, intricately interwoven forms that fill every available space, look very much like those of nearby Copán in Honduras, Quiriguá has long been supposed to be an off-shoot or a colony of that great city. And recent advances in translating hieroglyphs have proven the theory to be true. Tales of court intrigue, political alliances, betrayals and marriages, proud rulers and palace rebellion have begun to emerge from the hieroglyphs that archaeologists once thought spoke only of the stars and the gods. Archaeologists surmise that the city was a trade or trans-shipment center, part of the vast Maya trade network, and/or a political colony of Copán, and/or a plantation center for cacao (the Maya unit of currency was the cacao bean) or other export crops.

Quiriguá's stelae are the tallest and most massive yet discovered, and one of them (Stela E) is 35 feet tall and weighs some 65 tons. It's thought the Maya moved these huge blocks of sandstone from the quarry several miles away to the city by means of skids or log rollers. Other massive and inscrutable carvings at Quiriguá are the "zoomorphs"—bizarre, unknown animals, perhaps monsters from Maya legends or griffonlike mixtures of several animals, carved from gigantic boulders. The zoomorphs, found only here and at Copán, seem to have been some sort of Maya craze, fad, or fashion, for all of the large zoomorphs were sculpted in a 15-year period between A.D. 780 and 795.

Though most of it remains covered with jungle, Quiriguá is thought to cover many acres, and must have been a sizable city. However, until further archaeological work is done, the origins, purpose, and history of the city remain mysteries.

Located on a 75-acre forest preserve, once part of the holdings of the United Fruit Company, and now a kind of jungle island amid a sea of cultivated fields, the Quiriguá site is also remarkable for the variety of its birds—toucans, parrots, parakeets, motmots, woodpeckers, kiskadees, hawks, sparrows, and many other species flourish among the great trees and ruins, making this a point of interest to bird-watchers as well as students of Maya culture.

Esquipulas

Like Chichicastenango, the shrine of the Black Christ shows fascinating evidence of the continuing strength of the ancient religion of the Maya, and is another example of how the Catholic Church converted the Indians by incorporating the old gods into Christian doctrine and by building their churches in locations already held to be sacred by the Maya. Esquipulas is said to have been an important Maya trading and religious center, perhaps associated with nearby Copán. Maya stone sculptures still stand near the church, some of which are said to represent Ek-Balam-Chac, the Black Rain Puma. The Maya also worshiped other black gods (Ek Ahau, the Black Lord; Ek Chuach, the Tall Black One).

Whatever the links between the Black Christ and the black gods of the Maya, it is known that around 1590, as the ancient gods and places of worship were being ruthlessly destroyed by Christian missionaries, an Indian had a vision of Christ at the site of the present shrine. Whether to prevent an Indian revolt, or because whites were so hated and feared by the Indians that they would not worship a white Christ, the church authorities commissioned famous sculptor Quirio Cataño to carve a Christ from dark wood.

Finished in 1594, the Black Christ was quickly accepted by the Indians, and began building a reputation as the source of numerous miraculous cures. In 1738 the archbishop of Guatemala was cured of a chronic ailment by the Christ, ordered the present basilica constructed, and is now buried at the church's altar. Over the centuries the fame of the Black Christ has continued to grow, and each year hundreds of thousands of worshipers make pilgrimages from Mexico, Central and South America. Many of them come on foot, or by bicycle, and great numbers of them can be seen crawling the last few miles on their hands and knees, reciting prayers, in hopes of gaining the blessing of the Black Christ.

January 15 is a day of special veneration for the Black Christ, and during that period the town of Esquipulas is literally overflowing with thousands of pilgrims. Holy Week also brings great crowds to worship the image. However, the flow of the faithful never stops, and the town is always active with pilgrims (and those who profit from their faith by selling reputed relics, souvenirs, and small packets of soil from the area, which people mix with water and drink in hopes of miraculous cures)—and the pilgrims are not only Indians. Today the followers of the Black Christ come from every class of Latin American society, the majority of them non-Indians.

In addition to the spectacle of the pilgrims and the lovely image of the Christ, the church itself is one of the most beautiful colonial buildings in Central America (its construction was supervised by Diego de Porres), with exquisite silver and gold chandeliers, altar pieces and decorations, paintings by most of colonial America's most famous artists, and thousands of tributes placed there by those who have been healed by the Black Christ.

PRACTICAL INFORMATION FOR
THE ATLANTIC AREA

HOW TO GET THERE AND HOW TO GET AROUND. By trains.
If you are a railway buff (or a masochist!), and have a good cushion with you, trains for Puerto Barrios leave from the railway station, 18 Calle and 9 Avenida, Zona 1, 83–030/9, at 7:15 A.M. on Tues. and Sat. The fare is $1, and you should arrive in Puerto Barrios at 7 P.M. Trains for Guatemala City leave Puerto Barrios—the station is across the road from Hotel del Norte—at 6 A.M. on Wed. and Sun., arriving in the city at about 8 P.M.

By bus. Two companies service Puerto Barrios from Guatemala City. Though there are several trips a day, if you want to arrive in time to catch the boat to Livingston or Punta Gorda, Belize, you should buy your tickets a day or two in advance. Contact *Litegua,* 15 Calle 10–40, Zona 1, 27–578. Fare $3.50. From Puerto Barrios, 9 Calle and 6 Avenida, 0–481–002, 0–481–172. The trip will take 5 to 6 hours.

By car. Five miles beyond the Motel Longarone is the junction for the road to Zacapa, and at Estanzuela, a few miles after the turnoff, is the *Bryan Patterson Paleontology Museum.* Admission is free, and the museum is open 7 A.M.–6 P.M., Tues.–Sun. Even if you are not seriously interested in paleontology, the well-tended exhibits, and the short distance you have to drive from the Ruta al Atlántico, make this a very worthwhile side trip. If you want to arrange a tour and a short talk on the exhibits, write to Roberto Woolforlk, Museo de Paleontología, Estanzuela, Zacapa.

After returning to the Ruta al Atlántico, and continuing toward Puerto Barrios, you'll reach the junction to the ruins of Quiriguá, 50 miles from Motel Longarone. Turn right for 2 miles to the ruins, passing by tens of thousands of banana trees. Leave your car in the parking area at the entrance to the site, and walk through the well-kept garden visiting the huge stelae. It's a beautiful place to stroll through, but it gets very hot during the middle of the day, and photographers should visit in the morning when the stelae aren't in shadow cast by roofs that have recently been constructed over them to prevent more erosion.

If you're coming by train or by bus, you can walk to the ruins or take a bus. From the main road you have 60 miles to drive to Puerto Barrios, or 30 miles to the road north to Flores and Tikal.

By boat. From Puerto Barrios to Livingston. Leave daily at 10 A.M. and 5 P.M. Cost 30 cents. Buy your ticket at the office near the end of the road to the dock and walk 200 yards or so to the ferry. Get there early, because it is usually very crowded, and choose a seat away from the sides if the sea is rough. The trip takes about 1½ hours.

From Puerto Barrios to Punta Gorda, Belize, Tues. and Fri. at 7:30 A.M., and take about 3½ hours. Fare $2 for adults, $1 for children. The boat stops at Livingston about 8 A.M.

From Livingston to Puerto Barrios. Daily at 5 A.M. (arrive early!) and 2 P.M.

From Livingston to Punta Gorda. Tues. and Fri. about 8 A.M.

From Livingston to El Relleno (the bridge over the Río Dulce for onward travel to Tikal or a return to Guatemala City). The mail boat leaves on Tues. and Fri. at 11 A.M., takes about 2½ hours, and costs $1.70. You can hire a motorized canoe from the dock in Livingston or through La Casa Rosada, and then can swim near the hot springs before entering El Golfete and visit the Manatee Reserve on the north side of El Golfete. The fare will be about $20 for the group. Edgar Alfonso Campbell, who has 3 boats, is recommended.

From El Relleno to Livingston. The mail boat leaves early on Tues. and Fri., but you will have to check carefully the precise time if you want to go immediately to Punta Gorda, since this ferry leaves from Livingston at about 8 A.M. on those days. You can hire a launch at El Relleno to get to Livingston faster (less than 2 hours) if you want to catch the ferry to Belize.

ACCOMMODATIONS. There are some accommodations along the route from Guatemala City. Contact the **Motel Longarone,** km. 128 (041–0314); **Hotel Doña María, Hotel Royal** (in the village of Quiriguá). All are inexpensive.

El Relleno

(Bridge at exit of Lake Izabal, over Río Dulce)

Hotel Catamarán. On a small island a couple of miles down the Río Dulce, reachable by launch; in Guatemala City; 324–829. 12 rooms. Double: $13. Bungalows overlooking the water: $25. Restaurant, bar, small pool. Can arrange boat rentals.

Hotel del Río. On the south side of the Río Dulce, just after the Hotel Catamarán; in Guatemala City: 310–016. 14 rooms, all with air-conditioning. Double: $13. Restaurant, bar, pool, games room.

Turicentro Marimonte. On the south side of the river, a few hundred yards from the bridge; in Guatemala City, 314–437. 16 rooms. Double: $9. Restaurant, bar, swimming pool. Camping near pool.

Pensión Izabal. On the south side of the river at the foot of the bridge. Double: under $5.

Livingston

Hotel Tucán Dugú. On the right just after the ferry landing; 0481–572, 0481–588. 36 rooms and 3 suites. Double: $24. New 2-story hotel, each room with a balcony. Swimming pool ($2 fee for non-guests), large restaurant, bar.

La Casa Rosada. 500 yards to the left after the ferry landing. 5 rooms. Double: $5. General bathroom. Continental breakfast (70 cents) on the terrace. Private dock for sunbathing. Stock beer and soft drinks. Will arrange boats for trips to Río Blanco, beach across the bay, or up the Río Dulce. American-owned. Highly recommended.

Hotel Caribe. Near the ferry landing. 27 rooms. Double: $2. No fans.

Hotel Río Dulce. Near the ferry landing; 0481–059. 13 rooms. Double: $2. Shared bathroom, cold water.

Puerto Barrios

Hotel Henry Berrisford. 7 Avenida and 15 Calle; 0481–030. Double: $16. Private bath, cable TV.

Hotel Puerto Libre. At km. 292, 2 miles before Puerto Barrios, at the junction to Santo Tomás de Castilla; 0480–447. 26 rooms. Double: $11–$16. Rooms are air-conditioned and equipped with video TV and private bath. Swimming pool, restaurant with international menu.

Hotel del Norte. 7 Calle and 1 Avenida, on the shore of the Caribbean Sea; 0480–087. 34 rooms. Double with bath: $8; without bath: $5. Restaurant, bar. Choose a room with a view of the Caribbean Sea. If you are going to Livingston, you can park your car here ($2 for non-guests).

Hotel Europa. 8 Avenida between 8 and 9 Calle; 0480–328, 0480–127. Double: $7.50. Private bath, air-conditioning, restaurant.

Hotel Reformador. 16 Calle and 7 Avenida; 0480–533, 0481–531. 17 rooms. Double: $6. Restaurant, bar.

Hotel Español. 13 Calle between 5 and 6 Avenidas; 0480–738. 17 rooms. Double: $3. Restaurant for breakfast only.

Hotel Xelajú. 9 Calle between 6 and 7 Avenidas; 0480–482. 39 rooms. Double: $1.50. Restaurant.

RESTAURANTS. The major hotels in Puerto Barrios and Livingston have restaurants, but if you are staying elsewhere or continuing on, you might try:

Livingston

African Place. Near the cemetery; turn left at the top of the main street.

New York Greenhouse. Straight on at the top of the main street. Private house; evening meals have to be booked in the morning.

Raymundo. Opposite the Tucán Dugú.

Puerto Barrios

Bric-Brac. 8 Calle between 6 and 7 Avenidas. Chinese food. Open 24 hours.

La Caribena. 9 Avenida and 7 Calle.

Lisama. 9 Calle and 5 Avenida. Steaks and seafood. Open 24 hours.

El Timón. 7 Avenida between 7 and 8 Calles, across from the municipal market. Open 24 hours a day. International dishes.

BELIZE

For the Adventurous

by
ROBERT BRAATON

Robert Braaton is a writer who also works as a development consultant and has lived in a number of Central American countries, including Belize.

Although Belize is a Central American country, it is physically and linguistically isolated from the other Spanish-speaking countries of Central America. In addition, its predominant Caribbean coast and the cultural ties to the islands of the Caribbean have dictated that it be considered a Caribbean country. Its diminutive size, 8,866 square miles, coupled with the fact that it is still involved in a dispute with Guatemala, its only Central American neighbor, have contributed to the isolation.

The majority of its landmass is dominated either by the rugged Maya Mountains or lowland swamps. Two important factors have discouraged the development of the country and made the construction of roads difficult: physical isolation and small population (160,000) have stifled commerce and hindered the growth of tourism. A dependence on England and the lumber industry meant lack of agricultural development, industry, and self-reliance. Overshadowed by Mexico, its northern neighbor, isolated by

Guatemala, and "protected" by the barrier reef at sea, Belize has not been able to shake its image as a backwater country. But what to one person is undeveloped to another is unspoiled, and that unspoiled beauty has been attracting visitors for many years. The country and its people win a person over, and one begins to understand what has captured the expatriate residents who populate the country.

The sweeping white curve of the Barrier Reef beckons even from the air—and only from the air does one comprehend its size. The reef, which is 175 miles long, is second in size only to the Great Barrier Reef of Australia. From Ambergris Cay in the north to its southern end near the coast of Guatemala, the barrier reef is a beautiful living world sculptured by the vivid coral formations and populated by a seemingly boundless variety of fish. It can be explored however you choose: snorkeling, scuba diving, swimming, sailing, or light-tackle fishing.

Behind the protective barrier lay the cays (pronounced "keys"), hundreds of small islands, many only impenetrable mangroves and swamps. Although the majority of the cays are uninhabited, some have small settlements of fishing or day camps, and a few are a traveler's paradise. Lined with classic tropical beaches, stocked with piña coladas and moving to a Caribbean beat, these cays are the perfect place to return to after a hard day snorkeling. The ambience is conducive to everything from deep-sea diving to siestas in the hammock.

The interior of Belize does not so readily give up its treasures, but it is precisely that unspoiled nature which has enabled the country to establish a jaguar sanctuary and bird refuges. Because Belize has not suffered from the population pressures that other countries have, its wildlife population is abundant and varied—in all there are over 500 species. Five cats—jaguar, puma, ocelot, margay, and jaguarundi—are native to Belize. Birds are also plentiful and can be seen throughout the country as well as in the bird sanctuaries. Much of the jungle is unexplored, and many of its Mayan sites and limestone caves undiscovered. There is something for everyone who is fascinated by nature or archaeology.

The sheer number of pre-Columbian sites in Belize indicate that it was once a thriving part of the Maya empire. The ruins have been covered with jungle for more than a thousand years, and archaeologists have only recently begun to comprehend the extent of the civilization in Belize. Looters, who discovered most of the sites, have been forging ahead at unguarded sites stripping the country of its treasures. People interested in Mayan artifacts should note that it is a crime to remove them from Belize.

Belize, an underdeveloped and unspoiled country, beckons to those who want to make their own adventures. Belize is the place for those who enjoy their discoveries flavored by the process of getting there.

Past and Present

After the fall of the Mayan civilization, the population was redistributed, and the Maya empire faded into myth and memory—the jungle guarding all of its secrets. Its secrets were guarded well, for not until recently did the sheer number and sizes of sites in Belize move archaeologists to reclassify the area as a significant part of the Maya empire. The discovery of Caracol and the study of other sites, including Altun Ha, Xunantunich, and Lamanai, prove that the area was heavily populated and connected by roads with the great centers of Tikal and El Mirador. The indigenous people of Belize, the Mopan Maya, are descendants of those great Maya.

Belize was included in the area claimed by Spain in the New World. There is evidence that Hernán Cortés crossed southern Belize in the 1520s, and there is record of a conquistador named Montego attempting to conquer the area a short time later, but repelled by Nachankan and Belize Mayas. After that initial attempt the Spanish did not return again in force for nearly two centuries.

During that time the English pirates rediscovered Belize. The protection of its barrier reef and uncharted waters made it an excellent base from which to harass the Spanish main. The pirate Peter Wallace is credited with establishing the first settlement in Belize at the mouth of the Belize River in 1638. One of the theories about the origin of the name of Belize is that it is a corruption of the name Wallace. Or that the name derives from *balise,* the french word for beacon, alluding to the signal light that guided the freebooters back home. Yet another theory is that it comes from a Mayan word meaning "low-lying area to the east" or "muddy waters."

Whether the pirates can be credited with the naming of Belize is arguable, but it was definitely the lumbermen who began the colonization. In 1660, Bartholomew Sharp, a famous British pirate, began harvesting logwood for shipment to Europe for the production of textile dyes. The business proved lucrative, attracting other buccaneers and the first British settlers. The early 1700s saw the arrival of the first African slaves in Belize.

When the great artisans of England and Europe discovered the value and beauty of mahogany in the construction of furniture, the demand for the wood increased. This attracted more settlers, many arriving from Jamaica with their slaves. The slaves soon outnumbered the European settlers. Ultimately these first settlers and slaves formed the predominant ethnic group in Belize. These dark handsome people, known as Creoles, speak an English dialect which sounds warm and personal but just skirts comprehension.

Life was hard in the settlements, the work exhausting, and there was little means or opportunity to relax. Consequently the arrival of the cargo ship, which brought all the supplies, as well as rum and letters, was always greeted with a wild and outrageous celebration. This spirit can be experienced even today in the joyous celebrations of Belizean holidays.

The eighteenth century was marked by Spanish attacks on the British settlements, slave revolts, and attacks on the logging operations by the Mayans. In 1754 and again in 1759 the Spanish drove out the Baymen, as the settlers came to be called, and freed the slaves, but each time the settlers returned. Burnaby's Code, established in 1765, marked the formal beginning of government, and the Treaty of Paris of 1783 recognized British logging rights but prohibited agriculture in an attempt to block a permanent settlement. Even today this affects Belize; what agriculture exists in the country is primarily in the hands of the mestizos, who brought their knowledge from Guatemala and Mexico.

The end of the eighteenth century was marked by the defeat of overwhelming Spanish forces by 240 Baymen on Saint Georges Cay. This victory is a source of Belizean pride and is celebrated each year on September 10 as Saint Georges Cay Day.

This battle did not end Spain's claim to Belize, and with the independence of Latin America both Mexico and Guatemala claimed Belize. England rejected the claim and in 1859 negotiated a treaty with Guatemala by which Guatemala gave up its claim to Belize in return for the construction of a road by the British connecting Belize City and Guatemala City. Since the British did not comply with their part of the treaty, Guatemala reaffirmed its claim and each new government in Guatemala threatens to annex Belize by force. Although Belizeans take the claim lightly, England maintains a garrison of several thousand British soldiers in the country.

The nineteenth century brought the end of slave trade and later the abolition of slavery. It was also a period which marked the arrival of two important ethnic groups to Belize: the Garinagu in the 1830s and indigenous people from the Yucatán in the 1850s. Originating from the intermix of escaped slaves with island natives on Saint Vincent, the Garifuna (Island Caribs) were expelled from Saint Vincent by the British and sent to the island of Roatán off Honduras. And from there, in 1832, they crossed the Gulf of Honduras to Dangriga.

In the 1850s the devastation of the caste wars of the Yucatán drove thousands of mestizos and indigenous Mexicans into northern Belize. Bringing with them their knowledge of agriculture and a love of land, they came to own most of the land around Orange Walk and Corozal. With time they turned the area into one of the most important agricultural areas in Belize, and today sugar cane covers the countryside. The area still has cultural and linguistic ties to Mexico and Spanish is spoken throughout the area. This period also marked the declaration of Belize as a crown colony and the country spent the next century mired in colonialism. Lumber continued to be the base of the country's economy and little effort was made to develop a self-sufficient nation.

After World War II a sense of nationalism started Belize on the road to independence. The founding of the Peoples United Party, the establishment of adult sufferage, the introduction of the ministerial system, and the granting of self-government in 1964 led to complete independence in 1981. In 1984 the first general elections since independence were held, and Mr. Manuel Esquivel of the United Democratic Party (UDP) was elected Prime Minister. The dispute with Guatemala still remains, but both parties recognize the need to resolve the problem so each can focus on their own development.

As a result of the country's colorful history, the nation has become a cultural melting pot. In addition to the four principal ethnic groups, there are East Indians living in Belize City and the Toledo District to the south. There are also Jamaicans, Germans, Chinese, Lebanese, and Italians scattered throughout the country. Each brought their skills and added their culture to the country.

The Mennonites arrived in 1958 and established two communities, one in the north and one in the west. A very closed community, the Mennonites continue to speak a German dialect and ply the agricultural and crafts skills of their ancestors. They produce much of the vegetables consumed in Belize and their furniture can be seen in many Belizean homes.

There are several cultures minimally represented in Belize, including American expatriates and some Arabs, but they disappear in the masses where few people can track their ancestry to one ethnic group. A short walk down the street in Belize City will give one an idea of the extent of the racial mix: it's not unusual to hear conversations in Creole—the lingua franca—Garifuna, Spanish, and English.

EXPLORING BELIZE

Despite the fact that the barrier reef is Belize's greatest attraction, the country offers a wide variety of interesting and adventurous experiences for the traveler. The country divides itself naturally into three geographical areas—the cays, the coast, and the interior—each offering the opportunity for a unique experience. The gateway to all those areas is Belize City.

Belize City

Belize City is the only "city" in Belize—and, with a population of only 50,000, not a large one. The city grew at a false mouth of the Belize River in response to the logwood industry developing in the interior and the need for a shipping point. First mention of Belize Point appears about 1780, but the area had been intermittently inhabited since the early 1600s.

By 1839, Belize City was well established, as can be seen in the following description by John L. Stevens written in that year: "A range of white houses extended a mile along the shore, terminated at one end by the Government House and at the other by the barracks, and intersected by the Belize River. . . . "

Built on a peninsula and surrounded by a swamp, the city is vulnerable to the whims of nature, yet it was not until 1931 that the city was first devastated by a hurricane. Then in 1961, Hurricane Hattie roared through Belize, destroying many of the city's buildings and leaving over 250 people dead. Again the people returned to rebuild the city, but it was decided that the official capital should be moved to Belmopan, on the edge of the Maya Mountains, 50 miles west of Belize City. Still, today Belize City continues to be the center of the nation's commerce and social life.

The city, with its rickety, tin-roofed wooden dwellings built on stilts, is divided into 13 sections. The names of the sections—Mesopotamia, the Barracks, Port Loyola—each reflect some of Belizean history. The city is also crisscrossed by several canals necessary to drain the low-lying city and famous for the odor they give their life.

Remnants of Belize's illustrious past can still be seen throughout town despite repeated assaults by the forces of nature. The city is divided into the north and south sides by Haulover Creek, a false mouth of the Belize River. The south side is the oldest and most interesting part of the city and centers around Albert and Regent streets. Originally called Front and Back streets, they form the main business district of town. At the beginning of Regent Street is the governor-general's residence, known as the Government House, an elegant old structure built in 1814. Across the street is Saint John's Cathedral; built in 1857, it is the oldest Anglican church in Central America. Just up Regent Street from the cathedral is the Tourist Board. Also on Regent Street, overlooking Central Park, is the Supreme Court building; the lovely old building incorporates many of the classic elements of British colonial architecture. Finally, wedged between Regent Street and Haulover Creek at the foot of the swing bridge is the city market. Although it has a good fresh fish section, the market is generally characterized by neglect and a poor selection of vegetables.

Every day at 5:45 P.M., one has the opportunity to see the swing bridge "swing."

The two principal streets on the north side, Queen and North Front streets, intersect in front of the swing bridge. On one corner, facing the bridge, is the post office. Along Queen Street are numerous shops, restaurants, and the police station. The eastern tip of the north side peninsula is occupied by the Fort George Lighthouse and the tomb of Baron Bliss, the Portuguese patron of Belize. Originally the tip was occupied by Fort George, built in the eighteenth century on an island that was later connected to the mainland by fill. Today it is the site of the Fort George Hotel. This area also has some of the nicest old colonial houses of the city.

The city is full of contradictions: at once picturesque and dirty, friendly and dangerous; late-night strolls are not recommended. Although most Belizeans are honest, friendly, and hardworking, high unemployment and a stagnant economy leave many with time to drink, smoke marijuana, and hang out, eyeing tourists—especially women. Belize is the fourth-largest exporter of marijuana to the U.S., and its use pervades the country. Its aroma drifts through the streets, and if you are young or dressed very casually, chances are you will be approached by someone selling ganja. Concern is growing in the community and some efforts are being made to control the problem. Although violent crimes are few in Belize, pursesnatching, pickpocketing, and abusive hassling are common in the city.

An Excursion North

The Northern Highway is now a paved two-lane highway, and the 90 miles to Corozal can be traveled by car in just over 90 minutes. The Belize International Airport is located in Ladyville 10 miles from Belize City on the Northern Highway. Ladyville is also the location of the Belikin Beer Brewery. Since the construction of the new highway, it is necessary to take the old road from Sandhill to reach the ruins of Altun Ha.

In 1985 the Community Baboon Sanctuary was established to protect Belize's baboon population. The sanctuary is located on 18 square-miles bordered by the Belize River and can be reached by taking the Northern Highway to the Burrel Boom exit. Trails take visitors through an abundance of animal and plant life, and you're sure to hear the monkeys hoot!

A mile beyond Maskall on the western side of the Old North Highway is the Maruba Resort, an expensive hotel where tours and horseback riding excursions can be arranged.

Crooked Tree village, one of the first settlements in Belize, is located on a beautiful lagoon and surrounded by a bird sanctuary, which consists of several lagoons and marsh land. The area is inhabited by a large variety of aquatic birds, including egrets, storks, heron, ducks, and the large rare jabiru stork. The lagoons also offer excitement for the angler.

Orange Walk, 66 miles north of Belize City, was once a logging town but is now the center of the country's sugar industry. The 1970s boom days for the sugar industry are long gone, and a slump in sugar prices worldwide has caused widespread unemployment as the area looks for an agricultural product to revive the economy. During harvest time, from January to March, the roads are still crowded with cane trucks, but the future appears cloudy.

There are several minor but interesting Mayan sites around Orange Walk, but it is advisable to go with a tour or local guide, since it is in the principal marijuana-growing areas and the farmers don't like visits by strangers.

Corozal is the northernmost town and is located on Corozal Bay just south of Chetumal, Mexico. It has palm-lined beaches and a protected bay. The area offers excellent swimming and boating opportunities. The town's population is principally Spanish-speaking mestizos and is dependent on the sugar industry for much of its commerce. The only archaeological site of note in the area is Los Cerros, visible across the bay from the town.

There are frequent buses and taxis to the Mexican border just 8 miles north. A nice stopping place along this road is the Four-Mile Lagoon, a local swimming and picnicking spot. The Mexican port of Chetumal, the southern gateway to the Yucatán Peninsula, Cancún, Mérida, and the Mayan ruins, is only minutes from the border.

An Excursion West

The Western Highway is the gateway to the interior of Belize as well as to the southern region. Cemetery Road in Belize City becomes the Western Highway and cuts through the seemingly endless swampland that surrounds the city. The area is populated by scrub palm and white egrets.

Hattieville is the first populated area along the highway. It is inhabited by people who resettled there after the devastating Hurricane Hattie. Soon the jagged outline of the Maya Mountains appears to the south, the road begins to rise, and the roadside becomes populated with the first Caribbean pines.

At mile 30 is the Belize Zoo, a worthwhile stop. Although the variety of animals is limited to species found in Belize, the animals are healthy and friendly. The setting is lovely and the enclosures adequate, but the zoo is moving to a new location adjacent to the present one. The cat collection is outstanding. It all makes for a commendable start for a nation that is just beginning to comprehend the value of its wildlife.

Another 20 miles beyond the zoo lies Roaring Creek and the entrance to Belmopan. It is also the beginning of the Hummingbird Highway, which leads to Dangriga, where it joins the Southern Highway to Punta Gorda.

Belmopan is a sparsely populated, planned city established in 1970 after Belize City had suffered its last razing by a hurricane. Tourists are invited to visit the vault of the Archaeology Department in Belmopan—and it is well worth the time. Although the vault is small and not designed for display, it is filled with most of the Mayan masterpieces found in Belize. Donations are gratefully accepted, since there is never enough money for the department's work or its battle against those unscrupulous individuals who are ruthlessly looting the hundreds of small Mayan sites that cover the interior of Belize.

Another 12 miles west lies Georgeville and the road to Mountain Pine Ridge. The road is only partially graveled and requires four-wheel drive during the rainy season. Located in the Mountain Pine Ridge area is the best horseback-riding center in Belize: Mountain Equestrian Trails. Here you can arrange for riding tours of Belize's rural countryside. Augustine, the ranger station, is the site of the Rio Frio cave located 27 miles south of the highway. The huge cave has two entrances and some beautiful rock formations. The cave is not big by Belize standards; there are others—one of them the second largest in the world—which dwarf Rio Frio cave. Two miles before Augustine there is a series of granite-bottomed pools of the river Rio On that are great for dry-season picnicking and swimming. For the more adventurous there are trips to the 1,000-foot falls and the other caves and archaeological sites that dot the area. Here is some of the most beautiful scenery in Belize.

West again on the Western Highway there is the Belize College of Agriculture and Spanish Lookout—the Mennonite community—then the twin communities of Santa Elena and San Ignacio straddling the Macal River. San Ignacio, capital of the district of Cayo, is the center of commerce for the area, and the only large town in western Belize. The Western Highway enters Guatemala nine miles west of San Ignacio.

San Ignacio, with a population of nearly 5,000, still maintains the flavor of a Latin frontier town. That atmosphere is created and sustained by the cattle and logging industries, which are the primary sources of commerce in the area. San Ignacio is the most practical base from which to explore the area, since it has a variety of accommodations. Just one mile outside San Ignacio is the Maya Mountain Lodge and Educational Field Station for Cultural, Archaeological, and Wildlife Studies. Here you'll find a resident naturalist-ornithologist, a reference library, nature trails, and organized tours. San Ignacio is also home of the Panti Trail, a botanical garden designed for the study of Belize's healing herbs. Named after Don Eligio Panti, a Mayan bush doctor who has been healing people from all over Central America using only his system of ancient Mayan medicine, the trail provides an excellent opportunity to learn about the medicinal trees and plants of the region. Tours are offered on request and groups are guided by Dr. Rosita Arvigo, a professor of Botanical Studies and a practicing herbalist. Nine miles west, on the bank of the Mopan River, are the ruins of Xunantunich. El Castillo, the main pyramid, offers a commanding view of the entire area. One mile farther west lies the border town of Benque Viejo del Carmen. The town of 2,500 is inhabited primarily by the Spanish descendants of the nineteenth-century immigrants from Guatemala and the *chicleros,* who to this day wander through the dense jungle of Petén in search of chicle trees to tap for the principal ingredient in chewing gum. Despite the fact that Belize and Guatemala are politically at odds, the town is the center of a brisk trade, both legal and illegal, with its sister town Melchor de Mencos in Guatemala.

Excursion South

The Hummingbird Highway begins in Belmopan and winds for 50 miles southeast through the Maya Mountains. The highest section is only partially paved, principally one lane, and potholed. A quick stop at the lovely Blue Hole, beside the roadway 18 miles from Belmopan, breaks up the trip to Dangriga. Part of the cave system that honeycombs the area, the Blue Hole is a point at which an underground river emerges from under a granite wall and sinks again into the blue depths of the river system. Nearby Saint Herman's cave is one of Belize's many caves and an interesting stop on the way south. As with many of the caves in Belize, Saint Herman's shows signs of Mayan presence.

Dangriga, at the other end of the Hummingbird Highway, is a port town of about 8,000 inhabitants. It is the largest and most important settlement of the Garifuna people, a mixture of African slaves and Caribbean island natives who arrived from the island of Roatan in 1832. This event is celebrated each November 19 by a reenactment of the original arrival. The celebration begins the previous night with bands playing in the streets, Garifuna drum music, and dancing.

A government agricultural station and large citrus plantations are establishing Dangriga as a farming area. There is also a small fishing industry and boats to the cayes.

Just south of Dangriga is the Cockscomb Basin Wildlife Sanctuary and Forest Reserve. The region was established as a forest reserve in 1984, and in 1986 approximately 150 square-miles were dedicated as the world's first jaguar sanctuary. In addition to jaguars, the Cockscomb Basin is home to ocelots, margays, and scarlet macaws. There is a campground available for overnight excursions but a permit must be obtained beforehand from the Audubon Society in Belize City.

The Southern Highway is the newest section of Belize's highway system. This gravel road can become rutted and muddy, and at times traffic is interrupted during the rainy season. At Independence, formerly known as Mango Creek, one can take a dugout canoe to Placencia Peninsula, a long, narrow strip of land that encloses Placencia Lagoon. Placencia boasts some of the mainland's most beautiful beaches and has two principal villages: Seine Bight, a quiet Garifuna village in the north, and Placencia village, with the fair-skinned descendants of the English and Portuguese, in the south.

The Southern Highway ends in Punta Gorda, capital of the district of Toledo. Thinly populated and long isolated from the rest of Belize, Punta Gorda is an interesting mix of people, including Mayans, East Indians— who still grow much of the area's rice—Garinagu, Chinese, and Creoles.

Straight south of P.G.—as the town is known in Belize—is the Guatemalan village of Livingston; from there a short ferry ride to Puerto Barrios puts one on the road to Guatemala City. There is a ferry launch that makes regular trips—two times a week—between the towns. P.G. also marks the end of the Barrier Reef.

Excursions are available from here to Hunting Caye and Sapodilla Caye. Although there are no accommodations on the cays, they offer excellent snorkeling and diving. Their isolation offers peaceful enjoyment, as opposed to the populated northern cays.

Near Punta Gorda are the Mayan ruins of Lubaantun and Nim Li Punit; the latter is off the Southern Highway, while the former, located near San Pedro, requires a four-wheel drive. The interior villages of the area are principally populated by Mopan and Ketchi Maya, with the exception of Toledo, which was settled by southern refugees from the American Civil War.

The Cays

Ambergris Caye, the largest and most developed of the Belizean cays, is 35 miles from Belize City. The island is 25 miles long and a half mile wide, north to south, and is located about 200 miles south of Cancún, Mexico. San Pedro, the island's main attraction, is a small fishing village easily accessible from Belize City—20 minutes by plane. Flights leave several times daily; it's a two-hour trip by boat. The atmosphere on Ambergris Caye is very relaxed and casual, and hotel facilities range from first class to very modest. The many restaurants, gift shops, and bars—including one with a shark tank—are all within walking distance.

The Barrier Reef lies about a quarter mile off shore, directly in front of most of the island hotels. It provides some of the world's finest fishing and diving. The lagoons and mangrove thickets on the backside of the island provide excellent bird-watching and shell collecting.

The fishing off Ambergris Caye is great. One can troll for tarpon, mackerel, barracuda, or cast or deep-jig for snapper, grouper, trigger fish, jack crevalle, and others. Some of the greatest light-tackle bone fishing is available within 20 minutes of the local docks. Sailfish and marlin deep-sea fishing can be arranged through the many charter services on the island.

The types of diving activities range from shallow-water snorkeling to deep scuba diving. There are coves, cuts, drop offs, canyons, and coral forests—all available for divers within 20 minutes of San Pedro. Water temperature is approximately 80° to 82°F year-round. The waters of the Caribbean are extremely clear: visibility is seldom less than 50 feet. In the driest months of March, April, and May, visibility reaches 100 to 200 feet. Divers equipped with underwater cameras can film a wide range of scenes and colorful reef fish. The fish are easily approached; close-up views are possible without special lenses.

All equipment for snorkeling, scuba diving, light-tackle and deep-sea fishing, sailboating, and waterskiing is available for rent at the island's many dive shops, resorts, or diving excursion companies.

Caye Caulker, more commonly known as Caye Corker, is 17 miles northeast of Belize City. The cay has a small community of 600 people, who are fishermen or hoteliers. The lobster fishing has made the members of the Northern Fishermen Cooperative quite well-to-do. The accommodations on Corker are simpler and cheaper than those on Ambergris Caye, and consequently the cay is a favorite with the back-packer set. There are few restaurants, but cheap lobster abounds during the fishing season. Boats leave daily from the swing bridge or Jan's Service Station (Shell), and cost BZ$12 (U.S.$6) one way. A note of caution: pay only the boat owners for the trip, don't pay the boys who hustle for the boats.

Half Moon Caye is 70 miles east of Belize City. Part of the Lighthouse Reef atoll, the outermost of Belize's three atolls, the reef encompasses a large lagoon whose waters are the clearest in Belize—visibility up to 200 feet. In the middle of the lagoon is the famous Blue Hole (not to be confused with the inland Blue Hole), a large circular shaft extending down 400 feet into the seafloor. This mysterious world has been explored by Jacques Cousteau and documented in both books and films. Extending off the central shaft are several caves with stalactite formations, which imply that the caves were once above sea level. The hole's mysterious nature and reported legends of a sea monster in the depths only add to its attraction. At one end of Half Moon Caye is a lighthouse, built in 1848; at the other end is a bird sanctuary, the nesting ground of the rare pink-footed booby. Several resorts and tour agencies organize diving, sailing, and camping expeditions to the cay.

Turneffe Islands are 20 miles straight east of Belize City. Much of the atoll's 300 square miles is covered by mangrove swamps criss-crossed by waterways. A perfect environment for the sport fishing enthusiast, bone-fish, permit, and tarpon are abundant and the diving is good. Several of the islands have full accommodations or day camps.

Glovers Reef is the smallest of the Belizean atolls, about 20 miles east of Dangriga. The reef has only four tiny cays, but the immense lagoon offers great snorkeling and diving. Long Caye offers full accommodations; Middle Caye has a sheltered camp site for complete privacy.

About 10 miles southeast of Belize City, small uninhabited English Caye is a favorite for day trips. The reef is close to this tiny strip of sand and coconut palms, and the swimming is good.

One of the earliest settlements and first capital of Belize, tiny Saint Georges Caye is located only nine miles northeast of the city. It was the base from which the pirates and loggers plundered the Spanish fleets and Belizean forests. It is also the site of the famous battle of 1798 in which the Baymen defeated a large Spanish invasion force. The battle is celebrated today on September 10 as Saint Georges Caye Day, a national holiday. There is a small first-class hotel on the island.

PRACTICAL INFORMATION FOR BELIZE

FACTS AND FIGURES. Belize is located on the Caribbean coast south of the Yucatán Peninsula. In the north it is bordered by Mexico, on the west and south by Guatemala, and on the east by the Caribbean Sea. It has an area of 8,866 sq mi, which includes 275 sq mi of offshore cays. Belize has 168 mi of coastline. Its topography consists primarily of coastal lowlands and the rugged Maya Mountains, which push into central Belize from Guatemala. Although the mountains are rugged, they are not high: Victoria Peak in the Cockscomb Range is Belize's highest at 3,696 ft.

Belize lies between 15°–19° N. lat. with temperatures generally ranging from 80°–95°F in the lowlands to about 50°F in the mountains. Annual rainfall averages from 60 in in the north to 160 in in the south.

Belize presently has a population of approximately 160,000, composed principally of 4 major ethnic groups: Creole (African and English), Gari-funa (African and Island Carib), mestizo (Spanish and Amerindians), and Maya Indians. The remainder of the population consists of East Indians, some European and American immigrants, and Mennonites. Nearly one-third of the population resides in Belize City, and, overall, nearly 90 percent of Belize's population resides in city, town, or village, leaving about 75 percent of the country uninhabited. English is the official language, although Creole, Garifuna, and Spanish are spoken in some areas. Belize's 2 primary export crops are sugar and lobster, but the recent downturn in world sugar prices has devastated the sugar industry here. Although there is some cattle, citrus, and cocoa production, all other agricultural production is consumed locally. Tourism has had an important role in the economy of Belize, and the new government has made the promotion of tourism one of its priorities.

WHEN TO GO. Anytime. In Belize the tourist season (Dec.–Mar.) costs more but the weather is drier. Although it is hot year-round, the nights get cool during Dec. and Jan. The rainy season begins in June but does not get heavy until Sept. through mid-Nov. During the summer months snorkeling is good, since the water is clear and the rates are cheaper. During the rainy season the sandflies can be quite bothersome, especially on the cays. The hurricane season runs June through Oct., and although Belize has not been hit by hurricane since 1961, the possibility always exists.

TRAVEL DOCUMENTS. All visitors to Belize must have valid passports. Visitors arriving by motor vehicle should have a current license and certificate of registration for the vehicle. Internationally valid, third-party insurance is required.

MONEY. The Belize dollar has been tied to the U.S. dollar at a rate of BZ$2 per U.S.$1 for many years. Most tourist services are quoted in U.S. currency, but ask if you are unsure. Generally hotels will exchange currency, especially in the cays or outdistricts, but large conversions should be done at banks. Banking hours are Mon. to Fri. 8 A.M. to 1 P.M. and Fri. 3 P.M. to 6 P.M. Hotel accommodations are taxed 5 percent, but food is not. Some hotels charge a 10 percent service charge.

HOW TO GET THERE. By air. Miami, Houston, and New Orleans all have connections to Belize now. The Miami-Belize route is served daily by *Tan/Sahsa, Taca,* and *Eastern* airlines. Both Taca and Tan/Sahsa fly to Houston and New Orleans, each flying alternate days, so there is always a daily flight. *Continental* flies to Belize via Honduras. Flight time is 2 hours.

Taca and Tan/Sahsa, both Central American airlines, connect Belize to Mexico and the rest of Central and South America. Taca (offices at 41 Albert St.) has connections through Los Angeles to San Salvador; Tan/Sahsa (offices at Valencia's Blg., New Rd.) has connections through Honduras.

By sea. Traveling to Belize by commercial ship generally requires good planning and perseverance. The 175 mi of the Barrier Reef favor the small craft—that wonderland just beneath the waves makes it difficult for large cruise ships. Some do stop, but schedules are not regular and often there is only one stop on a package tour (see *Facts At Your Fingertips*). There is a regular ferry that services Punta Gorda and Livingston in Guatemala 2 times a week.

By road. It's 3 days from Brownsville, TX, to Chetumal, Mexico, the port of entry into Belize; from California it is 5 days. Although the Northern and Western highways of Belize are paved, heavy rainfall and poor surfacing have left big potholes. Except for the Hummingbird Highway, which is partially paved, the rest of the country's roads are gravel or dirt and require a good back, patience, and, at times, a four-wheel drive.

There are bus connections from Guatemala City through Flores to Melchor de Mencos, the Guatemalan port of entry. There you can catch a taxi to the town of San Ignacio for BZ$3. From the north there is regular bus service from Mérida, Mexico. In Chetumal, Mexico, taxis are authorized to enter Belize as far as Corozal; there is also a bus service to Corozal. From Corozal, it is a 3-hour bus ride to Belize City along the Northern Highway, now a paved 2-lane road.

TELEPHONES. Country code for Belize is 501. The country is divided into 12 code areas, and principal town codes are: 02, Belize City; 026, San Pedro; 03, Orange Walk; 04, Corozal; 05, Dangriga; 07, Punta Gorda; 08, Belmopan; 092, San Ignacio. There are no public telephones, but many businesses will allow you to make local calls for 25 cents to 50 cents. Dial 115 for international calls. Information is 113. Police, fire, and ambulance is 90 in Belize City. The Belize Telecommunications Office is located on Church Street in Belize City. Telegraph, telex, and telephone services are available.

ACCOMMODATIONS. Until the installment of the present government in Dec. 1984, the country's tourist industry received little support. Today the industry is receiving government support, but accommodations are still not of the quality found in more developed countries. But rustic accommodations do not mean uncomfortable ones. The tourist facilities capture the atmosphere of their environment and encourage participation. In a country where it is always comfortable to be outside and days are invariably filled with some activity, a room is just a place to get a night's sleep and store your things. All hotels in the expensive and moderate ranges have private baths with hot water showers, rooms are clean and comfortable, and some now offer satellite television. Even in Belize City the principal restaurants are located in hotels; consequently many hotels—particularly the beach resorts—offer a Modified American Plan, which includes breakfast and dinner. As one would imagine, the staple is seafood served in such a variety of ways as to satisfy anyone.

Hotel rates in Belize are generally expensive compared with other Central American countries. There is considerable range in the value per dollar of accommodations, particularly in the inexpensive category, so check around. *First-class* accommodations cost from U.S.$75 to $120 for a double per night Modified American Plan (breakfast and dinner included). *First-class* accommodations offering only European Plan (no meals) run about U.S.$75. *Moderate* hotels cost from U.S.$25 to $75 per night for a double without meals, but probably offer the best value for the money. Under U.S.$20 is *inexpensive;* these vary in quality. For those who are budget travelers there is a good selection in Belize City. Hotels are taxed 5 percent; some charge a 10 percent service charge.

MAINLAND

Belize City

Bellevue Hotel. *First-class.* 5 Southern Foreshore; 02–7051. Overlooking the mouth of the Belize River and the ocean, the hotel has a sense of the sea about it. It has 36 rooms, all air-conditioned, and a small restaurant. The fare is okay but expensive, there is a choice of European Plan or American Plan. The bar has a warm atmosphere and is generally populated by sailors and Belizeans. The Mayan Lounge is a popular local disco with a live band (reggae and Caribbean music) on the weekends.

Fort George. *First-class.* 2 Marine Parade; 02–7400 or 45600. Aging but well-established modern hotel. It has 41 rooms, all air-conditioned. Still considered the best in Belize, it is the meeting place of frequent travelers and is used by most major travel agents in the Americas and Europe. There is a small pool and sun-bathing area. The air-conditioned bar is the coolest spot in Belize, with a lovely view of the Caribbean. The restaurant is one of the finest in the country.

Villa Hotel. *First-class.* 13 Cork St. (in front of the Fort George); 024–5743 or 47 or 45. A new hotel with some nice colonial architecture, well recommended by seasonal travelers. 12 rooms, all air-conditioned. The bar-restaurant is simple and pleasant, and the cuisine is unarguably the best in Belize.

Château Caribbean. *Moderate.* 6 Marine Parade; 02–2813 or 26. Small hotel adjacent to Memorial Park, overlooking the Caribbean. All rooms air-conditioned, small restaurant—spartan bar.

El Centro. *Moderate.* 4 Bishop St.; 02–2413. Small hotel centrally located; good restaurant. Recommended.

Four Fort Street. *Moderate.* 4 Fort St.; 02–45638. Beautiful Victorian home converted to a guesthouse. Excellent restaurant, pleasant local.

Glenn Thorn Manor. *Moderate.* Barrack Rd. Small guesthouse-hotel. Clean, quiet, friendly atmosphere.

International Airport Hotel. *Low moderate.* In Ladyville near entrance to airport; 025–2150 or 2039. Basic accommodations for in-transit traveler. Bar and restaurant.

Mopan. *Low moderate.* Located at 55 Regent St. in the city's historical neighborhood; 02–7351, 3356. Surrounded by the governor-general's residence, the prime minister's lodge, Saint John's Cathedral, and the Tourist Bureau. There are 15 rooms, all air-conditioned. Delightful bar, interesting people, and friendly proprietors. Dining room offers simple but good fare; family atmosphere. Maya Airways agent on premises.

Río Haul Motel. *Low moderate.* Located out of town, at the foot of the Río Haul Bridge on the road to the airport; 024–4859. Clean, quiet, great for those traveling by car. Bar, restaurant. European Plan rates.

Even Belize's *inexpensive* hotels are costly by Latin American standards, but there are several hotels for the budget traveler or those who are just passing through the city on the way to a caye. Rooms are spartan but generally clean; each hotel has its own atmosphere due to location and clientele, so check around before you decide.

Belcove Hotel (9 Regent St. W.), small hotel on canal. One block from swing bridge. **Dominique's** (9 Gabourel Lane), small, simple and clean. **Golden Dragon** (on Queen St. near Majestic Theater), 14 rooms, all with air-conditioning and bath. **Luxury Hotel** (16 Queen St.), opposite the police station. **Mom's Triangle Inn** (11 Hanyside St.), 6 rooms, clean, with bath, some with air-conditioning; restaurant is gathering place for young travelers. **Taj Mahal** (16 Albert St.), centrally located; Indian restaurant.

Belmopan

Belmopan Convention Hotel. *Moderate.* Bliss Parade; 08–2130 or 2340. New hotel with 20 air-conditioned rooms, restaurant, bar, and convention facilities. Within walking distance of all Government ministries.

Bull Frog Inn. *Inexpensive.* 23–25 Half Moon Ave.; 08–2111. Simple accommodations; rooms with fans; bar and restaurant—the place to eat in Belmopan.

Circle A Hotel. *Inexpensive.* Next to Bull Frog Inn; 08–2296. Simple but clean, rooms with bath.

Cayo District

(San Ignacio/Xunantunich)

Chaa Creek Cottages. *Moderate.* Located 5 miles up the Macal River from San Ignacio, Box 53, Cayo; 092–2188. A delightful stop on the way to Tikal or a base for exploring Xunantunich, Mountain Pine Ridge, or the Macal River. Private cottages with fully equipped kitchens sleep up to 5 people each. Peaceful lovely setting.

Maya Mountain Lodge. *Moderate.* 6 Crist Rey Rd.; 092–2164. Several small cottages located in a rural setting outside San Ignacio. Restaurant on the premises; tours can be arranged.

San Ignacio Hotel. *Moderate.* The hotel sits on a hill overlooking the Macal River and town of San Ignacio; 092–2034 It is modern, well-constructed, and simply designed. Clean, comfortable rooms with fans, a restaurant, a bar, a swimming pool, and the town's only disco. Tours to Xunantunich and the caves and waterfalls of Mountain Pine Ridge can be arranged through the hotel.

El Indio Suizo. *Inexpensive.* Down the Mopan River 2 miles from Xunantunich, Benque Viejo del Carmen; 092–2025 or VHF 14845. Clean, simple individual cottages; communal dining. Excellent base for exploring the area. Offers horseback trips to Xunantunich, day trips to Tikal, hiking, rafting, bird-watching, swimming, and a warm family atmosphere.

Corozal

Nestor's Hotel. *Moderate.* 123 Fifth Ave.; 04–2354. 16 rooms; air-conditioning and private baths available.

Adventure Inn. *Low moderate.* This new resort hotel is located in Consejo, 6 miles north of the town of Corozal; 04–2187. It features well-designed rustic cabins with private toilet and washrooms and shared showers; a bar-restaurant with a comfortable tropical atmosphere. It offers windsurfing and motorboating and is the headquarters for "Adventure Belize" tours. On Corozal Bay.

Caribbean Motel and Trailer Park. *Inexpensive.* Known as Mom's, it has 10 cottages, all facing the sea at the south entrance to Corozal; 04–2045. The facility has hot and cold water and an outdoorsy atmosphere. American and Belizean food served at Mom's restaurant, adjacent.

Maya Motel. *Inexpensive.* Small "modern" hotel at south entrance to Corozal; 04–2082. 12 rooms with private bath and hot water; bar and restaurant.

Tony's Motel. *Inexpensive.* 17 rooms, clean, comfortable; nice location on the beach at south end of Corozal; 04–2055. Restaurant and bar.

The Capri. Also located at the south end of town; 04–2042. For budget travelers.

Dangriga

Pelican Beach Resort. *Low moderate.* Aging but quaint hotel on north side of Dangriga; 05–2044. A nice beach and excursions to nearby cays.

The only *inexpensive* hotel in Dangriga is the **Riverside** (34 Hay St.), but there are a few boardinghouse rooms available if one asks around.

Orange Walk

Baron's Hotel. *Inexpensive.* Modern hotel on the Northern Highway in Orange Walk; 03–2518. 30 rooms (5 with air-conditioning), private baths, lounge open in the evening. Best accommodations in Orange Walk.

For the budget traveler, there is also **Nueve Mi Amor** (19 Belize-Corozal Rd.; 03–2031—simple accommodations, some with bath, air-conditioning) and **Jane's** (21 Main St.; 03–2389).

Placencia

Rum Point Inn. *First-class.* Located between the villages of Placencia and Seine Bight on the Placencia Peninsula; 06–2017. The facilities consist of 5 ferroconcrete domes, each containing 2 double beds with baths. Tours available to the southern ruins and Tikal; also snorkeling, scuba diving, and sailing.

The **Sea Spray Motel, Ran's Travel Lodge,** and **Sonny's Resort** all offer *inexpensive* but clean accommodations.

Punta Gorda

Foster's. *Inexpensive.* Near the dock, this hotel is clean, simple, and cheap.

Mira Mar. *Inexpensive* (though more expensive than Foster's). 95 Front St.; 07–2033. The best P.G. has to offer. Restaurant.

Accommodations are occasionally tight in P.G. Also check the **Isabel.**

THE CAYS

Ambergris Cay

Atlantic Reef Resort. *First-class.* 10 thatch-roofed cabanas on a lovely white-sand beach just outside San Pedro; 026–2050. Bar and restaurant in a tranquil atmosphere. All facilities.

Casa Solana. *First-class.* A peaceful setting south of San Pedro; 026–2018. The 10 rooms have fans. There is a private dock, fishing and diving available. American Plan.

Paradise Hotel. *First-class.* A relaxed and casual atmosphere on the north edge of San Pedro village; 026–2083. 22 rooms with fans; suite, apartment, or full house also available. All with air-conditioning, TV, and kitchen. There is a bar, restaurant; excellent for swimming; provides one of the loveliest vistas in San Pedro. Fishing, diving, and tours available. European Plan.

Ramon's Reef Resort. *First-class.* Secluded palm shades, 15 thatched cabanas, each with private bath and ceiling fan, on outskirts of San Pedro; 026–2071. Bar and restaurant; dock and swimming pool. Picnic or day trips can be arranged; all diving and fishing facilities available. American Plan.

San Pedro Holiday Hotel. *First-class.* Located in downtown San Pedro on the beach; 026–2014. The holiday hotel offers 15 rooms with fans, food, and a gift shop that is the nicest on the island. There is a lovely beach and dock; all fishing and diving facilities are available.

Sun Breeze Beach Resort. *First-class.* 12 modern air-conditioned units just south of San Pedro village; 026–2191. Restaurant and bar; fishing and diving facilities. Both American and European plans and holiday packages available.

Victoria House. *First-class.* A small deluxe resort hotel 2 miles south of San Pedro village offering 16 rooms with fans, some with air-conditioning; 026–2067. Bar, restaurant, and all fishing and diving facilities available. All rates are American Plan (including all meals).

Ambergris Lodge. *High moderate.* Located in downtown San Pedro on the beach; 361–2345. The Ambergris Lodge offers 11 rooms with fans and an atmospheric bar and restaurant. Dive shop and all fishing and diving facilities are available. Both American and European plans.

The Hideaway. *High moderate.* Just south of San Pedro; 026–2141. 32 rooms with fans. Bar, restaurant, and swimming pool. The hosts are friendly; relaxed atmosphere.

Barrier Reef Hotel. *Moderate.* The hotel's 6 rooms are located in the picturesque Old Blake House, oldest house on the island, built in 1907, overlooking the town's central park and the ocean; 026–2075. The Jade Garden Restaurant specializes in Chinese and seafood dishes, and the Navigator Bar serves unsurpassed piña coladas.

Coral Beach Hotel and Dive Club. *Moderate.* Box 614, Belize City; 026–2013. Diving, fishing, and beachcombing tours are available. There is a restaurant, for guests only, serving family-style meals of fresh local seafood. You can catch your own fish and they will cook it for you.

Spindrift Hotel. *Moderate.* 40 modern rooms and some apartments overlooking the Caribbean; 026–2018. Private dock and all island facilities. Cable TV and air-conditioning in all rooms. The hosts, Don and Ruby LeBanc, offer a restaurant and bar, and there's a swimming pool under construction. An excellent value for the money.

Conch Shell Inn. *Inexpensive.* 4-room hotel right on the beach within walking distance of all facilities; 026–2022. Rooms have fans and private bath.

San Pedrano. *Inexpensive.* This small 6-room hotel on San Pedro's main street offers rooms with private baths and fans and a restaurant; 026–2093 or 026–2054. There is also an apartment available by the week. Both American and European plans are available in a quiet family atmosphere.

Fido's—Someplace Else. *Inexpensive.* Located on the beach; 026–2056. 6 rooms and an open-air bar. Barbecues, diving, and fishing are available.

There are several budget hotels available in San Pedro. They are very basic, but all are clean, most have fans and shared baths. These include **Milos Guest House,** the verandah overlooks the cemetery and ocean; **Rubies,** on the beach; and **Carlos,** on the main street.

Other Cays

Several of the smaller, more isolated cays have resort lodges—often the only facility on the cay—which offer a variety of activities: scuba diving, snorkeling, game fishing, windsurfing, sailing. The accommodations vary but generally range from good to excellent.

Gallows Point Inn. Directly east of Belize City, c/o 9 Regent St. W., Belize City; 501–02–3054. The lodge, protected by a reef to the east, offers anchorage for yachts and daily shuttle service. The facilities are nice, and tanks and tours are available.

Lomont's Glover's Reef Lodge. *Moderate.* Southeast of Belize City; The small reef is part of an atoll located outside the barrier reef and well situated for diving excursions to the world-famous Blue Hole and Lighthouse Reef. Facilities are simple but comfortable.

Pyramid Island Resort, known as Caye Chapel. *First class.* American Plan. Box 192, Caye Chapel, Belize; 02–44190 (Belize) or 800–535–8780 (U.S.) It is located just south of Caye Corker. The modern facility has its own airport with snorkeling, diving, and fishing available.

Turneffe Island Lodge. Located on the Turneffe Island east of Belize City; Box 781 McMinnville, TN 37110; 800–824–1000 (U.S.). This resort focuses on fishing but is also equipped for diving and is the resort closest to the Blue Hole and Lighthouse Reef.

Villa Adventure. *Inexpensive.* Located at the far end of the Caye Caulker. Provides tents for visitors; a casual, comfortable, and inexpensive way to stay on the island.

RESTAURANTS. All of the first-class restaurants are in hotels and, in the cases of several lodges or resorts, this is the only food available. Rice and beans are a staple of the Belizean diet and are found in many Belizean restaurants. Since the supply of fresh vegetables is limited, many canned vegetables are imported. But seafood and chicken (another Belizean favorite) are plentiful and the beef is good; if you like lobster, Belize is for you. The great majority of restaurants in Belize are *inexpensive:* dinner and drinks for 2 will cost under $20. Three restaurants, noted below, could be considered *first-class:* over $25 for dinner and drinks for 2.

BELIZE CITY

Admiral Burnaby's Coffeehouse. Regent St. Great place for American breakfasts.

Archie's. 14 Albert St.; 202–3171. Chinese and seafood, also steaks.

The Barracks. 136 Newtown Barracks. On the water; 024–5763. Steak, seafood, and Chinese cuisine.

Caribbean Restaurant. 36 Regent St. Good seafood and Chinese; T-bone steaks are a house specialty.

El Centro Restaurant. 4 Bishop St.; 02–2413. Good seafood.

Chateau Caribbean. *First-class.* 6 Marine Parade; 02–2813. Specializes in seafood and beef.

China Village. 46 Regent St.; 02–2633. Nice atmosphere and good service; tasty Chinese dishes, also seafood.

Dit's Saloon. 50 King St.; 02–3330. Typical foods; good bread pudding and cakes.

Fort George Hotel. *First-class.* 2 Marine Parade; 02–7400. An elegant atmosphere but the food's not exciting. Seafood, chicken, or steak served in 5-course dinner. Still "the place to go" in Belize.

Four Fort Street. 4 Fort St.; 02–45638. Nice atmosphere, good service, excellent lobster sandwiches.

Hong Kong Restaurant. 50 Queen St.; 024–5713. Simple setting; good location; good food.

Taj Mahal. 16 Albert St.; 02–2931. East Indian and vegetarian fare.

Macy's Cafe. 18 Bishop St.; 02–3419. Clean and cozy; good Belizean cuisine and warm smiles.

Mom's Triangle Inn. 11 Handyside St.; 024–5523. Good hamburgers and Belizean food; still *the* meeting place for young travelers. Sue, the owner, does radio work for travelers needing assistance.

New Chon Saan Restaurant. 55 Euphrates Ave.; 02–2709. Big portions, of authentic Chinese cuisine; take out.

Pizza House. 11 King St.; 02–3966. The only pizza shop in town—and it's good!

Villa Hotel Restaurant. *First-class.* 13 Cork St.; 024–5743 or 47. Probably the best restaurant in town. Simple menu but well done. Attention to details.

San Ignacio

Eva's Restaurant. Burns Ave. Belizean food; popular meeting place for travelers. **The Place,** next door to Eva's, offers excellent burritos and other snacks.

Maxim's. Corner West and Waight sts. Perhaps the best Chinese cooking in Belize.

San Ignacio Hotel. 18 Buene Vista St.; 092–2034. Dining room only open for meals.

Serendib. 27 Burns Ave. Newly opened. Specializes in Sri Lankan dishes. Excellent rices and curries; friendly owners.

COROZAL

In Corozal, try **Tony's Motel** and **Mom's** (both at the south end), good hamburgers and salads, or **Altun Ha** (75 4th Ave.), good ceviche.

ORANGE WALK

In Orange Walk there is **La Favorita** (15 Lovers Lane), **Golden Gate Restaurant** (10 Main St.), and **Nuevo Mi Amor** (on the highway south; 03–2031), perhaps the best.

DANGRIGA

In Dangriga it's the **Gateway** (34 Havana St.) or **Burger King Restaurant,** also on Havana St.

Punta Gorda

Mira Mar Restaurant. 95 Front St.; 07–2033. Specializes in Chinese and seafood dishes.

HOW TO GET AROUND. To explore the country, you will have to deal with the roads. The gravel and dirt roads get rough after the rains, and traffic on the Southern Highway is often interrupted during the rainy season. *Batty, Venus,* and *Novelos* bus lines service all the principal towns in Belize (the Tourist Board—see below—has schedules).

There are several small airlines and charter services available. All the main towns, as well as some of the cays, have their own airstrip. *Maya Airways* (6 Fort St., Belize City, or at the municipal airport, 02–2312 or 02–7215) services the entire country with regular flights to and from Corozal, Orange Walk, Dangriga, Big Creek (Placencia), Punta Gorda, Cay Chapel, and San Pedro (Ambergris Cay). *Tropic Air* (Municipal Airstrip, 02–45671) also flies to San Pedro.

There are several car rental agencies in Belize for those who want to explore on their own. Some rent cars, vans, and four-wheel-drive vehicles, prices are about the same (U.S.$50 per day, no mileage, for car or 4WD; $85 a day for van) in each agency. A four-wheel-drive vehicle is a must for most of the exploring in Belize. The rental agencies will also organize tours and furnish a driver and guide if asked (for formal tours see below). The rental agencies are: *Elijah Sutherland Car Rental,* 127 Neal Pen Rd., 02–3582 (perhaps the most experienced); *Smith and Sons Auto Rental,* 125C Cemetery Rd., 02–3779 (wide selection of vehicles including vans); and *S&L Guided Tours and Auto Rental,* 69 W. Collet Canal, 02–3062.

USEFUL ADDRESSES. The *Tourist Board* is located in Belize City on Regent St. next to the Mopan Hotel; 02–7213. *U.S. Consulate:* 29 Gabourel Lane; 02–7161. *British High Commission,* 34–36 Half Moon Ave., Belmopan.

TOURS. There are a wide variety of tours available, both in the states and locally, to explore Belize. Some of the more established: *Far Horizons,* Box 1529, San Anselino, CA 94960, 415–457–4575, focus on Mayan ruins; *See and Sea Travel Service,* 680 Beach St., Suite 340, Wharfside, San Francisco, CA 94109, 415–434–3400, group charters and diving tours; *Triton Tours,* 1519 Polymnia St., New Orleans, LA, 504–522–3382, diving and fishing tours; *Sail Belize,* Box 13023, Saint Petersburg, FL 33733, 800–237–6339, yacht rental and diving tours; *Out Island Divers,* Box 7, San Pedro, Belize, 501–026–2151 or 2083; *Explore Belize,* Box 46, San Ignacio, 501–092–2164; *Mountain Equestrian Trails,* Mile 8, Mountain Pine Ridge Rd., Central Farm P.O., Cayo District, Belize, 501–024–4253; the *Panti Trail,* Ix Chel farm, General Delivery, San Ignacio, Cayo, Belize; 092–45545. Tours can also be arranged through hotels; see "Accommodations," above.

ZOOS. *Belize Zoo,* mile 30 on Western Highway, west of Belize City. Lovely setting with outstanding collection of Belizean cats. Moving to site adjacent to present one. Open daily 10:30 A.M. to 4 P.M.

BEACHES. Because the mainland of Belize is very swampy and the coast is protected by the Barrier Reef, the mainland coast has few good beaches. One notable exception is the Placencia Peninsula, long famous for its beautiful white beaches. That is not to say Belize has no beaches. Many of the cays have classic palm-tree-lined white beaches filled with sea shells and other treasures for the beachcombers. All of the cay resorts have their own beaches and many of the uninhabited cays have lovely empty beaches for a very private experience. It should be noted that during the off season the sandflies can be quite bothersome.

SPORTS. Most people come to Belize for recreation related to the sea, and they are not disappointed. Not only do the Barrier Reef, atolls, and cays create an underwater wonderland to explore, but they also provide a feeding grounds for a great variety of game fish. See also "Tours," above and "Accommodations" for resorts and trips that cater to particular interests.

Bird-watching. Belize is a bird-watcher's paradise (a bird-watcher at an inland resort identified 62 species of birds in 1 day). There is a local chapter of the Florida Audubon Society (Box 354, Belize City) and 2 established sanctuaries for some for the 450 species that populate the country.

Boating. See "Accommodations" for resorts that offer boating among their activities; also see "Tours." Several yachts offer cruising and diving. The *Isla Mia* (a 75-foot motor yacht) can be contacted through Sea & Sea Travel Service, 680 Beach St., Suite 340, Wharfside, San Francisco, CA (415–771–0077); *Lucretia B.* (36-foot motor yacht), Fort George Hotel, Belize City; *La Strega* (80-foot), Sail Belize, Box 13023, St. Petersburg, FL (800–237–6339).

Diving. To many, Belize means diving. The combination of warm water (average temperatures about 80°F), exceptional visibility (up to 200 ft in some places), and a seemingly endless variety of aquatic plants and animals means there is something for everyone—from the beginning snorkeler to the experienced diver. The size of the area covered by the reef, the infinite variety of coral formations, the lovely atoll lagoons, and the eerie world of the Blue Hole and reef cutoffs ensure that no single visit is sufficient to see it all. Most of the diving is done through resorts. (See "Accommodations." Also contact: *The Dive Shop*, behind the Soccer Field, Cay Caulker, and *Out Island Divers* Box 7, San Pedro, Ambergris Cay, 026–2151.)

Fishing. The many rivers and lagoons of the mainland offer light-tackle fishermen plenty of action—including tarpon, snapper, and snook. The reefs are the home of barracuda, kingfish, snapper, grouper, several varieties of jacks, crevalle, and sharks, to name a few. And for the deep-sea fisherman there are marlin and sailfish. There is an international fishing contest held each year in March. For information on fishing licenses contact *Ministry of Natural Resources*, Government Offices, Belmopan, 08–2409.

The Mountain Pine Ridge area is perfect for **horseback riding** and **hiking**, both offered by some of the inland resorts.

Hunting. Although Belize is fast becoming aware of the value of preserving its natural resources, there is still sufficient wildlife to mean exciting hunting. The jungle and mountains of Belize are alive with deer (white tail and roe), peccary, and 5 species of cats, including jaguar and puma. Quail are plentiful in the bush, and the many lagoons are the home or migratory way station for many ducks. There are no restrictions on shotguns, but it is advisable to check with the authorities concerning rifles; contact Customs and Excise Dept., 02–7405. Contact Ministry of Natural Resources (see above) for license information. A few resorts cater to hunters but most can arrange hunting trips.

Spelunking. Belize is fast becoming a must-visit country for spelunkers. Many caves have been discovered in Belize, ranging from very small to the second largest in the world. Frequently in remote areas, they often contain underground rivers, immense caverns, and Mayan artifacts and ruins. There are some tours that are specifically for cave exploration.

CAMPING. Although there are few developed camp sites in Belize, the country begs to be explored by camping. Some established sites are avail-

able. In Belize City there is the *Caribbean Trailer Park* on New Town Barracks; facilities for vans, trailers, and tents. On the Western Highway there
is camping at *Ontario Village*. In the Mountain Pine Ridge area, camping
has been restricted to *Augustine,* a forestry station, near the Río Frío Cave.

SPECIAL EVENTS. Belize annually celebrates 3 important events in
its history: *Saint Georges Cay Day,* Sept. 10; *Independence Day,* Sept. 21
(both are occasions for a party Belizean style—i.e., good music, good rum,
and nonstop dancing); and the *arrival of the Garinagu people in Dangriga,*
on Nov. 19, celebrated with a reenactment of the original event and dancing and partying in the streets.

MAYAN RUINS. Altun Ha. Today the ruins are part of the village of
Rock Stone Pond. At the height of the classic Maya period, the site probably had a population of approximately 3,000; the surrounding area was
also quite densely populated. It was not until 1964 that a field team from
the Royal Ontario Museum, under the direction of David Pendergast,
began to excavate this site.

Altun Ha, located 33 mi north of Belize City along the Northern Highway, covers approximately 3 sq mi. The ceremonial center consists of 2
adjacent plazas bounded on each side by temples or mounds. The site is
unique in that it is nearly devoid of the carved stelae found so frequently
at other Mayan sites. But the caches from the unlooted tombs discovered
here were truly the treasures of kings. The list of objects includes jade,
polychrome pottery, carved shells, and hematite and flint objects. A tomb
in structure A-1 contained so much jade it became known as the temple
of the green tomb; another produced the greatest find of excavation—the
9¾-lb jade head of Kinich Ahau, the Maya sun god. The piece, the largest
object of carved Mayan jade ever discovered, is occasionally displayed in
Belize City.

Xunantunich. The ruins near the Guatemalan border on the Western
Highway are known as Xunantunich ("Stone Maiden of the Rock"). The
site is on an artificially leveled limestone ridge 600 ft above sea level. Its
location on the Mopan River indicates that it was a trading center and
important link between the interior and the sea. There were 3 carved stelae
and a carved altar found at this site, but the predominant attraction is El
Castillo pyramid, which rises 130 ft above the ruins. The Maya construction process of enclosing 1 pyramid inside another can be seen in this temple; it offers a commanding view of the river and surrounding area. Even
today the thousand-year-old structure is the tallest building in Belize. The
temple originally had a stucco frieze that extended all the way around the
structure; the reconstructed portion on the east side gives an idea of its
beauty. The site has never been completely excavated.

In the southern district of Toledo are 2 excavated Mayan sites, **Lubaantun** and **Nim Li Punit.** They are archaeologically significant in that their
masonry work was done without mortar. The largest stela in Belize was
found at Nim Li Punit.

East of Altun Ha in Orange Walk District near the village of Indian
Church is **Lamanai.** The site is reached by river from the Mennonite community of Shipyard. The river trip is enjoyable and from the top of the
principal pyramid one can see the marijuana fields, which are an important
part of the local economy. The site also has more recent historical struc-

tures, including an overgrown 19th-century sugar mill erected by English settlers and a 16th-century church built by Spanish missionaries.

Caracol, a large ceremonial site located in the Maya Mountains near the Guatemalan border, was only recently discovered and has been under excavation since 1986. Although almost impossible to reach during the rainy season, weather permitting a visit is worthwhile and the journey through the lush jungle of the Cayo district quite interesting. The outline of the **Los Cerros** mounds can be seen across the bay from Corozal; they have been only partially excavated. **El Posito** is located about 4 mi west of Guinea Grass. The site was once partially excavated and consequently one can see a wide range of Mayan structures, from preclassic all the way through the postclassic period. The pyramid that included the main temple has been reclaimed by the jungle, but it is still an interesting site to visit. **Cuello,** another site in the Orange Walk area, contains one of the earliest examples of Mayan architecture, dating to 2,500 B.C. The site also had polychrome pottery dating from the same period—some of the earliest ceramics found related to the Maya.

Besides these more important sites, the country is dotted with hundreds of minor ones. Some can be visited on tours set up by local tour agencies. It is not recommended that one visit small sites by oneself, since many are being looted and could present some danger. Looting is a very big problem in Belize, and it is not unusual to be offered a beautiful artifact on the street. The buyer should beware that removing archaeological artifacts from Belize is illegal.

Besides Belize, the Maya empire covered an area that today includes El Salvador, Honduras, Guatemala, and Mexico. Situated between the great ruins of the Yucatán and the sites of the Petén and the rest of Guatemala, Belize is ideally located to offer those amateur archeologists another chapter in the Maya story. The present government is putting emphasis on the ruins as a part of its overall promotion of tourism.

MUSEUMS AND GALLERIES. Although Belize has no true museums or galleries, a visit to the *Archaeology Department*'s vault in Belmopan is a must for any archaeology buff. It is filled with many Mayan masterpieces found in Belize. The *Bliss Institute,* # 1 Southern Foreshore, 02–7267, also has shows of Belizean art of culture; check the newspaper. Open weekdays 8 A.M.–5 P.M. At other times for special events. The small gallery at *Admiral Burnaby's,* Regent St., displays the work of local artists.

SHOPPING. Although local crafts are very limited, some fine souvenirs can be purchased. Wood carvings, black coral and tortoiseshell jewelry, and straw hats and baskets can be purchased at the *National Crafts Center,* 13 Vernon St.; *Cottage Industries,* 26 Albert St.; the gift shops of the *Fort George, Bellevue,* and *Villa* hotels; and from the artists themselves on the streets.

Photographic equipment and supplies (selection is limited) is available at *Brodie's,* on Regent St.; *Rosales Ampli-Foto,* 42 Albert St.; *Venus Record and Photo Shop,* corner of Albert and Bishop sts.; and the hotel gift shops. Business hours in Belize are 8 A.M. to noon and 1 P.M. to 4 P.M. Some stores reopen 7 P.M. to 9 P.M.

ENTERTAINMENT. There are many bars in Belize City, but certain ones seem to attract a very specific crowd. The *Fort George* hotel lounge is the meeting place of businessmen and first-class travelers; the bar at the *Bellevue* often has the sailing crowd; the *Upstairs Cafe*, 5 Queen St., is for the backpack crowd; and the bar in the *Mopan Hotel* has a wonderful atmosphere and a proprietor who attracts the more serious traveler.

There are several good discotheques, but some are in rough neighborhoods. Of particular note is the *Pub*, 91 N. Front St.; the music is loud with American records, and the air-conditioning is full blast. *Mayan Lounge*, Bellevue Hotel, open on weekends, features live local music and a mature crowd.

SECURITY. Theft and street crime are a problem throughout Belize. Particularily in Belize City, visitors should take precautions with wallets, purses, and jewelry, and avoid unfamiliar neighborhoods after dark.

As in many Central American countries, illegal drugs are also a serious problem in Belize, and penalties for possession are very stiff. Be warned that officials have been known to make examples of tourists caught with even small quantities of cocaine or marijuana.

LEAVING BELIZE. Departure tax for leaving Belize International Airport is U.S.$13.

HONDURAS

by
JOHN CHATER

John Chater is coordinator of a rural development project for Partners of the Americas, Honduras/Vermont. He lives in Tegucigalpa.

From the friendly, tranquil people to the ever-present military, from the mountain ranges that cover 80 percent of the country to the flat coastal areas—it is evident that Honduras is a country of strong contrasts.

For centuries a backward country with dictators and revolutions, Honduras today has an elected government and is well on its way to becoming a democracy. For many years Honduras was one of the poorest countries in Central America, but that is also changing. Here you see less of the great difference between the wealthy and the poor that you see in much of Latin America. What you do see is a growing middle class modeling itself on the values of the United States and a people trying hard to overcome the many problems caused by a corrupt colonial heritage. Each of the countries that surrounds Honduras—El Salvador, Guatemala, and Nicaragua—has a higher percentage of poor people. In Honduras, the wealthy often come from relatively poor rural families *(campesinos)* and still have their roots in the small pueblos from which their forefathers came. As a result, there is a developing social consciousness and a concern about finding solutions to the many problems that plague this country.

One-third of the land in Honduras is made up of rich farmland having optimal climate and abundant water. Much of this land is located in the Mosquito region, the Aguán Valley, and the department of Olancho, where the population is sparse and where much of the farming is still done using primitive methods.

Traditionally Honduras has been an agricultural country dependent on one major export crop—bananas. Since 1976, when hurricane Fifi destroyed a substantial part of the large banana plantations on the north coast, there has been a major push to diversify export crops. In addition to bananas, Honduras today exports coffee, citrus, cotton, beef, minerals, wood (Honduran mahogany is famous the world over), and vegetables. This transition has not been easy for the Honduran farmer, who is not used to producing quality products for a specialized market. Many mistakes have been made, but the farmers are learning from these mistakes and are beginning to make an impact on both U.S. and European markets.

One symptom of the major growing pains Honduras is experiencing today is a fascination for goods and products made in other countries, notably the United States. The Honduran middle class is just beginning to realize that its own country can produce quality goods at very reasonable prices. Although there is a 35 percent unemployment rate, the country has a strong and willing labor force. There are tailors, shoemakers, seamstresses, cabinetmakers, and many different artisans. With a little patience, the tourist can seek out these artisans and buy handmade products for good prices.

History

On July 30, 1502, during his fourth and final voyage, Christopher Columbus landed on the island of Guanaja, one of the Bay Islands (Islas de la Bahía) off the Caribbean coast of Honduras. Then he sailed to the mainland, to the Río Tinto Negro, where he took possession of the territory of Honduras in the name of the Spanish kings. Sailing east to a village now called Punta Caxinas and then on to the open sea, he encountered a storm so violent that his crew thought it was the end of the earth. When the storm finally passed, they proclaimed, "Gracias a Dios" ("thanks be to God"), and left, heading southward. Today this department of Honduras is named Gracias a Dios.

The Spanish began their conquest of Honduras 20 years later. Honduras was made a part of the military regime of the kingdom of Guatemala. The early Spanish discovered a wealth of minerals and fertile farmland. They discovered over 400 mines and established haciendas throughout the country. For many years Honduras was perhaps the wealthiest country in Central America and exported 500,000 pesos worth of gold a year to Guatemala. In these times of prosperity it was said that the men of Olancho shod their horses with shoes of gold.

As the Spanish conquered the country, they enslaved the natives and made them work in the mines and on the large haciendas. The Indians (for the most part peaceful) offered little resistance to the Spanish. There was one notable exception. Chief Lempira (for whom the Honduran currency is named) valiantly withstood the Spanish until finally Alonso de Cáceres, a Spanish commander, called for a truce and agreed to ride out to meet Lempira in a gesture of peace. Behind the commander was another man who, when in range, killed Lempira, thus ending the resistance of the Indians.

In 1821 Central America declared independence for the region, and a brief period of anarchy followed. But on September 15, 1821, the Central American Congress convened. In 1823 the Second Act of Independence was drafted, and it was decided that the various provinces represented would be free and independent, joined in a federation known as the United Provinces of Central America. A popular federal government was formed. Before long, civil war broke out and General Francisco Morazán fought heroically to defend the fragile new democracy. Morazán soon became president of the United Provinces of Central America and was able to hold them together until 1839, when the federation was finally dissolved. Morazán was forced into exile in 1840. Honduras then became an independent republic and established its capital in Comayagua. To this day the Honduran flag displays the five stars of the Central American countries.

José Azcona del Hoyo was elected president of the Republic of Honduras in 1986 and is serving a four-year term. The government is divided into three branches, the legislative, which consists of a national congress made up of representatives from each of the 18 departments; the executive, made up of the president and his cabinet ministers; and the judicial, which is made up of the supreme court and magistrates elected by the national congress.

Geography

Getting around Honduras by car 15 years ago was almost impossible, but today, thanks to an aggressive road-building program, the tourist can see a substantial part of Honduras by car. Since it's a fairly small country, about the size of Pennsylvania, one can stay comfortably in either San Pedro Sula or Tegucigalpa and take side trips of from one to three days and see almost all of the country—the major exception being the Mosquitia, which is still only accessible by air or boat.

Honduras has an area of 42,000 square miles and a population of just over 4 million people. Nearly two-thirds of the country is extremely mountainous, rich in minerals and natural resources. The country was once almost totally covered with forests. Many of these forests have been cut down, resulting in serious erosion made worse each year by the burning of millions of acres of land to allow a farming tradition begun by the Indians and continued by the Spanish colonizers. About 80 percent of the population live in these mountainous regions and eke out their living by planting corn and beans. Although these *campesinos* still practice slash-and-burn agriculture, the Ministry of Natural Resources and private international voluntary organizations, such as the Partners of the Americas, have begun aggressive programs to promote sustainable agriculture. By the use of contour plowing, soil-building techniques, and crop rotation the farmers are able to increase their crop production and rebuild their soils.

The Culture

The Mayan culture dates back thousands of years when they established the great city of Copán. Today the visitor to Copán can see the observation tower where the Mayans practiced astronomy, the stelae (monoliths) carved to commemorate their leaders, and the court where they played ball. The Mayans had invented an almost-perfect calendar long before the birth of Christ and had discovered the concept of zero a thousand years before the Chinese had. The Maya civilization disappeared with very little traces around about A.D. 900, bringing to an end a culture and history that is only now being rediscovered. In 1979, UNESCO declared the ruins at Copán a part of the cultural heritage of mankind.

The visitor to Honduras can see many masterpieces on display in various churches. Among the most famous classical Honduran artists of the eighteenth century is José Miguel Gonzáles; his works can be seen at the cathedrals in Comayagua and Tegucigalpa.

Pablo Zelaya Sierra, Honduras's best-known contemporary painter, was born in Ojojona, where there is a museum dedicated to his life and work. José Antonio Velásquez, a world-renowned primitive painter, is noted for his village scenes in which he depicts life typical of rural Honduras.

EXPLORING HONDURAS

No matter how one gets to Honduras, the cities of Tegucigalpa and San Pedro Sula will dominate one's perspective. To understand the country fully, one must visit both of these cities. The contrasts between them are immense and again typify the contrasts that lie throughout the entire country. San Pedro Sula, the country's main industrial center, is often referred to as the industrial capital, while Tegucigalpa is the governmental capital. San Pedro is flat and spreads out along the fertile Sula Valley in the tropical lowlands of the north coast. On the other hand Tegucigalpa is built into the hills of the central highlands. The climate in Tegucigalpa is nearly perfect, with an average temperature of 75° to 85° F year-round, and nights that are cool. San Pedro is much hotter. Life in the governmental capital reflects the flavor of the old Spanish way of life, the flurry of activity seeming to center around getting through the various governmental agencies (which always takes an inordinate amount of time), while life in the industrial capital seems to revolve around the excitement of the business negotiation.

Tegucigalpa

Tegucigalpa got its name from two Indian words, *teguz* ("hill") and *galpa* ("silver"). For many years Tegucigalpa was just a small mining town. As its wealth increased, so did its importance. In 1880, Marco Aurelio Soto, president of Honduras, decided to move the capital from Comayagua to Tegucigalpa, because Comayagua had been ruined in the civil war of 1873. The history surrounding Tegucigalpa is alive with stories of mule trains loaded with gold and silver being brought down from the hills. The first hotel, the Gran Hotel Central, was built in 1880. This hotel had hammocks for the travelers, and on the patio was a sign that was reflective of the style of life at this time: "Don't lay on the hammocks with your spurs on." Horseback riding was in fact the most common mode of trans-

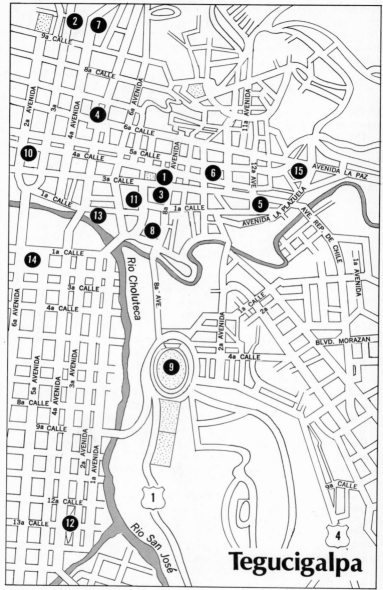

Tegucigalpa

Points of Interest

1) Cathedral
2) Shrine of Suyapa
3) City Hall (Palacio del Distrito Central)
4) Church Los Dolores
5) Church Menonita
6) Church San Francisco
7) Museum of History and Anthropology

8) National Congress Building
9) National Stadium
10) National Theater Manuel Bonilla
11) National University
12) Obelisk
13) Presidential Palace
14) San Isidro
15) San Miguel Market

portation, and travel developed directly from the horse to the car, because there has never been a railroad in the highlands of Honduras.

Tegucigalpa is part of the Distrito Central, which also includes Comayagüela, the city which lies just across the Choluteca River. Together these cities have a population of nearly 900,000, making this the largest metropolitan area in Honduras. Tegucigalpa retains the flavor of a small colonial city with its narrow, winding streets and brightly colored houses clustered in *barrios* built into the hillsides that surround the city. Around the center of the city lie many Spanish-colonial churches, government buildings, and schools.

The Plaza Morazán, commonly known as the Parque Central, is in the center of the Peatonal, a large mall closed to vehicle traffic. This is the hub of the old part of the city. Facing the park is the cathedral of San Miguel, constructed from 1756 to 1782 by Gregorio Nacianceno Quiroz. Its architecture is closely related to the Antiguan (Guatemalan) style of architecture, with a facade dominated by rusticated pilasters. It has seven niches with stucco images. The baptismal font was made by Indians in 1643 from a single block of stone. Also of great interest are the rococo gold pulpit, the handworked silver altar made by Vicente Gálvez, the cloisters, and the many pieces of colonial art. On the side portal that leads to the garden there is a bas-relief of Saint Joseph and Saint Anne with the Virgin resting on a flower that sprouts from their chests. There is a small museum in the cathedral.

Also within the center of the city is the church of San Francisco, four blocks east of Parque Central on Calle 4. The oldest church in Tegucigalpa, it was constructed by Franciscan friars in 1592 with donations from the wealthy miners. In 1740 it was rebuilt and transformed with Moorish characteristics.

The church of La Merced, one block south of Parque Central, faces the small Parque La Merced. Built in the late seventeenth century and restored in the late nineteenth century, this church is noted for its eighteenth-century baroque altarpieces, its rococo main altar from the school of Gálvez, and the collection of old paintings found in the sacristy.

The church of Los Dolores is three blocks west and two blocks north of Parque Central. The church, begun in 1732, features a baroque facade, gold altars, and fine paintings. The church of El Calvario, on Avenida 2 and Calle 5, was built in 1746, next to one of Tegucigalpa's finest cemeteries.

The National Palace (also known as Edificio de los Ministerios), between Calles 4 and 5 and Avenidas 3 and 4, was built as the convent of San Sebastián and remodeled in 1934 into offices for various governmental agencies.

The Presidential Palace is two blocks from the Parque Central on the banks of the river. This massive rose-colored fortress was built in a Moorish style. Up one block from the palace is the old university, built on Parque La Merced. Constructed in the mid-nineteenth century, this magnificent building is presently being renovated. Next door is the modern Congreso Nacional. Constructed on stilts, the building looks oddly out of place in this quaint older section of the city.

Teatro Manuel Bonilla—the National Theater—is located on Avenida 2 and Calle 4, close to the church of El Calvario. The theater was finished in 1912 after many years of construction.

Tegucigalpa has many interesting parks. Parque La Leona, for example, is a pleasant place to go and look out over the old section of the city. It is located on Calle La Leona, which winds up the mountainside to Barrio Leona, where there are many old houses worth seeing. Parque Picacho, on Calle Casamata about 1½ miles past the American ambassador's residence, offers an unprecedented view of the whole city: a particularly spectacular view at sunset.

About 4 miles out of town, just past the university, is the church of Suyapa, a large basilica still unfinished after 30 years of construction. Pilgrims are attracted from all over the country to worship here and to celebrate the Feast of the Virgin of Suyapa, the patron saint of Honduras. On the main altar is a tiny image—only a few inches tall—of the Virgin of Suyapa. This image is said to have miraculous powers. The annual *Feria de Suyapa* lasts eight days, beginning on February 3.

La Tigra

Just 12 miles from Tegucigalpa lies the mountain La Tigra and a 18,706-acre wildlife preserve. Because of the high altitude and humidity, a natural "cloud forest" covers the top of the mountain. This ecosystem is still in its pristine state. The dense trees, moss, ferns, and abundant wildlife make hiking and exploring here an incredible experience.

Valle de Angeles

Valle de Angeles is 15 miles from Tegucigalpa. Along the way, one can't help but marvel at the scenic mountains to the right. Here is a unique opportunity to see what the interior of Honduras really looks like, with *campesinos* cultivating almost all of the available mountainsides. During the dry-season these mountains are scarred by fires as the *campesinos* prepare their fields for cultivation using the traditional slash-and-burn technique.

Valle de Angeles has been set aside by the government of Honduras as a tourist zone, and thus many of the town's buildings have been restored to their original seventeenth-century state. You will enjoy walking through the village, stopping in the square, looking out over the mountainsides, and thinking about the Spanish miners transporting their gold and silver down from the mountains in long mule trains. There are many gift shops and handicraft studios, including those of the artisan training school located in Valle de Angeles, all worth visiting. Stop at one of the typical restaurants for a relaxing meal in this beautifully scenic village.

Santa Lucía

On the road back to town make sure to visit Santa Lucía. Nestled into the mountains, this old Spanish community is now the home of many people who work in Tegucigalpa but prefer to live in a rural community. Follow the cobblestone road down the hill to the old Spanish church, which is famous for its many religious paintings and the Christ of Las Mercedes, donated by King Philip II in 1572.

The fresh mountain air in Santa Lucía and the evening view of the lights of Tegucigalpa make a perfect ending to a day in Honduras.

Elsewhere Outside of Tegucigalpa

Francisco Morazán lived in Ojojona, an old Spanish mining town founded in 1579. The fine colonial church, El Calvario, has a painting of the crucifixion supposedly done by Murillo. Pablo Zelaya Sierra, one of Hondura's most famous contemporary painters, was born in Ojojona. The Ministry of Culture has turned his birthplace into a small museum located on the main square next to the church.

It was in San Antonio de Oriente that José Antonio Velásquez, Honduras's most famous primitive painter, got his inspiration. Many of his works are street scenes taken from this village and include paintings of the twin-towered church of San Antonio de Oriente perched on the mountainside, a black-robed priest, and a dog with his tail curling upward.

A 45-minute trip from Tegucigalpa on the road to Danlí takes you to the Pan American Agricultural School. Zamorano, as the school is called, provides students from all over Latin America with an excellent opportunity to learn about tropical agriculture. The expansive campus consists of beautifully arranged stone buildings, orchards of exotic species, ponds, and stables. You can even see a small herd of water buffalo that were brought to Honduras to determine their adaptability for use on small farms.

Located on the highway from Tegucigalpa to San Pedro Sula is the first capital of Honduras, Comayagua. It is the site of perhaps the most beautiful cathedral in the country. The city was founded in 1537 by Alonso de Cáceres, who was ordered by the Spanish governor of Honduras to build a city halfway between the Atlantic and the Pacific. He found the ideal location in this large fertile valley, which in the past few years has become one of Honduras's major bread baskets.

Still very colonial in nature, the town has low adobe and stucco houses with red-tile roofs, cobblestone streets, and colonial churches and plazas.

The cathedral, built from 1685 to 1715, was constructed by Indian workers, and their influence gives it a native touch. There are palm leaves on the first level of the facade, flowers and ears of corn sprouting from the plants that flank the door, and trees springing from the pilasters. Mystical Indian symbols can be found both inside and outside the building.

The crucifix in the cathedral was a gift from Philip IV, created by Cordoban sculptor Andrés Ocampo. The main altar was made in 1704, and the niches in 1639. The altar of Señor de Salame was made by Vicente Gálvez, who also made the main altar of the cathedral in Tegucigalpa.

The clock in the square tower, one of the oldest in the world, was constructed by the Moors for the palace of Alhambra in Seville, Spain, in the early twelfth century and was donated by Philip II. This clock still keeps time.

There are two museums in Comayagua: the Museum of Archeology and History and the Museum of Colonial and Religious Art. Both are well worth a visit.

Lake Yojoa, 2,000 feet above sea level and surrounded by beautiful mountains, is a favorite recreation spot for Hondurans, who come to enjoy fishing and water sports. The lake has very good bass fishing. Nearby is Pico Maroncho, a peak of over 9,000 feet, one of the highest in Honduras.

The area abounds with such wildlife as pumas, bears, jaguars, ocelots, and deer.

A lunch at one of the many little restaurants along the road beside the lake is always a treat. They all feature fresh fish, usually fried, served with french fries *(papas fritas),* and a small salad of tomatoes and cabbage or lettuce. One of the best of these little restaurants is the Black Bass, located on the west side of the road just as you begin to drive along the lake.

For a more leisurely lunch and a spectacular look at the lake, take the first left turn at the end of the lake (when coming from Tegucigalpa) to a resort called Motel Agua Azul. It is one of the most relaxing spots in all of Central America. You can dine overlooking the lake, swim in the cool water, or rent a boat to experience some excellent fishing.

Honduras's newest hydroelectric dam, and the highest dam in the Western Hemisphere, has created a new lake, Lake Cajón, that soon will be three times the size of Lake Yojoa. This new lake promises to become a sporting paradise and will be offering excellent boating, fishing, and sightseeing in some of Honduras's jungle.

Pulhapanzak

Farther on toward San Pedro Sula on the left is the turnoff for the Pulhapanzak waterfalls. The Río Lindo careens over a cliff and cascades more than 300 feet into a tropical jungle canyon. This site attracts many visitors who come to swim in the river, hike in the mountains, or see the nearby Maya ceremonial center. It is believed that this area is full of Mayan ruins which someday may be excavated.

San Pedro Sula

Founded in 1536 by Pedro de Alvarado, this city was little more than an agricultural town. Its importance increased with the development of the fruit companies, and recently San Pedro has mushroomed into the country's major industrial center. San Pedro Sula is the fastest-developing city in Central America. Located in the center of a vast fertile valley, which is almost all banana plantations, San Pedro Sula has become the commercial and distribution center for the entire area. Only 250 feet above sea level, it is extremely hot and humid with temperatures ranging from 80° to 100°F almost all year.

San Pedro is friendly and informal. There are a number of excellent restaurants and nightclubs, but not much else to see. The annual fair, *Semana Sampedrana,* brings a lot of excitement to San Pedro with beauty contests, horse races, art exhibits, song and dance contests, and an internationally famous cattle exposition. The fair takes place in the last week in June.

There is very little left in San Pedro of the old colonial city, although one can see an occasional building constructed about the turn of the century in the style of the early banana Republic. San Pedro serves as a good base from which to visit Copán, Fort Omoa, Puerto Cortés, Tela, La Ceiba, and the banana plantations.

Copán

A renewed effort is underway to rediscover the long-forgotten secrets of the Maya. During 1985 many of the stelae were cleaned and are now being protected from the elements, and many new excavated sections are being opened to the public. These efforts are being implemented by the government of Honduras under a program begun in 1979 by the Ministry of Culture and Tourism and the Honduras Institute of Anthropology and History.

Current thinking about the Mayan civilization is that there were four great regional centers: Tikal, Palenque to the west in Chiapas, Calakmul to the north in the Yucatán, and Copán to the south. Copán, in the opinions of many, is the most beautiful of all the Mayan cities. Situated on the banks of the Copán River, the city is 2,100 feet above sea level, resulting in warm tropical days, cool nights, and plenty of water year-round. Evidence indicates that the Maya first inhabited Copán 2,000 years before Christ. According to dates found on various monuments, the city reached its peak between A.D. 465 and 800. The rich soil of this area made it ideal for growing maize and the other staple crops necessary to sustain a great city.

By the end of the seventh century A.D. the astronomers of Copán had calculated the length of the tropical year, worked out accurate eclipse tables, meticulously timed the orbit of Venus, and devised a formula to correct the calendar which was much more accurate than ours today. Previously the Altar Q (letters refer to incomplete monuments, and numbers refer to those found broken) was believed to have been a "stone photo" of the Copán Academy of Sciences; however, it has been found that this statue represents the 16 kings of the Copán dynasty.

Several great explorers made expeditions to the ruins, including the Irishman John Gallagher (better known as Colonel Juan Galindo) in 1834. Then in 1839 the intrepid John Loyd Stevens, an explorer who was the U.S. ambassador to Central America, arrived with his associate, artist Frederick Catherwood. Stevens was so taken by the site that he bought it from a local farmer for $50 and later published the first detailed description of the city along with Catherwood's drawings in his book *Incidents of Travel in Central America: Chiagas and Yucatán*. This book is recommended to anyone interested in traveling in Central America. Other archaeologists soon followed: Englishman Alfred P. Maudsley made the first in-depth study of the ruins in 1881 and 1885, removing many of the sculptures to the British Museum. In 1891 the Peabody Museum made the first of four expeditions to Copán. The American Sylvanus G. Morley made his first trip in 1910 and soon became Copán's greatest student and admirer. In 1934 the Honduran government requested that the Carnegie Institute begin an extensive renovation of the ruins. Then 30 years ago the Honduran Institute of Anthropology and History took over supervision of the park. Excavation and restoration are still going on. In 1981 a group from Harvard uncovered some startling artifacts; one of them is said to be a Star of David or Solomon's seal. Although the main park covers only 70 acres, stelae and other artifacts have been restored and can be seen throughout the surrounding area.

Humo Jaguar, the twelfth king of Copán, built five stelae at different locations in the valley to mark out his domain. This king, who lived to be 82 years old, controlled an area of over 11 square miles. The five stelae have been restored and can be visited. Humo's son, Conejo, broke with Mayan tradition and did not destroy his father's monuments. He further broke with tradition when he changed the form of sculpture from bas-relief to an original form of high-relief done as figurative sculpture. These deeply carved stelae show realism and three dimensionality with complex ornamentation; they are distinctly different from the sculptures in other Mayan cities.

Copán's artists and architects used the nearby deposits of trachyte, a soft volcanic rock that they were able to carve using stone chisels. The Maya had no metal tools.

The Great Plaza

Entering the park from the western side, you first observe the Great Plaza, a wide grassy plain surrounded on three sides by tiers of stone. When built, this area was covered with painted stucco. The many stelae and altars were painted a variety of bright colors; it must have been an overwhelming sight for the crowds of Maya who flocked into the city for ceremonies.

A number of stelae (some of the most impressive Mayan sculptures in existence) are placed around this plaza. Most of these stelae show men, and in one case a woman, standing upright, facing frontward, with heels together and toes pointing outward; their arms are bent, and in the crooks of their arms they carry the ceremonial scepter, a stylized representation of a two-headed serpent, symbol of authority or power. On their heads are flamboyant plumed headdresses. Their waistbands, anklets, loincloths, sandals, earplugs, necklaces, and chest pendants are done in intricate and painstaking detail. The faces are sometimes grotesque, but often remarkably lifelike.

The Copán stelae were erected over pits in which offerings of jewelry, pottery, food, animals, and other objects were placed. The chamber under Stela A was left open. Among the hieroglyphs on this stela (dated A.D. 731) are several emblem glyphs—glyphs that represent a single city, in this case Tikal and Palenque—proving that Copán was in contact with these great cities. Nearby is an altar in the shape of a bundle tied with a cord. Perhaps this represents the bundles that the Maya traders transported over long distances to conduct trade throughout the Maya civilization.

Stela B (also A.D. 731) is something of an oddity, for this figure has a beard—very unusual for a Mayan. It is thought that this might be a result of foreign (maybe Mexican) influence. Over his head are curved shapes, initially thought to be elephant trunks but now believed to be the stylized beaks of macaws.

Stela C (A.D. 782) consists of two figures—one on each side—one with a beard and one without. It has been conjectured that this is the same person, portrayed on one side as a young man and on the other as an older man. This stela still shows traces of the original red paint. When John Stevens first saw these stelae over 100 years ago, he found many of them painted red and suggested it was this impermeable paint that had preserved the soft stones so well from the elements.

Stela D overlooks the entire plaza from the north end. The hieroglyphs on its back are significant because they record the day by using full-figure glyphs instead of the more common and simpler method of combining bars and dots. Here the figures—a toothless old man, a young man dancing with a toad, a young man with a monkey-faced arm, etc.—represent a total of 1,405,800 days. This is equal to the amount of time from the date the Maya used as point zero, August 10, 3114 B.C. The date of this stela is A.D. July 24, 736. This full-figure method of dating is rare, and the best examples are found here and at nearby Quiriguá.

Stela F is thought to represent a ballplayer; note his muscular legs and body padding. The elaborate feathered headdress is swept back and fastened with buttons in the back. Loops of rope hang down the back, encircling and framing the five blocks of glyphs.

Group G shows a two-headed serpent with humans emerging from its mouths, perhaps representing the birth of some great noble. Its date is A.D. 800, the last recorded period before the city was abandoned.

Stela H (A.D. 761) probably portrays a woman, though some archaeologists disagree; note the figure's skirt and womanly features. Throughout the history of the Maya there have been a number of powerful female rulers, and city-states often cemented relations by intermarriage between ruling dynasties. One explanation for this figure's unusual dress is that she was an outsider who married one of the rulers and then seized power after his death. Found under this stela were parts of a gold statue that came from distant Panama or Colombia.

The Central Court

This large grassy plaza separates the Great Plaza from the Ball Court and the Hieroglyphic Stairway. Here at the northeast corner stands Stela J (A.D. 702), covered with hieroglyphs. Note the basket-weave pattern on the back. This represents a woven-rush mat, a symbol of authority. The Mayan word for woven mat, *pop,* is also the word for throne, and the powerful first month of the Mayan 18-month year is named Pop. To date, archaeologists have only been able to decipher less than 20 percent of the total hieroglyphics. It's intriguing to scan these mysterious figures and think that they probably contain the answers to many of the most important questions about this enigmatic civilization, yet modern scholars are still unable to reveal their meanings.

The Ball Court

It was here that the Mayan athletes played before thousands of spectators. The object of the game seems to have been to bounce the ball up the slanted walls and hit one of the carved-stone goals at the top. As players were not allowed to use hands, arms, or feet and as the ball was large and made of solid rubber, the game must have been rough and demanding—something like a combination of football, soccer, and handball. There are scenes of ballplayers in action in the Copán Museum. This restored ball court is dated A.D. 775 and is built upon the remains of two former ball courts.

The Court of the Hieroglyphic Stairway

Located immediately south of the Ball Court, on its east side, the Hieroglyphic Stairway scales the tree-covered pyramid of Temple 26. It is 30 feet wide and 63 steps high. Each block is inscribed with a separate hieroglyph. King Ardilla, Conejo's successor, was responsible for designing this flight of stairs containing more than 1,250 hieroglyphic inscriptions. Dates inscribed on the stairway indicate that it was dedicated in A.D. 756. There are five great figures seated along the center of the stairway, which now contains a vacant space where a figure was removed and sent to Boston.

Nearby Stela N (A.D. 761) shows the influence of Conejo. The two figures on opposite sides of the stone round into one another. The deeply carved head with earplugs and the ceremonial bar are true sculptures, standing out from the background. The artists were no longer just carving on the stone but instead were making sculptures in which the physical nature of the stone disappears beneath the sculptural shape of the piece.

On the south side of the court are the remnants of a flight of steps that stretch the entire length of the court and lead up to the Temple of the Inscriptions, now shaded by a massive and lovely old ceiba tree. To the east of the temple at the top of the stairs, you will find the blank-eyed, snaggle-toothed, and wrinkled stone head of the Old Man of Copán. It is said that from time to time his frown turns to a smile.

The Western Court

The entire complex of interconnected structures and courts south of the Hieroglyphic Stairway has come to be known as the Acropolis. The Western Court is elevated 33 feet above the level of the Great Plaza. Between Temple 11 (Temple of Inscriptions) on the north side of the court and the floor of the court is what has come to be known as the Reviewing Stand, though this name is only speculation. A 50-foot-wide flight of steps decorated with giant conch shells leads down from the Reviewing Stand to the court. The steps are flanked by kneeling figures with human bodies and apelike faces with intertwining serpents. In front of the huge Temple 16 (the tallest pyramid at Copán), on the east side of the court, is the famous Altar Q showing the 16 kings of the Copán dynasty. To the south of the court is what appears to be a bandstand. It is a carved stone piece that some Hondurans insist is a sculpture of a marimba.

The Eastern Court

This rectangular plaza, 138 by 108 feet, is separated from the Western Court by the Jaguar Stairway, which is guarded by jaunty stone jaguars, each with one paw on hip and the other paw outstretched. Their black spots were once represented by round pieces of polished obsidian (you can see the indentations where the obsidian was placed). To the north and dominating the court is Temple 22 (Temple of Meditation), whose entrance is the gaping mouth of a two-headed serpent flanked by figures kneeling on skulls. Note the long-snouted sculptures of Chac, or Tlaloc ("he who makes the plants spring up"), the god of rain and fertility. The pervasive presence of this originally Mexican god at Copán is an indication that there was a strong influence from Teotihuacán. Temple 22 is one of the loveliest of all Mayan temples.

On this court's eastern perimeter you can stand atop a temple and look down to where the Copán River over the years has cut away a large section from the temple base, revealing older structures beneath it. To keep the Eastern Court from being further damaged, the river was diverted in 1935. To the south of the Eastern Court are the remains of various structures said to be the residential area for the Mayan nobility.

Recent research shows that in its last decades the city of Copán became more and more dependent on imported supplies and that the people in the surrounding towns were reluctant to continue supplying Copán. Thereafter the quality of life deteriorated to the point where the remaining residents left. It is hoped that, during the second phase of the current archaeological project, additional evidence will emerge to indicate more clearly the reasons for the abandonment of Copán.

The Town

Located a couple of miles from the ruins is the town of San José de Copán, known as Copán Ruinas or Copán. The Copán Museum is located at the head of the central square. The museum contains an excellent display of artifacts, including jade, polychrome ceramics, obsidian knives, and figurines of the Maya. There is a tomb depicting the traditional style of burial with treasure and food supplied for the life beyond.

There are a number of inexpensive hotels in Copán and, for those who wish to explore some of the outlying ruins, caves, or countryside, horses can be rented. Copán is about 2½ hours from San Pedro Sula on an excellent road.

La Lima

A few miles from San Pedro Sula lies the company town of the United Fruit Company. Once the banana capital of the world, La Lima is now a dusty remembrance of those bygone years. One can still see the well-laid-out wood houses constructed by the United Fruit Company for its managerial employees. There are also the beautifully manicured residences of the executives, an 18-hole golf course with huge palm and rubber trees, the research laboratory, the schools—one for the children of the workers and one for the children of management—and the hospital.

You can visit the banana plantations and see how the bananas are grown, harvested, and prepared for shipment all over the world.

The north coast provides a geographical contrast to the rest of Honduras. Along the 400-mile coast are stretches of beautiful beaches that provide relaxed, secluded swimming opportunities and excellent fishing. Natural ports dot this coastline.

Also along this coast are the vast plantations of the fruit companies where bananas, pineapples, and African palm trees dominate the landscape.

Puerto Cortés

This is the largest and most important port in Honduras and the most modern in all of Central America. The city of Puerto Cortés began its modern development because of the exportation of bananas, and life in this port city of 50,000 people revolves around the port. There is a new industrial free zone, where companies manufacture a variety of export products, from baseballs to luxury sailing yachts.

Puerto Cortés has the only containerized service in Honduras; they are able to receive huge container ships on which bananas and other agricultural products are exported. Most of the bananas are shipped by refrigerated truck and rail from the many plantations in the area and loaded directly onto the ships, where they remain under refrigeration all the way to the United States and Europe.

Just outside the city there are miles of white-sand beaches. The most popular beaches are Travesía, Colonia Vacacional, Rancho Mar, La Nasa, and others easily accessible by either bus or car. These beaches offer basic lodgings and are favorite weekend spots for Sanpedranos. Puerto Cortés has its annual fair featuring *Venice Night,* fireworks, gondolas, and dancing in the streets, during the third week in August. There are regularly scheduled buses between San Pedro Sula and Puerto Cortés.

Fortress of San Fernando de Omoa

This fortress is a short distance west of Puerto Cortés and an hour from San Pedro Sula along the coastal highway, which offers occasional glimpses of a very beautiful part of the Caribbean. The fortress of San Fernando de Omoa was built between 1759 and 1777. It was constructed under orders from the king of Spain to defend Caribbean ports from the frequent attacks by pirates. Thousands of lives (mainly blacks and Indians) were lost during the construction due to malaria, yellow fever, and other diseases that were rampant in the tropics. Material for the fort was brought from other Spanish forts as far away as the fortress of Santo Tomás de Castilla in Guatemala and from the island of Utila in the Bay Islands. The fortress withstood many attacks but was captured in 1779 by the British after a four-day battle. Its massive walls are still in very good condition, and the tourist is free to roam around exploring the many rooms of the fort as well as its cannons and piles of cannon balls.

Tela

Tela is a laid-back seaport town of 28,000 people, with narrow streets, dance halls, and some of the best white-sand beaches in Honduras. On the west side of town, across the bridge, lies the old seaport headquarters of the United Fruit Company. Many of the fine old homes in this compound have been turned into beach villas as part of the Telamar resort. There are shops, restaurants, a swimming pool, and private beach.

The Lancetilla Botanical Gardens, located just a little over 2 miles from Tela, feature trees and plants from all over the world. These gardens were begun by the United Fruit Company under the direction of Dr. Wilson Popenoe (the Popenoe House has become one of the landmarks in Antigua, Guatemala). When it appeared that disease would destroy the banana plantations, this project was initiated to experiment with new income-producing plants. Lancetilla is now a national park, and the visitor can spend as much time as she or he wants strolling through these magnificent gardens.

Also near Tela one can visit some interesting Garifuna villages. The Garifuna, descendants of slaves originally brought to the Caribbean from Africa, live in communities dotted along the coast. Today the Garifuna are famous for their traditional dances and excellent cooking. Coconut bread, *tapado de pescado* (a fish dish), and *sopa de caracol* are some of the dishes for which the Garifuna are famous. Also nearby are the beautiful beaches of La Ensenada, a former hideout for the English and Dutch pirates who constantly harassed the north coast.

There is regular bus service to Tela from San Pedro Sula, a trip that takes about two hours. When traveling by car, be careful not to miss the sign indicating the turnoff to Tela.

La Ceiba

This is the corporate headquarters for the banana and pineapple production of Standard Brands (now Castle and Cooke). La Ceiba is a city of 63,000 inhabitants and has the reputation for being a very lively, fun-loving city. There is a country club, built by Standard Brands, with a golf course and tennis courts.

Trujillo

Founded in 1524 by Francisco de las Casas, Trujillo is one of the oldest cities in Central America. Christopher Columbus and his crew celebrated the first mass on the American mainland near here. It was from the port of Trujillo that the gold from Olancho was shipped by the Spanish and, as a consequence, Trujillo was subject to frequent attacks by pirates. Three forts were constructed in Trujillo to defend against these attacks—San José, San Hipólito, and La Concepción. The remains of these forts can still be seen. In 1860 the infamous soldier of fortune William Walker was captured and executed near here, and his graves (there are two) are in the local cemetery.

The city, which still retains its colonial appearance, is surrounded by thick jungle, mountains, lagoons, and rivers. The hunting is excellent, as is the fishing. In nearby Calentura Mountain is the Cuyamel Cave, apparently used for thousands of years as a place of rituals and worship. It has been called the most important find of ancient ceramics in Mesoamerica, with pieces from periods ranging over millennia being discovered at various levels of the cave. There is also a very interesting museum in Trujillo.

Trujillo is located above a beautiful bay that is still unspoiled by large tourist developments and is therefore an excellent place for those who want to enjoy the tranquil beauty of this part of the Caribbean. On the road from La Ceiba there is a spectacular waterfall at Balfate; the water cascades over 200 feet into the river below, forming a small lagoon.

The road from La Ceiba to Trujillo is an improved gravel road, and it takes about four hours to make the trip. Work has begun on paving this road and it should be completed by late 1989. In the meantime the easiest way to get to Trujillo is to fly from La Ceiba, San Pedro Sula, or Tegucigalpa.

Bay Islands

Christopher Columbus landed on Guanaja on July 30, 1502, during his fourth and last voyage to the New World. The Spanish soon claimed that the inhabitants of the islands were cannibals, and sent them as slaves to work in the mines of Mexico and on the plantations in Cuba. These islands didn't remain deserted for long, and such notable pirates as Henry Morgan built permanent bases in Port Royal, Coxen Hole, and French Harbor.

Roatán, Guanaja, Utila, and the many smaller cays of the Bay Islands (Islas de la Bahía) provided the English and Dutch pirates with secure ports from which to launch their attacks on the Spanish. The Spanish merchant ships, filled with riches from the new world, were often overloaded and not very seaworthy; therefore they were excellent prey for the pirates, who had light, fast craft.

For 300 years these islands were frequently raided by the slave traders. The islands were depopulated at least three times by the Spanish. In the latter part of the eighteenth century the island's permanent settlers arrived. In the late nineteenth century and until 1920 the Bay Islands were major exporters of bananas and other fruit to the United States. Many trading companies were established, and they developed trading relationships directly with the U.S. and Europe. One can still see the remnants of the buildings constructed during this period, especially on Utila. As the Honduran government began to exert its control on the islands, it pressured the islanders to trade more with the mainland. At the same time trade with the U.S. began to wane to the point where today there is virtually no fruit production on the islands.

Today the islanders are mostly fishermen and merchant seamen working on U.S. merchant fleets or offshore oil rigs and returning to their families only after long periods of time at sea.

Visitors can easily imagine the rich history of these islands as they wander around or snorkel or dive in the crystal-clear waters. The reefs around the islands are alive with many varieties of fish, coral, and other sea life and offer unparalleled opportunities for both the novice and the experienced diver. The thought of discovering a sunken ship or buried treasure adds to the excitement.

Today the islands retain much of their English flavor. The people speak English and prefer to think of themselves as English or American rather than Honduran.

Roatán

The largest of the Bay Islands is a little less than 50 square miles in area. Roatán, with its substantial fishing fleet and shrimp-packing facilities, is by far the most popular of the islands. There is a road that connects the more than 20 communities. The airport has recently been enlarged and now has a blacktop runway. The capital of the island is the town of Roatán (Coxen Hole), which has a movie theater, travel agencies, boarding houses, and a few restaurants. French Harbor, along the south side of the island, has a large port with shrimp-packing facilities and the best restaurants on the island. Oak Ridge is another fishing town with excellent port facilities. Punta Gorda, a Garifuna town, lies directly across the island. The town of West End is a small settlement with some basic accommodations and excellent beaches, often quite deserted.

The islanders like to live near the water, and consequently most of the villages are on the water's edge. However, in the past few years many Americans have begun to settle here and have constructed substantial houses throughout the island, including parts of the interior.

Private taxis are very expensive. Often the same vehicle, when on its regular route serving as a bus, is much cheaper. There are diving resorts all around Roatán and a barrier reef that surrounds the island. The snorkeling and diving are excellent.

Utila

Once the site of some of the first banana and tropical fruit plantations, Utila is today a sleepy little island surrounded by beautiful beaches and spectacular underwater vistas. The main town is East Harbor, but there are also settlements on Pigeon Cay and Suc-Suc Cay and at West End. Accommodations here are very limited.

Guanaja

The easternmost of the Bay Islands, Guanaja, is smaller than Roatán, measuring slightly more than 21 square miles. The island's major town is Bonacca, built on what was originally two small cays about 500 yards from the mainland. Over the years the residents of Bonacca, who originally built their homes on stilts to get away from the sandflies, have been filling in the bay and creating one large island. Now with a population of over 2,000, the town has a series of canals, floating walkways, and houseboats that make it unique.

There are a few hotels in Bonacca, but the major resorts are on the island mainland. There are no roads on the island, so the tourist must travel by boat to get to the resorts. One will find that the resorts are well run, and although the focus is on diving, there are also many activities for the non-diver. The terrain offers a great opportunity for hiking and horseback riding. There are pine-covered mountains, waterfalls, beautiful beaches, and numerous reefs. It is claimed that Guanaja is the most beautiful of the islands.

The Mosquito Coast and Eastern Honduras

The Mosquito Coast (La Mosquitia) is located in the northeastern part of the country in the department of Gracias a Dios. It is mostly rugged jungle and is part of the least-known and least-explored section of Central America. This area still offers excitement and challenge to the adventurous explorer. Gold mining and gem hunting are among the interests here.

The Mosquito Coast of Honduras has numerous small fishing villages mostly inhabited by Black Caribs who are descendants of the Mosquito Indians and loggers. Because these Indians traditionally hated the Spanish, the English were able to move into this area in the early seventeenth century, setting up the kingdom of Mosquitia and using this as a mainland base from which to attack the Spanish. It wasn't until 1895, due to confrontations with the U.S., that England was forced to return this land to Spain. (*The Mosquito Coast,* the best-selling book by Paul Theroux, tells a fascinating story about the somewhat crazy adventures of a family that moves to the Mosquitia.)

The South Coast

This area located in the departments of Choluteca and Valle is hot and dry for most of the year. There are occasional torrential rains during the rainy season from May to November. This area is characterized by steep, severe mountain ranges tumbling down onto *sabanas* (flat pasture lands), and then onto the Gulf of Fonseca. The Gulf of Fonseca has a coastline of 60 miles and is bordered by El Salvador and Nicaragua.

The city of Choluteca is dry and hot. Choluteca is famous for its white doves, called *zanates,* and every evening the *zanates* roost in the trees along the city streets with much ceremony and noise. Their nesting habits are so precise at night that the people of Choluteca are able to set their watches by them. Choluteca is a cattle town and is surrounded by many cattle farms. These farms range from the most basic traditional agricultural systems to some very modern operations complete with milking parlors and sophisticated milking equipment. There are a couple of good hotels in Choluteca.

Amapala

The most famous place in the Gulf of Fonseca is the island of El Tigre, with its old part of Amapala. Amapala was once the major Pacific seaport for Honduras. With its natural deep-water channel, ships would moor off Amapala, where they were off-loaded by litners (small dugout boats) that transferred the cargo to the mainland. A few years ago the government of Honduras constructed a new port at San Lorenzo, leaving Amapala and virtually all of El Tigre abandoned. Well worth the visit because of its beautiful setting in the Pacific, a trip to Amapala has to be made by small boat; accommodations on the island are very primitive.

PRACTICAL INFORMATION FOR HONDURAS

Don't hesitate to inquire locally when questions arise; Hondurans are usually quite willing to help tourists.

WHEN TO GO. The weather in Honduras is pleasant throughout the year: it is typically sunny and warm. During the rainy season (May through Nov.) there are occasional rains, usually in the afternoon for an hour or so. The temperature in Tegucigalpa and the other highland areas averages 75° F year-round. It gets cool in the evenings. In San Pedro Sula and along the coastal areas it is hot and often humid, although it cools off a little in the evenings. The Bay Islands are hot, but are cooled by sea breezes.

Late Jan. and Feb. are the coolest months, while Mar. and Apr. are the hottest. During Easter *(Semana Santa)* it is customary for everyone to go to the beach, and seaside hotels are usually filled. The beaches are beautiful all year long and are often deserted.

Each town has its fiesta—a colorful fair, with feasts and celebrations—often lasting a full week. The tourist office (see below) has a festival calendar. The 2 largest and most popular of these fairs are the *Feria San Isidro* in La Ceiba during the third week of May and the *Feria Sanpedrana* in San Pedro Sula during late June.

HOW TO GET THERE. By car. A few years ago there was a steady stream of overland traffic through Honduras—mostly Americans on their way to Costa Rica or farther south via the Pan-American Highway. This stream of traffic has completely dried up, because of the problems in El Salvador and Nicaragua. For those who are contemplating driving, Honduras is a day's drive from Guatemala City. One route passes through El Florida. There is a short section of dirt road, but the border crossing is easier. This is the shortest route for those wishing to visit Copán. The other route is Aguas Calientes, near Nueva Ocotepeque. The border hours are 8 A.M. to 12 P.M. and 2 P.M. to 5 P.M. Those wishing to cross at other times have to pay extra. For those interested in driving, it is suggested that you consult the Mexican and Guatemalan tourist authorities before entering those countries.

By plane. Travel by air from Miami, New Orleans, or Houston is the most popular way to reach Honduras. *Tan–Sahsa,* the old standby, has daily flights from Miami and flights every other day from New Orleans and Houston. *Taca Airlines* also has regular service from Miami.

Airlines service Honduras's major airports at San Pedro Sula and Tegucigalpa. Flights to San Pedro Sula connect with flights to La Ceiba and to the Bay Islands. The airlines use 737s because the Tegucigalpa airport is too small to accommodate anything larger. Don't be surprised if your luggage arrives a day late. Often, especially during busy seasons of Christmas, Easter, mid-Feb., June, and Sept., the planes are very crowded and the airlines (especially Tan–Sahsa) send luggage the next day. A good piece of advice is to take a carryon bag with enough clothes for a couple of days. If you are a nonsmoker, beware. Tan–Sahsa permits smoking on board in all sections.

By bus. The *Ticabus* line did connect Tegucigalpa with Guatemala. Presently this service is reported suspended, but you can check this. Its offices are at Av. 2 Calles 6 and 7, Comayagnela. Bus transportation is available through Honduras to Nicaragua. You travel to San Marcos de Colon on the bus line *Mi Esperanza,* and can stay in a good hotel called Hotel Colonial. At the hotel you can arrange for a car to take you to the border and on into Nicaragua.

TRAVEL DOCUMENTS. To enter Honduras you need a valid passport and a round-trip airline ticket. You can obtain a visa at a Honduran consulate free of charge, or you can buy one at the customs station as you enter the country for a fee of U.S.$2. When you leave the country, there is an airport tax of L20.

Your visa is usually valid for 90 days and can be renewed at the offices of the Dirección General de Migración in Tegucigalpa, La Ceiba, San Pedro Sula, Santa Rosa de Copán, Siguatepeque, La Paz, and Comayagua. Once in the country, you should always keep your passport and travel documents with you.

HEALTH. Check with your own doctor regarding health precautions. Although no vaccinations are required, there is malaria in the coastal areas of Honduras, and, as with any third world country, dysentery is a problem; one has to be careful about food and water.

CURRENCY. The Honduran monetary unit is the lempira (L). The legal value at press time is L2 = U.S.$1. Often money is changed on the black market at higher rates; however, this practice perpetuates dollar flight, and the Honduran government is trying to keep its capital in the country where it can be put to work developing Honduras.

Honduran money comes in 1, 2, 5, 10, 20, 50, and 100 lempira bills. Wire transfers of money from other countries are relatively easy, but the Honduran bank handling the transfer will release the money only in lempiras.

Visa, American Express, and other credit cards are accepted in Honduras. But make sure to ask before you make your purchase.

ELECTRICITY. Be careful. Although most hotels use 110 volts AC, many wall outlets are 220 volts and often not marked. So before plugging in, check to make sure it's the same voltage as your appliance.

TELEPHONES. The country code for Honduras is 504. Hondutel (the national telephone company) uses six-digit telephone numbers.

ENGLISH-LANGUAGE PUBLICATIONS AND BOOKSTORES. There are no English-language papers printed in Honduras; however, one can buy the *Miami Herald* and occasionally *The New York Times* at major hotels and English-language bookstores. In Tegucigalpa there are the following English-language bookstores: *The Book Store* at Edificio Midence Soto in the center of the city, and *The Book Village* in Los Castanos shopping center on Blvd. Morazán.

USEFUL ADDRESSES. *American Express:* Transmundo Edificio Palmira in front of the Hotel Maya, Tegucigalpa. *Great Britain Consulate:* Colonia Palmira, Edificio Palao; 32–5480 or 5429. *United States Consulate:* Av. La Paz; 32–3120 or 3129.

Honduras Tourist Bureau: Box 154-C, Tegucigalpa, Honduras. The Tourist Bureau is very helpful and will give you listings of hotels, restaurants, and other touring information. Their main office is located downtown right next to the Congreso Nacional building. There are branches at each airport. There is also a branch located in San Pedro Sula on Calle 4, Av. 2 Suroeste, about 3 blocks behind the Gran Hotel Sula.

ACCOMMODATIONS. Rates are for double rooms: *Deluxe,* U.S.$75 and up; *Expensive,* U.S.$40–$60; *Moderate,* U.S.$25–$50; *Inexpensive,* under U.S.$20.

Choluteca

Hotel Camino Real. *Moderate.* Carretera a Guasaule; 82–0630. A hotel with 21 rooms, air-conditioning, telephones in the rooms, good restaurant, and bar. This hotel is located a few miles south of town on the Pan-American Highway.

Hotel La Fuente. *Moderate.* Barrio Los Mangos; 82–0263. This hotel has 41 rooms, a restaurant, bar, swimming pool, air-conditioning, and telephones in the rooms.

Hotel Pierre. *Inexpensive.* Av. Valle and Calle Williams; 82–0676. Located in downtown Choluteca, this hotel offers air-conditioning, restaurant, and parking.

Copán

Brisas de Copán. *Inexpensive.* Barrio El Centro. 7 rooms, parking, laundry, and fans.

Hospedaje Los Gemelos. *Inexpensive.* Barrio El Centro. 13 rooms.

Marina. *Inexpensive.* Barrio El Centro. 12 rooms, parking, restaurant.

San Pedro Sula

Hotel Copantl Sula. *Deluxe.* Carretera Salida a Chamelecón; on main highway from Tegucigalpa to Puerto Cortés; 53–2108, 53–4050. There are 205 rooms. The Copantl is the best hotel in San Pedro—in fact, the most luxurious hotel in Honduras. This new hotel-resort complex features spacious rooms, an excellent restaurant, large swimming pool, tennis and handball courts, bar, gym, and sauna.

Gran Hotel Sula. *Expensive.* Calle 1, Av. 3 and 4, next to park in downtown San Pedro; 52–9999; Telex: 5517. This excellent hotel has 125 rooms (many overlooking the Parque Central), suites, and poolside bedroom cabanas. In addition to a pool, the Gran Hotel Sula has the most popular coffee shop-cafeteria in town, plus a restaurant and a bar—the works. This is a popular place to meet, do business, and arrange a special tour.

Hotel Bolívar. *Moderate.* Calle 2 and Av. 2 Noroeste No.8; 53–3218, 53–1811. Constructed many years ago as San Pedro Sula's first luxury hotel, the building was constructed in the old Spanish-colonial style and retains this flavor. There are 70 rooms, and services include parking, restaurant, telephones in the rooms, swimming pool, conference room, and shops. Hotel Bolívar is located 2 blocks from the main plaza.

Hotel Colombia. *Moderate.* Av. 5 and 6, Calle 3 Surveste; 53–3118. This hotel has 25 rooms, air-conditioning, telephones in rooms, bar, and restaurant.

Hotel Los Andes. *Moderate.* Av. Circunvalcion No.84; 53–2526 or 4425. This excellent hotel has 40 air-conditioned suites, a bar, and a restaurant.

Hotel Palmira No. 1. *Moderate.* Calle 6, Av. 6 and 7 No.32; 54–3674. 25 rooms with parking, restaurant, and air-conditioning.

Hotel España. *Inexpensive.* Av. 3, Calle 13 Suroeste. This hotel has 19 rooms, a terrace, and fans.

Tegucigalpa

Hotel Honduras Maya. *Deluxe.* Colonia Palmira; 32–3191 or 3195. This hotel is one of the finest in the country and features 186 well-furnished rooms and suites. In addition, there are cocktail lounges, a large swimming pool, a sauna, and health spa. The restaurant and steak house are excellent, as is the shopping arcade. Gambling facilities are in the *Casino Royale.* The Maya is nicely situated near the city center and some of Tegucigalpa's best restaurants. There are many shops within easy walking distance.

Hotel Alameda. *Expensive.* Blvd. Suyapa, Box 940; 32–6920 or 6902. This new hotel has 75 rooms, nicely furnished in a Spanish-colonial style. There are shops, an excellent swimming pool, sauna, and gourmet restaurant (featuring international cuisine). This hotel is about 10 minutes from the center of the city. The lovely old-style setting makes this a relaxed, comfortable place to stay.

Hotel Plaza. *Expensive.* Located on Calle Peatonal, the downtown mall; 22–2111 or 6110. This renovated hotel has 83 rooms, a restaurant, sauna, and bar–disco. There is everything but a pool.

Hotel La Ronda. *Expensive.* Av. Jerez No.1104, Barrio La Ronda; 22–8151 or 8154. Located about 4 blocks from the central square, this hotel has 75 beds. There are also suites and apartments with kitchenettes available. There is a restaurant and bar with nightclub and dancing.

Hotel Istmania. *Moderate.* Av. 5, Calles 7 and 8; 22–1638. This hotel has 34 rooms. There is a bar and restaurant. The Istmania is located near the central part of the city.

Hotel Excelsior. *Inexpensive.* Av. Cervantes No.1407, 1 block from Hotel Honduras Maya; 22–2638. This is a very clean, quiet hotel, and the owner works hard to keep it that way. Services include restaurant, terrace, and conference room.

Hotel Granada. *Inexpensive.* Av. Guttenburg No.1401, Barrio Guana-caste; 22–2381. This hotel has 45 rooms and is a favorite hotel of the Peace Corp volunteers.

Hotel McArthur II. *Inexpensive.* Calle 8, Av. 4 and 5 No.454; 22–5906. This is an excellent hotel for a modest price. Services include parking, restaurant, bar, TV in room, laundry, air-conditioning. Credit cards are accepted.

BAY ISLANDS

Guanaja

Bayman Bay Club. *Deluxe.* Located on the island's north side, which is virtually uninhabited, this beautiful, secluded resort offers excellent accommodations, taxi service to and from the airport, and snorkeling and diving. There are 7 guest cottages—simple yet elegant—overlooking the tropical bay of this island paradise.

Posada Del Sol. *Deluxe.* Located on the south side of the island, this beautiful resort includes private beach, tennis courts, swimming pool, diving facilities, snorkeling, sailing, and fishing.

Inexpensive hotels on Guanajá include: **Hotel Miller, Boatel Playa,** and the **Holly Carter.**

Roatán

Although there is limited telephone service on the island, all the resorts mentioned can be contacted by mail for reservations. Accommodations are usually no problem except during the height of the winter vacation season.

Anthony's Key Resort. *Deluxe.* Sandy Bay; 32–5555 or (in U.S.) 612–546–8461. Recently renovated and enlarged to become the island's most prestigious resort, this resort is attractively laid out, featuring rustic cabins on the key, excellent diving facilities, and leisurely dining in small dining rooms overlooking the bay. Sailing, fishing, tennis, and moonlit beaches are all part of this tropical paradise.

Pirate's Den. *Deluxe.* Sandy Bay; cable Pirate's Den. This resort is located on a bluff overlooking the sea and has 34 rooms. Basic but comfortable, Pirate's Den offers a full range of services with an emphasis on diving.

Roatán Lodge. *Expensive.* Port Royal; 42–0302. This small (5-room), attractive resort overlooks Port Royal Harbor, where many famous pirates hid out after their attacks on the Spanish ships. Diving, snorkeling, sailing, swimming, and fishing.

Coco View. *Moderate–Expensive.* French Cay. This newly completed resort offers the best in diving and snorkeling. Coco View has gone out of its way to provide safe yet exciting opportunities for divers of all levels. A great place to go with either your family or your diving club.

Buccaneer Inn. *Moderate.* French Harbor. This motel-style resort has 5 ample rooms overlooking the bay. Each room is named for a famous pirate. There is an excellent restaurant, and the staff bends over backward to accommodate your swimming, sailing, fishing, and diving needs.

Utila

Utila, primitive in many respects, is a small island inhabited by the families of sailors and fishermen. There are 1 or 2 restaurants, a few bars, and some of the most incredible diving. Bring your own snorkeling or scuba gear. A dive master by the name of Gunther will rent you tanks, take you diving, and, when you are finished, sell you some very nice jewelry. For the adventuresome diver Utila is a real experience.

Sonny's Villa. *Inexpensive.* There are 6 basic rooms with baths and a "sometimes restaurant." Sunny's is a half-mile walk to some excellent snorkeling.

Trudy's. *Inexpensive.* Family-style hotel with 20 rooms and meals.

Lake Yojoa

Motel Agua Azul. *Moderate.* Agua Azul Sierra, Santa Cruz de Yojoa; 53–4750. This is perhaps the most tranquil resort in Honduras, overlooking the lake. One can sit on a large rambling veranda, relax, and take in an incredible view while enjoying an excellent fish dinner. This resort is the center of the country's famous large-mouth bass fishing.

Los Remos. *Moderate.* Located on the south end of the lake along the highway. Los Remos has 19 rooms and an open-air restaurant on a terrace overlooking the lake.

The North Coast

Tela

Hotel Telamar. *Expensive.* Box 47, Tela Nueva; 48–2196 or 2197. This resort, located in the old compound of the United Fruit Company, is managed by the Tourist Bureau. Located on the north coast's best beach, the resort comprises spacious villas, with fully equipped kitchens, and a small hotel, totaling 174 rooms in all. There are tennis courts, a pool, golf course, horseback riding, and a sauna. This resort is the favorite of Honduran families during Easter and is an excellent vacation spot year-round.

Hotel Tela. *Inexpensive.* Tela Vieja, Calle El Comercio; 48–2150. Parking, restaurant, and fans.

La Ceiba

Gran Hotel Paris. *Expensive.* Calle 8, Av. San Isidro and República; 42–2371 or 2391. This grand old hotel is the favorite of American adventurers, businesspeople, and tourists. There is always an interesting conversation around the bar as gold miners, cowboys, and scuba divers tell their tales. Services include air-conditioning, a pool, restaurant, golf, casino, and shops.

CAMPING. There are no campgrounds as such in Honduras; however, one can camp almost anywhere with the owner's permission. The beaches along the Caribbean, the river bank near the Copán ruins, the wildlands at Lake Yojoa, and the Bay Islands—all offer excellent camping opportunities.

There are 2 or 3 locations with facilities for RVs: *Parque Aurora* is one, and another is on the Pan American Highway just outside of Choluteca.

RESTAURANTS. Price categories are as follows: *Expensive,* $8–$15; *Moderate,* $4–$8; *Inexpensive,* under $4.

San Pedro Sula

La Carreta. *Expensive.* Av. Circunvalación, Calle Principal; 53–0789. Excellent restaurant.

La Fonda del Recuerdo. *Expensive.* Av. 6 Surveste.

Pat's Steak House. *Expensive.* Av. Circunvalación 5C. Excellent steaks and seafood. Probably the best restaurant in town.

Bolívar. *Moderate.* At Hotel Bolívar; 54–3224 or 3218 or 1811. Serves good international dishes in a quiet colonial atmosphere.

Don Udo's. *Moderate.* Av. Circunvalación, Hotel Andes; 53–4425 or 53–2526.

Granada. *Moderate.* Gran Hotel Sula; 52–9999 or 9992. The luncheon buffet is very popular; in the evenings there is music and dancing. Excellent.

La Gourmet. *Moderate.* Hotel Copantl Sula; 52–3066. International cuisine in an elegant setting. Recommended.

El Paso. *Moderate.* Ed. Farmacia Sula; 53–2116. Well-prepared dishes served in pleasant surroundings. Specializes in seafood.

Tegucigalpa

Chinatown Restaurant. *Expensive.* Blvd. Francisco Morazán. Excellent Chinese cusine.

Daymyo. *Expensive.* Blvd. Morazán. New Japanese restaurant.

Don Quijote. *Expensive.* Barrio Guanacaste, near Hotel Granada; 22–0070. Excellent Spanish-style paella.

El Arriero. *Expensive.* Av. República de Chile, Colonia Palmira. Excellent new restaurant specializing in beef.

El Novillo. *Expensive.* Av. 3, Calle 3, Colonia Alameda; 32–1128. Featuring Nicaraguan hospitality.

Estro Armónico. *Expensive.* Colonia Reforma, near bridge. The best restaurant in town. Cuisine made to order by chef Jean Louis and served in an atmosphere of classical music.

Gauchos. *Expensive.* Av. La Paz, in front of cinemas Alpha and Omega; 32–3682. Famous for its beef.

Hungry Fisherman. *Expensive.* Av. República de Chile No.401, Colonia Palmira; 32–6893. Excellent fish.

Kloster. *Expensive.* Blvd. Morazán; 32–7676. The most popular bar in town. The restaurant features well-prepared German food.

Pekin. *Expensive.* Calle 3, Av. República de Chile, Barrio San Rafael; 32–4586. Chinese cuisine.

Roma. *Expensive.* Av. República de Chile, Colonia Palmira. Italian.

Bungalow. *Moderate.* Blvd. Morazán. Typical Honduran food in a lovely open-air setting.

Cafe Allegro. *Moderate.* Av. Repúblic de Chile, 360B Colonia Palmira; 32–8122.

China Palace. *Moderate.* Calle 4, Av. Los Horcones; 22–1118. Good, basic Chinese food.

El Patio. *Moderate.* Calle 4, Av. 6; 22–1515. A favorite restaurant featuring *pinchos.*

Jack's Place. *Inexpensive.* Blvd. Morazán. Excellent sandwhiches.

Tito's. *Inexpensive.* Calle 5, Callejón Los Dolores; 22–3315. Good Italian pizza.

Tito's 2. *Inexpensive.* Blvd. Morazán.

Bay Islands

Roatán

Buccaneer Restaurant. *Expensive.* French Harbor. Excellent food served on a beautiful veranda.

Romeo's Restaurant. *Expensive.* French Harbor. Excellent food served overlooking the harbor.

Tela

Restaurante Cesar. *Expensive.* Right on the beach. Telamar, Tela Nueva; 48–2196. Typical Honduran cuisine.

Playa. *Moderate.* On beach; 48–2335. Good basic Honduran food. Inexpensive.

Marabu. *Expensive.* On the road to Telamar. Excellent seafood.

Lake Yojoa

Motel Agua Azul. *Expensive.* Take the turnoff to Pena Blanca and follow the signs to Motel Agua Azul; 53–4750. One of the best; excellent food in a peaceful setting overlooking Lake Yojoa.

La Ceiba

Recommended restaurants in the area include: **Chavelita's Restaurant** and **Seaview Restaurant.**

HOW TO GET AROUND. By air. *Sahsa, Aero Services,* and *Lansa* connect San Pedro Sula, Tegucigalpa, La Ceiba, and Bay Islands.

By car: Honduras has an aggressive road-construction program under way, and the tourist can now travel to all the major areas of Honduras on hard-surface all-weather roads. There are also many good secondary roads, but the tourist should seek local information before using them. The only section of the country not accessible by road is the Mosquito region. The only way to get there is to fly.

CAR RENTAL

All the car rental companies have booths at the airport. When you rent a car, make sure the car's registration is current and that the documents are in a safe place in the car. It is illegal to take Honduran rental cars out of the country. The car rental agencies are:

Budget Rent-A-Car–Tegucigalpa, Aeropuerto Toncontin, tel. 33–5170 or 5161, and Hotel Honduras Maya, 32–6832. In San Pedro Sula, Aeropuerto Villeda Morales, 52–2295, and Gran Hotel Sula, 53–3411.

Maya Rent-A-Car–San Pedro Sula, Av. 3 Noroeste, Calle 7 and 8 No.51, 52–2670. They also have an office in La Ceiba.

Molinari Rent-A-Car–Tegucigalpa, Hotel Honduras Maya, 32–8691, and Aeropuerto, 33–1307. In San Pedro Sula, Hotel Sula, 54–2639, and Aeropuerto, 56–2580. In La Ceiba, Hotel Paris, 42–0055.

National Car Rental–Tegucigalpa, Barrio La Granja, 33–2653; Hotel Honduras Maya, 32–3191; Aeropuerto, 33–4962). In San Pedro Sula, Hotel Copantl Sula, 52–6145.

Taxis are available on a flat-rate basis.

By bus: Tegucigalpa–San Pedro Sula buses are regularly scheduled throughout the day and night. The following bus companies provide this service: *El Rey* and *San Cristóbal* buses—Calle 9, Av. 5, Comayagüela, and Av. 7 Suroeste, Calles 5 and 6, San Pedro Sula; *Hedman y Alas*—Calles 13 and 14, Av. 11, Comayagüela, and Av. 4, Calle 9, Comayagüela; *Sáenz*—Calle 5, Av. 4 and 5, Tegucigalpa, and Av. 7 Suroeste, Calles 5 and 6, San Pedro Sula.

From Tegucigalpa, buses connect to Choluteca—*Mi Esperanza* buses, Av. 6, Barrio Villa Adela, Comayagüela; for Choluteca and San Marcos de Colón—*Cotrasul* buses, Av. Centenario, Comayagüela; to El Amatillo, Goascorán, Alianza, Langue, and Valle—Calle 2, Av. 7 and 8, Comayagüela; to Danli and El Paraíso—*Emtraoriente,* Colonia Kennedy, Mercado Jacaleapa, Tegucigalpa.

From San Pedro Sula there are regular buses to Puerto Cortés: *Impala,* Calle, 2, Av. 4 and 5 Suroeste, and *Citul,* Calle 7, Av. 5 and 6; to El Progreso, Tela, La Ceiba: *City-Unión-Progreseña* and *Caty-Tupsay-City,* Av. 2, Calles 5 and 6, Suroeste; and to the Copán ruins: *Etumi,* Calle 7 Suroeste. There are also buses that go to Santa Rosa de Copán and Nueva Ocotepeque, and on to the Guatemalan border.

NATIONAL PARKS. *Copán.* See "Historic Sites and Museums," below.

Lancetilla Botanical Gardens. Just over 2 mi from Tela. Trees and plants from all over the world. Gardens were started by the United Fruit Company to experiment with new income-producing plants when it was feared that disease would spoil the banana plantations.

La Tigra. A rain forest 16 km northeast of Tegucigalpa. There are armadillos, emerald toucanets, and a few quetzal birds. El Rosario, within the park, was a mining center from 1887 to 1954.

SPORTS. See "Accommodations," above, for resorts that cater to sports enthusiasts. **Baseball.** A very popular sport. There is a newly renovated baseball stadium in Tegucigalpa and sandlot fields all over the country where very enthusiastic and remarkably good games are played.

Fishing. There is a wide variety of fishing available in Honduras. Both the north coast and south coast offer excellent deep sea fishing. The Bay Islands are especially good. Varieties of fish include tarpon, mackerel, jewfish, sailfish, albacore and many others. Lake Yojoa is famous for its bass fishing. Eight to ten pounders are common, and even some bass over 20 pounds have been caught. The new hydro dam at Cajón is creating a lake that will be twice the size of Lake Yojoa and promises to provide excellent fishing in wild, untamed country. Two passport-size pictures are needed to get a fishing license.

Soccer. This game (*futbol* in Spanish) is the national sport and is played regularly all over the country. In Tegucigalpa there is the National Stadium, and in San Pedro Sula there is the Morazán Municipal Stadium. Every town has its soccer field, and on Sun. the local teams always play; usually both the players and the spectators are very spirited.

Golf and Tennis. Tegucigalpa, San Pedro Sula, La Ceiba, and La Lima all have country clubs where golf and tennis are available. You can obtain passes through your hotel. La Lima offers a lovely golf course that was originally constructed for the managerial personnel of the United Fruit Company. Some hotels have their own tennis courts. Racquetball is also becoming popular in both Tegucigalpa and San Pedro Sula. Ask at your hotel for information about locations.

Hiking and Climbing: Although not popular sports in Honduras, there are endless opportunities for both hiking and climbing. The terrain in Honduras ranges from fertile valleys, only accessible by horse or foot, to high mist-covered mountains connected by a series of roads and trails. The adventurous hiker can go from tropical jungle to small mountain village. One of the best areas to hike is in the rain forest at La Tigra, near Tegucigalpa. The *Club de Montanismo* (climbing club) of the Alianza Francesa de Honduras in Tegucigalpa is helpful to climbers and hikers and will be able to introduce you to local people with similiar interests.

Horseback Riding. There are stables in both Tegucigalpa and San Pedro Sula where horses can be rented. In the smaller communities the horse is still a very common means of transportation. In these small villages horses are best acquired through local contacts.

Hunting. Choluteca, the largest city in the southern part of the country, is known as the dove-hunting capital of the world. Hunters from all over are attracted by the plentiful white-winged doves and other species of game birds and ducks. The hunting season runs from Nov. 15 to Mar. 15, and the daily limit is 50 doves. The wilds around the city of Danlí and those of the departments of Olancho and Gracias a Dios are also favorites with hunters. There is an abundance of quail, dove, pigeon, deer, puma, wild boar, turkey, and jaguar. To bring guns into the country you must have prior permission from the Minister of Defence. Hunters should make arrangements through their tour guide. To get a hunting license contact the Association National Cazadorores, Tegucigalpa. The following information is required to obtain both gun and hunting permits: name, address, make of gun, model, serial number, and gauge. Two passport-type pictures and the above information must be given to either your travel agency or your tour guide. This should be done at least 2 weeks before departure. You must purchase all ammunition in Honduras.

Water Sports. The Bay Islands offer some of the finest snorkeling and diving in the world. These islands are surrounded by reefs that attract all kinds of sea life. The crystal-clear water affords the snorkeler and diver an experience he will never forget. The natural beauty, as well as the many sunken vessels that lie around these reefs since the days of the Spanish conquistadores, make for an exciting, adventuresome time.

Other popular water sports are also available; consult your hotel. Caribbean Sailing Yachts, located on Roatán, offer well-fitted sailboats that can be rented for as long as you want, with or without captain and crew. The 37 footers sleep 2 couples; the 44 footers sleep 3 couples.

HISTORIC SITES AND MUSEUMS. The rich history of Honduras means a wealth of sites for those visitors who are interested in exploring Central America's past.

Copán. About 2½ hours by a good road from San Pedro Sula. Considered by many to be the most beautiful of Mayan cities. See detailed description of ruins in "Exploring Honduras" section. It's recommended that you get to the ruins as early in the day as possible to miss the crowds (they're open 7 A.M. to 5 P.M.). Guided tours are available. There is a museum of artifacts from the ruins, a few miles away in the town of San José de Copán. The museum is at the head of the central square.

Comayagua. First capital of Honduras. The cathedral was built between 1685 and 1715 by Indian workers whose influence is evident in the design. The clock in the tower is one of the oldest in the world, originally constructed for Seville, Spain. There are 2 museums in town: *Museum of Archeology and History* and *Museum of Colonial and Religious Art.*

Fortress of San Fernando De Omoa. West of Puerto Cortés, about 1 hour from San Pedro Sula. This fortress was built between 1775 and 1777 under the king of Spain to defend the Caribbean ports from pirates.

Ojojona. Birthplace of Pablo Zelaya Sierra, one of Honduras's most famous painters, is on the main square. The church next door has a painting of the crucifixion, reportedly done by Murillo.

Omoa. *Castillo de Omoa,* an early Spanish fort built to protect the area from pirate raids.

Tegucigalpa. *Cathedral of San Miguel.* Across from the Parque Central, the cathedral was the built between 1756 and 1782. Note the baptismal font made by Indians from a single block of stone in 1643, as well as the gold pulpit and silver altar. There's a small museum here.

Church of San Francisco. Calle 5, 4 blocks east of Parque Central. Constructed in 1592 with donations from wealthy miners, the church was remodeled in 1740.

Church of Suyapa. About 4 miles out of town, the church is still unfinished after 30 years of construction. The tiny image of the Virgin on the main altar is said to have miraculous powers. The feast of the Virgin *(Feria de Suyapa)* begins on Feb. 3 and lasts 8 days, attracting pilgrims from all over the country.

National Museum of History and Antropology. Near Concordia Park. Mayan artifacts and a good collection of art and furniture dating back to colonial Honduras.

Trujillo. One of the oldest cities in Central America. Near here Columbus celebrated the first mass conducted on the American mainland. Remains of 3 forts can be found: *San José, San Hipólito, La Concepción.* Soldier of fortune William Walker was killed in Trujillo (there is a marker at the spot). His grave can be found in the local cemetery. Trujillo has a small museum.

Nearby is *Cuyamel Cave,* used for thousands of years as a place of ritual and worship. Here some of the most important ancient ceramics of Mesoamerica have been found.

Easiest way to get to Trujillo is to fly from La Ceiba, San Pedro Sula, or Tegucigalpa.

Valle De Angeles. About 14 miles from Tegucigalpa, this old mining town has many buildings restored to their original 17th-century appearance. Handicrafts and artists' works are available.

SHOPPING. Honduran gift shops feature a variety of gifts and souvenirs that are distinctly Honduran. There are also many exciting new lines of crafts that are being designed for the U.S. market and can be found in most shops. Honduran craftspeople are very versatile and produce most of their products from Honduras's vast selection of raw materials. Wood products, leather, fiber, jewelry, opals and gems, and hammocks are among the many items that you will see offered for sale, often at very low prices. Bargaining is the custom on the street but not in the shops.

Some of the many shops to visit for crafts in Tegucigalpa are: *Artesanía Carmen,* Av. República de Chile; *Artesanía Hondureña,* Av. República de Chile; *El Sique,* Av. Cervantes No.1218; *Artesanías Caoba,* Calle, 3, Av. 12 and 13; *Amano,* Frente Palacio Episcopal, downtown; *Galerías Maya,* Av. Repúplica de Chile; *Honduras Souvenirs,* Calle Real; *La Duquesa,* Av. 3, Calles 3 and 4; *Mundo Maya,* Hotel Honduras Maya; *La de Moda,* Hotel Honduras Maya; *El Coqui,* Calle 3, Av. 12 and 13; *Mayapán,* Calle 3, Av. 12 and 13; *Mundo Maya,* Av. 9, Calles 4 and 5; *Candú,* 2 locations—front of Hotel Honduras Maya and Av. Repúplica de Chile; also *Jolívez,* Av. 2, Calles 4 and 5, in Comayagüela.

Honduras has excellent artists, and their oil paintings, watercolors, and drawings can often be found in the above-mentioned stores. Galleries such as *Editorial Nuevo Continente* (Av. Cervantes No.1230A), *Galería de Arte "Clementina Suárez"* (Barrio La Hoya No.141), and *Estudio de Decoración "Victor España Noni"* (Calle No.1B No.214, Colonia Palmira) show the works of these artists.

In San Pedro Sula the *Mercado Artesanal* (Calles 6 and 7, Av. 8 and 9) has a wide selection of crafts.

NIGHTLIFE AND ENTERTAINMENT. Honduras is not famous for its nightlife. There are however a number of discos, some with live bands, and some of the larger hotels often have night-clubs with floor shows, particularily on weekends. Blvd. Francisco Morazán in Tegucigalpa is the center of nighttime action, and because it is the in place, there are always new nightclubs and bars opening up. Some of the most popular are:

The Metro, Blvd. Morazán all the way to the west end, is the newest disco and the most popular spot for the younger jet set.

Copas, Av. Paseo Argentina, a new video bar located just off Blvd. Morazán.

Casino Royal, at the Hotel Maya, is the spot for those interested in gambling. It features roulette, craps, and blackjack. Casino Royal also has a new location at Anthony's Key on Roatán.

The National Theater, *Teatro Manuel Bonilla,* on Calle 4, Av. 2 and 3, often has plays, ballets, chamber music, and other cultural events. Check the daily newspaper for listings.

In San Pedro Sula the *Guanacaste Bar* in the Gran Hotel Sula is very popular. The *Círculo Teatral Sampedrano,* the *Sociedad Pro Musica,* and the *Escuela de Música* give musical and theatrical performances at the Municipal Auditorium or at the Centro Cultural Sampedrano, 3 Calle 3 Noroeste, Av. 3 and 4.

Movies. Both Tegucigalpa and San Pedro have a number of good movie houses showing fairly recent movies in English with Spanish subtitles.

SAFETY. At press time the political situation in Honduras is stable and it is safe for tourists to travel on all roads open to the public. However, as in all Central American countries, it's always a good idea to ask if you see any situation that looks unusual. Although theft and street crime are not a problem in Honduras, visitors should take normal precautions with wallets, purses, and valuables.

EL SALVADOR

by
HELENA DE GUTIÉRREZ

Helena de Gutiérrez has worked for the National Tourism Institute of El Salvador as well as other social and economic development agencies for the country. She is president of the El Salvador/Louisiana Committee of Partners of the Americas and lives in San Salvador.

The Spanish conquistadores arrived in a land named Cuscatlán by the Pipil Indians who inhabited it: Cuscatlán means "land of precious things." Today El Salvador is still considered the land of precious things, although it's the smallest of the Central American countries. But El Salvador is small only in size; it is the most populated and industrialized of the Central American nations.

Rich in its natural beauty, the country offers a wide panorama of scenic contrasts: volcanic landscapes of dramatic beauty, crater lakes, miles of unspoiled Pacific coastline, coffee farms, and pine-covered mountains. The entire skyline of the country is dominated by more than 25 volcanoes, providing rich, fertile soil, ideal for coffee and other crops. El Salvador has been one of the leading coffee-producing countries of the world, though today this production has been reduced, due to a depressed economy caused by civil war.

The 200-mile-long Pacific coastline and its beaches range from pure white sand to volcanic black. The shoreline, fringed by palm trees, is practically uninterrupted. There is great fishing along the wide continental shelf.

The list of "precious things" is never ending. The climate is perfect: warm days, cool nights. There are lush tropical gardens with a wide variety of orchids and wildflowers, waterfalls, mangrove swamps, aromatic balsam groves, cloud forests, and exotic birds. The range of sports is quite varied: fishing, tennis, golf, waterskiing, surfing,—to name a few.

Another of El Salvador's treasures are several pre-Columbian ruins, which are testimony to a glorious past. Many archeological sites are being explored, and the various ceramics, stoneware, carvings, and tools are exhibited at the local museum. Pyramids, temples, ball courts, and other structures can be seen at Tazumal, San Andrés, and Cihuatán. Magnificent colonial churches and towns, as well as Indian villages in which traditional dances and religious rites are still practiced, are reminders of a more recent history. Many colorful handcrafted articles can be found, the artisans still using the techniques of their ancestors; among these are textiles worked on hand or foot looms, hammocks, ceramics, paintings, and leather goods.

San Salvador, the sophisticated capital city has a fast-paced lifestyle. It counts many movie theaters, discotheques, nightclubs, and a variety of restaurants—serving everything from local dishes to international cuisine—and of course numerous fine hotels.

To the Salvadoran, the most precious of all the country's treasures is its people. The Salvadorans are friendly, helpful, open, and reliable. They are also recognized worldwide as creative, industrious, and willing workers. The dense population encourages competition as well as sharing, perhaps due to the meeting of the best of two worlds: the Spanish and Indian cultures.

Visitors will find that, everywhere they go, a Salvadoran will always go out of his or her way to be of assistance, helping to find a place to stay or eat or provide an address. She or he will introduce family and friends and invite the visitor into his or her home,—"mi casa es su casa"—despite the fact that El Salvador has been undergoing difficult political and socioeconomic periods.

The Land

The total area of El Salvador is 8,124 square miles, about the size of the state of Massachusetts. The population numbers, 5,000,000 (more than 500 people per square mile).

On the north and east the country borders with Honduras, from the Trifinio Mountains to the Goascorán River estuary; in the northwest with Guatemala, from the Trifinio Mountains to the Paz River estuary; in the south with the Pacific Ocean; and the southeast with the Gulf of Fonseca, which separates El Salvador from Honduras and Nicaragua.

Two mountain ranges make up the physical aspect of Salvadoran territory: to the north the Central American Sierra Madre and to the south the Coastal Range. Between them there is an expanse of fertile valleys, extinct volcanoes, and plateaus. There are more than 25 extinct volcanoes, large craters showing petrified lava flows. Among these three, Santa Ana, San Miguel, and Izalco are considered dormant, since they show very little activity. Izalco showed strong activity from 1770 to 1957 and was called

Faro del Pacífico (Lighthouse of the Pacific) because ships enroute to the port of Acajutla were guided by the volcano.

Between the two parallel rows of volcanoes and mountains there is a high, hilly plateau about 2,000 feet above sea level, broken by a number of river valleys and dotted with deep, incredibly blue volcanic lakes, several of them in the craters of extinct volcanoes. Due to all the volcanic activity, the soil is rich and porous with volcanic ash and lava and extraordinarily fertile and productive.

Between the coastal chain and the Pacific Ocean is the coastal plain—hot, fertile, and, in the eastern part of the country, given over to the raising of cotton and livestock.

The coastline is generally low and sandy, except specifically the areas of the balsam coast and the Gulf of Fonseca, here with cliffs and ridges. The entire coast is dotted with bays, capes, estuaries, and islands.

The climate is wonderful throughout the year. There are only two seasons, the rainy season, which begins in May and ends in October, and the dry season from November through April. The rainy season is known as *invierno* (winter) and the dry season as *verano* (summer). Rainfall is usually in the evening or late afternoon; the rest of the day is sunny and dry. Occasionally, during July and August, there is a spell of continuous rain, called a *temporal,* which may last for two or three days.

The average temperature is 78°F, though it varies according to altitude, being warmer on the coast and dropping to a refreshing level in the highlands. In a delightful contrast, the weather is sunny and tropical but with low humidity. During the day one can wear a comfortable cotton suit and in the evening a light jacket or sweater is always welcome. The sun shines 360 days of the year, making El Salvador the perfect place for a sun-filled winter vacation.

El Salvador has more than 300 rivers; however, they are not navigable. The most important, and largest, is the Río de Lempa which originates in Guatemala near the Salvadoran border, flows through Honduras, enters Salvadoran territory, runs a length of 160 miles, and flows into the Pacific Ocean. Four hydroelectric dams have been built on the river, providing much of the country's electrical supply. Other important rivers are the Rió Grande de San Miguel in the east; the Río de Paz on the western border with Guatemala; the Río Goascorán bordering Honduras, and the Jiboa.

There are three kinds of lakes in El Salvador; those located inside volcanic craters, those created artificially by the erection of dams and hydroelectric plants built across the Río Lempa, and natural lakes. The most important crater lakes are Lake Ilopango, with an area of 28 square miles with a maximum depth of 814 feet, and Lake Coatepeque, 10 square miles and with a depth of 394 feet. The largest of the artificial lakes is Suchitlán (Cerrón Grande Dam), which is 52 square miles with a maximum depth of 262 feet. Guija is a natural lake, 44 square kms. in area, as are the lagoons of Olomega, Alegría, and Apastepeque.

The country's economy is mainly dependent on agriculture, the major crop being coffee. About 320,000 acres are given over to coffee production, and 320,000 acres of the southeastern lowlands are given over to the production of cotton, El Salvador's second major crop. A large amount of sugar cane (65,000 acres) and livestock are also produced.

El Salvador is one of the few balsam producers in the world. The product, erroneously named balsam of Peru, is used in the production of medicine and cosmetics. Due to the need to transport products from the fields, processing plants, and ports, El Salvador has the finest highway system in Central America.

History

The Olmec culture flourished over 4,000 years ago and lasted more than 1,000 years. Though centered around Veracruz, on the Caribbean coast of Mexico, the presence of the Olmec in El Salvador is evidenced by the Olmec Boulder, a rock near the town of Chalchuapa in Las Victorias—the four sides are carved in bas-relief and show figures of fierce warriors with the typical jaguar heads, characteristic of Olmec art.

The remains of the classic Maya period (A.D. 300–1000) can be found in ceramics and bartering tools, indicating a close commercial relationship between the El Salvador Maya and the Mayan centers in central Mexico. In the western region the culture continued its development under the Olmec influence. The archeological sites of this period are located in Quelepa, Tehuacán, San Andrés, Casa Blanca, and Guija. Visiting the sites, one can distinguish the different styles of this sophisticated civilization: the stepped-pyramid temples, ball courts, and paved plazas.

During the first centuries of the postclassic period (A.D. 1000–1525) these civilizations were invaded by the Pipiles, who originated in the Mexican plateau, descendants of the Toltecs and Nahua-speakers. They reached El Salvador about the eleventh century A.D., dominating the people and inhabiting the western region of the country, known today as Santa Ana, Ahuachapán, Sonsonate, La Libertad, Cuscatlán, La Paz, San Vicente, and Cabañas. Even now, in the remaining Indian villages of El Salvador, Nahua (a dialect related to the Nahuatl, spoken by the Aztecs) is still spoken.

The Pipil culture was tremendously influenced by the Maya. They worshiped gods of corn, rain, sun, fire, and other natural forces; they made use of hieroglyphic writing, a mathematical system including the concept of zero, and sophisticated astronomical calculations. They regulated their lives by means of the Mayan calendar and created distinctive pottery, stone carvings, gold and silver ornaments, and hundreds of large stone, plaster, and brick structures that still remain along the Salvadoran countryside. Their culture was centered around the cultivation of corn. The Pipil built a number of large towns—present-day Sonsonate and Ahuachapán were both originally Pipil trading centers.

Meanwhile, other Indian cultures built their civilization centers in eastern and northern El Salvador. The Lencas, for example, who share many Mayan characteristics, settled in Usulután, San Miguel, La Unión, Chalatenango, and Cabañas provinces. Recognized for their exquisite pottery, they must have been wide-ranging traders, as their wares are found throughout Mesoamerica. The Lenca have proved of great interest to archaeologists because they formed a dividing line between the cultures of the north—the Maya and Mexican people—and those of the south—tribes of Nicaragua, Honduras, Costa Rica, and Panama.

On May 31, 1522, a Spanish expedition led by Andrés Niño, disembarked on the island of Meanguera in the Gulf of Fonseca. In June 1524 the Spanish captain Pedro de Alvarado entered El Salvador by crossing the River Paz and began to war against the native tribes of Cuscatlán. The war of *conquista* was fierce, and many Spanish and Indian lives were lost. On April 1, 1525, a colony was founded near Cuscatlán and called San Salvador.

San Salvador was established on a site called La Bermuda, close by the city of Suchitoto, and remained in that place until 1540. This location was later considered inadequate, due to the poor and arid soil surrounding it, and the settlement was moved to the valley of Zalcoatitán (also known as Valle de las Hamacas, or Valley of the Hammocks, due to frequent earthquakes), a fertile valley located at the foot of the San Salvador volcano. On September 1, 1546, it received the title of city.

In the following years the country evolved under Spanish rule. Spaniards who settled here intermingled with Indians, and within 200 years the people of El Salvador were predominantly mestizos. As the population grew more homogeneous, caste distinction decreased in importance, enabling the people to develop an identity as Salvadorans, rather than Indians or whites, thus avoiding much of the divisiveness and culture antagonism that plagued other countries.

At the end of the eighteenth century El Salvador's crops of indigo, cacao, and cattle had become quite profitable. The population increased rapidly, and in 1786 the status of this territory within the kingdom of Guatemala was raised to that of an intendancy, making it an equal to neighboring states of Honduras and Nicaragua.

Toward the end of the first decade of the nineteenth century a sense of liberty rose among the Central American people. The French and American revolutions had popularized new ideas such as democracy and individual freedoms, and the decline of Spain as a world power paved the way for ideas of independence. When in 1821 the movement toward independence became too strong to resist, the Declaration of Independence of Central America was signed, with five Salvadorans among the signers. While the other Central American republics decided to join the Mexican empire of Agustín Iturbide, little El Salvador showed its independent nature by refusing. As Mexican troops poured into the country to force it to join, it had an extraordinary and audacious idea: it made a desperate plea to the United States to admit it into the Union as a new state. The United States, intent on cementing relations with Mexico, refused. When the empire broke apart in 1823, El Salvador joined Guatemala, Honduras, Costa Rica, and Nicaragua in forming the United Provinces of Central America.

The United Provinces was an experiment in unity that was not to prove successful. Liberals struggled with conservatives, church supporters with anticlericals, Creole landowners battled landless mestizos, and powerful Guatemala battled just about everyone else in its attempt to centralize power in that country. The United Provinces fell apart, but not before the federal capital had been transferred to San Salvador from Guatemala City in 1834. Today Salvadorans are still proud of the part their nation played in the independence movement and the struggles for Central American unity—statues of Arce (the first president of the United Provinces), Delgado (a priest who led uprisings against the Spanish), and other democratic thinkers can be seen in parks and plazas all over the country.

Struggles and dictators, conflicts and coups have continued thereafter. On October 16, 1979, General Carlos Humberto Romero was overthrown as president in a military coup and replaced by a civilian-military junta. In December 1980 the Christian Democratic leader, José Napoleón Duarte was appointed president of the junta. Agrarian, banking, and commercial trade reforms were instituted in El Salvador. Leftist revolutionary forces are trying to overthrow the present government; and there are dangerously active right-wing extremists. Because of this conflict, some areas of El Salvador are unsafe for visitors. You should inquire locally about the safety of any roads you wish to take (the guerrillas announce in advance roads that they might attack) and any places you want to visit.

In March 1982 elections for a 60-member Constituent Assembly led to a coalition government of several parties under Roberto D'Aubuisson, temporarily depriving the Christian Democrats of power. Elections were held again in May 1984, and again José Napoleón Duarte became president, this time earning 53 percent of the popular vote.

The current government system is of the representative type. The president is to be elected every five years and cannot be reelected for a second continuous term. The Legislative Assembly is made up by six deputies, and the government is organized into three major branches: judicial, legislative, and executive.

The population of El Salvador is 90 percent mestizo, 5 percent white, and 5 percent Indian. For the most part, the Indians live in the northern area of Sonsonate and in small villages like Panchimalco, where the women still wear traditional garb—colorful skirts and blouses and bright kerchiefs.

The Economy

Agriculture accounts for approximately 70 percent of El Salvador's export earnings and employs 30 percent of the population. Inflation was 16 percent in 1979 and by 1985 had risen to 22 percent. The textile industry is the most important in the country; others include shoe manufacturing, cosmetics, furniture, chemicals and fertilizers, pharmaceuticals, construction materials, cement and asbestos, food and beverage processing plants, and rubber goods. There are small deposits of various minerals: gold, silver, copper, iron ore, sulfur, mercury, lead, zinc, salt, and lime. In July 1975 a geothermal power plant began operating in Ahuachapán. Hydraulic resources are also being exploited as a means of generating power.

After the 1969 war with neighboring Honduras, El Salvador lost the Honduran market, but regained it in 1980, after renewing diplomatic relations with that country.

EXPLORING EL SALVADOR

San Salvador, the capital city, is located 2,230 feet above sea level, at the foot of the San Salvador volcano in the Valley of the Hammocks. Its population is approximately 1 million. The city moved to its present site in 1854. The present capital is a modern city, and its architecture conditioned to seismic shocks. (San Salvador has been destroyed twice by earthquakes.) The capital is centrally located and the country small in size; one can easily settle down in one of the city's many hotels and take day tours to practically anywhere in the country and return in time for dinner at one of the best restaurants, and then enjoy the nightlife at one of several discotheques or nightclubs. At press time the capital seems relatively safe for visitors, but you should keep abreast of the current political situation, and it's always a good idea to inquire locally about the safety at places you want to spend time at. We don't recommend walking the streets alone after 9 P.M.

The city is laid out in the shape of a cross, with its four main avenues meeting at city center beside Plaza Barrios. Avenida España runs from the north to Plaza Barrios, where it continues south as Avenida Cuscatlán. Calle Arce runs from the west to Plaza Barrios, where it becomes Calle Delgado and continues eastward. All streets north of Calle Arce and Calle Delgado have odd numbers, numbered consecutively as you move northward; for example, Calles 1, 3, 5, 7, etc. East of the central avenues (España–Cuscatlán) the streets are called Oriente, west they are called Poniente. Thus an address of 3 Calle Poniente is north of Calle Arce and west of Avenida España, while 6 Calle Oriente is south of Calle Delgado and west of Avenida Cuscatlán. The even-numbered avenues are east of Avenida España–Cuscatlán, while the odd-numbered avenues are west. North of the central streets the avenues are called Norte, and south they are called Sur. Thus an address on 25 Avenida Norte is west of Avenida España and north of Calle Arce. Fortunately the avenues and streets form an orderly, rectangular grid pattern (except for the *colonias*-suburbs), and once you become accustomed to the pattern, it's quite easy to find your way around.

San Salvador: A Walking Tour

Since most of the city's important public buildings are located around the Plaza Barrios, this is the logical place to begin a walking tour. Walking is not only the easiest but also the fastest way to get around this congested downtown area; here what were before perhaps only mild preconceptions about El Salvador's overpopulation become overwhelming reality as you make your way through the throngs of shoppers, peddlers, businesspeople, office workers, laborers, shoeshine boys, and street loungers.

Just south of the plaza you'll see the graceful colulmns of the greenish-colored National Palace. This is where the Legislative Assembly used to meet, although the building houses many government offices. Its attractive interior courtyard, with carefully tended trees and shrubs, is surrounded by tiers of balconies. Next to it is the huge Metropolitan Cathedral, massive and impressive, and still undergoing heavy reconstruction.

Around the corner on Calle Delgado is the lovely National Theater. Designed by French architect Daniel Beylard and completed in 1917, this neoclassic gem has been closed as a working theater for several years, serving in the interim as the mayor's offices, a radio station, a school of practical sciences, and a movie house. An upsurge of national pride and the need for a national showplace for the arts brought about its complete renovation, and it reopened in early 1979, including all the latest equipment yet retaining a European air with its gold leaf, marble floors, red velvet seats, exquisite woodwork, crystal chandeliers, and ornamental plasterwork. It

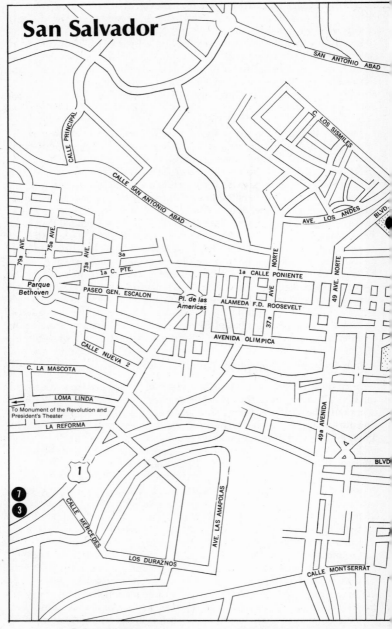

San Salvador

SAN ANTONIO ABAD

CALLE PRINCIPAL

CALLE SAN ANTONIO ABAD

C. LOS SISMILES

AVE. LOS ANDES

BLVD

79a AVE.

75a AVE.

73a AVE.

AVE.

3a

1a C. PTE.

NORTE

1a CALLE PONIENTE

49 AVE. NORTE

Parque Bethoven

PASEO GEN. ESCALON

Pl. de las Americas

ALAMEDA F.D. ROOSEVELT

AVE.

37a

AVENIDA OLIMPICA

CALLE NUEVA 2

C. LA MASCOTA

LOMA LINDA

To Monument of the Revolution and President's Theater

LA REFORMA

49a AVENIDA

BLVD

1

7

3

CALLE MERCEDES

AVE. LAS AMAPOLAS

LOS DURAZNOS

CALLE MONTSERRAT

Points of Interest

1) Central Market
2) Institute of Salvadoran Tourism (ISTU)
3) International Fairgrounds
4) Metrocentro
5) Metropolitan Cathedral

6) National Center of Arts
7) National Museum (David J. Guzmàn)
8) National Palace
9) National Theater
10) Plaza Barrios
11) Presidential Palace

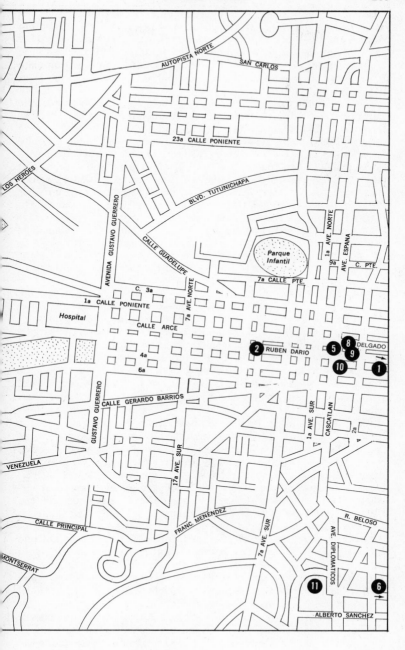

now consists of a main theater, which seats over 700, and four small recital halls. Try to attend a performance—ballet, classical music concerts, folk dances, and plays are scheduled regularly. If that's not possible, take a tour through the theater—its murals by Salvadoran artist Carlos Cañas are noteworthy, as are each of the different theaters, from the intimate Little Theater to the Grand Foyer. Take a look at the sumptuous presidential box.

Just around the corner from the theater, on 4 Avenida Sur and 2 Calle Oriente, is the Plaza Libertad with its winged monument to liberty. Across the street is the distinctive church of El Rosario. Built in a high arching design, it looks like a gymnasium from the outside, but inside it's quite peaceful and attractive—something like being inside a drum that's been sawed in half and laid on its side. Tiers of stained glass windows rise from both sides. Modern sculptures and altars mingle with traditional religious statues, and the sanctuary is calm and serene. Here is the grave of Father Delgado, the leader of the Central American independence movement. On the south side of the square is the Monumento a los Próceres de 1811, in memory of Delgado and the other leaders of the 1811 rebellion. The church of La Merced is nearby on 10 Aveniad Sur and Calle Modelo—the bell with which Father Delgado rang out that first call for Central American independence still rings from the tower of this church, the oldest in San Salvador.

A few blocks north on Calle Delgado between 8 and 10 Avenidas is the Central Market (Mercado Cuarte), which covers an entire block and is dedicated almost completely to the sale of handicrafts. Here you can wander through a maze of hundreds of little covered stalls, stopping to bargain for whatever catches your eye, including brightly colored sisal bags, finely woven hammocks, leather goods of every sort—especially saddles and handbags—tiny figurines from Ilobasco, cloth bedspreads and tablecloths from San Sebastián, piñatas, wood carvings, wicker furniture and baskets, pottery both painted and unpainted, and lots more. Don't hesitate to bargain.

The Central Market, located just behind the National Palace near 5 Avenida Sur and 6 Calle Poniente on Calle Gerardo Barrios, is not hard to find. Once you get within a few blocks, your nose will lead you, as well as the increasing number of loafers, street vendors, trucks with shouting drivers, squashed vegetables in the streets, women with baskets on their heads, screeches and shouts, and all the other distinctive signs that surround large marketplaces. This is not a great place for handicraft hunters; it's where the people of the city and surrounding towns do their shopping, mainly for fresh vegetables, fruit, meat, poultry, and seafood.

Also downtown are the offices of the Instituto Salvadoreño de Turismo (ISTU) on Calle Rubén Darío between 9 and 11 Avenida Sur. It would be wise to make this one of your first stops, since they will provide you with maps, bus and train schedules, descriptions of various towns and markets, and any advice or assistance you might need, from finding a hotel or apartment to locating a tiny mountain village.

From the center of the city Calle Arce heads east toward the slopes of the San Salvador volcano. After becoming Alameda Roosevelt, this main thoroughfare passes shopping centers, banks, restaurants, and once-luxurious mansions until it reaches an attractive park, watched over by the famous statue of El Salvador del Mundo, portraying Christ with his arms raised standing atop a globe of the world, looking over downtown San Salvador. Here Alameda Roosevelt forks, the road to the right becoming Paseo General Escalón, the one to the left becoming the Central American Highway, known as the Carretera a Santa Tecla. If you take Paseo Escalón, you'll find yourself climbing up a hill past magnificent houses. This is one of the city's most exclusive residential districts and is known as Colonia Escalón. If you have a car, you can drive through tree-lined streets, or spend a pleasant hour or two strolling around the neighborhood looking at the houses. After a leisurely walk you can stop for lunch or a snack in one of the neighborhood's excellent restaurants; many of the city's finest dining establishments are here, most of them right on or near the Paseo Escalón.

If you take a left at the statue of El Salvador del Mundo and head up the Carretera a Santa Tecla, you will pass a sports club on the left (Círculo Deportivo Internacional) and the Parque Nacional de Baseball a bit farther on. Just past the baseball stadium, you'll see a series of low buildings to the right. This is the El Salvador International Fairgrounds. Here every two years is an international fair. Exhibitors come from all over the world, and each country or industry has its own building on the grounds. Meanwhile, the fairgrounds aren't completely out of action: set up in one section is the Mercado Nacional de Artesanías. Here artisans from all over El Salvador come to sell their handicrafts and works of folk art. The selection is good, the quality is perhaps a bit better than that found at the Central Market, and the atmosphere much more subdued (although the prices are slightly higher).

Just around the corner from the fairgrounds on Avenida La Revolución is the Museo Nacional David J. Guzmán. This is the national archaeological museum, and though it is small, its collection is immensely interesting. The hill that leads past the museum climbs toward the Monumento a la Revolución, an expressionistic mosaic of a powerful man casting off his chains and raising his arms to the heavens. To one side is the Hotel Presidente, to the other the Teatro Presidente, one of the city's largest and best theaters, which features concerts, plays, ballets, movies, and beauty contests. From the Monumento a la Revolución there is a nice view of the city. The neighborhood that surrounds this hilltop is called Colonia San Benito, and it too is one of the city's nicest residential areas. As you stroll through its winding streets, you'll notice attractive houses and quite a few national emblems at embassy residences. San Benito also claims the Zona Rosa on the Boulevard del Hipódramo, a lovely area filled with sidewalk cafes, restaurants, discotheques, and small shops.

West of the Alameda Roosevelt is the Boulevard de los Héroes, so named in honor of those who fought against Honduras in 1969 in a war that lasted 100 hours. Along this boulevard there are many modern buildings, businesses, and restaurants, as well as the largest shopping mall in the country: Metrocentro. Across the street you'll find the Hotel Camino Real.

Another main street leading off the Boulevard de los Héroes is the Boulevard Juan Pablo II, named in honor of Pope John Paul II, who walked along this street on his visit to El Salvador in 1983. It leads from an old street downtown and connects with the Boulevard de Ilopango, where the largest industrial complexes in the country are located.

Excursions around San Salvador

There are many points of interest around the capital, which, while not within the city limits, are close enough to be easily reached on a short jaunt: inexpensive public buses run regularly and frequently to these places, and those with a car will be able to plan an itinerary that takes them to several of these places in a single day without ever having to retrace their steps. Because of the current conflict in El Salvador, inquire locally about the safety of all places you want to travel to.

Planes de Renderos, Parque Balboa, and Puerta del Diablo

Drive south from the city center along Avenida Cuscatlán, which becomes Avenida los Diplomáticos, so named because this is the road diplomats used to travel on their way to the Presidential Palace. At the first fork turn right toward Los Planes, past the Presidential Palace on the left, and the Parque Zoologico on the right; the zoo is small, but the selection of animals is good. The park is pleasant and especially recommended for children. Past the zoo is the Saburo Hirao Park and the Museum of Natural History. Dedicated to Salvadoran youth, they include recreational and outdoor educational facilities. The park covers 19 acres of land and includes a botanical garden and playground, specially designed for children. The museum, founded in 1976, is located in the southeastern section of the park. It is made up of 10 sections covering the different aspects of the flora and fauna and geologic composition of the country. As you wind up into the mountains, you pass through an attractively landscaped residential district—fine houses set on sloping lawns and gardens, often hidden by lush foliage. Continuing upward, you reach Parque Balboa, at about 4,000 feet above sea level. This is one of El Salvador's Turicentros—a series of national recreational parks—containing gardens, natural forests, soccer fields, and a roller skating rink. Near the parking lot you'll notice a number of tiny shacks with smoke pouring out of them; these are *pupusa* stands, and by all means you should stop and try them. Found only in El Salvador, *pupusas* are made of corn tortillas filled with cheese or pork rind or both and cooked on a griddle. They are indescribably tasty, especially when topped by the chili sauce that is kept in big jars at the center of the tables. They cost about 80 cents each, and three or four of these with a cold beer or soda make a quick lunch that's hard to beat. Try a variety, sampling one or two at each booth; *pupusa* aficionados know that each vendor's *pupusas* are different and will willingly list you their 10 favorite *pupusa* stands and describe the qualities of each.

After passing through Parque Balboa, continue up Mount Chulul a short distance to Puerta del Diablo, where two enormous crags stand like doorposts, framing a stunning landscape. The craggy peaks, reminiscent of an eighteenth-century Roman dream painting, are actually made up of a single rock, split in two by an ancient cataclysm. Stone steps lead to the summit, and the climb is well worth it, for as you stand at the peak the entire country seems to spread out before you—and a 360-degree vista that on a clear day takes in the blue Pacific rolling its whitecaps against the green coastal plain. To the east you can see the San Vicente volcano; far to the west is the Izalco volcano, next to the Santa Ana volcano. Beneath you, like a small toy town, is the Indian village of Panchimalco, with its dazzling white church, dating to the colonial period. For those so inclined, this is a spectacular and romantic spot for a picnic.

On the way back down, bear to the right out of the park and go to El Gran Mirador, another excellent lookout point. This gives you a view to the north, where you see the city climbing the lower slopes of the San Salvador volcano; to the right are the deep-blue waters of crater Lake Ilopango, and in the center is Guazapa Hill seen against the distant background of the mountains of the continental divide, near the border of Honduras.

Panchimalco

The old Indian village of Panchimalco is only 9 miles from the capital, but in spirit it is another world; in time, another century. Its inhabitants are Nahua-speaking Pipil, direct descendants of the warriors who put an arrow through Pedro de Alvarado's leg. The town is a refreshing and lovely place to spend a few hours, with its old cobblestone streets, tile-roofed adobe houses, and central plaza where two ancient traditions are symbolized by the 400-year-old church and the giant ceiba tree planted about the same time the church was built. The tree provides shade for the marketplace. Many tourists like to buy *pañuelos* as souvenirs. These plain soft cloths are woven by local women on handlooms. The great boulders at the base of Mount Chulul are said to have been rolled downhill by Indians in order to crush the advancing conquistadores.

The San Jacinto Teleférico

This amusement park–entertainment complex is set atop Mount San Jacinto and is reached by funicular. The ride up the mountain is by itself worth the price of admission, and is bound to raise your pulse a bit. The brand-new Swiss-made cable cars gently draw you up the mountainside, as housing projects, tiny villages, farms, coffee *fincas* (ranches), and forests pass by 400 feet below and the wind whistles through the window, rocking the tiny car to and fro. The entire city of San Salvador spreads out before you like a map, and the San Salvador volcano forms a massive backdrop. On the other side you can see the colors change as the wind sweeps across the surface of Lake Ilopango. On top of the mountain you'll stroll through pine forests until you reach a modern amusement park, with kiddy rides, mechanical and electronic games, and strolling figures out of Salvadoran folktales. On weekends there are shows, ranging from rock concerts to folk dances. In addition to hamburger stands, there is a comfortable restaurant–bar set among the trees at the mountain's peak, with tables on an open patio. You can climb the Teleférico just about dusk, watch the sun set over the shoulder of the volcano and the city lights sprinkle on as you ride through the gathering dark up the mountainside. Climb to the restaurant and sit out on the terrace with a beer and *pupusas* as the wind sweeps through the pines overhead and gaze at the city below—a peaceful, serene way to end the day. Just a short walk to the other side of the park will give you a grand view of the coastal plains to the Pacific. The Teleférico opened in late 1977; its entrance is only 10 minutes from downtown.

Lago de Ilopango

Just 9 miles east of the capital, this large volcanic lake is another favorite weekend recreation spot for Salvadorans. It's said the Pipil priests sacrificed four virgins to the gods of harvest here each year. The lake underwent great changes due to seismic activity in 1880, with the water level first rising, then falling precipitously and a 150-foot-high island erupting suddenly from the bottom. In 1923 the water rose again, damaging many lakefront homes. It still has the same mystic beauty that must have convinced the Pipil that the gods resided somewhere near. The lake has excellent beaches for swimming, and there are facilities for renting fishing equipment, boats, canoes, and water skis. The lake is surrounded by many private homes, sporting clubs (ask at your hotel and you might be able to get a guest pass), and restaurants serving fish fresh from the lake. Turicentro Apulo is here, with *pupusa* stands, a restaurant, changing rooms, cabanas, and camping facilities.

Cerro Las Pavas and Cojutepeque

About 15 miles past the turnoff to Lake Ilopango on CA-1 east, you enter the town of Cojutepeque ("hill of the wild dogs"). The town is especially interesting for its popular market, which is boisterous and colorful, filling the town's hilly streets with a profusion of tented booths and stalls selling fruits, vegetables, and other necessities. Though patronized mainly by local people, it does have some items of interest to tourists, including flowerpots, sombreros, and leather goods. Its sausage market is famous throughout the country; the local cigars are excellent, too. The town is built on the lower slope of a great hill, Cerro Las Pavas, which you can hike or drive up on a shady road that circles around the hill, offering a number of fine views. Hidden away at the top of the hill is the grotto of the Virgin of Fatima. The miraculous powers of the virgin are attested to by the hundreds of plaques on the walls of the grotto—some carved in marble, others in bronze, some crudely carved with a knife. It is said that the image of the Virgin came from Portugal, where recurrent letters appeared from her asking that she be sent here to Cerro Las Pavas. Holy souvenir salesmen nearby have everything a pilgrim might want.

Boquerón

Just a short drive from the capital will take you right up to the top of the San Salvador volcano, where you have an unparalleled view of the entire Valle de las Hamacas and into the crater. After driving to Santa Tecla, turn right at the sign for Boquerón. A fairly easy drive of about 7 miles brings you to a parking lot, and you must climb the last few hundred yards on foot—steep, but not too difficult. On top you're confronted with two equally magnificent views. On one side the panorama of the Valle de las Hamacas, with the capital city below, in the distance the twin peaks of the San Vicente volcano; to the right the towering pillars of Puerta del Diablo with the Pacific coast far away. On the other side there is a gaping abyss—the inside of the volcano, like some huge lunar crater, about 1½ miles across and 1,500 feet deep, with a second crater poking up from its floor, black and sinister, formed by the eruption of 1917. It is awesome and for some a bit frightening. The adventurous will want to descend into the main crater and scale the black rocky rim of the smaller crater, or hike around the rim of the larger crater (allow yourself four or five hours). Camping at Boquerón is definitely not recommended.

La Laguna Botanical Gardens

These gardens are located at the bottom of an extinct volcano's crater, southeast of Antiquo Cuscatlán on the road to Santa Tecla. The gardens cover an area of 7 acres, and it is perhaps the only garden in the world that has such a unique location and conditions. The woods covering the slopes serve as windbreakers and allow for underground water deposits. For more than a century three generations of one family have devoted their energies to the garden, planting and caring for hundreds of rare local and foreign species. Coffee plantations surround the gardens. For hundreds of years there was a small lagoon at the bottom of the crater, 2,625 feet above sea level; the last eruption, which took place in the eighteenth century, transformed the lagoon into a swamp. There are remains of this eruption on the grounds, such as petrified lava found among the plants.

Los Chorros

Los Chorros, another Turicentro, deserves special mention due to its remarkable beauty; those that have visited Boquerón might want to stop here for a picnic or a swim after coming down from the volcano. Located on the Central American Highway, 11 miles west of San Salvador, Los Chorros is a series of waterfalls spurting from the side of a mountain, falling into a misty gorge to a series of four man-made pools, each one overflowing into the next. The first is shallow, used by children or those who just want to wade, the other three are deep, clear, cold and delightful for swimming. Individual stones form a walkway across one pool, perfect for sunning. In the cliffs and hills around the pools, trails climb through a rain forest of ferns, vines, tropical flowers, and bromeliads. Down below by the pools there are snack stands and places for campers to park overnight or set up tents. It's peaceful and beautiful, but be warned that it gets crowded on weekends.

Excursions into the Countryside

Again, we suggest you inquire locally about the safety of all areas of El Salvador you wish to visit. The Instituto Salvadoreño de Turismo in San Salvador is the best place to go for safety advisories.

Two of El Salvador's most fascinating handicraft villages can be visited in a single afternoon, perhaps in conjunction with a trip to Cerro Las Pavas and Cojutepeque. Ilobasco is a potter's town, famous for its hand-painted clay figurines, which are found in markets and shops all over El Salvador. Realistic figures, smaller than a fingernail, portray people in various aspects of their daily lives: women carrying water jugs, men surrounded by coffee sacks, fruit vendors, and so forth, all small enough to fit under a cover no larger than a walnut shell—exactly how they are sold. Here in Ilobasco you can watch the craftsmen at work, painstakingly working their clay with tiny sculpting tools to capture infinitesimal details. The potters also make handsome vases, lamps, plates, and other items. There is a school in the town's main street, the Cooperative de Ceramistas, where local children learn the art of pottery making. It's fun to watch them at work, and the students welcome all those who stop in and watch. The town has several shops, each selling the same type of pottery. Before buying, however, visit several shops and compare prices and quality since they tend to vary.

San Sebastián is a charming town, but currently visitors are advised to avoid it. Conflict is being reported throughout the eastern provinces of Morazán and La Unión. Inquire locally before setting out on any excursions.

Cerro Verde and Izalco Volcano

On February 23, 1770, something strange happened in a field at the foot of Cerro Verde, a mountain over 6,000 feet high in western El Salvador: a small hole opened up, as one eye witness later described, puffing out small quantities of dust and pebbles. A cone formed around the orifice and within a few weeks it had risen to a height of over 4,000 feet, finally growing over 6,000 feet. For the next 200 years Izalco volcano was a fabulous sight, gushing out smoke during the day and shooting out flames and white-hot boulders at night, glowing rocks tumbling down its slopes. The volcano erupted with such regularity—every five minutes—and was visible so far out at sea that mariners used it to guide their way to safe harbor, so that it became known as Lighthouse of the Pacific.

Izalco was so magnificent that in the late 1950s, ISTU decided to build a resort hotel on the peak of neighboring Cerro Verde, where tourists would be able to peer into the glowing crater and watch the bubbling lava and fiery eruptions at close range. The handsome hotel was duly constructed, but just as it was about to open in 1957, the Lighthouse of the Pacific went out—Izalco ceased erupting and has not been heard from since, except for a few puffs of smoke, wafting up from its crater.

After years of hesitation, ISTU finally concluded that Izalco is spectacular enough even without the fireworks, and has opened the hotel. Located in the midst of an attractive and lovingly tended park, the hotel offers a view right into the crater of the volcano, and it is unforgettable—the lifeless, perfect cone is streaked with lava flows of an odd blackness with sinister wisps of smoke rising from the unseen fires at its core, and, stretching out beyond it, there is the wide green expanse of the coastal plain meeting the Pacific.

Intrepid visitors will want to climb its peak, and guides may be obtained through the hotel. It is a difficult climb over loose gravelly lava, making it particularly hard on your leg muscles, especially on the descent. But when you peer into the depths of the immense crater from the rim, it will all have been worth the effort.

The less adventurous will find great pleasure in walking through paths of cloud forests and topiary gardens. Many of the exotic trees and plants are identified by signs, and the views are always breathtaking. Not to be missed is the vista from the other side of the hotel: you can look out over vast coffee country, centered around the crater of the deep volcanic Lake Coatepeque, over 3,500 feet below. In addition to the Hotel de Montaña,

ISTU has created a national park in an area that includes Izalco and Santa Ana volcano. There are camping facilities, picnic areas, and a cafeteria (connected to the Hotel de Montaña). Although the last few miles to Cerro Verde are unpaved, the road is good. Those who want to travel by bus should first go to Santa Ana, where they can catch a bus that goes all the way to the top of Cerro Verde.

At the foot of the volcano there is another Turicentro, Atecozol, certainly one of the loveliest in El Salvador. It has two spring-fed swimming pools with dressing rooms, cabanas, a restaurant, and odd but interesting monuments—one to Atonatl, the Indian whose arrow wounded Alvarado on this spot during the invasion of 1524, and other monuments, such as a giant frog, Tlaloc, the god of rain and fertility, and Cuyancuat, a god with the head of a pig, a unicorn's horn, body of a snake, and feet of a tapir. Most attractive of all are the extensive grounds with indigenous trees of all sorts—the ceiba, the maquilishuat (El Salvador's national tree), the cortez blanco with its yellow flowers, the thick twisting amates, the lavender-bloomed cortez negro, and the famed balsam trees, which grow only in El Salvador, valued for centuries for their sweet healing sap. Always towering over the park is the perfect and majestic cone of Izalco.

Less than a mile from Atecozol is the Pipil Indian village of Izalco, also known as Asunción Izalco. Its weathered church has a lovely colonial facade and its interior, with images of Jesus, Mary, and saints, is interesting as an example of a typical Indian church. This village is known for its colorful Holy Week procession, its traditional Indian rituals in the second week in August, its native dances on Christmas Eve, and its feast of Saint John the Baptist, the third week in June, in which rituals are combined with a rough horseback game whereby the contestants try to knock each other from their mounts with chickens. A bell tower up the street from the church holds a bell set, a gift from King Charles V, with an amusing inscription challenging anyone who doesn't believe it weighs a hundred quintals (over a ton) to lift it up.

Lake Coatepeque

Easily reached on the way back from Izalco volcano, Coatepeque is a small, gemlike crater lake, which originated after a series of volcanic eruptions. As it has no outlet and has hot mineral springs flowing into it, its warm transparent waters have a high mineral content and are said to be medicinal. Its elevation is almost 2,500 feet above sea level, so the climate is superb, and the green hills that slope toward the water on all sides are planted with coffee. The water is a striking shade of blue with glints of silver across the surface, and the lake is so deep that its bottom has yet to be found, though areas have been measured at more than 1,200 feet. Only a 45-minute drive from the capital, Coatepeque has understandably become a popular weekend and holiday resort, with much of the area around the lake's shore occupied by beautifully kept cottages with resplendent lawns. Sailboats, speedboats, and water-skiers cut across the lake's surface. The fishing is excellent and the hot springs that gush into the lake are invigorating. There are two hotels, Hotel del Lago and Hotel Torremolinos, which serve a delicious crab soup—a must. The guapote (a local fish) is also a renowned delicacy.

With its enchanting setting, which offers so many pleasures and diversions, Coatepeque is an ideal place for an afternoon's excursion, or for a delightful weekend or holiday. Aside from a variety of hotels, it is also possible at times to rent private cottages for longer stays; those interested should inquire at ISTU.

The Pacific Coast

One popular map lists over 30 separate beaches along El Salvador's Pacific coast. In fact, the entire coast is virtually one long beach, broken every few miles by rocky headlands or the mouths of rivers or lagoons. Campers, surfers, fishing lovers, and beach nuts will want to start out at the west end of the country, somewhere around the Barra de Santiago, and wend their way down CA-2, the coastal highway, stopping off and investigating each beach until they reach the east end of the coast at Playa Playitas. During the trip they'll find a wide variety of beaches—shallow and deep, white and black sand, crowded and deserted, turbulent and calm—with a variety of accommodations for tourists. There are luxurious resort complexes and modest cabanas, where for a few colones a night you can hang a hammock between two poles under a thatched roof.

The stretch of highway winding along the cliffs overlooking the ocean between El Salvador's major port, Acajutla, and the old fishing town of La Libertad is known as La Costa del Bálsamo. This is the only place in the world where the famous trees that produce balsam of Peru grow. The misnomer for this substance produced exclusively in El Salvador came about when balsam in the early days of the Conquest was shipped first to Panama, where it joined other shipments coming from Peru, before being sent to Spain. The balsam resin is tapped from the trees by scoring the trunk with a machete, allowing a cloth to soak up the sap, and then boiling the cloths. The resin has been used for centuries as a curative for asthma and bronchial diseases, as a perfume, a natural antiseptic, and a base for soap. It was highly prized by buccaneers and privateers who cruised the Spanish Main as a miracle cure for the sword wounds that were their occupational hazards.

Steep hills with the highway gouged into the sides rise almost from the water's edge, and as you wind along the coast, you can peer over miles of black-sand beaches, broken by rocky points where ancient lava flows have poured into the ocean. Along this stretch are a number of private beach clubs, many of which allow foreigners to use the facilities for a small fee (it is not necessary to know a club member). Perhaps the best of these is Atami Beach Club, an idyllic spot on a high cliff, with tennis courts, a freshwater and two salt-water swimming pools, two excellent beaches, a restaurant, cabanas that can be rented for the day, and overnight rooms at very reasonable rates.

A few miles past Atami is El Zunzal, widely known as one of the best surfing beaches in the world.

La Libertad

La Libertad was once El Salvador's major seaport, but with the opening of the improved port facilities at Acajutla, it has become little more than a fishing town. But since it is only 19 miles from the capital by a good road, it's a favorite spot for the city folk. ISTU has opened a Turicentro here and improved the beachfront quite a bit, building snack stands and a swimming pool and renovating some of the old port buildings into great seafood restaurants, bars, and handicraft shops. The town itself is down-trodden, and the beach isn't as good as others, but it is an interesting place. Ask when the fishermen come in, and try to be there when they do. The town is an open roadstead—in its boom days as a port, cargo was lightered onto its pier—so there is no safe harbor for the fishermen's boats. When they bring home their catch, usually in the afternoon, each boat pulls up beside the high pier, a mechanical winch drops a line, the fisherman waits for just the right moment, and when his boat rises on the crest of a wave, he quickly attaches the winch's hook cables to his boat. Then the boat is hauled from the sea. It hangs in the air above the pier before it is swiv-eled, set down on crude rollers on the pier, and pushed back onto the beach. Even while the boat is being trundled up the pier, the townspeople and fish peddlers flock around, bargaining with the fishermen for their catch. It's a hectic and colorful scene.

Continuing east on CA-2 from La Libertad you pass a number of good beaches, such as Playa San Diego, that have bungalows and restaurants. As the road angles away from the shore, you begin passing through cotton country. Here, as throughout El Salvador, you will notice many oxcarts being driven down the highway, piled high with pineapples, watermelons, and other goods being taken to and from the market. At kilometer 51 you can see two unexcavated pyramids to the north of the highway. These hills are an archaeological site called El Amatal, but thus far have not been totally uncovered. Soon you pass the Cuscatlán International Airport near Comalapa. In the tiny town of Rosario de la Paz you might want to stop at Cafetería Jaltepec for what almost everyone agrees is the best *quesadilla* in the country (a Salvadoran specialty, *quesadilla* is a flat crumbly cheese-cake made from flour, eggs, milk, and cheese with a distinct cheese flavor very unlike cheesecake; it is delicious with a cup of strong Salvadoran cof-fee or hot chocolate).

Take a turnoff for Costa del Sol, and soon you will be passing a string of beaches—San Marcelino, Costa del Sol, Playa Los Blancos—where there is a mixture of private cottages, public beaches, and resort hotels. These hotels—Tesoro Beach, Izalco Cabaña Club, and Pacific Paradise—are the finest on the coast and only 15 minutes from Cuscatlán Internation-al Airport, so seekers of sand and surf can head right for the shore without having to stop in the capital. This long strip of white-sand beach faces the ocean on one side and an estuary, Estero de Jaltepeque, on the other, offer-ing visitors the chance to cruise through a maze of mangrove swamps, overgrown canals, and wide lagoons where you can see the ocean waves breaking on the sand bars that separate the lagoons from the sea. Here, there are countless varieties of wild birds, fish, and picturesque fishermen's houses on stilts scattered along the swampy banks. Guides are available with their boats to offer you cruises, and they may be hired through the hotels or at the town of La Herradura.

Also along the Costa del Sol, in the midst of the resort hotels, is Turi-centro Costa del Sol, a well-run Turicentro with cabanas that have elec-tricity and may be rented for the day or night (you must provide your own sleeping bag or hammock). There is also a bar, a freshwater pool, a restaurant that serves local food and oysters on the half-shell, trailer hookups and camping facilities—not to mention a broad, clean, and sparkling white-sand beach.

Returning to CA-2 and continuing east, you soon pass Turicentro Ichanmichén ("place of the little fish"), with a swimming pool, sports facilities, rocky pools surrounded by tropical trees—an attractive place to stop for a snack or a siesta. After passing through Zacatecoluca, you cross the Río Lempa on the Puente de Oro (which is under construction). The Lempa is El Salvador's longest and most important river because of the huge hydroelectric projects built on it to the north. Historically it's an important river also, for it seems to have formed a mutually recognized boundary between the Maya–Pipil tribes and the Lencas in the pre-Conquest days. Canoers, kayakers, and white-water addicts will not rest easy until they've made an expedition down the Lempa. The river passes through wild and beautiful country, with a wide variety of rare wildlife.

Just across the bridge is a road that will take you to Banía de Jiquilisco and more fine beaches that line the San Juan del Gozo Peninsula. The Bahía de Jiquilisco, itself, is known for its superb fishing. Continuing on CA-2, after Usulután (the capital of the ancient Lenca nation), you pass through a large barren field of lava from the slopes of the San Miguel volcano. Beyond Usulután is a turnoff that will take you to another wonderful beach, Playa El Espino.

Beyond the lava field the road angles back toward the ocean, and soon you reach the turnoff that leads to what is perhaps the most perfect beach in the country: Playa El Cuco. Wide, straight, and clean, it is about 6 miles long. The only beach that could possibly compete with it is El Tamarindo, a lovely little fishing village at the edge of the Gulf of Fonseca, a few miles east of El Cuco. Tamarindo is sheltered on the inside of the Punta El Faro and is calm and very safe for swimming.

Fishing enthusiasts who haven't tried their luck at Barra de Santiago, Estero de Jaltepeque, or Bahía de Jiquilisco will want to try it in the Gulf of Fonseca. All along the coast, the continental shelf stretches out 20 to 30 miles, making bottom fishing excellent. Sailfish, marlin, and tuna are plentiful. Surf-fishing fans will find abundant snapper, grouper, corvina, roosterfish, jack, bass, pompano, barracuda, and more.

Tazumal, San Andrés, and Los Ausoles

The most significant archaeological site yet excavated in El Salvador is that of the ruins of Tazumal, in the town of Chalchuapa. To get there you should take CA-1 west from the capital, turning toward Chalchuapa as you reach the city of Santa Ana. On the way you pass another extraordinary site that has been recently excavated and partially restored. Just beyond kilometer 33 on CA-1, crossing the Río Sucio, turn right, and only a few yards from the highway are the gray pyramids of San Andrés.

The site of Tazumal appears to have been inhabited for over 7,000 years, but the restored ruins now visible date from the early to postclassic period (A.D. 300–1200). In the nearby coffee fields are the sites of still earlier centers, such as Trapiche (500 B.C.–A.D. 200), Casa Blanca, and Peñate. Also nearby is Finca Las Victorias, where the intriguing Olmec Boulder was found.

The town of Chalchuapa has destroyed much of what was once Tazumal, but what remains is still impressive. The ruins are also quite confusing, because the archaeologist Stanley Boggs, who excavated and restored the site, did not try to restore the structures to their original state, but revealed different structures and styles from a period covering more than 1,200 years. For example, a temple dating from the early classic period sits next to a structure from the postclassic period, which shows great Toltec influences. The result is unharmonious and vaguely disquieting but fascinating as one observes the changes in style that occurred over a thousand-year period of Mesoamerican history. The people who built Tazumal must have had a wide range of contacts; pottery discovered in the ruins and nearby lake show the influences of Copán and the Ulúa Valley of Honduras, while the structures have stylistic similarities to Kaminajuyu, Teotihuacán, and Toltec cities, among others.

Although the exact purposes of the structures of Tazumal are unknown, we do know that it was a burial site—27 tombs have been excavated there. Some of the artifacts found in those tombs can be seen at the small museum that adjoins the site. It is advisable to visit the museum first, since there are charts and maps showing the layout of the structures in the area and information on its history. On display at the museum are the remains of a skeleton discovered at Tazumal; mushroom stones, which are said to symbolize the hallucinogenic mushrooms consumed by the Indians during religious ceremonies; exquisite jade carvings and polychrome pottery; heavy stone yokes; and elaborate metates, curved stones used for thousands of years to grind corn and still used throughout Mesoamerica today.

While in Chalchuapa you might also want to see the colonial church of Santiago. Its decorations, such as the stucco vegetables and fruits, show a strong Indian influence, for the builders of the church were Indians, laboring for their Spanish masters. Saint James (Santiago) sits on his horse atop the dome. Lake Cuscachapa, a small but attractive lake of volcanic origin, is close by, and many ancient artifacts have been found buried in its muddy bottom.

Close to Chalchuapa, near the town of Ahuachapán about 20 minutes away, are Los Ausoles ("the cauldrons"), an area of about 12 square miles in which there is so much geothermal activity that the earth seems to bubble like a vast pot of fudge. Geysers shoot into the air, steam hisses from the earth, mud boils over as if in a witch's cauldron, pools of water heat to boiling point, whiffs of sulfur percolate up through the mud. It's all a bit ominous and strange, but quite fascinating and lots of fun. Local women wash their clothes in some of the hot water pools as others splash in the natural hot bathtubs.

Northern El Salvador

Visitors should be warned about the current conflict in the northern areas. Inquire about present situations before you travel here.

Lake Guija, on the Guatemalan border in the northwestern corner of El Salvador, is the most beautiful lake in El Salvador, and has the added attraction of ancient ruins and countless thousands of petroglyphs scattered around its shores and islands.

The village of La Palma, just a few miles from the Honduran border, isn't only one of the most pleasant and scenic spots in the country, it's also the location of an increasingly famous artist's cooperative, which is turning out some of the most vibrant and original works of art and folk art in Central America. Fernando Llort, who studied in France, returned to his native El Salvador in 1972 and moved to La Palma. He began painting images of simple village life in a colorful, direct, and primitive style influenced by European traditions and by Indian and folk art. His work began attracting attention and Llort decided to set up a workshop and school, La Semilla de Dios, in hopes of helping the local people learn to express themselves through art. Soon other artists began to arrive in La Palma, and they too set up workshops and galleries. At present more than 250 artists make a living from the paintings and other crafts they sell through Llort's cooperative and elsewhere. Paintings in the characteristic Semilla de Dios style are available on wood, leather, canvas, embroidery, and exquisite miniatures painted on polished surfaces of small seeds.

PRACTICAL INFORMATION FOR EL SALVADOR

WHEN TO GO. Although the climate is moderately tropical, with an average year-round temperature of 78°F, many visitors find the most enjoyable season is from Nov. through Apr., when the country's sunny days and balmy weather make an ideal refuge from harsh northern winters. These months are known as summer, or the dry season, while the months from May through Oct. are known as the rainy season, winter. During the rainy season, however, the sun shines most of the time, with brief storms occurring in late afternoon or evening. As throughout Central America, the main determinant of temperature is altitude: the coast is very hot though often tempered by Pacific breezes, while the capital at 2,200 feet is more temperate and a sweater or light coat is welcome at night.

HOW TO GET THERE. By air. El Salvador's International Airport is the largest and most advanced in Central America and is serviced by the airlines *Taca, Aerónica, Tan–Sahsa, Copa,* and *Lacsa,* which operate flights to North and Central America. There are direct flights to and from Miami, New Orleans, Houston, Los Angeles, Mexico City, and all the Central American capitals.

By bus. A number of buses run daily between Guatemala City and San Salvador: these include *The Centro America, Futuro Express, Melva y Pezarossi, Mermey, Bisa, El Condor, Transesmer,* and *La Giralda,* which continues on to Puerto Barrios. The trip to or from Guatemala City takes approximately 5 hours.

Transportes El Salvador runs to Tegucigalpa, Honduras, on Mon., Thurs., and Sat.; from there, connections are available to Nicaragua and Costa Rica.

Condor International's "Rutas del Pacífico" leaves daily at 7 A.M. and 10:30 A.M. to Talismán, Mexico.

By car. Driving time from Guatemala City to San Salvador is about 4 hours, and the roads are good all the way. El Salvador has the best highway system in Central America.

ENTRY FORMALITIES. At press time a valid passport and visa are required of all U.S. citizens. To obtain a visa one must submit a police record, U.S.$10, one photo, and one's current employment status. This can be done in person at the Embassy of El Salvador or by mail. The address in the United States is: Embassy of El Salvador, 2308 California St., NW, Washington, DC 20008.

The importation of all animal products or by-products, such as ham, sausage, cheese, etc., is forbidden, and these will be confiscated and incinerated at the quarantine delegation of the port of entry. Products from the United States, Puerto Rico, New Zealand, Japan, Norway, and Central America are exempt. Fruits, subject to inspection by the quarantine inspectors, may also be confiscated, depending on their criteria. Pelts, skins, and leather are permitted as long as they have been tanned and are not coming from countries that have been affected by hoof-and-mouth disease and porcine fever, but they will be subject to a disinfecting treatment by the quarantine delegation at the port of entry. Plants and flowers may be imported as long as they are earth-free and have received proper treatment at the quarantine delegation. Dogs, cats, and birds may enter as long as they have a health certificate authorized by a veterinarian, and import permit papers that have been requested prior to entry through the Ministerio de Agricultura y Ganadería of El Salvador, which will indicate the necessary requirements according to the agricultural health laws. Vaccines required of dogs are rabies, hepatitis, leptospirosis, distemper, and parvovirus.

A vaccination certificate is not required of citizens or residents of the United States and Canada. Certificates of yellow fever vaccination are required of those arriving from countries that are affected by the disease.

When entering or leaving the country by land, avoid "off-work" hours: 12 P.M. to 2 P.M., and from 6 P.M. to 8 A.M. of the following day; Sat. from 12 P.M. until Mon. 8 A.M. all day during national holidays.

All vehicles entering or leaving the country by land must be fumigated to avoid possible contamination of fruit and plagues affecting the coffee plants within the Central American area. All tourists entering El Salvador by motor vehicle with foreign license plates must possess a document proving ownership of the vehicle and a valid driver's license; the vehicle may remain in El Salvador for a period of 30 days, which may be extended for another 30 days, not in excess of 90 days total, through a request made to the Dirección General de Renta de Aduana and transit authorities. Every tourist is required to export his vehicle when leaving the country, and to abide by the law that rules the importation of vehicles. Insurance is not required. Drive on the right.

CURRENCY. El Salvador's monetary unit is the colon (symbol C). U.S.$1 is equivalent to C5 at presstime. U.S. dollars are accepted practically everywhere; coins are not. Change will be returned in Salvadoran currency. Traveler's checks may be cashed at hotels and banks. It is recommended you carry small bills at all times, especially when going through the border by land because you must pay border taxes. Colones will not be accepted or changed in Honduras or Guatemala. There is an active black market in San Salvador where the dollar currently exchanges for C5.4. In front of the post office is the most popular spot to change money at this rate. Remember that this is illegal, and exercise caution if you change money in this way.

TELEPHONES. The country code for El Salvador is 503. When in San Salvador dial 14 for information; 19 to make an international call; 17 for the time; 23–7777 for a wake-up service.

MAIL AND COMMUNICATIONS. The post office in San Salvador is on Centro de Gobierno; 22–1922. Mail can be slow; at press time the postal service is on strike. When sending mail to El Salvador, be sure to specify Central America, so your mail doesn't end up in San Salvador, Brazil. You may prefer to use a courier service: *DHL,* 23–0300, telex 23–3105; *Cargo Express,* 23–9702; *TransExpress,* 24–4145; *World Courier,* 23–4428. To arrange for a cable, dial 16, or go to the cable offices at *ANTEL,* downtown, Calle Rubén Darío. English is widely understood.

USEFUL ADDRESSES. Excellent information on all aspects of Salvadoran life, including maps, hotel and restaurant listings, bus and train schedules, and much more can be obtained from the *Instituto Salvadoreño de Turismo* (ISTU), Calle Rubén Darío No.619, San Salvador, El Salvador; 22–8000. They're open Mon. to Fri., 8 A.M. to 4 P.M. There are also ISTU representatives at all border crossings who will help you in any way possible. The airport office (call 24–5454 or 6464) is open Mon. to Fri. 8:30 A.M. to 4:30 P.M.; the offices at the Guatemala and Honduras borders are open 8 A.M. to 12 P.M. and 2 P.M. to 6 P.M. In many ways, ISTU is the most helpful and efficient tourist board in all of Central America. If you plan to venture into the countryside, a representative will mark on your map the areas that are unsafe for tourists. Even if you have no questions, stop by and you'll find their suggestions and information invaluable.

U.S. Embassy, 25 Av. Norte No.1230; 26–7100.

U.K. Consulate, 17 Calle Poniente No.320; 71–1091 or 1026.

LAUNDRY. There are no laundromats in El Salvador, but there are laundry and dry-cleaning services in all the principal cities and in all the hotels.

BUSINESS HOURS. Although it does vary, most businesses are open 8 A.M. to 12 P.M. and 2 P.M. to 6 P.M. Stores are closed Sun.

ACCOMMODATIONS. In San Salvador the hotels range from deluxe to moderate. The deluxe hotels, among the finest in Central America, pamper their guests with comforts and services, such as large swimming pools, color televisions, wall-to-wall carpeting, spacious rooms with sumptuous furnishings, gourmet restaurants, bars, nightly entertainment, banquet and convention facilities, saunas, tennis courts, and more. These hotels are all associated with large international chains and are located in pleasant residential districts within 10 minutes from downtown. Prices for a double room range from US$60 to $120 (with the *Presidente* more costly than the others). The first-class hotels, which are closer to downtown and have clean and comfortable rooms, bars, restaurants, and, in many cases, swimming pools, range in prices from US$20 to $60. The city features a number of guest houses, usually large, old mansions with charming rooms. They are quiet and informal and excellent places to get acquainted with fellow travelers. Prices for a double range from US$4 to $20.

Out of the city accommodations are simpler and cheaper.

San Salvador

Deluxe

Camino Real. Blvd. de los Héroes; 23–3344. Telex C. REAL SANSA. An elegant Westin hotel 8 blocks from U.S. Embassy. Air-conditioned rooms and suites. Restaurant, coffee shop, bar and nightclub, swimming pool, television, shops. Tours available. Easy access to bus and taxis.

Presidente. Av. La Revolución, San Benito; 24–3044. Telex 20037 HPRE-SIN. El Salvador's most expensive hotel. All facilities, including restaurants and bars, pool, televisions, shops, and gym and sauna. Tours available. Easy access to taxis and bus.

First-Class

Alameda. Alameda Roosevelt and 43 Av. Sur; 23–9999. Air-conditioned hotel with restaurants and bar, pool, and gym and sauna.

Novo Aparthotel. 61 Av. Norte No.4617; 23–1661. Air-conditioned hotel with stoves and refrigerators available. Restaurants and bar.

Ramada Inn. 85 Av. Sur and Calle Juan José Cañas; 23–9233. Air-conditioned units. Pool, restaurants, bar. Close to public buses.

Ritz Continental. 7a Av. Sur No.219; 22–0033. Air-conditioned units with TVs. Pool, restaurants, bar, shops, gym. Tours available.

Siesta. Autopista Sur; 23–2500. Air-conditioned units with TVs. Restaurants, bar, pool. Convention facilities.

Terraza. 85 Av. Sur and Calle Padres Aguilares; 23–5444. Air-conditioning, TVs, pool, restaurants, and bar. Tours and public transportation easily accessible.

Guest Houses and Small Hotels

American Guest House. 17 Av. Norte No.119; 71–5613 or 0224.
Family Guest House. 1a Calle Poniente Bis No.325; 21–3578.
Austria. 1a Calle Poniente No.3843, Colonia Escalón; 24–0791.
Hospedaje Izalco. Calle Concepción No.666; 22–2613.
Hotel Custodio. 10a Av. Sur No.109; 21–3916.
Hotel Imperial. Calle Concepción No.659; 22–4920.
Hotel Internacional. 8a Av. Sur and Calle Delgado; 22–2121.
Hotel León. Calle Delgado No.521; 22–0951.
Hotel Panamerican. 8a Av. Sur No.113; 22–4823.
Hotel Roma. Blvd. Venezuela No.3145; 24–0256.

Out of Town

Prices for these hotels run from U.S.$10 to $25 for double rooms; *Tesoro Beach,* however, does cost U.S.$50; *Izalco Cabaña Club,* U.S.$32.

Cerro Verde

Hotel de Montaña. 28–1981. Simple accommodations. Restaurants and bar.

Lake Coatepeque

Hotel del Lago. 41–2160. Plain lodging. Restaurants, bar, pool.
Hotel Torremolinos. 41–1859. Lake resort with restaurants, bar, pool.

Pacific Coast

Tesoro Beach. Costa del Sol; 21–8626 or 3715. Beach resort with convention facilities, marina. Restaurants, bar and nightclub, pool. Air-conditioned units.

Izalco Cabaña Club. Costa del Sol; 23–6764. Beach resort with air-conditioned units, restaurants, bar, pool.

La Posada de Don Lito. La Libertad; 35–3166.

RESTAURANTS. In the capital, dining can be elegant and international or quick and simple (American fast-food chains have proved immensely popular with Salvadorans). The seafood restaurants are generally quite good, featuring red snapper, corvina, robalo, shrimp, oysters, crab, and lobster. A number of restaurants feature *platos típicos,* traditional Salvadoran dishes, such as *gallo en chicha* (cock), and the ubiquitous *pupusas.* A dinner for one person at the more expensive international restaurants will run about U.S.$10–$16; elsewhere you can eat as cheaply as U.S.$2. Alcoholic beverages cost U.S.$2–$3; beer is inexpensive: 40 cents–$1 for a bottle or glass. Wine, however, since it is imported, is quite expensive. One bottle may cost as much as U.S.$20.

Chinese

Chinatown. Paseo Escalón and 91 Av. Norte.
Chung San. Calle La Mascota and Calle a Santa Tecla; 23–3706.
Royal China. Paseo Escalón No.3698; 23–7408.
China Palace. Alameda Roosevelt No.2731; 23–7917.

International

Le Bistro. Calle La Reforma, San Benito.
Cafe Restaurante La Casona. Col. Maquilishuat, Calle La Mascota and Av. Masferrer; 24–6200.
Ciao. Calle La Reforma No.251, San Benito; 23–6272.
Los Entremeses de Federico. La Calle Poniente 822; 22–4507.
Estro Armónico. Paseo Escalón and 85 Av. Sur; 24–2609.
Gran Bonanza. 1a Calle Poniente and Blvd. de los Héroes; 23–4412.
Le Jardin. 15 Calle Poniente No.4430; 24–1227.
Madeira. 63 Av. Norte and 1a Calle Poniente; 23–6638.
Le Mar. Paseo Escalón No.4646; 23–9112.
Marcelinos. Calle La Reforma, San Benito.
Méditerranée. Blvd. Hipódromo No.131, San Benito; 23–6137.
Paradise. Blvd. Hipódromo, San Benito; 24–4201.
Siete Mares. Paseo Escalón, Balam Quitzé; 24–3091.

Italian

Beto's. Paseo Escalón No.4334; 24–3039.
Pizza Hut. Blvd. Hipodromo, San Benito; 24–6212.
Pietro's Pizza. Av. San Martín and 4 Calle Oriente No.17.
Pizza Nostra. Centro Comercial Granada; 23–9013.
Pizza Nova. Plaza Suiza; 24–1438.
Pronto Pizza. Paseo Escalón and 85 Av. Norte; 23–3639.

Mexican

Señor Pico. Paseo Escalón No.5026; 23–2067.
Can Cun. Paseo Escalón and 85 Av. Norte; 24–5719.
Las Brasas. Calle Libertad Poniente No.15, Santa Ana.
Las Carnes. Rancho Bosque Tecleño, Santa Tecla.
Gran Tejano. San Miguel; 61–1117.
El Parador. Km 102½ Ahuachapán; Calle Internacional; 43–0331.
El Torito, Paseo Escalon.
Vista al Lago. Km 12½ Calle a Apulo; 27–0208.

Seafood

Aloha. Calle El Progreso and Pasaje 4; 23–5550.
Chantilly. Paseo Escalón; 23–4180.
Cocterama. 21 Calle Poniente No.1633; 25–6649.
Conchamar. Blvd. de los Héroes; 26–5871.
La Hola. Zona Rosa, San Benito.
La Red. 17 Calle Oriente No.224; 22–3459.
Mar y Tierra. 27 Calle Poniente and 19 Av. Norte No.1052; 25–7214.
Macondo. Calle San Antonio Abad and Av. Lisboa.

Spanish

El Bodegón. Paseo Escalón and 77 Av. Norte; 23–1691.
La Posada de Abilio. Alameda Roosevelt No.2211; 23–0812.

Steak Houses

La Cabaña. Av. Olímpica No.3535; 23–9207.
La Carreta. 45 Av. Sur and 4a Calle Poniente; 24–2242.
La Diligencia. Paseo Escalón and 83 Av. Sur; 24–0756.
Doña Mercedes. Blvd. de los Héroes; 25–4112.
La Pampa Argentian, Final del Paseo Escalon.
La Ponderosa. Paseo Escalón and 75 Av. Sur; 24–0182.
El Tejano. Balam Quitze, Paseo Escalón; 24–3626.
Texas Meats. Calle La Mascota No.138; 23–3204.
La Vida en Rosa. Blvd. Hipódromo, San Benito.

Typical

Amanecer de Don Vicente. 79 Av. Sur, frente Rotonda.
Asados de Don Toño. Paseo Escalón and 91 Av. Sur.
La Casona. Final Calle La Mascota and Av. Masferrer; 24–6200.
Olga's. Paseo Escalón No.3952; 24–6859.
El Petate. Metrosur; 23–3259.
La Tortuga Veloz. Metrocentro; 24–3756.

HOW TO GET AROUND. By car. Stateside driver's licenses are honored in El Salvador, and some of the services offered by local agencies include 2- or 4-door vehicles, optional air-conditioning, free pickup and delivery, and bilingual chauffeur service. You can rent from *Avis, Hertz,*

Budget, and *Sure;* they have offices at the airport and most major hotels. Ask about the safety of any areas before visiting; the guerrillas from time to time declare traffic bans on certain roads and may attack them. Never travel down a side road that has no other traffic on it.

By bus. Since El Salvador is so small and San Salvador so centrally located, many find the easiest way to get around is to take public buses to a destination, spend the day exploring, and return to the hotel by public bus. This is much cheaper than taking taxis or renting cars. Bus service is frequent from 5 A.M. to 7:30 P.M. but nonexistent after 7:30 P.M. Buses have no set schedules, departing whenever they are full.

TOURS. There are a number of tour operators in the capital who offer a wide variety of interesting trips, from half-day city tours and visits to nearby points of interest, to full-day and overnight tours to all parts of the country. The tour operators are: *Alpha Tours:* Alameda Roosevelt and 55 Av. Sur. *Amor Tours:* Paseo Escalón No. 3913; 23–9384. *Izalco Travel Bureau:* Edificio Caribe, Local 9; 24–0402. *Rinsa:* 69 Col. Escalon; 23–5552. *Turex:* Plaza Orleans, Calle Arce and 19 Av. Sur; 22–1883. *Naquil:* 9 Av. Norte No. 406; 22–4375.

TURICENTROS. Turicentros are national parks established and run by ISTU. We do not recommend camping at any of them. *Amapulapa.* About 35 mi from San Salvador on CA-1 east: swimming pools, parks, waterfalls, flower gardens, restaurant, cabanas, trailer park.

Apulo. At Lagode Ilopango: swimming, diving, fishing, boating, restaurants, gardens, waterskiing, trailer park.

Atecozol. About 35 mi from San Salvador on CA-8, the road to Sonsonate: natural spring-fed pools, park and gardens, cabanas, restaurant, trailer park.

Cerro Verde. About 45 mi from San Salvador on CA-1 and CA-8, via Armenia: panoramic view of Izalco volcano and Lago de Coatepeque; flower gardens, hotel, bar, restaurant, cafeteria, trailer park at an elevation of 6,000 ft.

Costa del Sol. About 40 mi from San Salvador, taking CA-2 to Zacatecoluca and then the road to La Herradura: ocean beach, fresh-water swimming pools, bar, restaurants, football field, cabanas, trailer park.

Ichanmichen. About 35 mi from San Salvador on CA-2 to Zacatecoluca: natural spring-fed pools, gardens, forests, cabanas, restaurant, football field, trailer park.

Los Chorros. About 11 mi from San Salvador on the Pan-American Highway, Carretera a Santa Ana: waterfalls, exotic tropical gardens and forests, swimming pools, restaurant, trailer park.

Parque Balboa. About 7 mi from San Salvador on the road to Los Planes de Renderos: park, gardens, restaurant, roller skating rink, football field.

Sihuatehuacán. About 40 mi from San Salvador on CA-1 to Santa Ana: swimming pools, restaurants, open-air theater, roller skating rink, gardens, trailer park.

Other Parks and Gardens

Parque Saburo Hiras. Final Calle Los Viveros, Colonia Nicaragua; 22–7680. 19 acres with a botanical garden and playground specially designed for children.

La Laguna Botanical Gardens. Southeast of Antiguo Cuscatlán, on the road to Santa Tecla. Run by 3 generations of the same family for centuries, this garden is at the bottom of an extinct volcano crater. Petrified lava can be found among the plants—rare local and foreign species.

SPORTS. See also "Turicentros," above. **Golf.** The best courses are the private clubs, but they accept guest cards arranged through local tour operators (or check with ISTU); greens fees are reasonable. *Club Campestre Cuscatlán* (Final Paseo Escalón, No. 5423) has a 9-hole course, while *Club Salvadoreño Corinto,* by beautiful Lago de Ilopango, has 18 holes. The *Tesoro Beach Hotel* on the Costa del Sol has a 9-hole course. See complete listing of private clubs and recreation centers, below.

Car racing. El Salvador's professional racetrack, *El Jabali,* is located near the Nueva Carretera a Santa Ana, km 4½. If you go by car, take the highway to Santa Ana and turn off on the road to Quezaltepeque; after about 3 mi you'll see the track.

Surfing. El Salvador has some of the best surf beaches in Central America, as the colonies of surf bums along the coast attest. The favorite beaches are: *El Zunzal, Playa La Libertad, El Zonte.*

Soccer. There are games in the *National Stadium* on Wed. nights and Sun. afternoons, and often there are matches on other nights as well: check the sports page of the daily papers or call ISTU. The National Stadium "Flor Blanca" is located in Colonia Flor Blanca, 49 Av. Sur, San Salvador; 23–7243 or 7238. The biggest stadium, *Cuscatlán,* which is privately owned, is located at Finca Montserrat, Autopista Sur, San Salvador; 73–2231. There are stadiums in almost every city in the country since soccer is the most popular sport in El Salvador.

Tennis. New courts are opening all the time. In San Salvador, try the *Círculo Deportivo* (Calle Lorena and Carretera a Santa Tecla, km 4½), *Club Campestre Cuscatlán* (Final Paseo Escalón No. 5423), *Hotel El Salvador Sheraton* (83 Av. Norte and 13 Calle Poniente), with 18 tennis and 4 squash courts, *Hotel Presidente* (Colonia San Benito), and *Palacio de Los Deportes* (Final 11 Av. Norte and Campo de Marte). Outside of town are the courts at *Club Atami* (km 49½ La Libertad), *Club Salvadoreño Corinto* (Lago de Ilopango), *Club Salinitas* (Sonsonate), and the *Tesoro Beach Hotel* (Costa del Sol). Again, see club listings below.

Private Clubs and Recreational Centers

Admittance to the clubs can be arranged by the local tour operator.

Club Atami Beach Playa.
83 Av. Norte and 11 Calle Poniente;
23–7698.

Club Británico.
Paseo General Escalón and
85 Av. Norte No. 113;
23–3328.

Club Campestre Cuscatlán.
Paseo General Escalón and

Av. Masferrer No. 5423;
23–0444.

Círculo Deportivo Internacional.
Calle Lorena and
Alameda Manuel Enrique Araujo, km
4½;
23–7588.

Club El Bosque–Río Mar Club.
Inversiones Monei,
6 Calle Poniente No. 126;
22–7020 or 6768.

Centro Español.
Paseo General Escalón and
83 Av. Norte;
23–7306.

MUSEUMS AND ZOOS. The *Museo Nacional David J. Guzmán* is on Av. La Revolución, just off Carretera a Santa Tecla, on the road that leads up to Hotel Presidente Hyatt; 23–6246 or 5428. The museum's collection is small but choice, featuring pre-Columbian artifacts from all over El Salvador, including a chacmool from Casa Blanca near Tazumal, a superb solar disc from Cara Sucia, and the extraordinary Xipe Totec ("Our Lord of the Flayed Hide")—the Mexican god of fertility and penitential torture. The almost life-size figure represents a priest wearing the flayed skin of a human sacrificial victim (the mottled surface shows that the skin is being worn inside out). Like the seed of corn that loses its husk as it grows, Xipe Totec provides humans with food by giving his own skin, making him a kind of Indian-style Christ figure. The figure was found in a volcanic crater near Tazumal and bears a striking resemblance to a figure found in Teotihuacán, Mexico. Other objects in the museum include lovely metates (grinding stones), mushroom stones, stelae, and artifacts from the early history of El Salvador. The objects in the museum are nicely displayed and arranged. Open Tues. to Fri. and Sun. 9 A.M. to 12 P.M. and 3 P.M. to 5 P.M.; closed Mon. and Sat. afternoon.

El Arbol De Dios. Located at the end of Calle La Mascota on Av. Masferrer. This is a private institution dedicated to the development of art and handicrafts in El Salvador. The museum houses the work of Fernando Llort and numerous other artists from the town of La Plama in the district of Chalatenango. The museum also has an excellent restaurant-cafe and gift shop. Visiting the museum should be a priority for every tourist.

Parque Saburo Hirao. Final Calle Los Viveros, Colonia Nicaragua; 22–7680. The museum is located in the southeastern section of the park, which covers 19 acres and includes a botanical garden as well as a playground specially designed for children. The museum concentrates on the flora, fauna, and geologic composition of El Salvador. Open Wed. to Sun. 9:30 A.M. to 4:45 P.M.; closed Mon. and Tues.

Parque Zoológico Nacional. Calle Modelo; 21–4648. South of San Salvador, this small zoo has a nice selection of animals. Open Wed. to Sun. 9:30 A.M. to 5 P.M.; closed Mon. and Tues.

ARCHAEOLOGICAL SITES. *Tazumal,* in Chalchuapa, is west of San Salvador, using CA-1. On the way, you will also pass the ruins of *San Andrés;* these are just beyond km 33, past the Río Sucio, to your right, a few yards off the highway. Tazumal itself seems to have been inhabited from A.D. 300 to 1200. Nearby, the sites of *Trapiche, Casa Blanca,* and *Penate* were occupied as early as 500 B.C. The restorations of Tazumal show the varied styles of the entire period of habitation. A small museum displays pottery, the remains of a skeleton discovered here, jade carvings. The site is open daily 9 A.M. to 12 P.M. and 1 P.M. to 5:30 P.M. It's free. Inquire about buses from Santa Ana.

SHOPPING. Best buys in El Salvador are the distinctive and colorful native handicrafts; among the most popular items are the beautiful cotton macramé hammocks and plant hangers, woven baskets and wicker furniture, and endless variety of pottery, jewelry, handwoven textiles, and unique hand-painted scenes on leather, wood, or polished seeds. Antiques and religious relics are also favorites with bargain hunters—brass church candlesticks, wood statues called *santos,* and colonial furniture are among the treasures that can be found by shoppers. These items can be found in the city's modern shopping malls and department stores, boutiques, tiny shops, outdoor markets, and small sidewalk stands. However, the handicrafts are less expensive when bought where they're made, and of course it's far more interesting to actually see how the objects are made. Among the most fascinating handicraft areas are: **La Palma,** with its distinctive hand-painted leather, wood, and tin objects and its tiny seeds, each with a bright scene painted in miniature upon it (inquire about the safety of the area before visiting); **Ilobasco,** with its famous miniature ceramic figures; **Quezaltepeque,** where a variety of green and brown glazed pottery line the roads, drying in the sunlight; **Nahuizalco,** near Izalco volcano, renowned for its handmade wicker items; **Panchimalco,** where *pañuelas*—colorful scarves woven on small handlooms—can be bought; **San Sebastián,** the village of weavers, with its superb and inexpensive fabrics (again, inquire about the safety of the area before visiting).

In **San Salvador,** the shopper's first stop should be the *Mercado Cuartel* (Central Market), where handicrafts from all over the country are available. As in the villages, you are expected to bargain. The nearby *Flower Market,* with its incredible paper blossoms, as well as natural ones, is another must for shoppers. Another excellent handicraft market is the *Mercado Nacional de Artesanías* at the fairgrounds, on the road to Santa Tecla, near the Hotel Presidente Hyatt. Items will be slightly higher here. Most of the items available in the native markets are also available in the souvenir and curio shops in the deluxe and first-class hotels, though their prices will be much higher. A wide variety of handicrafts of the finest quality can be found in the city's large, reputable handicraft stores (that accept major credit cards). These include: *Nahanche,* at two locations, Metrocentro, across the street from the Camino Real, and Centro Comercial Basilea in the Zona Rosa; *Exporsal,* 51 Av. Sur No.134; *Nayarit,* Edificio Altamira, in front of El Salvador del Mundo; *La Casa de las Artesanías,* Calle los Andes, across the parking lot from Camino Real.

Numerous other shops can be found in the city's modern shopping malls, known as Centros Comerciales. Among the best are: *Centro Comercial Gigante,* Av. Olímpica, *Centro Comercial Caribe,* Plaza de Las Américas, *Centro Comercial La Mascota,* km 4 Carretera a Santa Tecla, and *Metrocentro,* Blvd. de los Héroes, across from the Camino Real. The shops in these centers are open Mon. to Sat. 8 A.M. to 12 P.M. and 2 A.M. to 6 P.M.; closed Sun. These shopping centers contain, in addition, a wide variety of shops, restaurants, supermarkets, bars, and nightclubs.

NIGHTLIFE AND ENTERTAINMENT. San Salvador has the same wide range of after-dark entertainment that you find in most large cities in the Western world—dining and dancing, nightclubs, discotheques, movies, theater, concerts, and frequent sporting events.

For dining and dancing by candlelight try the *Kahare* supper club at the *El Salvador Sheraton Hotel.* It features an orchestra and nightly shows. At the nightclub at the *Camino Real* the accent is on dancing, with live music sets alternating with recorded music intermissions.

Cafe Concert is a fun, informal bistro, with live music, singalongs, and entertainment that goes on until dawn. It's on Blvd. del Hipódromo No.235, Colonia San Benito, near the Hotel Presidente Hyatt.

There are a number of first-class movie houses in San Salvador that play mainly American motion pictures (with Spanish subtitles), many of them at prices of $1.50 or less. The listings can be found in the daily papers.

The National Theater, in front of Plaza Morazán, presents a variety of concerts, plays, recitals, and programs. The *National Symphony* presents regular concerts during its season—July through Dec. Ballet, folk dancing, chamber orchestras, solo performers, and folk music are also frequently found on the program. For information check with ISTU.

Many nights there are football (soccer) games at the *National Stadium* (see "Sports"). This is the most popular sport in El Salvador and it is worthwhile attending a game, even if you're not a soccer fan, just to see the intensity with which the Salvadorans approach the game. *Cockfights* take place at Palenque 1 and 2, 7 Av. Sur, 3 and 5 Calle Poniente, in Santa Tecla.

The *San Jacinto Teleférico* is 10 minutes east of downtown. This amusement park–entertainment complex is on top of Mount San Jacinto and is reached by funicular. The ride up the mountain is fun in itself. On top there are amusements for children, entertainment on weekends, a restaurant and bar, and spectacular views.

SAFETY. A visitor to El Salvador needs to be well-informed as to the current political situation. We have pointed out areas that, at press time, are experiencing conflict, but the situation in these areas can and does change. The smartest thing to do is to ask everyone (people at your hotel, taxi and bus drivers, people you meet) about all places you wish to visit. The guerrillas, in fact, do publicize which roads they want people to stay clear of, and many local people listen to the guerrilla radio. Main highways are usually safe during the day. We strongly advise that you *never* go down a side road that you don't see any traffic on. If you don't speak Spanish, the best thing to do is probably to avoid driving around altogether. Taxis aren't dirt cheap, but they'll make everything much easier for you. Again, if unsure about a place or a situation, ask. We don't recommend that you walk the streets alone after 9 P.M.

LEAVING EL SALVADOR. There is an airport exit tax of U.S.$10. Anything may be exported with the exception of archaeological artifacts, antiques, and gold and silver ingots.

NICARAGUA

by
PHILIP FINNEGAN

Philip Finnegan is currently special correspondent in Central America for U.S. News and World Report. *He previously served as* Time's *special correspondent in Cairo, covering North Africa.*

Since the first visits of the Spanish in the sixteenth century, Nicaragua has been known as a land of lakes, lagoons, and volcanoes, a natural beauty that has continued to delight visitors.

With a population of only 3 million in the largest Central American country (57,000 square miles, about the size of Iowa), Nicaragua is sparsely populated, a fact that helps preserve its beauty. Even this population is concentrated in the Pacific coast area. The Caribbean lowlands, which make up a third of the country's area, have less than a tenth of its population.

Yet even in the first descriptions of the country, there is a contradiction. The calm and beauty of nature is contrasted with occasional violence—earthquakes and volcanic eruptions.

Tension is inherent not only in the country's nature but also in its politics. For centuries Nicaragua has faced a national split between conservatives and liberals. Now that split is between the Sandinista revolution and opponents of the revolution. And, more than any other people in Central

America, Nicaraguans have been subjected to a turbulent history of foreign intervention.

History

Relatively little is known of Nicaragua's pre-Columbian past. Unlike Guatemala, Honduras, or El Salvador, there are no large temple complexes of ancient Indian cultures.

Enigmatic footprints are the first vestiges of human beings in Nicaragua. The footprints, at least 7,000 years old, show primitive people running in terror from a volcanic eruption. The little that can be determined from the footprints is that the climate of Nicaragua was very different at that time. The footprints of a bison, now extinct in Nicaragua, show that the climate was probably cooler than now, perhaps similar to the American Midwest.

Pre-Columbian Indians later constructed life-size statues of gods, humans, and animals using only crude stone axes and chisels, and left petroglyphs whose meaning still cannot be deciphered.

The area only began to emerge from the mists of obscurity shortly before the arrival of the Spanish. A group of Aztecs moved south from Mexico to form a trading colony in the Rivas area, close enough to ensure the protection of the Aztec empire but far enough to contact the Chibchan traders, who brought precious emeralds from Colombia.

The Niquirano tribe of Indians on the shores of Lake Nicaragua was profoundly influenced by the contact, beginning to speak some Nahuatl (the Aztec language), adopting their fashions of dress, and even imitating their methods of warfare. Many of the names of Nicaragua's most important areas are Nahuatl in origin, such as Managua, meaning "where the water is retained"; Matagalpa, "town of nets"; Xiloa, "water of Xilonem (goddess of corn)"; Chinandega, "town of stem huts"; and Jinotega, "place of sad people."

In 1519, only three years after the cruel Pedro Arias de Avila, commonly known as Pedrarias, founded the original settlement of Panama, he had become hungry for a larger territory and more Indians to rule. Moreover, the Spanish still hoped to find a sea route between the Caribbean and Pacific Ocean. Thus a mission was mounted to explore farther north.

When Captain Gil González de Avila reached Nicaragua in 1522, he found the most powerful Indian tribe of Nicaragua, at the time headed by Chief Niqarao. The chief and his tribe were pliable and quickly converted to Christianity; they sealed their demise with a gift of gold ornaments to the Spanish.

Two years later Francisco Fernández de Córdoba led another expedition of conquest in an effort to obtain more gold. The Niquirano helped the Spanish conquer other tribes. Cities were founded in Granada and León Viejo (Old León) near existing Indian settlements in an effort to exploit Indian labor in agricultural plantations.

Fernández de Córdoba had his own ambitions, hoping to conspire with Hernán Cortés, the governor of Mexico, to set up an independent governorship headed by himself in Nicaragua. Pedrarias learned of the plot to undermine his own power as governor of the area and sent an armed force after Fernández de Córdoba, who surrendered and was executed in León Viejo.

During the first years of the Spanish Conquest the chronicler Hernández Oviedo y Valdés described Nicaragua in glowing terms:

> It is one of the most beautiful and peaceful lands, for its abundance of corn fields and vegetables; of varied beans; of lots of different fruits, an abundance of cacao, a fruit that looks like almonds, used as currency among that people, for buying things, such as gold and slaves, clothes, food as well as so many other things.
>
> There is an abundance of honey and wax; as well as hunting animals, also pigs, deers, rabbits and other animals; and good fishing, from the sea as well as from the rivers and lakes; abundance in cotton, making clothes from it which the Indians of that land spin and weave.

The Spanish gradually broke down Indian society. The small Indian farms were converted into huge tracts in which Indian laborers would cultivate corn, beans, and cacao and raise cattle brought by the colonizers. The native population was decimated by disease and by the export of laborers to Peru for arduous work in the mines.

While the Spanish were transforming the densely populated Pacific coast, they had far less success in penetrating the sparsely inhabited Atlantic coast region, a huge, rainy jungle plain. The area's inhospitable, disease-ridden jungles and swamps hindered Spanish colonization. The untamed nature of the region as well as its numerous bays and lagoons made it a perfect haven for pirates, who attacked Spanish shipping in the Caribbean.

Occasionally these pirates would turn their attention to the east and attack Granada, a rich trading town. During one 20-year period, between 1665 and 1685, the town was attacked and burned by pirates at least three times, with one raid being led by the infamous pirate Henry Morgan.

Great Britain took advantage of the area's alliance with British privateers to create a British protectorate and proclaim a Mosquito Indian as king.

Spurred on by their success in dominating the east and by reports of disaffection in western Nicaragua, the British government mounted an expedition to attempt to gain the strategic link between two oceans for itself. In 1780, Horatio Nelson, then a young captain in the British navy, mounted an ill-fated expedition to capture Granada and Léon.

With Central American independence in 1821, rivalry between León and Granada only intensified. Granada, a trading and agricultural center, had a wealthier elite than did León, which had been the provincial capital. Social differences created a radically differing political outlook, with León favoring a unified Central America and reforms based on the American and French revolutions, while the conservatives of Granada favored the monarchical and clerical ideas inspired by Spain.

When the Central American Union broke down in 1838, the León–Granada conflict often erupted in armed conflict as the liberals and conservatives fought for power. With Nicaragua's strategic position it was only a matter of time before this instability attracted foreign intervention.

Both the United States and Britain became interested in building an interoceanic canal. To avoid a confrontation, the United States and Great

Britain in 1850 signed the Clayton-Bulwer Treaty under which neither power would solely control any canal in Nicaragua and neither country would occupy or colonize any area in Central America.

With the annexation of California to the United States and the great Gold Rush, Nicaragua became even more important to the United States. Cornelius Vanderbuilt recognized the area's potential as the easiest place to transit passengers quickly between the Atlantic and the Pacific, since the Panama Canal had not yet been built. In 1848 he set up a transit company that used steamers on the San Juan River into Lake Nicaragua, and from there coaches on a 13-mile overland route to the port of San Juan del Sur.

This concern of the American government and American commercial interests with the strategic value of Nicaragua as a transit point and a potential site of a transisthmian canal set the backdrop for one of the most bizarre incidents of Nicaragua and Central American history.

In 1855 the American adventurer William Walker, who only two years before had led a disastrous attempt to set up an independent state in the Mexican territories of Baja California and Sonora, was asked by the Liberal party to help them wrest control of their country from the Conservative party. Walker gathered 58 other adventurers, called the American Phalanx of Immortals, who quickly took control of the Conservative's stronghold of Granada.

Walker arranged for his own election as president within a year, and he began issuing a series of alarming decrees, instituting slavery, making English the official language, and taking out a foreign loan with the territory of Nicaragua put up as security.

The adventurer's downfall came when, not satisfied with controlling Nicaragua, he adopted the slogan "Five or none" and tried to seize the other Central American countries. Himself a native of Tennessee, Walker hoped that by unifying the five states into a republic supporting slavery, he would strengthen the U.S. southerners' cause against abolitionists in the North.

Walker's slogan was aptly chosen. Instead of five, he got none. Other Central American countries united and, backed by Britain and Vanderbuilt who had lost his transit company to Walker, defeated Walker at the town of Rivas in May 1857. Rather than surrender to the Central Americans, Walker and his supporters surrendered to American marines, who evacuated them back to the United States.

Walker did not accept his defeat easily, and in a subsequent attempt to set up his Central American republic, he was captured and executed by Honduran authorities in 1860.

With the Liberals discredited by the Walker episode, Nicaragua experienced a 30-year period of peace and economic growth under the Conservative party.

In 1893 the Liberal leader José Santos Zelaya overthrew the Conservative president. Zelaya's tough dictatorship stimulated the country's economic development. But anti-American policies, efforts to revive the Central American Union with himself as head, support for revolution in other Latin American states, and attempts to convince Japan and Great Britain to build a canal competitive to the Panama Canal, all led to his downfall.

When Zelaya executed two American soldiers of fortune in 1909, the incident served as a pretext for American intervention; about 400 marines were sent in to ensure his overthrow. After the immediate crisis was over, marines remained or were reinforced, in numbers ranging between 100 and 2,800, until all were finally withdrawn in 1933.

American interest in Nicaragua continued to increase with the signing of the Bryan-Chamorro Treaty in 1914 giving the United States exclusive rights to build a transisthmian canal.

American troops took on an active combat role in 1927 when Augusto César Augusto a popular leader of the anti-American forces, refused to lay down arms after a U.S.-sponsored settlement of the fighting between Liberals and Conservatives. Sandino's troops were bombed and hunted for over five years before an agreement was finally made whereby Sandino would lay down arms in return for a huge agricultural cooperative, occupying a fourth of the country.

The National Guard, led by Anastasio Somoza, resented Sandino's treaty with President Juan Bautista Sacasa—who was elected in 1932—and Sandino's alleged failure to lay down arms, so in 1934 Sandino was assassinated.

Within two years Somoza had deposed the president to begin a period of over 40 years of rule by himself, his sons, and associates. Thinking of his pro-U.S. policies, President Franklin Roosevelt remarked, "He may be a son of a bitch, but he's ours." When he was assassinated by a young poet in 1956, the transition was smooth for his elder son, Luis, to assume the presidency and for a younger son, Anastasio Somoza Debayle, to head the National Guard, until a decade later, when he too succeeded to the presidency.

Somoza amassed a huge fortune in the poor country. The list of Somoza assets is impressive—an airline, a shipping line, a port (now Puerto Sandino), hotels, a newspaper, a television station, factories, and more. The landholdings totaled an area the size of El Salvador.

When a 1972 earthquake in Managua left a half million people homeless, Somoza used the opportunity to enrich himself and associates through the diversion of money, food, and other relief goods sent.

The assassination in 1978 of leading critic Pedro Joaquín Chamorro, editor of the newspaper La Prensa, further strengthened opposition to the Somoza regime by uniting the bourgeois opposition into an organized protest movement.

When the middle-class opposition joined with the Sandinista National Liberation Front, which had fought the regime since 1961, the regime collapsed in July 1979, though not before considerable bloodshed throughout the country.

With the triumph, the Sandinista government put a high priority on social programs, eliminating polio through a nationwide vaccination campaign, cutting infant mortality to a rate a third of that before the revolution, and reportedly cutting illiteracy from 50 percent to 13 percent during a vigorous literacy crusade.

Nicaragua is facing serious economic problems as a result of a counter-revolutionary army, known as Contras, revolutionary dissatisfaction, and heavy indebtedness. Supermarket shelves are bare, with serious shortages of consumer goods. Factories have problems obtaining the foreign currency needed to buy raw materials necessary for production. Even agricultural production has been hit by the hostility of the private sector to the revolutionary government.

The economy remains heavily dependent on agriculture, the most important sector of the economy. Coffee remains the largest export, with cotton a close second, and sugar, meat, and bananas trailing behind.

Nicaragua today is deeply divided between those who favor and those who oppose the Sandinista revolution. Those favoring the revolution include many young people, peasants, workers, intellectuals, and the so-called popular Roman Catholic church. For those supporting the revolution, the election of Sandinista President Daniel Ortega in 1984 showed the overwhelming popularity of the revolution. Censorship and political restrictions are seen as necessary to defend the revolution against counter-revolutionaries supported by the United States.

Those opposing the Sandinistas include many private businessmen, conservative peasants, the hierarchy of the Roman Catholic church, the editors of *La Prensa* newspaper, and even former supporters who accuse the Sandinistas of taking the revolution too far to the left. These groups see Nicaragua's serious economic problems as evidence of economic mismanagement as much as of the country's civil unrest. They consider limitations on freedom as designed to gradually destroy the opposition press and political parties.

The two sides are irreconcilable in their differences. Even many families have split between supporters and critics of the Sandinista revolution. Although peace talks began at the Esquipulas II Summit in 1987, and have continued since then, the immediate outlook for Nicaragua appears to be continued political turmoil.

Managua

A booming capital of 800,000, whose population comprises over a quarter of Nicaragua's total, the city of Managua continues to expand at a rate double the rate of the country as a whole. Gone forever are the sleepy Indian villages that dotted the area at the time of the Spanish Conquest, though their memory is preserved in the names of the area.

Managua emerged into prominence as a mid-nineteenth-century compromise for the national capital with the hope of satisfying the Liberal stronghold of León and the Conservative stronghold of Granada.

The city's advantage was its approximate equidistance from both rivals. Otherwise, there have been a number of disadvantages.

The capital area has suffered two devastating earthquakes in this century—in 1931 and 1972. The later earthquake killed about 12,000 persons and leveled 250 city blocks. Scientists found that the whole site of Managua is heavily faulted and a major earthquake could be expected about every 50 years. The decision was then made to decentralize the city, with outlying areas developing their own services so that no earthquake could cause the same destruction. This explains why much of the downtown area is empty and overgrown with weeds, with a few destroyed buildings that were never bulldozed.

The city's location has been unfortunate in other ways. Unlike other Central American capitals, it is located in the lowlands, resulting in an extremely hot climate. Moreover, the proximity to water makes the area mosquito-ridden.

Perhaps the best place to begin a visit to Managua is at the Plaza de la Revolución. Here are many mementos of the capital's most turbulent moments in history. Towering over the square is the cathedral, once Managua's tallest building, now standing in ruins, devastated by the 1972 earthquake. The earthquake occurred shortly after midnight on December 23, so fortunately no one was in the building to be hurt.

Inside the cathedral huge columns and walls are cracked, while the roof is missing. Niches in the walls once held statues of Christopher Columbus, Queen Isabela, the conquistador Francisco Fernández de Córdoba, and other notables in Nicaraguan history.

Next to the cathedral is the National Palace, where yet another of the powerful shocks occurred for the regime of former dictator Anastasio Somoza Debayle. On August 22, 1978, a group of Sandinista guerrillas dressed as guardsmen seized the building and 1,500 captives, including the Minister of the Interior and one of Somoza's sons. After two days the prisoners were released when Nicaraguan newspapers printed a guerrilla communiqué, released about 50 prisoners, and paid a half million dollars. The operation raised the prestige and power of the Sandinistas, who within a year overthrew the Somoza government.

Diagonally across the square is the tomb of Carlos Fonseca, one of the founders in 1961 of the Sandinista Front. Fonseca was notable as the chief strategist and ideologist with the Front until he was killed in 1976 fighting Somoza's National Guard. At the grave an eternal flame burns in remembrance of Fonseca. The Spanish inscription on the grave proclaims that "Carlos is of the dead who never die."

Near Fonseca's grave there is a monument built in 1933 to the poet Rubén Darío, dressed in a Roman toga, a winged angel behind him. This is one of a number of tributes to this poet in Nicaragua. Behind the statue near Lake Managua stands the Rubén Darío Theater, where most of Managua's cultural activities take place.

For those interested in the Nicaraguan revolution, a number of monuments have been erected since 1979 commemorating various aspects of the revolution. On the Avenida Bolívar stands a monument to Pedro Joaquín Chamorro, a stark concrete monument with a bust of Chamorro on the outside and an amphitheater within. As editor of La Prensa, Chamorro was the Somoza regime's harshest critic. The location marks the site where Chamorro was assassinated with over 30 wounds in January 1978, an act that provoked massive anti-Somoza demonstrations.

A huge monument to Nicaraguan workers also stands on the Avenida Bolívar. The massive figure of a worker stands with a machine gun uplifted in the left hand and a pick in the right hand. "Only the workers and peasants will go to the end," notes an inscription on the monument, which was built for the sixth anniversary of the Sandinista revolution. To the left of the monument, a hill is visible on which is written in huge white letters FSLN, standing for the Frente Sandinista de Liberación Nacional (Sandinista National Liberation Front). Those interested in a concise history of the FSLN should visit the Museum of the Revolution, located in the complejo Eduardo Contrerra. Here one can read about Sandinista ideology, watch a documentary about the fall of Somoza, and see memorabilia from distinct periods of Nicaraguan history.

In front of the museum is the primary open market of Managua, the Mercado Roberto Huembes. Here one can obtain everything from freshly made tortillas to pedicures. It is one of the largest market complexes in Central America and well worth a visit.

The Nicaraguan government has also created a Literacy Museum, Parque Las Palmas, 1 Cuadra al Norte, to commemorate the revolution's literacy crusade in 1980. Some 55,000 volunteers, many high school students and Cuban volunteers, went into the countryside to cut illiteracy, reportedly reducing it from 50 percent to 13 percent.

Managua's prerevolutionary past is also of interest. Visitors should be sure to visit the footprints of Acahualinca, the first vestiges of ancient people in Nicaragua. The footprints of over a dozen persons, including men, women, and children, were preserved in mud. As the group fled in panic from the rain of ash from the Masaya volcano, 20 miles away, their footprints along with those of a deer, bison, and small bird were quickly covered over by ash, preserving them for posterity.

The footprints, discovered accidently a century ago when workmen were digging a well, are believed to continue for perhaps another hundred yards. Archaeologists did not have the funds to continue digging further.

There has been considerable controversy over the age of the footprints, but through the use of volcanic stratigraphy scientists have now determined that the footprints are from 7,000 to 9,000 years old. That time frame would mean that the footprints are those of hunters and gatherers, although previously it was believed that agriculture had not yet been introduced to Nicaragua at such an early date.

The National Museum in Colonia Dambach provides further insights into Nicaragua's pre-Columbian history. The collection shows pre-Columbian burial customs, ceramics, jade jewelry, and interesting group of large stone statues from Ometepe Island and the province of Chontales depicting both gods and Indian notables.

Managua has its natural beauty as well, with a lagoon in the midst of the city and another six lagoons ringing it. Formed, as others, by the collapse of a volcano, Tiscapa Lagoon, once the site of primitive Indian rites of human sacrifice, is now a pretty lake with a nice walk around it and a restaurant on the water where the fish can be fed.

Las Piedrecitas, a small park and walk overlooking the Asososca Lagoon, is pleasant with a striking view of the dark-blue waters. Asososca, which provides the water for Managua, is believed to have a depth of up to 300 feet. Its Nahuatl Indian name appropriately means "place of the blue water."

Xiloa Lagoon, 12 miles from Managua, has been developed into a popular beach with picnic tables, dressing rooms, public bathrooms, and restaurants. Although the azure water is calm and beautiful, its depth can make it dangerous for inexperienced swimmers.

Managua's new Comandante Edgard Lang Sacasa Zoo has a good sampling of the country's tropical wildlife, particularly from the rain forests. The zoo includes about 200 animals of 50 different species, including monkeys, crocodiles, peccaries (wild pigs), ocelots, pumas, leopards, deer, and parrots.

León Viejo

León Viejo (Old León) is well worth a visit because of its historical importance and the romance of its history. To get to León Viejo, turn off 25 miles from Managua enroute to León onto a dusty 10-mile road.

Founded in 1524 as the second Spanish town in Nicaragua, León served for 86 years as the capital of the area, until the city was finally destroyed in an earthquake caused by neighboring Momotombo volcano. Residents saw the city's destruction as only a belated divine judgment for evils that had occurred there—the beheading of the city founder, the assassination of the city's bishop, and 18 Indians torn apart by dogs.

Entering the barbed wire gate that leads to the site, the visitor approaches the main cathedral. In front of the cathedral stands the square where Fernández de Cordoba, city founder, was beheaded and 18 Indians were dismembered for rebellion against Spanish rule. Behind the cathedral is the house where the bishop was assassinated in 1549, stabbed to death in front of his wife by the sons of a governor he had severely criticized for oppression of Indians and extensive landholdings.

The Camino Real (Royal Road) served as the city's main street. On the street are private homes, the convent of La Merced, and the church of La Merced built in 1528. In the church is buried the infamous governor Pedrarias, who had ordered the deaths of the Indians and the city founder. The buildings, originally of adobe and brick, have been partially reconstructed with tiles placed on the walls to protect them from rain damage.

Around the core of the city, where the Spanish lived, there was a larger area of Indian workers—some originally lived in the area, while others were forced to move there to cultivate cacao and cotton as well as hunt and fish for the Spanish.

Towering over the site is Momotombo volcano, a perfect cone rising over 4,100 feet above sea level. Its eruption in 1610 was preceded by an earthquake that devastated León Viejo, forcing the inhabitants to move to the present site of León. Later it buried León Viejo under ash until the city was uncovered by archeologists 20 years ago.

Momotombo itself is legendary. Victor Hugo cited one anecdote: according to Spanish custom, priests mounted each of the volcanos in order to bless them, but those who mounted the ferocious Momotombo made up the sole mission that never returned. Even today the volcano often belches white smoke, a reminder that as recently as 1905 it erupted.

Momotombo's steam has been harnessed to provide some of oil-poor Nicaragua's power. Nicaragua is the third Latin American country, after Mexico and El Salvador, to utilize volcanos as an energy source.

León

León, the second-largest city in Nicaragua, has lost much of its colonial charm, but preserves the best colonial churches in the country.

The city served as the capital of Nicaragua for over 200 years. When the city was moved, the present location was chosen for its proximity to the Indian village of Subtiava, a village then speaking a now-forgotten tongue.

Befitting a capital of the province, León's cathedral is the largest in Central America. Its construction began in 1747, taking 69 years to complete. The cathedral is said to have been built by mistake when plans for a more modest church were mixed up with a larger church intended for Lima, a wealthier Spanish province in Peru.

Nicaraguan historians are inclined to dispute this, arguing that the cathedral's solid, squat construction and subterranean chambers are designed to withstand the shock of earthquakes and the weight of cinder from volcanic eruptions. Indeed, the cathedral has fared well, never suffering more than a cracking of its towers from earthquakes.

The huge baroque cathedral contains the tomb of Rubén Darío, guarded by a remorseful life-size lion, the symbol of a city whose name means "lion" in Spanish.

Three blocks north of the cathedral, the church of the Recolección, built in 1788, preserves a rather whimsical baroque style, with stone vines climbing the columns of the facade. The medallions carved into the facade are symbolic of the passion of Christ.

The church of San Juan Bautista in the Indian suburb of Subtiava is one of the most attractive colonial churches in Nicaragua. Inside is Nicaragua's finest colonial altar. A half block in front of the church are ruins of the large church of Vera Cruz.

On the Calle Central Rubén Darío, León preserves as a museum the house where Rubén Darío spent his infancy. Darío, the only Nicaraguan to achieve international stature in the creative arts, was influenced by the French symbolists. He created a modernist style that had considerable impact on writers of the time and leads many to consider him Latin America's greatest poet. The museum includes personal possessions and manuscripts of Darío.

Volcanic Springs

Continue on the highway to San Isidro. At the 115-kilometer marker (about 15 miles) outside León, turn left into the village of San Jacinto. Several blocks farther on is a stream bed active with volcanic springs, at the foot of the now-extinct San Jacinto volcano.

The boiling springs (*hervideros*) of San Jacinto show craters of red and black mud boiling and spurting up a foot into the air, as they release sulfurous gases. Residents say the springs are most active shortly after a heavy rain. Be careful not to get too close, though; there have been deaths from slipping into the boiling water.

Based on the activity for centuries of the boiling springs, scientists believe there may be considerable possibilities for thermal power.

Estelí and Selva Negra

At San Isidro turn left for the highway to Estelí, center of Nicaragua's tobacco industry. With a climate approximating the tobacco-growing areas of Cuba, and even with Cuban seeds, Nicaragua is producing high-quality handmade cigars for export. Pick up a box in the hotel gift shops or at the Managua airport.

Estelí's main square, across from the century-old cathedral, contains a number of interesting petroglyphs. The boulders, which have drawings of bird, animal, and human figures, were brought to the town from Las Pintadas, an important archeological site 5 miles west of the city.

A block from the main square there is a small museum commemorating the country's revolutionary past. Its modest collection includes arms used by Somoza's national guard and by the Sandinista Front during the revolution.

The cloud forest of Selva Negra is a pleasant area to spend a day, hiking on miles of trails, observing the rich wildlife, having lunch on a pretty artificial lake at the hotel, even spending the night before returning to Managua. To reach Selva Negra, drive past Matagalpa about 10 miles on the road to Jinotega. Turn right where one of Somoza's tanks destroyed in the revolution marks the entrance.

Selva Negra and Santa María de Ostuma nearby offer thousands of acres of virgin forest, though gradually coffee planting is transforming the area. Still it remains rich in wildlife such as ocelots, wart hogs, puma, jaguar, sloths, and spider monkeys, though gradually, with more agriculture, their numbers are dwindling.

The area remains one of the richest areas in Nicaragua for birdlife, including the cinnamon hummingbird, ruddy woodpecker, stripe-breasted wren, elegant trogon, shining hawk, emerald toucanet, banded cactus wren, long-billed hermit, and Boucard's hermit. The area even has a few of the quetzal, the holy bird of the Maya, beautiful with its long tail and its brilliant green, crimson, and white coloring. Early morning and late afternoon are the best times for bird-watching.

Matagalpa is an attractive town, the center of an important coffee- and cattle-producing area. About 3,000 feet above sea level, the climate is always cool. The town includes an attractive colonial-style cathedral built in 1874, and if you have lots of time, the Parque de los Monos has several interesting idols shaped in human form near its entrance.

Returning to Managua

Return to Managua by the Pan American Highway. About 10 miles from Matagalpa is the turnoff to Ciudad Darío, the birthplace of Rubén Darío. The original house has been preserved.

About 30 miles farther on is the battlefield of San Jacinto, where on September 14, 1856, William Walker's forces were dealt their first defeat during a six-hour battle with Nicaraguan troops, commanded by General José Dolores Estrada. It was the beginning of the end for Walker.

Tipitapa, on the southeast shore of Lake Managua, is only 12 miles from Managua. The town used to have thermal baths, but economic problems have forced their closure. Only a warm-water pool remains. The city is renown for its guapote, a tasty, fleshy fish. Stop for lunch or dinner.

Masaya

No visitor to Nicaragua should miss visiting the volcano of Masaya, one of 27 volcanos in the country, eight of which are active. The view into the crater as it pours forth steam is unforgettable.

The history of the area makes the experience all the more memorable. The Indians are said to have thrown maidens into the boiling lava in the crater, in an effort to appease Chaciutique, the goddess of fire. Offerings to the goddess have been discovered in lava tunnels in the area.

The Spanish conquerors thought they saw in the crater what they were searching for most, boiling gold. Several expeditions were mounted in the sixteenth century to try to mine that presumed gold, using devices such as a bucket that would close when immersed in the lava. The missions were given up when it was discovered that the lava was only molten stone.

To reach Masaya National Park, drive along the Carretera Masaya for 12 miles from Managua and take a turnoff to the right.

Approaching the Masaya volcano, also known as Santiago, you will drive over a huge 200-year-old lava flow that leads directly down from the crater.

About two miles from the entrance gate is the Cueste del Sacuanjoches, an area that abounds in Nicaragua's national flower, the sacuanjoche, a pretty yellow flower that grows on a bush.

Another two miles on a good road and you reach the rim of the crater. The massive crater, with its 1,870-foot diameter and depth of 590 feet, presents a striking view.

Over hundreds of years, as the volcano repeatedly erupted, the mouth of eruption changed. To see an older crater of the volcano, climb 185 steps to a lookout point marked with a large cross. From here, there is a dramatic view of Lake Managua and the craters of San Pedro and Nindiri volcanoes.

Continue driving on the road around the crater to the other side. The lookout point of Boca del Infierno ("Mouth of the Inferno") gives an even more imposing view of the crater. Smoke pours out from lava heated to over 1,800° F.

Return to Carretera Masaya, the main highway, and turn right, continuing just over a mile to the 26 kilometer marker (about 16 miles). Turn right into Nindiri, a village named after its Indian chief when the Spanish conquistadores arrived. It still has some palm-thatched huts and a colonial church built in 1798.

A small museum in the town contains a variety of pre-Columbian relics found in the Masaya area, including giant jars in which the Indians buried their dead, stone idols, and musical instruments.

Masaya, the city of flowers, is most notable for its Indian suburb Monimbo, where some of Nicaragua's best artisans work, creating a wide variety of crafts such as hand-knotted hammocks, carved masks, tapistries with pre-Columbian motifs, baskets woven of palm fibers, and wooden bowls and vases.

To get to Monimbo, you will pass by the ornate colonial church of the Ascensión built in 1833, and the church of San Sebastián, site of a massacre of several hundred persons, which led to a bloody uprising against the Somoza government in February 1978.

At the church of Magdalena are several shops that sell the embroidery, leather goods, and wood that Masaya is known for. The shopkeepers can direct a visitor to workshops where artisans are occupied at their trades. There are several shoemakers a block in front of the church of Magdalena, and some wood craftsmen on the Calle Central of Monimbo, though their work has now largely been mechanized with electric lathes and drills.

Some of the most interesting work done by artisans is found in the Barrio San Juan on the Calle del Estadio, near the Hospital Rafaela Padilla. Here artisans hand-knot hammocks, tapestries, and even rope.

Continue on about 6 miles to reach San Juan del Oriente, another village with artisans who make imitations of colorful pre-Columbian ceramics. The numerous workshops on the main road will be glad to let you watch their craftsmen shape the pottery. Products can be purchased either on the main highway to the south or at the village cooperative.

From San Juan del Oriente either continue on to Granada, about 7 miles north, or return to Managua through Niquinohomo, a rich coffee-producing area. Niquinohomo has the distinction of being the birthplace of the revolutionary leader, César Augusto Sandino, whose name has been given to the international airport, a port, and numerous streets and squares throughout the country, as well as assumed by the ruling Sandinista Front.

The house where Sandino spent his childhood has been turned into a museum, which includes some of his personal possessions and a flag signed by Sandino on February 2, 1933, marking his acceptance of the peace treaty ending his five years of guerrilla warfare. Appropriately enough the name Niquinohomo in the Chorotega Indian language means "valley of the warriors."

Granada

The first city founded in Nicaragua, Granada preserves some of the beauty of its past with lovely arcaded buildings, colonial churches, and attractive squares.

With its connections through the San Juan River and Lake Nicaragua to Caribbean and Europe nations, for centuries Granada was the country's trading capital, exchanging manufactured goods from Europe for Nicaragua's cattle hides, tallow, cacao, and indigo. Agriculture flourished as well in the area's rich volcanic soil.

As the country's wealthiest city, throughout the seventeenth century it was the frequent site of English, French, and Dutch pirate raids, plundering, burning, and even kidnapping its inhabitants.

The city was again burned during the mid-nineteenth-century struggle to expel William Walker, the American adventurer who had himself declared president.

In spite of these trials, the city remains the third largest in Nicaragua. The main square is attractive, bordered with arcaded buildings reminiscent of Spain.

The city includes Nicaragua's second most important collection of churches after León. The church and convent of San Francisco, built in 1585, is the oldest church in Nicaragua. Unfortunately much of the original design and facade was lost when William Walker's troops burned Granada. It was rebuilt in a new style in 1867.

The church of La Merced was built in 1781 but, like the church of San Francisco, suffered serious damage during the war against Walker. Its carved wood statues of the Virgen de los Dolores and Jesús Nazareno were originally brought from Spain over three centuries ago.

The church of Guadalupe served as a stronghold for the Walker forces, who turned it into a fortress and hospital as they struggled to retain control of Granada.

Las Isletas, a group of 323 islands offshore from Granada, are a must for all visitors to the city. Rich in wildlife and history, the islands can be reached by renting a motorboat for about $12 for a three-hour trip from the port of Asese, reached by driving past the Granada beach.

The islands are in an idyllic setting, most of them small and lush with vegetation. Residents live by growing mangos, coconuts, and a few oranges, but mainly by fishing for the tasty guapote and moharra fish that abound in the waters.

The area is one of the richest in Nicaragua for birdlife, including the uniform crane, green heron, little blue heron, black-crowned night heron, Mexican tiger bittern, American egret, Nicaraguan grackle, and Montezuma oropéndola. The birds can be spotted most often in the morning and late afternoon.

The beauty of the islands has been recognized by the wealthy of Nicaragua, who have built homes on many of them. Former dictator Anastasio Somoza Debayle had a home here.

To see all of the islands, ask to visit the fortress on San Pablo, the last of the island archipelago. A small fortress, originally built in the middle of the eighteenth century and reconstructed in 1974, marks the site where the Spanish installed a battery of cannons to protect Granada from attacks by pirates and the British, part of a series of fortifications built to protect the city. The eight cannon slits in the outer wall command the sea approaches to Granada. Several cannons remain at the site. The island with its two-room fort and view of distant Granada is a pleasant place for a picnic lunch.

Another boat excursion can be arranged from the port of Asese to Zapatera Island at a cost of about $30 for the day. Scantily populated, the island has been turned into a national park to preserve its rich archaeological heritage. The rocky island served as an Indian mausoleum. Here were erected huge stone statues weighing up to two tons, symbolizing the gods and notables of pre-Columbian Indians.

On the island, in the Sonzapote Peninsula and at the Punta de las Figuras, some of the massive bases of the statues remain intact, though most of the statues themselves have been moved to Granada for safekeeping, and some were taken during the past century to museums in the United States. At Sonzapote there are also royal tombs and a stairway that ascends to the summit of a hill.

The nearby Isla del Muerto ("Island of the Dead"), separated from the island of Zapatera by a small canal, has a large area of some of the best petroglyphs in Nicaragua, as well as tombs.

Ometepe, the largest island in Lake Nicaragua, is reached by boat from either Granada or from the port of San Jorge; regularly scheduled ferries run from each. As on Zapatera, Ometepe Island, with its two active volcanos, once had numerous stone carvings now removed for safekeeping to Granada and museums abroad. In front of the church of Altagracia some of these carvings of Indian chiefs and notables are preserved.

Lake Nicaragua, the largest lake in Central America, occupies an area of 3,100 square miles. It is the home for unusual freshwater fish, including lake sharks, measuring up to 10 feet in length, and sawfish. Although usually found in saltwater, these fish feed in the waters of the San Juan River delta, becoming used to a freshwater environment, and gradually swim upstream into the lake.

Fishermen will be interested to know that the tarpon, common to the southern part of the lake near San Carlos and in the San Juan River, is a favorite sporting fish. The average 60-pound fish provides a longer, tougher fight than any other fish in Central America.

The fortress of El Castillo de la Inmaculada Concepción on the San Juan River is of interest to tourists. (At the moment, it is closed as a military area. Visitors should check with Inturismo to see if the area is open.) The massive fort was built by the Spanish in 1672 in an effort to protect Granada from pirate attacks. The period when it was built was a time of tremendous danger because of pirates, who occupied and burned Granada at least three times between 1665 and 1685.

It was Horatio Nelson, then a young captain, who led the capture of the fortress in 1780, as part of a British plan to take Granada and León and assure the British access to the transisthmian route while dividing Spanish possessions. The assault failed when disease obliterated the British force, which had to abandon the fort after five months.

Pacific Beaches

Nicaragua has a wide variety of Pacific coast beaches—ranging from those of remote fishing villages to well-developed tourist facilities close to Managua.

Undoubtedly Nicaragua's most popular beach is Pochomil. Easily accessible from Managua over 35 miles of good road, Pochomil has been developed with picnic tables, dressing rooms, public bathrooms, several restaurants, and a nice hotel. The beach is clean and the surf calm.

For those who find a less developed beach more appealing, Masachapa may be preferable. Only a short drive from Pochomil, Masachapa combines a good beach with a fishing town. With the limited facilities in the area, hotels are primitive.

On the road from Pochomil to Managua, about 10 miles from Pochomil, stop at El Salto. Walk down a short path on the right side of the road to reach a small, but very pretty waterfall. On weekends many residents of Managua stop here to enjoy the waterfall and wash off the salt from swimming at Pochomil or Masachapa.

El Velero ranks as one of Nicaragua's most attractive beaches. Only 47 miles northeast of Managua, El Velero is reached by turning off the old Managua-León highway. Less frequented than other beaches due to an admission charge, it is well equipped with shaded picnic tables, a restaurant, and a very good hotel.

El Tránsito is about 7 miles south of El Velero by a dusty dirt road. It has few facilities other than a good hotel, but the beach is long and attractive, making it a quiet place to relax.

Poneloya, only 12 miles from León, has an attractive broad beach with a fishing village. Many wealthy residents of León keep holiday homes here.

Far to the south, 87 miles south of Managua, San Juan del Sur has a reputation as one of Nicaragua's most beautiful beaches. The beach, on a pretty half-moon bay with azure water, has a backdrop of mountains. Though attractive, the beach is no longer as clean as formerly, and hotels in the town are spartan. San Juan del Sur has a sense of glory faded, preserving a few fancy wood buildings on the beach. During its boom days the town served as a terminus of Cornelius Vanderbilt's transit company, which brought passengers by steamer up the San Juan River to Lake Nicaragua, and then 13 miles by coach over Central America's only macadam road to San Juan del Sur.

Atlantic Coast

At the moment, visitors to the Atlantic coast of Nicaragua need a special permission from the government (apply at Immigration, Pista de la Resistencia). Some areas, like Puerto Cabezas, are totally closed to visitors.

Bluefields, the most important town of the Atlantic coast, is named for Blewfields, a Dutch pirate who in the middle of the seventeenth century set up headquarters in the area. Besides being a refuge for bucanneers, the town served as the capital of the Mosquito protectorate of Britain, and the area was ceded to Nicaragua only in 1860. Its architecture reflects the influence of Britain rather than Spain. English is more widely spoken than Spanish. Protestantism rather than Catholicism is predominant.

To reach Bluefields, visitors can either drive or fly. Flights are often booked up to a month in advance, so the only choice may be a four-hour drive to Rama from Managua, and then a five-hour boat trip down the Escondido River. The trip can be rewarding since the boat travels through virgin jungle.

The jungle of the Caribbean coastal plains is lush with vegetation. With rainfall between 130 and 250 inches annually, trees grow in some areas up to 160 feet high. Wildlife living in the jungle include the boa, anaconda, jaguar, wild boar, deer, and spider and howler monkeys.

Most of the names of the Atlantic region are colorful Mosquito or Sumu Indian words that describe their relationship with the area, such as Kairasa, "river of the alligators," or Mairinlaya, "river of the women."

Across the Bluefields Bay, the Bluff serves as the port of Bluefields for lobster and shrimp fishing.

Corn Islands

About 40 miles east of Bluefields in the Atlantic Ocean are the Corn Islands (Islas del Maiz). The islands, small and beautiful, are a vision of paradise with their white sandy beaches, clear waters, and coconut-laden palm trees.

Large Corn Island, the biggest of the islands, is approximately 4 square miles and has about 2,500 West Indian-descent, English-speaking inhabitants who raise coconuts, extracting the oil, and who fish for shrimp and lobster. It has a nice hotel and an airstrip servicing the other islands.

The smaller island, with only about 200 inhabitants in its 1 square mile of land, is located 11 miles from Large Corn Island.

Scuba divers will be interested to know that only slightly over a mile from Large Corn Island is a Spanish galleon sunken in over 70 feet of water, and 7 miles south of the island is Blowing Rocks, volcanic rocks that cover submerged caves rich in marine life.

PRACTICAL INFORMATION FOR NICARAGUA

HOW TO GET THERE. As a result of American sanctions against Nicaragua, there are no direct flights from the United States. *Aeronica,* the Nicaraguan carrier, flies from Panama, Costa Rica, Mexico, and San Salvador. *Aeroflot* flies from Moscow via Cuba. *Copa* flies from Panama, Costa Rica, Guatemala, and El Salvador. *Cubana* flies from Cuba. *Iberia* flies from Madrid via Havana. *Tan/Sahsa* offers indirect service from Miami via Belize, Tegucigalpa, and also service from Costa Rica. *Air France, Lufthansa,* and *Varig* also fly into Managua. Although *Taca* has recently cancelled flights into Nicaragua, there is a possibility of their resuming in the future.

It is possible to enter Nicaragua via land, either by car or bus. *Tica* bus has direct service from San José, Costa Rica (9 hours including immigration). To enter through Honduras take a bus as far as San Marcos on the Honduran border and then catch a bus in Nicaragua to Managua.

TRAVEL DOCUMENTS. U.S. and U.K. citizens need only a passport to receive a visa upon arrival. A round-trip plane or bus ticket must be purchased to enter Nicaragua. Information can be obtained from the Embassy of Nicaragua, 1627 New Hampshire Ave. NW, Washington, DC 20009; tel. 202–387–4371.

CURRENCY. The currency is the *cordoba,* named since 1912 after the famous explorer Francisco Fernández de Córdoba. It comes in denominations of 1,000, 500, 100, 50, 20, and 10 cordoba notes as well as coins in denominations of 5, 1, .50, .25, .10, and .05 cordobas.

Upon arrival all foreigners will have to change $60 worth of currency at the official exchange rate (at press time) of 10.25 cordobas to the U.S. dollar. There is no limit to the amount of money that can be brought into the country, as long as U.S.$60 is changed at the point of entry. There is a very strong black market for dollars in Nicaragua; at the border towns, the exchange rate at press time is C100 to U.S.$1; in Managua, the exchange is C80 to U.S.$1 (subject to fluctuation).

Travelers should be aware of Nicaragua's tourism policy: all foreigners must pay for lodging in $U.S. Credit cards and traveler's checks are accepted at deluxe hotels; however, at moderate or inexpensive hotels, all lodging must be paid for in cash.

WHEN TO GO. Nicaragua is hot. In the western part of the country, where most of the people live, the dry season runs from Dec. to May, the wet season the rest of the year. Along the Caribbean coast it rains year-round. In the coffee highlands around Matagalpa, however, the weather is cool and refreshing. Bring your coolest clothes. Nicaragua is not a dressy country.

TELEPHONES. Pay telephones can be found throughout Managua as well as in the main TELCOR office a block east of the Plaza de la Revolución, the main town square.

To operate pay telephones, first lift the receiver, and when you hear a dial tone, insert a 1 cordoba coin and dial the number. When your party answers, then press the button and begin speaking.

City codes for the country are as follows: Managua 02, León 0311, Granada 055, Matagalpa 061, and Estelí 071. The country code for Nicaragua is 505.

MAIL. An airmail post card costs 5 cordobas to the United States and 6 cordobas to Great Britain. An airmail letter costs 5 cordobas to the United States and 6 cordobas to Great Britain.

Mail service is generally slow and not the most reliable. To communicate quickly by means of a cable or telex is often a better idea. Prepare the text and take it to the TELCOR office for transmission. TELCOR offices in Managua, León, Granada, Estelí, and Matagalpa are located on or within a block of the main town square.

USEFUL ADDRESSES. *U.S. Embassy:* Km 4½ Carretera Sur, Managua; 23881/5. *Inturismo:* Av. Bolívar Sur No.808, Managua; 27927. Inturismo can provide additional information about sights in the country, as can its branches in Granada at the Alhambra Hotel, and in Estelí on the north side of the main square of the cathedral.

ACCOMMODATIONS. In Managua there is a wide range of accommodations available, ranging from deluxe to dirt cheap, with all that implies. Elsewhere in the country hotels are few, frequently crowded, and often very basic, although in some small towns there are unexpectedly nice hotels.

In the major cities, such as Managua, Granada, and León, hotels must be paid in U.S. dollars. *Deluxe* hotels are $95 and up for a double room. *Expensive* ones range from $55 to $95. *Moderate* from $20 to $55. *Inexpensive* from $5 to $20. In addition, there is a 15% hotel tax added to your bill.

Outside of Managua, it is possible to find inexpensive "hospedajes" that will accept cordobas for payment; however, Inturismo, the national tourism board, is currently initiating a strong campaign for the payment of all lodging in dollars. Travelers should be aware of this policy.

Managua

Camino Real. Km 9 Carretera Norte; 31381. Telex 375–1403. *Deluxe.* A very comfortable, beautiful 117-room hotel near the airport. Large air-conditioned rooms, an attractive well-kept garden, pool, children's pool, restaurant, bar, cafeteria, tennis courts, and gift shops.

Intercontinental. Av. Bolívar Sur and 8a; 23531 or 23539. Telex 375–1054. *Deluxe.* Centrally located with 210 rooms. 2 excellent restaurants, cafeteria, bar, gift shops, pool, and air-conditioning make the hotel Nicaragua's finest. Shaped as a Mayan pyramid, the construction is so solid it survived the 1972 earthquake.

Estrella. Pista de la Solidaridad; 97010. *Expensive.* 40 large comfortable rooms with air-conditioning and a small pool and restaurant.

D'Lido. Km 3½ Carretera Sur; 24804. *Expensive.* 40 air-conditioned rooms in a pleasant but mosquito-infested setting around small pool with a coffee shop.

Las Mercedes. Km 12 Carretera Norte; 31210. *Expensive.* across the street from the airport, the hotel has 75 air-conditioned new rooms in a pleasant tropical garden setting, with a small pool, bar, and restaurant.

King Palace. Km 4 Carretera a Masaya; 74548. *Moderate.* 35 basic rooms with air-conditioning and a small restaurant.

Nuevo Siete Mars. 2a Av. Suroeste and 11a Calle; 24670. *Moderate.* Small but nice hotel, has 17 rooms some with air-conditioning, and a restaurant. Small central garden. Good value.

Hotel Morgut. 3 blocks east of Cine Cabrera. *Moderate.* Small, well-kept hotel. Each room with private bath, TV, and air-conditioning.

Palace. Km 7 Carretera Norte; 44119. *Moderate.* Nice rooms with air-conditioning or fans, very pleasant and clean.

El Colibri. One block north of Cine El Dorado; 27420. *Inexpensive to Moderate.* Small hotel with clean rooms, a friendly atmosphere, and a nice outdoor patio.

Guesthouses (Casas de Huespedes)

Bolonia. 11a Av. Suroeste; 60725. *Low moderate.* 23 basic rooms with fans. Very quiet.

Fieldler. 8a Calle Suroeste; 66622. *Low moderate.* Extremely clean, well-run guesthouse with 24 rooms with air-conditioning or fans. Highly recommended.

Tres Laureles. 9a Calle Suroeste; 24440. *Inexpensive.* A very small guest-house with only 3 rooms, but rooms are very clean and owner extremely helpful. Highly recommended.

Outside Managua

Bluefields. Cueto. Calle Neysi Ríos; 567. *Inexpensive.* Payment in cordobas. With 46 rooms, basic but the best in town.

Corn Island. Isleno. No telephone. *Moderate.* Has 17 beach cabanas with private baths, bar, dining room. Nice.

Estelí. Hotel Moderno. Costado Este Catedral 2 Cuadras al Sur; 2378. *Inexpensive.* A very nice hotel with 10 clean, well-kept, pretty rooms that include fans. Estelí's best hotel and best restaurant.

El Mesón. Del Mercado 1 Cuadra al Este; 2655. *Inexpensive.* Payment in cordobas. Has 7 good, well-kept rooms with fans. Restaurant.

Granada. Alhambra. Frente al Parque Central; 2035 or 4487. *Moderate.* 21 rooms, basic but traditional favorite. Attractive lobby, restaurant, and bar. Centrally located.

Granada. Calle 1a Calzada; 2974. *Moderate.* 22 well-furnished rooms opening onto small gardens. Restaurant and bar. Expansion plans call for opening of swimming pool, discotheque, and additional rooms soon. Nice.

Pension Cabrera. Calle Calzada. *Inexpensive.* Payment in cordobas. 10 small rooms, no air-conditioning, shared bathrooms.

León. Europa. 3a Calle and 4a Av. Sur; 2596 or 2575. *Inexpensive.* Payment in cordobas. 28 rooms some with air-conditioning, open onto small central garden. Best in town.

America. Mercado Central 1 Cuadra al Este; 3434. *Inexpensive.* Payment in cordobas. Has 7 very basic rooms but with separate baths and fans.

Matagalpa. Selva Negra. Km 139½ Carretera a Jinotega; no telephone. *Inexpensive.* Payment in cordobas. 28 cabins have stoves, refrigerators, fireplaces. Located in a beautiful forest. Restaurant on artificial lake.

Bermúdez. Parque Darío 2 Cuadras al Este; 3439. *Inexpensive.* Payment in cordobas. With 13 basic rooms.

Pochomil. Bajamar. Centro Turístico Popular Pochomil; no telephone. *Inexpensive.* 70 air-conditioned rooms, well kept, clean. Restaurant.

Poneloya. Lacoyo. Tel. 39. *Inexpensive.* Payment in cordobas. 22 rooms with those overlooking the sea having balconies and a nice view, but rooms are very basic with shared bathrooms and a lack of privacy since the walls do not extend to the ceiling. Still no choice since this is the only hotel in Poneloya.

San Juan Del Sur. Estrella. Tel. 210. *Inexpensive.* Payment in cordobas. On beachfront, basic with shared baths, but the best in town.
Hospedaje el Buen Gusto. Tel. 304. *Inexpensive.* Payment in cordobas. 9 very basic rooms with shared bathrooms.

El Tránsito. Centro Vacacional de los Trabajadores. Though designed for Nicaraguan governmental workers, also open to the public. *Inexpensive.* Payment in cordobas. Reservations must be made through INSSBI in Managua; 42983. 18 nice, clean rooms. Ask for a room with a view and porch overlooking the sea. Very pleasant.

El Velero. Centro Vacacional de los Trabajadores. Gates close at 6 P.M., so you must arrive before then. For weekends, reservations must be made through INSSBI in Managua; 42983. Very attractive complex with 42 cabins and 68 apartments. Cabins include refrigerator and stove. Restaurant, playground, as well as attractive beach. *Inexpensive.* Payment in cordobas.

RESTAURANTS. Dining in Nicaragua is very expensive. Expect to pay at least U.S.$25 per person in a good restaurant.
Typical Nicaraguan dishes are rarely served in restaurants. They can be sampled only from small stands in the Managua central market or numerous streetside vendors. Nicaragua is known for a variety of traditional dishes. *Bajo* is a mixture of beef, green and ripe plantains, and yucca. *Vigorón* is yucca with chicharrón (fried pork skins), served with cole slaw. *Nacatamales,* Nicaraguan hot tamales, are another favorite.
Perhaps the tastiest main dish, which is available in restaurants, is *guapote,* an excellent full-fleshed fish, usually served without its spine.
Nicaragua also has its own distinctive drinks, which can be sampled at small venders' stands. *Tiste,* a drink of cacao and corn, is delicious, as is *posol con leche,* a corn and milk drink. *Chicha* is a slightly fermented corn drink.

Chinese

China Palace. Frente Plaza del Sol; 31710. Open daily 12 P.M. to 3 P.M. and 6 P.M. to 10 P.M. Serves Chinese favorites including chop suey, sweet and sour sauces, wontons, and other typical dishes, as well as international favorites such as grilled steaks, pork, and shrimp. With 40 tables, service can be slow when crowded.
Other Chinese restaurants are: **Chang Gai,** Planes de Altamira, 73012; **Chop Suey International,** Plaza de Compras, 72340; and **Pan American China,** Ciudad Jardin, 44886.

French

La Marseillaise. Colonial Los Robles; 60526. Open daily 12 P.M. to 3 P.M. and 6 P.M. to 11 P.M., closed Sun. Wonderful French food in a pleasant, cozy setting. Limited menu offers steaks, lobster, and shrimp—all excellent. The chateaubriand is superb. With only 13 tables, reservations are almost a must for either lunch or dinner. Otherwise, there is a bar where one can wait for a table.

International

Regency. Intercontinental Hotel; 73010. Open daily 12 P.M. to 2:30 P.M. Open only for lunch with an excellent buffet and piano playing as background.

Volcan Masaya. Carretera Masaya; 24670. Serves a variety of international as well as local dishes.

Usual international favorites also served at other hotel restaurants, including **La Brasserie** (Intercontinental), **Le Pavillon** (Camino Real), and **La Choza** (Las Mercedes).

Mexican

La Cabaña-Rincón Mexicana. Intercontinental Hotel; 23136. Open daily from 6:30 P.M. to 12:30 A.M. Some of the best food and ambience in Nicaragua. Tacos, enchiladas, quesadillas with guacamole, and steaks are served to live entertainment with guitars and Spanish singing. With 32 tables, a pleasant place to spend an evening eating, drinking rum, and enjoying the entertainment, as do many Nicaraguans.

Seafood

The Lobster's Inn. Km. 6½ Carretera Sur; 70224. Open daily 12 P.M. to 3 P.M. and 6 P.M. to 10 P.M., closed Tues. Known with justification as Nicaragua's finest seafood restaurant. The lobster and shrimp are excellent. Though air-conditioned, the 20-table restaurant can get hot when crowded.

Costa Brava. CST 6½ Carretera al Sur; 61868. Open daily from 12 P.M. to 3 P.M. and 6 P.M. to 10 P.M. The specialties are the seafood—lobster and shrimp, grilled or in garlic sauce—but steaks are also served. A relaxed open-air atmosphere under a protective roof, generally with a cool breeze even on hot days.

Steaks

Los Ranchos. Km 3 Carretera Sur; 31379. Open daily 12 P.M. to 3 P.M. and 6 P.M. to 11 P.M., closed Tues. Excellent churrasco, about the best in Central America, as well as other steaks, chicken, and seafood. A nice 50-table setting with traditional Spanish music with guitar players and singers performing. Enjoyable both for food and entertainment, though it can get very crowded in the evening.

Los Gauchos. Km 3 Carretera a Masaya; 25540. Open daily 12 P.M. to 3 P.M. and 6 P.M. to 10 P.M., closed Thurs. Though steaks are the specialty, Los Gauchos also serves shrimp and chicken in a 36-table setting.

Traditional Food

Los Antojitos. Across from the Intercontinental Hotel; 24866. Open daily 12 P.M. to 10 P.M. Offers typical dishes such as refried beans, fried bananas, grilled steak, and shrimp in a pleasant outdoor setting.

There are several small, more informal places in Managua popular for their congenial atmosphere and inexpensive food. These are bar–restaurants that serve the local "Victoria" beer as well as "platos tipicos."

Sara's Comedor. One block north from Hospedaje Dorado on Calle Pablo Corea Q. An old garage converted to a restaurant; popular with an international crowd. Open evenings for food and beer.

Walpa Tara. De Montoya Media Cuadra Arriba; 23237. Cold beers and a variety of typical dishes.

Yerba Buena. Pista Benjamín Zeledón. Offers special drinks, coffee, and simple dishes. Has a bookstore and a good selection of information on the Sandinista Revolution.

Fast Food

A variety of American-style fast food is offered at: **MacDonald's** (not the golden arches), Camino de Oriente, 72285; **Pizza Maria,** Ave. Principal, Ciudad Jardín, 60619; **Pizza Deli,** Centro Comercial San Francisco, 75321; **El Eskimo,** 18a Av. Suroeste, 61868, cafeteria-style.

GRANADA

Terraza Las Palmas. On the lakefront near the Parque Central; no telephone. Open from 9 A.M. daily. A small lakeside restaurant that serves tasty guapote and grilled chicken.

Hotel/Restaurant Granada. Calle La Calzada. Serves a variety of international and Nicaraguan dishes.

Also, the **Drive Inn,** for sandwiches and beer; and **Restaurant Asia** for great steaks and Chinese food.

LEÓN

El Potro. In front of the old San Vicente Hospital; 2995. Open daily 11 A.M. to 10 P.M., closed Mon. Serves good shrimp, lobster, and steaks.

La Merienda. Avenida 2a Poniente y Rubén Darío. Serves a variety of fish dishes as well as the Nicaraguan specialty *gallo pinto* (rice and beans).

Try **Dragón de Oro,** Calle del Telecor, and **Los Angeles,** also on Calle del Telecor, for Chinese food and steaks.

La Terraza Kiloa 87. Located above the Teatro Karawal; 2442. Bar and restaurant serving typical dishes against a nice view of the city.

MATAGALPA

Selva Negra Hotel. 10 mi outside of town; no telephone. Good food in a pleasant setting on an artificial lake in an attractive forest.

TIPITAPA

Entrerios. Calle Central. With 12 tables, serves famous guapote and shrimp. The only one remaining of a number of good restaurants that used to serve visitors to the thermal baths.

HOW TO GET AROUND. Upon arrival at the Sandino International Airport, take a taxi into the city for about 100 cordobas (U.S.$10).

The best way to get around the country is by renting a taxi with driver. Taxis from major hotels are more expensive than taxis from cooperatives. Cheaper yet are those hailed on the street. For about $60 you can rent it for a day to go out of the city—a real bargain. Inside the city the rate is 10 cordobas a ride per person (about a dollar).

Rental cars are more expensive, but all the major agencies are represented in the country: *Avis,* Av. Sandino No.606, tel. 24881 or 24882; *Budget,* Pérez Alonso Blg., 2nd fl., 66226; and *Hertz,* km 4 Carretera Sur, 66462 or 66464. Avis and Budget also have desks at the Intercontinental Hotel, while Hertz has one at the Camino Real.

Buses are inexpensive, but usually very crowded. From Israel Lewites Terminal (on Pista de la Resistencia, near 25a Av. Oeste, Managua) buses depart for León, Jinotepe, Chinandega, Rivas, and Massachapa. From Sub-Centro Sureste Terminal (Pista Carlos Fonseca Amador and Pista Mártires 1 de Mayo) buses depart to Granada, Masaya, Matagalpa, Jinotega, and Estelí. From the Mercado Oscar Benavides (Colonia America 3) buses leave for Rama Chontales.

TOURS. *Turnica,* the Nicaraguan government tour operator, offers a wide variety of tourist and study trips to learn about the country with up to 2 weeks of travel in the country, including the Atlantic areas of Bluefields and the Corn Islands. Groups of at least 7 must apply for such trips.

Shorter day tours of Managua, the Masaya volcano, Granada and Las Isletas, Matagalpa, Léon and Poneloya, and Pochomil beach are offered for groups of 3 persons or more.

Information about these tours can be obtained from Turnica, Plaza España, Managua; 60303, telex 1299 TURNICA.

Inside the United States details can be obtained from Turnica San Francisco, 1551 Dolores St., San Francisco, CA 94110; 415–648–1991, telex 380460.

PARKS. *Masaya National Park,* open Tues. to Fri. 8:30 A.M. to 4:30 P.M. and Sat. to Sun. 9 A.M. to 5 P.M., closed Mon. The park, 12 miles from Managua, includes spectacular views inside the crater of the Masaya from the volcano summit.

Xiloa Lagoon, always open. The park, 12 mi outside of Managua, has swimming opportunities, and one can rent paddle boats to explore this volcanic lagoon.

SPORTS. Boating. Paddle boats can be rented on Jiloa Lake, 12 mi from Managua.

Fishing. Tourists can obtain 1-month fishing licenses for U.S.$20 from INPESCA (Instituto Nicaraguense de la Pesca), 4 Carretera Sur, Managua; 61427 or 60477. The fishing office can also provide information on best places to fish, though tarpon, known to fishermen for their long, tough fight, are found at the San Juan River and Lake Nicaragua.

Hunting. The Pacific coast and the northern areas of the country offer hunting opportunities for white-winged doves and pigeons. Turnica can arrange group tours for hunters.

Scuba diving. There are good opportunities for scuba diving in the Corn Islands, with submerged caves, a sunken Spanish galleon, and a wide variety of fish and marine life. To take advantage of this, a group tour should be arranged through Turnica, the Nicaraguan tour operator (see "Tours" above).

Spectator sports. *Baseball* is by far the most popular Nicaraguan sport, popularized by American marines stationed in Nicaragua in the 1920s. *Soccer* and *basketball* are also popular. The Institute of Sports, tel. 51933, can provide information on game times and places.

ARCHAEOLOGICAL SITES. *Footsteps of Acahualinca,* Managua.
Open daily Mon. to Sat. 9 A.M. to 12 P.M. and 1 P.M. to 5 P.M., closed Sun. The first vestiges of ancient man in Nicaragua show over a dozen persons fleeing from a volcanic eruption between 7,000 and 9,000 years ago.

León Viejo, 35 mi from Managua. The remains of the second Spanish settlement in Nicaragua, includes the remnants of houses, churches, and government offices.

Zapatera Island, the second-largest island in Lake Nicaragua is a rich area for monumental Indian statuary. The island, now a national park, includes royal tombs, a stone stairway ascending a hill, and a large stone table for sacrifice.

MUSEUMS. *National Museum,* Colonia Dambach, Managua. Open
daily Tues. to Sun. 9 A.M. to 12 P.M. and 2 P.M. to 5 P.M., closed Mon. No charge. The museum lost a considerable part of its collection during the 1972 earthquake and the fires that followed it. However, it still includes a number of massive pre-Columbian stone statues from Chontales and Ometepe Island, pre-Columbian ceramics, metates for grinding, and jade jewelry.

Museum of the Revolution, Complejo Eduardo Contrerra, Managua. Open daily 9 A.M. to 1 P.M. Collection includes photographs, manuscripts, and personal possessions of César Augusto Sandino and the founders of the Sandinista front, as well as a documentary film on the victory of the revolution.

Literacy Museum, Parque Las Palmas 1 Cuadra al Norte; 96186. No charge. Open Mon. to Fri. 8 A.M. to 11 A.M. and 2 P.M. to 5 P.M., closed weekends. Shows the accomplishments of the revolution in using literacy brigades to cut illiteracy in 1980 from 50 percent to 13 percent. Includes photographs and personal possessions of brigade members who died fighting illiteracy.

Rubén Darío Museum. Rubén Darío Street, León; 2388. Open Tues. to Sat. 8 P.M. to 12 P.M. and 2 P.M. to 5 P.M. and Sun. 9 A.M. to 1 P.M., closed Mon. Admission is 25 cordobas. Collection includes manuscripts, personal possessions, and various curios of one of Latin America's greatest poets.

Nindiri Museum, in the village of Nindiri, near Masaya. Open daily 9 A.M. to 12 P.M. and 2 P.M. to 5 P.M., inquire next door for the caretaker. Admission by donation. Includes a small but interesting archaeological collection of pre-Columbian ceramics and sculptures discovered in the Masaya area.

Museum of the Revolution. Estelí. Open Mon. to Fri. 8 A.M. to 12 P.M. and 2 P.M. to 5 P.M. and Sat. 8 A.M. to 12 P.M., closed Sun. No charge. A tiny museum a block from the main town square, it includes a number of photographs illustrating revolutionary history from the time of César Augusto Sandino and a tiny collection of arms used in the revolution.

General César Augusto Sandino Museum. Niquinohomo, Department of Masaya; tel. 41. Admission is 25 cordobas. Open Tues. to Sat. 9 A.M. to 12 P.M. and 2 P.M. to 5 P.M. and Sun. 9 A.M. to 1 P.M., closed Mon. Museum located in the house where Nicaragua's most famous revolutionary spent his childhood, includes historical items and personal possessions of Sandino.

SHOPPING. Nicaragua has a wide variety of handicrafts. From the Atlantic coast, beautiful jet-black coral necklaces, wood figures made of seashells, and belts of boa and other snake skins. From Masaya, colorful masks, baskets woven of palm fibers, tapestry, iguana skin shoes, wood carvings, and wood dishes. From San Juan del Oriente, attractive imitations of pre-Columbian pottery, generally in reddish ceramic. From San Juan de Limay, soapstone carvings of animals and humans. From Matagalpa and Jinotepe, attractive jet-black ceramics.

Handmade Nicaraguan cigars, such as Joya de Nicaragua, are high quality, made of tobacco from seeds of Cuban origin. They are available at hotel shops or the airport gift shops.

Nicaraguan Flor de Caña rum is delicious and available at any grocery store. A higher-quality version, aged five years, is available at duty-free shops.

The best general selection of Nicaraguan handicrafts is found in Managua. For the widest choice and the best value the *Mercado Roberto Huembes* has about 40 different small stands. (Open daily 8 A.M. to 5 P.M. and Sun. 8 A.M. to 2 P.M.) Even if prices are marked, visitors can bargain somewhat.

The *Casa de las Artes del Pueblo* (tel: 61368; open Mon. to Fri. 9 A.M. to 5:30 P.M. and Sat. 9 A.M. to 3 P.M., closed Sun.), is affiliated with the Nicaraguan Ministry of Culture but also offers an excellent selection of all crafts at good prices. Music and books can also be obtained from the Ministry of Culture. The Association of Sandinista Cultural Workers has a gift shop located at the Asociación Sandinista de Trabajadores de la Cultura.

Major hotels in Managua, including the *Intercontinental* and *Camino Real,* have good gift shops.

Masaya. The *artesans market* (open Mon. to Fri. 8 A.M. to 12 P.M. and Sat. 8 A.M. to 12 P.M. closed Sun.), in the suburb of Monimbo across from the church of Magdalena has several shops that sell the embroidery, leather goods, and wood that the city is famed for.

San Juan del Oriente. On the main street the cooperative (open Mon. to Fri. 7 A.M. to 12 P.M. and 1 P.M. to 4 P.M. and Sat. 7 A.M. to 1 P.M.)

offers a good selection of the town's attractive ceramics with pre-Columbian motifs.

ENTERTAINMENT. *Rubén Darío Theater,* near the Plaza de la Revolutión, offers occasional musical, theatrical, and dance performances. Call 23630 or 23632 for details of programs.

NIGHTLIFE. Undoubtedly Managua is the quietest of Central America's capitals, with relatively little nightlife. However, there are several discotheques, including *Lobo Jack,* Camino de Oriente, 72315 or 61527, *Bambana,* Calle Julio Bultrago, and *El Infinito,* Caminode Oriente. 60526. The Asociación Sandinista de Trabajadores de la Cultura has nightly entertainment: Wed., Reggae; Fri., jazz; other nights arranged weekly. Entrance costs 50 cordobas during the week, 70 cordobas Fri. and Sat.

SAFETY. Tourists should exercise the usual caution when traveling in Managua. Women should not walk alone at night. There are occasional security problems in outlying rural areas of Nueva Segovia, Matagalpa, Chontales, and Boaco provinces. However, the main towns, such as Estelí and Matagalpa, are very safe.

In eastern Nicaragua, though Bluefields and the Corn Islands are completely safe for visits, permission is still required from Immigration, Pista de la Resistencia. Less secure areas, such as Puerto Cabezas, are generally closed to nonresident visitors.

LEAVING NICARAGUA. Exit fee is $11. You may be asked to pay about $10 in dollars, the rest in cordobas.

COSTA RICA

The Garden of the Americas

by
NEVILLE HOBSON

Neville Hobson has been resident in Costa Rica since early 1981. An Englishman, he has lived in many countries before living in Costa Rica, including Germany, India, and the United Arab Emirates. He is currently a business and tourism writer and translator based in San José, principally working in the corporate publishing field.

Ask most Americans and Europeans where Costa Rica is, and the reply invariably will be, "It's that island in the Caribbean." No, that's Puerto Rico. Costa Rica is in the Central American isthmus, with Nicaragua to the north and Panama to the south. Its 2.7 million people live in a land area about the size of the state of West Virginia—a little under 20,000 square miles. But packed into such a small country live a people who are fiercely proud of their history, culture, and achievements.

Just about every visitor to this country agrees that it is a very special place, and very different. But exactly what *is* so special about Costa Rica?

Ticos, as Costa Ricans are called, are a polite, peaceful people. Perhaps what makes Costa Rica so special is the people's desire to "quedar bien"—"to leave a good impression." Or could it be the exuberant friendliness they express so naturally, with a marked willingness to get to know visitors and help them where they can? Whatever the reason, one thing is for sure—it is a rare visitor who does not return home impressed with the Ticos' warmth and hospitality.

As a tourist destination, Costa Rica offers a wealth of sights and sounds to experience. And its unique history provides a colorful backdrop to every place you will see: sun-drenched Pacific beaches, tropical jungles of the Caribbean coast, and the cosmopolitan cities and high mountains of the Central Valley. Visitors are astonished by the cleanliness of the country, its incredible natural beauty and wildlife, and even by the fact that you can drink water straight from the tap!

Although it formed an integral part of the Spanish empire, the country developed along lines very different from Spain's other colonies in the New World, particularly after independence. This can be seen today by the strong sense of national identity—Ticos pride themselves first as being Costa Ricans rather than Central Americans, or even Latin Americans—and by the fact that the country has largely avoided the political turmoils that unfortunately beset so much of Latin America, and Central America in particular.

However, it is a fact that the strife and turmoil in the region conjures up a less than rosy picture in the minds of most Americans and Europeans. People not well acquainted with Costa Rica often equate the problems in countries such as El Salvador and Nicaragua with all of Central America. Ironically, Costa Rica recently became well-known around the world because of its pivotal role in the Central American peace process during 1986 and 1987. The culmination of Costa Rica's efforts, which brought differing sides in Central America to the negotiating table, was the Nobel Peace Prize awarded to President Oscar Arias in 1987.

Costa Rica does not have an army—it was abolished in 1949 (security is entrusted to a small but efficient national police force). Over 20,000 Americans and thousands of other nationalities have retired or settled here, due in part to generous benefits and incentives offered by the government, and more and more foreign investment capital is coming into the country.

When visiting, you'll hear a wide variety of superlative statistics, such as "Costa Rica has more teachers than policemen," and "The only thing that doesn't grow is what you don't plant," among others. They're all true. For example, in education, Costa Rica ranks with many developed countries (the literacy rate is a very respectable 90 percent). Its telecommunications system is generally regarded as one of the best in the world. Known as "The Garden of the Americas" because of its rich soils and pacific disposition, this country has long been an agricultural innovator. The last 40 years in particular have seen steady social development and further political maturity.

History: First Encounters with the Old World

In mid-September 1502, on his fourth and last voyage to the New World, Christopher Columbus was sailing along the Caribbean coast of Central America when his ships were caught in a violent tropical storm. Seeking shelter, he found sanctuary in a bay protected by a small island. Ashore, he encountered natives of the Carib tribe, wearing heavy gold disks and bird-shaped gold figures, who spoke of great amounts of gold in the area.

Sailing farther south, Columbus met more natives, also wearing pendants and jewelry fashioned in gold. He was convinced that he had discovered a land of great wealth to be claimed for the Spanish empire. The land itself was a vision of lush greenery; popular legend has it that, on the basis of what he saw and encountered, Columbus named the land Costa Rica ("rich coast").

The Spanish Colonial Era

The first Spaniard to attempt conquest of Costa Rica was Diego de Nicuesa, in 1506. But he found serious difficulties due to sickness, hunger, and Indian raids. These hardships were encountered by other Spaniards who entered the region.

The first successful expedition was made by Gil González de Avila in 1522. Exploring the Pacific coast, he converted to Catholicism more than 6,000 Indians of the Chorotega tribe. A year later, he returned to his home port in Panama with the equivalent of $600,000 in gold. But over 1,000 of his men had died of disease, starvation, and Indian raids.

Many other Spanish expeditions were mounted, but all were less than successful, often because of rivalries between various expeditions. By 1560, almost 60 years after its discovery, no permanent Spanish settlement existed in Costa Rica (this name was then in general use, although it meant an area far larger than its present-day boundaries), and the natives had not been subdued.

Costa Rica remained the smallest and poorest of Spain's American colonies, producing little wealth for the empire. It tended to be largely ignored in terms of the Conquest, and instead began to receive a wholly different type of settler—hardy, self-sufficient individuals who had to work to maintain themselves.

The population stayed at less than 20,000 for centuries (even with considerable growth in the eighteenth century), and was mainly confined to small isolated farms in two highland valleys. Intermixing with the native Indians was not a common practice, and the population remained largely European.

By the end of the eighteenth century, Costa Rica had begun to emerge from isolation. Some trade with neighboring Spanish colonies was carried out (in spite of constant harassment by English pirates, both at sea and on land), and the population had begun to expand across the Central Valley.

However, seeds of political discord, which were to affect the colony, had been planted in Spain when Napoleon defeated and removed King Charles IV in 1808 and installed his brother Joseph on the Spanish throne. Costa Rica pledged support for the old regime, even sending troops to Nicaragua in 1811 to help suppress a rebellion against Spain.

By 1821, though, sentiment favoring independence from Spain was prevalent throughout Central America, and Costa Rica supported the declaration of independence issued in Guatemala on September 15 of that year. (Costa Rica did not become a fully independent sovereign nation until 1836, after annexation to the Mexican empire and then 14 years as part of the United Provinces of Central America.)

Foundations of Democracy

The nineteenth century saw dramatic economic and political changes in Costa Rica. For the major part of that century, the country was ruled by a succession of wealthy families whose grip was partially broken only toward the end of the century. The development of agriculture included the introduction of coffee in the 1820s and bananas in the 1870s, both of which became the country's major sources of foreign exchange.

In 1889 the first free popular election was held, characterized by full freedom of the press, frank debates by rival candidates, an honest tabulation of the vote, and the first peaceful transition of power from a ruling group to the opposition. This event was the foundation of the political stability that Costa Rica now enjoys.

During the early twentieth century each successive president fostered the growth of democratic liberties and continued to expand the free public school system, started during the presidency of Bernardo Soto (1886–1890). By the 1940s economic growth was healthy due to agricultural exports, but the clouds of discontent were again gathering.

In 1948 the president refused to hand over power after losing the election; the result was a civil uprising by outraged citizens, led by the still-popular José ("Pepe") Figueres Ferrer. In a few short weeks the rebellion succeeded and an interim government was inaugurated.

New Beginnings

On May 8, 1948, Figueres accepted the position of president of the Founding Junta of the Second Republic of Costa Rica. One of his first acts was to disband the army, creating in its stead a national police force.

Significant changes took place during the 1950s and 1960s, including the introduction of new social welfare policies, greater expansion of the public school system, and greater involvement by the state in economic affairs. The 1970s saw further economic growth.

But the bubble burst in 1981 with rampant inflation, crippling currency devaluation, and diminishing confidence in the country from abroad. The following year Costa Rica, owing $4 billion, had the dubious distinction of being the biggest per capita debtor in the world.

Today Costa Rica's economic situation is much healthier. Although difficulties still abound, as is the case with many developing countries, government policy over the last five years has helped the country maintain economic growth (one of the few Latin American countries that can claim this). While monetary stability has not been achieved, this has distinct benefits for tourists: dollars go far here when exchanged for a deflated local currency.

EXPLORING COSTA RICA

Costa Rica is divided into seven provinces: San José, Heredia, Alajuela, Cartago, Puntarenas, Guanacaste, and Limón. The capital, San José, is a bustling cosmopolitan city with a population approaching 1 million; it

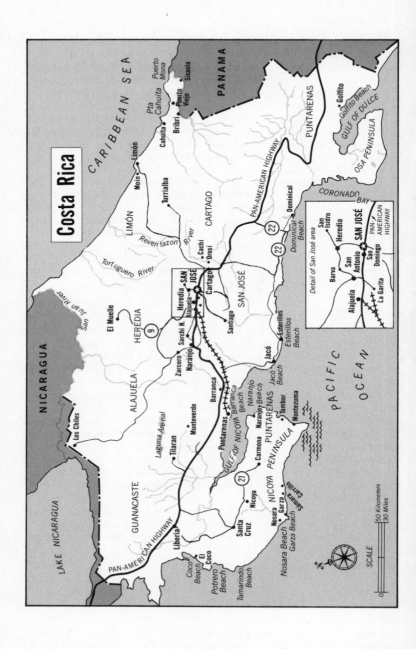

is the political, social, historical, and cultural center of the entire country. Each province has its own special features, from the rolling plains of Guanacaste to the cool mountains of San José. Looking at each province and what they offer the visitor, you'll soon why Columbus named this country "Costa Rica."

Province of San José

The province of San José is completely surrounded by the other six provinces of Costa Rica. Mainly mountainous, it is the country's most populous province.

The city of San José will undoubtedly be the focal point of your visit to Costa Rica. It's a modern city with a variety of architectural styles, from new high-rises in the downtown business district to Spanish colonial buildings in many of the older central residential districts, to wide boulevards and expansive residences in the newer outlying suburbs.

The largest city in the country, San José is surrounded by mountains. It's laid out in an angular way with streets and avenues crisscrossing north–south and east–west.

A few words about street addresses. Throughout this chapter, you'll see that addresses are given by avenida (avenue) and calle (street). Avenues run east–west, and streets north–south. Avenida Central (sometimes written as Avenida O) and Calle Central (or Calle O) are the starting points for all other roads. Even-numbered avenues are to the south of Avenida Central with odd-numbered ones to the north. Correspondingly, even-numbered streets are to the west of Calle Central with odd-numbered ones to the east. An address that's given as Avenida 1, Calles 3 and 5 means that the place is located on Avenida 1 between Calles 3 and 5.

Sounds simple so far? Well, it is, but most Ticos don't use avenue–street descriptions when going somewhere. They'll say that such-and-such a place is "two blocks west of the central post office and half a block north, next to so-and-so's pharmacy." Even more confusing for the visitor is the method of describing a location from where a place *used* to be! But don't worry, you'll soon get the hang of it (if not, go back to your hotel for a cool rum and Coke and try again tomorrow!).

There are many things to see in San José. Strolling the streets will allow your senses to take in the flavor of the city, but watch your feet—most sidewalks in the city center are not in very good repair. For resting your feet and people-watching, there are a number of parks in the city center, such as the Parque Central on Avenida 2 with its large bandstand, and the spacious Parque Nacional across from the Legislative Assembly between Avenidas 1 and 3 and Calles 15 to 19.

The National Theater, Avenida 2, Calles 3 and 5, is a beautiful structure; begun in 1890, it was built with donations from wealthy coffee growers. The building is topped with allegorical figures—representing dance, music, and fame—carved by an Italian sculptor. On either side of the main entrance are more statues: Calderón de la Barca and Beethoven, also by an Italian sculptor; the statues of comedy and tragedy are in the vestibule. Costa Rican sculptor Juan Ramón Bonilla created the sculptural group Heroes of Misery, which also stands in the vestibule. The theater has been declared a national monument and is in use constantly.

On Avenidas Central and 2, Calle 17, is the National Museum. The collections are housed in the old Bellavista Fortress, used as headquarters for the Costa Rican army until its abolition in 1949. Exhibits include art, furniture, and natural history. Other displays of historic interest are at the Plaza de la Cultura, with its impressive underground display of pre-Columbian jade pieces, and the Jade Museum, Avenida 7, Calle 9.

One sight worth investigating is the small, Spanish-Colonial city zoo in Barrio Amón (entrance at the far end of Avenida 11, three block behind the National Insurance Institute building). Plans have been in hand for some years to transfer the zoo to new premises in Santa Ana, some 12 miles west of the city; unfortunately, lack of funds has prevented this. Another classic example of Spanish-Colonial architecture is the National Liquor Factory by Parque España (Avenidas 3 and 7, Calle 11), one of the oldest commercial buildings in San José.

Province of Alajuela

The province of Alajuela is one of the largest and most diverse in Costa Rica. Located in the western part of the Central Valley, it is an important agricultural region and a major producer of coffee.

Costa Rica's second city, Alajuela, is 15 minutes from San José. It retains much of the flavor of a small town, yet is a fast-growing metropolis. The country's favorite son, Juan Santamaría, who is credited with defeating William Walker's invading forces in 1856, was a native of Alajuela. His life is recounted in displays at the Juan Santamaría Museum. The city has four churches noted for their architecture. There are two principal parks: one, in front of the cathedral, has enormous mango trees and a bandstand; the other is Juan Santamaría Park.

Close to Alajuela is Poás Volcano National Park. A good paved road leads up to the crater, one of the largest and most spectacular in the world.

At the Laguna de Fraijanes Park you can see a multitude of wild flowers, fish, ducks, herons, and other wildlife in a natural environment. The park also has wooden pathways, games areas, amphitheaters, and a forest with cabins for picnicking.

The agricultural town of Sarchí is well known as the center for handicrafts, such as the famous multicolored wood ox carts.

The pretty town of Zarcero has a colorful temple with a garden that produces beautiful flowers year-round. The town is in a mountain valley and surrounded by tall cypress trees and abundant natural wells. In the temple's garden one can also see many works of art carved out of cypress.

La Garita is a true flower and fruit garden. Here, there are many tropical plant nurseries, two zoos, a number of typical restaurants, and a play park for children.

Province of Cartago

Southeast of San José, Cartago is a province of high mountains and picturesque valleys begging to be photographed. It's also an important agricultural area, producing coffee and sugar cane as well as a number of newly introduced products such as macadamia nuts.

About 30 minutes from San José, the city of Cartago was once the country's capital. Home of the shrine of Costa Rica's patron saint, Nuestra Señora de los Angeles, Cartago lies in the shadow of Irazú volcano. Close by is the spectacular Orosí Valley, enclosing the roaring Reventazón River and the impressive Cachí hydroelectric complex. Orosí has one of the country's oldest and most picturesque colonial churches.

On the banks of the artificial lake created by the Cachí Reservoir, the Costa Rican Tourist Board has built Charrarra. This comprises a swimming pool, restaurant, docking facilities for outboard- and inboard-engined boats, covered refreshment areas in an enchanting eucalyptus forest, camping facilities, and a parking area.

Province of Puntarenas

This province extends from the highest point in northwestern Costa Rica over to the southern tip of the dry Nicoya Peninsula and then along the Pacific coast through tropical wetlands and down to the Panamanian border.

In the southern part of the province is Manuel Antonio National Park, a half-hour drive over the hill south of Quepos, 95 miles southeast of San José. The park has numerous hiking trails through thick, wildlife-filled jungle, up high cliffs with breathtaking views, over to a shaded waterfall, and down to white sandy beaches with calm crystalline waters. The park has guides, a small museum, rustic bathrooms, outdoor showers, picnic and camping areas, and lots of blissful peace—although the quiet is often interrupted by chattering monkeys.

Located on a spit of land jutting out into the Gulf of Nicoya on the Pacific coast, the city of Puntarenas is about two hours from San José. A major port town, Puntarenas has many beaches close by, some of dark volcanic sand. Fishing is a busy industry, and boats can be chartered to fish for marlin and to sail. Puntarenas is the base for sightseeing cruises, which take in a meandering circuit of the Gulf of Nicoya and its many little islands dotted about.

Also in this province is Monteverde, the highest point in northwestern Costa Rica, which was founded in 1951 by 30 American Quakers who arrived at this secluded 4,200-foot green mountain plateau after an exhaustive search for a place to live and work as they saw fit, in peace. It is now a thriving, spread-out community of 1,500 people and innumerable dairy cows. Monteverde is a three and a half-hour drive northwest of San José along the Pan-American Highway, with the last 22 miles over an extraordinarily bumpy country road. But the redeeming features of this last stretch are the superb views to right and left of both the Nicoya Peninsula and the gulf below. Beyond the Quaker settlement (whose mainstay is cattle raising, milking, and cheese making) is the large Monteverde Cloud Forest Reserve, sanctuary to diverse species of plants, insects, birds, and mammals. At the reserve are guides, a nature museum, a biological station, maps, and numerous hiking trails.

Province of Limón

This is the province of sprawling banana plantations and thick tropical jungle. To get to some of the interesting places, travel from Puerto Limón. The road leading north from Limón goes only as far as the new international port of Moín, 12 miles away. Beyond that, it's by boat up the intricate Tortuguero Canal system, stretching about 80 miles up the coast to the border with Nicaragua. The system is a mix of natural and artificial waterways crisscrossing the thick jungle. Running parallel to the sea, the canal banks are from 25 to 150 feet apart. Villages (some with stilted homes) dot this fluvial highway. The fishing in this area is without doubt among the best in the world. Some of the saltwater species are tarpon (average weight 80 pounds!), snook, jacks, wahoo, tuna, dorado, jewfish, grouper, mackerel, and snapper. Fresh-water species to catch in the rivers, canals, and lagoons include guapote (jungle bass), machaca (a toothy, tarponlike fish), and mojarra. As you fish in these areas, you're likely to be watched over by chattering monkeys, brilliantly colored birds, or an alligator basking in the sun along the banks. A number of companies offer trips through the canals, and some offer complete jungle cruise packages, including overnight stays at comfortable lodges.

Often described as a typical Somerset Maugham port town, Puerto Limón is Costa Rica's own little slice of Caribbean sparkle, and a major port in itself. It has a population of 60,000, largely made up of the descendants of Jamaican and Chinese immigrants. Limón hosts the country's most spectacular carnival every October 12, Columbus Day. One of the best ways to get to Limón is the eight-hour train ride from San José; the winding route meanders through the mountains and down into the tropical jungle.

The dirt road south of Puerto Limón plays hide-and-seek with expansive, palm-lined, white-sand beaches. It takes you to the picturesque fishing villages of Cahuita and Puerto Viejo; and even farther south to the remote virgin beaches of Cocles, Punta Uva, Manzanillo (for great surfing), and Punta Mona near the Panamanian border. Inland, by rough road, are the Indian villages of Bribri and Sixaola. Hotels throughout the area are best described as rustic. It rains a lot, which is marvelous for the bananas, coconuts, and monkeys, but puts a damper on area tourism development.

Province of Guanacaste

Hot, dry Guanacaste is Costa Rica's wild west, with rolling hills and expansive plains and large cattle ranches. The whole province is a treasure trove of both pre-Columbian and Spanish colonial history, and along its Pacific coast are many of the country's most beautiful beaches. Traveling through the province is made simple by the paved Pan American Highway, providing easy access to cities like Liberia, the provincial capital, and Santa Cruz, the "folklore capital" of Costa Rica. Not far from Liberia is Arenal volcano (best accessed by four-wheel-drive jeep) with Arenal Lake and the hydroelectric dam, the largest in Central America.

The folkloric town of Nicoya is an excellent base from which to take day trips to the beaches of Junquillal, Ostional (where thousands of giant green sea turtles come ashore to lay their eggs between May and October), Nosara, Garza, Sámara, or Carrillo. The town has a quaint seventeenth-century church and a mixture of Spanish colonial, rustic, and modern architecture. Most of Guanacaste's beaches are within reach of Santa Cruz. Between this city and Nicoya lies the small town of Guaitil, whose inhabitants are known for their skills in making ceramic articles, as did their ancestors, the Chorotega Indians.

Province of Heredia

The mountains surrounding the city of Heredia are filled with what are known as typical villages, such as Santo Domingo, San Luis, San Isidro, Barva, and San José de la Montaña. They all have little churches in Gothic or baroque styles surrounded by adobe houses.

A must-see in the city of Heredia is the old parish church in front of the park. This attractive building was constructed in the seventeenth century. Its walls are unusually thick with massive buttresses, giving it a singular appearance. The church is surrounded by pleasant parks and shaded malls. Close by is the small fortress, a symbol of the city. A curious fact about the fortress is that its loopholes open inward, which, instead of impeding the entrance of enemy projectiles, actually helped!

About 12 miles from San José is the spa of Ojo de Agua, the most popular in Costa Rica. Its facilities include swimming pools, soccer pitches, weightlifting equipment, and tennis, basketball, and volleyball courts, as well as an artificial lake with row boats. By the pool areas there are restaurants. Ojo de Agua's name is derived from the shape of the spring—like an eye.

The Río de la Hoja Forest is ideal for those who want to pass quiet and peaceful moments in contact with nature. With its dense growth of cypresses and other coniferous trees, the forest has many natural pathways and trails leading into the forest itself.

PRACTICAL INFORMATION FOR COSTA RICA

WHEN TO GO. Costa Rica enjoys a temperate climate, with temperatures remaining almost constant throughout the year. The Central Valley has an average daytime temperature of 70° F (21° C) that varies little during the year. For true tropical temperatures, both the Caribbean and Pacific coasts are 10°–15° F hotter than the Central Valley. The Caribbean coast tends to be humid, while the Pacific is dry. The rolling plains of Guanacaste Province have some of the highest temperatures, 80° to 90° F year-round.

In the cities of the Central Valley (San José, Alajuela, Heredia, and Cartago), it can be chilly in the evenings any time of year. Even though Costa Rica is a tropical country and only 10 degrees north of the equator, San José, for example, is nearly 4,000 feet above sea level.

There are two distinct seasons in Costa Rica: the rainy (May to Nov.), and the dry (Dec. to Apr.). In the rainy season, when it rains it really *rains*! But this is also one of the most attractive times of year as the entire country becomes a vision of green. Typically in this season it rains in the afternoons and the mornings are bright and sunny. In the dry season, the sky is normally a piercing blue without a cloud in sight. As to which is *the* best time to visit Costa Rica, this is invariably a matter of personal preference, and depends also on what you want to do when here. Many residents and visitors alike say that the best time to visit is late Nov. to late Feb.: the rains have finished (apart from an occasional shower) and the whole country is still a panorama of green.

In practical terms, certain times of the year are better than others for the visitor because of local holidays. It's not essential to have hotel reservations except at peak times (Christmas, Easter, and certain other holidays) when finding hotel rooms in the capital and at the beaches without a confirmed reservation may be difficult.

HOW TO GET TO COSTA RICA. Many airlines serve Costa Rica, either directly or via connections in other cities. All commercial and charter flights from abroad arrive at the Juan Santamaría International Airport 12 mi west of San José, linked to the capital by the 4-lane Pan-American Highway.

These airlines fly directly to Costa Rica from destinations in the United States, Europe, and Central and South America: *Lacsa* (Costa Rica's national airline), *Mexicana* (Mexico-based), *Sahsa* (Honduras-based), *SAM* (Colombia-based), *Taca* (Guatemala-based), *COPA* (Panama-based), *Aerónica* (Nicaragua-based), *KLM* (Holland-based), *Varig* (Brazil-based), *Eastern* (U.S.-based), *Pan American* (U.S.-based), and *Iberia* (Spain-based).

Most of the world's major airlines fly to hubs in the United States, Europe, and South America, from which connections can be made with one of the airlines serving Costa Rica direct, as listed above. Major hubs with direct flights to Costa Rica include—in the U.S.: Miami, New Orleans, and Los Angeles; Europe: Amsterdam and Madrid; South America: Caracas, Venezuela; Bogotá, Colombia; Quito, Ecuador; and Rio de Janeiro, Brazil.

Up-to-date travel information should be sought from your travel agent or the office of any of the airlines listed above.

From Other Central American Countries

Traveling by **air** between San José and the major cities in the rest of Central America—Managua, Nicaragua; Tegucigalpa and San Pedro Sula, Honduras; Guatemala City, Guatemala; San Salvador, El Salvador; Belize City, Belize; and Panama City, Panama—can be done easily via many of the airlines serving Costa Rica (see above).

However, the same can no longer be said for traveling overland by **bus.** Until November 1984, the San José-based company *Ticabus* offered comfortable services from San José in both directions—southeast to Panama City, and northwest through to Guatemala City—at a fraction of the cost of going by air. Because of the uncertain political situation in the other Central American countries (particularly in Nicaragua and El Salvador), at press time Ticabus has suspended most services, only traveling between San José and Panama City. The only way to get from San José to, say, Managua is to take the regular bus (although still comfortable) to the border crossing at Penas Blancas. From there, you'd have to cross into Nicaragua and take a bus from there to Managua. Expect long delays and extremely personal attention from the military-supervised customs and immigration officials on the Nicaraguan side. To book a trip to Panama City call Ticabus in San José at 21–8954 or 21–9229 (the terminal is at Calle 9, Avenidas 2 and 4). The round-trip fare is about $30.

There is no **passenger shipping service** as such between Costa Rica and elsewhere in the isthmus. Panama is the shipping crossroads of the hemisphere, but no scheduled passenger service exists from either Colón or Panama City to Central America. The exception to this is the recent advent of luxury **cruise liners** that include Costa Rica's Puerto Limón on the Caribbean coast and Puerto Caldera on the Pacific coast as ports of call—see the "Tours," below, for more details. None of the liners stops anywhere else in Central America. If you're an adventurous traveler, you can always try to book passage on one of the many "tramp" steamers plying the ports up and down Central America. A number of them, in particular the boats shipping bananas for export, have limited passenger accommodation. However, it must be stressed that personal safety (for political reasons in some of the other Central American countries) has to be a major consideration before embarking on a trip of this nature.

TRAVEL DOCUMENTS. A new immigration law passed in 1986 made entry into Costa Rica among the most strictly controlled in the world. Among its provisions was the requirement that *every* visitor from any country had to have a visa. However, the outcry both locally and abroad was such that the new law was suspended. It was sent back to the legislature for revision, where it remains at press time. The following were the requirements for entry into Costa Rica as of mid-1988, but before departure check requirements with your travel advisor or a Costa Rican embassy or consulate.

Citizens of the following countries do *not* need visas to enter Costa Rica; they must have a valid passport, an onward or return air ticket, and evidence of funds of at least $200: Austria, Bahamas, Belgium, Bolivia, Brazil, Colombia, Denmark, Finland, France, Holland, Israel, Italy, Japan, Yugoslavia, Liechtenstein, Luxembourg, Norway, Portugal, South Korea, Spain, Sweden, Switzerland, United Kingdom, and West Germany.

Citizens of Canada, the United States, and Panama may enter Costa Rica with just a *tourist card* and some other identification (driver's license or social security card, for example); a passport is not necessary. Tourist cards may be obtained from Costa Rican embassies and consulates; or, upon production of a valid ticket, from any of the airlines listed above. A tourist card costs $2 and allows a visitor to remain in Costa Rica for 30 days. The card can be renewed monthly for up to three months upon presentation at the principal Immigration Office (*"Migracion"* in Spanish) in San José, located east of the Supreme Court of Justice, Calle 21, Avenidas 6 and 8.

Citizens of all other countries require a visa to enter Costa Rica and must pay a deposit upon entry, refunded when they leave.

Although AIDS is not a serious problem in Costa Rica, tourists planning to stay longer than 30 days must show proof that they are free of HIV (Human Immuno-deficiency Virus) and the AIDS virus (double-check the exact ruling on this with your travel advisor or Costa Rican embassy).

An important point concerning dependent children under 18—a child of any nationality becomes subject to Costa Rican child welfare laws if he or she is here for longer than 30 days. This means that if you wish to leave after that time with your children, both parents have to obtain permission from the child welfare organization *(Patronato Nacional de Infancia)* to take children out of the country. This is essential; if you don't get permission, your children will be refused exit at the airport. (If you are divorced and traveling with children, it is *imperative* that you bring with you written permission from the other parent allowing you to travel with the children. That permission must be notarized by a Costa Rican consul in your country of residence.)

Tourist cards, passports, etc., should be carried at all times while in Costa Rica. The influx of undocumented refugees from Nicaragua and El Salvador in particular means that one may be stopped in the street by plainclothes immigration inspectors, especially in San José, who will request your identification. Not having papers could mean being escorted to the immigration office for verification checks. This is not by any means unpleasant, just inconvenient and time-consuming.

No health problems exist in Costa Rica, and you will not need to have inoculations before coming. This may be different if you're planning to visit from a country in which there are health problems (such as malaria); it is recommended that you consult with your travel agent, or check with the nearest Costa Rican embassy or consulate for up-to-date regulations.

WHAT TO PACK. Costa Ricans tend to dress informally, although for visits to the theater or going out to dinner, more formal attire is expected, such as a jacket and tie for men and a cocktail or similar dress for women. Generally shorts are not worn in the cities except in sports areas.

A note about dry cleaning: Although offered by most major hotels it is not usually of the quality Westerners expect. Recommended, however, is *Martinizing,* a franchise of the U.S.-based company, located in San José on Sabana Norte (tel. 31–6486).

Although dollars go far in Costa Rica, many imported items are terribly expensive because of high import duties (100 percent and above in some cases). Among the items it is recommended that bring with you are: contact lenses and solution, brand-name sunglasses, water purifiers, film and camera equipment, and electronic equipment. Visitors are normally allowed to bring items such as cameras and portable radios into Costa Rica without paying duty.

CURRENCY. Costa Rica's monetary unit is the colon (pronounced "co-LOAN," symbol C). The colon's value against the U.S. dollar is adjusted regularly by the Central Bank, which has followed a policy of monthly "mini devaluations" since 1985. All prices quoted in this chapter are in U.S. dollars at the rate of C75 = U.S. $1.

Currency denominations are as follows:

Bills of C1,000 (red), C500 (purple), C100 (gray), C50 (light green), C20 (brown), C10 (blue), and C5 (dark green).

Coins of C20, C10, C5, C2, C1, C0.50 and C0.25.

Money can be changed (legally) only through hotel cash desks or the national banking system. There are four state-owned banks: *Banco de Costa Rica, Banco Anglo Costarricense, Banco Nacional de Costa Rica,* and *Banco Crédito Agrícola de Cartago,* and around 20 "private" banks within the state-run system; check the Yellow Pages under "Bancos" for addresses. Banks are open Mon.–Fri., 9 A.M.–3 P.M. Some banks offer after-hours service up to 6 P.M. Recent developments in local banking include 24-hour automatic teller machines at branches dotted around the capital, and electronic funds transfer (including from abroad). If you hold a MasterCharge or Visa credit card you may be able to use the Banco Anglo's teller machines for cash withdrawals. Check with the bank's head office on Avenida 2 across from the National Theater, tel. 22–3322. If you have major currencies other than U.S. dollars (Swiss francs, pounds sterling, or other Western European currencies), the exchange rate may not be advantageous as the banks will first change your currency into dollars and then into colones. Best bets: to change Swiss francs, try the Banco Nacional (Swiss Bank Corporation correspondent); for pounds sterling, try the Banco Anglo (UK Midland Bank correspondent). If you have problems, go to the Central Bank (occupying the block surrounded by Avs. 0 and 1, Calles 2 and 4; tel.: switchboard, 33–4233; foreign department, 33–6045; exchange rate information, 21–2510).

There is a thriving black market for changing dollars that pays four or five colones above the official rate. Salesman abound on most street corners, especially in the center of San José around the Central Bank building. But be extremely careful—changing money this way is illegal. If you get caught you'll find the authorities unsympathetic and you'll spend at least a night in jail. The police occasionally mount crackdowns on illegal money changing, where you could find that the salesman you're dealing with is really an undercover detective.

U.S. traveler's checks issued in dollars are acceptable at many establishments, as is every major credit card.

ELECTRICITY. Electric current in Costa Rica is 110 volts. Before plugging in any electrical appliance, check that it is set to this voltage, and not to 220 volts.

TELEPHONES. Costa Rica's telephone system is one of the best in Latin America, with further improvements being made continuously. As Costa Rica is such a small country, there are no city codes; you just dial the number. All numbers are 6 figures, normally written as 2 digits and 4 digits separated by a hyphen; however, you may still see numbers displayed in the old way of 3 sets of 2 digits, each set divided by a hyphen.

To call outside Costa Rica, you dial 011 plus the code of the country you are calling and then the number. You can dial direct (without operator assistance) to more than 60 countries. The country code for making a call *to* Costa Rica is 506.

Throughout the country there are public telephones that accept coins of C2, C5, C10, and C20. In San José most public phones are the pushbutton type, and have instructions (in Spanish) clearly displayed. You can make international calls from public phones (if you have enough coins!); the best place in San José is at the offices of Radiográfica Costarricense, on the corner of Av. 5, Calle 3. The operators speak English. For local information, call 113; international information, 124; time, 112; telegrams, 123; international operator, 116.

Emergency telephone numbers: police, 117; fire department, 118; Red Cross, 21–5818; hospitals: San Juan de Dios—22–0166, National Children's—22–0122, Mexico—32–6122.

MAIL AND COMMUNICATIONS. The postal service in Costa Rica is extremely efficient. International mail service is highly reliable, although the same precautions you would take when sending something valuable in most other countries is also advisable here. Air mail to most European countries and to the United States takes about 5 days.

There are post offices in cities and towns throughout the country. The main post office in San José is at Calle 2, Av. 1 and 3.

The system of mailing addresses in Costa Rica is geared primarily to post office boxes (*apartados* in Spanish), although a letter written to a physical address will be delivered, too. Demand for postal boxes exceeds availability, especially in San José; it's not uncommon for box renters to rent out the use of their box to friends or business associates. Most hotels will, of course, allow you to receive mail at their postal box.

The postal service introduced a 4-figure postal, or zip, code system a few years ago. Although not yet in widespread use, the codes do exist and result in speedier delivery of mail when included in addresses. We have included the codes in all local mailing addresses shown in this chapter.

The telex system in Costa Rica is excellent, and the country has the highest density of teleprinters in Central America. In San José a public telex office is located in the offices of Radiográfica Costarricense (tel. 33–5555) at Av. 5, Calle 3. Courier and FAX service is also available.

TAXES AND TIPS. By law hotels are required to include a 10 percent sales tax and 3 percent tourism tax on all bills. In restaurants 10 percent sales tax is added to bills.

Restaurants are obliged by law to add a 10 percent tip to all bills when the billed amount exceeds C10 (about $0.14). As in most countries, it is the custom to leave an extra tip for exceptional service.

In hotels you would tip the bellboy for carrying baggage; about $2 for three bags would be fine. You do not have to tip taxi drivers.

USEFUL ADDRESSES. Costa Rica maintains diplomatic relations with most countries. All those with embassies or consulates in San José are listed in the telephone directory. Among them are:

United States: Box 10053, 1000 San José; Av. 3, Calle 3, 33–1155. (The American embassy will be moving to a new location in custom-built offices in the western suburb of Pavas. Construction was still in progress as of mid-1988.)

United Kingdom: Box 10056, 1000 San José; Centro Colón, 11th floor, 21–5566.

Canada: Box 10303, 1000 San José; Edificio Cronos, Av. 0, Calle 5, 23–0446.

You can obtain more information about Costa Rica (including a number of descriptive brochures in Spanish or English) from any of the offices of the Costa Rican Tourist Board *(Instituto Costarricense de Turismo—ICT): Head Office:* Box 777, 1000 San José; 23–1733. Telex 2281 INSTUR CR. *Plaza de la Cultura, San José:* Av. Central and 2, Calle 5, San José; 23–1733 (ext. 277) or 22–1090. *Juan Santamaría International Airport:* 41–8542.

ACCOMMODATIONS. Costa Rica offers a wide variety of places to stay to suit every taste and price range, from deluxe hotels to small pensions to trailer parks. It's all a matter of preference. Would you like to stay downtown in the capital, in a $300 luxury suite overlooking the bustling city? Or perhaps you'd prefer a cozy room with a fireplace, in a lakeside chalet in the cool mountains, with just the sound of the wind whispering in the pine trees? Or do you want to leave the hills behind and head for a tropical bungalow at a Pacific resort? Indeed, the variety of accommodations in Costa Rica is enormous. Many hotels have pools and tennis courts, as well as other sporting and recreational facilities.

Since the early 1980s, hotel occupancy rates in Costa Rica have been as low as 40–75 percent, due principally to a perceived image abroad of the country's location in the midst of the so-called Central American "war zone." While this misconception is a blow to the travel industry in general, it's good for last-minute or adventurous travelers who arrive without reservations, or for those who seek privacy. As a rule, there are more hotel rooms available than guests; therefore reservations, while best for peace of mind, are not generally essential (except at peak holiday periods, such as Christmas and Easter, when they *are* essential).

The hotel listing below is organized alphabetically by province and then alphabetically by city, town, or beach—in order of the following price ranges (based on double occupancy): *Super Deluxe,* over $165 (one hotel only); *Deluxe,* $101–$165; *Expensive,* $61–$100; *Moderate,* $30–$60; *Inexpensive,* under $30.

Province of Alajuela

Alajuela

Alajuela Hotel. *Inexpensive.* Av. Central and 2, Calle 2, Alajuela; 41–1241. Located in the center of Alajuela a half block from the Parque Central, this folksy hotel is a favorite with foreign retirees who often rent rooms or utility apartments by the month (with a 25 percent discount).

Province of Cartago

Palomo de Orosí

Motel Río. *Inexpensive.* Mailing address: Box 220, 7050 Cartago; 73–3128, 73–3057. Located in the breathtaking Orosí Valley near the picturesque village of Orosí. This motel is comprised of a series of large comfortable cabins with furnished kitchenettes, all facing a roaring, trout-filled river.

Province of Guanacaste

Coco Beach

Hotel La Flor de Itabo. *Moderate.* Mailing address: Box 32, 5019 Playa de Coco; 67–0003. Playa de Coco, or Coco Beach, can be reached by paved road all the way from San José, 155 miles distant. It's one of Costa Rica's favorite seaside spots. The beach's finest hotel—La Flor de Itabo—is air-conditioned, has hot water, U.S. satellite TV, pool, restaurant, and bar. Horseback riding, sport fishing, and scuba diving trips can be arranged.

Flamingo Beach

Planned as a resort project in the late 1970s, today Flamingo Beach is Costa Rica's most exclusive beach area. Its gently-sloping, snow-white beach is 1 mi long, and several smaller beaches dot the north and south ridge areas. The temperature is nearly always in the low 80s F with a refreshing sea breeze at night.

The beach's south ridge boasts dozens of private mansions, valued upwards of $250,000, owned by people from a wide variety of countries, mainly Europeans. On the north ridge are a brand-new luxury hotel, 2 condominium complexes (that can be time-shared or rented by the week), three excellent waterside restaurants, barbecue areas, swimming pools, and tennis courts. There is a full-service yacht marina on the lee side of the ridge, and a yacht and racquet club complex is under construction. Charter yachts are available for sport-fishing, scuba, and snorkeling trips. Fishing tournaments, including the annual International Sailfishing Championship in August, attract champion sportfisherfolk from around the world.

Flamingo Beach is easy to reach by road from San José (take the Pan-American Highway to Liberia, then a good-quality compacted dirt road; the road trip takes about 6 hours). Or you can fly by chartered light plane (45 minutes from San José).

Flamingo Beach Hotel. *Expensive.* Mailing address: Box 692, 4002 Alajuela; 39–1584 (San José office), or 68–0444. Developed by the same owners as the Presidential Suites condo, Flamingo Beach Hotel opened its doors in late December 1987. This is the first phase of the hotel, with 22 of the planned 90 rooms now open. Each large room is beautifully furnished and comes with satellite TV and telephone. (Planned for opening in mid-1988 are an additional 23 rooms, an air-conditioned ballroom, and 2 conference rooms outfitted with the latest communications and computer systems.) The hotel has 2 pools: a covered 1 for children, and an adult pool with a cozy wet bar.

Presidential Suites. *Expensive.* Mailing address: Box 692, 4002 Alajuela; 39–1584 (San José office) or 68–0260. Telex 7512 HERRATEL CR. Opened in 1985, each of these 12 furnished apartments has 2 bedrooms, 2 baths, fully equipped modern kitchens, living rooms, and dining areas. Their balconies overlook Flamingo Beach and the neighboring beaches of Brasilito and Conchal.

Tiempo Compartido Flamingo. *Moderate to Expensive.* Mailing address: Box 321, 1002 San José; 39–1952. Furnished 1- 2-, and 3-bedroom condominium villas are for rent (and sale) in the hills above the marina, in varied price ranges. The villas have spacious bedrooms, bathrooms, living and dining rooms, kitchens with pantries, private phone lines, and U.S. satellite TVs. Close by are the complex's pool, tennis courts (opened in early 1986), bar, and the exquisite *Les Ambers* French restaurant. Charter yachts offer dive trips to nearby Catalina and Bat Islands as well as sport fishing out in the Pacific where the billfish lurk.

Garza Beach

Hotel Villagio La Guaria Morada. *Moderate.* Mailing address: Box 860, 1007 San José; 22–4073 (San José office) or 68–0784. Telex 3185 GUIONE CR. In terms of luxury, tropical comfort, and peace, the Italian-owned Villagio is arguably Costa Rica's finest beachfront resort. While it's a long, dusty ride by road, Trans Costa Rican Airline (reservations 32–0808) offers $20 twice-weekly flights to nearby Nosara airstrip. There are 30 spacious bungalows scattered around beautifully landscaped grounds, all with ocean views. The gourmet Italian restaurant and bars are in an enormous open-sided structure with three unique thatched roofs, one on top of the other. In front of this attractive building are the pool and, at the edge of the beach, a discotheque. Available for charter are two fishing boats and a ski boat; Villagio's superb Italian chef will prepare the fish you catch for dinner. Delicious! In all, the hotel's exotic decor, ambience, and service are a delight. Bask in the sun on the pure white-sand beach as you sip your fruit cocktail.

Hermosa Beach

Condovac La Costa. *Expensive.* Mailing address: Box 5210, 1000 San José; 21–8949/33–1862 (San José office) or 67–0283/67–0267. The name Condovac is derived from Condominium Vacation, an ambitious tourism investment project begun in 1965 with local capital. The results today are impressive. Scattered along the north end of beautiful Hermosa Beach (*hermosa* means "beautiful") are 101 white stucco villas, with red-tiled roofs, climbing up the sharply sloped hill through tropical foliage. When not in use by their owners, the villas are rented by the day. Each is fully air-conditioned and can sleep five, and features a well-equipped kitchenette and terrace with dazzling views of the Gulf of Papagayo. Within the complex are 2 elegant restaurants, 3 bars, a discotheque, 2 pools, and many sports facilities including tennis, horseback riding, sport fishing, and water skiing.

Junquillal Beach

Hotel Antumalal. *Expensive.* Mailing address: Box 49, 5150 Santa Cruz; 68–0506. 20 modern rooms with ceiling fans in 10 attractive bungalows flank the hotel's pool (with wet bar) and tennis courts. Above, atop a gently sloping hill, is an open-air restaurant with a conical thatched roof, the tallest in Costa Rica. Stables are on the hotel grounds, with horses available for hire to ride the trail over the ridge to the long desolate beach to the south, or for exploring farther inland.

Villa Serena. *Expensive.* Mailing address: Box 17, 5150 Santa Cruz; 31–5043 or 68–0737. Children under 14 not permitted. A serene complex of four private bungalows, gourmet restaurant, small pool, and sauna. There are tennis courts (facing east-west, a distinct handicap for one of the players before and after midday); on hand for use in the public living room-cum-library are many videotapes of opera, ballet, feature films, and documentaries. The complex is tastefully landscaped with palm trees and brilliant bougainvilleas.

Liberia

Capital of the large but sparsely populated province of Guanacaste, Liberia is located just off the Pan American Highway, 145 mi northwest of San José and 45 mi southeast of the Nicaraguan border. This clean spread-out city of 22,000 is surrounded by vast cattle ranches and grain fields in rolling savannah plains, bringing to mind images of the old American Wild West. Although the Llano Grande International Airport is capable of handling wide-body jets, such as the 747 or L-1011, no international flights serve Liberia; all go to and from San José. The best accommodations in and close to Liberia are as follows:

Las Espuelas. *Moderate to Expensive.* Mailing address: Box 88, 5000 Liberia; 66–0144. Telex 6502 SPUR CR. This attractively landscaped hotel, a little over a mile south of the city on the Pan-American highway, is a favorite spot for tour groups from San José and abroad, and has excellent conference and meeting facilities. It has 39 air-conditioned rooms, three suites, pool, restaurant, and two bars. The entrance is shaded by an enormous guanacaste tree (from which this province received its name), and the interior courtyards are dotted with pre-Columbian figures.

El Sitio. *Moderate.* Mailing address: Box 471, 1000 San José; 23–7986 (San José office) or 66–0211. Just west of Liberia, on the way to the former polo field (now the Hipódromo Racetrack), is El Sitio. 36 of its 54 large rooms are air-conditioned. It has both adult and children's pools, a playground, horse riding facilities and trails, restaurant, and two bars. The entire hotel is decorated "à la cowboy."

La Siesta. *Inexpensive.* Mailing address: Box 15, 5000 Liberia; 66–0678. For those who want reasonable accommodations in downtown Liberia, this pleasant modern hotel is just the place. It has 25 air-conditioned rooms, a small pool, and a restaurant.

Motel Bramadero. *Inexpensive.* Mailing address: Box 70, 5000 Liberia; 66–0371. On the Pan-American Highway by the turnoff to downtown Liberia, this motel has 21 rooms—6 air-conditioned—pool, meeting facilities, and a lively restaurant and bar. The Bramadero has long been the favorite of Liberian businessmen, government employees, and cattle ranchers, who often gather for seminars, luncheon dates, and bull sessions.

Nuevos Boyeros. *Inexpensive.* Mailing address: Box 85, 5000 Liberia; Located on the Pan-American Highway. With 62 air-conditioned rooms on two floors, this is Liberia's liveliest hotel. It has two pools, a playground, gardens, meeting facilities for 500 people, an attractive seafood restaurant, bar, and the city's only coffee shop open 24 hours a day. The coffee shop is very popular, frequented by long-distance truck drivers, businessmen, and tourists (sometimes in busloads) traveling between Managua, Nicaragua, and San José.

Nicoya

Hotel Curime. *Inexpensive.* Box 51, 5200 Nicoya; 68–5238. Leaving downtown Nicoya for the beaches, one comes upon Curime's restaurant, bar, and 20 cabins among landscaped grounds at the point where the paved road ends and dirt road begins. Each cabin has two bedrooms (with one double bed and two singles), sitting area, refrigerator, and air-conditioning.

Nosara Beach

Forty-five miles southwest of Nicoya is Nosara, where one of the highest number of Americans in Costa Rica live, as well as many Europeans. Large condominiums and about 75 foreign-owned homes have been built within the 1,500-acre development, some in the lowlands near the beach and others nestled in the hills up to 450 ft. above sea level. Over 600 homesites are Many for sale, all with power and water lines. 35 mi of gravel roads meander throughout the complex. 10 minutes away, in the village of Nosara, is an airstrip, with scheduled flights twice a week via Trans Costa Rica Airlines. The community-oriented Nosara Civic Association maintains the area roads, tennis courts, shuffle board decks, horse riding and "monkey jungle" hiking trails, as well as a newsletter. Visits to Nosara, and private air transportation to the airstrip 10 minutes away, can be arranged through the Turi Nosara Center, Box 186, 1150 San José; 32–5626 (San José) or 68–0749 (Nosara).

Hotel Playas de Nosara. *Moderate.* Box 4, 5233 Nosara; 68–0495. Perched atop the lush green peninsula jutting out between the beaches of Guiones and Nosara is this cozy hotel with a sweeping 180-degree sea view. It has 12 simply furnished airy rooms in 6 hillside units, all with private balconies from which you might spot howler monkeys frolicking in the surrounding jungle, or pelicans gracefully skimming the surface of the blue Pacific Ocean below. At the top of the bluff is an open-air bar and restaurant (with fresh seafood specialties) amid tropical plants and flowers. A casual, friendly atmosphere prevails.

La Capulina de Roland. *Inexpensive.* Lista de Correos, 5233 Nosara. The Belgian owner renovated the area's oldest big house, and now rents basic rooms and a rustic "honeymoon cabin" to adventurous travelers.

Ocotal Beach

El Ocotal. *Deluxe.* Mailing address: Box 1013, 1002 San José; 23–8483 (San José office) or 66–0166. Telex 3032 OCOTAL CR (San José); 6503 OCOTAL CR (hotel). An elegant fishing resort three and a half hours from San José or 40 minutes from Liberia airport, El Ocotal has 6 large villas climbing up a hill to a restaurant with cuisine fine enough to match its spectacular views of the Pacific Ocean. Each villa has tall, sloping hardwood ceilings, air-conditioning, two double beds, TV, refrigerator, room service, direct-dial phones, and private terraces overlooking the Gulf of Papagayo. There are two pools and tennis courts (with lighting for night play).

The surrounding area abounds with deer, monkeys, anteaters, iguanas, and parrots. The American owner is an expert fisherman-sailor who charters first-class sport-fishing yachts outfitted with the finest equipment. Nearby waters are teeming with sailfish, blue and black marlin, dolphin, and roosterfish. Many secluded beaches, some visited only by an occasional sea turtle, are but a 10-minute boat ride away.

Pan de Azúcar

Hotel Sugar Beach. *Inexpensive.* Mailing address: Box 66, 5150 Santa Cruz; 68–0787. This tranquil American-owned hideaway is on Portrero Bay, northeast of the Flamingo Peninsula. Its 6 large rooms have 2 double beds, spacious bathrooms, ceiling fans, and seaside terraces. The small restaurant specializes in seafood, and the bar serves a wide variety of exotic cocktails. The surrounding still-virgin jungle is alive with wildlife.

Potrero Beach

Hotel Playa Potrero. *Inexpensive.* Mailing address: Box 45, 5150 Santa Cruz; 68–0669. The charm of this beachfront hotel lies in its bar's clientele, who make up this "Peyton Place South" they now call home. Many expatriate Canadians and northwestern Americans have migrated to Potrero, living inland on lots that are part of a retirement home investment project. The hotel's 11 modest rooms have 2 double beds and are equipped with cooling fans. In front of its restaurant, bar, beach boutique, and pool are 3 miles of shallow, sandy beach, perfect for calm swimming, wading, or collecting shells.

Santa Cruz

Hotel Sharatoga. *Inexpensive.* Mailing address: Box 33, 5150 Santa Cruz; 68–0011. This 39-room air-conditioned hotel, a favorite of Costa Rican businessmen, is located a few blocks from downtown Santa Cruz. As it is always hot and sunny here, the pool is very refreshing; the open-air bar and restaurant are good.

Tamarindo Beach

Hotel Tamarindo Diría. *Expensive.* Mailing address: Box 4211, 1000 San José; 33–0530 (San José office) or 68–0652. This hotel on the Pacific is about 40 minutes by air from San José or 23 miles overland from Santa Cruz. The well-designed 3-story building and open-air restaurant (fresh seafood!) is between the long Tamarindo Beach and vacation cottages. All 60 hotel rooms are air-conditioned. First-floor rooms view landscaped tropical gardens with pre-Columbian statues and colorful bushes; upper-level rooms have private balconies from which to view the beach and Cabo Velas Peninsula, where fugitive financier Robert Vesco still maintains a hideaway home. The 2 pools are flanked by comfy shaded sitting areas, a few short paces from the sea.

In addition to bar, conference room, games room, and boutique, the hotel runs a small travel agency. They can arrange fishing, scuba, snorkeling, and waterskiing trips, rent sailboats and wind-surfers, and direct surfers to secluded Langosta Beach around the corner to catch the big waves. The hotel's agency also offers boat tours through the mangrove-filled estuary nearby, and night tours from Nov. to Feb. to observe giant sea turtles spawning on the beach.

Province of Heredia

Ciudad Cariari

Central America's poshest country club community, Ciudad Cariari—or Cariari City—is just 10 minutes from Juan Santamaría International Airport and 20 minutes from downtown San José. Within this secure and spread-out community are: the Cariari Country Club (18-hole championship golf course, 10 lighted tennis courts, olympic-size pool, gymnasium, sauna, whirlpool baths, playgrounds, convention facilities, restaurants, and bars); 2 hotels (the Hotel Cariari and Sheraton Herradura); 2 plush condominium complexes (Residencias del Golf and Villas Cariari); dozens of millionaires' homes; the Costa Rica Academy (American system, grades K through 12, taught in English); a small shopping center; a nondenominational chapel; and 2 mi of secluded jogging trails and colorful flowers nearly everywhere you look.

Hotel Cariari. *Expensive to Deluxe.* Mailing address: Box 737, 1007 San José; 39–0022. Telex 7509 CARIARI CR. (Reservations in the U.S.A. can be made by calling toll-free 1–800–CARIARI.) The Cariari has hosted such distinguished guests as President Ronald Reagan, King Juan Carlos of Spain, Henry Kissinger, David Rockefeller, and Joe DiMaggio. As the Central Valley's first and finest resort hotel, it offers its guests all the amenities imaginable, including free U.S. satellite TV in all 160 rooms and suites. Elegant and excellent dining can be savored at the hotel's restaurants—the *Marisqueria* (seafood specialties), *La Flamme* (international).

There is also the *Boruca Coffee Shop* and the poolside bar, *Chapuzón Wet* (with several underwater bar stools). In the hotel, too, are travel and car rental agencies, a gift shop, and combined newspaper stand and bookstore. *Las Barandas* discotheque is a highly popular night spot, attracting the smart set from San José.

The Cariari runs its own efficient bus service to and from downtown San José, with comfortable minibuses departing the hotel every few hours throughout the day. The fare is a real bargain—about $0.18, compared with over $6 for a taxi! (One can use the bus service even if you're not a hotel guest.) Staying at the hotel means that you can also enjoy all the facilities of the Cariari Country Club.

Sheraton Herradura. *Expensive to Deluxe.* Mailing address: Box 7–1880, 1000 San José; 39–0033. Telex 7512 HERRATEL CR. (Reservations in the U.S. can be made by calling 1–800–SHERATON.) To celebrate its 10th anniversary in 1985, this hotel was given a $1 million facelift—with excellent results. In January 1986 it was announced that the Herradura had joined the international Sheraton family, and renamed as the Sheraton Herradura Hotel and Spa.

With 10 modern conference rooms, the hotel has become the place for large international gatherings. The 150 rooms and 27 suites are large and elegantly decorated, all with free U.S. satellite TV. The restaurant *Bonanza Grill* specializes in charcoal-broiled export-quality meats, while the *Bon Vivant* serves European cuisine. There are also 3 bars, 2 pools, and a casino. In addition to the use of the nearby Cariari Country Club facilities, guests have privileges at the Hacienda Los Reyes in Alajuela, which offers golf, tennis, horse riding, pool, and sauna. Bus services from the hotel to both the Hacienda and downtown San José is available.

In late 1985 the hotel inaugurated its *Vida Spa* total health treatment center, offering its clients electrogalvanic and whirlpool baths (filled with therapeutic herbs from the Black Sea), pinewood sauna, gymnasium, professional masseuse, nutrition center, and beauty clinic.

San Antonio de Belén

Belén Trailer Park. *Very Inexpensive.* Box 143, 4005 San Antonio de Belén; 39–0421. This is Costa Rica's only year-round trailer park, not only offering complete hookups for electricity and water but also providing showers, toilets, washers, and dryers. 21 sites are available, some being used for retirees' mobile homes. American-run since opening in 1972, the park has suffered from considerable reduction in business since the 1979 revolution in Nicaragua, for fewer and fewer people are now driving the length of Central America.

San José de La Montaña

Hotel de Montaña El Pórtico. *Inexpensive.* Mailing address: Box 289, 3000 Heredia; 37–6022. 11 miles northwest of San José, at an altitude of 6,000 ft, this snug hideaway is a favorite among peace-and-quiet-seeking locals and foreigners alike. Getting there is half the fun—on winding back roads that lead up toward Barva and Poas volcanos, passing through patchwork-quilt fields dotted with dairy cows. (The overwhelming sense of déjà vu one feels at times in Costa Rica is nowhere more poignant than in this area—you could be in Switzerland or Scotland or Germany. . . .) In addition to its fresh pine-scented air, El Portico has a delightful restaurant overlooking a duck pond with a sweeping downward view over the Central Valley. The hotel offers 15 cozy rooms, fireplaces (it can get chilly), pool, sauna, whirlpool, conference room, and numerous hiking trails.

Province of Limón

We have divided up this province into 3 areas—Puerto Limón, the northwestern area, and the southeastern area.

Puerto Limón

Hotel Acón. *Moderate.* Mailing address: Box 528, 7300 Limón; 58–1010. Smack in the center of town is the Acón, with 39 air-conditioned rooms in a modern 4-story building. Its small restaurant is excellent. The large second-floor discotheque is both popular and noisy, so choose your room carefully!

Condomar Las Olas. *Moderate.* Mailing address: Box 701, 7300 Limón; 33–5160 (San José office) or 58–1414. 2 miles northwest of Limón on the coastal road to Portete is this hotel—the only one in all of Central America built entirely over water. Its 48 long rooms all have large balconies facing the Caribbean Sea. The breezy restaurant's service is a bit slow, but does offer delicious Spanish and Caribbean food as well as great views across the sea. Its downstairs bar opens onto a beflowered patio, where the crash of waves—*olas* means "waves"—is heard from all sides.

Matama. *Moderate.* Mailing address: Box 230, 7300 Limón; 58–1123. A small hotel amid jungle, this little gem has an aviary, assorted caged animals (including a tapir, puma, leopard, and alligator), wild orchids, and literally thousands of coconut trees on the sloping grounds. The restaurant is superb and usually crowded. There is a pool, and for rent down the hill across the main road are 6 cabins fronting Playa Bonita.

Hotel Park. *Inexpensive.* Ave. 3, Calles 1 and 2, 7300 Limón; 58–3476. A meeting place for adventurous international travelers, this downtown hotel has 24 basic rooms, 6 with views and sounds of the bay below. The restaurant is large and airy with inexpensive delicious meals. Vargas Park—with palm trees, landscaped paths, an elaborate bandstand, and 3-toed sloths draped among the trees—is 2 blocks away, along the cement sea wall.

Northwest of Limón

Casa Mar. *Deluxe* (price includes airfare, 3 meals, and fishing). Mailing address: Box 825, 1007 San José; 41–2820. Casa Mar is open only during the tarpon and snook season (Jan.–June and Aug.–Oct.). It is located on a lagoon 15 minutes from the quaint village of Barra del Colorado, 12 miles south of the Nicaraguan border. It offers 12 comfortable rooms, restaurant-bar, games room, library, gift shop, as well as great fishing in the lagoon, canals, sea, or the San Juan River. Fishing boats are 16-footers, and come with bilingual guides.

Río Colorado Lodge. *Deluxe* (price includes airfare, all meals, drinks, and fishing). Mailing address: Box 5094, 1000 San José; 32–4063 (San José office) or 71–8852. Telex 3379 RIOCO CR. Open year-round, this jungle fishing lodge's 12 comfortable rooms have twin beds and hot showers. The cheery dining rooms serve excellent meals family-style. There's also a recreation room, open bar, outdoor riverside patio, aviary, zoo, and well-stocked tackle store. Its modern fishing boats (both 16- and 23-footers) and experienced bilingual guides make the Río Colorado Lodge among the best sport fishing experiences in Central America.

Tortuga Lodge. *Moderate.* Mailing address: Box 812, 1007 San José; 71–6861. Not just for fishing enthusiasts, this jungle retreat is located across the canal from the village and national park of Tortuguero. The lodge, with its 10 rooms and open-air restaurant-bar, is tucked away in its 71 acres of virgin land, full of hiking trails. Trips can be arranged to tour the canals and backwater lagoons, watch thousands of sea turtles laying eggs on Tortuguero Beach, visit the national park and turtle research station, or simply fish in the area.

Southeast of Limón

Hotel Cahuita. *Inexpensive.* Cahuita; 58–1515. Located 2 blocks from the center of the village of Cahuita, this easygoing establishment has 19 basic rooms above the first-rate family restaurant (with a constantly blaring TV!) and friendly owner's home. The 8 new rooms behind the wood structure are charming indeed, with screens, fans, and private baths. Wake to the sounds of roosters and pounding surf. The entrance to Puerto Vargas National Park and to the miles of snowy-white palm-lined beaches are only steps away.

Province of Puntarenas

Puntarenas

Hotel Colonial. *Moderate.* Mailing address: Box 368, 5400 Puntarenas; 61–1833. Set back on the road into the town of Puntarenas between the ocean and estuary is this spacious and elegant hotel. It offers 55 air-conditioned rooms each with 2 double beds and wall-to-wall carpeting, and there are tropical gardens, 4 pools, formal restaurant and bar, and tennis courts, as well as charter yachts for fishing or island-hopping in the Gulf of Nicoya.

Portobello. *Moderate.* Mailing address: Box 108, 5400 Puntarenas; 61–1322. Also located on the estuary side of the road into town, this hotel boasts something that 2 other nearby resorts don't have—a beach on their own property. Well, sort of . . . The Italian owners hauled in tons of white sand and created their own artificial beach. The hotel's 32 units are scattered about the landscaped grounds. Meals and drinks can be enjoyed outside around the pool or in the open-sided restaurant-bar. Flowers bloom everywhere.

Costa Rica Yacht Club. *Inexpensive.* Mailing address: Box 1000, 5400 Puntarenas; 22–3818 (San José office) or 61–0784. The club is next to the Hotel Colonial, and operates a 28-room hotel, open-air restaurant-bar, pool (in an abstract shape with bridges), and marina. Club members have preferential rates. It's a great place to meet friendly yachtspeople, and perhaps latch on to a trip round the Gulf of Nicoya.

Hotel Tioga. *Inexpensive.* Mailing address: Box 96, 5400 Puntarenas; 61–0271. Fronting the Pacific Ocean near the tip of this finger of land, the Tioga is a popular 4-story hotel. It has a small semi-indoor pool in the lobby courtyard, flanked by a coffee shop, bar, and 46 air-conditioned rooms (the ones in front are noisier, but have private balconies from which to view the goings-on in the gulf). Across the street is the main bathing beach, usually very crowded.

Bahia Gigante

Turística Bahía Gigante. *Inexpensive to Moderate.* Mailing address: Box 1866, 1000 San José; 22–9557 (San José office) or 61–2442. Several modern spacious bungalows and luxurious hillside condominium units are available for rent in this fast-growing seaside resort complex still under construction. Located on the Nicoya Peninsula, it is just 6 mi south on the dirt road from the Salinero Ferry terminal at Playa Naranjo. Within Bahía Gigante's protected bay is a small but growing marina with 150-ft dock. The hotel has a refreshing oversize pool, fed by an 80°F freshwater spring. The airy 13-sided *Rancho Restaurant* and bar serve delicious food and drinks. From the hotel's stables, riders can explore more than 9 mi of road and seemingly infinite hillside trails that crisscross through the complex's hundreds of acres of dry-jungle property, offering breathtaking views across the sea. Many land and water recreational activities can be enjoyed, such as beachcombing, sunbathing, swimming, scuba diving, snorkeling, waterskiing, windsurfing, sailing, motor boating, and deep-sea fishing.

Barranca Beach

Hotel Río Mar. *Inexpensive.* Mailing address: Box 250, 5400 Puntarenas; 63–0158. The hotel's 48 rooms are basic, but the atmosphere is invigorating. Its huge popular restaurant–bar is always full of friendly folks, barefooting it at the closest public beach. It's located less than 2 hours' drive from San José where the Barranca River empties into the Pacific Ocean. The ocean in these parts is often visited by sharks, but this doesn't seem to bother the avid surfers as they paddle out to catch the big waves, which—according to surfers—provide the longest and best rides in Central America. International surfing tournaments and festivals are held regularly at Barranca, in front of Dona Ana Park, operated by the Costa Rican Tourist Board.

Dominical Beach

Cabinas Punta Dominical. *Inexpensive.* Mailing address: Box 196, 5557 San Isidro de El General; 25–5328. 4 modern cabins, each accommodating 4 persons, are perched on a point in the jungle overlooking rocky Dominicalito Beach below, at the southern tip of the long Dominical Beach. Over a dirt road, it's located 22 mi southwest of San Isidro de El General, or 35 mi southeast of Quepos, which has an airport. The large, airy restaurant–bar serves good, inexpensive food. Electricity comes from a generator that runs from 5:30 A.M. to 9 P.M. Swimming, fishing, surfing, and horseback riding are available.

Esterillos Beach

Hotel El Delfin. *Moderate.* Mailing address: Box 2260, 1000 San José; 71–1640/77–1640. A luxurious new 2-story 15-room hotel on a secluded 7-mile-long beach, this resort—83 mi from San José—is a classic. The restaurant is gorgeous and serves delicious international cuisine. Each room has ceiling fans, hot water, soothing piped-in music (not Muzak!), and private terraces. There are tennis courts, pool, games room, library; horseback riding and fishing trips can be arranged. For swimming, the pool is best and safest, for the sea here is known for its dangerous rip tides and strong undertow.

Golfito

Gran Hotel Miramar. *Inexpensive.* Mailing address: Box 60, 8201 Golfito; 75–0143. The 27 rooms with ceiling fans and bath are nothing to write home about, but the Osa Peninsula is, and this is its best hotel. Close by is the quaint old banana town of Golfito (off the beaten track a bit, but accessible by dirt road from the Pan American Highway), which used to be a major port for shipping bananas until United Fruit Company (now United Brands) closed down their operations in 1985. Also nearby are beautiful Corcovado National Park and, for surfing lovers, the beaches of Pavones. The hotel's enormous open-sided restaurant–bar overlooks Golfo Dulce ("sweet gulf"), and is usually crowded with a mix of locals and tourists.

Jacó Beach

Jacó Beach Hotel. *Moderate.* Mailing address: Box 962, 1000 San José; 32–4811 (San José office) or 64–3032/64–3064. Telex 2307 IRAZU CR. This is Costa Rica's most commercial beach hotel, 83 mi southwest of San José, reached by paved road all the way. The hotel is in the middle of a 3-mile-long gray-sand beach. And 3 minutes away is a private airstrip (incoming planes invariably have to buzz the runway to shoo off grazing cattle!), or you can ride the hotel's bus for the 2-hour trip to and from San José.

The hotel has 150 air-conditioned rooms in two buildings, the newer wing boasting an elevator—the only one on the Pacific coast! Some rooms overlook the large pool, numerous chaises lounges and umbrella tables, tennis and volleyball courts, flowering landscaped walkways, and the sparkling blue Pacific Ocean. Facilities include *El Muelle Restaurant* (relaxed but formal dining on the second floor), *Jacó Beach Coffee Shop* (near the pool), *La Gran Via Bar* (in the airy lobby near the beach boutique), and the oceanfront *Disco Rancho* night spot. Rather tired-looking horses can be rented on the beach.

Manuel Antonio

Hotel La Mariposa Libre. *Deluxe.* Mailing address: Box 4, 6350 Quepos; 77–0355. Adults only. Perched high on the bluff between Quepos and Manuel Antonio National Park is the lush Pacific hideaway of La Mariposa Libre. Its 10 split-level villas are tucked amid landscaped tropical foliage, each with its own balcony. The spacious villas are tastefully decorated and have huge bathrooms with unique indoor gardens that attract hummingbirds and butterflies (the hotel's name means "the free butterfly"). This U.S.-owned resort serves gourmet cuisine in its elegant dining area, just above the pool and bar.

Apartotel Karahe. *Moderate.* Mailing address: Box 100, 6350 Quepos; 77–0170. Family-oriented Karahe rents fully furnished utility apartments, just a 5-minute walk down the path to Espadilla Beach, or a 20-minute stroll down the road to Manuel Antonio National Park.

Cabinas Manuel Antonio. *Inexpensive.* Mailing address: Lista de Correos, 6350 Quepos; 77–0212. This is the closest hotel to Manuel Antonio National Park. Each of its 18 rooms has several bunk beds and a porch facing the sea a few steps away.

Cabinas Ramírez. *Inexpensive.* Mailing address: Lista de Correos, 6350 Quepos; 77–0275. Formerly the Mar y Sombra, this spot has 17 modern, comfortable rooms, with ceiling fans, set back under sprawling jungle shade trees. The nearby restaurant–bar on the beach is the area's most popular, with tables inside and out. The sound of surf is drowned out most evenings by the blaring music and lively barefooted dancers. This is the closest hotel to the surfing area at north Espadilla Beach.

Monteverde

Hotel de Montaña. *Moderate.* Mailing address: Box 70, 1001 San José; 33–7078 (San José office) or 61–1846. This intimate 12-room country inn is the area's most commercial—with travel packages, including transportation and meals, the latter served family-style in a cheery dining area with fireplace and views. It is one of the first buildings you come to on the way to the Cloud Forest, after the village of Santa Elena. It's quite far from the forest, although transportation can be arranged.

Pensión Florimar. *Inexpensive.* Mailing address: Box 10–1605, 1000 San José; 61–0909. The owner of this friendly 5-room pension is one of the original Quakers who founded Monteverde. It is the closest lodging to the entrance to the Cloud Forest, less than a mile away.

Pensión Quetzal. *Inexpensive.* Mailing address: Box 10165, 1000 San José; 61–0955. This cozy mountain retreat has 10 modern rooms with shared baths above the restaurant and sitting area, where there's a fireplace, library, piano, and gift shop. The American owner, who is also the manager and cook, serves hearty meals, and packs lunches for those who go trekking through the forest.

Montezuma Beach

Cabinas Mar y Cielo. *Inexpensive.* Mailing address: Lista de Correos, 5361 Cobano; 61–2472. Getting to this beach is quite fun. From Puntarenas you cross the Gulf of Nicoya by public launch, follow the bumpy, dusty road southwest to Cobano, and then to Montezuma. The hotel, whose name means "sea and sky," has 6 basic rooms with private baths, all facing the open sea, above *Chico's Restaurant* and bar. There are several quiet beaches nearby, divided by rocky points that are the home to crabs and lobster. Close, too, is a huge waterfall, which forms a natural, freshwater bathing pool before it empties into the Pacific.

Naranjo Beach

Oasis del Pacífico. *Moderate.* Mailing address: Box 200, 5400 Puntarenas; 61–1555. A 5-minute drive southeast of the Salinero Ferry terminal takes you to this secluded resort fronting on a shell-filled beach and the calm gulf. The 36 rooms with ceiling fans surround 2 pools, tennis courts, attractively landscaped grounds and waterfront restaurant and bar. Hammocks are strung beneath thatched shelters on the beach, where horses can be hired. Well-outfitted charter fishing boats operate out of the hotel's small marina.

Hotel El Paso. *Inexpensive to Moderate.* Mailing address: Box 232, 2120 San José; 33–3214 (San José office) or 61–2610. This new, unpretentious hotel rents 15 rooms—with or without private baths, air-conditioning, or view—at a variety of prices. It's located just a 5-minute walk from the Salinero Ferry terminal. El Paso's restaurant specializes in rice and beans—a Costa Rican staple—and the bar is usually crowded before the ferry leaves for Puntarenas.

Palmar Norte

Motel Tico Alemán. *Inexpensive.* Lista de Correos, 8150 Palmar Norte; 75–0157. Located on the Pan-American Highway, 75 mi from the Panamanian border, this 18-room motel is the area's best, but it's basic. It's a perfect rest stop for tired long-distance drivers. The only game in the nearest town of Palmar Norte is bingo.

Tambor Beach

Hotel La Hacienda. *Moderate.* Mailing address: Box 398, 2050 San José; 25–9811 (San José office) or 61–2980. Arrive by land, sea, or air at this small, rather elitist resort. With 19 rooms and 5 villas, La Hacienda is situated in the middle of a very wide, 10-mile-long brown-sand beach fronting Bahía Ballena on the Nicoya Peninsula. Surrounding the hotel inland is a huge cattle hacienda with hundreds of humped Brahman bulls. Outside the spacious hotel rooms are long verandas, strung head-to-toe on the waterfront side with hammocks. The naturally fed saltwater pool is right next to the bar and has submerged bar stools. Gourmet meals are served in a large porch area, at the outdoor bar or in a landscaped picnic area, where barbecues and croquet matches are often held. A horse corral is next to the hotel, with spirited horses to whisk you along to the beach. The hotel also has its own landing strip.

Province of San José

The listings below begin with hotels. They are followed by apartotels, utility apartments—rented by the day, week, or month—which are highly popular with long-term visitors; these units can work out substantially cheaper than regular hotels.

City of San José

Aurola Holiday Inn. *Expensive to Super-deluxe.* Mailing address: Box 7802, 1000 San José; 33–7233. Telex 3545 AUROLA CR. (For reservations in the U.S.A., call toll-free 1–800–HOLIDAY.) This new 5-star hotel, which opened in Feb. 1986, is located in downtown San José on Morazán Park, 4 blocks north of the Plaza de la Cultura. If you think all Holiday Inns are alike, you're in for a surprise. This unique 17-story building is a highly visible city landmark with its dazzling polarized reflective-glass windows. The Aurola offers 188 beautifully decorated rooms, 8 spacious suites, 4 junior suites, and the ultraluxurious presidential suite complete with private bar, sauna, and whirlpool. (This is the only hotel in Costa Rica we have classified as super-deluxe based on price—the presidential suite is $300 a night.) Every room is fully air-conditioned with U.S. satellite TV and telephone. The hotel offers heated pool, convention facilities, underground parking, restaurants and bars, casino, discotheque, a health club (featuring sauna, gymnasium, and whirlpool baths), and car rental and travel agencies. The 17th-floor *El Mirador* restaurant is ideal for intimate, stylish dining: Impeccable service is provided by a skilled staff, a strolling minstrel will serenade you, you can choose from an extensive wine list, and the nighttime views across the city are stunning. For staying in great style right in the center of San José, this is the place.

Irazú. *Moderate to Deluxe.* Mailing address: Box 962, 1000 San José; 32–4811. Telex 2307 IRAZU CR. With 350 rooms and suites in varying price ranges, this is Costa Rica's largest hotel. Foreign tour groups and conventions are its mainstay. The Irazú has a pool, tennis courts, sauna, seminar facilities, ballroom (with lively dinner dances every Fri. night), coffee shop, formal restaurant, bar, casino, and car rental and travel agencies.

Ambassador. *Moderate to Expensive.* Mailing address: Box 10186, 1000 San José; 21–8155. Telex 2315 AMBASSADOR CR. 64 rooms, 7 suites, an Italian restaurant, as well as coffee shop, bar, and seminar facilities make up this west-of-downtown hotel, on Paseo Colón near shops, restaurants, office buildings, and 3 movie houses.

Corobicí. *Moderate to Expensive.* Mailing address: Box 2443, 1000 San José; 32–8122. Telex 2700 COROCI CR. The new Corobicí is the old Playboy Hotel, which filed for bankruptcy in 1981 and was bought by the Cariari Hotel Group in mid-1985. Substantial effort and money was spent in completely refurbishing the hotel; it has been well worth it. It is located near La Sabana Park to the west of the city, on the main highway heading west. The top 4 floors of this 11-story structure still need to be completed. 134 rooms and 4 suites are now in use, and more are being built. Facilities include conference rooms, pool, sauna, casino, car rental and travel agencies, gift shop, newsstand, and several restaurants and bars, as well as one of the city's favorite discotheques, *The Place*.

Balmoral. *Moderate.* Mailing address: Box 2344, 1000 San José; 22–5022. Telex 2254 BALMOR CR. Frequented predominantly by Latin American businessmen and tour groups from the Caribbean islands, the busy Balmoral is on Av. Central, on the eastern edge of San José's commercial district. It has 150 comfortable rooms, sauna, an elegant upstairs restaurant-bar, cheery coffee shop (serving great breakfasts, and lively street-level piano bar (ideal for people-watching), car rental and travel agencies, beauty parlor, gift shop, and casino.

Bougainvillea. *Moderate.* Mailing address: Box 69, 1000 San José; 33–6622. Telex 3300 BOUGAI CR. This new, elegant Dutch-owned hotel has 57 air-conditioned rooms, pool, gift shop, bar, and superb restaurant. It's just a few minutes north of downtown San José, 2 blocks from the unique El Pueblo shopping center, which has several fine restaurants, a half-dozen good bars, 3 discotheques, boutiques, and even a roller skating rink.

Don Carlos. *Moderate.* Mailing address: Box 1593, 1000 San José; 21–6707. Because of its spirited owner, this small hotel is quite unique. Carlos Balser was born in the U.S. in 1902, raised in Belgium and Germany, and has lived in Costa Rica since 1928. He is fluent in 7 languages and an expert on pre-Columbian art, examples of which are seen throughout his 10-room pension-style hotel. Located in quiet Barrio Amón just to the west of the National Insurance Institute Building, the hotel offers U.S. satellite TV in the public lounge, a small garden lounge, and coffee shop. There is no restaurant, but a stroll of no more than 5 blocks will take you to at least a half-dozen of San José's excellent restaurants.

Europa. *Moderate.* Mailing address: Box 72, 1000 San José; 22–1222. Telex 3242 EUROPA CR. The Europa is a downtown favorite of international businessmen, and the site of many conferences and seminars. It has a small pool surrounded by palm trees (in the center of town!), gift shop–newsstand, bar, and quiet restaurant.

Gran Hotel Costa Rica. *Moderate.* Mailing address: Box 527, 1000 San José; 21–4000. Telex 2131 HOTELRICA CR. When inaugurated with much pomp and circumstance in 1930, the Gran Hotel Costa Rica was the tallest building in Central America. This classically staid hotel is full of atmosphere and tradition. Its 100 rooms and small suites face either Av. 2, the National Theater, or Av. Central. An elegant restaurant is on the top floor and a colonial-arched open-air coffee shop–bar is at the plaza level on a terrace. A new illuminated glasslike elevator takes you to the lively underground lounge, which has a dance band performing on most nights.

La Gran Via. *Moderate.* Mailing address: Box 1433, 1000 San José; 22–7737. This is the economy-minded businessman's hotel, located on Av. Central facing the north side of the Gran Hotel Costa Rica. It has a small coffee shop on the second floor, overlooking the hustle and bustle outside.

Tennis Club. *Moderate.* Mailing address: Box 4964, 1000 San José; 32–1266. Visiting sports fanatics prefer this 26-room hotel for its variety of facilities—basketball, 7 tennis courts, pool, whirlpool baths, sauna, bowling alley, bar pool, and Ping-Pong tables. Some rooms come with a stove, refrigerator, and private balcony. There are conference rooms, a bar, restaurant, and grill. Across the street is La Sabana Park with many public sports facilities, including miles of wooded jogging trails.

Torremolinos. *Moderate.* Mailing address: Box 2029, 1000 San José; 22–5266. Telex 2343 HOTOMOL CR. Located in a quiet residential area 2 blocks north of the Centro Colón office block at the west end of the city, this 2-story, 75-room hotel boasts U.S. satellite TV in all rooms, a beauty parlor, barber shop, car rental and travel agencies, conference facilities for up to 150, a heated pool, and sauna. There is a good restaurant and cozy bar.

Amstel. *Inexpensive to Moderate.* Mailing address: Box 4192, 1000 San José; 22–4622. Telex 2820 AMSTEL CR. The Amstel has long been a traditional favorite of repeat San José visitors. Located a few steps from Morazán Park (and 5 lively bars), the 55 rooms are modern and spacious, although those facing outward can be rather noisy, especially at night. Below are a gift shop–newsstand, tour operator, bar, and outstanding restaurant, always packed at mealtimes—lunchtime here is a particular favorite for local businessmen.

Diplomat. *Inexpensive to Moderate.* Mailing address: Box 6606, 1000 San José; 21–8133. Telex 2287 HDIPLO CR. This friendly, centrally located hotel has 30 pleasant rooms of varying sizes and prices. The second floor restaurant–bar is a favorite lunchtime gathering spot for Costa Rican businessmen, in to enjoy the restaurant's daily specials.

Presidente. *Inexpensive to Moderate.* Mailing address: Box 2922, 1000 San José; 22–3022. Telex 2872 PRETEL CR. This 47-room hotel is located on Av. Central in front of the Balmoral Hotel. Downstairs has a tour operator, quiet bar–restaurant, and casino.

Johnson. *Inexpensive.* Mailing address: Box 6638, 1000 San José; 23–7633. Considering the many excellent downtown accommodations offered at such low prices, the 57-room Johnson is a real bargain. The Central Market area it's located in is a bit rough, but colorful and aromatic!

Musoc. *Inexpensive.* Av. 1 and 3, Calle 16, San José; 22–9437. The rooms are basic and the bathrooms are shared, but the Musoc has long been a favorite of young traveling adventurers and U.S. Peace Corps volunteers. It has extremely low rates, with inexpensive restaurants nearby, and is located right next door to the city's largest bus terminal, the Coca-Cola Station. In addition, the hotel has a huge parabolic antenna on the roof, with which it picks up more than a dozen foreign TV stations from satellites.

Park. *Inexpensive.* Av. 4, Calles 2 and 4, San José; 23–3688. This rollicking American-owned hotel is just off the southwest corner of the Parque Central. The guests who rent the rooms (principally retired Americans) reflect the lusty charm of the area. When its *Boardwalk Cafe* (6 A.M. to 3:30 P.M.) is closed, the *Park Bar* is very much open and alive.

Pensión Costa Rica Inn. *Inexpensive.* Mailing address: Box 10282, 1000 San José; 22–5203. A combination of good value, cleanliness, and central location has made this another favorite of repeat visitors to Costa Rica. The Chinese owner gives weekly and monthly discounts, so its 35 rooms are often full. It offers a TV room and morning coffee; there is no restaurant. The inn is located on the southeast side of Morazán Park.

Escazú

Casa Maria. *Inexpensive to Moderate.* Mailing address: Box 123, 1250 Escazú; 28–2270. About 1 km east of the Central Park in Escazú is the American-owned Casa Maria guesthouse. A modern, spacious house with a definite family feeling, it has seven comfortable guest rooms on 1 acre of quiet, secluded gardens with a barbecue area and large pool. U.S. satellite TV is available in the TV room. Appetizing meals served in the dining room include many Costa Rican and Nicaraguan dishes.

Posada Pegasus. *Inexpensive to Moderate.* Mailing address: Box 370, 1250 Escazú; 28–4196. A 20-minute drive through the northwestern suburb of Escazú will take you to this quiet, intimate mountain hideaway overlooking the city. The American owner shares his extensive library with guests, who might choose to read in a hammock or out on the large veranda. The air is cool and dry, and the view is nothing less than spectacular. The restaurant serves fresh, all-natural foods; tennis and swimming are available close by. Discounts are given for extended stays.

Pico Blanco. *Inexpensive.* Mailing address: Box 900, 1250 Escazú; 28–3197. Up into the hills in the western Escazú suburb overlooking San José is another quiet mountain retreat—Pico Blanco. The British landlord offers 3 rooms and 2 cabins, and serves delicious meals in the restaurant with superb views across the Central Valley. Both decor and ambience are very "English pub." Enjoy standing at the small bar with your ice-cold beer chatting with the regulars.

Apartotels

The following is a listing of the best apartotels in San José. Suites usually have bedrooms, bathrooms, sitting–dining rooms, and kitchens. Most of them have color TVs (1 or 2 with U.S. satellite TVs) and telephones, daily maid service, and linens. Some have pools. All of them can be rented by the week or month, and we have classified all as *moderate.*

Apartotel Don Carlos. Box 1593, 1000 San José; 21–6707. Location: Los Yoses.

Apartotel La Castilla. Box 4699, 1000 San José; 22–2113. Location: Av. 2 and 4, Calle 24.

Apartotel El Conquistador. Box 303, 2050 San José; 25–3022. Location: Los Yoses.

Apartotel Napoleón. Box 8–6340, 1000 San José; 23–3252. Location: Av. 5, Calle 40.

Apartotel Ramgo. 32–3823. Location: Sabana Sur.

Apartotel San José. Box 5834, 1000 San José; 22–0455. Location: Av. 2, Calles 17 and 19.

RESTAURANTS. Awaiting you in Costa Rica is a true smorgasbord of culinary delights. Such a selection of cuisines to choose from—Italian, French, Spanish, German, Japanese, Chinese, Korean, Argentine, Lebanese, Mexican, the United States (McDonald's and Kentucky Fried Chicken!)—plus, of course, Costa Rican. A number of restaurants—especially the posh ones in San José—have brought in professional chefs from Europe and offer truly delicious meals served with style and elegance.

Compared with North American and European standards, restaurant prices in Costa Rica are bargain basement! A succulent inch-thick T-bone can be enjoyed for less than $7. But if you want wine with it, be sure to have a thick bankroll or lots of credit on your gold card; all wines are imported and carry a hefty luxury tax—meaning that a bottle of rather ordinary plonk can cost the equivalent of $15–$20!

The following list of restaurants in San José includes those that are most popular with locals and foreign residents alike. Price categories (based on a 3-course meal for 2, excluding liquor) are as follows: *Expensive,* over $40; *Moderate,* $20–$40; *Inexpensive,* under $20.

If you're staying outside San José, you'll probably be eating at your hotel (see "ACCOMMODATIONS").

In the city center there are close to a dozen first-class restaurants within a few streets either side of Av. Central, and heading west along the Paseo Colón, you'll encounter some of the city's poshest.

A long-time favorite, especially with foreign residents, is **Chalet Suizo** (Av. 2, a half block west of Hotel Amstel; 22–3118). *Moderately priced,* the specialty here is delicious Swiss cheese fondue. The owner, Monsieur Robert, has been resident here for decades.

For elegance and style, try the restaurants at **Le Chambord** (Av. 9 and 11, Calle 3; 33–7172). *Expensive,* but worth every penny. Reservations are essential. There's also a wine and cheese cellar (extensive wine list), and you can top off your evening by joining the "in" crowd at *Regine's* disco in the basement.

For a wild evening à la Mexican, **Los Antojitos** (Paseo Colón, across from Hotel Ambassador, 22–9086; and Los Yoses, 25–9525) is the place. *Moderately priced,* pitchers of draft beer and Mexican-style dishes appear with lightning speed. In the evenings strolling mariachi groups will serenade you.

Many hotels downtown have excellent restaurants. Probably the most well known (and well frequented) is at the **Hotel Amstel** (Av. 1, Calle 7; 22–4622), which is always crowded, especially at lunchtime. *Moderately priced.* (See the "Accommodations" category for more hotel restaurants.)

Other very good restaurants in San José include the following:

La Bastille. *Expensive.* Paseo Colón. French-international. An established favorite, with a good wine list.

Le Chandelier. *Expensive.* Paseo Colón, west of Hotel Ambassador; 21–7947. Previously called *Le Coq Hardi;* one of the best French restaurants in San José.

Club Londres. *Expensive.* Paseo Colón, across from Centro Colón; 22–7896. Tastefully decorated with excellent service and good wines.

Greta's II. *Expensive.* Lourdes de Montes de Oca; 25–2153. International cuisine, masterminded by excellent Belgian chef. Super sauces.

Île de France. *Expensive.* Calle 5, south of Hotel Balmoral; 22–4241. French. Intimate, and popular with embassy people.

The Lobster's Inn. *Expensive.* Paseo Colón; 23–8594. As the name implies, seafood, especially lobster.

La Masía de Triquell. *Expensive.* Av. 2, Calle 40; 21–5073. Specializes in Spanish cooking.

Rías Bajas. *Expensive.* El Pueblo shopping center; 21–7123. Outstanding seafood served in elegant surroundings. Good wine selection.

Trigals. *Expensive.* Paseo Colón; 33–2843. Superbly comfortable, with excellent food and wines and first-class service.

Beirut. *Moderate to Expensive.* Corner of Av. 1, Calle 32; 57–1808. Lebanese and other Middle-eastern dishes.

Greta's I. *Moderate to Expensive.* Los Yoses; 53–3107. Offers special dishes of the day. Cozy and informal.

Maybo. *Moderate to Expensive.* San Pedro. The top Italian restaurant in a 1985 competition. Antipasto table.

Trattoria Ursonia. *Moderate to Expensive.* Paseo Colón. Beautifully decorated dining room offering delicious Swiss dishes.

Villa Franken. *Moderate to Expensive.* San Pedro, 1 block east and 75m south of the Banco Popular; 24–1850. A true German restaurant; try the delicious homemade sauerkraut.

Waikiki. *Moderate to Expensive.* Av. 0, Calles 17 and 19; 21–7403. Full range of Japanese dishes; sushi is the specialty.

Los Anonos. *Moderate.* Escazu; 28–0180. A favorite family restaurant, specializing in grilled meat dishes.

El Balcón de Europa. *Moderate.* Av. Central, opposite Hotel Balmoral. International. Old-established, with a large variety of dishes.

La Cascada. *Moderate.* Escazu; 28–0906. With an inside waterfall, specializing in grilled and barbecued meats.

Casino Español. *Moderate.* Av. 1, Calle 7; 22–9440. Old-Spanish atmosphere, specializing in seafood.

El Chicote. *Moderate.* Sabana Norte; 32–0936. Meat dishes. Very good, especially succulent steaks.

La Cocina de Lena. *Moderate.* El Pueblo shopping center. Typical Costa Rican dishes (try the *gallo pinto*), cooked over a wood fire.

Fulusu. *Moderate.* Av. Central and 2, Calle 5; 23–7568. Korean, Chinese, and Japanese dishes, with enormous servings.

La Goya. *Moderate.* Av. 1, west of Hotel Amstel; 21–3887. Great *bocas* served with drinks. A favorite after-office rendezvous.

Kamakiri Steak House. *Moderate.* 2 locations (Kamakiri complex, 33–6966; and Omni center, 22–8484). Specializes in grilled and barbecued meats.

Lamm's. *Moderate.* Escazu; 28–2539. Terrace dining, offering large grilled sandwiches and other "gringo" food. Very popular.

Lancers. *Moderate.* El Pueblo shopping center; 22–5938. English-Scottish decor, specializing in steaks and other meat dishes.

Paprika. *Moderate.* Los Yoses. Well-presented dishes. Popular spot for young executives.

Villa Bonita. *Moderate.* Pavas; 32–9855. Chinese dishes, and excellent international cuisine. Good service.

Las Tunas. *Inexpensive.* Sabana Norte. Good local specialties as well as hamburgers, etc. Both indoor and terrace dining.

Valerio's. *Inexpensive.* Los Yoses. Lively and busy, offering a wide range of pasta dishes, pizzas, etc.

Fast Food

San José has a number of familiar fast-food restaurants with both indoor dining and take-out service. These include *Pizza Hut,* with 7 branches around the capital and home delivery service; *McDonald's,* with 5; *Kentucky Fried Chicken,* with 3; and one *Hardee's.* Other not-so-familiar fast-food stops include *José Tako, Mister Pizza, Archi's Fried Chicken,* and *Pizzalegre.*

HOW TO GET AROUND. From the airport. When arriving at Juan Santamaría International Airport, you have a choice of transportation to get to your hotel, which invariably will be in San José. The airport taxi service is good, and many hotels have their own buses to pick up incoming guests. The closest hotels to the airport are the Cariari and the Sheraton Herradura, about 10 minutes down the highway. Generally it should take at most 20–30 minutes to reach hotels in downtown San José (taxi fare about $8).

There is public bus transportation, which includes the airport as a stop, although buses do not run later than about 11:30 P.M. Services generally are reliable, although the physical condition of many of the buses (especially city buses) leaves a great deal to be desired. Many bus drivers give the impression that they are in training for the Le Mans 24-hour race, and it can be quite frightening for a passenger on a fully loaded bus as it zips along at high speed in some of the narrow city streets. (A local saying is that the first thing that wears out on a bus is not its brakes but its horn!)

By bus. In San José, buses cover the whole city, and service is efficient. Bus stops are clearly marked. Intercity service runs from San José to all major parts of the country. Bus stations are located as follows:

To the province of Heredia—Av. 5, Calle 1.

To the province of Alajuela and the *northern part of the province of Puntarenas*—Av. 9, Calle 12.

To the province of Guanacaste—Coca-Cola Station and surrounding streets, between Av. 1 and 5, Calles 14 and 18.

To the southern part of the province of Puntarenas—Tracopa Station, Av. 18, Calle 2.

To the cities of Cartago and Turrialba—Av. Central and 2, Calle 13.

To the province of Limón—Av. 3, Calle 19, across from the Atlantic railway station.

By car. Driving licenses from your own country should be valid here, but check with your travel agent when booking your trip. Be sure to have a certified translation of your license in Spanish. An International Driving License, obtainable from automobile associations in many countries, would be useful. The maximum speed limit on highways is 80 km per hour (55 mph). Gas (petrol) stations are open seven days a week, generally from 6 A.M. to 6 P.M., with some open 24 hours. Gasoline (one grade of leaded only) costs about $1.50 a gallon.

When driving in Costa Rica bear in mind that "machismo" on the roads is the norm. Costa Rica has the dubious distinction of being third in traffic deaths per capita, one reason new traffic laws introduced in January 1988 included compulsory use of seat belts for front-seat passengers.

Renting a car in Costa Rica is easy, but driving in San José is not recommended. The city center streets are very narrow, designed and layed out long before the modern automobile, and have become extremely congested in recent years. Parking space is at a premium, and it can take three times as long to drive into the center and park than to walk or take a bus. However, renting a car to explore the countryside is a good idea.

Car rental companies offer efficient service. Among the rental companies are the following: *Ada,* 33–7733; *Ancla,* 27–0164; *Avis,* 32–9922; *Budget,* 23–3284; *Dollar,* 33–3339; *El Indio,* 33–2157; *Global,* 23–4056; *Hertz,* 23–5959; *National,* 33–4406; *Econorent,* 22–8428; *Pan American,* 20–1081; *Poas,* 23–4249; *Elegante,* 21–0284; *Rent-A-Car,* 21–7116; *Tico Rent,* 22–8920; *Toyota,* 23–2250.

Rental costs traditionally have been very high in comparison to other countries. New taxation levels in force since early 1986 have led to reductions in rates. But the prices offered by the various rental companies do vary enormously (for example, 1-day rental for a 2-door Toyota Starlet sedan varies between $17 and $30). It definitely pays to shop around.

By taxi. Costa Rica has surprisingly efficient taxi service. Operating throughout the country, most taxis are radio-controlled, carry a "Taxi" sign on their roofs, and have a distinctive white triangle sticker on both front doors that carries the license plate number. Nearly all cars are red (except those serving the Juan Santamaría International Airport, which are orange). Rates vary, especially outside San José. By law, all taxis now have meters installed, although many drivers don't use them. In San José the minimum metered rate is C40 (about $0.53) for the first kilometer and C12 per kilometer thereafter. If your taxi doesn't have a meter, or if it's not being used, agree on a rate before starting. Taxi drivers are notorious for overcharging passengers.

Taxis can be hailed in the street or called by telephone. The following are the major companies in San José: *Coopetico,* 21–2552; *Coopeirazú,* 27–1211; *San Jorge,* 21–3434; *Alfaro,* 21–8466; *Coopetaxi,* 35–9966; *Taxis Unidos* (airport service), 21–6865; *Coopeguaria,* 26–1366.

Taxis can also be hired on a daily basis—if you want to go sightseeing or if you don't particularly want to rent a car. Again prices vary and are subject to negotiation: as a general guide, you could expect to pay about $100 for car and driver for a day, although it would be more if your trip included visits to many different places. Although some do, most drivers do not speak English.

By rail. There is also a limited rail network. Crossing the country from east to west, all trains have their main stations in San José. The Pacific Station is located at Av. 20, Calle 2 (tel. 26–0011). The Atlantic Station is at Av. 3, Calle 17 (tel. 23–3311).

By ferry. There are 2 ferries operating on the Pacific coast, both of which carry cars and passengers. The *Salinero Ferry* (tel. 61–1069) crosses from Puntarenas to Playa Naranjo on the Nicoya Peninsula. The *Tempisque Ferry* (tel. 62–0147) crosses the head of the Gulf of Nicoya.

By plane. For getting around to popular visiting spots quickly, the internal airline *Sansa* (tel. 33–3258, 21–9414, or 33–0397)—a subsidiary of the country's international airline, Lacsa—has scheduled flights to many parts of the country from Juan Santamaría International Airport. A new airline, *Trans Costa Rica* (tel. 32–0808), also offers low-cost flights to certain areas. A number of charter companies operate plane rental services at the Juan Santamaría International Airport (tel. 41–2713 or 1444) and the Tobias Bolanos Airport (tel. 32–1010 or 0660 or 1474).

TOURS. The Costa Rican Tourist Board (ICT) has its principal office in a tall office block on Av. 2 in downtown San José, with a public information office underneath the Plaza de la Cultura where brochures and helpful information from multilingual staff can be obtained. The ICT also maintains offices in the U.S. (Miami and Los Angeles) and in Paris (for all addresses and telephone numbers, see "Useful Addresses," above).

Most hotels in San José have tour desks, where you can ask about the many tours available and make reservations. Tour-group members are picked up at hotels by tour company buses, vans, or Jeeps, depending on the tour. Bilingual guides are onboard to help you as you explore the country by highway or byway. You will be returned to your hotel at the end of a tour.

A recent boost to the country was the addition of Costa Rica as a port of call by some of the world's luxury cruise liners, such as the *Queen Elizabeth II,* which made her first visit to Puerto Limón on the Caribbean coast on January 21, 1986. Cunard, the owner of the *QE II,* intends to continue making calls here; information on future cruises can be obtained from any Cunard office or your travel agent, or Cunard's office in San José (tel. 23–5111). Other Cunard liners, such as the *Vistafjord,* have also visited the country, calling at the Pacific coast port of Caldera. (See also "Facts at Your Fingertips.")

There are dozens of tour operators in San José. The leading ones—which will mail you brochures, usually in English, upon request—are as follows:

Calypso Cruises. Box 6941, 1000 San José; 33–3618.

Coco Island Adventure. Box 130, 5400 Puntarenas; 22–0866.

Costa Rica Expeditions. Box 6941, 1000 San José; 23–9975.

Excai Tours. Box 7347, 1000 San José; 23–0155.

Geotur. Box 469, 1011 San José; 26–1503.

Horizontes Nature Tours. Box 4025, 1000 San José; 22–2022.

Ob-la-di, Ob-la-da Ranch. Canton de Mora, 6100 Colón; 49–1179.

Panorama Tours. Box 7323, 1000 San José; 33–3058.

Swiss Travel Service. Box 7–1970, 1000 San José; 32–6742.

TAM Travel. Box 1864, 1000 San José; 23–5111.

Tikal Eco Tours. Box 6398, 1000 San José; 33–0233.

Tropical River Adventures. Box 472, 1200 San José; 31–4140.

Viajes Especiales. Box 662, 1007 San José; 33–8591.

Many tour operators offer the same standard tours, but each with their own variations, guides, and transportation. Generally tours last a half day or a full day. The most popular tours are the following:

San José City Tour. A good orientation lesson in getting to know what's where in San José. Stops on the tour usually include the National Theater, metropolitan cathedral, the Plaza de la Cultura, various museums, the Supreme Court of Justice, the University of Costa Rica campus, and shopping areas.

Irazú Volcano and Cartago. Leaving San José and heading southeast, you'll pass Ochomogo, the geographic center of this hemisphere—you'll have to look hard to see the concrete marker some distance off the highway to your right—on your way to the old capital, Cartago. The tour includes a visit to the magnificent basilica of Nuestra Señora de los Angeles with its unique grottolike shrine to Costa Rica's patron saint, and Las Ruinas, the old cathedral destroyed in the Irazú volcano eruption of 1912. From here, the tour heads toward Irazú, climbing up through the beautiful countryside dotted with oxen pulling plows through fields of black volcanic soil. Soon you're at the crater mouth, 11,260 ft above sea level where, on a clear day, you can see both the Caribbean Sea and the Pacific Ocean just by turning your head. (Irazú is a national park; for a fuller description see "Parks, Gardens, Forests," below.)

Poás Volcano. Northwest of San José through Heredia is Poás volcano, which has one of the largest craters and highest-shooting steam geysers in the world. The drive to Poás is enchanting: you'll be on winding roads through green fields passing chalets and small farms. The paved road leads right to Poás, where there are picnic areas and a restaurant, among other things. (Poás is a national park; for a fuller description see "Parks, Gardens, Forests.")

Sarchí. The Poás volcano tour often includes a side trip to Sarchí (although it is also a tour by itself), home of Costa Rican artisan crafts. The villagers have been famous for their hardwood ox carts since the beginning of the century. Traditionally they hand-paint unique geometric designs on each one. Today they also turn out colorful cartwheels for wall decorations, wood carvings, cutting boards, jewelry, rocking chairs, and much more.

Orosí Valley. This tour starts out in San José, goes through Cartago, and then south into this enchanting valley of sugarcane and coffee farms, adobe homes, contented cows, and tranquillity. Stops might include the Mirador lookout point and picnic grounds with breathtaking views; Cachí hydroelectric dam and Cachí Lake, man-made as a result of the dam and perfect for waterskiing; the 300-foot Bride's Veil waterfall; the Ujarras ruins, site of one of Costa Rica's oldest Spanish settlements; and the village of Orosi with its 400-year-old church and religious art museum (see "Museums," below).

Jungle Train. With a blast of steam and the waving of many arms, you begin clickety-clacking your way toward the Caribbean Sea on one of the world's wildest train rides! The 8-hour journey will take you from cool coffee country at 5,000 ft down through the tropical jungle to the seaport of Limón. The 101-mile-long narrow-gauge track was engineered by American Minor C. Keith between 1871 and 1890. Your trip will take you through green valleys and cloud-draped mountains, over roaring rivers, through pitch-dark tunnels, rain forest jungle, and out to the balmy coast. There are 52 whistle-stops en route, at which swarms of locals ascend to ply their wares to passengers. Your tour will be on a newly refurbished private club car with cushioned seats, bar, and clean bathroom, tacked onto the end of the train. The most popular tour ends at Siquirres, about three-quarter of the way. From there, a bus takes you to a vast banana plantation to see how bananas are grown, treated, cut, graded, washed, labeled, and packed for export. A typical dinner follows in Turrialba on the way back to San José.

White-Water Rafting. For a country its size, Costa Rica boasts an incredible 500 miles of white-water rivers. Several tour operators run 1-, 2-, and 4-day adventures down rivers such as the Corobicí, Sarapiquí, Reventazón, Pacuare, General, and El Grande de Orosí. Trips are available to suit all preferences and skill levels, and trained guides use the best equipment to provide safe yet exhilarating rides for everyone. Kayak trips are also available.

Pacific Island Cruise. Several yachts in Puntarenas run trips out of the estuary into the sparkling Gulf of Nicoya. The most popular tour is that offered by Calypso Cruises on the 50-footer *Calypso.* A stop is made at one of the many islands dotting the bay for sunning on a white-sand beach, swimming, and snorkeling, which is topped off with a fresh seafood lunch.

Tortuguero Canal Excursion. A trip along the canal is like a scene from *The African Queen,* but instead of a Bogart-style vessel, you'll be comfortably transported in a canopied motorboat complete with bar and toilet. The Tortuguero Canal runs parallel to the Caribbean Sea for 80 mi, between Puerto Limón and the border with Nicaragua. Several tours, of varied durations, are available. Stops might include the nesting grounds of 350-lb turtles or any of the area's fishing lodges. Take binoculars (and insect repellant!), for the jungle wildlife is incredible.

Many other tours are offered for such activities as shopping, a night on the town, horseshows and cattle auctions, sport fishing, and visits to the national parks. Specialty tours are also available, such as trips to flower gardens, weekend farmers' markets, or new agroindustrial projects. In fact, there is an enjoyable tour to somewhere for everyone!

PARKS, GARDENS, FORESTS. Costa Rica has long been known as the "garden of the Americas." This land bridge is home and shelter to nearly 12,000 species of plants, 237 of mammals, 848 of birds, and 361 of amphibians and reptiles. Within this small country are more species of butterflies than in all of Africa, and more species of birds than in continental North America.

The Costa Rican national park system was begun in 1970, and now—at nearly 1.3 million acres—the 28 units encompass over 10 percent of the country's land area: a higher percentage than any other country in this hemisphere. In addition, the Costa Rican Tourist Board operates 10 recreational parks, and there are many privately owned gardens, forests, and amusement parks. Any travel agent in San José can provide complete information about all the sights to see in this category. Or you can visit the Costa Rican Tourist Board's public office at the Plaza de la Cultura in San José (tel. 22–1090).

National Parks

All national parks are open to the public. Some are in somewhat inaccessible areas; others—such as Coco Island—require special permission in advance. Listed below are the most popular parks for tourists to visit. Each one has a visitors' station, camping and picnic areas, toilets, hiking trails, and sometimes a small museum. The Costa Rican National Parks Service has brochures on some of the national parks. Write to: Servicio de Parques Nacionales, Ministerio de Agricultura y Ganadería, P.O. Box 10094, 1000 San José.

Barra Honda National Park. Close to the town of Nicoya, 200 mi west of San José, Barra Honda is renowned for its extensive network of limestone underground caves, 19 of which have been explored to date. The deepest cave, Santa Ana, which descends over 780 ft, contains a great number of beautiful stalactites, stalagmites, columns, and other cave formations. Outside the subterranean world, the park, which covers 5,670 acres, is a sunny, lowland dry-tropical forest with wildlife consisting mainly of birds and monkeys.

Braulio Carrillo National Park. This 77,600-acre mountainous park is densely covered with forests with numerous rushing rivers that have carved deep canyons, some of which are boxed in by sheer vertical walls. Within the park area are 2 extinct volcanoes—Barva and Cacho Negro. Only 16 mi northwest of San José, Braulio Carrillo is predicted to become the country's most-visited national park since the entrance is just off the nearly completed paved highway running from San José to Guápiles near Limón. The park contains an estimated 6,000 species of plants and nearly 400 of birds, including the rare quetzal, considered the most beautiful land bird.

Cahuita National Park. About 22 mi southeast of Puerto Limón on the Caribbean coast is the 2,600-acre Cahuita National Park. A snorkeler's dream, it includes a beautiful 1,400-acre coral reef off the beaches, with multitudes of brilliantly colored fish. Over 500 species of fish are native to these waters. Beachfront campsites nestle beneath thickly grouped palm trees, and you are guaranteed to see or hear screeching howler and white-faced monkeys.

Chirripó National Park. With an area of 124,000 acres, Chirripó—together with nearby Costa Rican–Panamanian Friendship Park—constitutes the area of greatest ecological diversity in the country, including the largest virgin forest. Chirripó Peak, reaching a height of 12,530 ft, is the highest mountain in Costa Rica; its lakes were formed 25,000 years ago by glacial activity. The peak is popular with mountaineers, who can find resting spots at numerous primitive shelters on their route. This park is not far from San Isidro de El General, 94 mi from San José on the Pan American Highway in the direction of Panama.

Coco Island National Park. Located in the Pacific Ocean 350 mi southwest of Puntarenas (or halfway between Costa Rica and the Galápagos Islands), the 10-square-mile island is completely given over as a national park. It's an important breeding ground for a number of species of seabirds that do not nest on land anywhere on the Costa Rican mainland. The island is famous for the stories of buried pirate treasure from the 17th century; over 500 expeditions have been mounted in search of hidden booty and treasure chests. No luck so far! Annual rainfall is more than 275 in., creating a number of cascading waterfalls, some of which plunge into the sea from spectacular heights. The whole island is covered in evergreen forest. The sea is incredibly beautiful—usually a turquoise blue color—with coral reefs and a rich marine life, including sharks, dolphins, and tuna.

Guayabo National Monument. Located 12 mi north of Turrialba, Guayabo is Costa Rica's most important archeological site and the only public park of its type. An advanced Indian culture is believed to have evolved in the region as early as 500 B.C. Dotting the area are many stone structures, built prior to A.D. 1400; they consist of cobbled streets, bridges, mounds, house foundations, and other samples of an indigenous culture. Only a small part of the area has been excavated so far; some archeologists feel that the remains of an ancient culture perhaps as rich as that discovered at Copán, Guatemala, are still buried, awaiting discovery.

Irazú Volcano National Park. Known locally as "nature's deadly powder keg," Irazú volcano stands 11,260 ft above sea level. It has a long history of violent eruptions, the last ones occurring between 1962 and 1965. Because of these eruptions, Irazú has a lunarlike landscape with little or no vegetation. A paved road leads right to the summit, about 40 minutes' drive from the city of Cartago. The volcano has two craters, the largest of which is 3,450 ft across and nearly 1,000 ft deep with a lake at the bottom whose waters constantly change color. The drive up to Irazú takes you through fertile agricultural countryside, with pleasant little restaurants along the way.

Manuel Antonio National Park. Located 100 mi south of San José, this 716-acre Pacific coast park is well known for its lush jungle vegetation that tumbles down to the high-tide line on its white-sand beaches. It is one of the most beautiful parks in the whole system. Camping and picnic areas line the beaches, and there are many hiking trails. The park contains varied wildlife, such as the squirrel monkey, howler monkey, and two-toed sloths.

Palo Verde National Park. The park, together with the Dr. Rafael Lucas Rodríguez Caballero National Wildlife Refuge, is in the province of Guanacaste, 18 mi west of Cañas at the mouth of the Tempisque River. Covering 23,400 acres—plus 18,170 acres of wildlife refuge—Palo Verde received its name from the attractive Jerusalem thorn (palo verde) tree. Made up principally of marshy wetlands, mangrove swamps, and deciduous forests, the park and refuge are home to more than 280 species of birds, including the largest concentration in Central America of herons, storks, egrets, ibis, ducks, and other birds.

Poás Volcano National Park. About 8,800 ft above sea level, Poás is one of the most spectacular active volcanoes in Costa Rica. The crater is nearly 1,000 ft deep and nearly 1 mile across. There is a secure viewing platform right on the crater mouth, where you can see the active fumaroles in the crater, which at times give off enormous clouds of steam and sulfurous smoke and ash.

Poás is the most developed and visited of the national parks, with a good-quality paved road right to the crater. A well-thought-out walking trail leads from the crater through a cloud forest to the second crater, called Botos Lake, nearly 1,000 ft higher; a dead crater, now filled with filled, it has thick vegetation growing to the water level. In the park is a newly built auditorium, where audiovisual presentations are given on this and other parks. The building also contains a restaurant, as well as a seismic room, where you can see sensitive instruments recording the slightest movement beneath the earth (there's no need to be nervous!). This national park is north of the city of Alajuela.

Santa Rosa National Park. Halfway between Liberia in Guanacaste and the Nicaraguan border is Santa Rosa—Costa Rica's number one historical national park. It contains a ranch house converted into a museum with maps and other documents about the battle of Santa Rosa in March 1856, when Costa Rica defeated the American William Walker and put an end to his plans of invasion. With an area of 54,150 acres, Santa Rosa has over 600 species of plants, 75 of mammals, and 260 of birds. There are thousands of insect species—including 2,000 of moths! Several hiking trails lead to Nancite and Naranjo beaches, which offer superb scenic landscapes.

Amusement Parks

El Bosque Encantado. Located in sunny La Garita, 20 minutes from San JosÉ, this amusement park (whose apt name means "the enchanted forest") is Costa Rica's equivalent of Disneyland. In addition to many children's rides (such as mini motorbikes, motorcars, and boats), the park offers horseback riding, 3 pools, a "space capsule," and restaurant. Built with children very much in mind, cutout figures of Cinderella, Snow White and the Seven Dwarfs, and other Disney characters dot the grounds. El Bosque Encantado is open Tues. to Sun.; for information call 48–7050.

Parque Nacional de Diversiones. The National Amusement Park is located west of the Hospital Mexico, just outside San José. It operates under the motto "The healthy child helps the sick child," and contributes funds to the National Children's Hospital in San José. The park has many indoor and outdoor rides (some suitable only for older children), an electronic games area, roller skating rink, boating lake, restaurants, and picnic areas. Open Wed. to Sun.; for information call 31–2001.

Gardens

Lankester Gardens. About 4 mi outside Cartago on the road to Paraíso is this beautiful park. Established in 1940 by British botanist Charles Lankester, it is now run by the University of Costa Rica. More than 800 species of plants are grown here, including the park's specialty—orchids; one of the largest collections in the world is here. Open daily.

Beaches

Costa Rica has many excellent beaches on both the Caribbean and Pacific coasts. On the Caribbean side you can visit beaches that have lush vegetation right to the shore; while on the Pacific coast you can choose between luxurious beach resorts or almost-deserted idyllic hideaways.

Just about every beach in the country that's accessible has a hotel or some type of accommodation, either right by the beach or close to it (see "ACCOMMODATIONS," above). What is the "best beach" is really a matter of personal preference. White sand, black sand, brown sand, rocky, pebbly, secluded, busy—Costa Rica has them all. Rather than try to classify beaches in this manner, we have simply listed the beaches that are generally regarded as the most popular; descriptions of them, where appropriate, will be found under "Accommodations."

One of the things many travelers finds so appealing about Costa Rica is that it is still undeveloped and that all of the beaches do not have a sophisticated, artificial infrastructure, with high-rise hotels and other ultramodern complexes. Yet there can be a disadvantage to this in that getting to many of the beaches—especially those in the province of Guanacaste—can be a long, dusty journey. Most roads from the closest towns to beaches are not paved, although many of them are of compacted dirt so that relatively high driving speeds can be maintained. It's very important make sure your gas tank is full when leaving the last major town, because there are no garage facilities at the beaches.

Here is a list of some of Costa Rica's most popular beaches:

Caribbean Coast. *Province of Limón:* Moín, Playa Bonita, Cahuita, Puerto Viejo, Vizcaya, and Puerto Vargas.

Pacific Coast. *Province of Guanacaste:* Ocotal, Hermosa, Coco, Potrero, Penca, Conchal, Tamarindo, Flamingo, Langosta, Avellanas, Pan de Azúcar, Junquillal, Nosara, Garza, Sámara, and Coyote.

Province of Puntarenas: Mal País, Montezuma, Ballena, Curú, Barranca, Mata Limón, Tivives, Tárcoles, Agujas, Herradura, Jacó, Esterillos, La Palma, Manuel Antonio, Dominical, Piñuela, Puerto Jiménez, and Zancudo.

Many travelers consider the beaches on Costa Rica's Pacific coast to be the best in the world. Miles and miles of pure white sand, unspoiled by high-rise hotels. But that's not to say that a visit to the beach means roughing it. Far from it! Most beaches boast small cosy and comfortable hotels. There are many beaches to choose from. Some are just a few hours from San José. Others, particularly those in the province of Guanacaste, take longer to get to by car (less than an hour by chartered plane), but the trip is extremely worthwhile.

SPORTS AND RECREATION. Costa Rica is a nation of sports lovers. Every town and village across the country has at least a soccer pitch, which you will see in constant use every day, especially on weekends. In San José there is La Sabana Park on the west side of the city, which includes public pools, an artificial lake complete with fountain and boat rides, miles of jogging trails, volleyball, basketball, and tennis courts, the National Gymnasium, soccer pitches, and the National Stadium in which championship and international matches are played. Southeast of the city center is the Plaza González Víquez public park; although smaller than La Sabana, it offers many facilities. See also "Accommodations," for resorts that have sports facilities.

Basketball and volleyball. These sports are regularly played in high schools, and many towns and cities have public courts. Matches between semiprofessional teams are played in the National Gymnasium at La Sabana Park in San José.

Bull fighting. Costa Rican bull fights have a very important distinction—the bull is never killed or even injured. At the end of every year there is a festival held at the *Zapote Bullring,* in eastern San José, in which hundreds of spectators climb into the ring with the bull and literally tease him, with lots of tail-pulling and shouting!

Cycling. Bicycle touring and racing is very popular, with many competitions and races held throughout the year. The most important is the Vuelta de Costa Rica, which circuits the whole country over a 2-week period, attracting many international cyclists as well.

Golf. There is an 18-hole course at the *Cariari Country Club* (tel. 39–2455 ext. 26). And 9-hole courses are at the *Costa Rica Country Club* (tel. 28–2155) and *Hacienda Los Reyes* (tel. 48–0004). The 2 9-hole courses are private, although guest membership facilities are available. Green fees are surprisingly inexpensive, and clubs can be hired.

Horseback riding. Many excellently trained horses are kept at *La Caraña Stables,* in Colón about 15 mi west of San José (45 minutes by bus). Every year international competitions are held here. Also in Colón is *Ob-la-di, Ob-la-da Ranch* (tel. 49–1179), which offers trips that combine trail rides with visits to some of the splendid waterfalls around town. Horses can also be rented at the *Cariari Country Club* (tel. 39–2455).

Motor racing. Every Sun. at *Autodromo La Guacima* (no phone; located 20 minutes west of San José), there are many activities, such as car races, quarter-mile races, autocross, motocross, and motorbike speed trials. Events are usually advertised in the local press.

Soccer. This is Costa Rica's national sport, played throughout the country in the largest cities as well as the smallest villages. Every Sun. there are matches between the teams of the First Division league. Details are given in the daily newspapers, or your hotel can provide you with information if you wish to see a match, usually played at the Saprissa Stadium in the northeastern suburb of Tibas, the National Stadium at La Sabana Park, or at the Alajuela League Stadium in Alajuela.

Sport fishing. Long considered by sport fishermen and magazine writers alike as one of the world's best fishing areas, Costa Rica offers a variety of both saltwater and freshwater sport fishing. Along the coastal waters of the Caribbean can be found the world's best tarpon and snook fishing; while the Pacific coast is regarded as one of the world's best areas for sailfish and marlin (a world record was set here with a catch measuring over 15 ft and weighing an estimated 1,000 lb). On both coasts there are a number of fishing lodges and hotels, such as Casa Mar and Río Colorado Lodge on the Caribbean, and El Ocotal and Flamingo on the Pacific (see "Accommodations" for details).

Squash. In San José you can play at the *Monterreal Squash Club* (tel. 32–3241), located near La Sabana Park. It is not necessary to be a member. The Monterreal also offers racketball courts.

Surfing. Many beaches on both coasts are suitable for surfing. Among the best surfing beaches are: *Pacific*—Boca de Barranca at Dona Ana Beach, Playa Hermosa de Jacó, Tamarindo, Langosta, and Playa Grande; *Caribbean*—Playa Bonita, Portete, and Puerto Viejo.

Tennis. Played mainly at private clubs and hotels, one has to be a member, or invited by one and pay a fee to play at the clubs. There are public courts at La Sabana Park in San José and the Ojo de Agua spa near San Antonio de Belén, 12 mi west of San José.

White-water rafting. See "Tours," above.

ARCHAEOLOGICAL SITES. The Guayabo National Monument, 12 mi north of Turrialba outside Cartago, is part of the national park system; for details see "Parks, Gardens, Forests," above. Archaeological displays are often mounted in the Jade Museum in San José; see "Museums," below.

MUSEUMS. The Costa Rican government helps to maintain 15 museums—9 in San José and 6 in the provinces.

San José

Entomology Museum. University of Costa Rica, San Pedro; 25–5555 ext. 23218, or 24–1213. Open Wed. and Thurs. 1 P.M. to 4 P.M. Admission free. This unpretentious museum, located in a quaint old house on the university campus, maintains its temperature at a constant 62° F for the sake of the insects. A wide variety is preserved in formaldehyde or behind hermetically sealed glass: spiders, termites, bees, fruitflies, locusts, cockroaches, beetles, butterflies. There is also the preserved cadaver of a gargantuan hook-nose beetle—only slightly smaller than a football!

Jade Museum. National Insurance Institute Building, 11th floor, Av. 7, Calle 9; 33–4570 or 23–5800 ext. 2584. Open Mon. to Fri. 9 A.M. to 3 P.M. Admission free. Opened in 1977, this museum displays 6,000 pieces of diverse types of jade, clay, stone, and gold found in Indian grave sites (the Indians believed in life after death, and all these objects were to accompany them to their new destinations). They are very well displayed in didactic form, using modern graphic design with subtle illumination. Contemporary art works are exhibited in an adjacent hall. The museum also exhibits archaeological objects from the various regions of Costa Rica, and has a separate wing for temporary archaeological exhibitions.

La Salle Museum of Natural Sciences. In front of Ministry of Agriculture and Livestock, southwest of La Sabana Park; 32–1306. Open Mon. to Fri. 7:30 A.M. to 3 P.M. and Sat. 7:30 A.M. to 12 P.M. Admission free. Founded in 1959, this museum exhibits over 1,500 samples of the world's fauna (including many now extinct), such as hundreds of mounted butterflies; stuffed birds, reptiles, animals, and fish (in conditions similar to their natural habitats); encased shells, minerals, and fossils; even a 44-foot-long whale skeleton in a flowering courtyard.

Museum of Costa Rican Art. East side of La Sabana Park; 22–7247 or 7155. Open Tues. to Sun. 10 A.M. to 6 P.M. Admission free. This little museum has been housed since 1978 in the Spanish colonial-style building that was formerly the international airport terminal. Its second floor has mural walls depicting Costa Rica's history from pre-Columbian times to the present. Its art collection includes paintings, carvings, and sculptures by the foremost 19th- and 20th-century Costa Rican artists.

Museum of Judicial History. Judicial Investigation Organization (OIJ) headquarters, Av. 6, Calle 15; 23–0666. Open Mon., Wed., and Fri. 8 A.M. to 11 A.M. and 1 P.M. to 4 P.M. Admission free. Exhibits include weapons, counterfeit money, portraits of past presidents of the Supreme Court of Justice, and information on criminal case evidence, the Napoleonic Code, judicial history, and the death penalty, which is now abolished.

Museum of Printing. Imprenta Nacional, La Uruca; 31–5222. Open Mon. to Fri. 9 A.M. to 3:30 P.M. Admission free. Antique printing equipment and old publications are on display.

National Museum. Av. Central and 12, Calle 17; 21–0295 or 33–1788. Open Tues. to Sun. 8 A.M. to 4:30 P.M. Small admission. This historic museum was founded in 1887 to study, preserve, and exhibit Costa Rica's historic past as well as its flora and fauna. The collections are now housed in the former Bellavista Fortress, which served as hilltop headquarters for the Costa Rican army until the abolition of military forces in 1949. Exhibits cover pre-Columbian art (pottery, stone, gold); the Spanish colonial era (furniture and art); national history (such as details of the 1856 military campaign against William Walker's fillibusters); portraits of all past presidents; the development of coffee; natural history (mounted butterflies and stuffed animals and birds); and religious art (statues and effigies). The labyrinthine fortress is itself of great architectural interest. The museum publishes a variety of books and magazines on the country's natural history and archeology; copies may be purchased at the museum.

Pre-Columbian Gold and Currency Museum. Av. Central and 2, Calle 5 (Plaza de la Cultura); 23–0528. Open Tues. to Sun. 10 A.M. to 1 P.M. and 2 P.M. to 6 P.M. Admission free. Founded in 1950 and reinaugurated in September 1985 in its current location, the museum displays over 1,800 pieces of indigenous gold artifacts, one of the world's most extensive and valuable collections of its type. Guided 90-minute tours show visitors figurines, amulets, jewelry, and other gold objects unearthed from Indian grave sites, some over 2,000 years old. The museum's numismatic collection consists of 3,000 coins and tokens, coin-making machines, and antiques from the old Costa Rican Mint. The museum is run by the Central Bank of Costa Rica.

Alajuela

Juan Santamaría Historic Museum. Av. 2, Calles Central and 2; 41–4775 or 42–1838; open Tues. to Sat. 2 P.M. to 9 P.M. Admission free. Dedicated in 1975, this museum is devoted to Costa Rica's favorite son—the young drummer boy from Alajuela. The museum highlights the battle of Santa Rosa in 1856 as well as the historical and cultural history of Alajuela. On display are portraits, weapons, maps, military uniforms, documents, colonial furniture, and period objects, as well as a detailed account of William Walker.

Barva

Coffee Museum. 4 blocks north of church of San Pedro de Barva, Barva de Heredia; 37–1975. Open Mon. to Sat. 7 A.M. 4 P.M. Admission free. Located in a ranch house built in 1834, in the heart of one of the country's major coffee-producing regions, the museum displays old coffee-processing equipment, such as mills, classifiers, pulp extractors, toasters, and bins.

Liberia

Casona de Santa Rosa Historical Museum. Santa Rosa National Park, 15 mi northwest of Liberia, Guanacaste. Open daily 8 A.M. to 4:30 P.M. Admission free. This restored ranch house is within the region's popular national park (see park description in "Parks, Gardens, Forests"). The displays recount the story of battles that took place here, such as the one in 1856 to oust William Walker.

Orosi

Museum of Religious Art. Next to church, Orosi, beyond Cartago; 51–3151. Open Tues. to Sat. 8:30 A.M. to 5 P.M. Admission free. Located in an ancient Franciscan monastery, this museum displays religious art, colonial furniture, silver objects, paintings, sculptures, and ecclesiastical frocks. The adjacent church, over 400 years old, is one of the earliest Spanish colonial churches.

San Blas, Nicoya

San Blas de Nicoya Religious Art Museum. South sacristy of church of San Blas de Nicoya, Guanacaste; 68–5109. Hours vary. Admission free. Nicoya was one of the first areas in the country to be explored by the Spanish, in the early 1500s. This colonial-style building contains religious images, processional candlesticks, silver, bronze, and copper liturgical objects, and other works depicting the religious traditions of this rural area.

Tres Ríos

Nuestra Señora de Pilar Religious Art Museum. South side of church of Tres Ríos, near Cartago; 29–5109. Hours vary. Admission free. Founded in 1977, this museum highlights Cartago's religious, cultural, and artistic heritage. On display are 60 objects of religious art, including incense containers, palliam, humeral veils, liturgical capes, and many effigies.

SITES OF HISTORIC INTEREST. The National Theater, San José. Plaza de la Cultura, Av. Central and 2, Calles 3 and 5; 21–1329 5341. Open Mon. to Fri. 9 A.M. to 6 P.M. and Sat. to Sun. 9 A.M. to 5 P.M. Small admission for touring the building. This magnificent structure deserves special mention. Although not strictly a museum, it is at the heart of Costa Rica's culture and history. Built between 1890 and 1897, the National Theater is a classic Renaissance-style structure. The facade features recessed statues of Beethoven and Calderón de la Barca, and on the roof arch there are allegories of dance, music, and fame by the Italian sculptor Pietro Bulgarelli. The theater's main staircase displays elaborate Versailles-style ornamentation; the overall visual impression is similar to that of the Paris Opera House or the Royal Palace in Madrid. The foyer, with its triptych ceiling supported by 20-foot-high marble columns, is magnificent. All around is gold lamination. The 3-story Grand Auditorium, a perfect horseshoe shape, features an enormous shimmering crystal chandelier suspended from the high ceiling; the orchestra pit can be raised up and down to suit the theater's needs. The theater is often used for international conferences and state receptions. A cultural programs are offered year-round, including the many concerts given by the National Symphony Orchestra and the Youth Symphony Orchestra, as well as the many visiting international opera companies, solo performers, and Spanish zarzuelas. The National Theater is surely the most elegant theater in Central America.

SHOPPING. In San José you will find a wide variety of things to buy to commemorate your visit. Don't be surprised to see many of the same types of goods in just about any city, especially clothing (many well-known brands are made in Costa Rica). Handcrafted items represent good value; it's especially worth a trip to the handicraft center of the country at Sarchí, beyond Alajuela and Grecia heading west of San José. There you can buy items, such as plates, bowls, tables, and chairs, handmade from many of the country's beautiful rare woods, like cocobolo, cedar, and laurel. Sarchí is also the home of the famous decorative ox cart; small ones on sale are suitable for use as portable bars.

In the center of San José, along Av. Central, there are shops and jewelry stores that offer reproduction pre-Columbian gold and silver pieces. You'll also come across street vendors plying similar wares—be prepared to bargain! Handcrafted ceramic and wood articles can be found in the artisan markets. For leather goods the northern suburb of Moravia has a number of shops. San José's Central Market offers a wide variety of small stores displaying well-crafted wares.

As a general rule, bargaining in shops (as opposed to haggling with street vendors) is not an acceptable custom. Courteous attention is given by shop assistants, although they tend to be zealous at times, descending upon you the second you cross the threshold. While this is fine for getting immediate attention, it can be irritating if you want to just browse.

ENTERTAINMENT AND NIGHTLIFE. From the classical culture at the National Theater to thumping rock music at many discos; from Costa Rican folklore dancing to *Swan Lake;* from hilarious Spanish-language comedies to the latest Rogers and Hammerstein musical presented in English—some type of cultural event is going on in San José all of the time.

The best way to find out what is happening where is through the English-language weekly *The Tico Times,* published every Fri. In the city center it's usually on sale at The Candy Shop (Plaza de la Cultura side of Gran Hotel Costa Rica), The Bookshop (Av. 1, Calles 3 and 5), and La Librería Francesa (Calle 5). Another English-language publication listing events is *Guide* magazine, published monthly and free at every major hotel.

The *National Theater* presents cultural programs throughout the year, in conjunction with the National Theater Company, the National Dance Company, and the city's 2 excellent orchestras. Most evenings there are presentations of one of one sort or another; check the press for information or call the theater at 21–1329. Often there are early concerts on Sun. at 10:30 A.M.

If you're in San José in Apr. and May or Sept. and Oct., you'll have the opportunity to see a musical or comedy in English put on by the *Little Theater Group,* which is the oldest theater group operating in Costa Rica. The group is based at the Costa Rican–North American Cultural Center in Los Yoses. Check *The Tico Times* for presentation dates or call the cultural center at 25–7344.

If you speak even a few words of Spanish, one way of really getting to understand the Costa Rican spirit and personality is to go to one of the many theaters in San José that put on Spanish-language plays. The cultural section of the major daily newspaper, *La Nación,* includes listings of most theatrical presentations. Among San José's best theaters are: *Teatro*

Melico Salazar (tel. 33–5172), *Teatro del Angel* (tel. 22–8258), *Teatro Carpa* (tel. 34–2866), and *Teatro 56* (tel. 22–6626).

If you wish to see a movie, there are nearly a dozen comfortable movie houses around the city—as well as another dozen "flea pits." Nearly every film shown here is in its original language with Spanish subtitles. Check the press for listings. Smoking is not permitted in movie houses nor in theaters. Or you may wish to relax in your hotel room and watch TV. There are 6 Costa Rican channels (in Spanish) broadcasting in color. Over the past few years, cable service has been established in San José, providing subscribers with an astonishing variety of programming in English (up to 20 channels) beamed from satellites high above the Pacific. Many hotels have this service, which includes such popular American channels as Cable News Network, ESPN, Headline News, TBS, Discovery Channel, and many more.

Nightlife

In San José there are literally hundreds of nightclubs, lounges, discotheques, and bars. Closing hours depend on many factors, such as how many customers are still left. On weekends many places keep on going way past the early morning hours, some until daybreak. As you'll find out, Costa Ricans love to party!

San José is a safe place in which to be out and about at night. However, a word of caution. As in any large city in any country, you should take the usual precautions, such as not flashing a bankroll anywhere you go. There are only 1 or 2 districts in the city you'd be well advised to avoid completely at night: the area around the Cine Libano at Av. 7, Calles 10 to 14; and a 3-to-4-block area south of Av. 4 at Calle 4—both rather low-class red light districts.

The following list includes those places most popular with residents and resident-foreigners alike.

Bars

In the city center the *Key Largo* (Av. 3, Calle 7, at Parque Morazán; 21–0277) is the largest and best-known "gringo bar" in Costa Rica; housed in a splendid colonial mansion, it has a distinct Bogart flavor (his pictures are on the walls). American-owned, the Key boasts three huge bars, a restaurant, and plush casino. Live music every night; open from noon till 6 A.M. daily.

Also American-owned, but of a far different flavor, is *Risa's* (Calle 1, Avs. 0 and 1). San José's yuppie bar, Risa's two compact rooms are nearly always crowded. One room houses a bar area with stools, the other contains tables and upholstered chairs for comfy seating. The decor is a tasteful balance of pastels and natural woods, and a tiny kitchen in the back serves up an astonishingly wide variety of good food. Open every day from 11 A.M. (Sun. from 1 P.M.) to midnight.

Other popular bars include *Los Murales* (Gran Hotel Costa Rica; 21–4000); and *Las Palmas* (Aurola Holiday Inn; 33–7036).

Close to downtown, a $1 taxi ride away in El Pueblo shopping center, are to be found a number of super bars. *Montego Bay* and *Kakatua* specialize in bands playing calypso and reggae every night. To see Costa Rican folklore dancing and singing (up to 15 different artists most nights) try *Salón Musical de Lety;* for quieter moments, *Momentos* is a romantic interlude.

In the eastern suburb of Los Yoses is *Friday's,* frequented mainly by aspiring yuppies, wealthy exiled Nicaraguans, and upbeat professors from nearby University of Costa Rica. It offers good American-style food and over 50 exotic cocktails. Beer is served in yard or half-yard glasses.

Discotheques

Costa Rica's largest and most popular American-style disco is *New Leonardo's* (Centro Colón on Paseo Colón; 23–7310). After undergoing a number of ownerships and name changes, it was recently refurbished and is packed most nights. Live Latin bands are featured on Wed. Smaller but equally popular, especially with teenagers, is *Top One* (Kamakiri complex on Av. 9 and 11, Calle 0; 22–8484), which is usually bursting at the seams.

In El Pueblo shopping center are *Infinito* (23–2195), featuring three separate discos in one to suit your taste: rock, Latin, and salsa; and *Cocoloco* (22–8782), with Latin bands on midweek nights. Other downtown discos include *Disco Salsa 54* (Calle 3, Avs. 1 and 3), playing enticing salsa music; and *El Tunel del Tiempo* (Av. 0, Calles 11 and 13) with its head-spinning, light-spiraling tunnel entrance. On the fringes of the city are *The Place,* in the Corobici Hotel, and *Las Barandas,* in the Cariari Hotel; *Graffiti* in San Pedro; and in the west, *Ramses* in Escazú.

SAFETY. San José is a safe place in which to be out and about at night, with the exception of 2 distinct areas (discussed above in "Nightlife"). You can even stroll through La Sabana Park at midnight without fear—can you say the same for Central Park in New York or Hyde Park in London? Even in the countryside you can walk anywhere at anytime without apprehension. One hears stories about other Latin American countries, particularly in South America, where, if you're driving, you always have a revolver in the glove compartment, just in case. Not in Costa Rica.

The above is not intended to give the impression that Costa Rica is an idyllic paradise where there is no crime of any kind. There are robberies and occasional muggings—but events like that still make headlines because of their rarity. The main thing you have to be watchful for are be purse snatchers in the streets, especially in very busy areas. Don't walk around wearing expensive jewelry or sporting solid-gold Rolexes; you will attract unnecessary attention. Deposit large amounts of money, traveler's checks, or other valuables with your hotel for safekeeping in their safe.

The most important thing is—just be aware. With practical forethought and sensible behavior, you'll be assured that your trip to this "garden of the Americas" is as enjoyable and memorable as you thought it would be when you planned it!

LEAVING COSTA RICA. Tourists must pay a $5 exit tax upon leaving Costa Rica. If you have stayed longer than the time permitted by your entry documents, you must obtain an exit visa costing about $10 and taking 48 hours to obtain. Special exit requirements apply to dependent children who have been in Costa Rica for longer than 30 days (see "Travel Documents" earlier in this chapter).

PANAMA

by
TITO DEL MORAL

Tito del Moral is a Panamanian journalist and author presently living in Florida. Among his many credits, he is the founder of Critica, *a daily newspaper, now in its twenty-seventh year of publication. Ambassador from Panama to Bolivia, Ecuador, and the Dominican Republic, Del Moral has been specializing in Latin American tourism for the past ten years. He holds merit awards for his work from several countries.*

The Republic of Panama, with its ever-present summer, offers the visitor a wealth of activities. Very few countries of this size, with a limited 77,432 square kilometers and 2 million inhabitants, offer the amazing variety of races, customs, and natural and man-made attractions that this country does. The largest financial center of Latin America, Panama is a multibillion-dollar banking and commercial center. It also has much to offer to families of business travelers: beautiful beaches; abundant fishing; diving in lakes, rivers, and two oceans; hunting in tropical forests and mountains; and that wondrous engineering masterpiece—the Panama Canal. All of this, together with the comfort of first-rate hotels available to all budgets, make Panama, without a doubt, an incomparable place to spend an unforgettable vacation.

This small American isthmus, which joins the Pacific and Atlantic oceans, is a lively crossroad of many races. The first impression the visitor gets of cosmopolitan Panama is certainly of a melting pot: Spanish, Chinese, Hindus, blacks from the Antilles, North Americans, and native Panamanian Indians—colorfully dressed in the typical costumes of their villages. Although the official language of Panama is Spanish, in the principal cities (Panama City on Colón) most people speak English as well.

Some History

Panama, which according to some experts in the native aboriginal languages means "abundance of fish," was discovered in 1501 by the Spanish explorer Rodrigo de Bastidas. Vasco Núñez de Balboa, who accompanied Bastidas on his exploration of the Isthmus of Panama, crossed tropical virgin forests of the isthmus and came upon a hill from which he could see a huge mirror of water in the distance—thus the discovery of what was originally called the South Sea and later the Pacific Ocean.

A year later, during his fourth and last trip to the New World, Christopher Columbus visited the isthmus and tried unsuccessfully to establish a colony. It was at this time that the Continental period of the Conquest began in Panama, then known as Tierra Firma ("firm soil"). The first colony was founded in the forested region of Darién and later moved to the shores of the Pacific. Pedro Arias de Avila, better known as Pedrarias, thus founded the settlement of Panamá.

From this point on, the colonization of America made headway with the discovery of Peru and other nations of North, Central, and South America. Through the Cruces Trail linking the two oceans, Panama, on the Pacific side, and Portobelo, on the Atlantic side, anchored an indispensable pathway for the transportation of gold from Peru, coins from the Indies, and the provisions and supplies that arrived from Spain. Panama became an emporium of the world. In the 1850s American financiers gained permission to build a railroad across the isthmus, increasing Panama's strategic importance. Later the country became even more important with the opening of the Panama Canal in 1903, which greatly enhanced the cosmopolitan importance of this nation and carried on Panama's tradition of being a bridge of the world.

Some South American countries and Panama became independent from Spain in 1821, Panama abstained from joining the proposed Central American Confederation of Nations. Instead, as recommended by Simon Bolívar, the Liberator, it voluntarily joined (along with Venezuela, Colombia, Peru, Ecuador, and Bolivia), what was originally known as Great Colombia—Bolívar's dream for a united Latin American nation. The Central American Confederation and Great Colombia eventually broke apart, and every nation followed its own independent course with the exception of Panama—which, faithful to Bolívar's ideals, remained united to Colombia. Several Panamanian separatist movements failed, and finally, as a result of the proposed opening of the canal, Panama, supported by the United States which was interested in the strategic significance of the isthmus and the canal, obtained its independence. (See the Panama Canal section later in this chapter.)

At present, Panama is governed by a democratic system of government elected by popular vote. (The current president, Eric Arturo Delvalle, was vice president when his predecessor resigned in 1985; the military remains a powerful force.) Although Panama is located in a zone of conflict, the

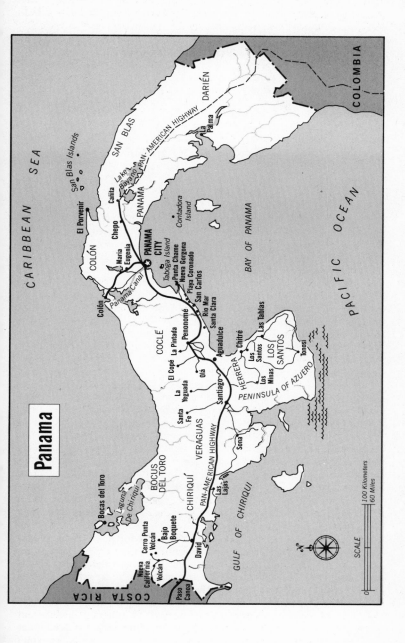

country is peaceful and avoids the political problems that afflict its immediate neighbors—except in those instances in which it has been able to
intervene as a good-will mediator.

Although the Republic of Panama has boundaries on one side with
Costa Rica, Central America, and on the other side with Colombia, South
America, the Panamanians do not think of themselves as being a part of
either South or Central America. They simply consider themselves as inhabitants of the Isthmus of Panama—a link that joins the three Americas
and, through the Panama Canal, joins all continents with the Americas.

EXPLORING PANAMA

Old Panama City

Stone ruins are all that remain of Panamá Vieja (the original settlement
of Panama City), burned and sacked in 1671 by Henry Morgan, the English pirate who reached Panama by crossing the Chagres River. Visitors
will first see the imposing Cathedral Tower, its stone spiral stairway leading to what once was the Bell Tower. In the huge atrium, where the main
altar was located, a few standing stone structures outline the large space
that was reserved for the faithful. Next to the main altar are remains of
another structure, possibly the sacristy, with its walls still standing. Stone
pathways mark what was once the Ascension Cathedral and lead to the
ruins of the City Hall, the San Juan de Dios Hospital, and the Santo Domingo and San José convents. There's no sign of the Spanish military fortress that was erected to defend the city. Continuing through Via Cincu-
entenario, you'll see several small bridges both at your left and right.
Among them is the legendary Obispo Bridge, a truly engineering and architectural marvel, joined from one end to the other by stones laid in perfect structural precision. Stop a moment at the Bohío Turístico ("Tourist
Hut"), a picturesque restaurant built of native wood and straw and decorated in typical Panamanian style. Pass the bridges and you'll reach the
Home of the Slaves and next to it see a stone of several tons with a circular
mound: this is the Sacrificial Stone where slaves were displayed before
being sold to bidders. (It's said that there were five times as many slaves
as Spaniards in Panama in 1610.) The words of a prominent Panamanian
educator inscribed in Spanish on a metal plaque in the lower part of the
Ascension Cathedral capture the feel of Panamá Vieja: "These ruins are
worthy of admiration because they keep in the silence of the past, the glory
and wealth that are gone forever."

Driving west, you'll pass a statue of Father Morelos, a national hero
of the Mexican independence, erected in front of the Pacific Ocean. It was
a gift from Mexico to Panama. Golf Heights and Paitilla are perhaps the
most exclusive residential sections of the Panamanian capital, a stark contrast to the Old Panama ruins. The magnificent residences—the most
humble of which approximates $400,000 in cost—are surrounded by gar-
dens of lush tropical vegetation. Beyond Golf Heights is San Francisco
de la Caleta, a heterogeneous area of condominiums and private homes.

Continuing toward Avenida Balboa, facing the Pacific Ocean, you'll
pass the imposing ATLAPA Convention Center; next to it is the luxurious

Marriott Caesar Park Hotel. The ATLAPA [Atlantic and Pacific] Convention Center is considered by many to be the most modern center of its kind in Latin America. Constructed at a cost of approximately $50 million, the ATLAPA Convention Center has a capacity for 16,000 persons. It is a huge complex with a modern theater-auditorium with 3,000 seats, a 3,445-square-foot convention hall, without any columns, for exhibitions, and facilities for general or private meetings. It represents all of the modern technological advances of the twentieth century combined with a decor that reflects the Panamanian cultural heritage. For more information on ATLAPA and the general rental costs, contact the General Manager, Panamanian Institute of Tourism, Box 4421, Panama City; 26–7000, 63–6500, or 26–4002, telex 3359 ATLAPA PG.

Once on Avenida Balboa, turn west to begin a tour of Panama City's "Manhattan."

Panama's "Manhattan"

Condominiums of 20 or more floors form a group of beautiful modern buildings that are by themselves proof of the tremendous ability and creativity of the Panamanian architects and engineers. You'll notice the circular structure of the majestic Holiday Inn. The apartments at Punta Paitilla range in cost from $180,000 to $200,000. At the end of this luxurious residential complex is the beautiful building of Panama's Union Club, an exclusive membership club.

Leaving Punta Paitilla and crossing Avenida Balboa once more, the visitor enters what could be called the "Wall Street of Panama." Enter Via España, and you see the Continental Hotel on the left, and in front, on a hill overlooking the city, many luxury stores.

Filled with a veritable ocean of cars, Via España continues past banks and more banks until it reaches the section of town known as Calidonia—predominantly Jamaican and very commercial. The people here are said to be descendants of the West Indians who worked on the railroad and the canal. Everywhere, however, the people in the streets have the carefree attitude typical of the tropics and exhausting heat. You won't find the rush and haste of the big cities of other parts of the world because Panamanians have a common philosophy: "take it easy." They seem, for the most part, to be happy-go-lucky individuals who try to enjoy life as best they can without much agitation.

Avenida Central

Continue along Avenida Central, which is Panama City's main street (Via España turns into this); to Plaza Cinco de Mayo. In the center of this square is a monument to the Martyrs of the Corps of Firemen of Panama. Opposite the square is the building that housed the old railroad station, now the Anthropological Museum of Panamanian Man. The structure and columns of this building are of North American architectural influence, typical of the southern United States. At the opposite corner is the International Hotel.

In the lobby of the museum is the bullet-proof "Popemobile" that Pope John Paul II used during his visit to Panama in 1983. The museum features displays of the human origins of Panama. You can purchase post-

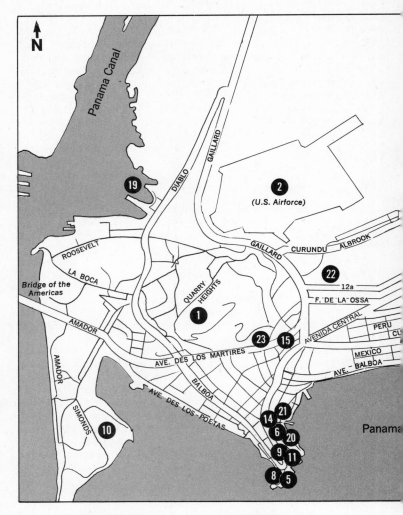

Points of Interest

1) Ancon Hill
2) Albrook Airport
3) Atlapa Convention Center
4) Balboa Monument
5) Las Bólvedas

6) Cathedral
7) Continental Hotel
8) Court of Justice Building
9) Flat Arch
10) Fort Amador
11) Golden Altar
12) Holiday Inn

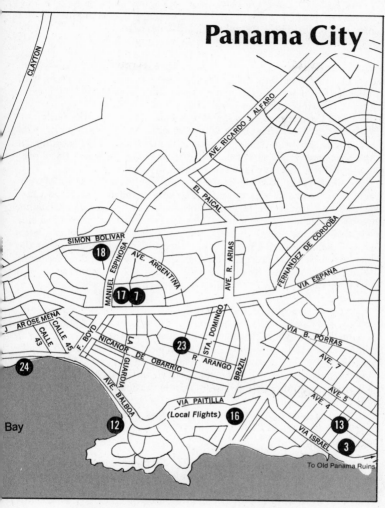

Panama City

13) Marriott Ceasar Park
14) La Merced Church
15) Museum of the Panamanian Man
16) Paitilla Airport
17) Panama Hilton
18) Panama University

19) Pier Balboa
20) Presidential Palace
21) Public Market
22) Railroad Station
23) Shopping Centers
24) U. S. Embassy

cards, literature, and reproductions of archaelogical items at the museum. The sale and exportation of original archeological pieces is prohibited.

Avenida Central, itself, is always in the center of a constant human and vehicular hubbub. There are stores on both sides of the avenue and numerous flashy signs announce sales. There are lottery saleswomen and salesmen, shouting newspaper boys selling the daily papers, all kinds of noisy horns, passenger buses covered with pictures of a variety of subjects—from landscapes to the religious to the feminine, street vendors competing with established businesses, and other signs of bustling activity. All of it creates a happy, colorful atmosphere typical of tropical Panama.

Avenida Central runs into Santa Ana Park. In back of the park, and almost hidden by luxuriant trees, is the church of Santa Ana, built in 1676. Since this park is a popular place for Panamanian political meetings, it is said that here is the heart of Panamanian democracy—a country of people who believe themselves to be intrinsically democratic.

Continuing along Avenida Central, you'll pass the restored La Merced (burned in 1963), and beyond that is Plaza Independencia or Plaza Catedral, cradle of Panama history; busts of the Founding Fathers of Panama have been erected here. Opposite the park is the cathedral; on one side is the old Main Post Office Building, where the original offices of the Panama Canal were located. Opposite the cathedral, and still operating, is the Central Hotel with its iron grille balconies. Since the end of the nineteenth century, chiefs of state from many nations have stayed at this hotel, and the French and North American pioneers of the Panama Canal made it their home.

A block or so from the Central Hotel is the Presidential Palace, also known as the Palace of the Herons because of the herons kept in the Moorish patio at the main entrance. Travel agencies can make arrangements for tourists to visit the building. The magnificent rooms are worth a look, particularly the Yellow Room with the superb murals painted by the Panamanian painter Roberto Lewis, which depict in beautiful natural colors the various periods of Panama history—from the Spanish Conquest to Republican times. It would not be unusual for the president of the Republic, himself, to make an appearance and say hello.

Casco Viejo

The Casco Viejo section of Panama City still maintains a colonial flavor. Lining the narrow streets are two-story white houses with ornamental iron balconies, reminding the visitor of Old Panama. Las Bóvedas is an old Spanish fortress with its merlons and observation towers still standing. The promenade along the top offers impressive views of the bay and city. In the lower part of Las Bóvedas are the dungeons, with their original iron doors, where the prisoners were jailed. At the center of Las Bóvedas, also known as Plaza de Francia, is an obelisk with the emblematic "cock of freedom" at the top—an homage to the frustrated French excavators of the Panama Canal and to Fernand de Lesseps (also builder of the Suez Canal).

At Las Bóvedas Promenade is the imposing old building that houses the Palace of Justice and the Supreme Court. On the opposite side the French Embassy continues to operate in its legendary mansion. Almost next to it, the French restaurant Casco Viejo offers the diner an opportunity to go back in time while having lunch or dinner in a typical colonial residence with old dining rooms and ornamental iron balconies. A new addition to the quarter is the Las Bóvedas restaurant, serving fresh seafood in the dungeons where prisoners once languished.

Avenida A passes the church of San José with its famous Golden Altar. At one time this altar belonged to the Ascension Cathedral in Old Panama. It was saved from pirate Morgan's pillage by a priest who painted it black. The legend goes that when Morgan saw the unsightly altar, he was puzzled. Looking at the priest, he said laughingly: "I don't know why I think you are more of a pirate than I am." Thanks to the cleverness of this priest, we can now admire this wonderful piece of art, totally covered with gold—a magnificent jewel of the colonial period. Near the church is still another marvel of Spanish colonial engineering, the centuries-old Arco Chato ("Flat Bridge"), a 50-foot-long, 35-foot arch with no internal supports. It's said that supporters of the proposed Panama Canal felt that the durability of this bridge proved Panama free of volcanic shocks and earthquakes—a fact which meant that Panama would be a better site for the canal than Nicaragua.

Plaza Bolívar is the site of the church of San Francisco. Next to it, in a public school, is the room where the Amphictyonic Congress of Panama was called by Simon Bolívar in 1826 in an effort to unite the Latin American nations. The room is as it was in the eighteenth century. In front of the school, in the center of the park, is a statue of the Liberator.

From Plaza Bolívar you can take a detour to Avenida B to see the effervescent public market, with a multitude of cars and hand carts in the streets unloading the products brought from the interior of the country: mangos, avocados, grapefruit, pineapples, bananas, and other tropical fruit and vegetables.

You'll reach Plaza Porras, named after a famous president of Panama called by Panamanians "the great old man." Opposite the monument of him, by Spanish sculptor Victorio Macho, is the Ministry of Foreign Relations of Panama, and, in the opposite corner, is the Spanish Embassy. Parallel to Avenida Perú is beautiful Avenida Cuba, and in front of Plaza Porras, the colonial building of the Cuban Embassy.

The Panama Canal

Seventy-one years after its construction, the Panama Canal continues to be the main tourist attraction of the country—since it is considered by many to be the eighth wonder of the world and the most important engineering work of the century. The canal could be defined as a water ladder where ships are raised, step by step through three sets of locks to a height of 85 feet, to cross from the Atlantic to the Pacific and back again. The route is approximately 50 miles long and the crossing operation takes eight to ten hours. Since this modern waterway is used by nearly 14,000 ships each year, the visitor is always able to observe the operations of raising and lowering the ships that pass from one lock to the other until they are leveled to the entrance of the corresponding ocean. To facilitate sightseeing, there are viewing posts on the Atlantic side at Gatun, where Gatun Lake, considered the largest man-made lake in the world is located, and at Miraflores, on the Pacific side. Bilingual guides are available to explain to the visitors the workings of the canal and to provide literature on its operation and history.

The Public Relations Department of the Panama Canal Commission is the Panamanian–North American organization in charge of managing and running the canal. This entity has a theater at the Miraflores Lock to show movies and slides on the full operation of the canal. The history of the canal is depicted in beautiful frescos on the walls of the administration building of the Canal Commission. Literature and slides are also available by the commission's Public Relations Department. Local travel agencies offer tours for those who are interested in getting more in-depth information on the workings of the Canal.

Frenchman Lucien Bonaparte Wyse saw a remarkable opportunity—he obtained a concession to build a canal along the railroad route. He in turn sold this concession in 1878 to Ferdinand de Lesseps, builder of the Suez Canal. Thus, the canal stands where it does today not because it is the best route, but only because the railroad was built there first, giving easy access to the route; the railroad is there only because the old Spanish mule trail had been there for over 300 years.

Lesseps was determined to build a sea-level canal—as he had done at Suez—instead of a lock canal, which would have been easier. Disease, scandal, corruption, rain, mud, and jungles took their toll—including 16,000 to 20,000 lives—and the company went bankrupt. (One of the workers, during 1886 and 1887, was an unknown French painter named Paul Gauguin.)

By 1900 it was apparent that only the U.S. had the resources to complete the huge project. The U.S. was keenly aware of the necessity of a canal because of their experiences in the Spanish-American War of 1898, when they had to send warships all the way around the tip of South America to reach Cuba, a voyage of 13,400 miles and 60 days. However, the commission set up by the U.S. Congress to survey possible canal routes advised that it be built through Nicaragua, where, because of the San Juan River and Lake Nicaragua, there would be much less digging required. The French, desperate to have the U.S. buy their concession and property in Panama, began intensive lobbying, claiming that Nicaragua was not safe for a canal because of its earthquakes and volcanoes. Chief lobbyist for the French was de Lesseps's former chief engineer, Philip Bunau-Varilla.

When, in 1902, due to the determined (and often unscrupulous) lobbying of Bunau-Varilla, the U.S. decided to buy out the French company, the treaty it negotiated with Colombia gave the U.S. only administrative control over the projected canal, while sovereignty over all the land remained Colombia's. Colombia, perhaps hoping the French concession would run out so their property would revert to Colombia, refused to sign the treaty. At the urging of powers in the U.S., and with assurances from Bunau-Varilla that the U.S. would support them, a group of Panamanian businessmen-revolutionaries declared themselves independent from Colombia. U.S. Marines landed immediately and kept Colombian troops from marching on Panama to put down the rebellion. Bunau-Varilla, desperately wanted the honor of signing the treaty as representative of Panama. Without consulting the Panamanian government, he changed the treaty so that instead of giving the U.S. administrative control for 100 years it gave them "sovereign rights in perpetuity over the Canal Zone." The U.S., astonished at such generosity, quickly signed the treaty before the representatives from the newly independent Panama arrived in Washington. Bunau-Varilla then bullied the new government of Panama, which had no real idea of the value of what they were giving away, into accepting the treaty.

The problems created by Bunau-Varilla's machinations and the heavy-handed Big Stick wielding by Teddy Roosevelt and the U.S. have led to over 75 years of friction and misunderstandings between the U.S. and Panama, continued assertions by all Latin American countries that the treaty is illegal and immoral (certainly Bunau-Varilla had no right to either alter or sign the treaty), and the recent acceptance by the U.S. government of the necessity of returning sovereignty over the Canal Zone to its rightful owner, Panama.

The main obstacle to building the canal was the rampant diseases of the Panamanian lowlands. In 1904 Colonel William Gorgas undertook one of the great sanitation campaigns in history, clearing brush, draining swamps, eliminating areas where mosquitoes bred and swarmed, and trying to eradicate the mosquitoes that carried yellow fever and malaria. Within two years, yellow fever had been wiped out, as well as the rats which carried bubonic plague, and malaria steadily declined. Army engineer Colonel George W. Goethals was placed in charge of the canal construction, and on August 15, 1914, the S.S. *Ancon* made the first complete passage through the new canal.

With the execution of the Torrijos-Carter treaties in 1977, the military and naval territory of the United States and other areas formerly known as the Panama Canal Zone reverted to the Republic of Panama. The United States has reserved the right to keep certain areas until 1999 for strategic military and security purposes. No decision has been made as to whether the land of the Canal Zone will be available for sale or lease when ownership reverts to Panama.

The average toll a ship pays to traverse the canal is $21,600. This represents a savings to the shipping lines of more than twice the amount it would cost them to have the ships sail around the distant and stormy Cape Horn at the southern tip of the continent. To this date the transatlantic *Queen Elizabeth II* has paid the highest toll: $97,696.38. The lowest toll, 36 cents, was paid by Richard Halliburton for the right to swim across the canal.

Although it was thought that by the 1980s the canal would be old and obsolete, the introduction of electronic systems and other technical improvements has modernized this waterway in a manner its builders never dreamed of. A massive computer center directs the major operations of the canal, and the course of every ship that crosses it is observed from the control center through a closed-circuit TV network. The actual canal, however, still employs its original gears and mechanisms.

A three-party commission of experts from the United States, Japan, and Panama is presently carrying out studies to determine the alternatives for making the canal available to ships over 100,000 tons, which cannot cross at the present time because of their dimensions. Two possible options have been found: to build a new sea-level canal at a cost of more than $20 billion or to widen the present canal with new sets of locks to meet the needs of modern ships.

Since the canal is located only minutes away from Panama on the Pacific side and Colón on the Atlantic side, it can be visited at all times of the day. However, it is possible to admire the formidable spectacle of the canal at night, with its constant activity and millions of lights, by obtaining a special permit through a travel agency.

The yacht *Fantasia del Mar,* among others, offers a partial tour of the Panama Canal.

BEYOND PANAMA CITY

Colón

With a population of approximately 100,000 inhabitants, most of them Jamaicans and many descendants of the Afro-Antillians who worked on the construction of the Panama Canal, the second city of the Republic, as Colón is called, has been less than fortunate in its urban cultural development. Nonetheless, in spite of its small size, it is one of the best-planned cities of the Republic, and its streets and avenues are easily found by number.

Colón was set on fire at the end of the nineteenth century as a result of the political rivalry between the Colombian liberals and conservatives at the time Panamanians were once more negotiating their separation from Colombia. The city was reconstructed and new buildings replaced the old wood houses that were consumed by the fire. Here, more than anywhere else in the country, the North American and French influence of the last century and the beginning of this century is in evidence.

Colón was reconstructed to resemble, almost exactly, the old city of New Orleans in the United States: the same large two-story houses with enormous balconies and the same types of columns, wide sidewalks, and ample arcades. But the city has not been able to develop like New Orleans due to economic and geographic conditions. It borders, on one side, the Atlantic section of the Panama Canal and, on the other sides, the military and naval zones of the United States. Consequently it has had no room to expand.

Some time after the inauguration of the canal, World War I was declared, and the canal proved its strategic and economic importance to the United States—which was able to move its troops through it at a time when massive transportation of soldiers across the Pacific or the Atlantic took days or weeks and air transportation was not feasible. The canal permitted fast mobilization of the troops, and Colón profited with an economic boom. This occurred once more, even to a larger extent, during World War II.

The once powerful Coco Solo Naval Base, located on one of the most beautiful bays of the Atlantic, has opened its doors to the expanding city of Colón, and the base has become a beautiful residential area. France Field, also a once-powerful air base, has been used to expand the Colón Free Trade Zone. France Field, located on the other side of the entrance to the canal, is gradually becoming an industrial assembly area for everything—from bicycles to general manufactured products. The Free Zone awards special contracts to foreign companies engaged in these activities and gives them help in setting up operations at France Field.

The Colón Free Zone is only an hour and a half away from the city of Panama. Basically devoted to the import-export business, it is considered the second Free Zone of the world—after Hong Kong. Here, bulk goods are imported duty-free for reexport to neighboring countries. In the same fashion that Panama's International Financial Center provides financial resources to many Latin American countries, the Free Zone supplies goods from all over the world. Annual operations amount to $4 billion. It is predicted that a new container port center close to the Free Zone will triple the commercial activities here. Although all business conducted at the Free Zone is wholesale, in certain cases businesspeople may be granted special permits to purchase retail; the merchandise is then forwarded to the airports or ports of exit of the visitors. More than 10,000 of the local population work in the Free Zone.

Colón has several hotels for tourists and businesspeople. The Washington Hotel, for instance, although built during the construction of the canal, still maintains its imposing facade and its classic internal comfort. Most of the rooms have a view of Cristobal Bay and from your window you can see the ships preparing to enter the canal on their way to the Pacific and those that are leaving it for the Atlantic.

At Cristobal Bay, as in the Bay of Panama, there are always from 20 to 30 ships waiting their turn to cross the canal. This is a marvelous spectacle, particularly in the evening. From the watchtowers at Gatun Locks you can watch the raising operations of a ship entering Gatun Lake to continue its trip toward the locks in the Pacific sector.

You can travel to Colón from Panama City along the canal by riding the trains of the Panama Railroad. The train ride takes you through the sections that were flooded when the canal was first opened and by the small island of Barro Colorado, which is maintained by the Smithsonian Institution for research on tropical diseases and the study of Panamanian fauna. The trip is beautiful and inexpensive.

You can also get to Colón from Panama City very economically in approximately an hour and a half by express bus or car on the Transisthmian Highway. And you can take a plane if you are in a hurry; the flight, although more expensive than train, bus, or car, takes only a few minutes. The Free Zone's general management makes available transportation by air or land to groups of businesspeople who wish to obtain information concerning the operations of this international trade zone. The zone's management should be contacted by telephoning 45–1033, 45–1186, or 45–2414 or writing to the General Management, Colón Free Zone, Colón, Republic of Panama.

Shopping in Colón is inexpensive. The stores offer a large variety of goods and most of them are located along Avenida del Frente, where you can also find very good restaurants. Articles from all over the world, particularly the Orient and Europe, are in abundance and at tempting prices. An added advantage to shoppers is the fact that the owners of these stores also operate through the Free Zone. Consequently tax-free purchases can be sent to the airport when you depart or to your country of origin, where you can pay the mailing charges COD. We recommend a shopping tour to the tourists who visit the city of Colón.

Near the city of Colón are beach resorts, entertainment, and all kinds of comfortable facilities. Historic Portobelo, for example, is relatively close. This legendary port town still preserves its stone ruins and the cannons of Fort San Lorenzo. A visit to Portobelo's church with its famous Black Christ, a life-size carved wood sculpture, is an experience that should not be missed. Nobody knows for certain the origin of this sculpture, but everyone worships the Christ to whom many miracles are attributed. The legend goes that the sculpture washed ashore on the beaches of Portobelo after the Spanish galleon that was carrying it sunk during the times of the Conquest. It is asserted that every time someone tries to take the sculpture away from Portobelo the sea becomes so agitated the Christ has to be returned to its small church. The annual procession in honor of the Black Christ is held on October 21. Many thousands of faithful worshipers from all over the country and abroad come dressed in the same purple color as the garments that cover the sculpture. Thousands and thousands of gold charms representing the miracles cover the body of the Christ, the cross, and the section of the altar where the sculpture is located. These are offerings from the faithful who claim their prayers have been answered. The atmosphere is extremely impressive: the strength of this sculpture and the painful look reflected on the face are no less moving.

Paradise Islands: Contadora

For those who wish to get away from the world for a complete rest, Panama has more than a thousand islands, several of which offer all kinds of comfort and attractions for a pleasurable retreat.

The most famous of these islands is Contadora, where many international organizations and business groups have conducted meetings. Many world celebrities have also made the island a favorite retreat. Contadora has a beautiful beach hotel with a casino, swimming pool, tennis courts, and a golf course. Family cottages with all kinds of modern facilities are available. Arrangements can be made for scuba diving, fishing, deep-sea fishing, sailing, and water skiing.

Contadora is only a 17-minute flight from Panama City. Flights are available continuously and the round-trip fare is about $40 for adults, $20 for children under 10. A day-long excusion, which includes lunch and a tour of Contadora by water launch, costs about $85. Travel agencies also offer economical package plans that include the round-trip flight and luxury rooms at the hotel for two nights, double occupancy.

Taboga

Facing Panama City, little more than 45 minutes by ferry boat, is the island of Taboga. Tourist boats leave daily from Pier 18 at Balboa on the Pacific side, at the entrance of the Panama Canal. Round-trip excursion fare is $18 and includes pick-up and drop-off at downtown hotels. On the way to Taboga, known also as the Island of Flowers, ferries pass under the impressive bridge that crosses the canal, the Americas Bridge. No cars are allowed in the colonial-style village of Taboga. Its best hotel is equipped with modern facilities; a superb restaurant serves fresh seafood and the famous corvina ceviche, marinated in lemon.

Isla Grande

Isla Grande, in the Atlantic, is 50 miles from Panama City, by car or railroad, then boat. This is a favorite retreat for fishing enthusiasts and offers great facilities.

San Blas Islands

The beautiful islands of the San Blas archipelago are only a 40-minute flight from Panama City. These islands of rustic huts, palm trees, and beautiful beaches are the home of the Cuna Indians, whose women are famous for hand-stitching. Their popular and colorful *molas* are in great demand to be both displayed and worn. The Indian women use the *molas* as dresses, and, with the gold jewelry they wear on the nose, their arm and ankle bracelets, and strings of necklaces, they are a unique, most charming sight. An excursion to these islands is well worth it—even if only to purchase *molas* and other Indian handicrafts. Daily flights leave Paitilla Airport in Panama at 6 A.M. and return at 5 P.M. The excursion fare is $85 for adults, $43 for children from 3 to 5 years of age, and includes a fresh seafood lunch and exploration by canoe of various islands with a local guide. You may extend your stay in San Blas by overnighting at the Anai Hotel, which offers comfortable accommodations. A stay at the Anai is enchanting and exotic—and not as complicated as pronouncing the name of the island on which it is located: Wichubwala. This sojourn will enable you to enjoy the pre-Columbian atmosphere of a rustic hotel with a first-class restaurant, fresh seafood, bar, and saltwater pool.

Panama Countryside

After crossing the canal from Panama City, passing over the Americas Bridge, and turning onto the Pan American Highway, there are about 370 miles to Paso Canoa on the Costa Rica border. From this point on, nothing but beaches. From Punta Chame, a peninsula 50 miles from Panama City, to Farallon, there are 40 miles of beautiful beaches, where you can enjoy surfing, swimming, snorkeling, and sunning: Punta Chame, Gorgona, Playa Coronado, San Carlos, Turiscentro San Carlos, El Palmar, and Río Mar. All have accommodations, including cabins, restaurants, and bars. Santa Clara Beach, about 74 miles from the city, is considered to have the nicest sand. Here the Pan American Highway turns inland to Penonomé, Aguadulce, and the central flatlands, such as Chitré, Los Santos, Las Tablas, and Santiago—where people are very proud of their Spanish heritage. It is from this region that we get most of the country's folklore and many of its crafts. Artisans talented in woodcarving, pottery, and weaving (which results in the famed Panama hats) live in this area. Many historic churches dating back to the time of the Spanish conquerors can be found throughout this region. Along the coast on the Azuero Peninsula, from Chitré to Punta Mala and around to Tonosí, you will find beaches and more beaches, guest facilities, and hotels. Chitré, Las Tablas, and Piamonte are visited yearly in February for the Carnival celebration. Beautiful and luxurious costumes are featured in the annual parade.

From Santiago de Veraguas the Pan American Highway takes you in two hours to David, in Chiriquí Province, where you are an hour from the mountains. Fishing in the Gulf of Chiriquí is famous. Chiriquí means "valley of the moon" in Indian dialect, but the province of Chiriquí is not a valley. It is a coastal plain, bounded on one side by the Central Cordillera. On the coastal side stop at the beach town of Las Lajas. David is the third city of the Republic. The high farms of Chiriquí are of a Swiss-chalet-type architecture; Chiriquí is a cattle country as well as the nation's prime Thoroughbred-raising area.

The Mountains

When in Panama visitors can keep their trips varied—staying part of the time in low-lying and coastal regions, where temperatures range all year between 75° and 80° F, and part of the time in the higher regions of the country, where temperatures stay around 60° F. A good hunting excursion in the mountains of Chiriquí or trout fishing in the rivers is quite a change from always fishing the aggressive swordfish of the Pacific.

Although Boquete, at 3,281 feet above sea level, does not have the snows of the Alps, the natives of this region call their town the "Switzerland of America" because of the many mountains that surround it with tropical green hues of all types and rainbows.

Volcan, located in the same high region of Chiriquí, has its Hotel Dos Ríos at a cost of $35 a person. This hotel also offers all kinds of facilities for trout fishing and hunting. The beautiful sight of the various types of orchids that are found everywhere is an enchanting experience. A visit to the Thoroughbred stud farms located in the area is a must.

Bambito, also in Chiriquí, has Hotel Bambito, a luxurious mountain resort with 60 rooms, a restaurant, and convention center for up to 200 persons, with a heated enclosed pool, sauna, and Jacuzzi.

The Darién

From the jungles of the Darién in eastern Panama, Balboa first sighted the Pacific Ocean. Since then, the area has remained almost as wild and unexplored. Its population today is probably less than it was in pre-Columbian days; virtually its only inhabitants are the Chocó Indians, who have lived along the jungle rivers for centuries, and groups of blacks, descendants of slaves brought over from Africa by Spaniards. Small numbers of Cuna Indians live along the Caribbean lowlands. The few settlements in the province can be reached only by boat or airplane. Intrepid travelers can visit Darién on their own by going to La Palma and asking around for rides into the interior on a small airplane or river launch. This involves a bit of roughing it and the ability to improvise—people have been known to wait for days to get rides.

The Chocó Indians of the Darién are ethnologically fascinating, as they live much like the earliest humans in a hunter-gatherer society. Theirs is a survival economy, with food hunted and gathered day by day—tapir, deer, peccary, agouti, paca, monkey, wild fowl, and armadillo are hunted, generally with a gun (interestingly, often each village has just one gun, with one man using it one day, another the next, each hunter sharing his game with all), though in some isolated areas bow and arrow and blowguns are still used. Their agriculture is limited to what they eat—rice, plantains, yucca, bananas, corn, cane. The men fish with spears and poisons, as well as nets and hooks. Their villages, usually about 15 thatch-roofed open-sided huts on piles, are found scattered along the rivers. Each hut is the home of an extended family or clan, with women usually living with their husband's family.

PRACTICAL INFORMATION FOR PANAMA

HOW TO GET THERE AND HOW TO GET AROUND. By plane. *Air Panama International, Eastern,* and *Pan Am* serve Panama from Miami year-round. The following airlines also have scheduled passenger flights to Panama: *AVENSA* (Venezuela); *Aerolineas Argentinas* (Argentina); *Aeromexico* (Mexico); *Aeroperú* (Peru); *Aviance* (Colombia); *Copa* (from various Latin American countries); *Cubana de Aviacion* (Cuba); *Ecuatoriana* (Ecuador); *Iberia* (Spain); *KLM* (Netherlands); *Lacsa* (Costa Rica); *Lloyd Aereo Boliviano* (Bolivia); *Sahsa* (Honduras); *Taca* (El Salvador); *Varig* (Brazil).

Domestic Airlines. All domestic flights leave from Paitilla Airport. *Servicios Aereos Generales* has sightseeing flights, charter services, cargo service within Panama and abroad; tel. 26–1104 or 64–5155. *Transpasa* offers charter flights throughout Panama; tel. 26–1548. *ANSA* offers daily service to the San Blas Islands; tel. 26–7891. *Aeroperlas* has daily flights to Contadora Island from 8 A.M. to 6 P.M., and flights to Bocas del Toro and Chiriquí on Fri., Sat., and Sun.; tel. 60–3201 or 69–4555. *Chitreana de Aviacion* has two daily flights to Chitre, Los Santos, Guarare, and Las Tablas; tel. 26–4116 and 26–3069. *Alas Chiricanas* offers daily flights to Chiriquí and Bocas del Toro; tel. 64–6448 or 64–7759. *Parsa* serves towns in the Darién province, La Palma, Sambu, Jaque, and others as requested; tel. 26–3883 and 26–3803.

Airports. The international *Omar Torrijos Airport* at Tocumen is one of the best and most modern in Latin America, with duty-free stores, restaurants, a bar, cafeterias, and slot machines in the waiting rooms. Located 20 minutes from Panama City; 66–7222. Taxis will take you into town for around U.S.$20. There is also bus service from the airport to Panama City, costing about U.S. 35 cents. Buses leave Plaza 5 de Mayo every 15 min. for the airport and take about 1 hr.

The *Paitilla Airport,* for domestic and private flights, is located in central Panama City, close to the Punta Paitilla residential area; 26–1868.

The western part of Panama is served by an airport in David; 75–2951.

By bus. Buses connect Panama City with San José, Costa Rica; cost is about U.S.$40. Contact *Ticabus,* ground floor of Hotel Ideal, Calle 22 B. Air-conditioning rarely works. *Panaica* also runs buses to San José, for slightly less money; their office is on Calle Monteserin. *Sirca* buses run between Panama City and San José and also to Managua. Don't plan to travel between San José and Panama City in one day.

Buses also connect Panama City with Colón. The bus terminal is near the Hotel International. There are also express buses (and slower buses) to David.

Panama City's buses run along the major streets, such as Via España to Av. Central. Passengers pay when leaving. To get off, yell "Parada!"

Buses also run from Colón to Portobelo every hour—leaving from the corner of Calle 11 and Av. Domingo Díaz.

By train. The *Panama Railroad* connects Panama City with Colón, running beside the canal. The scenic trip is inexpensive. In Panama City the train station is on Av. de los Mártires, northwest of Plaza 5 de Mayo. The trip takes about an hour and a half.

By car. Most major car rental companies offer their services to Panama's visitors. A valid foreign driver's license can be used for up to 90 days; minimum age for driving cars or motorcycles is 18 years. Full information may be obtained at your hotel. The rental car agencies have desks at the Omar Torrijos Airport near the customs exit. *Budget Rent-a-Car:* Holiday Inn, Via España, 63–8474, 64–1410 *HERTZ:* 63–6903. *Value Rent-a-Car:* 62–0111. *International National* (Japanese Cars): Via Brasil, 64–8643. *Avis Rent-a-Car:* 25–1597. *Econo Rent-a-Car:* 63–7600. *National Car Rental:* 64–8277, 64–8858. *Dollar Rent-a-Car:* 23–8726, 64–3798.

By taxi. Taxis, which charge by the zone, are available in Panama City. Always determine your fare in advance.

By ferry. Ferries leave from Balboa Port, Pier 18, at the entrance of the Panama Canal, for Taboga. The scenic round trip costs U.S.$5; there is a snack bar, and drinks are served. The first ferry leaves Balboa at 6 A.M.; the last ferry leaves Taboga at 6:15 P.M. Boats are available for group charter.

TRAVEL DOCUMENTS. This information is subject to change; please check with tourist information offices or your travel agent before your trip. A valid passport is needed to visit the Republic of Panama. U.S. citizens don't need visas; they can travel with $2 tourist cards, but must carry proof of citizenship such as birth certificates or passports. All other nationalities need visas. Proof of citizenship is needed to reenter the U.S.

CURRENCY. The balboa and the U.S. dollar are regular currency in Panama. Both have the same value. A 5 percent sales tax is charged, food and medicine exempted. To the numismatic collectors: the balboa is considered the largest coin in the world; the littlest one is the Panamanian half cent. The Banco Nacional of Panama (Central Branch) at Via España sells collections of the current coins and silver and gold coins of commemorative events such as the visit of Pope John Paul II.

TELEPHONES. 507 is the country code for Panama. To call international long distance when you're in Panama, dial 106; national long distance, 101.

LANGUAGE. The official language in Panama is Spanish, but because of the special relationship with the United States, most Panamanians in Panama City and Colón are bilingual.

WATER. Panama's water is drinkable.

CLIMATE. Temperatures range between 80° F and 85° F during the day, though it gets cooler at night and is about 10° to 20° cooler in the mountains. The climate is divided into 2 seasons: dry and rainy. The latter is from Apr. to Dec., and it rains with frequency. The average rainfall per annum is 65 in. along the Pacific coast and 120 in. on the Atlantic. The dry season, called "summer," is the favored vacation time. Temperatures range from 73° F in the highlands to 81° F on the coast during daytime and a cool 52° F to 65° F at night. Panama is an informal country. Dress is normally casual.

USEFUL ADDRESSES AND PHONE NUMBERS. The *Panama Tourist Bureau* is located in ATLAPA Convention Center, Via Israel, next to the Marriott Hotel. For more information call 26–4002 or 26–7000; telex 3359 ATLAPA PG. The *U.S. Embassy* as at Av. Balboa and Calle 37, Box 1099; 27–1777. To call the *police* phone 104. To call the time, 105. The number of *Santo Tomás Hospital* is 25–1436 or 27–4122.

ACCOMMODATIONS. The cities of Panama offer the more elaborate and expensive accommodations. Based on a room for 2 people, we have divided hotels into price categories as follows: *Expensive,* U.S.$65–$90; *Moderate,* U.S.$45–$65; *Inexpensive,* U.S.$30–$45.

Panama City

Panama City has many modern hotels, and together with the travel agencies they offer interesting package plans that include hotel accommodations, shopping trips, and tours.

Hotel Continental. *Expensive.* Box 8475, Panama 7; 64–6666. On Via España, in the center of Panama City's commercial and financial district; this is a good hotel for the business traveler. Restaurants, casino, bars and nightclubs, pool.

Holiday Inn. *Expensive.* Box 1807, Punta Paitilla, Panama 1; 69–1122. On Panama Bay overlooking the entrance to the canal; 1 mi from downtown. Restaurants and bars, casino, pool and poolside bar.

Marriott Caesar Park Hotel. *Expensive.* Box 6–4248, El Dorado, Panama 6; 25–4077. Directly across from ATLAPA Convention Center. Restaurants, bars, disco, casino, pool, tennis courts, gym, and sauna.

Ejecutivo. *Moderate.* Box 5370, Panama 5; 64–3333. 100 rooms with air-conditioning and color TV; restaurants and bar; secretarial services.

Granada. *Moderate.* Box 8457, Panama 7; 64–4900. Restaurant, pool, bar, casino.

Soloy. *Moderate.* Av. Perú and Calle 30, 27–1133. 200 rooms and 20 suites. Pool, restaurant, casino, bar.

Hotel California. *Inexpensive.* Via España and Calle 43, Panama 3; 63–7884. 20 rooms with private bath, air-conditioning, telephone.

Hotel Centroamericano. *Inexpensive.* Av. Ecuador and Justo Arosemena, Panama 5; 27–4555. 40 rooms, private bath, air-conditioning, telephone, restaurant, color TV.

Caribe. *Inexpensive.* Av. Perú and Calle 28 Este, Panama 5; 25–0404. Near business district. Air-conditioned rooms with private baths, TVs, and phones. Restaurant, bars, rooftop swimming pool. Caters mostly to locals.

Internacional. *Inexpensive.* Plaza 5 de Mayo, Panama 1; 62–1000. Restaurants, bar, casino. Air-conditioned units with TVs.

Riande Continental. *Inexpensive.* Apartado 4499, Tocumen 5; 20–5930. Adjacent to airport, 30 min. from Panama City. All rooms air-

conditioned; restaurants, bars, casino, disco; landscaped tropical court
with swimming pool; tennis courts.

Colón

Washington Colón. *Expensive.* Box 482; 47–8944. Historic Spanish mis-
sion-style hotel in palm-fringed setting on edge of Colón Bay, near canal
entrance. Restaurant and cocktail lounge with garden terrace; casino; tennis; pool and health club.

Countryside

Bambito. Hotel Bambito. *Expensive.* Mountain resort with restaurant,
disco, pool, sauna, Jacuzzi.
Cabana Kusicas. 71–4245.

Boquete. Hotel Central Boquete. *Inexpensive.* 70–1323. Rooms with
and without baths.
Hotel Fundadores. *Inexpensive.* 70–1298. Rambling place, with rushing
stream below it.
Panamonte. *Inexpensive.* Boquete Chiriquí; 70–1327. Very good hotel
in Chiriquí Highlands. Simple, comfortable rooms.
Pension Virginia. *Inexpensive to Moderate.* 70–1260. Large, quaint
house. Rooms with and without baths. Restaurant.
Hotel Wing. 70–1230.

Chitré. Hotel Hong Kong. *Inexpensive.* 96–4483.
Hotel El Prado. *Inexpensive to Moderate.* 96–4620. Considered by many
to be the best in the area.
Hotel Rex. *Inexpensive.* 96–4310.
Hotel Santa Rita. *Inexpensive.* 96–4610.
Hotel Toledo. *Inexpensive.* 96–4644.
Hotel Versailles. *Inexpensive.* 96–4422.

Contadora. Contadora Hotel. *Expensive.* c/o Apartado 1880, Panama
1; 60–3333. Self-contained resort. Restaurants, cocktail lounges, pools, casino, tennis courts, beach. Cottages available.

David. Hotel Nacional. *Inexpensive to Moderate.* Av. Central, Aparta-
do 37; 75–2211. Hacienda-style hotel near the Pacific coast. Traditionally
David's finest. Many rooms with private baths; air-conditioning. Beach
and river swimming.
Hotel Ecko Plaza. *Inexpensive.* Av. 4; 75–4068.
Hotel Fiesta. *Inexpensive.* Via Interamericana; 75–5454. Restaurant,
bar, pool. Air-conditioning.
Hotel Panama-Rey. *Inexpensive.* Calle 3 Oeste; 75–0253. Restaurant,
bar, pool.
Hotel Saval. *Inexpensive.* Calle D Norte; 75–3543.

Gorgona. Gorgona Jayes. *Inexpensive.* Apartado 7431, Zone 5;
23–7775, 55–4249, 64–3487. Good hotel with restaurant, pools, beaches,

tennis courts, discotheque, horseback riding. Air-conditioning. Economical packages available.

Santa Clara Beach. Sirena. *Inexpensive.* 28–2555. Bungalow accommodations.

Los Santos. Hotel La Villa. *Inexpensive.* 96–4845. Air-conditioned rooms. Swimming pool, bar, restaurant.

Las Tablas. Hotel Julienne. *Inexpensive.* 94–6312.
Hotel Oria. *Inexpensive.* 94–6315.
Hotel Piamonte. *Inexpensive.* 94–6372.

Taboga Island. Hotel Chu. *Inexpensive.* Owned by a hospitable Panamanian family of Chinese origin. Good restaurant.
Taboga Hotel. *Inexpensive.* Taboga Island 4421, Panama; 23–8521. Resort retreat on excellent beach, 12 miles by launch from Balboa. All rooms air-conditioned with balconies and ocean views.

Volcan. Hotel Bambito. *Expensive.* c/o Apartado 8–0555, Panama 5; 71–4265, 4251, 4219; in Panama 23–5084. Nice hotel located at 5,000 ft in the highlands; rooms available with fireplaces. Restaurant, tennis, pool, sauna.
Hotel Dos Ríos. *Inexpensive.* 71–4272. 55 rooms. Good for fishing and hunting.

San Blas Islands. Anai Hotel. *Moderate to Expensive.* Rustic hotel with great restaurant; bar and saltwater pool.

RESTAURANTS. Panama City, a cosmopolitan area, has restaurants of all nationalities to suit all tastes. The prices, like everywhere else, vary. For example, luxury hotels have first-rate restaurants and the prices are high: U.S.$10–$15 for an entrée. Among the best are: **The Belvedere,** with international cuisine, at the Holiday Inn of Punta Paitilla, tel. 69–1304; **La Corvina** at the Marriott Hotel, 26–4077; **El Pescador** at the Continental Hotel, 64–6666.

Highly recommended is **Las Tinajas** restaurant offering Panamanian food with typical folklore shows and girls wearing the famous Panamanian *polleras.* It features national and international music with renowned artists in a fun-filled atmosphere. The prices are moderate and it is centrally located, close to the main hotels and the banking center; 63–7890. **La Cascada** is an outdoor restaurant decorated with many cascades and huts. It specializes in charcoal-grilled meats, yucca, fried plantain, fried pork, and tamales. Moderate prices. American atmosphere. Very good service. Av. Balboa and Calle 25; 62–1297. **El Trapiche,** with its intimate atmosphere, represents a cozy corner of the interior of the country. Moderate prices. Specializes in typical Panamanian food; 69–2063.

Chinese restaurants are generally first rate and they are famous for their oriental food at very reasonable prices; 2 persons can dine with wine for only $15. Among the best are: **Palacio Rey Kung,** Calle 46 and Via España, 69–0956, and **Panachina,** centrally located near the Continental Hotel; 23–9937. **Lung Fung,** with a totally Oriental construction, has perhaps the best food and atmosphere, Entrada Urb, Los Angeles; 60–4011. Of the same style is **Interchina,** at Galerias Comerciales Obarrio; 69–0026.

For Japanese cuisine, try **Matsuei,** opposite the Granada Hotel; 64–9547.

For Hindustan food, the **Shamiana,** Centro Comercial, La Alhambra; 63–8586.

For Jamaican food, **Montego Bay Restaurant,** on centrally located Av. Perú; 69–1867.

For vegetarians, **Mi Salud Restaurant,** on Calle 31, 25–0972, in a centrally located residential section, and Mirella near the Continental Hotel, 69–1876.

Specializing in Spanish cuisine: **Panamar Club,** on the outskirts of the city at the end of Calle 50; 26–0892—this restaurant has an ocean view and is good for lunch although a little far for dinner; **El Cortijo,** in a residential area, Calle D-1, El Cangrejo, diagonally across from Hotel Granada, 69–6386; **La Cocina Vasca,** centrally located in a good section of the city, 64–3032; **Sarti,** close to the Continental Hotel in the banking sector, 23–7664, specializing in seafood (especially Paella); and **El Mesán de la Paella,** on Calle 50.

Las Rejas is excellent and expensive, specializing in international and Peruvian cuisine. Calle 1 and Via Brasil, 23–8228. **Los Toneles** specializes in charcoal-grilled meats and Argentinian *parrillada* with a delicious homemade sangria. Moderate prices. Via Fernández de Cordoba on the outskirts of the city; 61–8537.

Panama, with a name which means "abundance of fish," definitely has an incredible quantity and variety of fish, and the restaurants that specialize in seafood are a real treat for visitors. We'll mention some that deserve a high recommendation because of service, quality, and location. The delicious corvina fish, found only in this area of the Pacific, has a soft white meat and very few bones. The famous Panamanian ceviche is prepared by cutting the corvina into small pieces and marinating it in pure lime juice, adding pepper to suit the customer. **Lobster's Inn** specializes in charcoal-broiled seafood. Av. Balboa, opposite the Bay of Panama; 64–4841. **La Casa del Marisco** specializes in lobster and corvina. Expensive. Also on Av. Balboa; 23–7755.

Other good restaurants that specialize in international cuisine are: **El Pavo Real,** a luxury restaurant specializing in European food and crepes. Expensive. Calle 51 Este, Campo Alegre; 69–0504. **Le Trianon** is for French food. Marriott Hotel; 26–4077. **La Terraza Barbacoa,** serving charcoal-grilled meats and salads, is outdoors by the Panama Hilton Hotel swimming pool; 23–1660. **Le Bistro** is a typically French-style restaurant in a good section of the city; 69–4025. **Le Saint Tropez** is European. The owner of the restaurant prepares an excellent duck à l'orange and an exquisite filet mignon. Very good wines. Panama's banking area, Calle F El Cangrejo No. 10 and Via Argentina; 69–2582. **American Legion,** for international food, in Fort Amador with a view of the Panama Canal on the Pacific side; 52–5505. **Shalom** is for Mediterranean and Israeli food. Located in the modern Punta Paitilla shopping center. No reservations are necessary.

Outside Panama City restaurants are less expensive (a good meal running U.S.$7–$10). Inquire at your hotel for locations.

TOURS. The following Panama City travel agencies are certified by the Panama Tourist office and offer a variety of tours—giving visitors an easy way to explore the city, the Canal Zone, and Portobelo, enjoy Colón free zone shopping, experience the San Blas Islands, Taboga Island, and more. Day tours and overnight trips are offered. *Agencias Giscome.* Calle L2–27, Box 3124, Panama 3 (62–0111; Telex 3678 GISCOME PG). *Happy Tours, Inc.* Plaza 5 de Mayo–Hotel Internacional, Box 6–4628, Panama 6 (62–7810; Telex 3639 HAPPYTOURS PG. *Interclub Travel Service.* Calle Eusebio Morales. Box 8649, Panama 5 (64–5977/6116; Telex 2474 INT-CLUB PG). *Margo Tours.* Calle 53, Paitilla, Centro La Florida, Box 473, Balboa, Panama. (64–9796; Telex 3181 GODAL PG). *Receptour, S.A.* Ave. Frederico Boyd and Calle 51, Box 8880, Panama 5 (69–6702/6703; Telex 2322 RECEPTOUR PG). *Revis Travel Agency S.A.* Calle 35 y Ave. Peru, Box 11050, Panama 6 (25–6574; Telex 2852 REVIS PG). *Turista Internacional, S.A.* Centro Comercial Plaza, Paitilla 8 Box 5929, Panama 2 (64–3711/3572; Telex 2310 TURISTA PG). *Magic Tours Corp.* Box 1626, Panama 1. (61–8890; Telex 2516 ACOSA).

During the December to April dry season the yacht *Fantasia del Mar* is one of several offering tours of the canal. The boat leaves at 8 A.M. from dock 17, port of Balboa; returns at 12:30 P.M. Adults $20, children $10. For further information telephone 64–7595 or 32–5395. Or see Argo Tours, above. Food and drink available onboard.

CRUISES. Cruises are available year-round from the United States to the Panama ports of Cristobal or Balboa, crossing the canal from both the Pacific and Atlantic oceans. The *Royal Princess* and her twin, the *Island Princess,* or the charming *Sun Princess* depart from Los Angeles, New York, Fort Lauderdale, or San Francisco. For additional information call your travel agency in the United States or Cunard Cruises agencies. See also *Facts at Your Fingertips.*

Exploration Cruise Lines, at 64–9796, offers a transcanal cruise from $799. You can see the San Blas Islands, historic Spanish main gold ports, plus the beautiful Pearl Islands and primitive Indian villages in the lush Darién jungle. All the comforts and facilities, dining rooms serving delicious meals, lounge with bar, and spacious sun decks. If you're considering any Panama Canal cruises, you can write to Margo Tours, Box 473, Balboa, Panama.

BEACHES. Since the weather in Panama is always warm and the sun shines bright almost all year, practically every day of the year is fine for getting a tropical tan. (Sunbathers should of course use a lotion to avoid a sunburn—the sun is strong here.) The beaches in Panama are free, and good not only for swimming and sunbathing but also for picnics and spending a quiet day with the family. Below are some we recommend:

Amador. This is the closest beach to the center of of Panama City. Amador was the site of the military fort of the same name. During World War II the Americans used this location as an observation point and defense of the interoceanic waterway since the area is located at the Pacific entrance of the Panama Canal. To get to Amador, you drive through what used to be called the Panama Canal Zone and is now occupied by military forces from Panama and the United States and canal management civilian personnel. The beautiful white building that houses the South Command of the U.S. Marines is located near the entrance to the causeway that leads to Amador Beach.

The Amador Officer's Club is located on the causeway. Although this club is supposedly only for U.S. military personnel, with proper identification foreign visitors are welcome, particularly North Americans, war veterans, and persons in civil or active service. The Officer's Club has a magnificent restaurant with good food and drinks which is very reasonable. (For example, brunch is only $4.50.) There are Bingo nights during the week. Along the causeway you will also see the great breakwaters and, parked alongside, dozens of cars with visitors who bring their picnic lunches and enjoy an extraordinarly beautiful view—the activity at the entrance to the Panama Canal with ships coming and going and 30 to 40 ships at the bay, waiting their turn to cross.

The main section of Amador Beach has a steel net, which protects the area from sharks. There are stands that sell soft drinks, barbecued meat, and sandwiches at very reasonable prices. Most people prefer to bring their own coolers. We recommend to those visitors who rent and drive their own cars to do likewise, and we guarantee they will enjoy a wonderfully different day in a unique corner of the continent.

Taboga. This charming island is an hour away by ferry boat from the port of Balboa, and is another beach resort that, although relatively small, is family-oriented and cozy. Both the Taboga Hotel and the Chu Hotel have good rooms and restaurants.

There are powerboat rides, waterskiing, and scuba diving at the two main beaches. At the Taboga Hotel you can rent a small hut facing the beach for only $5 a day. On weekends there's always a musical combo playing at the beach.

The inhabitants of this island are fervent Catholics and there are those who will assure you that the paternal and maternal forebearers of Saint Rose of Lima and Saint Martin de Porras were originally from this island. July 16, the day of the Virgin del Carmen, patron saint of the island, is celebrated with a unique procession: the image of the Holy Virgin is placed in a boat filled with flowers which sails around the island followed by hundreds of fishing boats, outboard boats, and yachts. It is an impressive spectacle, and if you wish to participate in the festivities, you should make reservations in advance.

Gorgona. Gorgona has extensive beaches, excellent for surfing. It is 2 hours by car from downtown Panama along the Pan American Highway, which crosses a good portion of the interior of the country. There are many inexpensive country restaurants and facilities for the bathers at Gorgona.

Coronado. A luxurious resort an hour and a half by road from Panama City. See also "Sports."

Contadora. Only a 17-minute flight from Panama City, with a fine hotel and numerous water sports available.

María Chiquita. Located on the Atlantic coast at approximately 2 hours by car through the Transisthmic Highway that goes from Panama City to the city of Colón. It is an excellent location for fishing, has restaurant facilities, and low-cost cottages. Close by is historic Portobelo with its Spanish forts. Scuba diving is particularly interesting here because at the time of the conquistadores, Portobelo was the trade center between Europe and America. Some scuba diving enthusiasts have found silver doubloons at the bottom of Portobelo Bay, where Sir Francis Drake was buried in a lead box after dying of tropical fever. However, none of the native or foreign treasure hunters has ever discovered evidence of this dramatic grave—perhaps you could?

San Blas Islands. A series of 365 islands replete with crystalline water, beautiful beaches, huts, and palm trees. Daily flights leave Paitilla Airport in Panama City. Day trips and lodging available.

Bocas del Toro. Excellent Atlantic beaches, is 175 miles from Panama City. Good spot for exploration and water sports, particularly scuba diving, and harpoon and deep-sea fishing. There is a great abundance of lobsters and turtles in Bocas del Toro and interesting tours of the reefs. Transportation to Bocas del Toro is by air. In this province of Panama you can visit large banana plantations and watch the processing, packaging, and shipment of bananas.

Las Lajas. Near the city of David in Chiriquí Province, Las Lajas is a beautiful beach where you can find, in a relatively short distance, the sea, mountains, many rivers, and a modern environment. Las Lajas can be reached by car from Panama City through the Pan American Highway. Along the way the traveler will see all the interior of the country, almost to the Panama–Costa Rica border.

SPORTS. Baseball. Every weekend, national and sometimes international baseball games are held for enthusiasts at the Juan Demostenes Arosemena Stadium, located in the center of the city, and at other popular fields. Panamanian baseball players have excelled in the past and are presently excelling in the great leagues of the United States–the National League and the American League. In first place among these is Rod Carew, who just won the right to the Hall of Fame after completing the 1985 season with 3,063 hits credited to his career. This placed him as number 13 among the 16 greatest batters in more than 100 years of U.S. baseball history. Other outstanding Panamanians in the great leagues are Juan Berenguer, Omar Moreno, and Benjamin Oglivie.

Boxing. Since the 1920s, with Panama Al Brown, up to the 1970s and 1980s, with Roberto Duran, the famous Mano de Piedra (Iron Hand), Eusebio Pedroza, and others, Panama has had 14 world boxing champions. For this reason, boxing is one of the favorite sports of the Panamanians. Panama always has boxers in the ranking lists of the World Boxing Council or the World Boxing Association. During a visit to Panama a boxing enthusiast may well be able to watch future world champions in action at the modern New Panama Gym, 20 minutes by car from the main hotels in downtown Panama.

Cock Fights. There are cock fights every Sat. and Sun. in Panama City and in the interior of the country. The closest cockpit is *Club Gallístico de Panama,* approximately 12 minutes from the main hotels of Panama, on the outskirts of the city.

If you wish to watch a cock fight in a typical country atmosphere, you can drive through a magnificent expressway to *Club Gallístico de los Arcontes* in the town of La Chorrera, about 20 miles from Panama City. Along the way you will pass Americas Bridge, the bridge that crosses the Panama Canal, and will also enjoy a view of the perennial lush greenery of this country. A piece of advice: when you are watching a cock fight, do not raise your arm when betting takes place. Bets are based on an honor system and you only need to raise your arm to indicate that you are accepting a bet. It's a matter of dignity to honor it, and you would have to pay the other bettor the amount proposed. There's no proof other than your own word and that of the other person.

Fishing and Diving. See also "Beaches," above. Because Panama is bordered by the Atlantic and Pacific oceans and Gatun Lake and several rivers are located right in the midst of the Panama Canal, the country is ideal for water sports. More than 40 world fishing records for various marine species have been made in Panama. *The Guiness Book of World Records* indicates that a world record for scuba diving was also reached in Panama: during the same day a person was able to scuba-dive in the Atlantic in the morning, at Gatun Lake at noon, and in the Pacific Ocean in the afternoon.

Although travel agencies offer well-organized water sports packages (see "Tours," above), you can get more information for day or overnight fishing trips by contacting *Tropical Charters;* 26–5166 or 87–3795. Another sports center, *Buzo,* specializes in water sports and equipment; 61–8003. Also try *Panama Surf* at the Paitilla Shopping Center.

You can also get information on boat or yacht rentals for fishing trips in the Pacific from the *Yacht and Fishing Club of Panama,* 25–3911, or the *Balboa Yacht Club,* 52–2524. Many young enthusiasts from Panama's best families are willing to serve as hosts, and others will be glad to rent you their boats and help you get the necessary equipment for enjoying your favorite water sports.

For deep-sea fishing arrangements, contact the *Pacific Club* at 69–6071; *Contadora Marina,* 64–2758; *Piñas Bay's Tropic Star Lodge,* 20–1400; *Macarava Fishing Co.,* 60–4470; and *Lago Club,* 69–6071.

You can take a Quick Resort Scuba Course at *Scuba Panama* and later, accompanied by an instructor, take the "Dives in Two Oceans" tour or "The Lake" tour. Scuba Panama (open daily 8 A.M. to 12 P.M. and 2 P.M. to 6 P.M.) is located at Calle 33 Este between Av. Cuba and Justo Arosemena; 27–2516, telex 2429 RCA, PG.; or write Box 666, Balboa. Scuba Panama has five different packages, including hotel accommodations, scuba course, and equipment, which take visitors to Taboga, Portobelo, Isla Grande, Contadora, and San Blas Islands. Prices run from $70 and up.

Golf. After an hour and a half drive from Panama City on an excellent road is Coronado Beach, a beautiful summer resort of luxurious homes and condominiums. *Coronado Golf Club,* the best in the Republic and one of the most beautiful in Latin America, is located here; tel. 64–2314. Although this exclusive club is only for members and their families, this is one place where the typical Panamanian hospitality is shown at best. Visitors are welcome and if they are members of a golf club in the United States or elsewhere, they will be treated as members by showing their membership card. An 18-hole golf course, panoramic restaurants, and a large bar offer the visiting golfer a pleasant day. Almost everyone here is bilingual. Although there are no hotels in Coronado itself, there are good restaurants, and through your travel agency you can rent a furnished bungalow or condominium at reasonable prices.

The *Panama Golf Club* also welcomes visitors and is closer to the city than Coronado; 66–7777. Golf is also available at Contadora; 63–5311.

Horse Racing. The modern Presidente Remon Racetrack, a 20-minute drive from the center of Panama City, is open 3 days during the week,

Sat., Sun., and during national holidays. A total of 11 races every day. You can bet your favorite play: winner, place, show, one-two, combinda, duplets, peregrina trifect, and pick six. The Presidente Remon Racetrack has an up-to-date betting system—OUTOTRK LI—similar to that of the New York Racing Association tracks at Belmont Park, Aqueduct, and Saratoga. At Presidente Remon there are both afternoon and evening races. The evening program is from 3 P.M. to 8:30 P.M., and the regular program from 1 P.M. to 7:30 P.M. At least 14 classic races are held every year featuring the best national and international studs mounted by renown jockeys from the United States, Mexico, Venezuela, Puerto Rico, Chile, and Peru. There are several restaurants, bars, and a beautiful clubhouse at the racetrack, where horse racing enthusiasts, horse owners and Thoroughbred stud owners gather. Admittance to the racetrack is $2.50 per person. The logo displayed at this Panamanian racetrack reads: "PRESIDENTE REMON RACETRACK—CRADLE OF THE WORLD'S BEST JOCKEYS." This might seem rather exaggerated unless you remember that Panamanian jockeys such as Lafitt Pincay, Jacinto Vasquez, and Jorge Velasquez, have on many occasions occupied first place in U.S. racetrack statistics.

Yachting Competitions. Because of the climate and abundance of water, Panamanians practice water sports year-round. Waterskiing, windsurfing, boating (either for fishing or simply enjoying a day at sea) are most popular, and powerboat regattas are held at Panama Bay at various times of the year. The *President of the Republic Powerboat Classic* is an international event that takes place in Dec. This regatta is entered by Panamanians and world champions who travel to Panama from places as far away as Los Angeles, California, bringing with them their powerful boats to compete for a large trophy (about 5 ft in height) and a cash prize that fluctuates every year. Thousands of Panamanians and foreign visitors watch this famous competition in the Pacific Ocean along Av. Balboa. The regatta starts at the Yacht and Fishing Club in the Bay of Panama, crosses the entrance of the Panama Canal, turns around at Taboga Island Bay, and returns to the goal line at the point of departure.

CASINOS AND LOTTERY. All large hotels in Panama City have state-run casinos, and the largest portion of the income they generate is used for charity to support public institutions such as childrens' homes. Casino concessions are not granted to private organizations; the places that are designated for gambling, such as luxury hotels, must have at least 200 rooms. Admission to all casinos is free; minors and persons considered "undesirable," are not allowed.

There's blackjack, seven eleven, poker, and roulette at the casinos, and a large variety of automatic machines popularly known as *traganiqueles* (nickel-swallowers). These machines pay 100, 200, or more times the amount of the bet, and bets ranging from 5 cents to $1 can be placed. When you hit the jackpot, you can win hundreds to thousands of dollars. Winnings, regardless of the amount, are not taxable, and the cashiers pay them without any discounts.

The Gambling Control Board presents shows at the nightclubs of the hotels that meet the legal requirements for casino operation. Therefore, after playing seven eleven or roulette or trying your luck at the automatic machines, you can celebrate your good luck or forget your losses by enjoying a show.

In addition to the casinos, there is another state-controlled game that is conducted for charity purposes. The national lottery, a true institution to the Panamanians, is operated under the same strict control of the casinos. Drawings are held outdoors at the Lottery Square between Av. Peru and Cuba before the public. At the scene there are Panamanian bands and expositions of artifacts that can be purchased at very reasonable prices as souvenirs. Lottery drawings are held on Wed. and Sun. A lottery ticket costs 55 cents, and the prize depends on the amount played at that particular drawing. A 55-cent lottery ticket for a normal drawing can pay $1,000 if you have the 4 numbers of the first prize, $300 if you have the 4 numbers of the second prize, and $150 if you have the 4 numbers of the third prize. In other words, you have 3 opportunities to win the big prizes. For extraordinary drawings, which have 5 digits, the cost of the ticket is $1.10. Prizes range to $400,000.

In addition to the big prizes, the lottery also has consolation prizes for the first 3 numbers or the last 2 or 3 numbers of the drawings. If you have the last number of the winning 4, you get a refund for the cost of your ticket.

You can also buy tickets for another type of drawing called Chance. To win at Chance, you must have the last 2 numbers of the winning 4. A Chance ticket is 25 cents and the first prize pays $11, the second $3, and the third $2.

The sale of lottery tickets is not authorized outside of Panama. All winning tickets are paid tax-free to the bearer and the exact amount is paid without any discounts. Lottery and Chance tickets can be purchased in the streets of Panama or in lottery agencies in the city and the rest of the country. For foreign visitors in transit, there's an agency at Omar Torrijos Airport. Lottery salespersons have a special identification card, so it is safe to purchase tickets in the streets of Panama.

SIGHTS OF HISTORIC INTEREST. *Arco Chato (Flat Arch).* Arched bridge in midst of ruins of the church of Santo Domingo, Av. A, Panama City. The durability of this over-200-year-old bridge was used as an argument to build the Panama Canal in this country rather than in Nicaragua, which suffered from devastating volcanos and earthquakes.

Las Bóvedas. Calle 1, Panama City. Ruins of old Spanish fortress; original iron doors of the dungeons are still intact.

Panama Canal. Considered by many to be the eighth wonder of the world—a truly beautiful and fascinating sight. View from Gatun on the Atlantic side or from Miraflores, by the Pacific gateway. Bilingual guides. The Canal Commission has a theater at the Miraflores Locks which shows educational films; the commission offers a variety of information about the canal. History of the canal is in frescos on the walls of the commission's administration building. Yacht tours are available (see "Tours"). Contact travel agencies for tour information (also see "Tours") and to make arrangements to visit the canal in the evenings. Buses travel between Panama City and Miraflores.

Panamá Viejo. Ruins of the original city, founded by Pedrarias, burned by the pirate Henry Morgan in 1671. Wander among the ruins of the cathedral, the city hall, the San Juan de Dios Hospital, convents, home of the slaves. You can reach Panama Viejo by bus on Via España or Av. Balboa.

Presidential Palace. The most impressive building in Panama City. It is also known as the Palace of Herons, since the birds are kept in a fountain area at the entrance. Beautiful patio areas; famous Yellow Room with murals by Panamanian painter Roberto Lewis depicting the history of Panama. Between Calle 6 and 7. Contact travel agencies to arrange for tours.

Portobelo. Legendary port town with ruins of Fort San Lorenzo. The church here contains the famed Black Christ, saved from a sinking ship during the Conquest. It is said that no one can remove the Christ from Portobelo because the sea itself becomes agitated. Procession in honor of the Black Christ is held each October 21. Buses connect Portobelo and Colón (see "How to Get Around").

San José Church. Av. A, Panama City. Houses the famous Golden Altar, saved from the pirate Henry Morgan by a priest who painted it black.

ART GALLERIES AND MUSEUMS. Watercolors, oils, acrylics, etchings, and miniscultures can be found at the Panama galleries. Many of the galleries have permanent exibitions of Panamanian painters. The colorful styles of paintings reflect the high sensitivity, strength, and feeling of the native artists. Other Panamanians, such as Al Sprague, known for his folklore paintings, have been highly recognized throughout the world during recent decades. We recommend some painters, especially Herrera Barría, Dutary, Trujillo, Alicia Viteri, Chong Neto, Cedeno, Broce, Alcántara, Lewis. Originals and reproductions can be found at the following galleries:

Arte Consult. Calle 50; 69–1523 or 69–5815.

Arte Habitante. Calle 42 No.43, Bella Vista; 25–0632 or 25–0577.

Et cetera. Calle 50 No.50; 64–8058 or 69–6046.

Gaiería Cano. Paseo Camino Real, Plaza Paitilla, Av. Balboa and Via Italia; 69–0469.

Museums

Museo de Arte Contemporáneo. Av. Ancon and Calle San Blas; 52–4608.

Museum del Hombre Panameno (or Archeological Museum). Plaza 5 de Mayo, close to the International Hotel. Historical artifacts that demonstrate the rich cultural heritage of Panama.

The Museum of Colonial Religious Art, is in Santo Domingo Church, next to the Flat Arch, between Calle 3 and Av. A. An impressive collection of early art and artifacts.

The Museum of Natural Sciences. Calle 29 and Av. Cuba. Has exhibits on the geology, flora, and fauna of Panama.

SHOPPING Panama has always been a world trade center, and with the international comercial interests focused on the Panama Canal, modern-day traders have created a shopping bonanza unequated in the Western Hemisphere. Panama City's Av. Central, the new shopping areas around the hotels, and the airport's duty-free stores, all offer fantastic selections of imports at prices much lower than in your hometown. French perfumes and porcelain, English bone china, Swiss textiles and watches, and Dutch diamonds come across the Atlantic. And from the Pacific come electronic watches and cameras as well as brass, silk, and ivory from China and India.

Visitors also enjoy the native arts and handcrafts, from straw hats and bead necklaces *(chaquiras)* to reproductions of ancient gold jewelry. You may also buy a brilliant *mola,* the famous handwork of the Cuna Indian women; 50 hours of work are needed to create a pair of molas for a blouse. These garments are greatly prized by knowledgeable collectors and can be bought from the Indians on the San Blas Islands. Panama hats, though available throughout Panama, are actually made in Ecuador; there is no bargain buying them here. The *"montero"* Panamanian straw hat is an attractive alternative.

Inexpensive, duty-free shopping is available along Av. del Frente in Colón.

In Panama City

Shopping Areas

Plaza Paitilla. On Av. Balboa in the Punta Paitilla residential area. A beautiful mall with luxurious stores featuring fashions and goods from all over the world. High quality, but expensive. Several restaurants, and from 5 P.M. happy hours and fashion shows.

Obarrio Gallery. Many stores not expensive. Pharmacy, theaters, restaurants, entertainment. Located on Via España and Via Brasil. Near the Continental and Panama Hilton hotels.

Plaza Regency. In the heart of Panama on Via España, near the National Bank; several stores with European clothing. High-quality merchandise. Good prices.

Panama Hilton Hotel Arcade. Located in the hotel; many stores, restaurants. Good prices.

El Dorado Shopping Center. 10 minutes from the Panama hotels area. El Dorado has everything: good stores, fashionable quality merchandise, a supermarket, restaurants, entertainment, slot machines, and a racetrack agency. It is a nice place for a visit. Not expensive.

Av. Central. Best for shopping at bargain prices. Many stores. Good-quality merchandise. Everything you'd like to buy is here—merchandise from India, Europe, South and Central America, China.

La Florida and Plaza New York. Located on Calle 50 in the heart of the banking district. Several fashionable clothing stores.

Jewelry

Reprosa. Beautiful jewelry store featuring pre-Columbian gold artifacts and reproductions of the work of ancient man. There are stores at various locations: Av. Samuel Lewis, 69–0457; Panama Hilton Hotel, 69–4304; Marriott Caesar Park Hotel, 26–2490; Albrook Mall, 27–3797.

Nat Mendez Jewelry in Punta Paitilla Mall; 62–2800. Ask to see the beautiful Panamanian *mosqueta* made of pearls and gold.

Pretelt Jewelry. Baccarat, Cartier, Christofle, Lalique, and other exclusive names. Located in the heart of the city, Torre Banco Union; 69–1624 or 69–3453. Also duty-free at the Omar Torrijos Airport; 66–4704.

Riviera Jewelry. Rolex, Piaget. Located in the Hotel Continental Arcade and on Av. Samuel Lewis in front of Torre Banco Union; 64–8469 or 23–6254.

Mercurio Jewelry. Silver gifts. Located on Av. Samuel Lewis; 23–7326.

Oriental Shops

Salomon's, the best, is on Av. Central and in the Hotel Continental. *Sol de la India,* also on Av. Central and in the Panama Hilton Hotel. *Arcade Estrella del Este* is on Av. Central.

Home and Gifts

Luria's, located in El Dorado Shopping Center. *Hogar Ideal,* on Via España. *Casa Bella,* on Via España and Via Argentina.

Stereos and Photography

Audio Foto, on Via España in front of the Hotel Continental. *Camera Center,* also on Via España, offers Samsung, Sony, JVC, and many other brands.

NIGHTLIFE. When it comes to after-dark entertainment, no one is disappointed in Panama. The excitement begins at dusk and goes on through the night. The list of attractions is dazzling. You can see native talent doing the *Tamborito,* a Panamanian folk dance, watch a cockfight or a belly dance, enjoy a classical concert at the Anayansi National Theater, take in a glamorous show girl extravaganza at one of the hotels, disco to a brassy beat under a multitude of blinking lights, or dance to romantic big band sounds from Latin America, North America, and Europe, or head for sizzling casinos where the action continues till dawn. Major hotels have casinos (see "Casinos and Lottery" and "Accommodations," above).

Le Palace. One of Panama's newer night spots, located opposite the Ejecutivo Hotel. Open Mon. to Thurs., 3 shows each night from 9 P.M. Fri. and Sat., 4 shows.

Open House. Close to the Ejecutiva Hotel. Disco music. It's casual.

Bacchus. Via España. Close to the Granada Hotel. Happy hours. Music and dancing.

Disco 2000. Via Brasil. Music and dancing.

Holiday Inn. Heavy action in the lobby bar. Happy hours every day from 5:30 P.M. to 10:30 P.M., Sun. from 5:30 P.M. to 9 P.M.; shows with top international artist in the Inna Nega from 10:30 P.M. to 12:30 P.M.; "Tropical Night" with a poolside buffet and a Panamanian dance show with beautiful *polleras,* Wed. from 11:30 P.M. to 1:30 P.M.

Marriott Caesar Park. Happy hours at the hotel's Bar Mi Rincon every night from 5 P.M. to 8 P.M.; with music from midnight to 1 A.M. The *Stelaris* disco is also active nightly. For more information call the hotel.

Hotel Continental. El Sotano disco. The "world's most fabulous Wurlitzer organ" is a great attraction. Panamanian night every Thur. with buffet, cockfight, dancing. On Via España in front of the Panama Hilton Hotel.

Magic. Disco. On 50 St.

LEAVING PANAMA. There's a $15 departure tax.

USEFUL PHRASES AND VOCABULARY

PRONUNCIATION

Spanish is a relatively easy language to learn. Here are a few basic rules on pronunciation.

		as in:	example:
1) **Vowels** are pronounced precisely, with exceptions noted below:			
a		father	mas
	exception: ai/ay	life	aire, hay
	au	out	autobús
e		then	necesito
	exception: ei	weigh	seis
	eu—no equivalent word in English, but sounds like:	eh-oo	neumático
i		police	repita
	exception: before a, e, o, u	yes	viaje, bien, edificio, ciudad
o		none	nnoche
	exception: oi	boy	oigo
u		good	mucho
	exception: before a, e, i, o	was	cuarto, puedo, cuidado, acuoso
	(silent when used with: qui, que, gul, gue)		aquí, queso, guía, embrague

2) **Consonants** are pronounced similarly to English, except:

c	before a, o, u	kick	casa, poco, película
	before e, i	see	dice, décimo
g	before a, o, u	go	gazpacho, langosta, gusto
	before e, i	house	gerente, ginebra
gu	before a	guava	agua
h	(silent)	Esther	hablo

j		hill	mejor
ll		young	llame
ñ		onion	señor
q	(always followed by silent "u")	pique	mantequilla
rr	rolled	thr-r-ee	arroz
x	as in English, except in a few proper names when between vowels or beginning a proper name	hut	México, Oaxaca,
		zest	Xochimilco Xochicalco
y	before vowels when meaning "and"	yet me	ayer y
z		lose	azul

3) **Accent marks** are used to indicate which syllable is stressed, or to distinguish between two words, i.e., el (the) or él (he).

GENERAL VOCABULARY

Good morning/good day.	Buenos días.
Good afternoon.	Buenas tardes.
Good evening/good night.	Buenas noches.
I am glad to see you.	Mucho gusto en verle.
I don't speak Spanish.	No hablo español.
Do you speak English?	Habla usted inglés?
A little bit.	Un poquito.
How do you say in Spanish?	Cómo se dice en español?
Do you understand me?	Me entiende usted?
I understand.	Entiendo.
I don't understand.	No entiendo.
What did you say?	Cómo dice?
More slowly, please.	Más despacio, por favor.
Repeat, please.	Repita, por favor.
Write it down, please.	Escriba, por favor.
I don't feel well. I am sick.	No me siento bien. Estoy enfermo.
I need a doctor.	Necesito un médico.
How are you?	Cómo está usted?
Fine. And you?	Perfectamente. Y usted?
Very good.	Muy bien.
I have the pleasure of introducing Mr. . . .	Tengo el gusto de presentarle al señor . . .

Pleased to meet you.	Mucho gusto en conocerle.
The pleasure is mine.	El gusto es mío.
Pardon me. Excuse me.	Perdóneme. Con permiso.
Do you have a match?	Tiene usted un fósforo?
Can I take your photo?	Puedo tomar su fotografía?
Where is the . . . ?	Dónde está . . .?
I don't know.	No sé.
Where can I change my money?	Dónde puedo cambiar mi dinero?
Where do you come from?	De dónde es usted?
Can you tell me?	Puede usted decirme?
What do you wish?	Que desea usted?
What is the matter?	Que pasa?
Sit down, please.	Siéntese, por favor.
You are very kind.	Usted es muy amable.
It doesn't matter.	No importa.
Call me/phone me.	Llámeme por teléfono.
Is Mr. . . . in?	Está el señor . . .?
What is your name?	Cómo se llama usted?
Let's go.	Vámonos.
Good-bye.	Adiós.
Till we meet again.	Hasta la vista.
Until later/so long.	Hasta luego.
Many thanks.	Muchas gracias.
Don't mention it/You're welcome.	De nada.

address	dirección
American	americano
aspirin	aspirina
better	mejor
boat/ship	barco
book	libro
bookstore	librería
boy	niño, muchacho
building	edificio
bullfight	corrida de toros
bullfighter	torero
business	negocio
chair	silla
church	iglesia
cigarette	cigarro
clean	limpio
cleaning	limpieza
come here	venga acá
come in	entre
depart	salir, partir
do	hacer
dry	seco
dry-clean	lavado en seco
expensive	caro
eye	ojo
eyeglasses	lentes, anteojos
few	pocos

film	rollo, película
find	encontrar
forbidden	se prohibe
from	de
garden	jardín
gentleman	caballero, el señor
girl	niña
go	ir
good	bueno
guide	guía
handbag	bolsa de mano
hard	duro
heavy	pesado
high	alto
hospital	hospital
house	casa
husband	esposo
know	saber
lady	la señora, dama
look	mire, vea
look out	cuidado
lost	perdido
man	hombre
more	más
me	mi
my	mio, mia
name	nombre
new	nuevo
no more	nada más
no/non-	no
of	de
office	oficina
old	viejo
painting	pintura
please	por favor
policeman	policía
pretty	linda, bonita
quick	rápido, pronto
rain	lluvia
school	escuela
see	ver
single	solo, sencillo
smokers	fumadores
smoking	fumar
suitcase	maleta
sweet	dulce
there is, are	hay, son
thick	grueso
thin	delgado
time	tiempo
too	también
trip	viaje

United States	Estados Unidos
up	arriba
very	muy, mucho
wallet	cartera
watch	reloj
water	agua
weather	clima
welcome	bienvenido
wet	mojado
wife	esposa
with	con
with me	conmigo
without	sin
woman	mujer
yes	sí
young lady	la señorita
your	su

Index

Index

Fodor's Travel Guides

U.S. Guides

Alaska
American Cities
The American South
Arizona
Atlantic City & the
  New Jersey Shore
Boston
California
Cape Cod
Carolinas & the
  Georgia Coast
Chesapeake
Chicago
Colorado
Dallas & Fort Worth
Disney World & the
  Orlando Area

The Far West
Florida
Greater Miami,
  Fort Lauderdale,
  Palm Beach
Hawaii
Hawaii (Great Travel
  Values)
Houston & Galveston
I-10: California to
  Florida
I-55: Chicago to New
  Orleans
I-75: Michigan to
  Florida
I-80: San Francisco to
  New York

I-95: Maine to Miami
Las Vegas
Los Angeles, Orange
  County, Palm Springs
Maui
New England
New Mexico
New Orleans
New Orleans (Pocket
  Guide)
New York City
New York City (Pocket
  Guide)
New York State
Pacific North Coast
Philadelphia
Puerto Rico (Fun in)

Rockies
San Diego
San Francisco
San Francisco (Pocket
  Guide)
Texas
United States of
  America
Virgin Islands
  (U.S. & British)
Virginia
Waikiki
Washington, DC
Williamsburg,
  Jamestown &
  Yorktown

Foreign Guides

Acapulco
Amsterdam
Australia, New Zealand
  & the South Pacific
Austria
The Bahamas
The Bahamas (Pocket
  Guide)
Barbados (Fun in)
Beijing, Guangzhou &
  Shanghai
Belgium & Luxembourg
Bermuda
Brazil
Britain (Great Travel
  Values)
Canada
Canada (Great Travel
  Values)
Canada's Maritime
  Provinces
Cancún, Cozumel,
  Mérida, The
  Yucatán
Caribbean
Caribbean (Great
  Travel Values)

Central America
Copenhagen,
  Stockholm, Oslo,
  Helsinki, Reykjavik
Eastern Europe
Egypt
Europe
Europe (Budget)
Florence & Venice
France
France (Great Travel
  Values)
Germany
Germany (Great Travel
  Values)
Great Britain
Greece
Holland
Hong Kong & Macau
Hungary
India
Ireland
Israel
Italy
Italy (Great Travel
  Values)
Jamaica (Fun in)

Japan
Japan (Great Travel
  Values)
Jordan & the Holy Land
Kenya
Korea
Lisbon
Loire Valley
London
London (Pocket Guide)
London (Great Travel
  Values)
Madrid
Mexico
Mexico (Great Travel
  Values)
Mexico City & Acapulco
Mexico's Baja & Puerto
  Vallarta, Mazatlán,
  Manzanillo, Copper
  Canyon
Montreal
Munich
New Zealand
North Africa
Paris
Paris (Pocket Guide)

People's Republic of
  China
Portugal
Province of Quebec
Rio de Janeiro
The Riviera (Fun on)
Rome
St. Martin/St. Maarten
Scandinavia
Scotland
Singapore
South America
South Pacific
Southeast Asia
Soviet Union
Spain
Spain (Great Travel
  Values)
Sweden
Switzerland
Sydney
Tokyo
Toronto
Turkey
Vienna
Yugoslavia

Special-Interest Guides

Bed & Breakfast
  Guide: North America
1936...On the
  Continent

Royalty Watching
Selected Hotels of
  Europe

Selected Resorts
  and Hotels of the U.S.
Ski Resorts of North
  America

Views to Dine by
  around the World